CONTENTS

Page

PREFACE AND EXPLANATIONS V

GENERAL INTRODUCTION — ORIGIN AND ORTHOGRAPHY OF THE NAME, XI

PART I. A GENEALOGICAL MEMOIR OF SAMUEL RUNELS, 1703–1745 . 1

PART II. A GENEALOGICAL MEMOIR OF JOB RUNELS, OR RUNALS, 1713–1762 117

PART III. A GENEALOGICAL MEMOIR OF JOHN RUNELS, OR RUNALS, 1718–1756 171

APPENDIX "A." THE EARLIEST REYNOLDS FAMILIES OF NEW ENGLAND, WITH A PARTIAL GENEALOGY OF ROBERT REYNOLDS, OF BOSTON, 1632–1659 252

APPENDIX "B." GENEALOGICAL NOTICES OF OTHER REYNOLDS FAMILIES ORIGINATING IN NEW ENGLAND 270

APPENDIX "C." GENEALOGICAL NOTICES OF REYNOLDS FAMILIES THAT SETTLED IN AMERICA OUTSIDE OF NEW ENGLAND . . 273

APPENDIX "D." GENEALOGICAL NOTICES OF OTHER RUNNELS FAMILIES IN NEW HAMPSHIRE 274

APPENDIX "E." NOTICES OF OTHER RUNNELS FAMILIES IN MAINE, 279

APPENDIX "F." A GENEALOGY OF VALENTINE RUNNELS, IN MASSACHUSETTS 281

APPENDIX "G." MISCELLANEOUS NOTES ON A FEW OTHERS, AS YET UNCONNECTED WITH THE FOREGOING FAMILIES 284

ADDENDA 289

ROLL OF HONOR 295

INDEX I 301

INDEX II 317

A Genealogy of
Runnells and Reynolds Families

in America

WITH

RECORDS AND BRIEF MEMORIALS

OF THE

EARLIEST ANCESTORS

SO FAR AS KNOWN,

AND OF MANY OF THEIR DESCENDANTS,
BEARING THE SAME AND OTHER NAMES

IN THREE PARTS, WITH AN APPENDIX

BY

Rev. M. T. Runnels, A.M.

Pastor of the Congregational Church in Sanbornton, N.H.

*"And the Lord said unto Moses, Write this for a
Memorial" in a book." —Exodus xvii, 14.*

HERITAGE BOOKS
2012

HERITAGE BOOKS

AN IMPRINT OF HERITAGE BOOKS, INC.

Books, CDs, and more—Worldwide

For our listing of thousands of titles see our website
at
www.HeritageBooks.com

A Facsimile Reprint
Published 2012 by
HERITAGE BOOKS, INC.
Publishing Division
100 Railroad Ave. #104
Westminster, Maryland 21157

Originally published
Boston:
Alfred Mudge & Son, Printers
No. 34 School Street
1873

International Standard Book Numbers
Paperbound: 978-0-7884-1324-7
Clothbound: 978-0-7884-9268-6

PREFACE AND EXPLANATIONS.

A few words, both apologetic and explanatory, are here premised, inasmuch as this book of genealogies is believed to contain some features peculiar to itself, — at least, in the extent to which they are carried out; while, from previously observing the difficulty which persons of no more than ordinary intelligence have found in tracing the records of books of this kind, so familiar to the genealogist, the author has been convinced that explanations and directions for using cannot well be made too minute or explicit.

The first design of this collection was simply to furnish a *register* of all the children, both of sons and daughters, of those who, being descended from the three ancestors assumed in the respective "Parts," originally bore their surname, in some one of the various styles of its orthography. This register is now very nearly complete. A few supposable omissions among the earlier generations it is now impossible to supply, — and for the very few among later generations, it is not advisable longer to wait.

Entire uniformity and impartiality have also been observed in the registry of these descendants. The well-approved plan of the "Slafter" and "Spalding Memorials" has been substantially followed. Consecutive numbers are used on the left margins of the pages all through the book, no two individuals ordinarily appearing with the same number, and many being entered twice, or with two numbers, both as *members* and as *heads* of families. All descendants, bearing the original patronymic, can therefore be readily traced by observing the following simple directions. For finding any name of a Runnels or Reynolds, consult Index No. 1, where all the Christian names, only, are alphabetically arranged, to which each person may append the surname with whichever mode of spelling he may choose! Where several of the same Christian name are given in the Index, the year of birth, when known, preceding each name, will assist in determining which person of the common Christian name is meant. The number after each name is the consecutive number at which, in the main body of the book, the person is first entered as a child, in all cases except of the original ancestors themselves. When the individual was not married, or being married was not known at the time of reporting to have had children, as also in case the personal record is comparatively short; everything respecting that individual is stated at this only place of entry, as a child. Otherwise a higher, bracketed [——] number, directly after the name, refers to the place farther on in the book, where that same individual is entered as the head of a family, the smaller bracketed number there following the name, referring back again to the first number, as found in the Index. Here, too, after name and bracketed number, the pedigree of the individual is briefly indicated in parenthesis by the use of small exponential figures, the first over the name in question, thus, " Samuel^5," showing the generation to which the individual belongs, the next being the father with exponent one less, then the grandfather with exponent one less, etc., back to the first ancestor whose name appears with the exponent ^{1}, thus, Samuel^1. All other information, besides the birth of the individual, is given at this point, in larger type, with sketches of history, in some cases, more or less extended, the whole preceding the list of children entered with the first consecutive numbers found in the Index, as before stated. Any line can thus be traced backward by following the *smaller* bracketed numbers after *parents'* names, and forward by following the *larger* bracketed numbers after *children's* names.

While collecting material for the male lines, as above, it was found that a large amount of valuable genealogical information was being obtained respecting families of other names in the various female lines. The author has thought that by arranging these records in groups under their respective mothers, or ancestresses who first bore the Runnels or Reynolds name, a greater variety and enhanced value would be given to the work, as a whole. Of course it was absolutely impossible to trace out all these side lines, for no

single book could contain them. Nor has such fulness or complete-
ness been aimed at, as in the main lines just alluded to. The
writer has, therefore, restricted himself to those families with which
he was previously acquainted, whose records could be incidentally
obtained without delaying or embarrassing the main purpose in
view, and whose members have furnished their records, of their
own accord, with desires that they be inserted. If any are disposed
to complain because these female lines are not better filled and
more fully carried out, they must bear in mind that it was impossible to bestow exhaustive pains upon this part of the work without
" giving heed to endless genealogies," contrary to the apostle's
direction ; also, that everything which was furnished, has been
scrupulously published ; and where much was not given, much
cannot reasonably be required.

All descendants of the original ancestors, however, in these
female lines, and the names of all persons who intermarried with
the various families noticed in the book, are catalogued in Index
No. 2. The surnames are alphabetically entered, and under each
the Christian names also in alphabetical order, followed by the
consecutive number belonging to each name, or that under which
it may be found, with the added cardinals 1, 2, 3, etc., as in the
book, for children of the third generation from the original Runnels
or Reynolds daughter whose line is traced ; with added cardinals
in parentheses (1), (2), (3), etc., for children of the fourth generation ; with added Roman figures I, II, III, etc., for children of
the fifth generation, and with added Romans in parentheses (I),
(II), (III), etc., in a few instances, for children of the sixth
generation. (See these directions more fully illustrated in the
" Addenda.")

Many more notices of individuals and other biographical sketches
perhaps equally worthy of insertion might have been secured ; but
the author has confined himself to such as were previously known,
or came providentially to hand without special or direct efforts to
obtain them. These are inserted chiefly to relieve the monotony
of bare genealogical tables. A greater number would have swelled
the book to an inordinate size. The sketches are more full in several cases where material previously published, in some form, was
found pertaining to the individuals in question ; and where, espec-

ially, different phases of life, in different periods or localities, could be illustrated ; as, for example, of Revolutionary life in [82], [186], [215], and [2208] ; of pioneer life in [123], [458], [1924], and [2434]. Here, too, as in respect to the fulness of the female lines, must the principle obtain, that only where much is given can much be required. In every case the substance, at least, of all information sent has been incorporated.

A few epitaphs, anecdotes, and scraps of poetry are introduced, not as a matter of literary pretension, but for variety's sake, and to gratify, in some cases, the desires of those whose buried treasures may thus more vividly be kept in memory.

In accordance with the wise saying ascribed to John Quincy Adams, that "Posterity delights in details," more full and minute citations from old registries of deeds, probate records, and other public documents, are here given, than are customary in most similar works, for the reason that the proof of many genealogical points, established, is thus presented ; while all the information which can be gathered respecting one's earlier ancestors is naturally gratifying, and barren facts or dates thus grouped together, though of no general interest except to immediate descendants, frequently suggest far more than can be expressed in words.

No effort has been made to trace our ancestry to the old country, as such attempts are rarely attended with sufficient satisfaction to warrant the requisite outlay of time and money. Our family history in America is all we need, while the "Roll of Honor" is a silent but eloquent reminder of what sacrifices our fathers and their sons have made in the several national struggles.

A few minor explanations are here appended. If two different dates were found, — as of births on *town* conflicting with *private* records, — or if a similar uncertainty existed as to names, etc., the more probable is given first, and the other directly after, in parenthesis. Sometimes, however, a word in parenthesis is only explanatory of what precedes, and such cases are to be determined by the sense alone.

In the female lines, the children of Runnels or Reynolds daughters (as well as sons), though marrying into other families, and thus changing the name, are yet entered with consecutive numbers ; but the surname is designed invariably to follow the oldest child of the given family, in parenthesis, and likewise to be supplied with all the other children (consecutive numbers) of that family, unless repeated. Other family names, introduced by marriage, also appear in parentheses after each oldest child of that name in the *next* generation; and on returning to the *previous* generation, the previous surname is usually repeated, in parenthesis, after the Christian name of the next child. Several deviations from this rule will indeed be observed, through an oversight in preparing copy, the most important of which will be corrected, in " Errata," at the close of the volume.

All Christian names, appearing in the direct line of descent from common ancestors, are printed in small capitals, except by mistake in a few instances; they were also designed to be given in full, though we still have only the initials of middle names from some families.

The term " unmarried " is never, or rarely, employed. The fact may be inferred, if nowhere stated to the contrary, except in those families of which the records are evidently not filled, and mere names are given. Where one place of settlement or residence is stated in immediate connection with the head of a family, it may be left as a matter of inference that the children were all born in that place, unless otherwise stated. On the other hand, places of parents' residence are sometimes to be inferred from the given places of children's births.

Consecutive numbers are always referred to in brackets.

The usual abbreviations for the names of States are employed, and usually but once each after each family name, when the place of residence is first given. Every town afterwards mentioned is supposed to be in the same State, if without special designation.

Other abbreviations are those in common use, as " b." for " born," " m." for " married," " d." for " died," etc.

A mark of interrogation (?) after a name or date implies uncertainty.

Previously to 1752, the year, in England, commenced on the 25th of March; hence, for many years afterwards, writers and transcribers of dates occurring between Jan. 1 and March 25, were accustomed to signify both years, thus: " Mar. 5, 1744–5," *i. e.* " 1744 " according to the " Old Style " of reckoning, " 1745 " according to the " New Style."

The estates and moneyed transactions of our fathers were often much larger than they seem to us, judging from the figures ; the value of money in former times — except during the Revolutionary war — being much greater than at present.

A blank " Family Record " is inserted at the end of each book, thus enabling different families to supply deficiencies in their records, or continue them in future years.

Some patrons of this work, especially among the female lines, may be liable to a lack of general interest and a feeling of disappointment in the same, because their personal acquaintance is confined to a very limited circle of the numerous families and individuals here recorded. But such must bear in mind that the book could never have been printed except by thus collecting the greatest possible number of families, all of whom could claim a direct connection with some common ancestor. They must also content themselves with the charitable conclusion that all other parts of the work, though uninteresting to them, may yet prove gratifying to other persons in other family groups.

The labor of compiling and arranging these records has been great, but to the compiler himself exceedingly pleasant. No less than eight hundred letters have been written, and at least an equal number of circulars sent out. Much time has also been spent in the inspection of public documents in town and county archives, and many pleasant visits have been enjoyed at the homes of numerous " cousins," all of which are thankfully remembered.

To all those who have kindly aided him in the supply of material, the author would here express heartfelt gratitude, — next to Him who only hath " made him to prosper." To the printers, also, for their kindness and courtesy during the eight months occupied in going through the press, with continuous additions and emenda tions ; for the remarkable fewness of errors and mistakes, considering the character of the work ; and for the highly satisfactory mechanical execution of the book itself, — the thanks of all interested are justly due.

M. T. R.

SANBORNTON, March 15, 1873.

GENERAL INTRODUCTION,

WITH

REMARKS UPON THE ORIGIN AND ORTHOGRAPHY OF THE NAME.

THE true genealogist is not solely or chiefly influenced by a feeling of family pride. He distinguishes, as a late writer in the " Boston Journal " has happily done, " between a pride of ancestry and a taste for pedigree." " The former is senseless ; but the latter, he claims, is at least harmless." Adopting the noble sentiment of Burke, that " those who do not treasure up the memory of their ancestors, do not deserve to be remembered by posterity," he would yet by no means expose himself to the quaint sarcasm of Sir Thomas Overbury, that " those who rest their claim to consideration on the merit of their ancestry, and not their own individual worth, resemble a hill of potatoes, — the best portion is under ground ! "

It, therefore, matters not that his ancestors or their descendants are unknown to fame. He desires to glorify the God of his fathers by rescuing their names, however humble, from oblivion, by commending their Christian virtues, and by transmitting their history, whatever it was, to those who shall come after. He is thus enlarging the field of actual knowledge to the " rising generations " of the several families represented, and his inquiries, as another has said, are " fraught with instruction in affording us an insight into the habits of life and social ways of periods long past, and in fixing in the memory historical epochs and events," by enabling different persons to associate at least the chronology of such events with their own forefathers or relatives who may have been incidentally connected with them. He (the genealogist) would also

afford to each family circle of the more recent generations a permanent, though brief, memorial of the loved who have passed from
their embrace, — "not lost, but gone before," — feeling assured
that the treasured *name*, even of the youngest child in a family
record, is, to some hearts, no unmeaning expletive.

Actuated by such motives, the author's original design in preparing the present work was to collect and present a complete list, with
brief biographical sketches, of all persons, arranged by families,
who bore or still bear the cognate surnames of Runnels, Runnals,
or Reynolds, and are proved to have been descended from the common ancestor whose name stands at the head of each Part.

On commencing his investigations, however, he was soon con-
fronted by the troublesome fact that his own and his ancestors'
name is one of the most difficult to trace and connect in the way
proposed. Assuming that those records which contain actual sig-
natures, like wills, deeds, etc., and the records of towns where the
individuals lived, were to be regarded as most reliable for the orthography of the name, he found *such* records unanimous in giving
it "Runels" or "Runnels" in the earlier generations of Part I;
though clerks, or transcribers of *other* records, had spelled the
name variously, either by confounding it with the several ancient
methods of spelling the English "Reynolds," by using the vowels
indiscriminately in either of the two syllables; or, by doubling the
consonants *n* and *l.* Hence he found, for the varied orthographies
of Part I, nineteen in all: "Runels, Runnels, Runeles, Runells,
Runnells, Runiles, Runils, Runnils, Runills, Runiels, Runniels,
Runails, Runnals, Runnalls, Rennals, Rennalls, Renolls, Rennolds,
and Reynolds."

Only one branch of this family (Part I) is now known to retain the more ancient "Runels"; several branches, or rather
individuals, in later times have adopted "Runnells," while several other branches, mostly in the later generations and in
the family of Stephen [10], have taken refuge from all confusion
in the more common and less ambiguous "Reynolds." As, however, "Runels" was found to be the only well authenticated name
of the common ancestor Samuel [1], and as "Runnels" is the orthography more generally used by his descendants, the author felt
obliged to regard this as the standard, though leaving each family

at liberty to retain its own method of spelling, whether traditional or assumed.

Similar remarks would apply to the other Parts of the book. Among the records consulted for Parts II and III (mostly in New Hampshire), were the following sixteen varied orthographies, besides a greater part of those already given: " Runals, Runnalds, Ranals, Ranells, Renels, Renells, Renals, Reneles, Rennels, Renolds, Rennalds, Ronals, Roneles, Ronels, Roniels," and the evident contraction " R'nls."

The Reynolds and Runnels families of the " Appendix " also afforded fourteen additional variations, as follows: " Raynolds, Roynalds, Reinolds, Renold, Ranalls, Renes, Renls, Rennell, Renalls, Reanols, Ronalls, Runolds, Runnall, and Runalls." Thus there are furnished no less than *forty-nine* different ways of spelling the names under consideration, while a glance at the last citations (or the " Appendix " at the close of this volume) will show that even the " Reynolds " orthography is not of undeviating usage. This latter name, indeed, is generally admitted to have been derived from the old German " Reginald "; and it cannot certainly be determined whether Runnels (or Runels), as above, is a corruption of this English Reynolds, as is claimed by some, or whether it has an independent Scotch derivation. Probability favors the latter supposition The *word* " Runnel " is a Scotch term, meaning a small brook, or rivulet. It is found in the poetry of Sir Walter Scott; see " Introduction " to " The Bridal of Triermain " : —

> " For here, compell'd to disunite,
> Round petty isles the runnels glide."

Also, Canto 2d, of the same poem : —

> " See how the little runnels leap,
> In threads of silver, down the steep,
> To swell the brooklet's moan."

Nor is this an obsolete Scotch word, as claimed by some; for in one of the later works of Hugh Miller, LL. D., " The Cruise of the Betsy, with Rambles of a Geologist; or, Ten Thousand Miles over the Fossiliferous Deposits of Scotland," printed in 1858, are the following allusions: p. 326, " While at the bottom of the hollows, washed by the runnels, which, in the slow lapse of years, have been the architects of the whole, we find cairn-like accumulations of water-rolled stones, the disengaged pebbles and boulders of the deposit" (boulder clay) ; p. 514, " The sun broke out in great beauty after the showers, glistening on a thousand minute runnels, that came streaming down the precipices, and revealing through their vapory haze the horizontal lines of strata." See, also, pp. 51, 301, 330, 334, and 376.

As confirming the above supposable derivation, Bowditch, in his " Suffolk Surnames," calls " Runnells " " a name taken from the face of nature"; instancing " Rev. Mr. Runnells, teacher" (probably mistaken for trustee, see [2046]) " at the New Hampton Institute, N. H., 1858."

Another possible derivation of the name has been suggested from the old Norwegian " Ronald," as we find the name of " Baron Ronald Urka," who was present at the death of King Haco, the last of the Norwegian invaders, who died at Orkney in the thirteenth century. Hence we have North and South " Ronald sha" among the present names of the islands of the Orkneys; as, also, the unfortunate hero of one of Walter Scott's minor poems, " Lord Ronald." This derivation is, however, less probable ; and Runnels might as reasonably originate in Reynolds as in Ronald, except as the latter was afterwards a Scotch rather than an English name.

But the fact that the Runnels families are undoubtedly of Scotch extraction (see Introductions to Parts I and III, and [3936]), would seem to favor an independent Scotch derivation for the name itself, probably from an object in nature, as shown above. Reynolds, to be sure, in pronunciation, often *sounds* like Runnels, and the latter, on that account, is thought to be a very reasonable corruption of the former; yet we must, evidently, go farther back than any of the dates or records cited for the Runnels families of this work, to prove their identity with the name or race of Reynolds. The conclusion to which the writer has arrived is this, that Runnels is, for the most part, Scotch, while Reynolds is English and Irish. He has found numerous families by the name of Reynolds in Lowell, Lawrence, Salem, Boston, and Hartford, which were of Irish origin, and some of them were evidently of very recent arrival ; but no Scotch families have been discovered bearing that name.

The old Reynolds families, noted in the Appendix, are of undoubted English origin; and their descendants have quite generally and tenaciously held to the original spelling of their name, — with slight occasional variations, as before noted, — at least, there is no documentary evidence that any of them have changed the name to Runnels. On the other hand, many branches of the Runnels families, as will be seen in various parts of this book, have changed to Reynolds, on the supposition that this was the original name of which Runnels was only a corruption. Hence the case stands that many of the Reynolds name are found among Runnels families, but none of the Runnels name are found among Reynolds families; and the conclusion is that, aside from the changes just noted, the two names, though sounding alike in rapid pronunciation, are really separate and distinct.

No " coat-of-arms " of Runnels or Reynolds families has come to the author's knowledge, except that noticed under [2003], claimed to have been obtained in England from a book of heraldry in the library of the royal college.

Not being versed in the science of heraldry, the writer confesses that he cannot interpret *all* the terms employed in this description, of which an exact copy is here given for the gratification of those who are skilled or interested in armorial ensigns, and who also may be better able than himself to judge of its genealogical importance.

" *Arms;* Argent (white) ; masoned ; sable (black), upon a chief indented of the last (black). A plate charged with a rose, gules (red), barbed and seeded, etc. ; between two fleurs d lys. Or (gold). — *Crest;* a fox passant, gold, holding in its mouth a rose, as in the arms, slipped and leaved, vert (green). — *Motto :* " Murus aheneus esto." — (Underneath) " Runnells." — (On the back) " The family of Runnells is originally from the town of Biddeford, in the county of Devon. There are five descents in Sir Wm. Seager's visitation, in 1619."

This latter statement, seeming to point to an English rather than a Scotch origin, might lead one, in view of the foregoing conclusions, to question the historical accuracy of the whole document; unless we fall back on another fanciful derivation of the name which has been suggested, viz., that the first who bore it, and for whose services this coat-of-arms was created, was a courier, or bearer of despatches, of remarkable swiftness and shrewdness, during the wars of the Roses, 1455–1485 ; that he was enlisted on the side of the house of Lancaster, hence the *red* rose in the fox's mouth, and that he was accustomed literally to " *run ells* " — perhaps two English ells — at a stride ! But even on the supposition that this is a true derivation, it is far more likely that the first " Runnells," or " Runner of Ells," was a tall, gaunt Scotchman, rather than a stout and burly Englishman ! though he may have afterwards settled in Devonshire, and his descendants have been multiplied there, against the time of " Sir William Seager's visitation " !

The compiler of the following records has never known, or been at all anxious to prove, that —

" The boast of heraldry, the pomp of power,"

could be claimed by any of his name in lands and generations far removed.

PART I.

BEING A

GENEALOGICAL MEMOIR

OF

SAMUEL RUNELS,

OF BRADFORD, MASS.,

1703—1745.

INTRODUCTION.

No connection can be established, either by records or tradition, between Samuel Runels, of Bradford, Mass., 1703–1745, and any of the numerous Reynolds families which, according to Savage, had previously settled in different parts of New England (see Appendix) ; nor can a connection be found with any others of the Reynolds or Runnels name in this country, except with the brother, who is said to have accompanied him hither, and with Job and John Runels, or Runals, of Durham, N. H., 1733, who are also presumed, on good traditional authority, to have been his younger brothers. (See Introductions to Parts II and III.)

Among the descendants of Samuel, tradition is uniform in ascribing to him and his family a Scotch descent, and in introducing them to this country by the way of Nova Scotia (New Scotland).

A common legend has been repeated, with varied embellishments, in at least three distinct branches of his family, that he, with an older brother, " between the ages of 16 and 20," escaped from an attack of Indians, or pirates, upon their father's residence " near Halifax," and " came in an open boat " either " to a British ship," or " all the way to Salem." This immediate Nova-Scotian origin of Samuel seems also confirmed by an allusion in his will. The term " Eastern parts " would not then have been applied to the " District of Maine," as that was a part of Massachusetts. No place east of Essex County would naturally be meant, which was itself farther west than Arcadia, or the present provinces of Nova Scotia and New Brunswick.

His grandfather, too, either as owner or occupant, had evidently gained *for* him a *right* to those lands. It is, therefore, reasonable to infer that this " Grandfather Runels " may have been among those Scotch settlers who came to Nova Scotia with La Tour, a French Protestant, in 1628. They landed at Port Royal (now Annapolis), and built the so-called " Scotch Fort " on the east side of the Basin (Granville), the remains of which were visible as late as 1829.

When Sir William Phips of Massachusetts captured Port Royal, May 20, 1690, the English dismantled, but did not garrison, the fort; and we are told by Haliburton (Hist. of Nova Scotia, Vol. I, p. 72), that " In this defenceless state the unfortunate Arcadians *in that neighborhood* were attacked by two piratical vessels, the crews of which set fire to a number of houses, slaughtered their cattle, hanged some of the inhabitants, and deliberately burned one family, whom they had shut up in their dwelling-house to prevent their escape."

No similar depredations were committed in Nova Scotia, according to history, for several years before or afterwards. If, therefore, the substantial verity of our legend be assumed, the subsequent facts of his history would favor the conclusion that Samuel may have found his way as a refugee from the scene just described, and a homeless adventurer to the shores of Essex, in the year 1690. Subsequent tradition, in a New-England family, would naturally confound the barbarities of pirates with those of Indians, as also the name of the more recent with that of the original key and capital of Nova Scotia.

Of the older brother nothing is known except, traditionally, that he " settled in the South," and that grandsons of *both* the brothers were associated together, at West Point, as fellow-soldiers in the old French war. He is supposed to have been the ancestor of those more recently bearing the name of Runnels in the Southwest, among whom were Col. Harmon Runnels, of the Revolutionary war; his son, Gov. Runnels, of Mississippi, who died Dec. 15, 1857, in Houston, Texas; and his grandson, the present Ex-Gov. Runnels, of Texas, after whom a county in that State is named.

FIRST GENERATION.

1. SAMUEL[1] was b., as supposed, about the year 1674, near Port Royal, N. S. ; m. Abigail Middleton, probably of Haverhill, Mass., 1700-2. The old Haverhill record has " Samuell Renolls and Abigall Middeltine." But this orthography is of no authority in opposition to the earlier and more numerous citations of the name on the Bradford Records, *both* christian names and the wife's orig- inal *surname* being also incorrect. All their children, except the second, are given on the Bradford Records as " sons and daughters of Samuel and Abigail Runels." It is inferred *either* that she was at her father's home in Haverhill at the birth of her second child, *or* that they lived first in Bradford, afterwards in Haverhill, and then in Bradford again, where they were finally settled, as proved by the following abstract of Deed and Will from the Essex Records in Salem, Mass.

" Dec. 26, 1710. John Bointon to Samuel Runels in Bradford, Husband- man, in consideration of £7, part paid and part secured by bill, a certain piece of land lying in the township of Bradford, 20 acres as it is bounded, be it more or less ; bounded on the N. E. corner on a little small red oak marked and on the South side of a frog pond ; and so running on the East side upon land of Thomas West till it come to Boxford line ; and on the South on Boxford line to the stump of an old tree, with stones by it, on Boxford line ; and from that stump, on the West side, by land of Richard Kimball, unto a stake and stones on the N. W. corner."

We have no evidence of real estate as possessed in Massachusetts at an earlier date by a member of this family ; implying that though married some eight or ten years previously, this ancestor did not have a " home of his own," in Bradford, till 1710-11. It is evident, too, from this deed, and the price paid, that his original twenty-acre lot must have been comparatively wild and less valuable land at the time of purchase. The northern bounds are not given, but its loca- tion on Boxford line is made certain. This was afterwards known in Bradford as the " Job Runnels Place," where the " Job Runnels apples," excellent for their keeping qualities the year round, were found growing. J. Warren Chadwick now owns the same site, near Chadwick's or Little Pond. The land was transferred from John Runnels [22] to James Buswell, and by the latter to Jona. Chadwick. The *old* Runnels house was standing as late as 1840, on a knoll a few rods southwest of Mr. Chadwick's, with the famous apple-tree near it. The stump of the " little small red oak," alluded to as the northeast-corner bound, afterwards a gigantic tree, was dug up in June, 1871, and a piece of the same is now preserved by the writer as a choice relic. Five other deeds show that this original farm in Bradford was nearly doubled by Samuel [1], and that he purchased a tract of land in Newbury of Nathaniel Dole. He was also assessed for taxes in Boxford, 1712–17, one of those years, as per record, £2 6s. His descendants in Concord, N. H., have a tradition that he was interested in the early settlement of that town ; hence he is mentioned in Dr. Bouton's History as " signing a petition to Gov. Shute for the granting of Penacook, 1721 ; " " enrolled as a settler, 1725 ; " " taking a home lot near the present city, 1727," and " having a house erected, 1731." His home lot, " No. 16, 1st Div." was " fenced and improved," — afterwards deeded to William Stickney. His house, built but " not inhabited " by him, stood nearly opposite the old Abbot Fort, Main Street, on the spot now occupied by the house of Woodbridge Odlin, Esq. He also owned five acres on the " Sugar Ball Plain." (Hist. of Concord, p. 126.)

The Church Records say that " Samuel Runnels was admitted to full communion with the Congregational Church in Bradford, Nov. 27, 1709, was baptized, and owned ye Covenant said day." Ever after he brought his children very early to baptism as " children of the Covenant," the names of his five youngest appearing on the same Church Records, as below. His Will was dated " March 5, 1744–5," and " Proved, at Ipswich, Nov. 25, 1745." Abstract as follows : —

"I, Samuel Runels, of Bradford, etc., yeoman, * * bequeath to Abigaill my dearly and well beloved wife one cow, four sheep and my mare for her own use, also household goods and wearing apparel, and the free use and improvement of the East end of my house during her natural life. I give to my sons, Stephen and Job all my lands in Bradford, (they paying the legacies here mentioned) also to Stephen the East end of my house to come in possession after the decease of my wife, and to Job the West end of my house which he now lives in. As to *my lands that may fall to me in the Eastern parts*, by *my Grandfather* or *Father Runels*, I give them to my four sons, Stephen, Samuel, Job and Ebenezer to be equally divided between them for quantity and quality.

" I give unto my beloved son Samuel Runels 25 shillings lawful money, and that to be his portion in my estate with what I have already given him.

" I give and bequeath unto my son Ebenezer Runels the sum of £35 lawful money (or other payable bills of credit equivalent thereto) or to his lawful heirs, when he comes to the age of 21 years, to be paid by my Executors in equal parts, and that to be his portion out of my estate.

" I give to Sarah Lakeman, or her heirs, £10 in six months after my decease ; and to my grand son, William Atwood, or his heirs, £5 lawful money to be paid when he is 21 years of age.

" I constitute my beloved sons, Stephen and Job, sole executors (to whom I give my live stock except what I have given to my wife by will), ordering them to pay my honest debts and funeral charges and legacies above mentioned, and to give their mother, my now present wife, a decent burial at her decease."

The " Enventory" of his estate was taken by Thomas Kimball
l two others, Dec. 3, 1745, and is still to be seen among the old
ers of Ensign Enos Reynolds [64]: " Amounting, whole, in
.s of ye last Tenor, £222 17s. 3d." Among the items speed are " About 30 acres of land with buildings thereon, £160."
)ne pare of oxen £9." " Thirteen barriels of syder, with bariels
" " Waring apareal £5 7s. 6d.," and various " Utensiels for
sbandry." He d. and was buried in Bradford.
The writer was so happy as to *discover* his grave, in the old
adford cemetery, in 1871! The rich satisfaction was also
orded of resetting the prostrated gravestones and re-marking
eir inscriptions, which read, upon the headstone, " Here lies
ried the body of Sergt. Samuel Runels who died the 27th of
tober, 1745, aged 51st years"; on the footstone, " Samuel
inels." Date of death corresponds with that upon the Town
cords; but a mistake of " 5 " for " 7 " was undoubtedly made
the age, as well as in the *manner* of expressing it. He must
ve been more than 51 years old, as appears from the birth of his
lest son, and the age of his second son's wife, buried at his side.
lling it " 71 years," the year of his birth, not otherwise ascer-
ined, is reasonably fixed at 1674. This synchronizes with his
pposed arrival from Nova Scotia in 1690. We also learn, only
om the above inscription, that he bore the military title of
Sergeant." His widow d. Oct. 11, 1753, in Bradford (Town
cords). Their children were all b. in Bradford except the
cond.

2. STEPHEN [10], b. May 14, 1703.
3. SAMUEL [17], b. Dec. 17, 1706, probably in Haverhill, as his birth
    appears on the Haverhill, and *not* on the Bradford Records; the
    only child given on the former under his parents' names.
4. JOHN, b. March 9, 1710; d. within a year and one month.
5. JOHN, b. April 8, 1711; d. July 6, 1713. The baptism of "John,
    child of Samuel and Abigail Runels," appears on the Ch. Rec-
    ords "Apr. 1, 1711." If this is *not* a mistake, it belongs, evi-
    dently, to the older John, who must therefore have d. between
    Apr. 1 and 8, 1711. It is probably, however, designed for "Apr.
    10 or 11, 1711," and so marks the baptism of this younger child.
6. JOB [20], b. June 18, 1712; bap. July 27, 1712.
7. SARAH [30]. b. Oct. 31, 1716; bap. Nov. 4, 1716.
8. ABIGAIL [43], b. Nov. 11, 1722; bap. 1722.
9. EBENEZER [45], b. Nov. 20, 1726; bap. the next day.

SECOND GENERATION.

10. STEPHEN[2] [2] (Samuel[1]), m. Esther Hovey, of Rowley, and was admitted to full communion with the Congregational C. in Bradford, as "Stephen son of Samuel," "Aug. 3, 1729." lived in B. and there acquired some property as "a cooper, "Jan. 14, 1735–6," under which date Zechariah Hardy deed him, "for £140 a piece of land in Boxford, which was forl Nathaniel Hardy's." This marks the probable time of his set in Boxford as a farmer, and about the same time he first ap among the tax-payers of that town. From the Essex Pro Records: "Inventory of Stephen Runnels, late of Boxford, man, deceased, intestate, prized, Apr. 12, 1753, and witnesse Esther Runnels his widow"; who also "rendered account, a ministratrix of her husband's estate, Mar. 24, 1755." His es however, seems never to have been fully settled till after his Stephen's death; as "Sept. 3, 1771, a Committee was appoi: by Nathaniel Ropes, Judge of Probate, to divide and set off, for quantity and quality, one third part of all the real esta: Stephen Runnels unto *his widow, Esther Runnels, now Hovei* her right of dower in said real estate, to and for her use and provement during her natural life." According to the Box Records, she had m., 2d, Luke Hovey, of Boxford, "published . 16, 1755," thus regaining her maiden name.

He did not come in possession of a part of his father's hous Bradford, as by terms of the will, his own death preceding th: his mother by some months, "Mar. 10, 1753," aged 50. (Box Town Records.) Children: —

11. STEPHEN [62], b. 1729, in Bradford; bap. as "son of Stephen, Oc 1729" (Brad. Ch. R.).
12. MARTHA, b. 1732, in Bradford; bap. as "dau. of Stephen, Dec 1732," and probably d. young, as her name is not remembere the family.
13. ESTHER [72], b. 1734, in Bradford; bap. as "dau. of Stephen, 29, 1734."
14. ASA, b. 1737, in Boxford; d. young.
15. WILLIAM [74], b. June 28, 1740, in Boxford.
16. DANIEL [82], b. Sept. 15, 1742, in Boxford.

17. SAMUEL[2] [3] (Samuel[1]), was admitted to full commu: with the Cong. Church in Bradford, as "Samuel son of Samu

" Mar. 3, 1728." He m., 1st, Mrs. Anna Sessions, Feb. 18, 1730. Her crumbling gravestones were accidentally found, 1871, in the old Bradford cemetery, near the grave of Samuel [1]. Inscriptions with difficulty deciphered as follows : Head, " Here lies buried the body of Anna, the wife of Mr. Samuel Runels Iu'" (Jun.), " who died 20th of September, 1746, and in the 56th year of her age." Foot, " Anna Runels." This makes the year of her birth 1690, while the date of her death agrees with the Bradford Recs. He m., 2d, Hannah Emerson, of Haverhill. Nov. 19, 1747. (Haver. Recs.)

He is called a " House Wright," "June 3, 1738," when Maxwell Hazeltine conveyed to him, for £36, " a parcel of marsh or meadow, scituate lying and being in Rowly, on Plumb Island." " May 1, 1747," he bought of Eben Sherwin "for £650, old tenor, two pieces of land in Boxford, 51 acres."

From these and *seven other* deeds, we infer that within twenty years after his first marriage he added to the small property given him by his father (and probably by his own industry at his trade) some forty acres of land in Bradford and at least eighty acres in Boxford ; also.that his estate at first was near that of his father's and the line of the two towns, at Little Pond, where he lived, perhaps at a home furnished by his first wife as the widow Sessions, till between 1747 and 1749. He then became, probably at his second marriage, a resident of Boxford, on the other side of Little Pond, at the homestead still occupied by some of his posterity.

Two deeds are also found of " Apr. 2 " and " May 20, 1777," the latter giving him possession of a small "tract of marsh" in Newbury ; and the following deed will show to his Concord (N. H.) descendants the origin of their Horse Hill estate : " July 26, 1777 ; John and Benja. Jones of Beverly to Samuel Runnels of Boxford, *Gentleman*, for £48 a certain lott of land situated in Concord, in the county of Hillsboro' and State of N. Hamp., being a certain 80 acre lot in said township, lying at or near Horse Hill, so called." Tradition says that he was a lieut. in the old French war of 1756, with his son as a drum-major. He d. Apr. 12, 1783, aged 76 ; and " Feb. 3, 1784, administration of the Estate of Samuel Runnels, late of Boxford, gent., deceased, was granted to Samuel R , his son." His Inventory was given in, " Apr. 6, 1784." Property amounted to £699 4s., including farm, personal property, and one quarter part of a " gondola," rated at £2 5s., defined by Coffin (History of Newbury) as a " hay boat," and probably used by Samuel [3] on Merrimack River for visiting his Plum Island and Newbury purchases.

Return of commissioners, appointed for division of his estate, was made " May 8 " ; and " assignment made by Judge of Probate to Samuel Runnels and Anna Page, *his only children,* July 6, 1789." Children : —

    18. SAMUEL [93], b. Dec. 19, 1730, in Bradford (1st wife); bap. as " Son of Samuel Jun., Dec. 20, 1730 "

    19. ANNA [102], b. 1748–9, probably in Boxford; but bap. at the Bradford Church, " Feb. 26, 1749," as a " daughter of Samuel and Hannah R."

20.   JOB[2] [6] (Samuel[1]), had settled as a farmer in Bradford with his father, as noticed in the latter's will, 1745 ; also, before this, " June 6, 1743," he had purchased of William Eastman for " £219 14s., old tener, 15 acres and 34 perches of land in Bradford, adjoining his father's." He doubtless bought out his brother Stephen's share of the original homestead, which ever afterwards, increased as above, was called after his own name. (See under Samuel[1].) He was admitted to full communion with the Cong. Church in Bradford, Oct. 3, 1736. His 1st wife, Abigail, whom he m. 1733, d. Oct. 14, 1753. He m., 2d, Mary Woodman, Oct. 5, 1758. The following is an abstract of his Will, made at Bradford, Mar. 9, 1770, and proved at Salem, June 3, 1776, soon after his death (aged 64), of which we have no nearer date : —

" To my wife Mary the use of one cow and four sheep during her widowhood, — to be kept by my two sons, — and the household goods that she brought with her: the remainder of the goods (household) to be divided equally between my two daughters *Marther* (Martha) and Sarah, with £6 13s. 4d. to be paid to each of them by my two sons, within three years after my decease. All my real estate in Bradford or else where to my sons, in equal division. To my three daughters Abigail, Phebe and Elizabeth, five shillings apiece, with what they have already had, to be paid at my decease. Also, to the heirs of my daughter, Mary Bussel, deceased, the sum of five shillings apiece, to be paid at my decease. My two sons, John and Thomas, are appointed Executors " [Clerk of Probate wrote the former " *Job*," by mistake] and are directed " to give my wife, above named, a comfortable support in sickness and health during her life, and a decent burial at death, in case she dies my widow."

Receipts given by the above legatees, except Sarah, June 4 and 10, 1776, alluding to " the last Will and testament of our honored Father, Mr. Job. Runnels." Children all b. in Bradford, as per Records.

21. ABIGAIL [109], b. Oct. 12 ; bap. Oct. 13, 1734.
22. JOHN, b. Feb. 27, 1736 (Town Rec. says, by mistake, 1735) ; bap. Feb. 29, 1736 (Ch. Recs.). He was in both the old French and the Revolutionary wars. Admitted, with Sarah his wife, to full communion with the Bradford Church, Nov. 20, 1774. He m., 1st, Sarah Kimball, June 8, 1758, after his first military service. She d., and he m., 2d, " late in life," Mrs. Rebecca Kimball, of Boxford, 1807. He d. at the old homestead, 1821, aged 85.
23. MARY [115], b. July 22 ; bap. July 24, 1737.
24. PHEBE, b. May 8 ; bap. May 10, 1739 ; m. Abraham Kimball (per receipt as above).
25. THOMAS [120], b. Feb. 26 ; bap. Mar. 1, 1741.
26. ELIZABETH, b. 1743 ; bap. June 12, 1743 ; d. young.
27. ELIZABETH, b. July 1, 1748 ; m. " Mikel Kimball " (as per receipt). " Michael Kimball and his wife owned Covenant but came not to the Lord's Table, Sept. 30, 1764 " (Brad. Ch. Recs.).
28. MARTHA, b. July 3 ; bap. July 29, 1750.
29. SARAH, b. May 10, 1759 (2d wife) ; bap. May 13, 1759 ; m. Nathaniel Griffin, of Bradford, Dec. 31, 1778.

30.   SARAH[2] [7] (Samuel[1]), was admitted to full communion with the Cong. Church in Bradford, as " Sarah, dau. of Samuel

Runnels, July 2 (4), 1732 "; and was m. by the Rev. Joseph Parsons to Nathaniel Lakeman, of Boxford, Jan. 23, 1734. Resided in Bradford, where all their children were b.

31. ELIZABETH (Lakeman), b. Nov. 28; bap. Nov. 30, 1735; d. Jan. 20, 1756.
32. SAMUEL, b. Jan. 7; bap. Aug. 12, 1737.
33. SARAH, b. Oct. 25, 1738.
34. MARY, b. July 9; bap. July 13, 1740; d. before 1758 (see 42, below).
35. ABIGAIL, b. July 21; bap. July 25, 1742.
36. NATHANIEL, b. Aug. 11; bap. Aug. 19, 1744.
37. EBENEZER, b. Apr. 12; bap. Apr. 20, 1746.
38. ESTHER, b. Mar. 16, 1748(7); bap. Mar. 20, 1748.
39. DANIEL, b. July 29, 1750.
　　The three following are not upon the Town Records, but appear among the church baptisms as the "sons and daughter of Nathaniel Lakeman."
40. AMOS, b. 1752; bap. Nov. 5, 1752.
41. JOB, b. 1755; bap. Feb. 9, 1755.
42. MARY, b. 1758; bap. Sept. 17, 1758.

43. ABIGAIL[2] [8] (Samuel[1]), m. William Atwood, of Bradford, Dec. 24, 1739. She d. prior to the date of her father's will, 1745, leaving the son then mentioned.

44. WILLIAM (Atwood), b. Jan. 20, 1740, in Bradford.

The circumstances of his early training were unfavorable, as is often the case, his father soon marrying again and having numerous *other* children. He therefore became a sort of Ishmael in the world, and no descendant of his can ever arise to charge us with disrespect to his memory, if, for variety's sake, we venture a little episode at his expense, as related by Mr. Alfred Poor, genealogist, of Salem, Mass. " He was very fond of ' the ardent,' but, like many others in the same situation, did not abound in means for gratifying his appetite. One ingenious device of his, however, was this : he would go to a country store with two bottles of the same size and shape, one in each side pocket of his slouched overcoat, — one filled with water and the other empty. Lurking in the back store for a while, he would watch his opportunity and slyly fill the empty bottle. On leaving the premises, if detected, he would stoutly deny the theft at first : but when hard pressed, would draw the bottle of water from his pocket and deliver it, with great apparent disgust, to the storekeeper, exclaiming, ' Here, take your miserable rum; I don't want it !' With real satisfaction the trader would turn its contents into his cask, thinking that so much was saved from his thievish customer, while William, with the genuine article, would coolly make his escape!"

45. EBENEZER[2] [9] (Samuel[1]), learned a different trade from either of his older brothers, — that of a blacksmith, — and probably in the neighboring village of Haverhill, where we find him, "Jan. 7, 1748" (by mistake on the county records, "1744," as he was then a minor) receiving, by deed from "agents of the town of Haverhill, for £33 10s. (N. T. in hand before), a certain piece of parsonage land, on Merrimack River, and containing about 8 acres"; "Mar. 6, 1748," just after his first marriage, he buys of Edmund Mooers, for "£750, O. T., a lott of land with a dwelling house there on"; "Apr. 7, 1748," with "Abigail his wife," he conveys to "William Greenleaf, for £220, O.T., one half an acre in Haverhill,

formerly of the parsonage land so called "; and " Apr. 17, 1749,"
to Samuel White, for " £75, about ¼ of an acre, at a place
commonly known by the name of the River Parsonage Lots."
He must have received a dowry by his wife, or else have worked
quite successfully at his trade before 1748, since the amount received from his father's estate by will at " twenty-one years of
age," could only have helped him to the *first* or *parsonage* purchase
(above), out of which the two last deeds show that he was making
what would be called, in these days, a " handsome speculation,"
while reserving the second purchase for his own homestead. Eight
other deeds are found conveying real estate in Haverhill *to* him,
and eleven others, *from* him to others, also in Haverhill, and all
prior to 1784, showing that his business relations were quite extensive in that place. The following also marks the time of his
purchasing the estate, afterwards given to his son Samuel [54] in
Hollis: " Feb. 5, 1777," Ebenezer and Thomas Jaquith and wives
(their marks), " to Ebenezer Runels, for £666 13s. 4d.
255 acres of land, partly in Hollis, N. H., and partly in Dunstable, Mass." As a blacksmith in Haverhill, he had, for the
times, a large establishment, devoting himself mainly to the oversight of his numerous employés. Was engaged considerably in
the ironing of vessels, and was also partner in a ship-building
interest at Newburyport, according to tradition among the
descendants of his oldest son in Maine. His residence in
Haverhill was situated on the present Washington Square;
house, where now the Lafayette and Washington Blocks, with
garden in rear and extending east to the Little River; shop,
opposite the house, in rear of the present Christian Baptist
Meeting-house. He m., 1st, Abigail Sollis, of Beverly, 1747.
She d. Oct. 3, 1765, and the next year he m., 2d, Hannah Smith,
of Haverhill, who was b. May 31, 1742, in H., and there d. Mar.
29, 1814, aged 72. The writer has a copy of his Will, dated Feb.
10, 1795, agreeing with the Essex Prob. Recs.; abstract as follows: —

" I give unto my oldest son, Benjamin, £10 lawful money, to be paid out
of my estate in three years. To Stephen, £15, ditto, in two years. To
my son, Ebenezer's children, Ebenezer and Abigail, £20 each. To my
daughter, Mary Ayer, £5, in one year. To my daughter, Abigail Hagget,
one feather bed, one mahogany case of drawers, and £10, in two years.
I give to Samuel 40 shillings, and require him to pay to his mother 30 shillings yearly, during her natural life." [This in consideration of the Hollis
property which he had previously received] " To Nathaniel, £50, to be
paid in two years. To Daniel and Ebenezer, equally, one half the house
and garden I now possess. To Hannah, £30, in one year after my decease.
To Thomas, a piece of land in Haverhill, with house thereon, in which he
now lives. To Daniel and Thomas, equally, the shop, shop lot and tools,
ordering them to pay Stephen 50 shillings each, within two years. Finally,
to my wife, Hannah, and my son Thomas, jointly, all other property in
Haverhill, making them Executors of my will, and ordering them to raise
money as needed, by the sale of my Pepperell farm (so called), dividing
the balance equally among all my children."

Account of Executors was rendered " Dec. 14, 1795." Property prized, in all, " at $4,632.73," including his " Pepperell farm

at \$1,686.67," and his " Mansion house, and land adjoining in Haverhill, at \$1,000." The words " Memento Mori" are on his gravestone in the old Haverhill cemetery, which also gives his death, " Aug. 4, 1795," aged 69. Children, b. in Haverhill, — an equal number by each of his two wives.

46. BENJAMIN [123], b. Mar. 31, 1748.
47. EBENEZER [133], b. Apr. 21, 1750.
48. JOHN, b. Aug. 14, 1752; d. Sept. 14, 1753.
49. STEPHEN [136], b. July 3, 1754.
50. JOHN, b. June 18, 1756; d. June 16, 1760.
51. MOLLY (Mary) [146], b. July, 1758.
52. ABIGAIL [158], b. Dec. 7, 1760.
53. THOMAS, b. Dec. 14, 1763; d. Nov. 16, 1765.
54. SAMUEL [163], b. Mar. 15, 1767.
55. THOMAS [171], b. Feb. 7. 1769.
56. NATHANIEL STEVENS [180], b. June 23 (22), 1771.
57. DANIEL, b. Oct. 22, 1773; d. Sept. 22, 1774.
58. DANIEL [192], b. Dec. 18 (Fam. Rec. says " Sept. 22 "), 1775.
59. EBENEZER [198], b. 1778; not found on the Haverhill Recs.
60. HANNAH, b. Apr. 22, 1783; d. Feb. 22, 1787.
61. HANNAH [201], b. July 12 (4), 1787.

THIRD GENERATION.

62. STEPHEN[3] [11] (Stephen[2], Samuel[1]), m. Hannah Pearl, of Boxford, April 11, 1754. As appears from the following and one other deed, he inherited and occupied, as a farmer, his father's real estate in Boxford, adding to the same and selling from it: "April 13, 1763, Stephen Runnels of Boxford, yeoman, to James Lendall, for £20 14s. 2d., a certain tract or piece of land in B., 4½ acres, more or less, being one half of what I bought of Daniel Wood." He d. probably in the summer of 1771, aged 42, as we have from the Essex Probate Recs. "Administration of the estate of Stephen Runnels, late of Boxford, deceased, granted to Hannah Runnels, who gave bonds with Samuel Runnels and Richard Pearl, *this Sept.* 23, 1771." Inventory presented Oct. 24, 1771. Real estate, £257 13s.; personal property, £122 2s. 7½d.: Total, £379 15s. 7½d. His widow did not render her account as administratrix till "Mar. 2. 1779," the troublous times of the Revolution, and the absence of her oldest son no doubt preventing. At this latter date, "£42" are added to the above figures as the "Increase" of his estate, bespeaking *her* good management. At the same time the guardianships of "Eunice Runnels, a minor, aged 18," of "Billey, 16," and of "Hannah, 14," are granted to John Pearl; also, of the younger children, "Phebe aged 12, Esther aged 10, and Sarah aged 8," granted to their mother. Commissioners appointed to divide the property, Apr. 21, 1779; who made their report June 8, 1779. She probably d. late in the year 1789, as widow Hannah Runnels is among the tax-payers of that and previous years (but not afterwards) on the Boxford Records, where also are found the births of their children.

63. ABIGAIL [205], b. Aug. 21, 1755.
64. ENOS [215], b. Feb. 20, 1757.
65. HANNAH, b. Nov. 29, 1758; d. young.
66. EUNICE [228], b. Jan. 6, 1761.
67. BILLEY, b. Jan. 24, 1763. Was in the Revolutionary war, having enlisted when a mere youth, winter of 1779-80. He was known to have been taken prisoner by the British, and d., as supposed, in a prison-ship near New York, 1781, aged 18.
68. HANNAH [238], b. Dec. 30, 1764.
69. PHEBE [243], b. Dec. 8, 1766.
70. ESTHER, b. Sept. 1768; d. Mar. 2, 1789.
71. SARAH, b. Nov. 1770; d. Aug. 1, 1789, in Salem, N. H.

72. ESTHER[3] [13] (Stephen[2], Samuel[1]), m. Moses Sargent, of Methuen, Nov. 29, 1767. She was his second wife, and succeeded to the care of his five children by his former wife Elizabeth ; to these was added her only child.

73. ASA (Sargent), b. Sept. 25, 1768 (Methuen Records).

74. WILLIAM[3] [15] (Stephen[2], Samuel[1]) ; m., 1st, Rebekah Foster, of Andover, Mass., 1771–2, and moved from North Andover to Methuen in 1774. He had previously taken land in Londonderry, N. H., — conveyed to him, in company with Ebenezer Runnels, of Haverhill, in 1769, — of which his part, sixty acres, was deeded away in 1773. (Rockingham Records.)

This shows that he may have *contemplated* settling in Londonderry, with his brother Daniel [82]. He was in the Revolutionary war, — how long, cannot be ascertained. At Methuen again, "June 14, 1779," as under that date, "William Runnels, of Methuen, yeoman [deeded], to Jesse Tyler for £30 a piece of meadow in M., including some islands of upland lying therein." (Essex Records.)

Tradition in the Messer family informs us that he was exposed to great privations in the army, suffering especially from hunger on a certain march, when " one day he picked up a piece of pork-rind and a pealed onion, supposed to have been dropped by a party of Indians along the road ; at first hid away his treasure, for fear his hungry companions might rob him of the scanty provision, and afterwards ate it in a place of seclusion from the rest." This may have been on Col. B. Arnold's disastrous march through the wilderness to Quebec, in the fall of 1775.

After the war, and prior to 1790, — as by six other deeds, — additions were made to his real estate in Methuen, of nearly one hundred acres. His 1st wife d. Nov. 20, 1808, aged 62, at Methuen. He m., 2d, Mrs. Olive Smith (formerly Messer), of Methuen, Dec. 26, 1809 ; who d. Sept. 8, 1837.

He d. July 10, 1822, at Methuen ; is styled " Elder William Runnels " on his gravestone, and this epitaph is added : —

> " Though I have lived to eighty-two,
> God gives long life to very few ;
> Let none presume, then, on old age,
> But in religion now engage."

His children — as per Town Records — were all b. in Methuen, except the oldest : —

75. REBEKAH [248], b. Apr. 3, 1773, in Andover.
76. STEPHEN, b. Apr. 2, 1775; m. Abigail Sargent, of Methuen, Sept. 30, 1804. Jesse Webster deeded to him a " farm in Salem, N. H., Dec. 3, 1807 " (Roc. Recs.). His gravestone in Methuen gives him the title of " *Coln*. Stephen Runnels," he there dying "July 21, 1831," aged 56.
77. DANIEL [256], b. Apr. 29, 1777.
78. ABIGAIL [259], b. Feb. 16, 1780.

79. ESTHER, b. Sept. 8, 1782; m. Leonard Carlton, of West Boxford, and there d. Apr. 8, 1868.
80. JOHN [267], b. Oct. 30 (Fam. Rec. " 28 "), 1786.
81. SARAH [277], b. May 18, 1791.

82. DANIEL[3] [16] (Stephen[2], Samuel[1]), had settled in London-derry, N. H., as early as 1765, since he was said, " June 20, 1765," to be " of Derryfield, now resident in Londonderry, Joyner," and received by deed from James Karr, of Goffstown, " for £553 17s., one seventh part of a certain tract of land lying in Hopkinton, on the north side of Contoocook River, 3303 acres." He made two other purchases in Londonderry in October of the same year, — called " Daniel Runnels of L., carpenter "; while two convey-ances of land to others, by himself and wife, in 1773 and 1774, are also recorded among the Rockingham deeds, at Exeter, N. H. He m. Hannah Spofford, Apr. 14, 1767, who was b. March 16, 1746, and d. in Derry, Jan. 23, 1829, aged 83. His homestead was one mile north of the centre meeting-house in Derry, not far from the celebrated Beaver Pond, and the spot where the first sermon was preached to the early settlers of Londonderry. It is now (1872) owned by his grandson, William Reynolds [284]. Parker's Hist. of Londonderry, p. 152, states that he was one of the undertakers of the work (with Joseph Morrison) of building the new meeting-house in the east parish, 1769. His military history, during the Revolutionary war, is gathered as follows, chiefly from the " Adj. General's Report of New Hampshire," Vol. II. " Dec. 2, 1775, General Sullivan, at Winter Hill, called for thirty-one companies of New Hampshire men (commonly called the ' six-weeks' men ') to take the place of the Connecticut troops who had left. Daniel Runnels, of Londonderry, was the captain of Co. 3 " (p. 278).

Same account in the " New Hampshire Provincial Papers," to wit, that the " Committee of Safety, Dec. 2, 1775, ordered Daniel Runnels and fifteen others to enlist a company of sixty-one able-bodied men to serve in the Continental army under General Washington, and to join them immediately to General Sullivan's brigade."

In April, 1776, he signed the " Association Test," with others of his fellow-townsmen. September of the same year, two more regi-ments were raised to reinforce the Continental army in New York. Col. Thomas Tash commanded the second regiment, and " Daniel Runnels was captain of Co. 7, Sept. 26, 1776." He next appears as " Daniel Runnels, captain of Co. 1 in Col. Nichol's regiment," which went with Gen. Stark to Bennington. He was undoubtedly engaged in that renowned battle, his regiment being " sent by a circuitous route to gain the rear of the left wing of the enemy," Aug. 16, 1777. Parker's History confirms this, informing us that " a company of seventy volunteers " (Co. 1 above) " was enlisted in Londonderry, July 20, 1777 "; that it was " commanded by Capt. Daniel Reynolds, and was in the battle of Bennington." Oct. 18, 1777, he was ordered to pay off the roll of his company. General Whipple had command of a New-Hampshire brigade sent to operate against the British under Gen. Sullivan, in Rhode Island, in the summer of 1778. In this brigade, "Daniel Reynolds was captain of Co. 3, Col. Peabody's regiment." Here *this spelling* of the name appears for the first time in the military history of New Hampshire; though it is afterwards ordered that "Capt. Daniel Runnels be paid as an officer in Col. Stephen Peabody's regiment, raised for the defence of Rhode Island, April 28, 1778."

In the spring of 1779, a regiment was ordered from New Hampshire for service in Rhode Island under Col. Hercules Mooney, of Lee, in which "Daniel Reynolds was captain of Co. 2," at first, " May 29, 1779"; and afterwards "Major" of the same regiment, as under dates of " Sept. 4 and 18, 1779."

One regiment only, and the last, for the Revolutionary struggle, was raised in New Hampshire in 1781, "the prospect of peace relaxing military operations." Of this, "Daniel Reynolds" was "*Colonel.*" A " note" here, in the military history, remarks (Adj. General's Report, Vol. II, p. 364), that " he had served his country on various occasions," as above; that " his name was often written Runnels, and hence there has arisen some doubt as to the offices held by him; but there is now no doubt that Capt. D. Runnels and Col. D. Reynolds are one and the same man, from Londonderry." Whether the change of his patronymic was first made in 1778 by himself, or by the regimental clerk, it seems to have been adopted by him about that time, and to have been followed, generally, by his townsmen and his descendants ever since.

We may add that but few Revolutionary records are more praiseworthy than his. His gradual *growth* in acknowledged merit and distinction as an officer, and his *perseverance to the end*, give him a high rank among the revolutionary soldiers of New Hampshire.

Col. Reynolds was honored by his town by being elected first representative to the General Court of New Hampshire, 1780–84 inclusive, also in 1786 and 1788. He was one of the selectmen of Londonderry in 1785, 1787, 1789–92 inclusive, and in 1794. He d. at his home, greatly beloved and respected, Dec. 13, 1795, aged 53. Inventory of his estate taken Dec. 21, 1796. His children were all b. in Londonderry, now Derry.

83. STEPHEN [282], b. Jan 10, 1768.
84. SALLY [291], b. Oct. 22, 1769.
85. DANIEL [303], b. Oct. 7, 1771.
86. HAMILTON DAVIDSON [311], } b. July 4, 1773.
87. POLLY [314],
88. HANNAH [325], b. March 16, 1776.
89. JOSEPH, b. Oct. 20, 1778; a farmer in Derry, where he d. May 17, 1849, in his 71st year.
90. THOMAS K. [334], b. Oct. 20, 1780.
91. ESTHER S., b. Jan. 18, 1783; d. at Derry, Apr. 27, 1836, aged 53.
92. BETSY, b. March 30, 1785; d. Mar. 16, 1818 (gravestone says, " Mar. 5, 1817"), aged 33.

93. SAMUEL[3] [18] (Samuel[2], Samuel[1]), being the only son of his father, was closely connected with him for many years in various other relations. They were fellow-soldiers in the old French

war, occupied the same house and homestead in Boxford, and are named as joint purchasers of real estate in six deeds before 1772. " Samuel Runnels and Samuel Runnels, jun., both of Boxford," with " gentleman " attached to the former, and " yeoman " to the latter, or " husbandmen " to both. " Behold, how good and how pleasant it is for " father and son *thus* " to dwell together in unity ! " " Oct. 23, 1764," they bought of Stephen Merrill, for £20, " a certain parcel of flatts and crick grass, laying in Newbury, and known by the name of Dole's Banks," thus adding to the purchase of their father and grandfather in that vicinity ; but they seem to have enlarged their estate far more in Bradford than elsewhere, probably near the " old place," making, among other purchases, " June 20, 1769," " a certain measurage or tract of land lying in Bradford, commonly known by the name of Dismal *Hole*, containing about six acres of woodland, for £63 16s.," to which, three years later, four and one half acres were added for £26 7s., " near a place known by the name of Dismal *Hall*."

The following reminiscence of his service in the French war is handed down by tradition from his own lips, substantially. He " was on duty with his fellow-soldiers," probably in the vicinity of Lake George, N. Y. (Gen. Johnson *vs*. Dieskau, 1755), when " the French made a sudden attack upon the British troops ; and the latter, being few in number at that point, fell back behind a breast-work of fallen trees. There they stood their ground under a brisk fire from the enemy, who made desperate and long-continued efforts to dislodge them, but were finally obliged to retire. After the action," as he used to say, " he could cover with his two hands " (*spread* as to the fingers, no doubt) " no less than forty ball-holes in the log by which *his own head* had been protected." After this service, he m. Joanna Platts, of Bradford, Mar. 14 (published Feb. 26), 1757. She d. in Boxford, " Dec. 16, 1809, aged 75," and was hence b. in 1734, probably a daughter of " Jonas Platts," a part of whose estate, " ten acres in Bradford," they deeded " to N. Wallingford, for £114 13s. 4d., Jan. 17, 1773."

" Mar. 12, 1790," he conveyed a lot of land in Concord, N. H., to William Stickney, for £43 7s. 6d., — the " home lot," doubtless, near Concord Street, on which his grandfather " erected a house in 1731."

Having received a lieutenant's commission, he served in the revolutionary war as a " minute man," the gun which he used in that capacity being still in the possession of his great-grandson, Cyrus Runnels, of Concord, marked " 1757," and originally more than six feet in length !

Hence the Boxford Records give his name as *Lieut*. Samuel Runnels, both in the " tax-lists " from 1784 onwards, and among the " families." His taxes in 1790 were, in the column of " Heads " (two in number), " 5-6 " ; " Real," " 9-11 " ; " Personal," " 3-6 " ; probably shillings and pence ; and if so, his taxes were remarkably low. Yet he seems to have become somewhat reduced in pecuniary affairs, as his " Inventory," rendered April 30, 1810, was only

$456.55. He survived his wife but about three months, and d. Mar. 12, 1810, in the eightieth year of his age. "May 8, 1811," receipts for $23.43, as paid by his administrator, are given from each of the four following children: Jonathan Runnels, Jonas Runnels, Benajah Burns and Anna, his wife, and Amasa Peabody and Louisa, his wife, the last acknowledging this amount "out of the estate of our honored father," but "excepting" (as not relinquished) "our share in his pew in Boxford-West meeting-house." His children were all b. in Boxford: —

94. JOSEPH [341], b. Oct. 19, 1758 (though Bouton's Hist. of Concord gives "Nov. 18, 1759").
95. JONATHAN, b. Dec. 16, 1760; d. within five years.
96. RHODA [352], b. Apr. 30, 1763.
97. JONATHAN [362], b. Aug. 8, 1765.
98. LOIS (Louisa) [364], b. Apr. 18, 1768.
99. SAMUEL [366], b. July 20 (17), 1770.
100. HANNAH (Anna), b. Jan. 6, 1773; m. Benajah Burns, miller, 1808; and d. Dec. 1, 1860, at East Haverhill, Mass., in her 88th year, where also he d. July 27, 1865.
101. JONAS [372], b. Aug. 20, 1775.

102. ANNA[3] [19] (Samuel[2], Samuel[1]), is styled "Anna R., spinster, of Boxford," "Aug. 10, 1770," in deed, with others, of a piece of land and a meadow in Methuen, to Jacob Whitcher, of M. Afterwards m. Joshua Page, of Haverhill, son of Joshua, b. May 4, 1746, in H., and there d. May 28, 1806, aged 60. She d. Aug. 1, 1806, aged 58. "They lived in the west part of Haverhill, near the brick-yard," where their children were born: —

103. HANNAH (Page).
104. SAMUEL.
105. CALEB.
106. JOSEPH; d. young.
107. SALLY.
108. MOSES.

109. ABIGAIL[3] [21] (Job[2], Samuel[1]), was admitted to the Bradford Congregational church, Jan. 11, 1756, and was m. by the Rev. Joseph Parsons, third minister of Bradford, to Jeremiah Kimball, Jr., of B., Dec. 6, 1757. Children: —

110. RICHARD (Kimball), b. June 14, 1760.
111. JEREMIAH, b. June 26, 1762.
112. BETTE, b. Mar. 1, 1764.
113. SARAH, b. Aug. 7, 1769.
114. AMOS, b. Sept. 3, 1774.

115. MARY[3] [23] (Job[2], Samuel[1]), m. Daniel Buswell ("Buzzil"), Jan. 25, 1759, and d. Dec. 9, 1765, aged 28 (Brad. cemetery). He was b. in Bradford; bap. Aug. 24, 1735; d. Aug. 12, 1813. Children: —

116. BETSEY (Buswell), b. Jan. 31, bap. Mar. 2, 1760; m. Ezra Trask, mason, of Bradford, Nov. 22, 1787. They lived in Bradford (house now occupied by their youngest child), where she d. Dec. 14, 1835, in her seventy-sixth year. Children: —

1. SOPHIA (Trask), b. Dec. 29, 1788 ; m. Thomas Morrison, of Derry, N. H. ; 2 children.
2. MARY (Polly), b. Nov. 18, 1790.
3. MATILDA, b. Jan. 25, 1793 ; d. July 16, 1804, aged 11½ years.
4. ELIZA, b. Mar. 13, 1795 ; m. David Burpee ; 1 child.
5. SARAH, b. May 4, 1797 ; m. Joseph Page, of Newburyport ; 1 child.
6. ANN, b. Mar. 1, 1799.
7. IRENA, b. July 16, 1804 ; m. William Elliot, of Beverly ; now resides in Bradford ; 1 child.

117. SARAH, b. 1761 ; bap. as dau. of Daniel Buswell, Mar. 8, 1761 ; d. before June, 1776, not being mentioned with the other three children in receipt of their guardian appended to the will of Job Runnels [20].

118. DANIEL, b. April 3, 1763 ; bap. same day ; a soldier in the revolutionary war, — last three years ; m. Ede Bodwell, of Haverhill. Apr. 1, 1789. She was b. Feb. 18, 1772, in Methuen. They first settled in Bradford ; but after birth of their second child, moved to Antrim, N. H., where he d. Sept. 3, 1859, aged 96, and she d. Mar. 12, 1870, aged 98. Children : —
1. ABIGAIL (Buswell), b. Aug. 22, 1789 ; a tailoress for many years in Haverhill, Mass., where still residing (1871).
2. SALLY, b. May 31, 1791 ; m. Sewall Spalding ; 11 children, " two daughters, seven sons, and lastly, two daughters more."
3. CHARLOTTE, b. Mar. 17, 1794, in Antrim ; m. and settled in Iowa ; 4 children.
4. THOMAS, b. Feb. 1796 ; d. Oct. 1825, aged 29.
5. JOSHUA, b. 1798 ; d. aged 1 year and 3 months.
6. PRISCILLA, b. Oct. 1799 ; m. Aaron Parker, of Boxford ; 6 children.
7. ZELINDA, b. 1801 ; d. Dec. 1821, aged 20.
8. ANN SEATON, b. Aug. 1803 ; m. John Robinson ; d. 1851 (7), at Concord, N. H.
9. WILLIAM ALFRED,
10. ELIZA ELMA, } b. Aug. 1807 ; William A. settled on his father's place in Antrim ; m. Betsy Ann McMasters, and d. 1850, aged 43. Two of his sons, (1) THOMAS ALFRED and (2) ISAAC, were in the late war, and both d. in service, the latter being a musician with his uncle, Isaac J. Eliza E., d. May, 1808. aged 9 mos.
11. ELIZA MESSER, b. Aug. 1809 ; m. Thomas Thompson ; resides in Antrim ; 2 children.
12. ISAAC JAMES, b. July, 1811. Enlisted as leader of a band in one of the New York regiments for the late war of the rebellion, and d. of yellow fever in Florida.

119. JAMES, b. Nov. 25, 1765. Left an infant at the death of his mother ; he was adopted by his uncle, John Runnels [22], and inherited from him the ancestral farm, on which he lived till 1815. He then moved to Andover, and there d. 1856, aged 91. He m. Sarah Pearl, of Boxford, 1793. Children : —
1. SALLY (Buswell), b. 1794 ; d. 1820, aged 26.
2. ELIZA, b. 1796 ; d. 1819, aged 23.
3. ASCENATH, b. 1798 ; d. 1832, aged 34.
4. JOHN RUNNELS, b. Dec. 18, 1800 ; now residing in Bradford, having m. Harriet H. Payson, of Pembroke, N. H., July, 1827, who was b. June 17, 1807. Children : (1.) CHARLES ELLIOT, b. May 20, 1830, in Bradford, and there d. Mar. 1, 1851, aged 21. (2.) JAMES EUSTACE, b. Jan. 17, 1834. in Pembroke, N. H. ; was a shoe merchant in Martha's Vineyard ; enlisted in the 3d Mass. Regiment, 1861 ; served six months in North Carolina, was sick of consumption, and d. at Bradford, Sept. 16, 1865, aged 31. He m. Julia A. M. Gibbs, of Middleboro', 1861(2), who was b. Aug. 15, 1839, and d. Nov. 28, 1867, aged 28.

5. BENJAMIN PEARL, b. Jan. 1803; a shoe manufacturer; residing in Haverhill; 3 sons and 1 daughter.
6. CHARLES SPOFFORD, b. 1805; a Congregational clergyman, formerly settled in West Fairlee, Vt.; removed to Chicago, Ill., about 1856, and there d. soon after; m. Caroline Martin; 4 daughters.
7. FIDELIA, b. 1807; residing in Boston.
8. MARIANNE, b. 1809; m. Stephen Drew, of New Haven, Ct.; 1 son and 1 daughter.
9. JAMES OTIS, b. 1811; a broker in Boston; resides in Wakefield; 1 daughter.
10. EMILY, b. 1813; m. James Callaham, stone-cutter, of Andover; 5 children.

120. THOMAS[3] [25] (Job[2], Samuel[1]), m. " his wife Phebe," in Bradford, about 1763. "Thomas Runnels owned covenant, but came not to the Lord's table, Nov. 18, 1764." This seems to have been in order to have his first child baptized. As the birth of his second daughter is taken from the Methuen Records, we infer that he had moved to that town *prior* to 1771. He there lived till *after* " March 3, 1777," as under that date we have (Rockingham deeds), " I. Young, conveying land in Salem, N. H., to Thomas Runnels, of *Methuen*." He had removed to Salem, " Mar. 21, 1781," as we then find " Edward Patee" deeding " land to Thomas R. of *Salem* "; and that he was *living* and still owning land in Methuen as late as 1785, is implied in one of the deeds of William [74].

Nothing further can be ascertained respecting him or his daughters. It is presumed that they left no families; hence, in the want of sons, *his* branch, as well as his father's, in the Runnels name, becomes extinct. Children : —

121. " MEHITEBALL," b. Oct. 28, 1764, in Bradford; bap. "Nov. 18, 1764" (Ch. Recs.).
122. PHEBE, b. Feb. 26, 1771, in Methuen, called "a dau. of Thomas and Phebe," like her sister.

123. BENJAMIN[3] [46] (Ebenezer[2], Samuel[1]), having learned the blacksmith's trade of his father, and m. Hephzibah (or "Hipsey") Bradley, of Haverhill, in 1768, he emigrated the next year to the " District of Maine," and first settled at Pondleborough, on the Kennebec. Removing up the river two or three years later, he was among the first settlers of what is now Augusta, then a wilderness, and is said to have owned one hundred acres on the site of the present city, which he afterwards sold for two dollars per acre! While there he was drafted into the revolutionary army about 1776, and remained " not more than two years." Served as a blacksmith with the army in New York, and was employed in forging the chain which was thrown across the Hudson to keep British ships from going up the river. Meanwhile his family remained at Augusta (the Indian Cushnoe), greatly annoyed by their savage neighbors. On one occasion, *seven* Indians came to their house, ransacked it, and spent the night, to the terror of his wife and children. She always said her life was spared only by the resolute intervention of a squaw, who was one of the company, in her behalf. Preferring

the country about Ticonic Falls, farther up the river, he moved thither for his final settlement, 1778. Added to his trade the business of a lumberman and speculator. Erected the first framed house on the site of Waterville village, and about the year 1793, built a small vessel, — claimed to be the first launched on the upper Kennebec, — and run it to Augusta, twenty miles, before being rigged. He also built the first mill in Waterville. and, subsequently, the first at Pittsfield, up the Sebasticook. Was the first representative from the combined towns of Waterville and Winslow to Boston, and became the possessor of so much land in Winslow, where he lived. as to obtain the sobriquet of "King Runnels." But he was afterwards much reduced in property by the failure of one Shepard, an English contractor, — after whom Shepard's wharf, in Hallowell, is named, — and by other misfortunes, especially by losing a contract of his own for furnishing masts to be sent to England. The timbers were cut too short, in attempting to lade them upon the short vessels sent to transport them. With his affairs in a very unsettled state, he d. suddenly, of apoplexy, in Winslow, June 22, 1802, aged 54. His wife had d. Dec. 25, 1798. The beautiful spot selected by her for a family burial-place, on the east bank of the Kennebec, a mile or two above Waterville, is now neglected and almost forgotten ; the gravestones are crumbling to dust, and a thrifty young cedar is drawing its nourishment from the ashes of the departed ; while the majestic river, still flowing near at hand, and roaring from the distance, as of old, serves only to intensify the reflection, so readily suggested, that of all *human* works and devices upon earth, " there is none abiding." Children :

124. JAMES [376], b. Jan. 1769, in Haverhill, Mass.
125. MARY [380], b. May, 1770, in Pondleborough, Me.
126. JOHN [388], b. Nov. 19, 1771 (gravestone), in Pondleborough.
127. BENJAMIN [395], b. Apr. 1773, in Augusta, Me. (as since named).
128. STEPHEN [401], b. Feb. 1775, in Augusta.
129. RUTH [404], b. Dec. 1776, in Augusta.
130. ABIGAIL [414], b. March 4, 1778, in Winslow.
131. RACHEL [423], b. March 24, 1782, in Winslow.
132. DAVID [433], b. Oct. 5, 1783, in Winslow.

133. EBENEZER[3] [47] (Ebenezer[2], Samuel[1]). He "followed the sea and d. in the West Indies, July, 1774," aged 24. Had m. and "left two children in this country," who were living, according to their grandfather's will, in Feb. 1795, but are supposed soon after to have died without issue.

134. EBENEZER, b. about 1771.
135. ABIGAIL, b. about 1773 ; is said to have m. and lived in Chester, N. H.

136. STEPHEN[3] [49] (Ebenezer[2], Samuel[1]), was enrolled, according to the " History of Haverhill, Mass.," p. 382, among the " Minit men, trained in Capt. Jas. Sawyer's Co., by voat of the town, Mar. and April, 1775 " ; also in the " List of eight months' service men, raised immediately after the battle of Lexington, 1st Co.," ninety-four in all, thus early commencing his Revolutionary

career. Afterwards, his name appears, p. 391, among "those who lost guns at the battle of Bunker Hill, from Haverhill," twenty-one in number, — an evidence of hard fighting. Also, "Drafted for the Continental service, in 1775-6," p. 393. His brother, Nathaniel S. [56], used to say he was "six years in the revolutionary war, a sergeant, and present at the surrender of Burgoyne." Others make his time as a soldier but three or four years. In the New-Hampshire Provincial Records we have "Corporal Stephen Runnels, belonging to the Continental army," to whom the "Treasurer is ordered to pay 40 shillings discount out of the taxes to be accounted for, out of his depreciation, Feb. 13, 1783." Hardly intelligible; but the *date* favors the longer term of service. He was a blacksmith, like his father, and by reason of the latter's investment in Hollis, N. H., he changed his residence to that place in 1777, where also he became affianced to Chloe, dau. of Moses Thurston. Afterwards, when absent as a New-Hampshire soldier, he was accustomed to send *to her* his wages, which she faithfully kept in her possession, intending to purchase her marriage outfit with the money. As the currency was depreciating, and likely soon to be worthless, she was advised by a friend, at one time, to lay it out in rye; but she listened to no such suggestion, and when at last she came to "buy her furniture," was obliged to pay "$7 for a white cream pitcher," and for other things in like proportion! Having m., as proposed, in 1782, they followed their brother-in-law — the Rev. Stephen Fuller, who m. Phebe Thurston — to Vershire, Vt. (1789), where he d. suddenly, July 22, 1798, aged 44. "He had a loving disposition and great muscular powers." She afterwards moved to Fletcher, Vt., but finally settled on the wild lands owned by her husband, in Topsham, Vt , and there d. Dec. 13, 1807, aged 49. The five oldest children b. in Hollis; the others in Vershire.

137. STEPHEN, b. 1783; d., by scalding, at the age of 13 months.
138. MARY CROCKER [445], b. Aug. 4, 1784.
139. STEPHEN [458], b. Sept. 1, 1785 (Hollis Recs.), 1786 (Family Recs.), yet "13 months younger than Mary."
140. CHLOE, } b. Dec. 10, 1787 (Hollis), 1788 (Family).
141. HANNAH, }
      Chloe d. Aug. 29, 1804, at Fletcher, Vt.; Hannah d. 1808, at Topsham, Vt.
142. MOSES THURSTON [472], b. Mar. 5, 1790, at his uncle Fuller's, in Vershire.
143. SARAH [475], b. June 14, 1793.
144. SOLLIS [489], } b. April 5, 1797.
145. SEWALL [500], }
      Named after their two grandmothers, — the one being a Sollis, the other a Sewall, before marriage.

146. MOLLY (Mary)[3] [51] (Ebenezer[2], Samuel[1]), was m. to William Ayer, of Haverhill, June 9, 1778, at Hollis, N. H., by Rev. Daniel Emerson. He was b. Oct. 1753, in Haverhill; was a soldier in the Revolution, and lived as a farmer in Bow, Concord, Hillsboro', and finally, Fishersfield (now Newbury), N. H., where and in which vicinity many of their descendants remain. He d.

June 6, 1827, aged 74 ; and she d. Apr. 22, 1842, aged 84, both in Newbury. Children : —

147.   WILLIAM (Ayer), b. Mar. 2, 1779, in Hollis; a farmer, Bradford and Hillsborough, N. H.; m., 1st, Abigail Eaton, of B.; m., 2d, Mehetabel Gay, of H., and d. 1870, aged 91.   Children : —
1.   HANNAH, b. Aug. 22, 1805; m. John Robbins, Aug. 4, 1824; d. July 29, 1858, aged 53.
2.   DELIA, b. Aug. 3, 1807; m. Hiram Monroe, May 17, 1850. Hillsborough.
3.   MARY R., b. May 17, 1811; m. Leonard West, May 8, 1834. Bradford Centre.
4.   CAROLINE S., b. Aug. 13, 1816; m. William J. Murdough, July 17, 1838. Bradford Centre.
5.   ROENA F., b. Dec. 22, 1818; m. Elisha H. Eaton, Mar. 17, 1840.
148.   JOHN, b. June 4, 1780, in Bow; a farmer; m. Annis Brockway; d. March 9, 1819, at Bradford, aged 39.   She d. 1872. Children : —
1.   JAMES, b. Feb. 8, 1804 (3). Res. Danvers, Mass.
2.   WILLIAM, b. Mar. 29, 1806. Res. Hillsborough.
3.   JOHN HODGMAN, b. Oct. 1809; d. Mar. 1813, aged 4 years 5 mos.
149.   MARY (Polly), b. Feb. 8, 1782, in Concord; m. Humphrey Jackman, and settled in Abbotsford, C. E. She d. Dec. 1861, in her 80th year. Nine children, of whom the six following — three sons and three daughters — are still living.
1.   GILMAN (Jackman).   2. ELMOND.   3. HUMPHREY.   4. ELIZA.   5. CLARISSA.   6. LAVINIA.
150.   BETSY, b. Nov. 17, 1783, in Concord; m. Moses Boynton; lived in Thornton, N. H., and d. Aug. 21, 1867, aged 84. 11 children :—
1.   HAZEN (Boynton), d.   2. WILLIAM.   3. BETSY.   4. MOSES.   5. SAMUEL.   6. NANCY, d.   7. NATHANIEL.   8. CLARISSA, d.   9. ELEAZER, d., and two others, who d. young.
151.   JAMES, b. May 12, 1788, in Concord; a farmer, residing, first, in Fishersfield, till 1814; afterwards, in Washington, N. H., where he d. Mar. 29, 1863, aged 75. He m., 1st, Lucy Brockway, Feb. 19, 1811; m., 2d, Mary Harriman, June 5, 1833. All his children by 1st wife, and the two oldest, b. in Fishersfield. The whole number of his grandchildren, 1870, were 18; then living, 16. Whole number of his great-grandchildren, 6. Children : —
1.   LEONARD, b. Oct. 3, 1811.
2.   HAZEN, b. June 5, 1813.
3.   LUCY, b. June 22, 1815.
4.   MATILDA, b. July 13, 1817.
5.   SIMON, b. May 4, 1819; m. Hannah N. Gilman, of Gilmanton, N. H., Nov. 13, 1845. She d. May 13, 1872.
6.   MARY B., b. Apr. 7, 1821; m. Simeon D. Glidden, now of Manchester, N. H.
7.   ROXANA P., b. Aug. 8, 1823.
8.   HARRIET, b. June 18, 1825; d. Oct. 20, 1866.
9.   JONATHAN B., b. Sept. 23, 1827; d. June 19, 1863.
10.   CYRUS, b. Dec. 20, 1829.
11.   JOHN ALVIN, b. Aug. 1, 1832.
152.   MOSES, b. Feb. 8, 1790, in Concord; m Abigail Proctor, Feb. 18, 1810. She was b. June 3, 1787, in Washington, N. H. Places of residence various, as appears from their children's births. He d. July 19, 1868, in Putney, Vt., aged 78. Children : —
1.   ELMOND, b. June 22, 1812, in Washington; a farmer, Putney, Vt.
2.   MARY, b. April 26, 1814, in Newbury; m. Daniel Farnsworth, Aug. 9, 1849, in Langdon, N. H. He was b. Jan. 23, 1813, in Washington; a farmer, now residing in Claremont, N. H. Children all b. in Washington, N. H. (1.) LUCY M. (Farns-

worth), b. Apr. 14, 1851; d. Mar. 3, 1854, in her 3d year. (2.) ADDIE, b. Mar. 11, 1853. (3.) VERONA, b. May 4, 1854.

3. LOUISA, b. Apr. 27, 1816, in Newbury; m. to Otis G. Watkins, by Rev. Moses Adams, Apr. 6, 1847, at her father's, in Rockingham, Vt. He was b. Dec. 31. 1817, in Chester, Vt.; after marriage, a farmer in Springfield, Vt., till 1850, when they moved to Baraboo, Sauk Co., Wis., and there still reside. Children: (1.) GEORGE R. (Watkins), b. Jan. 13, 1848, in Springfield Enlisted Feb. 6, 1865, in Co. E, 49th regiment Wisconsin volunteers; discharged June 26, 1865, at St. Louis, Mo. (2.) ALBERT E., b. Aug. 17, 1849, in Springfield. (3.) ELIZA ANN, b. Dec. 15, 1851, in Baraboo, Wis., as were the remaining children. (4.) OLON AYER, b. Mar. 27, 1853. (5.) LUCY VIOLA, b. Mar. 19, 1854. (6.) MARY ELDORA, b. Jan. 24, 1856. (7.) ORICK WILLIAM, (8.) OTIS GOULD, Jr., twins, b. Feb. 2, 1860; Otis d. Aug. 3, 1860. (9.) EMMA JANE, b. Nov. 18, 1861.

4. MOSES, Jr., b. July 8, 1817, in Washington, N. H.; a farmer, Putney, Vt.

5. WILLIAM P., b. Dec. 27, 1818, in Washington; a farmer, Putney, Vt.; m. Mrs. Elizabeth S. (Johnson) McMullen, Feb. 25, 1867. She was b. June 23, 1830, in Putney. Children: (1.) ANDREW J., b. Dec. 14, 1867. (2.) WILLIE E., b. Dec. 25, 1869.

6. NANCY, b. June 5, 1821, in Springfield, Vt.; m. Erastus T. Corser, farmer, of Chester, Vt., Aug. 14, 1850. He was b. Jan. 26, 1812, in Compton, C. E. She (1st wife) d. Sept. 24, 1854, in Chester, aged 33, leaving (1.) MARIA N. (Corser), b. Oct. 10, 1851.

7. GEORGE WASHINGTON, b. Sept. 28, 1822, in Springfield; d. Dec. 19, 1870, in Putney, aged 48.

8. ROYAL, b. Mar. 27, 1824, in Rockingham, Vt.; a farmer; m. Nancy Jackson, of Abington, Mass., Nov. 9, 1848; settled in Fairfield, Sauk Co., Wis., in 1855, soon after the organization of the town, in which he has served four years as town treasurer and assessor, and is at present (1872) chairman of the board of town supervisors; also, one of the county supervisors. Enlisted Feb. 7, 1865, Co. E, 49th regiment Wisconsin volunteer infantry; discharged with the regiment, Nov. 14, 1865. Children: (1.) LUCY A., b. Oct. 13, 1849, in Abington, Mass.; d. Jan. 22, 1863, at Fairfield, Wis., in her 14th year. (2.) ABBIE E., b. May 4, 1852, in Rockingham, Vt.; a school-teacher. (3.) CARRIE F., b. Jan. 30, 1857, in Fairfield, Wis. (4.) ELLA VESTA, b. May 19, 1859. (5.) CHARLES J., b. Nov. 23, 1861.

9. MARTHA M., b. May 15, 1825, in Rockingham; m. George W. Barnes, farmer, of Hillsboro', N. H., Nov. 19, 1851. Present residence, Fairfield, Wis. Child: (1.) GEORGE (Barnes), b. Feb. 20, 1862, in Fairfield.

10. JOHN Q., b. Oct. 31, 1826, in Rockingham, Vt., and there d. Apr. 29, 1828, in his 2d year.

11. ALEXANDER A., b. July 4, 1828; d. May 3, 1829, in Rockingham, aged 10 mos.

12. ABBY A., b. Sept. 16, 1829, in Rockingham; m. William R. Glover, farmer, of Baraboo, Wis., Apr. 23, 1853. Children: (1.) IRA F. (Glover), b. Aug. 30, 1854, in Baraboo. (2.) JANET, b. Sept. 26, 1859, in Greenfield, Wis., and there d. Sept. 10, 1864, aged 5.

13. LUCY, b. Apr. 26, 1832, in Grafton, Vt.; m. Erastus T. Corser, 2d wife, now of Dummerston, Vt., June 21, 1855. Children: (1.) FRANK E. (Corser), b. Mar. 31, 1857, in Chester, Vt.; d. Jan. 20, 1862, in Bartonsville (Rockingham), Vt., in his 5th year. (2.) ALFRED, b. Jan. 29; d. Dec. 22, 1861, in Bartonsville. (3.) ADELBERT M., b. June 30, 1863, in Bartonsville.

(4.) GEORGE E., b. July 8, 1865, in Bartonsville. (5.) MARY E., b. July 5, 1868, in Dummerston.

153. SARAH, b. Nov. 25, 1791, in Hillsborough; m., 1st, Enoch Howlitt, of Hillsboro'; m., 2d, Zabina Colburn. Child: —

1. ZERAH (Colburn), b. Jan. 13, 1832, in Saratoga, N. Y. He was named after his uncle, the celebrated arithmetician. His father d. a few years after his birth, and his mother returned to Hillsborough, N. H., where, during his boyhood, he earned his living on a farm, proving himself an insatiable reader, but enjoying no means for an early education besides a few months' attendance at a district school, and a short clerkship in a factory. He first entered a machine shop in Lowell, Mass., April. 1846; but "his professional career commenced on the Concord railroad, under the late Charles Minot, then its manager, who was attracted by the brightness and practical ideas of this singular youth. In a few months he had mastered the anatomy and physiology of the locomotive engine, tabulated the dimensions and proportions of those under his observation, and published a small, but excellent and still useful. treatise on the subject." The locomotive was ever after his chief study. Was superintendent of the works of Mr. Souther, in Boston, — for a few months of the Tredegar Works, at Richmond, Va., and for a year, or more, of the New Jersey locomotive works at Paterson, N. J., "during which engagement he made some improvements, still standard, in the machinery of freight engines." But he "early found that the *literature* of engineering was his true calling." His writings were various in scope, and vigorous in practical treatment. "On the locomotive, the steam-engine and boiler at large, steam navigation, bridges, railway works and mechanical engineering in general, he became a first-rate authority. His thoroughly practical education in the workshop, his extended observation of engineering works, his intimate acquaintance with professional literature, his remarkable quickness of comprehension, his more remarkable memory, and his mechanical talent and inborn engineering ideas, combined to give him a distinction that no engineer in the world will deny him, — the best general writer in his profession." In 1854. he started in New York the "Railroad Advocate," which he afterwards enlarged and entitled the "American Engineer." He was commissioned, with his associate, Mr. A. L. Holley, by several railroad presidents, in the autumn of 1857, to visit Europe, and report upon the systems of railway management in use there. In 1858, he returned to London, began to write for the "Engineer," and soon became its editor. In addition to his editorial labors, he wrote several pamphlets on boiler explosions, heat, etc.. the originality of which attracted great attention. He received two medals for papers before the "Institution of Civil Engineers," one on "Iron Bridges," the other on "American Locomotives and Rolling Stock." He also served one year as president of the "Society of Civil Engineers." But the high tension which he always maintained upon his mental powers too early destroyed the balance of his over-wrought brain, and he d. soon after his last arrival in this country, April 20, 1870, aged 38, under a cloud of temporary insanity, having accomplished more than most men in thrice as many years of active life. Had he early received the advantages of a systematic and liberal education, it might have proved difficult to prescribe the limits to his usefulness or his fame. Extraordinary instances of his powers of memory are related. He could state *exactly* the height of the summit of every railway

of which reports had ever reached his eye, together with their leading gradients and other material features. He was highly esteemed for his social traits, his amiability and kindness. While residing in London, he delighted to bestow valuable attention upon American engineers visiting England, by whom his memory is cherished with affection. He was m. and left one child, (1.) SARAH, now living with her mother in New York. (The above is an abstract of *two* published sketches of his life; one of which, from the pen of Mr. Holley, appeared in the "New York Times" of May 2, and the "Scientific American" of May 14, 1870.)

154. CLARISSA, b. May 30, 1793. in Hillsborough; m. Benjamin Nichols, farmer, of Bradford, N. H., Nov. 1811. He d. Aug. 11, 1851. Children : —

1. JOSEPH (Nichols), b. April 20, 1813; d. Sept. 3, 1854, aged 41.
2. NANCY AYER, b. Apr. 5, 1815; m. William Dunfield, 1837. He was b. in New Brunswick; was the runner of a saw-mill, in Hillsboro', fifteen years; enlisted, at the age of 51, in Co. A, 7th regiment N. H. volunteers; served one year, and a half; was discharged on account of ill health, and d. June 7, 1871, in Newbury. Children: (1.) WILLIAM N. (Dunfield), b. Jan. 19, 1838, in Bradford; a carpenter; m. Laura E. Garfield, May, 1861; enlisted in Co. H, 16th N. H. volunteers, Sept. 1862, and d. of disease in New Orleans, La., June, 1863, aged 25, leaving, I. WILLIE C., b. Aug. 15. 1862. (2.) GEORGE T., b. June 3, 1840, in Washington, N. H.; a farmer; m. Sarah L. Robbins, of Bradford, N. H., Mar. 1861. Enlisted in Co. B, N. H. 16th regiment, Sept. 1862; served out his time, and now lives in Bradford. Children: I. CARRIE E., b. Dec. 10, 1861. II. LIZZIE E., b. Apr. 15, 1867; d. Mar. 4, 1871, in her 4th year. (3.) LIZZETTE L. (adopted child), b. Sept. 9, 1848; d. July 4, 1858, in her 10th year.
3. HUBBARD NEWTON (Nichols), b. Nov. 10, 1816; a farmer in Bradford; m. Mary Ayer [155, 3], Apr 2, 1840. Children: (1.) CALISTA, b. Apr. 12, 1841; m. Francis Smith, of Bradford. Child: I. MARY (Smith), b. July, 1867. (2.) BENJAMIN, b. Sept. 8, 1842; m. Jane Dole, of Claremont; resides in Missouri; 1 child. (3.) HENRY H., b. Apr. 21, 1844. (4.) WILLIAM A., b. Nov. 6, 1845. (5.) MARY A., b. Mar. 21, 1847; d. June 2, 1849, aged 2. (6.) SORANUS G., b. June 6, 1848; d. Apr. 9, 1851, in his 3d year. (7.) CHARLES N., b. May 1, 1850. (8.) GEORGE, b. May 18, 1852. (9.) FRANK, b. Aug. 22, 1854; d. Apr. 14, 1855, aged 8 mos. (10.) ALILIAN, b. July 24, 1858. (11.) NELLIE, b. Apr. 3, 1860. (12.) JEFFERSON D., b. June 18, 1862. (13.) SILAS D., b. Sept. 21, 1865; d. Mar. 30, 1871, in his 6th year.
4. HIRAM (Nichols), b. Sept. 12, 1818. Learned the stone trade in Virginia and Quincy, Mass.; m. Harriet Brockway, of Hillsborough, Apr. 4, 1843, and settled as a farmer and stoneworker in Bradford, one mile from his father's. Aug. 1, 1870, he was thrown from a mowing machine, and his right hand and wrist were so badly injured that amputation was necessary. Is still enabled to prosecute his work by the use of artificial means. Children: (1.) JOHN O., b. Dec. 28, 1846. (2.) HATTIE E., b. July 28, 1851. (3.) GEORGE H., b. Oct. 20, 1854. (4.) ETTA F., b. Dec. 27, 1856. (5.) CLARA J., b. Nov. 14, 1861
5. MARY (Nichols), b. Aug. 16, 1820; m. Henry D. Nichols, Aug. 7, 1844, at Bellows Falls, Vt. He was b. July 22, 1823; a workman in an iron foundry; death occasioned by the falling of a tree at Hillsborough, Feb. 9, 1858, in his 35th year. Children: (1.) EUGENE S., b. Feb. 28, 1846, in Keene, N. H.; m.

Clara J. Reed, of Winchendon, Mass., Apr. 14, 1867; resides in W.; workman in iron foundry. (2.) GEORGE A., b. May 25, 1849, in Keene. (3.) CLARA J., b. Aug. 18, 1853, in Hillsborough. (4.) HENRY B , b. Aug. 10, 1855, in H.

6.   CLARISSA (Nichols), b. Apr. 16, 1822; m. Jacob C Bailey. carpenter, Nov. 28, 1845; residence in Bradford Village, N. H. Children: (1.) HERMAN ALONZO (Bailey), b. Sept. 19, 1847. (2.) CYRUS NICHOLS, b. Jan. 16, 1853. (3.) ELVA JULIA, (4.) EVA JANE, twins, b. Feb. 26, 1855; Eva J. d. Apr. 1857, aged 2. (5.) WILLIS NEWTON, b. Sept. 9, 1866.

7.   EDWIN (Nichols), b. June 22, 1824; a farmer, retaining his father's homestead in Bradford; m. Almira Stuart. June 3, 1847. She was called to suffer the amputation of her foot, Nov. 3, 1871, as the final result of a sprain some four years previously. Children: (1.) ELLA F., b. June 23, 1848. (2.) EMMA J., b. Sept. 27, 1849. (3.) NANCY M., b. Jan. 29, 1850. (4.) LUCY A., b. July 25, 1853. (5.) ALICE J., b. Dec. 30, 1854. (6.) LOREN E., b. June 1, 1856. (7.) GILMAN S., b. Feb. 27, 1864. (8.) MINNIE K., b. Feb. 20. 1867.

8.   ELIZA (Nichols), b. Feb. 13, 1826; m. Samuel Bates, carpenter, of Bradford Village, Nov. 2, 1848. Children: (1.) BYRON (Bates), b. June 15, 1851. (2.) CLARABEL, b. Aug. 28, 1868.

9.   JULIA (Nichols), b. July 10, 1828; resides in Bradford.

10.   SARAH J., b. Oct. 15, 1830; m. Samuel W. Colby, of Warner, N. H., farmer, Aug. 21. 1866.

155.   BENJAMIN, b. Jan. 15, 1795, in Hillsboro', N. H.; settled as a farmer on his father's place in Newbury (where he still resides), having m. Sally McCrellis, of Goshen, N. H. Children: —

1.   JOHN, b. Nov. 5, 1819; m. Miss J. T. Gillingham, Nov. 30, 1843; a carpenter, Claremont, N. H.

2.   HANNAH, b. Feb. 17, 1821; m. J. Peabody Bly, Oct. 26, 1843; Newbury, N. H.

3.   MARY, b. May 11, 1822. See [154, 3].

4.   ANN CAROLINE, b. Nov. 13, 1823; d. July 30. 1824, aged 8 mos.

5.   ANN CAROLINE, b. Dec. 25, 1824; m. Jona. W. Buswell, May 31, 1849; New London, N. H.

6.   HENRIETTA, b. Sept. 25, 1826; m. Henry Fisher Stowell, farmer, of Washington, Feb. 20, 1850; residence, first, Unity; now Claremont, N. H. He was b. May 14, 1826, in Lempster. Children b. in Claremont. (1.) BENJAMIN FRANK (Stowell), b. Sept. 5, 1851. (2.) ELGIN WARE, b. Mar. 26, 1854. (3.) ANNIE GRACIA, b. Nov. 3, 1864.

7.   ALMA ANN, b. Feb. 6, 1828; m., 1st, Frederick Brackett, Mar. 12, 1846; m., 2d, Abner Stowell, Sutton, N. H.

8.   WILLIAM, b. Mar. 19, 1829; m. E. A. Bailey, Nov. 30, 1854; a farmer in Newbury, on the homestead.

9.   ADALAIDE, b. Oct. 18, 1830; m. Daniel W. Barney, Mar. 26, 1850; resides in Illinois.

10.   ALMEDIA, b. June 20, 1832; d. Aug. 28, 1835, aged 3.

11.   ADALIZA, b. Oct. 30, 1833; d. Mar. 14, 1835, in her 2d year.

12.   BENJAMIN FRANKLIN, b. Sept. 22, 1835; m S. P. Bailey, Mar. 31, 1857; a farmer, residing in Unity, N. H.

13.   SALLY BANDEN, b. Sept. 29, 1837; m. Ezekiel F. Barnard, Nov. 26, 1859; Newbury.

14.   ADDISON, b. May 28, 1839; m. Sarah A. Barnard, Aug. 15, 1863, in Bradford; now residing at Sutton Mills, N. H. She was b. Oct. 8, 1841. Children: (1.) ELTON, b. Aug. 5, 1864. in Washington. (2.) LOREN, b. Sept. 7, 1866, in Sutton. (3.) ANNIE, b. Aug. 1, 1868. (4.) SHERMAN, b. May 30, 1870.

15.   ZEROIDA, b. Mar. 21, 1841; m. Daniel G. Peaslee, Mar. 11, 1863; Bradford.

16. LA FAYETTE, b. Dec. 1, 1844.
156. NANCY, b. July 30, 1798, in Hillsboro'; m., 1st, Jouathan Brockway; m., 2d, Thomas Spalding, of Newbury, and d. Nov. 10,
1868, aged 70.
157. SAMUEL, b. May 15, 1800, in Newbury, and there d. Aug. 30, 1803,
aged 3 years 3½ months.

158. ABIGAIL³ [52] (Ebenezer², Samuel¹), m. Benjamin Haggett, of Bradford, Mass., June 30, 1785, and d. about 1823, aged
63. Children : —

159. LYDIA (Haggett), b. about 1789; m. James Pevere (1st wife), 1810,
and d. soon after.
160. POLLY, b. 1793; m. James Pevere (2d wife), 1815, and d. of consumption.
161. EBENEZER, b. 1796; was a hack-driver in New York city when
last heard from.
162. HANNAH, b. 1800; d. about 1830, in Bradford.

163. SAMUEL³ [54] (Ebenezer², Samuel¹), received from his
father's estate the farm in the south part of Hollis, N. H., which
the latter had purchased in 1777 ; also the mill site on Nashua
river, where he built the saw and grist mills (two runs of stones),
since known as " Runnels' Mills," near the so-called " Runnels'
Bridge." He also added a carding mill, which was carried on by
his sons. These mills were sold to the Nashua Manufacturing Co.,
Aug. 1865, shortly before the death of his son Ebenezer. He
scrupulously fulfilled the terms of his father's will relative to his
mother, paying her regular annual visits till her death in 1814.
He m. Abigail Smith, of Nottingham, Sept. 20, 1791, at Hollis.
She was b. Jan. 29, 1768. He d. June 5, 1834, aged 67, in Hollis,
and the following appears on his gravestone : —

" Sickness sore, long time he bore,
Physicians were in vain ;
Till death did seize, and God did please,
To ease him of his pain."

She d. Dec. 30, 1848, aged 81, and her gravestone bears this
inscription (Hollis cemetery) : —

" How wide the torrent rolls
That bears us to the tomb !
Which ends our toils and sorrows here,
And bears our spirits home."

Children, b. in Hollis : —

164. FREDERICK [503], b. June 28, 1792.
165. EBENEZER [511], b. July 8, 1794.
166. HANNAH, b. July 27, 1796; d. Mar. 18, 1836, in her 40th year.
167. PERSIS, b. Aug. 29, 1798; m. Horace Whitney, Nov. 1835; lived in
Nashua, and d. at her father's, in Hollis, July 2, 1842, aged 44.
168. BETHIA [518], b. Dec. 1, 1800.
169. SUSAN [525], b. Jan. 29, 1803.
170. SAMUEL, b. June 22, 1805; d. July 27, 1806, aged 13 months.

171. THOMAS[3] [55] (Ebenezer[2], Samuel[1]), inherited most of his father's property in Haverhill, and successfully continued the same business there for many years. Was m. to Lucy Lapham, of Bradford, Sept. (Aug.) 9, 1792. He d. Oct. 30, 1846, in his 78th year; and she d. Dec. 28 (29, gravestone), 1859, at the advanced age of 91 years 10 mos. 9 days. Their children were all b. in Haverhill: —

172. SOPHIA, b. Apr. 11, 1794; d. Mar. 12 (11), 1815, aged 21.
173. JOHN [529], b. May 7, 1796.
174. BETSY [533], b. Mar. 12, 1798 (called "Elizabeth" on the Town Records).
175. LOUISA [540], b. Apr. 25, 1800, (Town Records give "Oisa, b. May 10")
176. KING LAPHAM [552], b. Mar. 20, 1802.
177. WARREN [559], b. Feb. 10, 1804. (At first "Ebenezer" on the Town Records, and "altered by desire of Mrs. R., Apr. 9. 1804.")
178. MOSES CLEMENT [565], b. Nov. 20, 1805.
179. MARY, b. Nov. 1, 1807; m. Simon Pearson, of Byfield, Nov. 1828; d. Mar. 31, 1831, in her 24th year.

180. NATHANIEL STEVENS[3] [56] (Ebenezer[2], Samuel[1]), followed the natural current of emigration from Haverhill, Mass., to Haverhill, N. H., where he m. Polly Merrill, Dec. 1, 1796. Moved back to Haverhill, Mass., in 1804, but returned in 1806, and finally settled in Piermont, N. H., in 1818. Here he lived, as a farmer, greatly beloved and respected, and d. Aug. 24, 1857, aged 86. She d. Oct. 6, 1838. Children b. in Haverhill, N. H., except the two youngest: —

181. MIRA [570], b. Sept. 12, 1797.
182. HARRIET [577], b. Mar. 6, 1799.
183. EBENEZER [582], b. Dec. 17, 1800.
184. SALLY HAZEN; b. Nov. 24, 1802; d. Dec. 28, 1823, aged 21.
185. ARTHUR [589], b. Nov. 26, 1806.
186. MARY MERRILL [592], b. Jan. 29, 1809.
187. HANNAH SMITH, b. June 6, 1811.
188. BARTLETT [601], b. July 18, 1813.
189. GEORGE [604], b. Aug. 17, 1815.
190. CHARLES SWAN, b. June 15, 1818, in Piermont; d. by drowning in Connecticut river, July 18, 1830, aged 12.
191. HAZEN [616], b. Sept. 13, 1820, in Piermont.

192. DANIEL[3] [58] (Ebenezer[2], Samuel[1]), continued the business of a blacksmith at Haverhill, Mass., with his brother Thomas, but a short time after their father's death (see his will), when he moved to Warner, N. H., and there settled for life, following the same trade, and retaining the "Runels" orthography. He m., 1st, Chloe George, in the summer of 1799, the couple standing, as its prospective occupants, on the sills or sleepers of the newly-framed *house*, in which they afterwards lived together till her death, May 23, 1829, aged 50. She was b. Jan. 14, 1779, in Hopkinton, N. H. He was m., 2d, to Mary Bailey, of Newbury, Vt., by Rev. G. W. Campbell, Oct. 4, 1831, and d. Dec. 21, 1838, aged 63. Children by first wife, and all b. in Warner: —

193. DANIEL GEORGE [618], b. Jan 8, 1801.
194. HANNAH, b. Sept. 17, 1802; d. Apr. 10, 1834, in her 32d year.
195. SALLY, b. Aug. 24, 1810; d. Nov. 1, 1828, aged 18.
196. CHARLES. b. May 23, 1817; d. at Burlington, Ia., July 19, 1838, aged 21.
197. GEORGE [625], b. Feb. 3, 1823.

198. EBENEZER[3] [59] (Ebenezer[2], Samuel[1]), was m. to Hannah Lane, of Newburyport, by Rev. John Giles, Sept. 22, 1808 (Town Records). She lived with her mother at Newburyport, while he was absent as a sea-captain. He was taken by the British during the war of 1812-15, with his vessel, crew, and cargo; was imprisoned in England, and afterwards heard of in the State of Georgia, though never seen by his friends. Children: —

199. ALMIRA, b. June 18, 1809, in Newburyport (Town Records). Was insane, and d. at Haverhill.
200. EBENEZER, b. 1811; d. in infancy at Haverhill.

201. HANNAH[3] [61] (Ebenezer[2], Samuel[1]); m., 1st, Benjamin Cole, of Haverhill, Mar. 9, 1806. He was "drowned with five other persons in Merrimack river when returning from Newburyport," May 24, 1807, aged 25. Hence this epitaph on his gravestone in Haverhill cemetery: —

"Death's sudden stroke dissolved my feeble frame;
Reader, prepare, your fate may be the same.
Renounce your sins, by faith to Jesus fly;
Then, welcome death, — 't is gain for you to die."

She m., 2d, Henry Clement, of Salem, N. H., Jan. 12, 1812, and lived in Thornton, N. H., and Boxford, Mass. He d. Dec. 14, 1843. She d. at Boylston, Mass., Oct. 1, 1864, aged 77. Children: —

202. MARY RUNNELS (Clement), b. July 18, 1813, in Thornton; was m. by Rev. Peter Eaton, at West Boxford, to Gilman Hull, Sept. 19, 1843. He was b. Jan. 28, 1809, in Northwood, N. H.; now a shoemaker, residing at Georgetown, Mass.
203. SARAH LOUISA, b. Dec. 14, 1819, in West Boxford; m. Lyman Whipple, farmer, of Somerville, Apr. 24, 1845; afterwards resided at Boylston; now at Shrewsbury, Mass. Children: —
    1. WILLIAM HENRY (Whipple), b. May 7, 1846, in Somerville; was in the army of the late war fourteen months, Co. K, 57th Mass. regiment; m. Mina A. Hill, of Marlboro', Mass., Aug. 31, 1869, and now resides in Worcester. Child: (1.) GEORGE ALBERT, b. Nov. 15, 1871.
    2. LYMAN HOLBROOK, b. Sept. 6, 1849, in Boylston.
    3. MARY LOUISE, b. Apr. 24, 1852, in Boylston; m. George K. Adams, of Northboro', Mass., Jan. 1, 1872.
    4. JOHN ALBERT, b. Dec. 11, 1858, in Boylston.
204. WILLIAM HENRY, b. June 20 (14), 1824, in West Boxford; d. Dec. 28, 1833, in his 10th year.

FOURTH GENERATION.

205.   Abigail[4] [63] (Stephen[3], Stephen[2], Samuel[1]) ; m. Abel
Gage, of Pelham, N. H., Jan. 13, 1780 ; d. Aug. 2, 1825, aged 70.
She was truly a *mother*, rightly guiding her household, and wisely
training her children.   Her advice and assistance were much
sought for in her neighborhood, in cases of sickness and difficulty.
Her husband was b. in Pelham, Nov. 18, 1755, — the day of the
great earthquake, — and d. Sept. 3, 1846, in his 91st year.   He
served as a soldier in the Revolutionary war, during the year 1776,
for which service he received a pension the last twenty-eight years
of his life.   Kept school several seasons in different parts of the
town, in private houses, before school-houses were built, and when
" reading, writing, and ciphering " were the only branches taught.
He was active in all his employments, and possessed the confidence
of his fellow-townsmen in so large a degree that he was elected as
selectman more than half the years between thirty and sixty of his
own age.   Was also a devoted member of the church to which he
belonged, and held the office of deacon about forty-five years, till
the infirmities of age admonished him to resign.   Having *heard*
that granite ledges had been riven in pieces with wedges, in some
distant locality, he resolved to try the experiment on his own farm,
which abounded in granite, and was surprised at his success.   His
tools were of a *primeval* pattern, like the material on which he
wrought ; but it is claimed that he was *the first* in this part of the
country to attempt stone quarrying, and to start that important
business, which has reached such a height in Concord, N. H.,
Quincy, Mass., and other places.   The centre meeting-house in
Dracut, built about 1782, and the present town-house in Pelham, as
it was originally, afford specimens of his earliest work.   A ten-
dency to mechanical pursuits, a taste for vocal and instrumental
music, and a marked religious character, are noticed in this family,
through their several generations.   The parents, all the children,
who lived to mature age, and a large majority of the grandchildren,
have professed their faith in Christ.   Children, all b. in Pelham : —

206.   Sarah (Gage), b. Jan. 20, 1781 ; m Henry March, farmer, of Lon-
        donderry, May 11, 1819 ; d. Sept. 8, 1827, in her 47th year.
207.   Billy Runnels, b. Feb. 20, 1783 ; a farmer ; m., 1st, Abigail Hall,
        of Pelham, July 23, 1805, who d. Apr. 19, 1808 ; m., 2d, Rebecca

Wilson, of P., Nov. 11, 1813, who d. 1816; m., 3d, Nancy Anderson, of Londonderry, where he then resided, Jan. 1818. He d Mar. 7, 1837, aged 54. Children : —

1. CALEB (Gage), b. Oct. 2, 1805 (first wife); a blacksmith, Manchester, N. H.; m. Susan Claggett, of Londonderry, June 25, 1830. Children: (1.) MELINDA CLAGGETT, b. Dec. 4, 1831. (2.) LEANDER, b. Nov. 23, 1833; a blacksmith, Manchester; m. Cordelia B. Kenne, May 3, 1857, and d. Aug. 20, 1865, aged 32. Children: I. SUSAN ARDELL, b. Feb. 14, 1860. II. CHARLES HENRY, b. Sept. 8, 1863. (3.) GEORGE F., b. Apr. 30, 1839 ; a fancy painter, Montreal, C. E.   (4.) WILLIAM CLAGGETT, b. Jan. 10, 1842; a printer, Manchester, N H.; m. Nellie Jones, Mar. 2, 1860. Children: I. FREDERIC WILLIAM, b. Apr. 5, 1866. II. FRANK HERMON, b. June 9, 1868.

2. CHARLES, b. Mar. 5, 1815 (second wife); a carpenter; Bedford, N. H.; m. Mary Newton, of Henniker.

3. WILLIAM WASHINGTON, b. Dec. 30, 1818 (third wife); a trader in dry goods. Boston, Mass.; m. Sarah W. Griffin, Sept. 27, 1846. Children: (1.) CHARLES AUGUSTUS, b. Aug. 8, 1847. (2.) ALICE AUGUSTA, b. Oct. 15, 1854.   (3.) ANNIE S., b. Sept. 27, 1856. (4.) ABBIE FRANCES, b. Oct. 5, 1858. (5.) WILLIAM WASHINGTON, b. May 31, 1864.

4. LEANDER, b. Oct. 2, 1820; a boot and shoe maker, Braintree, Mass.; m. Mary Denton Allen, of B., June 18, 1845. Children : (1.) WILLIAM L., b. Dec 20, 1845; "enlisted for the late civil war in the 42d regiment Mass. volunteers; served his time, and returned." (2.) RICHARD ALLEN, b. Apr. 2, 1848; d. Jan. 30, 1851, in his 3d year. (3.) CHARLES HENRY HALL, b. June 28, 1850; d. June 9, 1863, aged 13. (4.) RICHARD ALLEN, b. July 16, 1852. (5.) ELIZABETH DENTON, b. July 16, 1854 ; d. Oct. 7, 1854. (6.) FREDERIC ALLEN, b. Aug. 15, 1855; d. Oct. 11, 1855.

5. ABIGAIL, b. June 20, 1822; m. Charles Henry Hall, of Braintree, Mass., blacksmith, May, 1850; now residing in California.

6. AARON HARDY, b. Nov. 13, 1824; resided in Londonderry; there m. Hannah Humphrey, of L., May, 1850; "joined the Union army in the West; became captain of a company; was a brave soldier and officer for two or three years, and after the war removed to California." Four children; two d.

7. JOHN ANDERSON, b. June 25, 1827; a boot and shoe maker, Derry, N. H.; m. Martha Tenney, of Londonderry, May 6, 1851. Children: (1.) ELLA F., b. May 23, 1852. (2.) M. FLORENCE, b. Jan. 15, 1855. (3.) CHARLES F., b. Jan. 20, 1857; d. Feb. 28, 1860, aged 3 years. (4.) NANCY JANE, b. June 9, 1861. (5.) LYDIA P., b. July 20, 1863; d. May 4, 1865, in her 2d year.

208. MEHETABEL. b. Jan. 30, 1785; d. Feb. 5, 1789, aged 4.

209. HANNAH, b. Apr. 26, 1787. See [231.]

210. MEHETABEL. b. Feb. 5, 1789; d. July 31, 1861, aged 72.

211. AMOS, b. Mar. 22, 1791; a shoemaker; m. Celenda Hovey, of Boxford, Mass., — where he then resided, — Mar. 1815. She d. July 4, 1830. Children: —

1. WARREN, b. Mar. 17, 1816; a carpenter, Bradford, Mass.; m. Caroline Bartlett Foster, of Pembroke, Nov. 15, 1842. Children: (1.) ELLEN ISABEL, b. May 6, 1846. (2.) MARY KIMBALL, b. Oct. 25, 1849; d. Jan. 4, 1866, in her 17th year. (3.) GEORGE WARREN. b. Sept. 11, 1852; d. Oct 22, 1863, aged 11. (4.) CARRIE MADORA, b. Mar. 11, 1857. (5.) HATTIE TENNEY, b. Oct. 3, 1859; d. Oct. 21, 1863, aged 4. (6.) HENRY WILLIS, b Sept. 19, 1863.

2. ABIGAIL, b. Mar. 21, 1818; m. James Carlton, carpenter, of Boxford, Mass., Apr. 26, 1837. Children: (1.) CHARLES WARREN

3

(Carlton), b. Sept. 21, 1838; d. Apr. 22, 1857, in his 19th year. (2.) CELENDA HOVEY, b. Sept. 27, 1840; m. Charles Robert Anderson, mechanic, of West Boxford, Mass., Sept. 21, 1860. Children: I. WILLIAM H. (Anderson), b. Jan. 13, 1862. II. CHARLES CARLTON, b. Jan. 12, 1863. III. FRANK HERBERT, b. July 7, 1865. IV. DAVID ALBERT, b. Nov. 16, 1867. (3.) LEWIS A., b. Mar. 22, 1851.

3.　HARRIET REYNOLDS, b. Mar. 4, 1820; m. Daniel Chamberlain, of Boston, mathematical instrument maker, Nov. 24, 1842. Children: (1.) EDWARD GAGE (Chamberlain), b. Apr. 13, 1845. (2.) CELENDA GAGE, b. July 13, 1849; d. Apr. 18, 1850, aged 9 mos. 5 days. (3.) HARRIET ELIZA, b. June 8, 1852. (4.) GEORGE WILLIAM, b. Sept. 24, 1854. (5.) ABBIE GRAY, b. July 14, 1857. (6.) DANIEL ARTHUR, b. Aug. 2, 1860.

4.　GEORGE, b. Aug. 26, 1822; d. Nov. 23, 1863, aged 41.

5.　MARY ANN, b. Nov. 24, 1824; d. July 5, 1830, in her 6th year.

6.　AMOS, b. Mar. 20, 1827; d. July 2, 1830, in his 4th year.

7.　CELENDA, b. June 1, 1829; d. July 5, 1830, aged 13 mos. and 4 days. The three youngest children died, thus, at nearly the same time with their mother.

212.　STEPHEN, b. Aug. 4, 1792; a farmer and carpenter; m. Olive Bradford, of Salem, N. H., Dec. 22, 1818; d. May 9, 1834, in his 42d year.　Children: —

1.　CAROLINE, b. Jan. 5, 1821; m. Russell Richardson, stone-cutter, of Pelham, Mar. 31, 1841.　Children: (1.) RUSSELL OZRO (Richardson), b. Aug. 15, 1842; a shoe manufacturer, Lynn, Mass.; m. Margaret S. Emerson, of Windham, N. H., Jan. 1865.　Child: I. FREDDIE EMERSON, b. Feb. 29, 1872.　(2.) LOUISA CAROLINE, b. Mar. 29, 1845; m. John E Farnham, of Lynn, Mass., — in the shoe business, — Nov. 27, 1867. (3.) ORLANDO W., b. June 8, 1848; in the shoe business, Lynn; m. Emma McMaster, Jan. 1871.　Child: I. CHARLEY, b. Oct. 1871.　(4.) JUSTIN W., b. Oct. 3, 1851.　(5.) CHARLEY B., b. Apr. 4, 1853; d. July 24, 1856, in his 4th year.　(6.) ALBERT H., b. Oct. 21, 1855.　(7.) FRANK W., b. Aug. 9, 1859; d. Feb. 14, 1860, aged 6 mos.

2.　WILLIAM BRADFORD, b. Sept. 29, 1823; a carpenter; residence, first, in Methuen, Mass., now in Providence, R. I.; m. Louisa Dearborn, Sept. 2, 1846.　Children: (1.) Louisa D., b. July 16, 1848.　(2.) SARAH F., b. Apr. 24, 1850; d. Apr. 4, 1851, aged 11 mos. and 10 days.

3.　LAURA ANN, b. Jan. 31, 1827; fitted herself for a teacher, and for several years was principal of the New Hampton (N. H.) Female Seminary; m. the Rev. Moses H. Bixby, about 1860 (second wife).　He had previously been a missionary in Burmah, Asia, and returned to that field the same year, with his wife, "to open a new mission," where "they spent about eight years very successfully," until failing health compelled him to return to America.　He is now pastor of a church in Providence, R. I.　Children: (1.) WILLIAM (Bixby), b. Sept. 1863, in Burmah; d. 1867.　(2.) EARNEST MERLE, b. Sept. 1866, in Burmah.

4.　REBECCA EVELINE, b. July 24, 1829.

5.　ASCENATH, b. Aug. 25, 1834; joined the Burmah mission with her sister, as an assistant, about 1866, and still labors there.

213.　DEBORAH, b. Nov. 21, 1795; m., 1st, Joel Butler, farmer and cooper, of Pelham, Apr. 8, 1823, who d. Nov. 1827; m., 2d, Seth Cutter, Jr., farmer and stone-cutter, of Pelham, Oct. 23, 1832, and d. Sept. 14, 1864, in her 69th year.　Children: —

1.　JAMES MILTON (Butler), b. Feb. 5, 1824; a carpenter, Nashua, N. H.; m. Sarah Jane Steele, of Hudson, N. H., Oct. 2, 1862.

Children: (1.) ARTHUR MILTON, b. June 22, 1863; d. Apr. 7, 1869, in his 6th year. (2.) ALBERT STEELE, b Dec. 30, 1864. (3.) CLARA ADELLA, b. Aug. 15, 1866. (4.) BLANCHE MARIA, b. July 17, 1870.

2. HENRY, b. Oct. 10, 1826; a carpenter, Hudson, N. H.; m. Belinda Smith, of H., Apr. 29, 1856; "was a soldier in the Union army, and did good service." Children: (1) LINNIE FRANCES, b. June 29, 1857. (2.) EMMA MARIA, b. Aug. 28, 1859. (3.) CHARLES HENRY, b. Dec. 28, 1861; d. Sept. 12, 1864, in his 3d year. (4.) NELLIE MARTENAH, b. Dec. 13, 1866.

3. AMELIA (Cutter), b. Sept. 12, 1834.

4. ABIAH, b. Feb. 1, 1837; m. Kimball Webster, surveyor, of Hudson, Jan. 29, 1857. Children: (1.) LIZZIE JANE (Webster), b. Jan. 11, 1858. (2.) ELLA FRANCES, b. Aug. 19, 1859. (3.) KIMBALL C., b. June 26, 1861; d. Aug. 22, 1861. (4.) JAMES, b. June 26, 1861; d. same day. (5.) ELIZA BALL, b. July 14, 1862. (6.) LUTINA RAY, b. July 26, 1865. (7.) JULIA ANNA, b. Oct. 26, 1867. (8.) MARY NEWTON, b. Aug. 9, 1869.

214. ABEL, b. Nov. 23, 1798; m. Anna Moody Johnson, of Hudson, Dec. 6, 1826, and has since occupied the farm on which his father commenced in Pelham, nearly one hundred years ago. Engaged in school-teaching, for winter employment, during seventeen years, in one district five terms, and in another, adjoining, four terms. Was afterwards superintendent of the schools in Pelham for several years, and has been a teacher in the Sabbath school nearly fifty years, including twenty-three years as superintendent. Without serving an apprenticeship, he took up the trade of carpenter; has built quite a number of houses, barns, and other buildings, in Pelham and elsewhere, and assisted in building the first bridge across the Merrimack River, between Lowell and Centralville (then Dracut), in 1826. Children, b. in Pelham : —

1. ANGELINA MATILDA, b. Jan. 6, 1828.

2. ARTHUR AUGUSTUS, b. Mar. 9, 1830; a carpenter, Portsmouth, N. H.; m. Mary Frances Lucy, of Stratham, Oct. 25, 1854. She was b. June 28, 1836. Children: (1.) ARTHUR EDWARD, b. Dec 2, 1858. (2.) MARY ANNA, b. June 9, 1860. (3.) ELLEN ISADORE, b. May 12, 1862.

3. WALTER EDWARDS, b. June 16, 1833; d. Apr. 8, 1861, in his 28th year.

4. LYMAN BERKLEY, b. June 27, 1835; a carpenter, Methuen, Mass.; m. Sarah Tyler Clark, of M., Apr. 21, 1858. Children: (1.) EMMA ADDIE, b. June 19, 1861. (2.) CARRIE ALICE, b. Aug. 3, 1863. (3.) JULIA ANGIE, b. Sept. 18, 1865.

5. HENRIETTA PHILENA, b. Aug. 16, 1837.

6. ROSCOE WISNER, b. Sept. 2, 1839; was a trader, Boxford, Mass.; m. Abbie R. Cole, of B., Nov. 24, 1863. She was b. Dec. 14, 1840. He d. Feb. 9, 1869, in his 30th year. Children: (1.) HERBERT EDWIN, b. Aug. 9, 1865. (2.) ALICE MAY, b. Feb. 4, 1868.

7. EMMA ISADORE, } b. Sept. 24, 1841; Emma Isadore d. Aug. 17,
8. ELLEN ISABEL, } 1861, aged 20.

9. SYDNEY PAYSON, b. Dec. 11, 1843.

10. OTIS ALLEN, b. Nov. 13, 1846.

215. ENOS[4] [64] (Stephen[3], Stephen[2], Samuel[1]), enlisted for the war of the Revolution at the age of eighteen, and, like other volunteers from northern Massachusetts, was at first enrolled with New Hampshire regiments. Hence his name appears on the military

records of New Hampshire, first under the head of "Losses at the Battle of Charlestown, June 17, 1775," — "Enos Runnels, Capt. Moore's Co , Stark's regiment, £1 17s. 6d.," — which losses were made up to the soldiers out of the State treasury. Again, on the "Pay roll of Capt. Henry Dearborn's Co., Col. B. Arnold's Detachment," we have the signed receipt of "Enos Runnels, of Boxford, Joiner," to "Two months' pay, £4, Sept. 18, 1775 " This proves that his enlistment, under Arnold, must have occurred in July, or immediately after his release from the Charlestown campaign (see below). Two deeds of his, "Apr. 20, 1779," forcibly suggest that sacrifice of home and property, — a portion, at least, of his paternal acres, — which he felt obliged to make, in order that he might serve his country faithfully to the last; while his reception at home, on a furlough, — probably just before this date, — afforded an incident of tender interest, as an absence of nearly four years, his hardships and exposure, and the terrible disease, small-pox, from which he suffered at Quebec, had left him in disguise, so that his mother at first supposed he was a *stranger*, while drinking at the family well in the door-yard! His final term of service expired not long before his marriage to Sarah Simmons, of Boxford, "published Feb. 2, 1782." He appears to have settled first, in Andover, where the birth dates of his two oldest children are found, as below ; the others upon the Boxford records, on which "Enos Runnels" is found for the first time among the "Tax payers," in "1785." Later in life he changed the spelling of his name to "Reynolds," and this is retained by all his descendants. He held two commissions as "Ensign," the first signed by John Hancock, governor, June 17, 1786 ; the second, for a special service of four months, in 1787, "suppressing the rebellion in the western counties," of which he used to speak as his "Shay hunting"! He d. Aug. 11, 1845, in his 89th year. His excellent wife survived him nearly ten years, and d. June 25, 1855.

The following is extracted from the "Boston Atlas " of Aug. 16, the "Boston Post" of Aug. 21, and the "Christian Register" of Aug. 30, 1845 : —

"The life of this Revolutionary soldier was more than commonly eventful. His first engagement was at Bunker Hill. He was in Stark's regiment, and that portion of it that started from Medford early in the morning and reached Bunker Hill ' along in the forenoon.' It marched to the redoubt, which was then full. Orders were given for it to take post on the left when the rail fence was commenced, and Mr. Reynolds aided in making it. Here he fought during the battle." . . . "His next service was as a volunteer in the expedition of Arnold to Quebec. He encountered the full hardships of that perilous enterprise. The night of his keenest sufferings on an island in the river was bitterly remembered. For thirty-three days on this march he did not sleep in dry clothes." "In December (1775), he was taken prisoner at the fall of Montgomery, and remained in the hands of the British till the succeeding October, though he always spoke with touching gratitude of

Gen. Carleton for his humanity towards himself and fellow-prisoners. Afterwards enlisting for three years, he served in the northern army of Gen. Schuyler. Again taken prisoner by the Indians, and delivered to the British, he was lodged at Ticonderoga, but soon executed a daring plan of escape, with one or two others, swam the lake, rejoined the army under Gates, and saw Burgoyne surrender at Saratoga At the time of Arnold's treachery he was stationed at West Point, and performed guard duty in the same room with Maj. Andre on the last night of his life." "The war being over, Mr. Reynolds devoted himself to the labors of peace. He struggled manfully through all the trials that awaited the brave men of the Revolution." "He was first vice-president of the whig State convention in Faneuil Hall, Sept. 1842." "He was emphatically a good man and a practical Christian. Even the spirit of detraction never dared to utter an insinuation against his integrity of character or purity of purpose. It was his constant aim to make his life conform to the precepts of the gospel. His bodily strength was for several years prostrated by paralysis, but his mind was clear and his faith unshaken to the last. Through the intense sufferings of a six months' illness, he was never heard to utter a word of impatience ; and a few hours before his death, he said, with earnestness, ' It is so, it is so !' in response to the lines, —

> ' Jesus can make a dying bed
> Feel soft as downy pillows are.' "

"His decease left a melancholy void in the family, of which he was the head, and the object of love and veneration ; in the town, of which he was a valued citizen ; in the neighborhood, which he enlivened by his hospitality, and instructed by his wisdom and historic lore ; and in the church, of which he was an exemplary member."

His granddaughter [636], in Texas, from amid scenes of peculiar national trial, pays the following tribute, — under date of Dec. 4, 1870, —

"TO THE DEPARTED HERO.

> "Peace be to thee, dear honored sire ;
> Calmly thou sleepest in thy narrow home,
> Bright gem in freedom's starry crown.
> Thy mission here on earth is done ;
> Thy children's children speak thy fame,
> Wafting thy praise on wings of love,
> To freedom's children, ever sung,
> And generations yet unborn."

Children : —

216. STEPHEN [629], b. Nov. 18, 1782, in Andover.
217. FREDERICK, b. Feb. 9, 1785, in Andover. He was a carpenter, lived at West Boxford, and d. Apr. 9, 1867, aged 82.
218. MATILDA, b. Apr. 13, 1787, in Boxford, as also the following children. She m. Jedidiah Barker, of Boston, at B. (his 2d wife), Nov. 24, 1816. See [244].
219. ELIPHALET [635], b. Apr. 4, 1789.

220. SAMUEL SPOFFORD [643], b. Nov. 14, 1791.
221. WILLIAM, b. Jan. 20, 1794; d. Mar. 25, 1818, aged 24.
222. SARAH [652], b. Feb. 19, 1796.
223. HARRIET, b. Feb. 11, 1799; resides at the paternal home, West Boxford (1872).
224. REBECCA ADALINE, } b. July 31, 1801; { d. Sept. 1801.
225. HANNAH EVELINE, }   { d. June 17, 1803, in her 2d y.
226. REBECCA EVELINE, b. Nov. 11, 1803. "Was distinguished," says her pastor, "for force of character, energy of will, integrity of conscience, and a spirit of self-sacrifice, with intellectual traits no less remarkable." She visited the Sandwich Islands *alone* at two different times, being absent from home four months on the first journey, 1851–2; and on the second, occasioned by her brother's sickness, see [629], from Aug. 1855, till May 31, 1856. She d. Jan. 3, 1865, in her 62d year.
227. MARY ISABELLA [657], b. Feb. 20, 1807.

228. EUNICE[4] [66] (Stephen[3], Stephen[2], Samuel[1]), m. Samuel Marston, of Methuen, Mass., Sept. 6, 1779. Their six oldest children were b. in Methuen, where they appear to have lived at first; but in 1793 they moved to East Andover, Me., then a wilderness, abounding in bears and other wild beasts. Theirs was among those "industrious and intelligent families from Essex Co., Mass.," who are said to have settled in Andover originally, as farmers, about the year 1790, and to have given character to its subsequent population. They struggled with the hardships of pioneer life, and enjoyed but limited privileges for many years. Children : —

229. HANNAH (Marston), b. Oct. 29, 1781; m. Sherebiah Arnold, May 15, 1809, and d. May 19, 1860, in her 79th year. He was b. July 15, 1778; d. Feb. 17, 1860, in his 82d year. Children : —
   1. SAMUEL M. (Arnold), b. Oct. 31, 1811; m. Mary W. Carlton, Jan. 15, 1837, and d. Feb. 8, 1855, in his 44th year. Children : (1.) SHEREBIAH M., b. Nov. 8, 1837; d. Feb. 9, 1858, in his 21st year. (2.) SAMUEL B., b. May 5, 1839; m. Jane Harlow, Oct. 1866. Children : I. FLORA, b. Apr. 1868. II. ALICE E., b. Mar. 1870. (3.) MARY E., b. Dec. 31, 1840; m. George Lord, of Fairfield, Me., July 3, 1864. Children : I. EDITH VIOLA (Lord), b. 1869. II. MATTA E., b. July, 1871. (4.) EUNICE RUNNELS, b. Mar. 2, 1843; m. Andrew Currie, of Richmond, N. B., 1864. (5.) LOTTIE C., b. Jan. 5, 1845; m. Alfred Sampson, of Lisbon, Me., 1867. Child : I. MITIE (Sampson), b. 1867. (6.) JOSEPH A., b. Oct. 11, 1846. (7.) MARTHA M., b. Aug. 8, 1848. (8.) CLARA A., b. Oct. 23, 1850; d. 1852, aged 2. (9.) EDITH V., b. Sept. 7, 1853; d. Oct. 10, 1854, aged 13 months.
   2. EUNICE RUNNELS (Arnold), b. Nov. 27, 1813; d. July 6, 1838, in her 25th year.
   3. HANNAH C., b. Feb. 21, 1815; m. Stephen B. Judkins, Aug. 5, 1835.
   4. BETSY T., b. Sept. 21, 1819; see [231, 2].
   5. MARIA G., b. Dec. 14, 1822; m. Charlie B. Davis, Jan. 11, 1872.
230. DEBORAH (Marston), b. Apr. 24, 1783 (4); m. Joseph S. Carlton, 1802. He d. Apr. 1849; she d. Aug. 1851, aged 68. Children : —
   1. DEBORAH (Carlton), b. Nov. 19, 1804; m. Eben Harnden, Sept. 1829. Children : (1.) EBEN (Harnden), Jr.; resides in Weld, Me. (2.) WILLIAM; resides in No. 6, Franklin Co., Me. (3.) ELIZABETH; resides in Weld. (4.) SAMUEL. (5.) JOHN. (6.) THOMAS; resides, with the two last, in Phillips, Me.

(7.) JOSEPH; resides in Weld; also three other children, names not given, who have d.

2. JOSEPH (Carlton), b. Sept. 13, 1806; m. Mary Sweat, Jan. 1842. He resided in Illinois, and d. Oct. 1861, aged 55. Seven children.

3. WILLIAM M., b. Aug. 12, 1808; m. Adaline Winship, Aug. 1851; resided in Concord, N. H., and there d. Feb. 1860, in his 52d year. Children: (1.) ELIZABETH. (2.) ELIJAH. (3.) MARY.

4. SAMUEL S., b. Oct. 29, 1810; m. Julia Thompson, Oct. 27, 1842; d. Dec. 10. 1850, aged 40. Children: (1.) ARI. (2.) SEWALL. (3.) MARCILLA. (4.) LEVI. (5.) VIOLA.

5. THOMAS, b. 1815; m. Hannah Parker, May. 1841; residence, Weld, Me. Children: (1.) CHARLOTTE, b. June, 1842; d. Apr. 1844, in her 2d year. (2.) DANIEL R., b. Jan. 1844; resides at Plattsburg, N. Y. (3.) BETSY P., b. Jan. 1845; d. Feb. 1866, aged 21. (4.) LEROY P., b. Feb. 1847; resides at Winthrop, Me. (5.) ABBIE E., b. Oct. 22, 1849; d. Aug. 1867, in her 18th year. (6.) JOHN F., b. Jan. 1851; resides at Boylston, Mass. (7.) LOUISA, b. Jan. 16, 1853. (8.) LEONA E., b. Sept. 14, 1855. (9.) EVENS A., b. Feb. 9, 1857. (10.) ELMER E., b. Feb. 11, 1859. (11.) ETTA A., b. Feb. 13, 1861. (12.) WILLIAM P., b. July 18, d. Sept. 15, 1866.

6. SALLY, b. 1817; m. William Dow, June, 1842; residence, Pittsfield, Ill. Eight children.

7. CHARLOTTE, b. 1820; d. Apr. 1832, aged 12.

8. ALBION, b. Feb. 1822; m. Roxanna Thompson, Oct. 1846; resided at Strong, Me., and d. Jan. 1870, aged 48. Eight children.

9. CATHARINE B., b. Sept. 22, 1824; m. Benjamin J. Masterman (1st wife), 1848; d. Mar. 1851, in her 27th year. Two children.

231. SAMUEL (Marston). b. Feb. 25 (23), 1786; m. Hannah Gage [209], of Pelham, N. H., Jan. 26, 1815. He was a farmer in Andover, and d. Jan. 25, 1856, aged 70. Children: —

1. SAMUEL, b. Dec. 19, 1815; m. Lucinda Cutting, Nov. 27, 1838. Children: (1.) LUCINDA MELVINA, b. Aug. 11, 1839; m., 1st, Nathaniel R. Thomas, of Andover, July 4, 1861. He d. May, 1863, and she m., 2d, Henry W. Dunn, Nov. 1865. Children: I. WARREN NATHANIEL (Thomas), b. May 5, 1862. II. HENRY CLAUDE (Dunn), b. Aug. 4, 1866. (2.) SAMUEL WARREN, b. May 20, 1844; resides in Andover; m. Abbie M. Littlehale, May 20, 1871. (3.) DAVID ALONZO, b. Oct. 6, 1846. (4.) HANNAH ERMINA, b. Jan. 28, 1853. (5.) ASCENATH PERRIS, b. Oct. 14, 1859.

2. ABEL GAGE, b. Apr. 19, 1817; residence, Andover; m., 1st, Betsy T. Arnold [229, 4], Jan. 18, 1844, who d. Sept. 18, 1845, aged 26; m., 2d, Ann M. West, Dec. 29. 1846. Children: (1.) HANNAH M., b. Apr. 9, 1845 (1st wife); m. Joel Merrill, of Andover, Dec. 19, 1868. (2.) LEANDER A., b. Oct. 19, 1847 (2d wife). (3.) JOHN W., b. May 5, 1849. (4.) CELINDA G., b. Aug. 1, 1851. (5.) FRANCENA P., b. July 24, 1853. (6.) NORA M., b. Jan. 4, 1856. (7.) ARVILLA W., b. Aug. 24, 1858; d. Nov. 20, 1865, aged 7. (8.) WALTER E., b. Dec. 4, 1860. (9.) LAURA C., b. Mar. 21, 1863. (10.) MARTHA H., b. July 23, 1865. (11.) ELLEN I., b. Jan. 21, 1867.

3. HANNAH PEARL, b. July 11, 1819; m. Thomas Howarth, 1840. He was then a clothier in Andover, Mass.; afterwards lived in Virginia, where she d. Children: (1.) ELIZABETH (Howarth). (2.) THOMAS J.

4. WILLIAM RUNNELS (Marston), b. Feb. 23, 1821; m., 1st, Lucy A. Hall, Sept. 20, 1846, who d. Jan. 29, 1867; m., 2d, Ann M. Delano, Oct. 12, 1868. Children: (1.) LUCY V., b. Sept. 13,

1848; m. Daniel Crowley, Aug. 13, 1869. Child: I. RALPH L. (Crowley), b. Dec. 2, 1871. (2.) CHARLES H., b. June 16, 1851. (3.) ALMA G., b. Dec. 2, 1852; m. Harvey L. Newton, Sept. 15, 1870. (4.) WILLIAM H., b. Apr. 9, 1856. (5.) EMMA A., b. June 13, 1857. (6.) ETHEL M., b. July 15, 1859. (7.) NELLIE F., b. Oct. 8, 1862. (8.) MARY F., b. Apr. 13, 1864; d. Feb. 5, 1867, in her 3d year. (9.) LETTIE A., b. July 6, 1866. (10.) ELMER N., b. Aug. 2, 1869 (2d wife). (11.) HERBERT H., b. Dec. 30, 1871.

5. CHARLES HARDING, b. Mar. 17, 1823.
6. LEANDER ARNOLD, b. Apr. 23, 1825; m. Clarissa B. Merrill, Aug. 21, 1852, who d. Apr. 24, 1867; residence, Andover, Me. Children: (1.) IDA H., b. Apr. 17; d. Apr. 20, 1854. (2.) CATIE S., b. Dec. 13, 1855. (3.) CLARA E., b. Sept. 9, 1857. (4.) GEORGE L., b. May 18, 1864.
7. ABIGAIL G., b. Apr. 1, 1827; m. Benjamin J. Masterman, 2d wife, [230, 9], 1852, and d. Aug. 1855, aged 28. Children: (1.) ALICE (Masterman), b. 1853; d. 1861, aged 8. (2) EVA, b. 1855: d. same year.
8. MATILDA BARKER, b. Feb. 3, 1829; m. Asa A. West, Mar. 18, 1854. Children: (1.) ARVILLA (West), b. June 18, 1855; d. Feb. 18, 1863, aged 7 yrs. 8 mos. (2.) DIONTHA, b. Aug. 20; d. Oct. 12, 1857. (3.) ANNA P., b. Aug. 12, 1860; d. Feb. 20, 1868, in her 8th year. (4.) LIZZIE F., b. Nov. 5, 1864. (5.) SCOTT C., b. Sept. 21, 1866.

232. WILLIAM RUNNELS (Marston), b. Apr. 8, 1788; supposed to have d. young.
233. SARAH (Marston), b. Sept. 4, 1790; m. a Proctor. Child: —
   1. DOLLY A. (Proctor); m. Asa A. Proctor, 1845. Children: (1.) CHARLES A. (Proctor), b. 1847. (2.) MARY A., b. 1849; d. Aug. 22, 1863, aged 14.
234. MOLLY (Marston), b. Feb. 18, 1793; m. John Sweat, Oct. 29, 1811. Children: 1. JOHN A. (Sweat). 2. MARY A. 3. SARAH B. 4. ELIZABETH R. 5. PERSIS. 6. BENJAMIN. 7. HIRAM. 8. JAMES. 9. JOSHUA. 10. SOPHIA. 11. MARTHA.
235. ANNA (Marston), b. Sept. 2, 1795, in East Andover, Me.; m. Daniel Sweat, Nov. 10, 1814. Children: 1. ANN (Sweat). 2. FREDERIC; resides in Canada. 3. DANIEL; d. 4. CHARLOTTE; resides in Vermont. 5. ELVIRA; resides in Paris, Me. 6. CLARA; resides in Roxbury, Me. 7. MATILDA.
236. CHARLOTTE (Marston), b. July 12, 1801, in East Andover; m., 1st, Eben Nutting, in East Cambridge, Mass., May 7, 1835. He d. and she m., 2d, Jonathan P. Stevens, of Andover, Me., May 20, 1845. Child: —
   1. JASON S. (Nutting), b. June 7, 1836; d. Jan. 9, 1865, in his 29th year.
237. ELIZA (Marston), b. May 7, 1806, in East Andover; m. Ebenezer Cutting, Apr. 8, 1824. Children: —
   1. EBENEZER M. (Cutting), b. Aug. 14, 1825; m. Dolly F. Bodwell, Mar. 4, 1850; residence, Andover. Children: (1.) OSCAR WINFRED, b. May 19, 1851. (2.) ELLA ADELIA, b. Feb. 6, 1853; d. July 9, 1864, aged 11. (3.) MOSES NELSON, b. Dec. 5, 1854; d. July 16, 1864, in his 10th year. (4.) KATIE ELVIE, b. Dec. 22, 1856. (5.) ADRA LORA, b. Jan. 4, 1859; d. Aug. 4, 1864, aged 5 yrs. 7 mos. (6.) AGNES EDA, b. Mar. 26, 1862; d. Aug. 5, 1864, aged 2 yrs. 4 mos. 10 days. (7.) CHARLEY BROWN, b. Mar. 3; d. Sept. 11, 1864. (8.) NELLIE ADELIA, b. July 13, 1866. (9.) FRED MILTON, b. Apr. 10, 1870.
   2. WILLIAM H., b. Aug. 30, 1826; m. Sarah E. Pulcifer, Mar. 1852; residence, Weld, Me. Children: (1.) ELLA J., b. May 27, 1853. (2.) ALURA E., b. Nov. 28, 1857; d. Aug. 8, 1861, in her 4th

year. (3.) WILLIAM A., b. Feb. 2, 1863. (4.) SHERMAN U.,
b. Jan. 5, 1866.

3. CHARLES H., b. May 7, 1828; m. Abigail A. Roberts, Mar. 4, 1851;
residence, Andover. Children: (1.) BETSY E., b. Nov. 27,
1853; d. Apr. 16, 1854, aged 5 mos. (2.) LUELLA A., b. May
3, 1856. (3.) CHARLES E., b. Mar. 10, 1859; d. Feb. 9, 1861,
aged 2. (4.) NELLIE E., b. June 16, 1861; d. Jan. 6, 1862,
aged 6 mos. 20 days. (5.) LIZZIE E., b. Dec. 17, 1862; d.
Sept. 13, 1871, in her 9th year. (6.) CORA M., b. Apr. 27, 1866.
(7.) GEORGE M., b. Apr. 16, 1868. (8) WILLIAM W., b. Jan.
13, 1870.

4. ELIZA C., b. Apr. 28, 1830; m. Sylvester Roberts, of Andover,
July 1, 1851. Children: (1.) LAURETTA E. (Roberts), b. June
5, 1855. (2.) CHARLES H., b. Aug. 13, 1858

5. DAVID (Cutting), b. Apr. 1, 1832; m. Almira Roberts, June 15,
1856; residence, Andover; enlisted in Co. C, 20th Maine regiment, July, 1862, and d. Jan. 8, 1863, in his 31st year. at
Washington, D. C. She d. Mar. 17, 1862, leaving, (1.) IDA
MIRA, b. Dec. 30, 1857. (2.) DAVID HOMER, b. Apr. 26, 1860.

6. SARAH B., b. July 3, 1834; m. Samuel Akers, June 15, 1858.
Children: (1.) ARTHUR W. (Akers), b. June 1, 1859. (2.)
LESLIE M., b. Aug. 29, 1860. (3.) ETTIE P., b. May 30, 1863.
(4.) FRED C., b. Feb. 22, 1865. (5.) HENRY S., b. May 30, 1868.

7. SAMUEL E. (Cutting), b. Nov. 20, 1836; m. Hattie J. Morse,
Apr. 5, 1866. Children: (1.) WALTER J., b. Oct. 18, 1867; d.
July 25, 1868, aged 9 months. (2.) ROSE E., b. July 30, 1869.

8. EUNICE C., b. Jan. 6, 1839; m. John D. Newton, May 6, 1858.
Children: (1.) JOHN F. (Newton), b. Apr. 17, 1859; d. Feb.
14, 1861, in his 2d year. (2.) J. ORVILLE, b. Apr. 5, 1864.
(3.) CHARLIE M., b. Sept. 15, 1869.

9. HARRIET M. (Cutting), b Feb. 23, 1841; m. George Newton,
Oct. 10, 1863; d. Sept. 13, 1864, in her 24th year.

10. PERSIS B., b. Feb. 20, 1843; m. Carlton Hutchins, of Andover,
Mar. 7, 1861. Children: (1.) EDWARD C. (Hutchins), b. Dec.
22, 1861. (2.) EDGAR H., b. Mar. 7, 1865. (3.) EBEN F., b.
Feb. 26, 1867. (4.) JOHN L., b. Aug. 1, 1869.

11. GEORGE M. (Cutting), b. Mar. 17, 1845.

12. MOSES P.. b. Jan. 29; d. Mar. 13, 1847.

13. LOUIS(A) M., b. Apr. 15, 1848; m. Alonzo N. Rand, of Lynn,
Mass., July 10, 1866. Children: (1.) LLUELLYN A. (Rand),
b. Oct. 18, 1867; d. Jan. 1868, aged 3 months. (2.) JOHN G.,
b. Aug. 3, 1871.

14. CALEB O. (Cutting), b. June 3, 1850.

238. HANNAH[4] [68] (Stephen[3], Stephen[2], Samuel[1]), m. James
Kimball, farmer, in 1786, and settled in Nelson, N. H. Her name
is found in a list of twenty persons who joined the Congregational
church at N., in 1794, the first year of the Rev. Gad Newell's ministry. She d. Nov. 9, 1797, in her 33d year. The children of
James and Hannah Kimball — he having eight others by a second
wife — were all b. in Nelson, as follows: —

239. HANNAH (Kimball), b. Aug. 22, 1787; m. Calvin Greenwood, of
Nelson, farmer and mechanic, Apr. 9, 1807. He was b. Sept. 14,
1785, and d. Nov. 11, 1835, aged 50. She d. on her 77th birth-
day, Aug. 22, 1864. Children: —

1. ALVIN (Greenwood), b. May 9, 1808. Lives in Nashua, N. H.;
two children.

2. ORLAN, b. Mar. 28, 1810; m. Eunice Washburn, Sept. 2, 1834;

resided last in Nashua, and there d. Oct. 1845, in his 36th year. Children: (1.) FRANK WALDO, b. Aug. 11, 1835, in Ludlow, Vt.; m., 1st, Amelia B. Kennedy, of Canton, N. Y., Nov. 27, 1856; she d., and he m., 2d, Adda L., dau. of Henry T. Chickering, Nov. 2, 1871. He was in the late war nearly five years, enlisting in the 6th Mass. regiment, and participating in its trying march through Baltimore. Was afterwards drum major in the Mass. 26th, and finally a captain in the 83d (colored) regiment, in the U. S. regular army. (2.) URSULA NEWELL, b. Feb. 11, 1838, in Perkinsville, Vt.; m. H. M. Smith, of Manchester, N. H., Dec. 25, 1861. She is now a distinguished vocalist, residing in Boston, Mass. Her rendering of "Gratias Agimus Tibi," "with clarionette obligato by Thomas Ryan," at the "World's Peace Jubilee," Wednesday afternoon, July 3, 1872, was scarcely, if at all, inferior to the performance of Madame Peschka-Leutner, on the same occasion. Child: I. ALFRED E. (Smith), b. May 27, 1863. (3.) CALVIN WASHBURN (Greenwood), b. Sept. 29, 1843; served four years in the army, Mass. 26th regiment, with which at New Orleans, La., and onward to Sabine Pass; and afterwards with Gen. Sheridan, at the Winchester, and succeeding battles, in Virginia; now residing in Nashua, N. H.; m. S. Anna Hammond, of Nashua, Oct. 20, 1869. Child: I. MAUDE SARAH, b. Feb. 14, 1871.

3. GEORGE, b. June 22; d. July 18, 1812.
4. MARY LOUISA, b. Sept. 19, 1814; d. June 25, 1855, in her 41st year; one child, now residing in Minnesota.
5. OSCAR, b. Oct. 19, 1816; d. Apr. 1859, in his 43d year.
6. LUCINDA, b. Nov. 12, 1818.
7. GEORGE, b. Aug. 29, 1820; d. Apr. 10, 1858, in his 38th year.
8. DEXTER, b. Oct. 23, 1822; residence in Hollis, N. H. Four children.
9. CAROLINE, b. July 20, 1824; m. H. T. Chickering, of Concord, N. H., formerly freight-agent of the Concord Railroad, now (1872) of the Boston and Lowell Railroad, with residence at Somerville, Mass. Child: (1.) WILLIAM HENRY (Chickering), b. Aug. 26, 1854.
10. WALTER (Greenwood), b. May 12, 1828; resides in Wisconsin; had three children, who all d. of diphtheria, within a few weeks of each other.

240. ESTHER RUNNELS (Kimball), b. Sept. 1789; m. Abijah Wetherbee, of Walpole, N. H. Among their children is —
1. WILLIAM (Wetherbee), Esq., of Amherst, N. H.

241. SALLY (Kimball), b. Aug. 5, 1791; m. Ezra Sheldon, of North Billerica, Mass.

242. LOIS (Kimball), b. Oct. 28, 1797; m. Henry Wright, who d. 1852. She is now living with her son at Clinton, Mass. Eleven children; three only surviving; two in Clinton, and one daughter: —
1. SAVIRA (Wright), a teacher of the freedmen for six years, till 1870, being then stationed, in the same employment, at Montgomery, Ala.

243. PHEBE[4] [69] (Stephen[3], Stephen[2], Samuel[1]), m. Jonathan Dwinell, of Bradford, Jan. 1784. Children all b. in Bradford: —

244. ABIGAIL (Dwinell), b. Dec. 8, 1784; m. Jedidiah Barker, of Boston (1st wife), Sept. 9, 1808, and d. Dec. 15, 1815, aged 31. He was b. Aug. 29, 1784, in Haverhill; a boot and shoe manufacturer; m., 2d, [218], see, and d. in Boston, Aug. 14, 1868, aged 84. He was buried in Boxford, and on his gravestone are these words: "He giveth his beloved sleep," in allusion to the meaning of his

name "Jedidiah," "Beloved of the Lord." His children — by
first wife — were all b. in Boston: —

1. JAMES (Barker), b. July 28, 1809.
2. MARY STICKNEY, b. June 13, 1811; m. John Plummer Healy,
Dec. 23, 1847. He was a graduate of Dartmouth College, 1835,
and has since been a counsellor-at-law in Boston. Child:
(1.) JOSEPH (Healy), b. Aug. 6, 1849; graduated at Harvard
University, 1870.
3. JOHN SPRAGUE, b. Dec. 27, 1813.
4. WARREN WHITE, b. Nov. 27, 1815; m., 1st, Betsy Copeland
Sprague, in 1837, who d. Oct. 13, 1865. He m., 2d, Mrs.
Sarah (Baker) Sprague, Nov. 1866. Child, 1st wife: (1.)
CLARENCE SPRAGUE, b. Dec. 2. 1842.
245. JAMES (Dwinell), b. 1787; "married young, and soon died," —
about 1805–6.
246. POLLY, b. 1789; d. Apr. 1, 1816, aged 27.
247. STEPHEN, b. Nov. 16, 1791; d. Apr. 1864, at Groveland, Mass., in
his 73d year.

248. REBEKAH[4] [75] (William[3], Stephen[2], Samuel[1]). m. Joseph
Messer, farmer, Nov. 29, 1792(3), and settled soon after in New
London, N. H , then a wilderness, where their children were b. and
d., as per records of that town. She also d. at N. L., Dec. 29, 1844,
in her 72d year. Children : —

249. HEZEKIAH (Messer), b. Nov. 20, 1794; d. Mar. 26, 1795, aged 4 mos.
6 days.
250. MEHETABEL, b. Jan. 19, 1797; d. 1816, aged 19.
251. JOSEPH, b. Sept. 22, 1798; d. Mar. 24, 1799, aged 6 mos. 2 days.
252. WILLIAM, b. Oct. 19, 1800; d July 31, 1802, in his 2d year.
253. WILLIAM, b. Nov. 28, 1802; d. May 5, 1804, in his 2d year.
254. REBEKAH, b. May 31, 1805; d. Dec. 1824, in her 20th year.
255. JACOB, b. Dec. 17(15), 1807; a farmer, in New London; m., 1st,
Mary Putney, of N. L., Sept. 27, 1832, who d. Feb. 6, 1848; m.,
2d, Roxilana Pingree, Feb. 6, 1849, who d. July 10, 1855; m., 3d,
Laura Ann Putney, of N. L., Nov. 18, 1860, who d. Apr. 1863.
He d. Mar. 30, 1871, in his 64th year. Children, — 1st wife, —
b. in New London : —
1. PUTNEY, b. Feb. 1834; d. Apr. 10, 1836, aged 2.
2. EDWIN, b. Sept. 2, 1836.
3. MARY ANN, b. Nov. 15, 1842.
4. ADELBERT, b. Sept. 30, 1844; m. Albina J. Crockett, of N. London, Nov. 27, 1871.

256. DANIEL[4] [77] (William[3], Stephen[2], Samuel[1]), m. Lydia
Webster, of Salem, N. H., "May 1, 1806" (Town Recs.), May 6,
1807 (Family Recs.). She was b. May 18, 1787. From the Rockingham Deeds we have — proving former date of marriage correct —
"Apr. 27, 1807, Daniel Runnels, of Methuen, and *Lydia his wife*,"
deeded land in Salem, for $700, to Enoch Merrill ; "May 5, 1807,
Daniel R. of M., *Hatter*," to Stephen Runnels, of M., for $300,
thirty-one acres of land in Salem ; also "Nov. 10, 1807, Daniel R.,
of M., Felt maker," to Jesse Webster, "certain lands in Salem,
for $1,400." Yet he afterwards lived and carried on his trade in
Salem, where he d. Jan. 8, 1854, in his 77th year, and she d. Oct.
18, 1842, aged 55. Children b. in Salem : —

257. SALLIE WEBSTER, b. July 11, 1809; m. William Merrill, of S.,
Sept. 30, 1852, who d. Aug. 27, 1862. She now living at Salem.
258. ELIZABETH FOSTER, b. Feb. 19, 1811; d. Jan. 25, 1819, in her 8th year.

259. ABIGAIL[4] [78] (William[3], Stephen[2], Samuel[1]), m. Kimball Cole, of Boxford, May 10, 1804. His love letter, " hurrying up " the ceremony, is now in the possession of Mrs Mary H. Cole [660], West Boxford. He d. Jan. 14, 1822 ; she d. Apr. 7, 1861, aged 81. Children : —

260. SARAH FOSTER (Cole), b. Aug. 23, 1805; Mrs. Town; d. Mar. 8, 1834, in her 29th year.
261. REBECCA, b. Apr. 2, 1807; d. Feb. 19, 1834, aged 27.
262. EPHRAIM FOSTER, b. July 6, 1809.
263. MEHETABEL BARKER, b. June 9, 1811; Mrs. Sullivan; d. Feb. 9, 1835, in her 24th year.
264. ABIGAIL, b. Feb. 22, 1813; d. June, 1833, aged 20.
265. JOHN KIMBALL, b. Dec. 16, 1814.
266. WILLIAM RUNNELS, b. Jan. 15, 1817. See [660].

267. JOHN[4] [80] (William[3], Stephen[2], Samuel[1]), m. Prudence Harris, of Dracut, May 18, 1818, and settled as a farmer in North Andover, where he lived nearly fifty years on one retired and beautiful place, and there d. Jan. 11, 1868, aged 81. Children : —

268. RUFUS ANDERSON, b. Feb. 15, 1819 ; a farmer, occupying the old homestead in N. A.
269. MARY ELIZABETH, b. June 15, 1821; d. Jan. 19, 1823, in her 2d year.
270. MARY HARRIS [660], b. Jan. 19, 1824.
271. WILLIAM BARTLETT [666], b. Apr. 9, 1826.
272. ELIZABETH FOSTER [671], b. Feb. 11, 1829.
273. GAYTON OSGOOD, b. May 28, 1831; m. Kate L. Hill, June 14, 1860; a farmer, now living (1871) in Derry, N. H.
274. ABBY MINERVA [673], b. Sept. 23, 1834(3).
275. PRUDENCE LAVINIA [677], b. Feb. 27, 1837.
276. JAMES HARRIS, b. Oct. 23, 1839; a farmer in North Andover.

277. SARAH[4] [81] (William[3], Stephen[2], Samuel[1]), m. Benjamin Porter, May 10. 1821, at Boxford ; settled first in Merrimack, N. H. ; moved to Sebago, Me., in 1833, and afterwards lived in Buxton, Me., where she d. Apr. 11, 1865, aged 74. Children all b. in Merrimack : —

278. STEPHEN RUNNELS (Porter), b. Oct. 27, 1824.
279. JOHN TYLER, b. Dec. 18, 1826.
280. SARAH, b. Aug. 26, 1828.
281. MARTHA OSGOOD, b. June 4, 1830.

282. STEPHEN[4] [83] (Daniel[3], Stephen[2], Samuel[1]), was a carpenter, and occupied the old homestead at Londonderry. He was major of the New Hampshire 8th regiment (first battalion), in 1812, and served for the defence of the State in the war of that period. Afterwards a colonel in the New Hampshire militia. He m. Sarah Ela, of Londonderry, Feb. 1811, who was b. June 6, 1785, and d. Sept. 19, 1860, aged 75. He d. Apr. 15, 1848, aged 80. Children b. in Londonderry : —

283. ALFRED [679], b. Dec. 15, 1811.
284. WILLIAM [680], b. Mar. 4, 1814.
285. ELIZA, b. Aug. 25, 1816; d. June 14, 1844, in her 28th year. On her gravestone, Derry cemetery : —

"Yet again we hope to meet thee,
When the day of life is fled;
Then in Heaven with joy to greet thee,
Where no farewell tear is shed."

286. MARY ANN [691], b. July 2, 1818.
287. STEPHEN [695], b. Aug. 8, 1820.
288. SARAH [701], b. June 2, 1822.
289. LUCY [703], b. Jan. 16, 1826.
290. ELLEN MAR [708], b. July 15, 1828.

291. SALLY[4] [84] (Daniel[3], Stephen[2], Samuel[1]), m. Capt. Joseph Gregg, Feb. 1788, at Londonderry, N. H. He was there b. Jan. 22, 1763 ; a carpenter and joiner by trade ; settled early in Acworth, N. H., — see Hist. of Acworth, p. 223, — and there d. Dec. 30, 1840, aged 78. She d. at A., Aug. 11, 1842, aged 73. Children b. in Acworth, all but the first : —

292. HANNAH (Gregg), b. May 19, 1789, in Londonderry ; m. Ithiel Silsby, of Acworth. Feb. 20, 1812, who d. at Newton Corner, Mass., Aug. 27, 1868. Children b. in Acworth.
   1. LEVI HAYWARD (Silsby), b. Nov. 8, 1813.
   2. ANNA SHEPHERD, b. Sept. 15, 1815 ; d. Feb. 1816, aged 5 mos.
   3. ITHIEL HOMER, b. Dec. 12, 1817.
   4. HAMILTON REYNOLDS, b. Sept. 6, 1821 ; d. Sept. 2, 1846, aged 25.
   5. MARY BULLARD, b. Dec. 4, 1829.
293. JONATHAN (Gregg), b July 10, 1791 ; m. Philinda Edgates ; d. Oct. 1850, aged 59. Seven children.
294. POLLY, b. June 16, 1794 ; m. Aaron Bullard, and d. Aug. 19, 1837, aged 43. Eight children.
295. ESTHER, b. Aug. 26, 1796 ; d. Mar. 17, 1812, in her 16th year.
296. SALLY, b. Oct. 22, d. Nov. 18, 1798.
297. SOPHIA, b Jan. 15, 1801 ; d. Mar. 14, 1812, aged 11.
298. LUCINDA, b. July 8, d. Sept. 11, 1803.
299. CLARINDA, b. Oct. 12, 1804 ; m. John S. Cram ; resided in Hanover, N. H. Seven children.
300. ELIZA REYNOLDS, b. Sept. 4, 1807 ; m. Benjamin H. Pearson. Four children.
301. DANIEL R., b. Feb. 24, 1810 ; d. Dec. 8, 1811, aged 9½ months.
302. JOSEPH LADD, b. Mar. 7, 1813 ; m. Abbie Curtis. Three children, — two living (See History of Acworth.) He " was educated as a civil engineer, in which capacity he served with ability on the Fitchburg Railroad and on the Northern Railroad while they were building. He also once made a survey through the forests of Maine, from the Atlantic to the St. Lawrence. For some years he was employed on Southern railroads. He was assassinated at Jacksonville, Fla.," Mar. 19, 1859, at the age of 46, " by a young man who exclaimed, after he had fired the fatal shot, ' I have shot my best friend !' He was respected and beloved by all that knew him ; a noble son, a kind and indulgent husband and father, and an affectionate brother."

303. DANIEL[4] [85] (Daniel[3], Stephen[2], Samuel[1]), early left his father's home in Londonderry, and was first a teacher in Dover and Durham, N. H. Was afterwards deputy sheriff of Strafford Co. for several years, and crier of the court at Dover. Owned land at Alton Bay, where he was building a wharf, when he caught the cold that proved fatal, Oct. 24, 1809, at the age of 38. After his death, the widow and young children made it their home for some

time at Alton.   She, before marriage, was Elizabeth, dau. of James Leighton, of Durham, there b. Apr. 19, 1778, there m., winter of 1796–7, and there d. Sept. 12, 1851, in her 74th year.   Children b. in Durham : —

304.   HANNAH [711], b. Dec. 9, 1797.
305.   DANIEL [724], b. July 9, 1799.
306.   MARY, b. 1801 ; d. aged 12 months.
307.   EBENEZER THOMPSON [733], b. May, 1803.
308.   STEPHEN [740], b. Jan. 1, 1805.
309.   ADDISON [752], b. Jan. 15, 1808.
310.   ELIZA [759], b. July 23, 1809.

311.   HAMILTON DAVIDSON[4] [86] (Daniel[3], Stephen[2], Samuel[1]), was a " builder," and settled in Salem, Mass , where he m. Martha Eaton, in 1810.   He d. early in life   She was b. Aug. 17, 1785, in Marblehead, and d. July 14, 1869, at Roxbury, aged 84. Children : —

312.   LOUISA HAMILTON, b. Feb. 19, 1811, in Salem ; m. Capt. Joseph P. Thompson, mariner, of Salem, Sept. 1, 1834.   She d. Aug. 30, 1856, in her 46th year, at Roxbury, where he still resides (1869), Warren Street, Boston Highlands.
313.   WILLIAM JAMES [766], b. Oct. 9, 1814, in Salem.

314.   POLLY[4] [87] (Daniel[3], Stephen[2], Samuel[1]), m. John Rogers, of Acworth, who was b. Aug. 1763, in Londonderry, N. H., and moved with his father, Lieut. John Rogers, to Acworth, in 1768 (see Hist. of Acworth, p. 261).   They resided first in A., afterwards in Lempster, where she d. Oct. 16, 1829, aged 56.   He then lived and kept the " Monument House " in Lexington, Mass., where he d. Sept. 24, 1832, aged 69.   Children : —

315.   DANIEL (Rogers), b. 1797 ; d. young in Acworth.
316.   MARIA, b. 1799 ; m. Lorrin Way ; lived in Lempster, and d. May 7, 1859, aged 60.
317.   HANNAH OPHELIA, b. 1801(?) ; m. Rev. Joseph Hemphill (2d wife), Jan. 27, 1857, in Lowell, Mass.   He was b. Feb. 1, 1805 ; officiated as a clergyman of the Universalist denomination in Ridgeway, N. Y., and other places ; d. May 19, 1868, at Yarmouth Port, Mass., aged 58.
318   JOHN ADAMS, b. 1807(?) ; graduated at Union College, N. Y. ; studied law at Watertown, N. Y. ; was admitted to the bar in Albany ; practised law in New Hampshire, for some time in company with Lyman B. Walker, Esq. ; m. Hellen R. Eastman, and d. Feb. 23, 1867, at Ridgeway, N. Y.
319.   ELIZA JANE, b. 1809, in Acworth ; d. young in Lempster.
320.   MALVINA BORDWELL, b. 1811.
321.   STEPHEN REYNOLDS, b. Jan. 24, 1813 ; was a trader five years in Concord, N. H. ; now residing (1872) in Warner ; m. Rebecca Rogers, of Billerica, Mass., Sept. 1849.   She d. Oct. 25, 1851, at Concord, N. H., aged 27.
322.   SUSAN HEMPHILL, b. Feb. 28, 1814 ; m. Jesse Eaton, of Salisbury, N. H., June 10, 1832, in Lexington, Mass.   He was a farmer, tax collector for many years, and deputy postmaster in Salisbury, where he d. July 30, 1861.   She d. Feb. 22, 1872, in Warner, aged 58.   Children : —
   1.   SAMUEL (Eaton), b. May 5, 1833 ; m. Adello Fisher, of Prince-

ton, Ill.. where he resided as a merchant till 1872. Children :
(1.) FANNIE FISHER, b. Aug. 20, 1861; d. July 15, 1863, in her
2d year. (2.) GRACE HARPER, b. Oct. 23, 1863; d Jan. 30,
1864, aged 3 mos. 7 days. (3.) JESSIE REYNOLDS, b. Nov. 27,
1865. (4.) ANNIE LAWRIE, b. Dec. 12, 1867. (5.) MARY
ESTELLE, b. Apr. 1, 1870.

2. MARY ROGERS, b. Oct. 17, 1835; d. July 4, 1859, in her 24th year;
"a young lady of much promise."

3. HARRIET ELLA, b. Feb. 26, 1845.

323. HARRIET ELIZA (Rogers), b. 1816(?); m. Charles P. Talbot, now
of Lowell, an extensive manufacturer, firm of "C. P. Talbot &
Co.," — "Works" in North Billerica, Mass. Children : —

1. FANNIE MELBURN (Talbot), b. July, 1837, in Williamsburg, Mass.
2. EDWARD REYNOLDS, b. May 29, 1839. in Lowell; was in company
with his father, and resided at North Billerica. His sudden
death, Feb. 2, 1872, in his 33d year, threw a deep gloom over
the community. The "Lowell Daily Courier" of Feb. 6,
speaking of his funeral the day before, says : "It seemed as
though all the people of this place and the surrounding
neighborhood had assembled to pay the last tribute of respect. Never before was seen such a gathering in North
Billerica, or one which more fully bore out the words of the
poet, —

    ' One touch of nature makes the whole world kin.'

How anxious was each friend and neighbor to see what
remained of him who had won the love and esteem of all
classes ! " He was one of those "who never close the hand
against the widow and the fatherless, the poor, and him that
hath no helper, or to any benevolent or worthy object." At
a meeting of the working people in the employ of C. P. Talbot
& Co., held at the mills on Saturday, Feb. 3, very expressive
and sympathetic resolutions were passed. He had m. Eliza J.
Jaques, of Lowell, dau. of John Jaques, a native of Sanbornton, N. H., and left children : (1.) HARRIET, b. Dec. 10, 1867.
(2.) GERTRUDE, b. May 28, 1871.

3. JULIAN, b. May 27, 1841, in Billerica; is in business with his
father (1872), and a member of the Lowell City Council.

324. DANIEL (Rogers), b. 1818 (?); d. young.

325. HANNAH[4] [88] (Daniel[3], Stephen[2], Samuel[1]), m. Benjamin
Carter, a wheelwright, of Dover, N. H., Feb. 23, 1792, at Londonderry. She d. at Dover, Apr. 1809, aged 33. He d. July 5, 1826,
at Wakefield, N. H. Children b. in Dover : —

326. HANNAH (Carter), b. Jan. 28, 1793; m. Stephen Varney, 1813, who
was b. June 3, 1791, in Dover. Children : —

1. GEORGE CARTER (Varney), b. Aug. 18, 1814, in Meredith, N. H.
2. HANNAH REYNOLDS, b. Apr. 19, 1816, in M.
3. CHARLES, b. Mar. 18, 1819, in Boscawen, N. H.
4. MARY ELIZABETH, b. Aug. 3, 1822, in Boscawen.
5. BETSY, b. Apr. 19, 1826 in B. See [771].
6. WILLIAM HENRY, b. June 27, 1829.

327. DANIEL REYNOLDS (Carter), b. Oct. 19, 1794; d. Sept. 2, 1842, at
Rochester, N. H., in his 48th year.

328. CHARLES, b. Aug. 3, 1796; d. at Wakefield, N. H., Oct. 15, 1854,
aged 58.

329. GEORGE W., b. Oct. 12, 1798; d. at Wakefield, Mar. 14, 1831, in
his 33d year.

330. BENJAMIN, b. Apr. 2, 1800; d. Oct. 28, 1802, at Dover, in his 3d year.

331. BENJAMIN ADOLPHUS. b. Feb. 28, 1803; m. Margaret C. Haskell, Dec 3. 1826.
332. STEPHEN HAMILTON, b Mar. 1, 1805; d. at Dover, Oct. 21, 1806, in his 2d year.
333. HAMILTON, b. June 10, d. Oct. 9, 1807, at Dover.

334. THOMAS K.[4] [90] (Daniel[3], Stephen[2], Samuel[1]), was a carpenter, and m. Sally Moody Pillsbury, of Chester, N. H , Oct. 30, 1804, at Londonderry. He may have been the soldier enlisted as " Thomas Runnels in Capt. N. G. Bradley's Co , Sept. 15, 1814, for three months" (N. H. Military Hist.). His business was in Lowell, Mass., his family residing at Derry, where all his children were b. She d July 30, 1843, aged 60, probably at Derry, as she is there buried. He d. June 13, 1845, at Lowell, in his 65th year. Children : —

335. ELIZABETH LOUISA, b. Apr. 30, d. May 2, 1806.
336. MALVINA ABIGAIL, b. Oct. 7, 1809; m. John A. Coburn, of Boscawen, June 20, 1839, at Derry. He is a native of Wheelock, Vt.; a harness and trunk maker; has resided at Fisherville, N. H., since 1845.
337. ADALINE ANN, b. Mar. 21, 1815; was a teacher in South Boston, and there d. suddenly, Feb. 9, 1839. On her tombstone in the Derry cemetery: " Reader, choose this day whom you will serve, and prepare to meet your God; for He will call for you in an hour when you think not."
338. BETSY AUGUSTA [769], b. Jan. 11, 1819 ("1822," as afterwards given; but we do not feel at liberty to change the next date).
339. MOSES CROSS [771], b. Nov. 28, 1821.
340. SARAH FARRAR [776]. b. June 26, 1824.

341. JOSEPH[4] [94] (Samuel[3], Samuel[2], Samuel[1]). As early as " Sept. 21, 1780," he had conveyed to him by his grandfather and father, jointly, " two certain eighty-acre lots of land in Concord, N. H., lying at or near Horse hill;" and "Dec. 15," of the same year, "for £30, an additional six-acre lot in Concord."
Accordingly, having served in the Revolutionary war as a Massachusetts soldier, he m. Joanna Farnum, of Andover, Mass., in 1780 or '81 (1779 says one), and settled on one of the above lots, probably in the spring of 1781, being the second to make a clearing in that part of Concord. It is related that the same season he one day stuck a *willow twig* into the ground near his rude tenement, which he had used as a riding-stick from near the present village of West Concord. It grew into a wide-spreading tree, affording a delightful shade, till his children found it necessary to cut it down in the fall of 1871 ; when the stump, after a growth of ninety years, was found to measure, for its greatest diameter, seven feet and four inches ! He appears, by the Rockingham records, to have sold one of his eighty-acre lots to Charles Emery, " Dec. 31, 1807." His wife was b. Dec. 8, 1759 (Hist. of Concord says " Sept. 25, 1761"), and d. in Concord, " Nov. 16, 1833, aged 74." He d. Dec. 18. 1843, aged 85. Children b. in Concord : —

342. JOSEPH, Jr., b. Mar. 27, 1782; lived on the old place at Concord, and there d. Aug. 14, 1863, aged 81.

343. ISAAC [780]. b. Nov. 16, 1783 (Nov. 27, 1784).
344. THEODORE [786], b. Apr. 2, 1786.
345. SARAH, b. May 2, 1788; still residing at C.
346. JONATHAN [795], b. Jan. 28, 1791 (Fam.), Mar. 28, 1790 (Hist. of Concord).
347. JOSIAH, b. Apr. 10, 1792; still resides with his sisters on the homestead (1872).
348. FARNUM, b. Mar. 1, d. Mar. 3, 1794.
349. FARNUM [808], b. Jan. 25, 1795.
350. DORCAS, b. July 9, 1797; residing at C.
351. HAZEN [815], b. Sept. 21, 1801.

352. RHODA[4] [96] (Samuel[3], Samuel[2], Samuel[1]), m. Amasa Peabody, of Dracut, Mass., see [364], in 1786; lived first in Boxford, then in Dracut, where she d. suddenly, July 16, 1805, aged 42. Children b. in Dracut, except the oldest: —

353. SARAH (Peabody), b. May 6, 1787, in Boxford; m. Clark Pearsons, and removed to Vermont and Canada.
354. JONATHAN, b. 1789; d. in Dracut at mature age.
355. AMASA, b. Aug. 25, 1791; a blacksmith; m. Hannah Woodbury; lived first in Pelham, N. H.; afterwards in Bedford, and there d. Sept. 1830, aged 39.
356. TRYPHENA, b. Nov. 28, 1793; m. Daniel Goodhue, of Dracut, who was b. May 19, 1784; was a clothier; d. Jan. 20, 1862, in his 78th year. She is now residing (1870) with her son (6) in Dracut. Children: —
    1. OZIAS (Goodhue), b. Nov. 2, 1815; a carpenter; married.
    2. AGNES, b. Apr. 4, 1818; m. John Pierce, of Reading, Mass. Children· (1.) AUGUSTA A. (Pierce). (2.) JOHN M. (3.) FLORA E.
    3. ADALINE (Goodhue), b. Jan. 26, 1820; d. Aug. 28, 1825, in her 6th year.
    4. IMLA, b. Apr. 8, 1823; d. Aug. 28, 1825, in her 3d year.
    5. MARY JANE, b. Aug. 10, 1825; m. Joseph B. Hopkins, of Reading, Mass. Children: (1.) GEORGE W. (Hopkins), b. 1845; was a shoemaker; served in the late war, 50th regiment Mass. volunteers, and participated in the seige of Port Hudson, La., forty-five days, 1863; d. Feb. 20, 1869, aged 24. (2.) SARAH J. (3.) MARY A. (4.) EMMA E.
    6. DANIEL J. (Goodhue), b. Dec. 17, 1827; a farmer, residing in Dracut.
    7. CHARLES W., b. Sept. 5, 1831; a machinist; married; enlisted in Co. C, 6th Mass. regiment, nine months' men.
    8. DAVID H., b. Dec. 30, 1833; a shoemaker; m. Emma E. Bennett, who d. Dec. 16, 1861, aged 23. He enlisted in Co. C, Mass. 6th regiment, nine months' men, in 1863; was wounded in the foot, in a skirmish, taken prisoner, and d. in the Libby Prison, Richmond, Va., June 30, 1864, leaving one child (1.) EMMA E.
    9. SAMANTHA A., b. Aug. 31, 1836; d. Mar. 9, 1869, in her 33d year.
357. RUFUS (Peabody), b. Mar. 31, 1796; m. Betsey Town, and lived in Dracut.
358. FREDERICK, b. Sept. 15, 1798; m. Susan Frost; lived in Hudson, N. Y., and now residing at Alstead, N. H.
359. ELIZA, b. May 6, 1803; m. Charles Bancroft; resided first in Dracut, now at South Reading, Mass.
360. RHODA, b. 1804; d. 1805, in her 2d year.
361. RHODA, b. July 6, 1805; m. Alvin Flint, of Dracut; d. 1830, aged 25.

362. JONATHAN[4] [97] (Samuel[3], Samuel[2], Samuel[1]), followed
his older brother Joseph to Concord, N. H., though not sooner than
" June 7, 1794," as under that date himself and Samuel Runnels,
Jr., " both of Boxford, yeomen," deeded a shop from the Messrs.
Morse, for £30, " now standing on the widow Sarah Farnum's
land." He next appears as Jonathan Runnels, Jr. (why " Jr." is
not evident) ; called also " a trader," " Jan. 31, 1795," and receiving from D. Farnum " a piece of land and one-half of lot whereon
stands a grist-mill." He m. Ruth Farnum, of Concord, previously
to " May 30, 1799," as we then find him and " Ruth his wife"
deeding the last mentioned property to John Hart for $500, and
taking in exchange, at same price, " a piece of land with buildings
in Concord on road leading from Concord meeting-house to Boscawen." Having returned to Boxford before 1811, he there spent
his last days, and d. May 18, 1817, in his 52d year. She d. Apr.
6, 1827. Child : —

363. MOSES [821], b. Feb. 5, 1801, in Concord, N. H.

364. LOIS[4] [98] (Samuel[3], Samuel[2], Samuel[1]), m. Amasa Peabody, of Dracut, as his 2d wife, see [352], Dec. 28, 1806. She d.
Apr. 4, 1825, aged 57. He was b. May 23, 1755 ; d. Sept. 1830
(1811), aged 75 (or 56). They showed a commendable spirit in
desiring to retain their share in her father's pew in the Boxford
West meeting-house, see [93] ; but for what purpose — as they
were not residing in Boxford — is not apparent. Their only
child, but the tenth in his family, was : —

365. AMANDA MALVINA, b. Mar. 21, 1810, in Dracut; m. Joseph V. Fox,
    June 16, 1831. He was b. Oct. 10, 1805 ; d. June 13, 1843, in his
    38th year. She now resides (1870) at No. 45 Booth Corporation,
    Lowell. Children : —
    1. MARTHA M. (Fox), b. May 13, d. July 21, 1837, in Lowell.
    2. DIANA L., b. Oct. 6, 1838, in Groton, N. H. ; d. July 21, 1867, in
        her 29th year.
    3. GEORGE I., b. July 20, 1841, in Dracut; served in Co. C, 6th
        regiment Mass. volunteers (nine months' men), and d. of gun-
        shot wound, at Jerusalem, Va., June 18, 1863, aged 22.

366. SAMUEL[4] [99] (Samuel[3], Samuel[2], Samuel[1]), though purchasing a shop in Concord, N. H., with his brother Jonathan [362],
in 1794, did not settle there till Feb. 1798. Hence, " May 31,
1797," he is still called " Samuel Runnels, Jr., of Boxford, Mass.,"
and deeded from " James Walker, of Concord, for $1,100, one hun-
dred and eighteen acres, more or less, being the whole of Lot No.
98." This was the so-called " Walker lot," on which he settled as
above, near the Contoocook River. He had been a shoemaker in
his younger years, and had also pursued the study of mathematics,
fitting himself for a land-surveyor and purchasing instruments,
" Mar. 1796," with which he did much of the surveying in the
vicinity of his new home for many years. He was a captain in
the third company of infantry, eleventh regiment New Hampshire
militia. In 1814, a company of " Home Guards " was formed in

Concord, of persons exempt from doing military duty, and "Ex-Capt. Samuel Runnels was fourth sergeant." He was selectman of the town of Concord two years, 1816–18, and ever took an active part in the affairs of that part of the town where he resided. Was a famous hunter of *pigeons* in his time, capturing the birds in nets. United with the first Congregational church in Concord, Mar. 12, 1820, at the same time with his wife, and was a very constant attendant at the old North meeting-house, though living at a distance of seven miles. He is hence mentioned in the "Statesman" of Jan. 14, 1870, as one of the "portraits" in the "Old North Picture Gallery." He m., 1st, Anna Hardy, of Bradford, Mass., Sept. 1, 1795, who d. in Concord, Jan. 27, 1823; m., 2d, Abigail Hardy, of Warner, N. H., Dec. 1824 (Feb. 1825), who d. May 24, 1848. He d. Sept. 19, 1836, aged 66. Oldest child b. in Boxford; the others in Concord: —

367. SAMUEL [824], b. Dec. 6, 1796.
368. LOIS, b. May 26, 1798; resides at the old homestead (1870).
369. PRISCILLA, b. Aug. 26, 1799; m. Dodge Hayward, Apr. 1852, and resides in Concord.
370. ANNA, b. Aug. 17, 1803; see [780].
371. EDWARD [832] (adopted), b. May 5, 1836.

372. JONAS[4] [101] (Samuel[3], Samuel[2], Samuel[1]), resided in Boxford; a shoemaker; m., 1st, Anna (Nancy) Merrill, of Bradford, Nov. 25, 1802, who d. Mar. 1817; m., 2d, Sarah Davis, of Boxford, July, 1819, who d. Apr. 9, 1855, aged 74. He d. Jan. 8, 1853, in his 78th year. Children: —

373. JESSE [837], b. Aug. 31, 1808.
374. MARY EMELINE [840], b. July 1, 1811.
375. CATHARINE [845], b. Mar. 27, 1814.

376. JAMES[4] [124] (Benjamin[3], Ebenezer[2], Samuel[1]), was a farmer in Winslow, Me., and m. Sarah Whitten, of Hancock, Mar. 12, 1791; d. Nov. 25, 1796, in his 28th year, under the following painful circumstances: "Three weeks after the birth of his youngest child," while crossing the Kennebec in a boat, above Ticonic falls, on a dark evening, he was drawn into the rapids and carried over. His wife waited, in intense anxiety, all night. Boat found below the falls the next morning. Body recovered at Hallowell the following spring, — recognized only by a piece of paper in his pocket bearing his name, — and buried at H. He left, b. at "Ticonic" or Winslow: —

377. JOHN [848], b. Mar. 2, 1792 (Dec. 1791).
378. JEREMIAH HOLMES [859], b. May 15, 1794.
379. ABIGAIL, b. Nov. 4, 1796; d. July 1, 1797, aged 8 months, being strangled on the back of a chair, placed at her bed, in her mother's temporary absence, to keep her from falling.

380. MARY[4] [125] (Benjamin[3], Ebenezer[2], Samuel[1]), was usually called Polly; m., 1st, George Whidden (or Whitten), of Winslow, Me., — her father's clerk at the time, — Dec. 5, 1789.

He d. Jan. 29, 1809. She m., 2d, James Pratt, Nov. 1809, who
d. in 1848. She d. at Clinton, Me., where she had lived, Oct.
1850 (Nov. 1852), aged 80. All her children by first husband, —
the two oldest b. in Winslow, the others in Clinton : —

381. GEORGE (Whidden), b. Apr. 1791; d. at Winslow, Mar. 4, 1808,
aged 17.
382. OLIVE, b. Mar. 5, 1793; m., 1st, Nahum Kittredge, Jan. 1811; a
stone-worker, b. in Tewksbury, Mass., and d. Sept. 1829. She
m., 2d, John Elkins, of Lowell, Mass., Oct 19, 1837, who d.
Aug. 28, 1856, at New Durham, N. H.; m., 3d, Thomas Colby,
farmer, of Thetford, Vt., May 23, 1860, who d. Feb. 22, 1869.
She is now residing (1871) with her step-son, in Thetford (Post
Mills P. O.). Lived with her first husband in various places,
by whom seven sons, with ten years, one month and one day
between the births of the oldest and youngest.
  1. HENRY RUNNELS (Kittredge), b. Feb. 21, 1812, in Clinton; now
living in Lowell, Mass.
  2. GEORGE WHITTEN, b. Aug. 27, 1814, in Billerica, Mass.; d. at
Carlisle in 1841, by being buried in a well, aged 27.
  3. WALTER SWAIN, b. Apr. 2, 1816, in Billerica; now residing at
Strafford, Vt.
  4. LUTHER BRADLEY, b. Nov. 17, 1817, in Burlington, Mass.; now
living in Lowell.
  5. HORATIO GATES, b. Nov. 14, 1819, in Reading, Mass.; d. Aug.
29, 1846, in his 27th year.
  6. WILLIAM, b. Nov. 1820. in Reading; d. 1821, aged 6 mos. 19 days.
  7. TIMOTHY B., b. Mar. 22, 1822, in Burlington, Mass.; m. Matilda
C. Carter, Oct. 14, 1849; a quarryman and farmer; has resided
at Wilmington, Mass , Northfield, Vt., and now at Sharon. Vt.
Children : (1.) HORACE VESPER, b. Sept. 20, 1850, in Wilmington. (2.) GEORGE BRADLEY, b. Nov. 2, 1851, in W. (3.) HAR-
RIET MELVINA, b. Mar. 15, 1855, at Copperas Hill (Strafford?),
Vt. (4.) MARY ELIZABETH, b. Oct. 23, d. Dec. 7, 1857, in
Northfield. (5.) LAURA AMELIA, b. Feb. 13, 1859, in N. (6.)
MORANIA JANE, b. Feb. 28, d. July 15, 1861, in Northfield.
(7.) CHARLES HENRY, b. Nov. 27, 1863, in Sharon. (8.) TIM-
OTHY EUGENE, b. Mar. 28, d. Aug. 23, 1865, in Northfield.
(9.) EDWARD PAUL, b. Feb. 16, 1866, in N.
383. BENJAMIN (Whidden), b. Dec. 1795; was a soldier through the
war of 1812, being at Sackett's Harbor, N. Y., just before peace
was declared; settled at Presque Isle, Aroostook Co., Me., and
d. 1867, aged 72.
384. NANCY, b. Aug. 30, 1799; m. Benjamin Kendall, now residing with
her son, —
  1. WALDO (Kendall), at South Reading, Mass.
385. DAVID, b. Dec. 1801; was in the war of 1814, enlisting as captain's
waiter that year, and remained in different capacities as a soldier, till "the bells rang out for peace." Lived afterwards in
St. John, N. B., where he d. prior to 1860.
386. SARAH (Sally), b. Apr. 4, 1804; m. Reuben Simpson, of Clinton,
Me., Oct. 1826, where she ' Nov. 6, 1851, in her 48th year.
Children : —
  1. HARRIET (Simpson), b. Sept. 21, 1827; m. Enos H. Huzzy, of
Haverhill, Mass.
  2. GEORGE, b. Mar. 15, 1829; now residing at Wamego, Kansas.
  3. BRADFORD, b. Feb. 13, 1831; now living at Benton, Me.
  4. MARY ANN, b. Dec. 17, 1833; m. George Corson, of Rochester,
N. H., where residing, since 1848.

5. URIAH, b. May 5, 1835; now a driver of government teams in the far West.
6. OLIVE, b. Dec. 30, 1839; d. Oct. 18, 1863, in her 24th year.
7. DAVID, b. Nov. 4, 1841; same business as 5, above.
8. SARAH, b. Jan. 5, 1844; m. John Kilgore, of Leavenworth, Kan.
9. ELVIRA, b. Aug. 27, 1848; now living with her oldest sister in Haverhill.
387. SAMUEL (Whidden), b. July 4, 1807; lived in Ohio, and settled finally in Iowa.

388. JOHN[4] [126] (Benjamin[3], Ebenezer[2], Samuel[1]), resided first at Winslow, afterwards at Clinton, Me., having m. Mary Brown, of Hancock Plantation, Oct. 19, 1795. He d. Feb. 14, 1807, of tetanus, as the result of freezing his feet, aged 36. She inscribed his gravestone with her own hands in after years, at Benton, near Kendall's Mills, and there d. Mar. 1856. Two oldest children b. in Winslow, the others in Clinton: —

389. JOHN [865], b. Nov. 12, 1796.
390. OLIVER, b. Mar. 14, 1798; was drowned near Kendall's Mills, in the Kennebec, Nov. 28, 1818, in his 21st year, his body being recovered at Bath the April following.
391. DAMON [868], b. July 11, 1800.
392. ELNATHAN, b. Dec. 8, 1802; d. of brain fever, at Winslow, Dec. 1, 1824, aged 22.
393. JAMES [879], b. May 9, 1804.
394. BENJAMIN [884], b. July 15, 1806.

395. BENJAMIN[4] [127] (Benjamin[3], Ebenezer[2], Samuel[1]); a blacksmith by trade; m. Lydia Priest, of Winslow, May 21, 1799, and resided in W., where their children were all b. Like his brother James, he also was drowned at the Ticonic falls. While "dipping for shad and salmon," he was dragged in from a cliff, now shown on the Winslow side, June 3, 1810, aged 37. His body was found the next day in Waterville bay. She d. Jan. 23, 1840. Children: —

396. WASHINGTON [889], b. Mar. 5, 1800.
397. SYBIL [898], b. Jan. 9, 1802.
398. SOPHIA, b. Mar. 20, 1804; m., 1st, Henry Raymond; 2d, Hiram S. Crammer, of Cincinnati, O. Was living in Buffalo, N. Y., in 1840, where she is supposed to have died.
399. WARREN [902], b. May 25, 1806.
400. BETSY, b. 1808; d. 1824, aged 16.

401. STEPHEN[4] [128] (Benjamin[3], Ebenezer[2], Samuel[1]), settled in Winslow, and m. Lucy Priest, of W., sister of his brother Benjamin's wife, Apr. 11, 1798. He d. Aug. 21, 1824, in his 50th year. She d. "soon after the birth of her children": —

402. COLUMBUS [914], b. 1799.
403. SAMUEL [921], b. Jan. 30, 1802.

404. RUTH[4] [129] (Benjamin[3], Ebenezer[2], Samuel[1]), m, 1st, —— Drew, 1793; m., 2d, Joseph Proctor, farmer, of Clinton, Me., Feb. 1, 1797, who d. Dec. 23, 1856. She d. at Waterville, Me., July 24, 1847, in her 71st year. Children: —

405. JOHN (Drew), b. Sept. 5, 1794; was in the war of 1812; now residing in Pittsfield, Me.
406. JAMES (Proctor), b. Mar. 22, 1798; settled in the West, "on the Mississippi river."
407. ABIGAIL, b. Aug. 30, 1800, in Winslow; m. Willard Robbins, of Nashua, N. H.
408. JOSIAH, b. Jan. 21, 1804; d. "at Dunstable, N. H." (now Nashua), Oct. 22, 1841, in his 38th year.
409. AARON, b. Jan. 18, 1807; present residence, Waterville, Me.
410. ELIZA, b. Apr. 12, 1809. See [921].
411. SYRENA, b. Apr. 27, 1812, in Brookline, N. H., to which place her parents had moved; m. Samuel Robbins, of Nashua.
412. RHODA, b. Feb. 6, 1814, in Brookline; m. B. F. March, and now resides at Taylor, Ogle Co., Ill.
413. JEREMIAH, b. Nov. 19, 1818, in Dunstable, Mass.; now living in Waterville, Me.

414. ABIGAIL[4] [130] (Benjamin[3], Ebenezer[2], Samuel[1]), m. Robert Spear, of Winslow, Me., Apr. 17, 1796. He was b. Mar. 22, 1775; served in the United States army in the war of 1812-15, enlisting near the time of the birth of his youngest child; d. at Saco, Me., soon after the war. She d. at Winslow, May 31, 1859, aged 81. The five oldest children b. in Winslow; the three youngest at Moose Pond, now Hartland, Me.

415. WILLIAM (Spear), b. Sept. 7, 1797; settled in Athens, Me., and there d. Jan. 2, 1834, in his 37th year.
416. CHARLOTTE, b. Dec. 20, 1798; m. Asa Getchell, of Winslow, Dec. 23, 1815. Her son: —
    1. HENRY (Getchell) was in the late war, "19th regiment Maine volunteers;" present at the battle of Gettysburg. Her son: —
    2. SEBASTIAN S., in one of the New Hampshire regiments during three years' service, "participated in eighteen pitched battles without injury."
417. ELIZA (Spear), b. Sept. 17, 1801; m. Asa Merrow, of Farmington, Me.
418. NEHEMIAH, b. Jan. 10, 1804; now living in Winslow, near Waterville.
419. HEPHZIBAH, b. Feb. 27, 1808; m. Leonard Tibbetts, of Athens, Me., and d. Mar. 1858, aged 50. Her sons: —
    1. SUMNER (Tibbetts), and
    2. FREDERICK, were both lost in the late war, the former by disease, the latter being shot in battle.
420. ALFRED (Spear), b. Oct. 31, 1810; d. at Gardiner, Me., Nov. 1864, aged 54.
421. STEPHEN, b. July 17, 1812; resides at Athens, Me. His sons: —
    1. WILLIAM, and
    2. STEPHEN, were both lost in the war of the rebellion.
422. MARY ANN, b. Aug. 1814; m. H. Bragg, of Vassalboro', Me.; d. Dec. 3, 1835, aged 21.

423. RACHEL[4] [131] (Benjamin[3], Ebenezer[2], Samuel[1]), m. Joseph Emery, in 1801, who was b. Apr. 3, 1776, in Brookline, Mass. They made several removals, from Maine to Massachusetts, Vermont, and New York, and finally back again to Maine, as appears from the birthplaces of their children. He d. at Montville, Me., Feb. 17, 1849, aged 73. She d. at the same place, Feb. 17, 1856, aged 74. Children: —

424. HEPTZIBAH (Emery), b. Dec. 20, 1802, in Winslow; m., 1st, an Anderson; 2d, a Brashier; now residing at Montville, Me. (Freedom Vill. P. O.).
425. JULIA A., b. 1804, in Winslow; m. a Longfellow.
426. MELINDA (Belinda), b. 1806, in Brookline, Mass. See [902].
427. JOSEPH, b. 1808, in Montpelier. Vt.; d. the same year.
428. GEORGE W., b. Aug. 7, 1810, at Little Chazy, N. Y.; now living in Palmyra, Me.
429. MIRANDA, b. 1812, at Little Chazy; m. Samuel Crawford.
430. ALEXANDER, b. Jan. 1, 1818 (16), in Waterville; now resides near East Pittsfield, Me.
431. MARY, b. Aug. 5, 1822, in Augusta, Me.; m. a Baker, of Palmyra, Me.
432. SUSAN, b. Feb. 16, 1824, in Hallowell, Me.; m. a Furplus, of Bangor.

433. DAVID[4] [132] (Benjamin[3], Ebenezer[2], Samuel[1]), was one of the earliest permanent settlers in Pittsfield, Me., to which place his attention may have first been called by his father's mill; but he finally "went seven miles through the woods, by a spotted line, and commenced on a lot of wild land to make him a farm." He continued to reside in P. — lastly with his oldest son — till his death, July 30, 1871, in his 88th year, "like as a shock of corn cometh in his season." He m., 1st, Betsy Emery, of Hollis, Mar. 1802, who d. Dec. 16, 1814; m., 2d, Sarah McDonald, of Pittsfield, June, 1815, who d. Oct. 11, 1849. Children b. in Pittsfield: —

434. DANIEL [930], b. May 7, 1803 (1st wife).
435. ANNIE, b. June, 1807; d. Dec. 9, 1814, in her 8th year.
436. MARGARET DAVIS [937], b. Oct. 10, 1812 (13).
437. GREENWOOD [941], b. Dec. 21, 1816 (2d wife).
438. SYBIL [951], b. Mar. 15, 1819.
439. DAVID [957], b. Feb. 13, 1821.
440. ISAAC [960], b. Mar. 20, 1823.
441. THOMAS LEWIS [964], b. July 31, 1825 (24).
442. ELIZA WAITT [969], b. July 16, 1826.
443. SARAH ANN [973], b. Oct. 20, 1829.
444. MARY, b. Aug. 15, 1833; d. Sept. 9, 1859, aged 26.

445. MARY CROCKER[4] [138] (Stephen[3], Ebenezer[2], Samuel[1]), having moved to Fletcher, Vt., with her mother, after her father's death, m., 1st, Moses Melvin, of Cambridge, Nov. 1800. He d. 1811, and she m., 2d, William Elmer, of Orange, Vt., Feb. 15, 1812, who d. June 12, 1840, aged 65 years 8 months. Resided with her son [455], at Orange, till her death, June 18, 1863, in her 79th year. Her seven oldest children (first husband) were b. at Cambridge, Vt.; the five youngest in Orange: —

446. NATHAN (Melvin), b. Oct. 13, 1801; d. 1820, aged 19.
447. ANNA E., b. May 30, 1803 (Cambridge Recs.); m. Milton John Wolcott, of Vershire, Vt., Oct. 6, 1823, who was b. Sept. 16, 1802, in Holderness, N. H., and d. at V., July 14, 1862, in his 60th year. She d. Oct. 12, 1850, in her 48th year. Children b. in Vershire, except the two oldest: —
    1. SOLLIS ALCONDOR (Wolcott), b. Sept. 8, 1824, in Barnet. Vt.; m. Louisa Angeline Morey, Feb. 7, 1850, in Boston, Mass.; is now (1872) engaged in the railroad business at Dubuque,

Iowa Children: (1.) SOLOMON, b. Sept. 20, d. Sept. 28, 1851, in Chelsea, Vt. (2.) IDA ANN, b. June 29, 1856, in Northfield, Vt. (3.) EMMA JANE, b. Apr. 22, 1859, in Floyd, Iowa. (4.) MILTON DANIEL, b. Dec. 22, 1863, in Floyd. (5.) EDDIE SEWARD, b. May 15, 1866, in Dubuque. (6.) SOLLIS ALFRED, b. Mar. 25, 1869, in Dubuque. Also an adopted child, (7.) MARTHA, b. Jan. 6, 1848, in Boston.

2. EDWIN, b. Dec. 7, 1826; d. Jan. 27, 1827, in Barnet, Vt.
3. SEWALL ALBERT, b. Apr. 27, 1828; m. Elvina E. French, Apr. 3, 1851, at Manchester, N. H.
4. SARAH JANE, b. June 30, 1830; m. Stephen Titcomb, of Boston, Mass.
5. ALONZO, b. Sept. 14, 1831; m. Hannah D. Jones, Nov. 9, 1850, at Manchester, N. H.; d. Nov. 5, 1870, at New Hartford, Ia., aged 39.
6. ALPHONSO, b. Feb. 9, 1834; m. Lucy Ann Woodworth, Mar. 10, 1856, in Chelsea, Vt.; was first a farmer in Lyme and Orford, N. H.; now (1872) in the railroad business at Dubuque, Ia. Children: (1.) HORACE EDDIE, b. Dec. 10, 1862, in Lyme. (2.) CARRIE LOUISA, b. Jan. 2, 1866, in Orford.
7. CHARLOTTE LEMIRA, b. Sept. 7, 1836; m. William Philo, of New Hartford, Ia.
8. NORMAN MALTBY, b. Feb. 17, 1839; m. Martha Wolcott (1. (7.) above), Mar. 20, 1872, in Dubuque, Ia.
9. CHLOE ANNETTE, b. May 28, 1840; m. Morton Hammond, of New Hartford, Ia.
10. NEWELL NASON, b. Jan. 22, 1842.

448. MOSES (Melvin), b. Apr. 1, d. Apr. 6, 1805.
449. MARY, b. May 17, 1806; d. young.
450. STEPHEN, b. Sept. 19, 1807; d. Aug. 30, 1808, aged 11 mos. 11 days.
451. CHLOE, b. July 11, 1809; m. Sewall Peck, and resided in Licking Co., Ohio.
452. JACKSON, b. 1811; d. 1815, aged 4.
453. RICHARD (Elmer), b. Jan. 22, 1813; d. Mar. 6, 1815, aged 2.
454. LOUISA, b. Feb. 5 (9), 1815; m. Lyman Woodward, of Mansfield, Vt., and d. July 18, 1852, in her 38th year.
455. GEORGE WASHINGTON, b. Apr. 18, 1817; m. Emeline Fowler, Oct. 8, 1839. Children b. in Orange: —
    1. LOUISA H., b. Aug. 28, 1840; m. George Blanchard, of Barre, Vt.
    2. LUELLA MARIA, b. Mar. 4, 1845; m. Mason K. Griffith, of Tunbridge, Vt.
    3. MYRA L., b. Mar. 29, 1849; m. Origen Blanchard, of Barre, Vt.
    4. EVA ESTELLE, b. Sept. 8, 1852.
    5. FRANCES ADELLA, b. July 29, 1854.
    6. GEORGE EUGENE, b. Dec. 29, 1857.
456. ROXANA, b. Mar. 9, 1819; m. Hiram Cilley, of Topsham, Vt.
457. RICHARD FOWLER, b. Dec. 30, 1821; was married, and d. Jan. 9, 1854, at Orange, Vt., aged 32.

458. STEPHEN[4] [139] (Stephen[3], Ebenezer[2], Samuel[1]), m. Jane Brown, at Cambridge, Vt., Jan. 26, 1806, and located first as a farmer in Topsham, Vt., where his six oldest children were born. In 1818, he migrated to Ohio, and Apr 1, 1819, settled, as a pioneer, in McKean township, Licking Co. Built his log cabin in the woods, and moved into it the third day, without "chinking," flooring, or chimney, small timbers of split bass-wood being afterwards used for a floor. That year he planted two acres of corn among the logs, the product of which must needs be carried thirty miles to a grist-mill. Salt was brought from a distance of forty miles,

costing five dollars per bushel, and the clothing of himself and family, taken from New England, when worn out, was in part substituted by buckskin. In 1821 and 1822, money was so scarce that he could realize only twenty-five cents a day for labor, and wheat, hauled to a distance of forty miles, he sold at twenty-five cents per bushel, sometimes for unbleached cotton cloth at fifty cents a yard! Amid such hardships and privations, his farm was successfully cleared up ; but the completion of the Ohio canal, in 1832, made his circumstances easier, and he began to accumulate property. He took great interest in the educational enterprises of the new settlement. Having previously experienced religion, in 1827, under the preaching of a Baptist missionary from Connecticut, he became a faithful, devoted Christian, and was afterwards enabled to build a house, entirely with his own means, which was dedicated to the service of God. Benevolent and kind-hearted, he freely ministered to the wants of the poor, and was loved by all his acquaintances. He d. Oct. 30, 1844, aged 59. She d. Mar. 18, 1867. Children : —

459. EDWIN [979], b. Dec. 28, 1807.
460. LOUISA [991], b Jan. 2, 1810.
461. LUKE BROWN [993], b. Dec. 26, 1811.
462. LYDIA JANE [1003], b. June 17. 1813.
463. ADALINE, b. May 18, 1815; d. May 21, 1816, at Topsham, Vt., aged 1 year.
464. STEPHEN [1010], b. June 9, 1817.
465. SOLLIS [1016], b. May 10, 1819, in Licking Co , Ohio.
466. EMELINE, b. Apr. 24, 1821 ; d. Jan. 17, 1825, in her 4th year.
467. BENJAMIN FRANKLIN [1022], b. Apr. 6, 1823.
468. JAMES MONROE [1028], b. Sept. 4, 1824.
469. MARY MARIAH [1037], b. Sept. 4, 1826.
470. THOMAS BROWN [1046], b. Jan. 28, 1830, in Licking Co., as were each of the six youngest.
471. SAMANTHA, b. Nov. 18, 1832; d. the same day.

472. MOSES THURSTON[4] [142] (Stephen[3], Ebenezer[2], Samuel[1]), was named after his grandfather, Moses Thurston, of Hollis, N. H., who, "at a religious conference, Apr. 6, 1800, while addressing the throne of grace, being fervently engaged, was called into eternity, and, without struggle or groan, resigned his spirit to God who gave it, in his 80th year " (Hollis Cemetery). Thrown entirely upon his own resources in early life, he had bound himself to a Mr. Melvin, of Cambridge, Vt., till the age of 21, but bought the remainder of his time, the year before, for the purpose of studying with his uncle, Rev. Stephen Fuller, of Vershire. Thus fitting himself to teach school, he engaged in that employment, for several winters, in Cambridge, Vt., Haverhill, Mass., and other places. In 1816, he went into business at Cambridge Borough, with Mr. Trowbridge, and there continued as a successful merchant, under the firms of "Trowbridge & Runnels," "Runnels & Hunt," and "Runnels & Willey," for about ten years. Was the leading business man in the place, and did much for its welfare, especially in his efforts to build the Congregational meeting-house, in 1825.

His secular affairs then took an unfavorable turn.   He lost his health and most of his property by a series of misfortunes. He d. of a lingering consumption, Oct. 5, 1831, in his 42d year, "rejoicing in hope," and having united with the Congregational church by a profession of his faith in Christ, in his sick room, but a few weeks before his death.   His gravestone says, "An honest man, — the noblest work of God."   He m., 1st, Adaline Willey, of Jericho, Vt., at J., Nov. 25, 1819.   She d. at Hinesburg, Vt., on her way home from Saratoga Springs, Sept. 10, 1821, aged 23.   He m., 2d, Caroline Stearns, of Jaffrey, N. H., at Burlington, Vt., Feb. 10, 1825. She was a former pupil of his in Cambridge ; was b. Nov. 25, 1797, in Waltham, Mass., being in the seventh generation from Isaac Stearns, of Watertown, Mass., 1630. Children : —

473. MOSES THURSTON, b. May, 1828 ; d. aged 4 days.
474. MOSES THURSTON [1050], b. Jan. 23, 1830, in Cambridge, Vt.

475. SARAH[4] [143] (Stephen[3], Ebenezer[2], Samuel[1]), m. William Cox, Jr., of Vershire, Vt., Dec. 16, 1810.   He was a farmer in the east part of V., sold his estate to a copper-mining company prior to 1860, and removed to the neighboring village of West Fairlee, where he d. Apr. 11, 1869, aged 84 years 8 months, and she still resides (1872).   Children b. in Vershire : —

476. WILLIAM R. (Cox), b. Feb. 15, 1812 ; a farmer in Prophetstown, Ill., and there d. Dec. 16, 1856, in his 45th year.
477. HULDAH MALTBY, b. Dec. 11, 1813 ; m. John A. Gayety, iron factor, of Van Buren, N. Y., 1837. Children : —
  1. WILLIAM C. (Gayety), b. 1838 ; d. 1842, aged 4.
  2. FRANCIS, b. 1842.
  3. HULDAH ANN, b. 1844.
  4. EDWIN C., b. 1846 ; d. 1848, aged 2.
  5. SARAH ELIZABETH, b. 1848.
  6. MARY C., b. 1849.
  7. WILLIAM EDWIN, b. 1851.
478. MOSES THURSTON RUNNELS, b. Aug. 12, 1815 ; a farmer ; Lyme, N. H. ; now (1871) Thetford, Vt. ; m. Louisa Bunker, at Vershire, Mar. 30, 1841. Children : —
  1. ARABELLA OPHELIA, b. Apr. 13, 1844, at Vershire ; m. Jesse M. Cook, farmer, of Thetford, Feb. 24, 1869. He enlisted Aug. 14, 1861 (2), in Co. G, 9th Vermont regiment ; discharged June 13, 1865. Child : (1.) MABEL LOUISA (Cook), b. Oct. 25, 1871.
  2. PHEBE LOUISA (Cox), b. Nov. 5, 1847, at Lyme, N. H. ; d. Apr. 9, 1851, in her 4th year.
  3. HENRIETTA MARIA, b. Nov. 31, 1849 ; d. at Lyme, Apr. 6, 1851, in her 2d year.
479. SEWALL FULLER, b. June 10, 1817 ; a farmer in Vershire ; m. Lucina Bunker, 1843 ; d. Sept. 14, 1853, aged 36. Child : —
  1. FRANCINA, b. 1845.
480. SALINA SAWIN, b. May 29, 1819 ; m. Rodney Carr Tarbox, millwright, Nov. 12, 1839. Resided in Piermont, N. H., where he d. July 16, 1855. Children : —
  1. WILLIAM FELLOWS (Tarbox), b. June 16, 1841 ; d. Sept. 6, 1842, aged 15 months.
  2. RODNEY WALTER, b. Nov. 19, 1842 ; resides at Winooski, Vt.
  3. L......, b. May 23, 1846 ; d. May 21, 1849, aged 3.

    4. GEORGE MINOT, b. Nov. 7, 1847; d. Sept. 30, 1849, in his 2d year.
    5. LUCY ANN, b. June 29, 1852.

481. PHEBE M. (Cox), b. Jan. 7, 1821; d. Dec. 20, 1846, at Methuen, Mass., (?) aged 26.

482. ELIAS, b. Feb. 16, 1823; d. Aug. 18, 1825, in his 3d year.

483. SOLLIS RUNNELS, b. Feb. 10, 1825; a farmer in Vershire; moved to Prophetstown, Ill., and there d. May 19, 1868, aged 43. He had m. Luella F. George, of Vershire, 1850, who was b. May 22, 1825. Children : —
    1. WILLIAM ARTHUR, b. Aug. 17, 1851, in Vershire.
    2. MARY JANE, b. Oct. 15, 1853, in V.
    3. NETTIE Y., b. Jan. 27, 1864, in Prophetstown, Ill.

484. EDWIN FULLER, b. Sept. 22,. 1826; farmer in Vershire, Vt., and Prophetstown. Ill., moving to the latter place after his oldest brother's death, in 1857; m. Lucy George, of Vershire. Children : —
    1. LOUISA.   2. EVA.   3. DANIEL EDWIN.   4. ELLA.

485. STEPHEN RUNNELS, b. Aug. 20, 1828; d. Apr. 9, 1831, in his 3d year.

486. ELIAS WALTER, b. Sept. 16, 1830; d. Feb. 15, 1834, in his 4th year.

487. LUCY MARIA, b. Feb. 27, 1833; m. James Sleeper, Jr., farmer, of Sandown, N. H. Children :—
    1. SEWALL I. (Sleeper), b. Oct. 5, 1853.   2. CARRIE W., b. Nov. 10, 1855.   3. KATIE I., b Aug. 17, 1857.   4. ANNABELLE, b. Oct. 16, 1859.   5. LUETTA, b. Aug. 3, 1861.   6. CORA G., b. Jan. 6, 1863.   7. MYRTIE L., b. Dec. 8, 1865.   8. JAMES BURTON, b. Aug. 10, 1867.   9. ANDREW J., b. Oct. 26, 1868.

488. DANIEL WALTER, b. Sept. 22, 1834; a farmer in Vershire, south-west part of the town; m. Mary Ann Swan, Mar. 26, 1861, who was b. Oct. 15, 1841, in Tunbridge, Vt. Children : —
    1. JENNIE ARDELLE, b. Apr. 19, 1862.
    2. WILLIAM WALLACE, b. Apr. 17, 1864.

489. SOLLIS[4] [144] (Stephen[3], Ebenezer[2], Samuel[1]), was m. to Mary D. Parker, of Chelsea, Vt., by Rev. J. Johnson, Sept. 18, 1825. First located, as a merchant, in Cambridge, Vt., where his six oldest children were born. Removed to Burlington, Ohio (village of Homer), where the four youngest were born. Finally settled in Sigourney, Iowa, 1853, and still residing in that vicinity (1872). She d. at S., Mar. 23, 1862, — a woman of marked intelligence, and rare excellence of Christian character. Children : —

490. ANNIS C. [1056], b. June 17, 1826.
491. CAROLINE STEARNS, b. Jan. 11, 1828; d. at Burlington, O., May 1, 1837, in her 10th year.
492. JAMES LAWRENCE [1062], b. Oct. 4, 1829.
493. AZRO DENNISON [1068], b. Mar. 6, 1831.
494. MARY LUCRETIA [1070], b. Apr. 2, 1833.
495. EMELINE SOPHIA [1072], b. Dec 5, 1835.
496. HARRIET MARIAH [1076], b. Oct. 9, 1836.
497. FANNY WELLS, b. Nov. 4, 1838; d. July 16, 1840, in her 2d year.
498. EMILY ELIZABETH [1084], b. June 23, 1841.
499. JULIA FIDELIA [1087], b. Apr. 2, 1843.

500. SEWALL[4] [145] (Stephen[3], Ebenezer[2], Samuel[1]), m., 1st, Malinda Willey, at Cambridge, Vt., March 10, 1824. Settled first in Ohio, afterwards in Calumet Co., Wis., as a farmer. She d. Aug. 1, 1856. He is now residing (1872) at Grovesville, Wis., where he m., 2d, Mrs. Viann Waller, Sept. 6, 1859. Children, — first wife : —

501. HENRIETTA [1092], b. Oct. 12, 1825.
502. FRANKLIN [1103], b. Dec. 25, 1830.

503. FREDERICK[4] [164] (Samuel[3], Ebenezer[2], Samuel[1]), m. Hannah Chamberlain, at Hudson, N. H., Aug. 20, 1817, and settled in Concord, N. H., where he d. Feb. 5, 1833, in his 41st year. She was b. Sept. 25, 1787, in Andover, Mass., and is supposed to be still living with her daughter [509] in Wisconsin. Children : —

504. SAMUEL, b. Oct. 9, 1818; d. June 10, 1820, in his 2d year. This *may* have been the " child of Mr. Runnels," referred to in Bouton's Hist. of Concord, p. 378, as dying near that time by a singular casualty.
505. HANNAH, b. June 4, 1820; d. Mar. 8, 1846, in her 26th year.
506. MARY ANN, b. June 18, 1822; d. Sept. 19, 1844, aged 22.
507. SAMUEL B., b. Apr. 18, 1824; m., 1st, Roxana G. Savery, June 17, 1856; lived first at Wareham, Mass., afterwards at South Boston, where she d. of heart disease, Nov. 5, 1868. He m., 2d, Anna Trafton, of Boston, Apr. 10, 1871; is now a machinist in the Norway Iron Works, South Boston.
508. ELIZABETH S., b. July 18, 1826; m. Mouroe Cook, of Wakefield, N. H., June 11, 1854, and d. Nov. 21, 1856, aged 30.
509. LOUISA G. [1108], b. Feb. 23, 1827.
510. AMOS, b. Nov. 25, 1831; d. May 5, 1832, aged 5 mos. 10 days.

511. EBENEZER[4] [165] (Samuel[3], Ebenezer[2], Samuel[1]), inherited his father's farm and mills in Hollis, N. H., and m. Mrs. Lydia (Lawrence) Hale, of Littleton, Mass., " Dec. 30, 1828," according to the Hollis records, though another date is given by some of the family. She was b. Nov. 9, 1794, and d. at Hollis, Dec. 8, 1857, aged 63. He d. at H., Sept. 26, 1865, aged 71. Children b. in Hollis : —

512. LYDIA ABIGAIL, b. July 12, 1830; d. April 1, 1833, in her 3d year.
513. CHARLES SMITH, b. June 7, 1831; m. Fidelia Wheeler, of Hollis, Feb 6, 1867; resides on the old homestead in H.
514. DANIEL FREDERICK [1116], b. Mar. 25, 1833.
515. MARY ABIGAIL, b July 5, 1835; d. at Hollis, Mar. 25, 1859, in her 24th year.
516. LYDIA ELLEN, b. Oct. 30, 1837; m. John Henry Poole, merchant, of Boston, Nov. 26, 1863; residence in South Boston.
517. SARAH ELIZABETH, b. Oct. 14, 1840; d. Sept. 1, 1845, aged 5.

518. BETHIA[4] [168] (Samuel[3], Ebenezer[2], Samuel[1]); m. James R. Read, Dec. 19, 1822, at Hollis, N. H. He was b. Mar. 30, 1800, and d. Feb. 4, 1859, aged 59, having resided at Temple, Me., Medford, Mass., and Marion, Linn Co., Iowa. She d. Aug. 18, 1864, in her 64th year. Children : —

519. EBENEZER RUNNELS (Read), b. June 20, 1824.
520. HIRAM AUGUSTUS, b. Oct. 10, 1826; a carpenter; served three years in the last war, being sergeant in Co. H, 19th regiment Illinois volunteers.
521. CALVIN RICHARDSON, b. Mar. 3, 1829; a carpenter, now residing in Central City, Linn Co., Iowa; m. Lydia Ann Dewitt, Nov. 27, 1861, who was b. Apr. 12, 1841. Children : —
    1. GRACIE DARLING, b. May 23, 1863.
    2. CLAUDIE GERTRUDE, b. Jan. 10, 1866.
    3. TESSIE MARY, b. Dec. 5, 1871.

522. JAMES DEXTER, b. Aug. 28, 1831; a farmer; three years in the service of his country, sergeant of Co. K, in the 6th Iowa cavalry; m. Joanna Angeline Gardner, Dec. 8, 1853. She was b. Mar. 2, 1830. Children : —

    1. BERTHA ETTIE, b. Aug. 31, 1856.
    2. EFFIE JENETTE, b. Feb. 17, 1860.
    3. RAYMOND DEXTER, b. Oct. 22, 1862; d. Aug. 18, 1864, in his 2d year.
    4. LLEWELLYN JAMES, b. June 22, 1868.
    5. GERTRUDE DEXTER, b. May 2, 1870.
    6. ABBIE ETHEL, b. Feb. 21, 1872.

523. DANA DUNBAR, b. Dec. 15, 1833; a mason; m. Rhoda Adaline Crane, May 22. 1859, who was b. Feb. 18, 1840. Children : —

    1. WALTER SIDNEY, b. Apr. 9, 1860.
    2. ELMER AUGUSTUS, b. Nov. 1, 1861.
    3. HARRY LYMAN, b. Jan. 8, 1865.
    4. LOTTIE JOSEPHINE, b. June 13, 1868.
    5. HATTIE MAUD, b. Jan. 4, 1872.

524. HANNAH ABIGAIL, b. July 11 (14`, 1836; m. Lorenzo Jenks, who was b. Oct. 22, 1838, and d. at Marion, Iowa, Apr. 20, 1866, in her 30th year, leaving : —

    1. MARY ABBIE (Jenks), b. Apr. 8, 1861.

525. SUSAN[4] [169] (Samuel[3], Ebenezer[2], Samuel[1]) ; m. George Washington Sherburn, Sept. 1826 ; d. at Boston, Mar. 28, 1850, aged 47 ; buried in Nashua, N. H. Children : —

    526. SAMUEL (Sherburn), b. June 13, 1827.
    527. ABIGAIL, b. Mar. 25, 1829.
    528. GEORGE W., b. Jan. 24, 1832.

529. JOHN[4] [173] (Thomas[3], Ebenezer[2], Samuel[1]) ; m., 1st, Anna Page, of Haverhill, Mass., Dec. 13 (21, town records), 1817. She d. Oct. 12, 1826. He m., 2d, Mrs. Elizabeth Wilson, of H., Feb. 1, 1827, and has since deceased. Children b. in Haverhill : —

    530. THOMAS KING [1122], b June 29, 1819.
    531. LUCY ANN [1124], b. Aug. 26 (29), 1820.
    532. JOHN S. [1126], b. Feb. 18, 1826; an adopted son, being the nephew of his second wife.

533. BETSY[4] [174] (Thomas[3], Ebenezer[2], Samuel[1]) ; m. Peter Elkins Smith, of Haverhill, Mass., a native of Sanbornton, N. H., Aug 31, 1817. He was a blacksmith ; commenced his trade with Thomas Runnels [171], father of his future wife, in 1805, at the age of 13 ; moved to Amherst, N. H., in 1823 ; afterwards lived in South Merrimack, N. H., Cincinnati, O., and Covington, Ky., whence returned to Haverhill, or Bradford, Mass , in 1857. Their " Golden Wedding " was celebrated at Bradford, Aug. 31, 1867. Children : —

    534. SOPHIA RUNNELS (Smith), b. Aug. 16, 1818; m. Rev. Mr. Chamberlain, now of Iowa.
    535. CAROLINE ELIZABETH, b. Sept. 15, 1820; m. Rev. Mr. Jewell, now of Illinois.
    536. CHARLES OTIS, b. May 3, 1823; d. Feb. 4 (5), 1872, at East Taunton, Mass., of consumption, in his 49th year.
    537. JANE UNDERHILL, b. June 4, 1826; now Mrs. Sargent.

538. MARY LUCY, b. Nov. 28, 1832; now Mrs. Patterson; residing (1870) at Cummings' Mills, in Dorchester, N. H.
539. HERBERT AUGUSTINE, b. Oct. 17, 1835; a saloon keeper in Haverhill, Mass. (1869); m. Emma L. West [549], of Bradford, Sept. 7, 1869.

540. LOUISA[4] [175] (Thomas[3], Ebenezer[2], Samuel[1]); m. Richard H. West, of Haverhill, Dec. 1822; lived in Bradford. owning a now valuable estate near Haverhill bridge, where he d. Sept. 20, 1861, and she still resides (1872). Children b. in Bradford: —

541. ORESTES (West), b. Jan. 9, 1824; a shoe merchant in New York city, firm of "Studwell Bros. & West," 17 Murray Street; m. Mary A. Hyatt, in New York. Children: —
  1. GEORGE HYATT, b. Feb. 26, 1850; is a clerk in a wholesale boot and shoe establishment, New York; m. Ellennora Punchard, a native of England, Oct. 26, 1871.
  2. MARY LOUISA, b. Sept. 12, 1852.
542. ELBRIDGE G., b. Dec. 26, 1826; a shoe manufacturer, first in Farmington, N. H., now in Haverhill, Mass.; m. Abby Partridge, of Northampton, Mass. Child: —
  1. EDWARD HENRY, b. Apr. 1848, in Farmington.
543. ELLEN, b. Oct. 25, 1828; d. Sept. 30, 1830, in her 2d year.
544. CHARLES O., b. Sept. 1, 1830; resides with his mother in Bradford.
545. ANN H., b. Feb. 12, 1832; d. Sept. 17, 1849, in her 18th year.
546. WALTER, b. Jan. 14, d. Dec. 15, 1833.
547. MARY E., b. Oct. 17, 1835.
548. JAMES G., b. Jan. 18, 1837; a Union soldier in the war of the rebellion; d. at Andersonville, Ga., Aug. 26, 1864, in his 28th year.
549. EMMA L., b. Jan. 4, 1838. See [539].
550. SARAH PAGE, b. Dec. 9, 1840; d. Feb. 4, 1843, aged 2 years 2 mos.
551. BEN LAPHAM, b. Oct. 4, 1843; m. Charlotte Morse, of Boxford, Mass.; a shoe manufacturer, now living in Georgetown, Mass. Children: —
  1. RICHARD HAZEN. 2. ADELAIDE.

552. KING LAPHAM[4] [176] (Thomas[3], Ebenezer[2], Samuel[1]); m. Nancy Alden, at Dedham, Mass., June 9, 1831. She was a dau. of Paul and Rebecca (Newell) Alden, descended from the John Alden who landed on Plymouth Rock in 1620. He owned and carried on an extensive bakery in Fall River, Mass., for many years, where she d. Apr. 18, 1856, and he still resides. Children: —

553. FRANCES JONES, b. Jan. 26, 1833, in Dedham.
554. ROXANA ALDEN, b. Jan. 22, 1837, in Fall River, as were the other children; d. Nov. 9, 1840, in her 4th year.
555. FRAISETTE, b. Mar. 19, 1838.
556. EBENEZER, b. Apr. 13, d. May 1, 1840.
557. GEORGE, b. July 13, d. July 26, 1844.
558. CHARLES, b. Aug. 1, d. Aug. 22, 1846.

559. WARREN[4] [177] (Thomas[3], Ebenezer[2], Samuel[1]), m. Mrs. Ann Wells, of Utica, N. Y., June 1, 1830; resided first at Amherst, N. H., then at Fall River, Mass., as at present. Two oldest children b. in Amherst: —

560. HIRAM [1133], b. July 21, 1831.
561. HAZEN, b. June 18, 1834; d. at Fall River, Sept. 10, 1843, aged 9.
562. HARRIET ANN [1135], b. Nov. 18, 1838.

563. Amelia Elizabeth [1140], b. Sept. 17, 1840 (Sept. 16, 1841).
564. Warren Hazen [1145], b. Dec. 21, 1843.

565. Moses Clement[4] [178] (Thomas[3], Ebenezer[2], Samuel[1]), a blacksmith in Haverhill, Mass.; m. Eliza B. Perry, of Bradford, Sept. 29, 1825, who d. Nov. 26, 1867. He d. at H., Dec. 3, 1869, aged 64. Children : —

566. Eliza A. [1149], b. Feb. 20, 1827.
567. Sarah Jane [1151], b. July 24, 1829.
568. Moses W., b. July 22, 1835; m. Matilda Gerrish, of Dover, N. H., Nov. 17, 1856; d. at Bradford, Dec. 20, 1869, in his 35th year.
569. William, b. Nov. 5, 1838; d. Nov. 10, 1839, aged 1 year.

570. Mira[4] [181] (Nathaniel[3], Ebenezer[2], Samuel[1]), m. George Hibbard, of Piermont, farmer, Apr. 29, 1820, who occupied a valuable and attractive homestead on the Connecticut River, in the northwest part of P., now held by their eldest son. He d. about 1863. Children : —

571. Benjamin (Hibbard), b. Jan. 27, 1822.
572. Sarah A., b. Nov. 29, 1823; m. John H. Sawyer, of Bradford, Vt.; a farmer on the opposite side of the river from her father's.
573. Moses, b. Dec. 25, 1826; a farmer in Lancaster, N. H.
574. William, b. Feb. 1, 1828; also a farmer in Lancaster.
575. Hannah Jennette, b. Aug. 31, 1830; m. Edward Augustus Lambert (second wife), of Brooklyn, N. Y., Feb. 15, 1859. He is a native of New York city, where now (1870), an importer of paper and stationery, and president of the "Craftsmen's Life Assurance Company." Was mayor of Brooklyn, N. Y., 1853-4; an original trustee and commissioner for location of the "New York State Inebriate Asylum." Was active in efforts as a civilian in the late war of the rebellion, calling the first great war meeting on Fort Greene in Apr. 1861. An officer in the synods and general assembly of the Presbyterian church; treasurer of its home missions, and member of committee appointed in 1866 for its re-union. (From the "History of Brooklyn," "Presb. Re-union Memorial," etc.) Children b. in Brooklyn : —
   1. Edward Hibbard (Lambert), b. Aug. 20, 1860.
   2. Rufus Crook, b. Apr. 13, 1862.
   3. Jennette Hibbard, b. May 31, 1865.
   4. Annie Cuyler, b. Oct. 3, 1869.
576. Mira (Hibbard), b. Dec. 23, 1832 (3); was m. to Rufus Crook, of Brooklyn, N. Y., by Rev. I. Davis, at Piermont, Mar. 4, 1851. He was a native of Piermont; went in early life to New York, and became very successful in the business of a restaurant. Was a member of the Lafayette Avenue Presbyterian Church (Rev. Dr. Cuyler's), and one of the pioneers, a trustee, and a member of the committee in the noble enterprise of that society for building a church edifice. He d. Mar. 14, 1868. Children b. in Brooklyn : —
   1. Julia (Crook), b. Nov. 26, 1851; d. Mar. 23, 1854, in her 3d year.
   2. Louise, b. Feb. 10, 1855.
   3. Effie, b. Nov. 17, 1856.
   4. Gertrude, b. Aug. 8, 1858.
   5. Alice, b. Feb. 25, 1861.
   6. George Edward, b. Sept. 27, 1866.

577. HARRIET[4] [182] (Nathaniel[3], Ebenezer[2], Samuel[1]), was m. to Abner Tarbox, of Piermont, N. H., by Rev. Robert Blake, Mar. 12, 1829. He. d. Apr. 20, 1853. Children : —

578. CHARLES (Tarbox), b. Sept. 12, 1831 : a farmer in Piermont.
579. MIRA ANN, b. Feb. 23, 1835 ; m. Willard Williams, of Bradford, Vt.
580. HARRIET R., b. June 4, 1840.
581. SARAH JANE, b. Aug. 16, 1843 ; m. Alfred M. Robie.

582. EBENEZER[4] [183] (Nathaniel[3], Ebenezer[2], Samuel[1]), resided in Portsmouth, N. H., having m. Ann Jane Donnell, of York, Me., Aug. 1826. She was b. 1808, in St. Domingo, W. I. (or New York City). He repaired to California soon after the discovery of gold, and was there assassinated, at Sonora, Mar. 13, 1861, aged 60. She having remained in Portsmouth, there d. Nov. 27, 1861, aged 53. According to the Rockingham Probate Records, Joseph M. Edmonds, Esq., of Portsmouth, was appointed to settle his estate, 1863. He was highly esteemed as a citizen, and a member of the Christian Baptist Church, in Portsmouth. His children, b. in P., were : —

583. GEORGE, b. Aug. 1827 ; d. 1829, aged 2 years, by accident of scalding.
584. MARY ELIZABETH [1153], b. Feb. 13, 1829.
585   CHARLES EBEN, b. Nov. 22, 1830 ; went to California with his father, and there d. Mar. 31, 1858, in his 28th year.
586. ANN MARIA [1157], b. Sept. 11, 1832.
587. GEORGE HAZEN, b. May, 1834 ; was a printer by trade ; took a voyage at sea for his health in the capacity of steward, and was last heard from at Liverpool, Eng., 1858, when about embarking for the East Indies.
588. HANNAH JANE [1159], b. Feb. 7, 1837.

589. ARTHUR[4] [185] (Nathaniel[3], Ebenezer[2], Samuel[1]), inherited the farm occupied by his father in Piermont, N. H. ; sold the same after his father's death, and purchased another near the site of the old meeting-house in P., where residing. with new buildings erected (1872). Was m. to Luella Hall, at her father's, in Newbury, Vt., Nov. 5, 1838, by Rev. Mr. Dow. She d., after a wearisome and protracted illness of dropsy, Apr. 18, 1872. Children b. in P. : —

590. MARY MORRILL WORTHEN [1166], b. May 24, 1841.
591. EZRA BARTLETT, b. Aug. 4, 1847 ; m. Ella J. Merrill, of Bradford, Vt., Sept. 7, 1871, and settled with his father in Piermont.

592. MARY MORRILL[4] [186] (Nathaniel[3], Ebenezer[2], Samuel[1]), was m., 1st, to John Adams Worthen, of Bradford, Vt., Nov. 14, 1828, by Rev. Robert Blake, of Piermont. He d. Aug. 5, 1847, aged 43. She was m., 2d, to William Pollard, of Barnet, Vt., Nov. 18, 1858, by Rev. George Webber, of St. Johnsbury. He is a farmer, residing in Bath, N. H., on Connecticut River, near McIndoe's Falls. Children (first husband) all b. in Bradford except the youngest : —

593. MARY ANN (Worthen), b. Mar. 28, 1830; m. William Edwin Peckett, of Bradford, July 15, 1849; residing, 1872, in South Boston, Mass., 196 Dorchester Street. Children : —
 1. ADA ISABELLE (Peckett), b. May 28, 1850.
 2. GEORGE FRANKLIN, b. Nov. 4, 1861; d. July 8, 1863, in his 2d year.
 3. HATTIE LEWIS, b. Apr. 17, d. Aug. 4, 1866.
594. JOHN ADAMS (Worthen), b. Jan. 24, 1832; m. Lucy Flagg Crafts, July 2, 1854; resides at Melrose, Mass. (Wyoming Station). Children : —
 1. FRANK FAYETTE, b. June 13, 1855.
 2. SUSIE S., b. Jan. 17, 1859.
595. HARRIET, b. Dec. 17, 1833; m. John W. Lewis, of St. Johnsbury, Vt., Dec. 1863.
596. GEORGE B., b. Dec. 4, 1836; enlisted in the U. S. navy, at Charlestown, Mass., June 12, 1856; cruised on the coast of Africa for two years; was discharged at Portsmouth, N. H., June 12, 1860. The following November — having been on a merchant vessel to St. Helena, and thence to Vera Cruz, Mexico — he enlisted at the latter port on the U. S. steamer "Susquehanna"; cruised in the Mediterranean, and visited the Holy Land. Called home by the impending war, he re-enlisted on the U. S. steamer "Cambridge," and followed the fortunes of that vessel as corporal of marines. Was wounded at Roanoke Island, Feb. 8, 1862, but afterwards took part in the engagement with the rebel steamer "Merrimack"; in consequence of which, with his head wounded, ribs badly broken, and lungs diseased, he was sent to the Brooklyn, N. Y., hospital, in Nov. 1862. Received his final discharge, Feb. 9, 1863. Remained with his friends in Brooklyn, Bath, and Bradford, — a great sufferer in his country's cause, — and d. a true patriot, at Bradford, Sept. 15, 1863, in his 27th year. (Funeral attended by the writer.)
597. ARTHUR ENOCH, b. Jan. 5, 1839; m. Letitia Hancock, Nov. 8, 1860; was in the regimental band of the 3d Vermont regiment; served thirteen months, and narrowly escaped in the seven days' fight and retreat before Richmond, Va., 1862. Now residing in Melrose, Mass. Children : —
 1. GEORGE ARTHUR, b. Sept. 16, 1863.
 2. INEZ EMMA, b. Aug. 31, 1866.
598. MIRA JENNETTE, b. July 8, d. Aug. 26, 1841.
599. ADAMS MERRILL, b. Nov. 13, 1842; being adopted by Mr. John Poor, of Landaff, N. H., he has taken the name of Adams M. Poor, and resides in L ; m. Jane S. Clough, Jan. 27, 1864. Children : —
 1. FRANK CLOUGH (Poor), b. May 17, 1865.
 2. HATTIE CLARABELLE, b Apr. 18, 1867.
 3. MARY LOUISA, b. Mar. 27, 1869.
 4. EMMA ROWENA, b. Apr. 6, 1871.
600. JANE ELIZABETH (Worthen), b. Sept. 17, 1844; m. Luther B. Pollard, June 16, 1868. He is the son of her mother's second husband, and they now reside with their common parents, at Bath, N. H. Children : —
 1. JOHN WORTHEN (Pollard), b. May 28, 1869.
 2. MYRA HIBBARD, b. Oct. 27, 1870; d. Jan. 22, 1872, aged 1 year 3 months.

601. BARTLETT[4] [188] (Nathaniel[3], Ebenezer[2], Samuel[1]), m. Lucinda Elvira Clark, Nov. 15 (Oct. 12), 1837, at Hartford, Ohio. She was b. Oct. 12, 1819, and d. Nov. 17, 1860, aged 41. He was a carpenter, moved early in life to Ohio, and there d., at Alexandria, Licking Co., Aug. 20, 1849, aged 36. Children : —

602. MARY ISABELLA [1170], b. Sept. 6, 1839, in Hartford, O.
603. LUCY ORLINAH, b. Feb. 1, d. Mar. 17, 1846, at Alexandria, O.

604. GEORGE[4] [189] (Nathaniel[3], Ebenezer[2], Samuel[1]), migrated to Ohio, and m. Hannah Gorrell, at Mount Vernon, O.,
May 20, 1841. Moved back to New England, again to Ohio, and
finally to Sigourney, Iowa, about 1854, where he d. Jan. 4, 1869,
in his 55th year. Children : —

605. LYDIA [1175], b. May 16, 1842, in Alexandria, O.
606. NATHANIEL [1180], b. June 26, 1844, in Alexandria.
607. CHARLES, b. Sept. 1, 1846, in Bradford, Vt.
608. GEORGE FRANCIS, b. Jan. 10, 1849, in Alexandria.
609. FLORA, b. Sept. 18, 1851, in A.
610. EMILY, b. Dec. 8, 1853, in A.
611. MIRA, b. Mar. 26, 1856, in Sigourney, Ia.
612. MARY PICCOLOMINA, b. Oct. 7, 1858, in Sigourney; d. Oct. 29, 1870,
      aged 12.
613. MERRILL FREMONT, b. Oct. 26, 1861; d. Jan. 8, 1863, in his 2d year.
614. JESSIE, b. Mar. 25, 1864.
615. JOSEPH HAZEN, b. Jan. 31, 1867.

616. HAZEN[4] [191] (Nathaniel[3], Ebenezer[2], Samuel[1]). Having
made a successful expedition to California, he was m. to Harriet
A. Metcalf, of Piermont, N. H., by Rev. I. Davis, Dec. 20, 1853,
and lived in Piermont village till his lamented death, Oct. 10, 1857,
aged 37. He left one child : —

617. HAZEN FAYETTE, b. Sept. 2, 1857; now residing, with his mother,
      in Zumbrota, Minn.

618. DANIEL GEORGE[4] [193] (Daniel[3], Ebenezer[2], Samuel[1]),
succeeded his father as a blacksmith in Warner, N. H., and m., 1st,
Rachel Corser, of West Boscawen, Jan. 25, 1829. She was the
sister of Rev. Enoch Corser, and d. July 14, 1839. He m., 2d,
Dolly Weed, of Topsham, Vt., Dec. 6, 1840, and d. June 26, 1866,
in his 66th year. His children, — three by each wife, — b. in
Warner, were : —

619. SARAH GEORGE [1182], b. Aug. 9, 1830.
620. MARY CLOUGH [1188], b. Dec. 27, 1832.
621. DANIEL HENRY, b. July 8, 1835; d. July 25, 1837, aged 2.
622. DANIEL, b. Oct. 31, 1841; resides chiefly in Lowell, Mass.
623. HELEN, b. Apr. 30, 1845.
624. ELLA JANE, b. Jan. 1, 1849; now (1872) in the "Mirror" printing
      office, Manchester, N. H.

625. GEORGE[4] [197] (Daniel[3], Ebenezer[2], Samuel[1]), is now
senior partner of th efirm "Runels, Clough & Co.," stone-cutters
and dealers in granite, in Lowell, Mass., where he resides, with a
summer residence at Gloucester. They have one hundred and
fifty men in their employ, with stone-yards at Lowell, West Concord, N. H., Fitzwilliam, N. H., and more recently at Gloucester.
Amount of business from one hundred and fifty thousand to two
hundred thousand dollars per annum. This firm furnished all the
stone for the Masonic Temple, in Boston, 1867, and for Booth's

Theatre, New York, 1868. Were also furnishing, in 1869, for the new Custom House in Portland, Me., for the building of the "Equitable Insurance Company" in New York, and for several other edifices, both public and private. He m. Mary Ann Morrill, at Springfield, N. H., Dec 31, 1845. Children: —

626. EMMA, b. Dec. 21, 1847, in Lowell, Mass., and there d. July 9, 1871, in her 24th year. "At a meeting of the trustees and teachers of the Independent Union Mission," in Lowell, July 23, "her death was suitably noticed, and ready and hearty testimony borne to her fidelity and worth." In the resolution of sympathy communicated from the same meeting to her family and the press, she is said to have been "for several years a faithful, constant and successful teacher of the Sunday school," so that, in her death, "the mission experiences a serious loss."

627. CHARLES, b. Oct. 18, 1849, in Lowell.

628. HENRY, b. Mar. 27, 1852, in Waterbury, Vt.

FIFTH GENERATION.

629. STEPHEN[5] [216] (Enos[4], Stephen[3], Stephen[2], Samuel[1]), was for many years a merchant at Honolulu, Oahu, Sandwich Islands, and returned home with his sister, Rebecca E. [226], in very poor health, May, 1856. He d. at his father's homestead in Boxford, Mass., July 17, 1857, in his 75th year. He m. Susan Jackson, of Honolulu, in 1829. Children, all b. in Honolulu : —

630. MATILDA EUELA [1192], b. Oct. 8, 1830.
631. EVELINE, b. Dec. 25, 1831; d. Feb. 19, 1856, at Boxford, aged 24.
632. JOHN RICE, b. Nov. 21, 1833; d. at San Francisco, Cal., Apr. 16, 1855, in his 22d year.
633. HARRIETTE, b. Aug. 27, 1835; m. Roger Sherman Littlefield, of Boston (second wife), Aug. 16, 1864. See [642].
634. EDWARD JACKSON, b. Aug. 28, 1838; was educated in New England, and d. at Honolulu, Jan. 27, 1865, in his 27th year.

635. ELIPHALET[5] [219] (Enos[4], Stephen[3], Stephen[2], Samuel[1]), m Hannah Hall, of Dracut, Nov. 14, 1815. He d. in New York, Apr. 17, 1838, aged 49. She d. Aug. 1867. Children : —

636. SARAH CLEMENT [1195], b. July 18, 1817, in Boxford.
637. WILLIAM JAMES [1203], b. July 11, 1819, in Haverhill, Mass.
638. CHARLOTTE MATILDA, b. Aug. 20, 1821; a teacher in East Lyme, Ct. (1870).
639. MARY ANN, b. Nov. 21, 1827; m. John Butterworth, in Boston, Nov. 27, 1861. He was a native of England; a druggist; now residing (1870) at Boston.
640. WALTER SCOTT, b. Jan. 15, 1831; m. Mary Ann Outhank, of Charlestown, Mass., Aug. 9, 1858. He was a book-keeper in Boston; afterwards a teacher in Sabinetown, Texas, where he d. Jan. 15, 1860, aged 29. She was b. Aug. 29, 1838, in Concord, Vt.; now employed (1870) at Allen's photograph rooms, 13 Temple Place, Boston.
641. ELEANOR ANALETTE [1210], b. Feb. 7, 1833; she and the two last were probably b. in Bradford, Mass., as their births are on the Bradford Records.
642. HARRIET ISABELLA [1214], b. Mar. 15, 1837.

643. SAMUEL SPOFFORD[5] [220] (Enos[4], Stephen[3], Stephen[2], Samuel[1]), resided in Charlestown, Mass.; a morocco dresser; d. Dec. 3, 1855, at West Boxford, aged 64. Had m. Beulah Reed, of Concord, Vt., 1817, who d. Aug. 29, 1868, at Woburn, Mass. Children, all b. in Charlestown except [650] : —

644. CAROLINE MATILDA [1217], b. Dec. 20, 1818.
645. SAMUEL ARCHER, b. Feb. 1821; a merchant at Honolulu, S. I., where he d. Oct. 26, 1847, in his 27th year.
646. HARRIET ELIZA, b. Mar. 1823; d. at Charlestown, Mar. 1830, aged 7.
647. EDWARD EVERETT [1224], b. Dec. 26, 1825.
648. FRANCES ANN DRINKWATER, b. Nov. 13, 1827; m. William Eustis Skilton, in Charlestown, July 12 (13), 1854. He is an importer; residing at Charlestown (1870).
649. HARRIET AUGUSTA, b. Mar. 1830; d. 1832, aged 2.
650. CHARLES PEARL, b. Apr. 12, 1831, in Boxford, probably, as his birth appears alone on the Boxford Records; was an engineer, and d. at White Pine, Nevada Territory, Feb. 13, 1868, in his 37th year.
651. SARAH ISABELLA [1228], b. Mar. 1835 (7).

652. SARAH[5] [222] (Enos[4], Stephen[3], Stephen[2], Samuel[1]), m. Joshua Baldwin, of Charlestown, Mass., at West Boxford, Nov. 26, 1824. He was a morocco dresser; afterwards lived at Billerica, and now (1870) at Townshend Harbor, Mass. She d. Oct. 27, 1833, in her 38th year, at Charlestown, where their children were b. : —

653. SARAH EVELINE (Baldwin), b. Mar. 14, 1826; d. in Boston, Aug. 19, 1852, in her 27th year.
654. HARRIET MATILDA, b. Nov. 20, 1828; d. at West Boxford, May 5, 1847, in her 19th year.
655. WILLIAM, b. 1830; d. aged 2 months.
656. SUSAN ISABELLA, b. Sept. 13, d. Oct. 26, 1833.

657. MARY ISABELLA[5] [227] (Enos[4], Stephen[3], Stephen[2], Samuel[1]), m. William Lund, of Charlestown, Mass , May 2, 1831, and d. Apr. 27, 1834. at C., aged 27. Children, b. in Charlestown : —

658. MATILDA BARKER (Lund), b. Feb. 12, 1832.
659. MARY ISABELLA, b. Jan. 27, 1834; d May 19, 1865, aged 31. Her poetical effusions, as well as the testimony of her friends, give proof that she was both amiable and gifted, with rare qualities of mind and heart. We extract from a little volume entitled "Stray Leaves," published in 1867 (pp. 31-2), this beautiful "Birth-Day" tribute to her aunt, Matilda Barker [218], in 1864. Its allusions, as verified by the foregoing records, make it most an appropriate close to this generation of her grandfather's family : —

> " A greeting from the homestead
>   Is sent to you this day,
> To remind you that we're near in thought,
>   Though we seem so far away.

>   .   .   .   .

> " But not to these few hours alone
>   Are all our thoughts confined,
> For they are flying far through air,
>   For thoughts are free as wind.

>   .   .   .   .

> " At seventeen hundred eighty-seven,
>   We see them pause with care;
> For there they find a date is given
>   That marks a day most fair.

"For at that time one precious gem
　To a golden chain was given,
That, when completed, numbered *twelve*,
　But soon its links were riven.

"And still *this* glittering gem shines on,
　In sunshine and in shade;
And many a heart, by its bright light,
　Is warm and happy made.

"But He who gave its lustre rare,
　And keeps it still undimmed,
Will place it in a brighter chain,
　And take it back to him."

660.　MARY HARRIS[5] [270] (John[4], William[3], Stephen[2], Samuel[1]), m. William Runnels Cole, of Boxford [266], Jan. 17, 1855. He was a farmer; served the town of Boxford as selectman, clerk, treasurer, and school committee, and d. Nov. 18, 1865, in his 49th year, at West Boxford, where she still resides (1869). Children : —

661.　WILLIAM KIMBALL (Cole), b. June 3, 1856.
662.　ABBY LAVINIA, b. July 27, 1858; d. Dec. 26, 1865, in her 8th year.
663.　NORMAN SEAVER, b. July 3, 1860.
664.　MORRIS LEE, b. Apr. 29, 1863.
665.　MARY, b. Sept. 20, 1865; d. Sept. 22, 1867, aged 2 years, 2 days.

666.　WILLIAM BARTLETT[5] [271] (John[4], William[3], Stephen[2], Samuel[1]), is a farmer at North Andover, Mass., near Lawrence (1870), having m. Sarah Jane Cram (?), of Oxford, Mass., Nov. 27, 1850. Children : —

667.　CLARA JEAN, b. Jan. 13, 1852, in Gardner, Mass.
668.　SARAH BARTLETT, b. July 16, d. Sept. 16, 1854, in North Andover.
669.　CLARENCE WILLIAM, b. July 31, 1855, in North Andover.
670.　CHARLES BARTLETT, b. June 10, 1858, in East Boxford.

671.　ELIZABETH FOSTER[5] [272] (John[4], William[3], Stephen[2], Samuel[1]), m. William George Richardson (first wife), Oct. 23, 1850, at North Andover. He was a truckman residing in Boston. See [677]. She d. Dec. 22, 1855, in her 27th year. Child : —

672.　GEORGE ASA (Richardson), b. Aug. 9, 1852.

673.　ABBY MINERVA[5] [274] (John[4], William[3], Stephen[2], Samuel[1]), m. Joseph W. Poor, at West Boxford, Feb. 25, 1857. He is a blacksmith residing at North Andover, where were born : —

674.　WILLIAM GEORGE (Poor), b. June 13, 1858.
675.　MINNIE WHITE, b. May 9, 1863.
676.　LINCOLN, b. Apr. 18, 1865, the Tuesday after President Lincoln's assassination.

677.　PRUDENCE LAVINIA[5] [275] (John[4], William[3], Stephen[2], Samuel[1]), m. W. G. Richardson (second wife), see [671], Jan. 4, 1857, at West Boxford. He d., by a railroad accident, in Ohio, July 1, 1857. Child : —

678. LIZZIE WILLIAM (Richardson), b. Dec. 17, 1857, in North Andover;
d. of diphtheria, at her uncle's [273], in Derry, N. H., Feb. 1,
1870, aged 12. The following lines, composed by "M. H. C.,"
of West Boxford, soon after her death, will touch a tender chord
in many hearts. The writer was probably her aunt [660]; and
the person addressed in the third line, the aunt at whose house
she died : —

> " 'Kiss me, mother, I am going
>   Where the sick and weary rest;
> Kiss me, Katie, raise me higher,
>   Lay my head upon thy breast.

> " 'No, I fear not the dark river, —
>   Jesus passed its gloom before;
> Now I leave you: He will take me
>   O'er to yonder shining shore.'

> " And thus sweetly, gently passed she
>   From our weeping gaze away;
> Can we doubt her loving welcome
>   To the realms of endless day?

> " O, be trustful! Do not question
>   Why, of all, the dearest go;
> When we reach those blessed mansions
>   All these mysteries we shall know.

> " Only through *His* grace to strengthen,
>   Can we ever hope to win;
> Only cleansed in that dear fountain,
>   Can we hope to 'enter in.' "

679. ALFRED[5] [283] (Stephen[4], Daniel[3], Stephen[2], Samuel[1]),
was a graduate of Dartmouth College, in 1844, and had nearly
finished his course at the Theological Seminary, Andover, Mass.,
when loss of health, and especially of sight, by a severe affection
of the eyes, compelled him to abandon his studies and all hopes of
laboring for Christ in the profession of his choice. Retiring to
Derry, he took possession of the old homestead, and m. Maria
Louisa Cushing, of Scituate, Mass., Nov. 26, 1854 (Dec. 15, 1852).
She d. Oct. 15, 1857, aged 33. On her gravestone: " I shall be
satisfied when I awake with thy likeness." He d. of consumption,
Mar. 25, 1861, aged 49. His disappointment in not being permitted to serve his Master in the gospel ministry, seems largely to
have influenced him in the making of his Will, which is found, for
substance, as follows, in the Rockingham Probate Records, dated
" Feb. 4, 1861 " : —

" He bequeaths to his brother Stephen Reynolds certain portions of real
estate and $200; to Mary A. Taylor, wife of Robert Taylor, of South Bos-
ton, $100; to Sarah Moore, wife of George Moore, 2d, $25; to his sister
Ellen Kent, wife of Richard Kent, Jr., $25; to his nephew Edward P. Rey-
nolds, $100, against his he is twenty-five years of age, or, in case he dies, to
the American Board C. F. M.; to the last named Board, for Foreign Missions, $300; to the American Home Missionary Society, $300; to the

American Education Society, $200; to the American and Foreign Christian Union, $100. He wills his pew in Derry meeting-house, No. 34, to his brother Stephen; a good set of gravestones to his mother's grave, and the residue of his property, after all payments and just debts discharged, to the above societies in proportion to bequests."

He seems thus earnestly to have desired that promotion of the cause of Christian truth by means of his property, after death, which he could not secure by personal labor and sacrifice, according to his intentions, during his earthly life.

680. WILLIAM[5] [284] (Stephen[4], Daniel[3], Stephen[2], Samuel[1]) ; a farmer in Derry, having bought back the old homestead, — sold after his brother Alfred's death, — and there residing (1871). He m., 1st, Hannah Copp, of Chester, Aug. 5, 1835, — the mother of his six oldest children, — who d. Nov. 27, 1851 ; m., 2d, Annah Mariah Colby, of Derry, Oct. 5, 1855. Children, b. in D. : —

681. FRANK MELLEN [1232], b. Nov. 1, 1838.
682. WILLIAM, b. June 10, 1840; d. of consumption, at Derry, May 20, 1855, in his 15th year.
683. STEPHEN, b. Mar. 8, 1842; employed in a boiler foundery, at Cincinnati, O., 1869.
684. ELIZA SARGENT [1234], b. Sept. 15, 1845.
685. CHARLES LEWIS, b. Sept. 21, 1848; a teamster in Boston, 1869.
686. EDWARD PARKER, b. Sept. 27, 1851.
687. IRA AUGUSTUS, b. Mar. 26, 1859 (second wife).
688. IDA MARIA, b. Apr. 4, 1861; d. Aug. 15, 1863, in her 3d year.
689. LUCY COLBY, b. Oct. 9, 1864.
690. ERNEST, b. May 2, 1869.

691. MARY ANN[5] [286] (Stephen[4], Daniel[3], Stephen[2], Samuel[1]), m. Robert Taylor, Dec. 22, 1842. He was a native of Derry, N. H. ; for twenty years in the police department, Boston, and captain, or chief of police, the last years of his life. Home at South Boston, where he d. greatly lamented, Dec. 14, 1866, and she, as his widow, was still residing (1869). Children, b. in Boston : —

692. EDWARD REYNOLDS (Taylor), b. Nov. 30, 1843; of the firm of "Jordan, Marsh & Co.," in Philadelphia (1869).
693. FRANK MONTGOMERY, b. Sept. 17, 1845; now in business in Arkansas.
694. GEORGE WARREN ALEXANDER, b. Apr. 26, 1848; a clerk in Jordan, Marsh & Co.'s store, Boston (1869).

695. STEPHEN[5] [287] (Stephen[4], Daniel[3], Stephen[2], Samuel[1]), settled as a farmer and carpenter in Derry, N. H., — his farm having been set off from the original homestead, — and m. Sarah Sargent, a native of Candia, Aug. 24, 1848. Children : —

696. WALTER SWEENY, b. Dec. 27, 1849; a carpenter in Lawrence, Mass., 1869.
697. WILLIE WALDO, b. Apr. 12, 1855.
698. FREDERICK WARREN, b. Sept. 29, 1856.
699. HERBERT SARGENT, b. June 12, 1858.
700. ADIE ANNA, b. June 17, 1862.

701. SARAH[5] [288] (Stephen[4], Daniel[3], Stephen[2], Samuel[1]), m. George Moore, 2d, farmer, of Derry, N. H., Nov. 6, 1850. Child : —

702. MARY HELEN (Moore), b. Aug. 5, 1857, in Derry.

703. LUCY[5] [289] (Stephen[4], Daniel[3], Stephen[2], Samuel[1]), m. Joseph Montgomery, farmer, of Derry (Depot), Feb. 11, 1848, and d. June 7 (Jan. 13), 1860, aged 34, leaving : —

704. FANNY (Montgomery), b. Aug. 19, 1851.
705. LIZZIE, b. Aug. 27, 1853.
706. NELLIE, b. Sept. 2, 1856.
707. LUCY, b. Apr. 23, 1859.

708. ELLEN MAR[5] [290] (Stephen[4], Daniel[3], Stephen[2], Samuel[1]), m. Richard Kent, of Derry, Feb. 24, 1859. He was a teacher ; more recently a farmer and surveyor in Adrian, Mich., where were b. : —

709. LUCIE MONTGOMERY (Kent), b. July 5, 1860.
710. SALLIE LOIS, b. Jan. 2, 1863.

711. HANNAH[5] [304] (Daniel[4], Daniel[3], Stephen[2], Samuel[1]), m. Daniel Nason, Feb. 17, 1817. He was superintendent of the Boston and Providence Railroad, from the starting of the road till 1869, and resided in Boston thirty-seven years, latterly at 510 Tremont Street, where she d. of congestion of the lungs, Feb. 15, 1872, aged 74, and he, not knowing of *her* death in this world, d. of paralysis, Mar. 3, 1872. They were both buried in South Berwick, Me. Children : —

712. OLIVIA (Nason), b. July 10, 1818, in Berwick, Me.; m., 1st, —— Wilson; m., 2d, John L. Thompson, Richmond, Ind.
713. HANNAH, b. Sept. 22, 1819, in Alton, N. H.; m. William Washburn, of Richmond, Ind., and there d. Aug. 26, 1865, in her 46th year.
714. MATILDA, b. Mar. 8, 1821, in Alton; d. Mar. 7, 1827, at Salmon Falls, N. H., aged 6.
715. CAROLINE AUGUSTA, b. May 18, 1822, at Salmon Falls; as were all the rest, except the youngest.
716. ELIZABETH HOOTON, b. Feb. 11, 1824; d. Feb. 12, 1826, aged 2.
717. DANIEL, b. Oct. 22, 1825.
718. CORDELIA, b. June 27, 1827; Mrs. Jordan; d. at Boston, Feb. 8, 1865, in her 38th year.
719. SYLVESTER, b. Oct. 17, 1828; d. at Boston, Apr. 13, 1847, in his 19th year.
720. JAMES, b. Oct. 9, d. Nov. 7, 1830.
721. STEPHEN HAMILTON, b. Apr. 22, 1832.
722. JOSHUA PIERCE, b. Aug. 27, 1834.
723. RAYMOND LEE, b. May 17, 1840, in Boston, and there d. Jan. 24, 1863, in his 23d year.

724. DANIEL[5] [305] (Daniel[4], Daniel[3], Stephen[2], Samuel[1]), was a stone-cutter, residing in various places, as seen below ; now a farmer in Durham, N. H. ; m. Sarah Watson of Nottingham, N. H., Nov. 24, 1824, at Dover. She was b. May 26, 1803. Children : —

725. ABIGAIL JANE [1236], b May 24, 1826. in Dover, N. H.
726. DANIEL THOMAS [1244], b. Mar. 6, 1828, in Nottingham.
727. ADDISON, b. July 16, 1831, at Great Falls, N. H., and there d. Aug. 24, 1832, aged 13 mouths.
728. MARY FRANCES [1248], b. Jan. 28, 1834, at Great Falls.
729. SARAH ELIZABETH [1256], b. Feb. 23, 1836, in New Market.
730. WILLIAM ADDISON [1261], b. Apr. 7, 1839, in Durham.
731. NASON FREEMAN [1263], b. July 10, 1841, in Manchester.
732. ALFONZO SCOTT, b. June 20, 1846, in Boston; a soldier in the last war, with his two brothers; see [1261]; a farmer and shoemaker (1870), residing with his parents at Durham; m. Emma Wingate, of Madbury, June 1 (?), 1870.

733. EBENEZER THOMPSON[5] [307] (Daniel[4], Daniel[3], Stephen[2], Samuel[1]), m. Abigail Wyatt, at Gilmanton, N. H., Mar. 5, 1824. She was b. June 23, 1802, in Wenham, Mass., now living with her oldest child in Lowell (1870). He d. May 29, 1852, aged 49. Children : —

734. ALMIRA GOODWIN [1265], b. July 4, 1825, in Berwick, Me.
735. DANIEL [1271], b. May 26, 1828. in Alton, N. H.
736. ABBY PERKINS [1273], b. Aug. 30, 1831, in Alton.
737. CHARLES LEACH [1276], b. Nov. 10, 1834, in A.
738. HAMILTON [1278], b. May 1, 1836, in A.
739. HARRIET ANN, b. Sept. 2, 1838, in Durham, N. H.; d. at Allenstown, N. H., Jan. 5, 1840, in her 2d year.

740. STEPHEN[5] [308] (Daniel[4], Daniel[3], Stephen[2], Samuel[1]), a shoemaker, farmer, and now also (1870) station-master of the Boston and Maine Railroad, at Madbury, N. H.; m. Sally Garland, Sept. 1, 1831, at Durham, where she was b. Nov. 24, 1809. Children : —

741. MARY ELIZABETH [1283], b. July 22, 1832, in Durham.
742. LYDIA MARGARET [1286], b. Dec. 29, 1833, in Durham.
743. STEPHEN HENRY [1289], b. Mar. 17, 1835, in New Market.
744. JAMES ADDISON [1291], b. Nov. 7, 1836, in Durham.
745. HANNAH JANE [1293], b. Aug. 9, 1838.
746. CHARLES WILLIAM [1295], b. May 9, 1840.
747. SARAH MITCHELL, b. Dec. 12, 1841; a seamstress in Dover, N. H. (1870).
748. JOSEPHINE MARIA [1298], b. July 12, 1843.
749. JOHN TILTON, b. Aug. 3, 1845; a farmer, with his father, in Madbury, N. H.
750. GEORGE ALBERT, b. Sept. 18, 1847; trader and bookkeeper in Charlestown, N. H.
751. BERNICE ANN, b. June 17, 1849, in Dover, and there d. May 8, 1851, in her 2d year.

752. ADDISON[5] [309] (Daniel[4], Daniel[3], Stephen[2], Samuel[1]), resided at Somersworth, N. H., Canton, and Millbury, Mass., and finally in Worcester, Mass., where he was overseer in a woollen manufactory, and there d. Aug. 16, 1845, in his 38th year. He m Elizabeth Winship Rogers, at Somersworth, Jan. 13, 1833. She was the daughter of Samuel and Esther Rogers, of Bath, Me., and was there b. Sept. 4, 1812. Children : —

753. WILLIAM ADDISON [1300], b. Dec. 7, 1834, in Somersworth.
754. LIZZIE MARY [1306], b. May 25, 1836, in Millbury.

755. ALFRED WESLEY, b. Aug. 16, 1839; d. Apr. 25, 1840, at Millbury, aged 8 months.
756. EMILY JANE [1308], b. Sept. 25, 1841, in Millbury.
757. ALFRED WESLEY, b. June 30, d. Aug. 5, 1844, at Worcester.
758. LUCIUS ADDISON, b. Sept. 5, 1845; enlisted in the 36th Massachusetts regiment, Co. C, Aug. 27, 1862; taken prisoner, Dec. 15, 1863, and d. at Andersonville, Ga., from exposure and starvation, July 7, 1864, in his 19th year.

759. ELIZA[5] [310] (Daniel[4], Daniel[3], Stephen[2], Samuel[1]), m. (Rev.) Converse L. McCurdy, at Great Falls, N. H., Aug. 15, 1828, and d. Oct. 12, 1848, at Bristol, N. H., aged 39. He joined the New Hampshire Conference of the Methodist Episcopal Church, in the summer of 1834. Was stationed in New Hampshire, successively at Newington, Kingston, Manchester, Winchester, Chesterfield, Rindge, Concord, Lebanon, Haverhill, and Bristol. In 1849, was transferred to the New England Conference, and stationed in Massachusetts, at Palmer, Oxford, Natick, Cambridge, Charlestown (High Street), Boston (Church Street), Gloucester (Elm Street), Lynn (Boston Street), Marblehead, Barre, Leominster, and Athol Depot, where he was laboring in 1870. At that time, for nearly thirty-seven years, he had lost only three Sabbaths from inability to preach, and had enjoyed a remarkably successful ministry. Children : —

760. ELIZABETH R. (McCurdy), b. Mar. 14, 1830, at Great Falls; m. Marshall W. White, druggist and jeweller at Bristol, N. H., and has six children.
761. GEORGE SUMNER, b. Sept. 29, 1831, at Great Falls; d. May 20, 1832, aged 8 months.
762. CHARLES WESLEY, b. Feb. 26, 1833, at Great Falls; was in the war of the rebellion nearly four years, first lieutenant, 16th Illinois cavalry; now m. and lives at Sandwich, Ill.
763. HARRIET NEWELL, b. July 31, 1836, in Kingston, N. H.; d. July 18, 1837, at Durham, aged 11 months 18 days.
764. HANNAH NASON, b. May 6, 1838, in Manchester, N. H.; m. E. B. Kinsley, of Cambridge, Mass., who was a captain in the 59th regiment Massachusetts volunteers, and now holds the office of store-keeper in the Custom House, at Boston. Two children.
765. MARIANNE, b. Nov. 17, 1844, in Lebanon, N. H.; d. at Natick, Mass., Dec. 20, 1852, aged 8.

766. WILLIAM JAMES[5] [313] (Hamilton Davidson[4], Daniel[3], Stephen[2], Samuel[1]) ; m., 1st, Martha R. Pratt, of Roxbury, Mass., Aug. 15, 1843, who d. July 13, 1850 ; m., 2d, Harriet E Wheelwright, of New York, Mar. 27, 1861. He was a bookseller and publisher on Cornhill, Boston, till 1857 ; afterwards a representative in the Massachusetts legislature, for two years, from Roxbury, and a director of the First National Bank, Boston. He resided in Roxbury (now Boston Highlands), where he d. of heart disease, Jan. 17, 1865, in his 51st year, and where his widow still resides. Children, first wife, b. in Roxbury : —

767. MARTHA LOUISA, b. July 7, 1845.
768. WILLIAM JAMES, b. Feb. 1, 1849.

769. BETSY AUGUSTA[5] [338] (Thomas K.[4], Daniel[3], Stephen[2], Samuel[1]). She now writes her name " Augusta B."; m., 1st, David A. Gregg, Dec. 5, 1841, who d. Feb. 1, 1842; m., 2d, Augustus Bowers, Jan 19, 1854; a dealer in ready-made clothing, 472 and 474 Broadway, Albany, N. Y.   Child : —

770. WILLIE FRED REYNOLDS (Bowers), b. Apr. 17, 1862.

771. MOSES CROSS[5] [339] (Thomas K.[4], Daniel[3], Stephen[2], Samuel[1]), m. Betsy Varney [326, 5], of Boscawen, N. H., May 10, 1845.   Has resided for many years in Salem, Mass., as a wholesale grocer; residence, 14 Church Street.   Has been a member of the city government of Salem, — an alderman in 1855 and 1868, — also one of the directors of the board of trade.   She d. May 18, 1870, aged 44, in Salem, where their children were b. : —

772. ANNA ADALINE, b. Aug. 29, 1846; d. Sept. 18, 1854, aged 8.
773. HENRY ELWIN, b. Aug. 17, 1848.
774. MARY ELLA, b. June 5, 1851; d. at her father's, in Salem, Jan. 8, 1870, in her 19th year.
775. CARRIE AUGUSTA, b. Mar. 5, 1853.

776. SARAH FARRAR[5] [340] (Thomas K.[4], Daniel[3], Stephen[2], Samuel[1]), m. William Gilmore, of Ware, Mass., Feb. 4, 1842. He d. Jan. 27, 1854, at Lowell, Mass., where they had resided. She d. June 10, 1856, at Fisherville, N. H., aged 32.   Children : —

777. ELLEN AUGUSTA (Gilmore), b. July 14, d. July 31, 1843, at Lowell.
778   HELEN LEXERA, b. Oct. 7, 1844, in Lowell; d. May 30, 1864, in her 20th year, at Barre, Mass.
779. EDWARD CLARENCE, b. Oct. 5, 1846, in Lowell; was a soldier in the late war, enlisting first in the New Hampshire.5th regiment, Co. A, afterwards in the Vermont invalid corps; now residing in Boston, 74 Boylston Street.

780. ISAAC[5] [343] (Joseph[4], Samuel[3], Samuel[2], Samuel[1]), enlisted " Sept. 26, 1814, for sixty days, in the 2d regiment New Hampshire detached militia, John Steele, of Peterboro', colonel, company of Capt. Edward Fuller, of Pembroke." Was stationed at Portsmouth.   Afterwards settled on a portion of his father's homestead in Concord, N. H.; m. Anna Runnels [370], of C., Aug. 9, 1821, and there d. Dec. 16, 1851, aged 68.

Bouton's History of Concord says of Mrs. R. (p. 529), that she " often walked from her house, seven miles, to the old North Church on the Sabbath," to attend meeting.   " Would start at eight in the morning, and reach home again at 4 P. M., with occasional rides part of the way with neighbors overtaking her, on horseback or in wagons."   Children : —

781. SABINA, b. June 1, 1825.
782. FRANCIS, b. Apr. 2, 1828; m. Mary Jennett Brewster, Dec. 1859.
783. LUTHER, b. Jan. 20, 1835.
       Also, adopted by Mrs. R., after his death, the two following : —
784. FLORENTINE SCOTT, b. July 12, 1852; d. Mar. 27, 1869, in his 17th year.
785. GEORGIA ELLA, b. July 2, 1854.

786. THEODORE[5] [344] (Joseph[4], Samuel[3], Samuel[2], Samuel[1]), having moved back to the ancestral soil of Massachusetts, m. Mehetabel Philips, of Bradford, June 22, 1815 ; lived in Bradford and Boxford, and d. at his son Horatio's [1326], in Bradford Village, Sept. 25, 1869, in his 84th year. The " New Hampshire Statesman," noticing his death and his father's, adds : " The family is very remarkable for its longevity." The compiler of this Genealogy recalls a most interesting and satisfactory interview with him in 1868. Much valuable information was obtained. His combined intelligence and geniality seemed unusual for a man of his years. His children were : —

787. CYNTHIA [1311], b. Sept. 5, 1816, in Bradford.
788. LEONARD [1313], b. Feb. 5, 1818, in Bradford.
789. DANIEL LAKEMAN [1316], b. Feb. 29, 1820, in Boxford.
790. LORENZO [1322], } b. Mar. 9, 1822, in Boxford.
791. HORATIO [1326],
792. LUTHER [1329], b. June 27, 1825, in Bradford.
793. LEVERETT, b. Dec. 27, 1827; d. Aug. 1831 (2), in his 4th year.
794. GEORGE MOODY [1337], b. Oct. 2, 1829.

795. JONATHAN[5] [346] (Joseph[4], Samuel[3], Samuel[2], Samuel[1]), m. Lydia Pressy, 1812, who was b. Mar. 17, 1795, and d. 1861, aged 66. Settled first in Concord, near the present Mast Yard Railroad station, where all their children were b. ; afterwards migrated to Pennsylvania ; now living (1872) with his grandson [1359], to whom he has rented his farm, in Erie County. Children : —

796. BETSY KIMBALL [1339], b. Apr. 10, 1813.
797. ESTHER HERRICK [1342], b. Sept. 3, 1814.
798. GARDNER KIMBALL, b. Sept. 18, 1816; d. 1841, aged 25, "having just learned his trade."
799. STEPHEN CHANDLER [1347], b. Sept. 30, 1818.
800. RHODA HOIT [1354], b. Sept. 3, 1820.
801. ABIGAIL [1364], b. Apr. 7, 1823.
802. FULSOM BROWN [1376], b. Apr. 26, 1825 (6).
803. FRANCIS NEWELL [1382], b. Apr. 22, 1828.
804. MARY L. [1390], b. Oct. 13, 1829 (30).
805. BARTLETT DIMOND [1396], b. Mar. 15, 1832.
806. JOANNA FARNUM, b. Sept. 17, 1834 ; d. Sept. 26, 1837, aged 3.
807. OSMYN (Osmond), b. Oct. 10, d. Oct. 25, 1836.

808. FARNUM[5] [349] (Joseph[4], Samuel[3], Samuel[2], Samuel[1]), m., 1st, Jerusha Webber, of Boscawen, N. H., Mar. 27, 1823, who d. July 4, 1848, aged 46 ; m., 2d, Gracia Trussell, of Hopkinton, June 11, 1850 ; a farmer, now residing in Hopkinton. Children, first wife : —

809. JEREMIAH FARNUM [1402], b. Oct. 14, 1824.
810. MARIANNE JEWETT [1406], b. Apr. 12, 1827.
811. JERUSHA AUGUSTA [1410], b. June 19, 1831.
812. OSMYN EATON [1415], b. June 12, 1834.
813. HELEN CARROL [1418], b. May 18, 1839.
814. EDWARD GILMAN, b. Dec. 6, 1843 ; resides with his father, in Hopkinton ; m. Maria Jennie Mills, of H., Jan. 1, 1869 (Dec. 31, 1868).

815. HAZEN[5] [351] (Joseph[4], Samuel[3], Samuel[2], Samuel[1]), m.,

1st, Sarah Blanchard Fisk, of Concord, N. H., Apr. 19, 1832, who d. Oct. 30, 1840, aged 35; m., 2d, Sarah E. Corliss, of Millville (Concord), Apr. 19, 1842, who d. at Concord, as his widow, Jan. 17, 1870, aged 50. He was a deacon of the Concord West Congregational church, " elected Aug. 15, 1840," and d. June 27, 1859, in his 58th year. Children, second wife : —

816.   SARAH LAVANCIA, b. May 15, 1845; m. Orlando L. Manning, of Billerica, Mass., Apr. 27, 1863, who d. Dec. 29, 1867.
817.   JOSEPH DWIGHT, b. July 10, 1847.
818.   LYMAN BEECHER, b. Apr. 19, 1849.
819.   EVERETT HAZEN, b. June 7, 1851.
820.   JOHN CORLISS, b. Apr. 21, 1854.

821.   MOSES[5] [363] (Jonathan[4], Samuel[3], Samuel[2], Samuel[1]), settled in Pelham, N. H., as a blacksmith and farmer; m., 1st, Sabra Marshall, of P., June 5, 1826, who d. Aug. 31, 1827; m., 2d, Isabell Campbell, of Windham, N. H., Oct. 31, 1837. Children : —

822.   SABRA M. [1420], b. Aug. 6, 1827, in Dracut, Mass. (first wife).
823.   FARNUM J. [1422], b. Aug. 8, 1839 (second wife).

824.   SAMUEL[5] [367] (Samuel[4], Samuel[3], Samuel[2], Samuel[1]), m. Anner Abbot, of Concord, June 13, 1826, and settled on the upper part of his father's homestead, near Contoocook River and the present Mast Yard Railroad station. He was a member of the first Congregational Church in Concord, uniting May 7, 1820 ; also of the West Parish Congregational Church, from its organization. Superintended the Sunday schools held on Horse Hill for several seasons, and was one of the selectmen of Ward 1 (city of Concord), from Mar. 1863, till his death, Nov. 22, 1864, in his 68th year. His widow was a lady of marked intelligence and amiability, to whom the compiler feels indebted. She " passed quietly from earth," of acute paralysis, Jan. 23, 1872. Was one of the six females by the name of Runnels, whose names were among the original members of the West Concord Congregational Church, at its organization, Apr. 1833, and was the *first* of these to exchange the church militant for the church triumphant. The other five, whose common membership was thus continued with hers for nearly thirty-nine years, were Sarah [345], Dorcas [350], Lois [368], Priscilla (Hayward) [369], and Mrs. Anna [780], the three last being sisters of her husband. The children of Samuel and Anner, b. in Concord, were : —

825.   SAMUEL, b. Jan. 21, d. Jan. 22, 1828; entered by the desire of Mrs. R., and named thus for the present record.
826.   JOANNA, b. Aug. 28, 1829; d. Oct. 21, 1830, aged 14 months.
827.   CYRUS, b. Apr. 6, 1832; graduated at the Chandler Scientific School, Dartmouth College, 1855; was employed as a surveyor in Iowa and Illinois for nine years, but returned to the old homestead, after his father's death, where still residing (1872). Was a member of the Concord City Council, 1868–71.
828.   LOUISA JANE, b. Jan. 18, 1835; resides with her brother at the old home.

829. EMILY, b. May 24, 1838; m. Joseph M. Freeze, Oct. 6, 1863; residence, Lawrence, Mass.
830. ALMIRA [1424], b. May 16, 1841.
831. ANNER ABBOT [1431], b. May 1, 1844.

832. EDWARD[5] [371] (Samuel[4], Samuel[3], Samuel[2], Samuel[1]), is a farmer, and retains the place first occupied by the family in Concord. Was a member of the City Council of Concord in 1868; m. Lucy Maria Tucker, of C., Nov. 24, 1864, who was b. July 12, 1846, in Grafton, N. H., and d. at C., June 13, 1872, in her 26th year. Children: —

833. MARY JANE EDWINA VIOLA, b. Aug. 13, 1865.
834. GEORGE EDWARD ELLSWORTH LYON, b. Nov. 26, 1867.
835. HATTIE MARIA ABBY CELESTIA, b. July 21, 1869.
836. ARTHUR SAMUEL HANNIBAL LEWELLYN, b. Dec. 24, 1870.

837. JESSE[5] [373] (Jonas[4], Samuel[3], Samuel[2], Samuel[1]), m. Lydia Stiles, Nov. 28, 1832, who was b. July 5, 1812; a shoemaker; residence (1871) in Andover, Mass. Children: —

838. LYDIA EMELINE [1433], b. Dec. 29, 1836.
839. JOSEPH FRANKLIN, b. Mar. 20, 1839, who is also a shoemaker by trade.

840. MARY EMELINE[5] [374] (Jonas[4], Samuel[3], Samuel[2], Samuel[1]), m. Elijah Stiles, shoemaker, of Boxford, Mass., Nov. 11, 1829 He was b. in Middletown, Mass., Nov. 14, 1808; present post-office address, South Groveland, Mass. Children: —

841. CHARLES FRANKLIN (Stiles), b. July 14, 1832; m. Susan Towne, of Andover, Oct. 3, 1854; a shoe-manufacturer at South Groveland.
842. HENRY LEVERETT, b. Dec. 2, 1833; d. Sept. 27, 1840, in his 7th year.
843. JULIA JEANETTE, b. May 14, 1845; m. George Stanwood Dodge, of Boxford, Aug. 28, 1869. He enlisted, 1861, as a three-months' man, "the first soldier that went from Boxford" to the late civil war; afterwards in the 35th Massachusetts volunteers, for three years, till the end of the conflict.
844. HENRY EVERETT MERRILL, b. Aug. 20, 1852.

845. CATHARINE[5] [375] (Jonas[4], Samuel[3], Samuel[2], Samuel[1]), m., 1st, Israel Stiles, shoemaker, Apr. 23, 1837, at Boxford He d. in Woburn, July 2, 1852, and she m., 2d, William Jordan, shoemaker, Nov. 4, 1860, at Woburn. He was in the late war, 9th New Hampshire regiment, Co. C, from Nov. 15, 1863, till Mar. 25, 1864, and d. Dec. 16, 1865, aged 55. Her children were: —

846. EVERETT (Stiles), b. Feb. 23, 1845, in Woburn, and there d. Sept. 23, 1850, in his 6th year.
847. CAROLINE THOMPSON, b. July 1, 1850; residence, at present, with her mother, in Woburn.

848. JOHN[5] [377] (James[4], Benjamin[3], Ebenezer[2], Samuel[1]), enlisted in the "war of 1812," — autumn of that year, — and continued to its close; settled as a farmer first in Pittsfield, then in Hallowell, Me., and m. Philura Robbins, from New Hampshire, Dec. 25, 1818. He d. at H., May 3, 1864 (3), aged 72, and she d. May 30 (29) of the same year. Children: —

849. SARAH ANN [1435], b. Jan. 21, 1820, in Pittsfield.
850. GEORGE WILLIAM (or Washington), b. Jan. 18, 1822, in Hallowell,
      where also the rest of the children were b.; went to California
      in the fall of 1849; arrived at Sacramento, June 13, 1850, and is
      supposed to have d. in that vicinity, 1852, aged 30.
851. ELISHA WHITE [1446], b. May 1, 1825.
852. JAMES COX [1451], b. May 17, 1827.
853. FRANCES ELLEN, b. Sept. 8, 1829; m. James (Daniel) Norton, fish-
      dealer, of Newburyport, Mass., Mar. 1859, and d. Feb. 1861, in
      her 32d year.
854. MARY JANE [1461], b. Jan. 28, 1833.
855. JOHN EDWIN [1463], b. Mar. 29, 1835.
856. LURINDA MEANS, b. Feb. 14, 1838; d. of consumption, at Hallowell,
      Aug. 1859, in her 22d year.
857. WILLIAM HARRISON, b. May 1, 1839; d. Mar. 22, 1859, of consump-
      tion, at Hallowell, in his 20th year.
858. BENJAMIN FRANKLIN, b. Nov. 7, 1844; enlisted in the Maine 3d
      (8th) regiment of volunteers, June, 1861; served at Hilton
      Head, and d. at Yorktown, Va., of quick consumption, after
      receiving his discharge on account of sickness, Sept. 1862, in
      his 18th year.

859. JEREMIAH HOLMES[5] [378] (James[4], Benjamin[3], Ebenezer[2],
Samuel[1]), served his country one year and six months in the campaign of 1813–14, enlisting the next spring after his brother John
[848]. Went to Greenbush, N. Y., and thence to Sackett's Harbor, a little too late for the engagement under Gen. Brown (May,
1813). Was in the battle of Williamsburg (down the St. Lawrence), and at French's Mills; transferred to Buffalo and Canada
West; was in the rear guard at the battle of Chippewa, July 5,
1814, and the autumn following, received his discharge before the
close of the war. Married Salome Potter, of Gardiner, Me., Nov.
17, 1825, who was b. June 9, 1801; settled as a farmer near Hallowell, and there still residing (1870). Children: —

860. MARTHA POTTER [1465], b. Feb. 3, 1827.
861. MARY ANN, b. May 7, 1828; m. William Porter, truckman, of
      Newburyport, Mass., Feb. 10, 1854.
862. CHARLES FRANKLIN [1470], b. Apr. 23, 1832.
863. BENJAMIN PENCIN, b. Nov. 5, 1833; sailed from New York, Nov.
      1853, and this being his first experience at sea, he was thrown
      overboard in a gale, near Liverpool, Eng., and thus d. Dec. 25,
      1853, aged 20.
864. SANFORD ELI, b. Nov. 17, 1839; enlisted as a private in the Maine
      3d regiment, Co. E; left Augusta. June, 1861; was sick, first of
      diphtheria, then of measles, and finally of consumption; d. at
      Yorktown, Va., June 17, 1862, in his 23d year, having written
      home but two days before.

865. JOHN[5] [389] (John[4], Benjamin[3], Ebenezer[2], Samuel[1]),
lived as a farmer in what is now Clinton, Me., where his sons still
reside, and he with the older, on the original homestead; m. 1st,
Lydia Guptil, of Berwick, Nov. 1, 1820. She d. May 9, 1860, at
Clinton, and he m., 2d, Mrs. Sarah Bragg, of Benton, Mar. 20,
1861, who also d. Feb. 4, 1868. Children, first wife: —

866. JOHN [1474], b. June 15, 1828.
867. FREDERICK WINGATE [1479], b. July 20, 1830.

868. DAMON[5] [391] (John[4], Benjamin[3], Ebenezer[2], Samuel[1]), m. Hannah Brown, of Clinton, Me., Oct. 14, 1823. She was b. Apr. 2, 1805, in Ellsworth, Me. He lived and d. in that part of Clinton which is now Benton, where were b. the following children : —

869. AUGUSTA HANNAH [1483], b. Dec. 28, 1824.
870. CLARK DAMON [1486], b. Aug. 7, 1827.
871. CHARLES RANDALL [1488], b. Oct. 1, 1829.
872. EMELINE MORRILL [1493], b. May 25, 1832.
873 ELIZABETH MARIA, b. May 6, 1834; d. July 27, 1850, aged 16.
874. RIPLEY, b. Mar. 17, 1839; d. Feb. 19, 1843, in his 4th year.
875. ISRAEL FOX, b. Dec. 11, 1840; a trader; m. Mrs. Adaline Preston (formerly Garland), of Benton, Dec. 25, 1869.
876. ANNE, b. Jan. 18, 1843; resides in Lewiston (1870).
877. EMILY BROWN, b. Dec. 21, 1845; resides in Lewiston (1870).
878. ELIZABETH FLORENCE [1495], b. Sept. 21, 1850.

879. JAMES[5] [393] (John[4], Benjamin[3], Ebenezer[2], Samuel[1]), m., 1st, Mary Elizabeth Dwelley, of Prospect, Me., Jan. 12, 1829. She was b. Sept. 18, 1808, and d. Dec. 29, 1855, aged 47. He m., 2d, Rosilla Luce, of Union, Me., May, 1859. Had previously moved (1823) to Frankfort (North Searsport), where he chiefly resided, a farmer and teacher, for thirty-seven years ; also a lieutenant and captain in the Maine militia. Children, first wife : —

880. LYDIA ANN [1499], b. Jan. 12, 1831.
881. WILLIAM THOMAS CURTIS [1506], b. Oct. 3, 1835.
882. ATEMIZA, b. Aug. 16, 1840; d. at Frankfort, Aug. 6, 1841, aged nearly 1 year.
883. AURELIA ADELAIDE, b. July 6, 1850.

884. BENJAMIN[5] [394] (John[4], Benjamin[3], Ebenezer[2], Samuel[1]), settled, as a farmer, in Clinton, Me., and m. Lovina Baker, Sept. 15, 1833, who was b. Aug. 1, 1818. Children : —

885. MARTHA AMY, b. May 12, 1835; see [1479].
886. GEORGE FARRINGTON, b. Sept. 25, 1837; m. Emma Odlin, of Benton, Mar. 1862. Enlisted in Co. C, 24th Maine regiment, Sept. 1862; was sent to New Orleans; returned sick of chronic dysentery, Aug. 1863, and d. Apr. 6, 1864, at Clinton, in his 27th year.
887. HARRIET ANN, b. May 3, 1841; m. George Ricker, of Waterville, June 1, 1860, and d. May 10, 1861, aged 20.
888. ELVA ESTELLE, b. Mar. 18, 1859; d. Dec. 12, 1863, in her 5th year.

889. WASHINGTON[5] [396] (Benjamin[4], Benjamin[3], Ebenezer[2], Samuel[1]), was a farmer, first in Winslow, Me., till 1841, and then settled in South Albion, where he d. Aug. 17, 1867, in his 68th year. He m. Anne Stevens, of Winslow, Sept. 29, 1821, who was b. Jan. 5, 1797, and d. at South Albion, Aug. 30, 1869, in her 73d year. Children : —

890. CHARLOTTE [1508], b. Sept. 30, 1822.
891. WELLINGTON [1512], b. Nov. 28, 1824.
892. JOHN [1518], b. Apr. 1, 1827.
893. BENJAMIN FRANKLIN, b. Apr. 4, 1830; enlisted for the late war, July 14, 1862, in the Maine 19th infantry; Aug. 4, 1863, was transferred to the 1st Maine heavy artillery, Co. H; is marked

6

among the "Deceased Maine Volunteers," having d. Dec. 1864, in his 35th year.

894.   ADALINE, b. Feb. 14, d. Aug. 4, 1833.
895.   GEORGE WASHINGTON, b. Feb. 28 (27), 1837; a farmer, occupying the homestead at South Albion; m. Mary A. Dutch, at Belfast, Me.. Apr. 29, 1867, who was b. 1839.
896.   DANIEL, b. Dec. 11, 1839; enlisted in Boston, Mass., Apr. 8, 1864; served in the U. S. A. signal corps; discharged, Aug. 1865; now living (1871) at North Weymouth, Mass.
897.   ALMIRA (Myra) [1521], b. Sept. 28, 1843.

898.   SYBIL[5] [397] (Benjamin[4], Benjamin[3], Ebenezer[2], Samuel[1]), m. Isaac Doughty, mariner, of Hallowell, Jan. 27, 1823. He d. Aug. 1829; she d. at Waterville, Jan. 17, 1862, aged 60. Children : —

899.   MAHALA (Doughty), b. Feb. 23, 1824, in Hallowell; m. Reuben Emery, of Waterville.
900.   CLARISSA ANN, b. Feb. 1, 1827, in H.; m. Isaac Wiley, of Boston, and d. July 2, 1856, in her 30th year.
901.   LOUISA MARIA, b. Nov. 10, 1829, in Winslow; m. Alfred Norton, of Greenland, N. H., and d. Apr. 23, 1858, in her 29th year.

902.   WARREN[5] [399] (Benjamin[4], Benjamin[3], Ebenezer[2], Samuel[1]), m. Belinda Emery [426]. of Winslow, "Sept. 12, 1825" (Pub. Records), or, "Dec. 1826"; resided in Waterville, as a farmer, till her death, Aug. 1868, aged 62, since which he has lived chiefly with his son [905], in Boston. All their children were b. and nine of them d. in Waterville. Were ever parents more sadly " bereaved of their children"?

903.   GEORGE WARREN, b. Oct. 1, 1827; d. Dec. 25, 1850, aged 23.
904.   JULIA ANN, b. Jan. 28, 1828; d. Dec. 30, 1847, in her 20th year.
905.   HIRAM CRAMMER, b. Mar. 15, 1831; m. Mary F. Pattee, at Bath, Me., Apr. 13, 1854; studied medicine in Philadelphia and Boston, at the Harvard Medical School; commenced practice in Boston, 1868; office (1870) as "Dr. H. C. Reynolds," 1265 Washington Street.
906.   JOSEPH JACKSON, b. Apr. 14, 1833; d. May 18, 1845, aged 12.
907.   CHARLES ALFRED, b. July 31, 1835; was an engraver by occupation; moved to California (starting) Aug. 1853; returned June, 1860, and d. Nov. 14, 1862, in his 28th year.
908.   MOSES, b. Nov. 30, 1837; d. Oct. 1, 1838, aged 10 months.
909.   CALVIN, b. Sept. 16, 1839; d. Feb. 8, 1852, in his 13th year.
910.   MARGARET, b. July 20, 1843; d. Jan. 25, 1852, in her 9th year.
911.   MARY ANN, b. Jan. 12, 1847; d. Mar. 4, 1852, aged 5.
912.   CAROLINE. b. Apr. 27, 1850; d. Jan. 29, 1852, in her 2d year.
913.   WARREN HENRY, b. Dec. 1, 1852; was studying medicine with his brother in Boston (1870).

914.   COLUMBUS[5] [402] (Stephen[4], Benjamin[3], Ebenezer[2], Samuel[1]), migrated in early life to New Brunswick; resided at St. Stephen's, chiefly as a lumberman, and there m. Margaret Alward, 1822. He d. at St. S., July, 1864, aged 65. Children : —

915.   JANE, b. 1825; m. Phinehas Tyler.
916.   MARY ANN, b. 1828; m. William J. Walker, and d. 1851, aged 23.
917.   LUCINDA, b. 1832; m. Miles Towers; d. 1854, aged 22.
918.   ELIZA ALICE, b. 1835; m. William Hanson.

919. SUSAN, b. 1837; d. 1855, aged 18.
920. GEORGIANA, b. 1840; d. 1857, aged 17.

921. SAMUEL[5] [403] (Stephen[4], Benjamin[3], Ebenezer[2], Samuel[1]), was a farmer first in Winslow, Me., afterwards in Waterville, two miles north of the village, where he d. Aug. 30, 1869, in his 68th year. Had m., 1st, Charity Davenport, of Winslow, Aug. 8, 1820, who d. 1831 ; m., 2d, Eliza Proctor [410], of Winslow, Oct. 10, 1835, who d. Aug. 19, 1860, aged 51. Four children by each wife, as follows : —

922. LEVI, b. Nov. 21, 1822, in Winslow; was killed by being precipitated upon a cart wheel in motion, while assisting in the hay field, at Clinton, Aug. 8, 1836, in his 14th year.
923. EMILY, b. Sept. 17, 1824, in Winslow; d. Mar. 12, 1825, aged 5 mos. 25 days.
924. EMILY [1524], b. May 1. 1826, in Winslow.
925. ELIZABETH (Betsy) [1530], b. Feb. 11 1829, in Winslow.
926. MARY LAMSON, b. Oct. 16, 1838; m. William E. Nichols, of Waterville, May 15, 1861.
927. RANDOLPH MARSHAL, b. Mar. 20, 1840; d. Aug. 6, 1858, in his 19th year.
928. SOPHIA FRANCES, b. May 28, 1845 ; m. Shepard Eldridge, of Clinton, Feb. 14, 1870.
929. ABBIE ANNA, b. July 22, 1849.

930. DANIEL[5] [434] (David[4], Benjamin[3], Ebenezer[2], Samuel[1]), is a farmer in Pittsfield, Me., and m. Sybil McDonald, of P., Apr. 7, 1823. Theirs is a pleasant and hospitable home. Children, b. in P. : —

931. JULIA ANN [1535], b. Oct. 28, 1824.
932. WALTER MCDONALD, b. Mar. 8, 1826; d. Apr. 9, 1847, aged 21, being carried over Clinton falls, on the Sebasticooke, with a raft; body found after nine days.
933. GEORGE [1543], b. Oct. 1, 1829.
934. HARRIET SMILEY [1545], b. Apr. 29, 1833.
935. DANIEL NELSON [1552], b. Dec. 18, 1836.
936. MARGARET DAVENPORT [1557], b. Oct. 23, 1839.

937. MARGARET DAVIS[5] [436] (David[4], Benjamin[3], Ebenezer[2], Samuel[1]), m. Nathaniel Davenport, grocer, of Hallowell, Me., June 19, 1836. He was b. Feb. 29, 1792, and d. Nov. 19, 1866, in his 75th year. Children : —

938. STEPHEN FRANKLIN (Davenport), b. Jan. 22, 1838; a sewing machine dealer and repairer, occupying (1870), with his mother, the attractive residence left by his father, in Hallowell. He m. Lizzie A., dau. of Capt. S. C. Cox, of Hallowell, Oct. 10, 1871.
939. GEORGIANA, b. Jan. 24, 1842; m. Edwin Hartshorn, sign and ornamental painter, of Hallowell, May 19, 1863. Children : —
    1. ALBERT HENRY (Hartshorn), b. Nov. 4, 1864.
    2. FRANK DAVENPORT, b. Dec. 19, 1868.
940. AMMI (Davenport), b. Mar. 27, 1846; a clothing dealer (1870) in Gardiner, Me.; m. Abbie A. Clark, of G., Dec. 18, 1870.

941. GREENWOOD[5] [437] (David[4], Benjamin[3], Ebenezer[2], Samuel[1]), settled as a farmer and lumberman in the east part of

Pittsfield, Me., with real estate in and near the now flourishing
village of P. Has business connections, in the lumber trade, with
Portland and other seaports. He m. Louisa Mahoney, of Pittsfield,
May 13, 1839. Children : —

942.   ANGENETTE, b. Sept. 16, 1840; m. H. C. Chandler, boot and shoe
     merchant and postmaster in Pittsfield, Feb. 13. 1870, but d., to
     the great grief of her *many* friends, Aug. 8, 1870, in her 30th year.
943.   WILLIAM FRANKLIN, b. Feb. 18, 1842; was enrolled in a Massachu-
     setts company of sharpshooters ("Audrews's"), Capt. Saunders,
     Sept. 3, 1861; was at the battle of Ball's Bluff; discharged on
     account of sickness, Feb. 1862.
944.   GREENWOOD CHARLES [1560], b. Feb. 19, 1844.
945.   ALBION, b. Nov. 26, 1846.
946.   GEORGE MILTON, b. Feb. 12, 1849; d. of diphtheria, Nov. 26, 1861,
     in his 13th year.
947.   SERAPHINE, b. Oct. 3, 1850; d. of diphtheria, Nov. 16, 1861, aged 11.
948.   WARREN, b. Dec. 17, 1853.
949.   ANNIE LOUISE, b. July 15, 1857.
950.   CHARLES MILTON, b. July 28, 1859.

951.   SYBIL[5] [438] (David[4], Benjamin[3], Ebenezer[2], Samuel[1]),
m. Adoniram Millett, farmer, of Pittsfield, Me., Jan. 25, 1838.
Children : —

952.   MELISSA JANE (Millett), b. Feb. 1, 1839; m., 1st, Charles Willetts,
     of Worth, Mich., Dec. 1855, who d. Jan. 8, 1864; m., 2d, John
     Burgess, Mar. 1868. Her children were : —
     1.   ADONIRAM WILSON (Willetts), b. Aug. 1857.
     2.   FRANCIS COBURN, b. May 15, 1860.
     3.   CHARLES, b. Dec. 25, 1863.
     4.   ALONZO JOHN (Burgess), b. Jan. 1869.
953.   ALONZO DIXON (Millett), b. July 28, 1840; enlisted as a private,
     Co. D, 8th Maine volunteers, Aug. 1861; promoted to captain;
     discharged, Nov. 15, 1864. Settled in Waterville, Me., and
     there m. Martha Hubbard, June, 1865. Child : —
     1.   ALBRO, b. Aug. 3, 1869.
954.   JOHN COOK, b. Dec. 7, 1841; d. May 11, 1863, in his 22d year.
955.   ISAAC RUNNELS, b. Mar. 10, 1844; d. Jan. 4, 1852, in his 8th year.
956.   LUCY STINSON, b. May 11, 1845; m. Ira Libbey, carpenter, of
     Pittsfield, June 2, 1867. Children : —
     1.   HERBERT ALONZO (Libbey), b. July 1, 1868.
     2.   ARTHUR, b. Mar. 14, 1870.

957.   DAVID[5] [439] (David[4], Benjamin[3], Ebenezer[2], Samuel[1]),
m. Adaliza A. Farnum, at Pittsfield, Me., Dec. 14, 1845. She was
b. Feb. 5, 1823, in Warren, N. H. His business has been that of
lumberman, hotel keeper, and now (1871) of grocer and provision
dealer, firm of " Runnells & Son," at Flint, Mich. He also
continues in the lumber trade. Previous residences. after marriage, at Pittsfield and Lewiston, Me., and at East Tawas, Mich.
Children : —

958.   CARLTON KIMBALL [1562], b. Aug. 14, 1847, in Pittsfield.
959.   FRED AUGUSTUS, b. May 6, 1853, in Lowell, Mass.

960.   ISAAC[5] [440] (David[4], Benjamin[3], Ebenezer[2], Samuel[1]),
settled first as a farmer in Pittsfield, Me.; moved to Worth,

Sanilac Co., Mich., 1855, where both farmer and merchant till his death, July 4, 1859, aged 36, being drowned while endeavoring to rescue another drowning person. He m. Elizabeth Moor Dixon, of Clinton, Me., Dec. 17, 1846, who was b. at C., Sept. 24, 1821. Children : —

961. Horace Edward, b. Jan. 23, 1848, in Pittsfield; attended the "Business College" in Poughkeepsie, N. Y.
962. Shubal Dixon, b. Apr. 20, 1850, in P.
963. Alvah Ernest, b. Oct. 19, 1853, in P.

964. Thomas Lewis[5] [441] (David[4], Benjamin[3], Ebenezer[2], Samuel[1]), migrated to Michigan in 1851 ; a lumberman and explorer till 1864 ; since then, a farmer and dealer in real estate ; present residence, Birch Run, Mich. He has held various town offices. Helped organize a company for the 3d regiment Michigan infantry, 1861, with the office of lieutenant, but did not enter the service on account of sickness. procuring a substitute at an expense of five hundred dollars. He m., 1st, Rhoda Eliza Murr (Marr), at Metcalf, C. W.. Aug. 25, 1853. She was b. Nov. 17, 1830, in Townsend, C. W. ; d. at Worth, Mich., Jan. 11, 1865, aged 34. He m., 2d, Adelia Caroline Murr, first wife's sister, Apr. 17, 1866, at Worth. She was b. Aug. 29, 1837, in Metcalf, C. W. Children : —

965. Francis Lewis (first wife), b. May 28, 1854, in Worth, and there d. Jan. 7, 1865, in his 11th year.
966. Cora Ella, b. Dec. 21, 1856, in Worth.
967. Elizabeth Murr, b. Nov. 6, 1861, in Croton, Mich.
968. William Lewis (second wife), b. Aug. 22, 1868, at Birch Run, Mich.

969. Eliza Waitt[5] [442] (David[4], Benjamin[3], Ebenezer[2], Samuel[1]), m. William B. Sweetzer, of Pittsfield, Me., May, 1848. He was a farmer and lumberman ; moved to Worth, Mich., where she d. Sept. 2, 1859, aged 33, leaving : —

970. Charles (Sweetzer), b. Dec. 26, 1849, in Pittsfield; now residing in Hudson, Iowa.
971. Martha, b. May, 1852, in Pittsfield.
972. Eliza, b. May 29, 1859, in Worth.

973. Sarah Ann[5] [443] (David[4], Benjamin[3], Ebenezer[2], Samuel[1]), m. John Rogers, farmer, of Pittsfield, Me., Mar. 20, 1852 ; residence near her brother Daniel's [930]. Children : —

974. Ida Emma (Rogers), b. Dec. 16, 1852.
975. Dorabelle, b. Jan. 17, 1854.
976. George Lincoln, b. July 21, 1861.
977. Kate May, b. Apr. 16, 1864.
978. Bertha Alice, b. Apr. 1, 1868.

979. Edwin[5] [459] (Stephen[4], Stephen[3], Ebenezer[2], Samuel[1]). After moving with his parents to Ohio, at the age of 12, his schooling was obtained in log school-houses, of the rudest construction, to which he was accustomed to walk three and four miles by marked trees. The seats and benches in those "nurseries of learning"

were made of split timber, and oiled paper was used instead of glass for the intromission of light. To the kindness and thorough instruction of one Samuel Shaw, from Maine, who first taught him mathematics, he ever felt greatly indebted. Under the stimulus afforded by *that* teacher, he used to cipher by torch-light on pieces of hickory bark, and often till midnight. He afterwards attended school at the Granville academy, and began himself the occupation of teaching, in 1825, before he was eighteen years of age. Was almost constantly in the school-room, in his own and surrounding towns, till 1833 ; and, having gained notoriety as a teacher, he was afterwards, until 1846, frequently called to the most difficult schools, far and near, from which previous teachers had been ejected. Over three thousand different pupils, during these twenty years, were under his instruction, among whom were Samuel B. Curtis, William S. Rosecranz (both generals in the late war), Royal T. Wheeler, for many years a judge in Texas, and others who have since proved men of eminence. He was licensed to preach in 1836, and has exercised that vocation as opportunities occurred, though never as a settled pastor. Having chiefly resided as a farmer, near his father's original homestead, in Licking County, he has now become an extensive landholder, both in Ohio and Iowa. He m. Lydia Eaton, of Licking County, O., Dec. 26, 1833, where their children were b. : —

980. CELESTIA [1564], b. Nov. 9, 1834.
981. JOHN RYLAND, b. Feb. 17, 1836; m. Ruhama Brooks, in Licking Co., Feb. 2, 1860, who d. of diphtheria, Apr. 9, 1860. He enlisted in Co. K, 4th Iowa infantry, at Clarinda, Page Co., Iowa, Aug. 20, 1861, from purely patriotic motives, "refusing a commission"; d. of camp fever, at Rolla, Mo., Nov. 3, 1861, in his 26th year, being commended by his officers "for his great worth and moral excellence," as "a brave soldier, and one ever ready to discharge his duty, however arduous it might be."
982. ANGENORA, b. June 5, 1839; d. Jan. 23, 1846, in her 7th year.
983. CORWIN, b. Oct. 2, 1840; d. May 28, 1848, in his 8th year.
984. ORMOND [1567], b. Feb. 5, 1842.
985. MARY EXELINE, b. Nov. 13, 1843; d. Apr. 9, 1848, in her 5th year.
986. ANNIE PHILOMA, b. Apr. 4, 1845; m. Charles McFarland, of Mt. Vernon, O., Nov. 29, 1871.
987. ORANGE SCOTT, b. June 11, 1847; graduated at the Homœopathic College of Medicine, at Cleveland, O., Feb. 1871, and has commenced practice in Indianapolis, Ind., in company with Dr. J. B. Hunt. He m. Isadora Clark, at Columbus, O., June 20, 1872. She was b. Dec. 4, 1846, in C.
988. MOSES THURSTON, b. Dec. 26, 1848; a student at Oberlin College, 1870, — in medicine, with his brother, at Indianapolis, 1872, also attending lectures at the "Homœopathic Hospital College," of Cleveland, O. He has assisted his namesake, the compiler, very essentially in procuring the records of this Ohio branch of the family; and the sketches of pioneer life, under the names of his grandfather and father [458] and [979], are substantially from his pen.
989. SHERWIN TIP, b. Aug. 11, 1851.
990. EDWIN BURGET, b. Sept. 11, 1853.

991. LOUISA[5] [460] (Stephen[4], Stephen[3], Ebenezer[2], Samuel[1]),

m. Benjamin Franklin Wheeler, tanner, of Marietta, O., Apr. 1832, and d. at M., Mar. 13, 1834 (5), aged 24. He d. 1838, in Licking Co. Child : —

   992. LOUISA (Wheeler), b. 1833, in Marietta, and there d. 1835, aged 2.

   993. LUKE BROWN[5] [461] (Stephen[4], Stephen[3], Ebenezer[2], Samuel[1]), a farmer in Licking Co., O.; m., 1st, Joanna Brooks, Nov. 13, 1833, who d. Jan. 30, 1851; m., 2d, Esther Scribner, Sept. 17, 1851. Children, all by first wife except the youngest : —

   994. LOUISA M., b. Oct. 4, 1834; d. May 25, 1836, in her 2d year.
   995. ORLANDO LEMAN [1572], b. Apr. 15, 1836.
   996. JOSEPH ALONZO [1576], b. Dec. 11, 1837.
   997. STEPHEN WALTER, b. Jan. 8, 1840; m. Sarah Miller, in Licking Co., Sept. 3, 1863; was a member of the "142d Ohio National Guards," called out in the spring of 1864; d. at Bermuda Hundred, Va., of inflammation of the brain, caused by a sunstroke, Aug. 13, 1864, in his 25th year; "an experienced Christian."
   998. PURLONA JANE [1579], b. Jan. 1, 1842.
   999. JOANNA BROOKS, b. May 20, 1843; d. July 21, 1845, aged 2 years 2 months.
   1000. ALZENA [1581], b. Mar. 10, 1845.
   1001. LEWIS HARMON, b. July 25, 1847.
   1002. MIRANDA L., b. Nov. 15, 1852.

   1003. LYDIA JANE[5] [462] (Stephen[4], Stephen[3], Ebenezer[2], Samuel[1]), m. Solomon Brooks, carpenter, Sept. 13, 1832; resided first in Licking Co., O., where their children were all b.; now living in Marshall, Iowa : —

   1004. MARY JANE (Brooks), b. June 24, 1833; m. Rufus Tupper Carris, Apr. 16, 1854, in Licking Co., O. He was b. Nov. 20, 1832, in Orange Co., N. Y.; a farmer (1872) in Talleyrand, Keokuk Co., Ia. Children : —
     1. HILA ANN (Carris), b. Jan. 15, 1856, in Washington Co., Ia.
     2. ELDRIDGE GREENLEAF, b. Apr. 15, 1858, in Keokuk Co., Ia., as were the following : —
     3. ALBERT WYETH, b. Aug. 2, 1860; d. Apr. 6, 1861, aged 8 mos.
     4. WILLIAM HENRY, b. Apr. 20, 1862.
     5. ROSETTA MELVINA, b. June 18, 1864.
     6. JOHN SMITH, b. Feb. 5, 1866.
     7. ULYSSES SIMPSON GRANT, b. Mar. 23, 1868.
     8. EVA MAY, b. Apr. 3, 1870.
     9. MARY, b. Mar. 1, 1872.
   1005. ROSETTA M. (Brooks), b. Apr. 8, 1835; d. Dec. 27, 1855, at Marshall, in her 21st year.
   1006. ADOLPHUS L., b. Jan. 28, d. Mar. 13, 1839.
   1007. AMANDA M., b. Nov. 21, 1841; d. Sept. 2, 1848, in her 7th year.
   1008. DELILAH D., b. Feb. 19, 1847.
   1009. SARAH C., b. Nov. 28, 1849.

   1010. STEPHEN[5] [464] (Stephen[4], Stephen[3], Ebenezer[2], Samuel[1]), was a farmer; m. Malinda J. Brawder, in Marshall, Clark Co., Ill., Apr. 28, 1842; d. at Broadway, Union Co., Ohio, Apr. 16, 1862, in his 45th year. Children : —

   1011. MARY J [1584], b. Apr. 23, 1843, in Marshall, Ill.
   1012. VITALIS S. [1587], b. May 14, 1845, in Licking Co., O.
   1013. MARTHA J. [1589], b. Aug. 24, 1847, in Evansville, Ind.

1014. ELIZA L., b. July 4, 1851, in Evansville.
1015. ROSA E., b. Apr. 17, 1857, in Broadway, O.

1016. SOLLIS[5] [465] (Stephen[4], Stephen[3], Ebenezer[2], Samuel[1]), settled as a farmer, first in Licking Co., then in Delaware Co., O., and d. at his latter home, July 15, 1854, aged 35.   Had m. Eliza G. Nash, in Licking Co., Feb. 24, 1842.   Children : —

1017. CAROLINE STEARN, b. Nov. 24, 1843, in Licking Co., and there d. Apr. 6, 1848, in her 5th year.
1018. ALBINA JANE [1591], b. Oct. 23, 1845.
1019. RICHARD CORYDON, b. June 16, 1849.
1020. MARION PARKER, b. Mar. 27, 1852.
1021. SOLLIS, b. Dec. 1, 1854, in Delaware Co.

1022. BENJAMIN FRANKLIN[5] [467] (Stephen[4], Stephen[3], Ebenezer[2], Samuel[1]), was first a farmer in Licking Co., O., and moved thence to Page Co., Ia., 1859 ; m. Lucy Snow Wyeth, Jan. 23, 1852, who was b. Dec. 13, 1830, in Franklin Co., Mass.   Children : —

1023. IRVING, b. Mar. 15, 1855.
1024. WALTER, b. Apr. 12, 1856.
1025. FREMONT, b. Feb. 12, d. July 24, 1858.
1026. SARAH JANE, } b. Nov. 16, 1861.
1027. RYLAND,   }
        Ryland d. Feb. 19, 1862, aged 3 months.

1028. JAMES MONROE[5] [468] (Stephen[4], Stephen[3], Ebenezer[2], Samuel[1]), a farmer ; m., 1st, Emily Jane Menser, in Licking Co., O., Mar. 27, 1844 ; moved to Clarinda, Page Co., Iowa, where she d. May 23, 1855, and he m., 2d, Mrs. Eliza Ellen Burchard, Dec. 2, 1857.   Five oldest children b. in Licking Co. : —

1029. HARRISON, b. Feb. 11, d. Apr. 11, 1845.
1030. DENISON, b. Oct. 5, 1846 ; d. May 10, 1848, in his 2d year.
1031. THOMAS TAYLOR, b. Sept. 1, 1848.
1032. JUSTIN, b. Mar. 25, 1851.
1033. FRANCES JANE, b. Oct. 25, 1853 ; d. Jan. 27, 1854, aged 3 months.
1034. FRANKLIN BENJAMIN, b. Dec. 27, 1854, in Clarinda, Ia.
1035. PARLEY, b. Jan. 11, 1859 (second wife), in Licking Co., O.
1036. EMER, b. Jan. 10, 1864, in Buchanan Co., Mo.

1037. MARY MARIAH[5] [469] (Stephen[4], Stephen[3], Ebenezer[2], Samuel[1]), m. Matthew Eli Hopkins, farmer, of Appleton, O., Feb. 26, 1846, at Newway, Licking Co., O. ; settled at Benton Ridge, Hancock Co., O.   Children, all b. in Blanchard township : —

1038. CORTLAND RUNNELS (Hopkins), b. Apr. 23, 1848.
1039. AMANDA JANE, b. Sept. 21, 1849 ; m. Joab Moffith, farmer, of Blanchard township, O., Dec. 30, 1869.   Child : —
        1. EVA (Moffith), b. Nov. 16, 1870.
1040. MEROA MARIAH (Hopkins), b. Jan. 10, 1852.
1041. AMELIA CAROLINE, b. Nov. 8, 1853.
1042. CARY MEAD, b. Sept. 17, 1857.
1043. LAURA DUKES, b. Jan. 20, 1861 ; d. Aug. 20, 1862, in her 2d year.
1044. NORAH DELL, b. June 9, 1863.
1045. ALMA ETHAEL, b. July 28, 1867.

1046. THOMAS BROWN[5] [470] (Stephen[4], Stephen[3], Ebenezer[2], Samuel[1]), remained as a farmer near his father's old place in Licking Co., O.; m. Mahala D. Pumphrey, Oct. 23, 1860; d. Oct. 6, 1865, in Knox Co., O., in his 36th year. Children: —

    1047. SEWARD, b. Nov. 6, 1861.
    1048. CARLETON, b. Jan. 12, 1863.
    1049. ALSON WINTER, b. Mar. 23, 1864.

1050. MOSES THURSTON[5] [474] (Moses Thurston[4], Stephen[3], Ebenezer[2], Samuel[1]), moved with his mother to Jaffrey, N. H., 1832; graduated at Dartmouth College, 1853, and at the "Theological Institute of Connecticut," East Windsor Hill, 1856; labored for the "American S. S. Union," in Wisconsin, Texas, and Kansas, and at Boston, Mass., in all four years; was pastor of the Orford, N. H., West Congregational Church till 1865, and then of the Congregational Church in Sanbornton, where still residing (1872); m. Fannie Maria, dau. of H. S. Baker, Esq., of Haverhill, N. H., July 9, 1861. Three oldest children b. in Orford; two youngest in Sanbornton: —

    1051. CAROLINE STEARNS, b. May 16, 1862.
    1052. FANNY HUNTINGTON, b. Dec. 5, 1863.
    1053. MARY AINSWORTH, b. July 22, d. Sept. 24, 1865.
    1054. CATHARINE BAKER, b. Dec. 7, 1868.
    1055. MOSES THURSTON, b. June 13, 1870; d. suddenly, of brain disease, Oct. 24, 1871, aged 1 year 4 months. This darling child was *taken* at nearly the same age at which his father was *left* an orphan; and at the same age at which his grandfather was *taken*, his father was again *left*. The first and last of three successive generations, bearing the same venerated name, are thus joined in the spirit world. See [472]. As another striking coincidence, he died the *same day* on which his father, more than one hundred miles from home, in Jericho, Vt., was exhuming and removing, from a private to a public cemetery, the mortal remains of his grandfather, buried forty years before. His parents can only add, in the beautiful lines of Bryant: —

> "Oh! we shall mourn him long, and miss
> His ready smile, his ready kiss;
> The patter of his little feet,
> Sweet frowns, and stammered phrases sweet;
> And graver looks, serene and high,
> *A light of heaven* in that young eye;
> All these will haunt us, till the heart
> Shall ache and ache — and tears shall start.
>
> But he who now, from sight of men,
> We hide in earth, shall live again;
> Shall break these clouds, a form of light,
> With nobler mien and clearer sight;
> And in the eternal glory stand,
> With those who wait at God's right hand."

1056. ANNIS C.[5] [490] (Sollis[4], Stephen[3], Ebenezer[2], Samuel[1]), m. Hiram P. Perkins, at Dresden, O., Nov. 18, 1849. He was b. Sept. 29, 1815; residence, 1858, in Keokuk Co., Ia.; 1868, at Cole Camp, Benton Co., Mo. Children: —

1057. PARKER HAZEN (Perkins), b. Aug. 8, 1850.
1058. MARILLA E., b. May 24, d. May 26, 1853.
1059. ABIEL JACOB, b. Oct. 30, 1855.
1060. EDGAR MOORE, b. July 10, 1858.
1061. LAWRENCE TAFT, b. July 6, 1862.

1062. JAMES LAWRENCE[5] [492] (Sollis[4], Stephen[3], Ebenezer[2], Samuel[1]), m. Hannah Shoemaker, at Ashley, Delaware Co., O., Dec. 7, 1854 (3) ; resided at Sigourney, Ia., 1857 ; d. at Atchinson, Kansas, Apr. 29, 1865, in his 36th year. She has now returned to Ashley, O. Children : —

1063. ELLA, b. Sept. 1, 1855, in Ashley.
1064. JENNIE ELIZABETH, b. Aug. 3, 1856, in Sigourney, Ia.
1065. LILLIE, b. Aug. 19, d. Sept. 3, 1858, in Ashley.
1066. LAWRENCE ARTHUR, b. Nov. 13, 1861, in A.
1067. MARY, b. Feb. 19, 1865, in Atchinson, Kansas.

1068. AZRO DENNISON[5] [493] (Sollis[4], Stephen[3], Ebenezer[2], Samuel[1]), m. Mary Ann Glanden, of Sigourney, Ia., Dec. 31, 1862 ; moved to Yam Hill Co., Oregon, in 1864, where she d. an exceedingly happy death, Dec. 16, 1867, aged 23. He is still (1872) in North Yam Hill, Oregon, " carrying on the boot and shoe business." Child : —

1069. SOLLIS SHELTON, b. Oct. 13, d. Nov. 16, 1867.

1070. MARY LUCRETIA[5] [494] (Sollis[4], Stephen[3], Ebenezer[2], Samuel[1]), m. Charles W. Rosecrans, brother of Gen. William S. Rosecrans, at Sigourney, Ia., Feb. 12, 1862. She was remarkable, alike for her vivacity, intelligence and amiability ; d. at Lafayette, Ia., Jan. 1, 1863, in her 30th year. He d. June 18, 1865, leaving : —

1071. MARY LUCRETIA (Rosecrans), b. Nov. 27, 1862.

1072. EMELINE SOPHIA[5] [495] (Sollis[4], Stephen[3], Ebenezer[2], Samuel[1]), m. Joseph B. Moore, farmer, Aug. 31, 1858, at Sigourney, Ia., and settled in Liberty, Adams Co., Ill., where were b. : —

1073. ROBERT DENNISON (Moore), b. Feb. 5, 1860.
1074. MARY HARRIET, b. 1866.
1075. SOLLIS ALBERT, b. Nov. 7, 1869.

1076. HARRIET MARIAH[5] [496] (Sollis[4], Stephen[3], Ebenezer[2], Samuel[1]), m. John R. Hartzell, farmer, Nov. 18, 1855, at Sigourney, Ia. Children : —

1077. SOLLIS RUNNELS (Hartzell), b. Sept. 21, 1856.
1078. BRUCE P., b. Jan. 5, 1858.
1079. IRA S., b. Dec. 8, 1860.
1080. MARY E., b. Nov. 18, 1862.
1081. NELLIE M., b. Apr. 5, 1866.
1082. CHARLES DENNISON, b. Oct. 22, 1868.
1083. THOMAS ARTHUR HATCH, b. Dec. 31, 1870.

1084. EMILY ELIZABETH[5] [498] (Sollis[4], Stephen[3], Ebenezer[2], Samuel[1]), m., 1st, Edward Carris, Jan. 1, 1861, at Sigourney

He was b. Feb. 22, 1835, in Orange Co., N. Y.; was a soldier in the war of the rebellion, Co. C, 8th Iowa regiment, and d. at Sedalia, Mo., Feb. 28, 1862, aged 27. She m., 2d, James R. Turner, Sept. 8, 1866, at Sigourney. He was b. Nov. 4, 1835, in Trumbull Co., Ohio; was enrolled in Capt. Isaiah Moore's company, 17th regiment Illinois infantry, May 24, 1861; discharged June 4, 1864. They afterwards resided on a farm in Talleyrand, Ia., where they were both members of a Congregational church ten miles distant from their home; are now (1872) keeping a hotel at Keota, a new railroad town in Keokuk Co., Ia. Her children were : —

1085. FANNY EDITH (Carris), b. Nov. 18, 1861, in Keokuk Co.
1086. SEWALL A. (Turner), b. June 17, 1867.

1087. JULIA FIDELIA[5] [499] (Sollis[4], Stephen[3], Ebenezer[2], Samuel[1]), m. Joseph P. Seaton, at Carris' Corner, Ia., Sept. 15, 1863; have resided, since 1868, in Sigourney. Children : —

1088. AMANDA VIRGINIA (Seaton), b. July 20, 1865, in Van Buren, Ia.
1089. ALMA ETTA, b. May 23, 1867, in Van Buren.
1090. GEORGE EDWARD, b. June 13, 1869, in Sigourney.
1091. ROBERT E. LEE, b. Apr. 22, 1871, in. S.

1092. HENRIETTA[5] [501] (Sewall[4], Stephen[3], Ebenezer[2], Samuel[1]), m. Lewis P. Blood. of Liberty, O., Jan. 26, 1842; residence (1872) at Stockbridge, Wis., where he owns a valuable farm on the shore of Lake Winnebago. Children : —

1093. FRANKLIN (Blood), b. Apr. 3, 1843, in Ohio; was a soldier in the 21st Wisconsin regiment, from Oct. 16, 1864, till the close of the war.
1094. CHARLES SEWALL, b. Feb. 25, 1845; d. in Grovesville, Wis., Mar. 16, 1865, aged 20.
1095. NATHAN LEWIS, b. Jan. 5, 1847, in Wisconsin, as also the remaining children.
1096. SETH, b. June 6, 1849.
1097. EDWIN, b. July 6, 1851.
1098. AMANDA MELINDA, b. Feb. 4, 1853.
1099. ALMERON, b. July 3, 1854.
1100. ADDISON, b. July 8, 1857.
1101. GUY, b. Aug. 8, 1859.
1102. ADALINE, b. Jan. 5, d. Sept. 17, 1862.

1103. FRANKLIN[5] [502] (Sewall[4], Stephen[3], Ebenezer[2], Samuel[1]), is an enterprising and successful farmer at Grovesville, Wis.; m. Lenora Ellen Blood, of Elmira, Ill., Nov. 18, 1861. Children : —

1104. WILLIE FRANKLIN, b. Mar. 18, 1863.
1105. MARY LENORA, b. June 3, 1866.
1106. HERBERT SEWALL, b. Apr. 19, 1869.
1107. SETH ALBERT, b. Nov. 3, 1871.

1108. LOUISA G.[5] [509] (Frederick[4], Samuel[3], Ebenezer[2], Samuel[1]), m. Benjamin Franklin Carter, of Concord, N. H., Dec. 8, 1850, at Carthage, Me.; residence, 1870, at Menasha, Wis. Children : —

1109. FREDERICK RUNNELS (Carter), b. Mar. 23, 1852, in Carthage, Me.
1110. CHARLES FRANKLIN, b. June 22, 1854, in Concord, N. H.
1111. SARAH ELIZABETH, b. Sept. 15, 1855, in C.
1112. JOHN HALL, b. Oct. 31, 1857, in C.
1113. MARY LOUISA, b. Feb. 22, 1861, in C.
1114. HENRY WELLS, b. July 18, 1863, at Fond du Lac, Wis.
1115. BENJAMIN GARVIN, b. Dec. 17, 1865, at Empire, Wis.

1116. DANIEL FREDERICK[5] [514] (Ebenezer[4], Samuel[3], Eben
ezer[2], Samuel[1]), is a merchant in Nashua, N. H., firm of " Runnells
& Chase " ; owns a pleasant residence on Main Street, and is building a new store, 1872 ; m. Sarah E. Farley, of Hollis, Sept. 9,
1858. Children : —

1117. BELLE MAUDE, b. Sept. 30, 1861 ; d. Mar. 23, 1865, in her 4th year.
1118. FLORA, b. Mar. 20, 1863.
1119. MYRTA BELLE, b. Dec. 16, 1864 ; d. Oct. 30, 1866, in her 2d year.
1120. KATE SARAH, b. Nov. 24, 1868.
1121. FREDERICK DANIEL, b. Dec. 21, 1870.

1122. THOMAS KING[5] [530] (John[4], Thomas[3], Ebenezer[2], Samuel[1]), was a seaman, and mate of a vessel ; m. Elizabeth Lee
Davis, of Liverpool, Eng., 1839, who d. Dec. 1843 ; was finally
cast away at sea, his ship having sprung a leak ; d. from exposure,
Jan. 31, 1845, in his 27th year, and was buried on an island
between Norfolk, Va., and Baltimore, Md. Child : —

1123. SARAH ELIZABETH, b. Aug. 12, 1842 ; d. Nov. 16, 1844, aged 2 yrs.
3 months.

1124. LUCY ANN[5] [531] (John[4], Thomas[3], Ebenezer[2], Samuel[1]),
m. Joseph Elbridge Smith, of Haverhill, Mass., Apr. 27, 1846 ;
residence in H., 1870. Child : —

1125. MARY LUCY (Smith), b. Nov. 22, 1847 ; m. a Darling, of Haverhill, 1868.

1126. JOHN S.[5] [532] (John[4], Thomas[3], Ebenezer[2], Samuel[1]),
m. Abby H. Gage, a native of Haverhill, N. H., Nov. 5, 1846 ; a
soldier in the 14th Massachusetts regiment (first heavy artillery) ;
d. at Fort Whipple, Va., Sept. 18, 1863, in his 38th year, having
served his country two years and three months. His home was in
Haverhill, Mass., where his widow still lives (1870). Children : —

1127. THOMAS GAGE, b. Aug. 5, 1847.
1128. ELLEN FRANCES, b. Nov. 5, 1849 ; d. Apr. 28, 1850, aged 5 mos.
23 days.
1129. EMMA ESTELLE [1593], b. Mar. 20, 1851.
1130. ISADORE FRANCES, b. Sept. 16, 1853 ; m. George R. Huse, of
Haverhill, at Kingston, N. H., July 3, 1871.
1131. CORA ELLA, b. Feb. 18, 1855.
1132. ABBY ETTIE, b. June 23, 1859.

1133. HIRAM[5] [560] (Warren[4], Thomas[3], Ebenezer[2], Samuel[1]),
m.. 1st, Catharine Garret, in London, Eng., June 5, 1850, who d.
at Fall River, Mass., 1862 ; m., 2d, Hannah ——, May 4, 1864, in
Boston, Mass. Child : —

1134. HIRAM, b. Oct. 26, 1866 ; d. Apr. 28, 1868, in his 2d year.

1135. HARRIET ANN[5] [562] (Warren[4], Thomas[3], Ebenezer[2], Samuel[1]), m. John R. Fish, of Fall River, Mass., at Tiverton, R. I., who was b. July 29, 1833. Children : —

1136. CHARLES HAZEN (Fish), b. Sept. 7, 1856.
1137. HIRAM FRANCIS, b. Dec. 28, 1858.
1138. JOHN ELLSWORTH, b. July 29, 1861.
1139. FRANK HENRY, b. Sept. 20, 1865.

1140. AMELIA ELIZABETH[5] [563] (Warren[4], Thomas[3], Ebenezer[2], Samuel[1]), m., 1st, David Farrell, at Fall River, June 4, 1857, who was b. June 9, 1836, in Paterson, N. J., and d July 21, 1859, aged 23 ; m., 2d, Alfred Seymour Wingate, at Tiverton, R. I., Aug. 27, 1860, who was a native of Watertown, N. Y., and d. Aug. 1 (July 7), 1867 ; m., 3d, William Alfred Gosling, of New Bedford, Mass., upholsterer, Mar. 9, 1869, who was b. Apr. 7, 1843, in Stockport, Cheshire, Eng. Her children were : —

1141. WARREN MATTHIAS (Farrell), b. May 4, 1858, in Fall River.
1142. MARIA (Wingate), b. Oct. 27, 1862. in Adams, N. Y.
1143. HENRY HERRICK, b. Nov. 18, 1865. in Troy, N. Y.
1144. WALTER RAYMOND, b. Nov. 30, 1867, in Bristol, R. I.

1145. WARREN HAZEN[5] [564] (Warren[4], Thomas[3], Ebenezer[2], Samuel[1]), m. Harriet K. Dyer, Sept. 10, 1865, at Provincetown, Mass., who was there b. June 27, 1844 ; residence, Fall River, Mass. Children : —

1146. LUCY ANN, b. Apr. 15, 1865.
1147. WILLIAM HENRY, b. Feb. 14, 1867.
1148. GEORGE WARREN, b. June 12, 1870, in Fall River.

1149. ELIZA A.[5] [566] (Moses Clement[4], Thomas[3], Ebenezer[2], Samuel[1]), m. James Simpson, 1851, and d. Nov. 28, 1860, in her 35th year. Child : —

1150. CHARLES (Simpson), b. 1852.

1151. SARAH JANE[5] [567] (Moses Clement[4], Thomas[3], Ebenezer[2], Samuel[1]), m., 1st, William Taylor, 1849 ; m., 2d, Greenleaf Lull, 1863, and d. Nov. 26, 1866, aged 38. Child : —

1152. MARY E. (Taylor), b. May 29, 1851, in Charlestown, Mass.

1153. MARY ELIZABETH[5] [584] (Ebenezer[4], Nathaniel[3], Ebenezer[2], Samuel[1]), m., 1st, Nathaniel Donnell, of York, Me , 1847. He was a tin and sheet iron worker ; two years later, went to California, and there d. Jan. 12, 1851. She m., 2d, Levi P. Thayer, of Lowell, Mass., Aug. 1856 ; a boot and shoe maker ; residence (1872) in Lynn, Mass. Her children : —

1154. OCTAVIUS (Donnell), b. Feb. 1848; m. Ella Keene, of Lowell, Mar. 18, 1869 ; a machinist in the Charlestown navy-yard, 1872.
1155. EMMA FLORENCE (Thayer), b. Jan. 30, 1858.
1156. ANNA MARIA, b. July 10, 1862.

1157. ANN MARIA[5] [586] (Ebenezer[4], Nathaniel[3], Ebenezer[2], Samuel[1]), m., 1st, Charles Brown, shoemaker, of Seabrook, N. H., Apr. 15, 1852. He d. "in consequence of his service in the war of the rebellion," 1861. She m., 2d, Charles Elwood Pickering, Dec. 21, 1862. He is a railroad employé. Chief residence in Boston (1872), though she still retains her father's homestead in Portsmouth, N. H. Child : —

1158. ELLA MARIA (Brown), b. Jan. 30, 1855; d. Nov. 18, 1858, in her 4th year.

1159. HANNAH JANE[5] [588] (Ebenezer[4], Nathaniel[3], Ebenezer[2], Samuel[1]), m., 1st, Albert Foye, stone and marble cutter, of Dover, N. H., Mar. 8, 1853 ; resided in Portsmouth ; served in the late war, and d. Feb. 17, 1867. She m., 2d, Frederick Danielson, of Portsmouth, mariner, July 24, 1868. He had served in the Atlantic and East Gulf blockading squadrons, U. S. N., from 1860 to 1866, continuously. Present residence in Portsmouth, No. 55 Daniels Street. Her children, b. in Portsmouth, were : —

1160. HENRY ALBERT (Foye), b. Aug. 20, 1854.
1161. CHARLES EBEN, b. Apr. 10, 1857.
1162. EDWARD DREW, b. Feb. 29, 1860; d. Feb. 27, 1863, aged 3.
1163. NELLIE ALBERTA, b. Oct. 24, 1866.
1164. KATIE MABEL (Danielson), b. Oct. 8, 1869.
1165. GRACIE MARSHAL, b. Mar. 20, 1872.

1166. MARY MORRILL WORTHEN[5] [590] (Arthur[4], Nathaniel[3], Ebenezer[2], Samuel[1]), was m. to Asa Ames, by Rev. Mr. Bean, of Haverhill, N. H., Feb. 25, 1868. He is a farmer in Orford, N. H., where their children were born : —

1167. LUELLA PAMELIA, b. Dec. 12, 1868.
1168. ARTHUR EDWIN, } b. Dec. 29, 1870.
1169. EZRA ASA,
    The two last "look so much alike," that their grandfather finds it difficult to distinguish the one from the other.

1170. MARY ISABELLA[5] [602] (Bartlett[4], Nathaniel[3], Ebenezer[2], Samuel[1]), m George Munsell, M. D., at Kirkersville, O., July 3, 1858. He studied medicine in Alexandria, O., and there practised ; also in Hamilton, Ia., having moved to the latter place, 1860. Children : —

1171. HENRY C. (Munsell), b. Sept. 25, 1859, in Alexandria, O.
1172. EMMA, b. June 28, 1862, in Hamilton, Ia.
1173. ANNA, b. Jan. 29, 1865, in H.
1174. WILLIAM, b. June 10, 1868.

1175. LYDIA[5] [605] (George[4], Nathaniel[3], Ebenezer[2], Samuel[1]), m. John W. Stokesbury, farmer in Keokuk Co., Ia., June 11, 1863. Children, b. in Sigourney, Ia. : —

1176. GEORGE ARTHUR (Stokesbury), b. Nov. 26, 1864.
1177. MARY JANE, b. Sept. 19, 1866.
1178. FLORA ETHEL, b. Feb. 27, 1869.
1179. ELIZA ELLEN, b. Feb. 21, 1871.

1180. NATHANIEL[5] [606] (George[4], Nathaniel[3], Ebenezer[2], Samuel[1]), m. Ann Eliza Enos, of Oskaloosa, Ia., Sept. 11, 1865, and d. of typhoid fever, Jan. 12, 1868, in his 24th year, leaving : —

1181. CADY ALBERTA, b. Apr. 9, 1867.

1182. SARAH GEORGE[5] [619] (Daniel George[4], Daniel[3], Ebenezer[2], Samuel[1]), m. Jere C. Call, Apr. 2, 1850, who is foreman in a machine shop; residence in Lowell, Mass., 13 Railroad Street. Children, all b. in Lowell, except the third : —

1183. FRANK HANSON (Call), b. June 8, 1852; d. Feb. 19, 1858, in his 6th year.
1184. MARY ELLEN, b. May 24, d. Oct. 2, 1856.
1185. CHARLES HENRY, b. Oct. 15, 1858, in Warner, N. H.
1186. WILLIE F., b. May 7, 1863; d. Mar. 23, 1864, aged 10 mos. 16 days.
1187. EMMA FRANCES, b. Aug. 4, 1870.

1188. MARY CLOUGH[5] [620] (Daniel George[4], Daniel[3], Ebenezer[2], Samuel[1]), was m. to Charles S. Pillsbury, at her uncle's, the Rev. Enoch Corser's, in Boscawen, N. H., Dec. 24, 1863. He resides in Londonderry, N. H., 1872, as a farmer. Children : —

1189. CHARLES GEORGE (Pillsbury), b. Feb. 15, 1865, in Webster, N. H.
1190. ADAMS DIX, b. Mar. 23, 1868, in Londonderry.
1191. JOHN ARTHUR, b. Aug. 26, 1872, in Londonderry.

SIXTH GENERATION.

1192. MATILDA EUELA[6] [630] (Stephen[5], Enos[4], Stephen[3], Stephen[2], Samuel[1]), m. Henry Dan Wilmarth, at Boston, Mass., Jan. 17, 1855. He is a native of Taunton, Mass.; now (1871) a merchant in Boston, firm of " Talbot, Wilmarth & Co.," 67 Franklin Street. Children : —

1193. ARTHUR REYNOLDS (Wilmarth), b. Nov. 7, 1855, in Boston.
1194. EDWARD NATHAN, b. Jan. 2, 1865, at Jamaica Plain.

1195. SARAH CLEMENT[6] [636] (Eliphalet[5], Enos[4], Stephen[3], Stephen[2], Samuel[1]), m. Charles Kimball Blanchard, at Charlestown, Mass., May 30, 1844. He was b. Dec. 25, 1815; first went to Texas at the age of 19, and there chiefly resided, after marriage in Jasper Co., and at Milan and Hemphill, Sabine Co.; was county clerk most of the time, also a land agent As a true patriot, he " stood by the old flag`amidst threats and persecutions," in the late war, and d. at Sabine, Texas, Jan. 24, 1870, aged 54. Children : —

1196. MARJERY CATHARINE (Blanchard), b. June 6, 1845, in Jasper Co., Tex.; m. James T. Shaw, at Hemphill. July 24, 1864. Child : —
    1. EDWARD CHARLES (Shaw), b. Mar. 1868.
1197. MARY MARIA (Blanchard), b. Sept. 23, 1846, in Jasper Co.; m. William Stroud, Oct. 13, 1870.
1198. ISABELLA ARIETTA, b. July 10, 1848, at French Grove, Bureau Co., Ill.; d. Aug. 29, 1849, aged 13 mos. 19 days.
1199. ELIZABETH ROBINS, b. July 7, 1850, in Sabinetown, Texas; m. Charles W. Smith, Mar. 8, 1870.
1200. CLARA LILLA, b. Nov. 13, 1852, in Milan, Tex.
1201. CHARLOTTE HANNAH, b. May 24, 1855, in Milan.
1202. CHARLES WILLIAM, b. May 7, 1858, in Sabine Co.

1203. WILLIAM JAMES[6] [637] (Eliphalet[5], Enos[4], Stephen[3], Stephen[2], Samuel[1]), m Mary Frances Chesley, dau. of Col. A. P. Chesley, of Virginia, July 6, 1848. Was living (1870) at Danville, Vermillion Co., Ill. " Most of his time since moving West, has been devoted to the science and profession of music." Children : —

1204. ISABEL GERTRUDE, b. Apr. 12, 1849.
1205. WILLIAM WALTER SCOTT, b. July 7, 1851.
1206. IDA BLANCHARD, b. June 26, 1854.

1207. MARY EATON, b. Oct. 24, 1861.
1208. MAUD LELIA, b. Jan. 7, 1866.
1209. JAMES ALEXANDER, b. Aug. 12, 1868.

1210. ELEANOR ANALETTE[6] [641] (Eliphalet[5], Enos[4], Stephen[3], Stephen[2], Samuel[1]), m. Melzar Eaton, of Stoneham, Mass., Nov. 27, 1851, at Woburn. He was b. May 6, 1829, in W.; a surveyor of leather; enlisted in the Massachusetts 4th regiment heavy artillery, for ten months, till the close of the war, 1865. Children: —

1211. WALTER REYNOLDS (Eaton), b. Mar. 5, 1856.
1212. HARRY WILMARTH, b. Sept. 3, 1857.
1213. EDWARD MELZAR, b. Dec. 29, 1859.

1214. HARRIET ISABELLA[6] [642] (Eliphalet[5], Enos[4]. Stephen[3], Stephen[2], Samuel[1]), m. Roger Sherman Littlefield (first wife), July, 1858, and d. Apr. 21, 1861, aged 24 (?). He was b. Nov. 14, 1834, in Randolph, Mass., his mother, Lucinda Sherman, being a granddaughter of Hon. Roger Sherman, of Connecticut, a framer and signer of the Declaration of Independence. He enlisted as a private in the 1st regiment Massachusetts heavy artillery, 1861; was in twelve regular battles, twice wounded; promoted to captain in his regiment, and was present at the surrender at Appomattox Court House, Apr. 9, 1865. Was still in government service 1870, "Harbor Improvement," at Green Bay, Wis., where then residing. See [633]. Children (first wife): —

1215. CLARA ISABELLA (Littlefield), b. Apr. 8, 1859.
1216. WALTER, b. Jan. 1861; d. same month.

1217. CAROLINE MATILDA[6] [644] (Samuel Spofford[5], Enos[4], Stephen[3], Stephen[2], Samuel[1]), m. Isaac Wilder Blanchard, Apr. 28, 1840. He was b. Nov. 1815, in Charlestown, Mass.; a banker in the Eagle Bank, Boston, 1870, and residing at Charlestown, where their children were born: —

1218. SAMUEL WILDER (Blanchard), b. Apr. 3, 1841; d. Jan. 2, 1850, in his 9th year.
1219. ABBY HERSEY, b. Apr. 29, 1845; m. Joseph Warren Guppey, Dec. 6, 1865, who was b. July 13, 1834, in Dover, N. H.; assistant superintendent of the Erie railroad, 1870, with residence in New York city, where were born: —
    1. CAROLINE WARREN (Guppey), b. May 30, 1867.
    2. BENJAMIN WILDER, b. May 13, 1869.
1220. EMMA FRANCES (Blanchard), b. Mar. 21, 1847; d. Mar. 26, 1850, aged 3.
1221. CARRIE WILDER, b. Oct. 18, 1850; d. Nov. 21, 1856, aged 6.
1222. MARY THOMAS, b. Dec. 1, 1852.
1223. ISAAC ARCHER, b. Oct. 13, 1854; a deaf-mute; misfortune occasioned by disease of the brain; was being educated, 1870, at the "New York Institution for the Deaf and Dumb."

1224. EDWARD EVERETT[6] [647] (Samuel Spofford[5], Enos[4], Stephen[3], Stephen[2], Samuel[1]), is a morocco dresser, residing at Woburn, Mass., 1870; m. Sarah Maria Brown, of Chelsea, Mass.,

Oct. 20, 1851 (2), who was b. Oct. 9, 1833, and d. at Woburn, Sept. 8, 1870, in her 37th year. Children : —

1225. MARIA (Minnie) DUNN, b. Nov. 5, 1854, in Charlestown.
1226. FANNIE ELIZA, b. Feb. 4, 1857, in North Woburn.
1227. WILLIAM BROWN, b. Sept. 3, 1862, in N. W.

1228. SARAH ISABELLA[6] [651] (Samuel Spofford[5], Enos[4], Stephen[3], Stephen[2], Samuel[1]), m. Charles Allison McDonald, of Woburn Centre, Mass., Oct. 15, 1857. Children, b. in Woburn : —

1229. CHARLES EDWARD ALLISON (McDonald), b. Oct. 6, 1858; d. same year.
1230. BEULAH REED, b. Dec. 22, 1865.
1231. SAMUEL ALLISON, b. June 4, 1870.

1232. FRANK MELLEN[6] [681] (William[5], Stephen[4], Daniel[3], Stephen[2], Samuel[1]), is a teamster in Boston ; m. Lizzie Ray, of B , 1860, and there resides. Child : —

1233. FRANK, b. Sept. 1861.

1234. ELIZA SARGENT[6] [684] (William[5], Stephen[4], Daniel[3], Stephen[2], Samuel[1]), m. Gustavus Chamberlain, at Lowell, Mass., May 24, 1866. He is a farmer, 1870, at Fayette Ridge, Me. Child : —

1235. GRACE MABEL (Chamberlain), b. July 16, 1867, in Fayette.

1236. ABIGAIL JANE[7] [725] (Daniel[5], Daniel[4], Daniel[3], Stephen[2], Samuel[1]), m., 1st, Henry Sherman, of Boston, Mass , June 15, 1843.   He was freight master of the Providence Railroad ; a native of Edgecomb, Me., and there d. of consumption, Aug. 3, 1848.   She m., 2d, James Clinton Watson, farmer, of Northwood, N. H., Sept. 10, 1850.   Post-office address, " Northwood Narrows." See [1261]. Her children : —

1237. ANGELINE (Sherman), b. Apr. 7, 1844, in Boston; d. May 17, 1845, aged 13 months 10 days.
1238. CHARLES, b. May 3, 1845; d. Dec. 15, 1846, in his 2d year.
1239. CONVERSE MCCURDY, b. Jan. 10, 1847; now engaged (1871) in a woollen factory, at Amesbury Mills, Mass.
1240. CHARLES HENRY, b Aug. 16, 1848, in Edgecomb, Me.; now a merchant at Northwood Narrows, N. H., firm of "Lancaster & Co."
1241. EUNICE MATILDA (Watson), b. Aug. 14, 1852, in New Market, N. H.; d. Oct 7, 1853, aged 14 months.
1242. HERBERT, b. Jan. 8, 1859, in Northwood.
1243. GRACE, b. Dec. 31, 1862.

1244 DANIEL THOMAS[6] [726] (Daniel[5], Daniel[4], Daniel[3], Stephen[2], Samuel[1]), m. Hannah P. Eaton, of Kensington, N. H., Sept. 18, 1848, in South New Market. She was b. Dec. 31, 1830, at Kingston Plains. He is a shoemaker, now living at East Kingston, N. H. Children : —

1245. STANLEY WOODBURY, b. Oct. 8, 1849, in New Market; is in the shoe business near his father's; m. Mrs. Mary E. Currier, of East Kingston, Apr. 1, 1871, who was there b. July 7, 1849, and has one child by her former husband : —
    1. NETTIE ARDELL (Currier), b. Aug. 5, 1867, in East Kingston.

1246. EDSON RODOLF, b. Oct. 25, 1851, in Kensington.
1247. EUNICE MATILDA, b. Feb. 9, 1854, in K., and there d. June 14, 1855, aged 16 months.

1248. MARY FRANCES[6] [728] (Daniel[5], Daniel[4], Daniel[3], Stephen[2], Samuel[1]), m. David D. Tuttle, at Exeter, N. H., May 30, 1852. He was b. June 27, 1832, in Nottingham, N. H., where still residing, as a shoemaker. Children : —

    1249. WOODBURY DURGIN (Tuttle), b. Sept. 25, 1858; d. Aug. 19, 1869, in his 11th year, in consequence of a distressing accident, while descending from a tree, five weeks before.
    1250. IVORY BURTEN, b. June 15, 1860; d. Mar. 16, 1861, aged 9 mos.
    1251. MANSON, b. Nov. 17, 1861.
    1252. ALVAH, b. Dec. 6, 1863.
    1253. NETTIE JANE, b. Jan. 7, 1866.
    1254. MARY HANNAH. b. May 23, 1868.
    1255. CLARA DURGIN, b. Mar. 13, 1870.

1256. SARAH ELIZABETH[6] [729] (Daniel[5], Daniel[4], Daniel[3], Stephen[2], Samuel[1]), m. William H. Locke, at Lowell, Mass., July 7, 1857. He was b. May 25, 1835, in New Durham, N. H.; residing (1870) at Amesbury Mills, Mass., employed in a woollen factory. Children : —

    1257. WALTER HERBERT (Locke), b. Mar. 16, at Northwood, and d. Aug. 16, 1858, at Dover, N. H.
    1258. GEORGE EDGAR, b. Aug. 16, 1860, in Northwood.
    1259. WILLIE HENRY, b. Apr. 17, 1863, in East Kingston, N. H.
    1260. CORA BELLE, b. Oct. 1, 1866, in E. K.

1261. WILLIAM ADDISON[6] [730] (Daniel[5], Daniel[4], Daniel[3], Stephen[2], Samuel[1]), m. Caroline Frances Pendergast, of Northwood, Aug. 8, 1859, who was b. Aug. 13, 1840; his home is at Northwood, business that of a shoemaker and farmer. Enlisted with his two brothers [1263] and [732], Aug. 29, 1864, in the 1st New Hampshire heavy artillery, Co. E, Col. Long and Capt. Davis. The three brothers were mustered in together, Sept. 5, and discharged at Fort Sumner, near Washington, D. C., at the same time, June 15, 1865. James C. Watson, see [1236], was also enlisted in the same company, and discharged as above, and one brother and another brother-in-law of *his*, all three, with W. A. R., from Northwood. Child, of the last : —

1262. CHARLES EVERETT, b. June 6, 1860.

1263. NASON FREEMAN[6] [731] (Daniel[5], Daniel[4], Daniel[3], Stephen[2], Samuel[1]), was a shoemaker at East Kingston, but now (1871) resides at Amesbury Mills, Mass., engaged in the woollen factory, with his brother-in-law and nephew [1256] and [1239]

See also [1261]. He m. Faustina Marshal, of Islesborough, Me., Apr. 14, 1869, at Lowell, Mass. Child : —

1264. RALPH NASON, b. Apr. 16, 1870.

1265. ALMIRA GOODWIN[6] [734] (Ebenezer Thompson[5], Daniel[4], Daniel[3], Stephen[2], Samuel[1]), m. Oliver Wetherbee Holt, of Allenstown, N. H., Oct. 31, 1851. He was b. Dec. 31, 1821. Was a machinist in Lowell and elsewhere, but has now lost his eyesight and his reason in part. Her present home is in L. Children : —

1266. MIRA EVA (Holt), b. July 30, 1852, in Lowell.
1267. FRANK OLIVER, b. Apr. 16, 1855, in L.
1268. FREDDIE EUGENE, b. Nov. 26, 1859, in Andover, Mass.
1269. CHARLES HAMILTON, b. May 8, 1861, in Manchester, N. H.
1270. ABBY HATTIE, b. Sept. 8, 1863, in Lawrence, Mass.

1271. DANIEL[6] [735] (Ebenezer Thompson[5], Daniel[4], Daniel[3], Stephen[2], Samuel[1]), an engineer, formerly on the Vermont Central Railroad ; home at Northfield, Vt. ; now living at Lowell, Mass., "in the city employ." He m., 1st, Laura Ann Hassam, of Northfield, July 27, 1848, at Nashua, N. H., who d. Mar. 10, 1854, at Northfield ; m., 2d, Melissa Lewis, of East Lempster, N. H., Jan. 29, 1856, at Lowell, who d. at East Lempster, Apr. 19, 1857 ; m., 3d, Sarah Jane Cannavan, of Dover, N. H., Feb. 3, 1865, at Alton, N. H. Child, first wife : —

1272. HAMILTON EUGENE, b. Mar. 10, 1850, in Northfield ; a carpenter, in Lowell, 1870 ; m. Laura A. Jones, of Methuen, Feb. 3, 1872.

1273. ABBY PERKINS[6] [736] (Ebenezer Thompson[5], Daniel[4], Daniel[3], Stephen[2], Samuel[1]), m. John Augustus Reed, Feb. 5, 1852. He was b. May 11, 1825, in Bedford, Mass. ; employed, 1870, in the navy-yard at Charlestown, Mass., gun carriage department ; residence, 45 Warren Street. Children : —

1274. ABBIE HATTIE (Reed), b. Aug. 22, 1856, and d. Sept. 15, 1857, at Charlestown, aged 1 year and 24 days.
1275. ADDIE CORA, b. Oct. 28, 1859, in Charlestown.

1276. CHARLES LEACH[6] [737] (Ebenezer Thompson[5], Daniel[4], Daniel[3], Stephen[2], Samuel[1]), is a machinist, formerly of Lowell, Mass. ; at Cochituate, Mass., 1870 ; m. Halina Maria Loker, of Lowell, Jan. 1, 1864, at Boston. Child : —

1277. ANDREW JUSTIN, b. Aug. 31, 1866.

1278. HAMILTON[6] [738] (Ebenezer Thompson[5], Daniel[4], Daniel[3], Stephen[2], Samuel[1]), is a shoemaker, having lived (1870) at Alton, N. H., near his father's old place, for fifteen years, except two years in Iowa, prior to 1866. He m. Corysand A. Glines, dau. of Rev. Josiah Glines, of Alton, June 14, 1857. Children : —

1279. CORA EVA, b. Sept. 24, 1858, in Alton, and there d. May 23, 1862, in her 4th year.
1280. CHARLES HAMILTON, b. Mar. 31, 1861.

1281. CARY HOMER, b. July 1, 1864.
1282. WILLIS, b. Apr. 19, 1866, in Hardin, Clayton Co., Iowa.

1283. MARY ELIZABETH[6] [741] (Stephen[5], Daniel[4], Daniel[3], Stephen[2], Samuel[1]), m. Levi Leighton Elder, of Falmouth, Me., Dec. 28, 1858, at Dover, N. H. He is a stone-cutter; was in business at Concord, N. H., in 1870. Children: —

1284. WILLIE LINCOLN (Elder), b. May 27, 1865, in Portland, Me.
1285. ANNIE GERTRUDE, b. Apr. 1, 1867, in Portland; d. at Madbury, N. H., Aug. 28, 1869, in her 3d year.

1286. LYDIA MARGARET[6] [742] (Stephen[5], Daniel[4], Daniel[3], Stephen[2], Samuel[1]), m. John M. Davis, of New Market, N. H., shoemaker, Mar. 27, 1853, at Dover. He was b. Nov. 15, 1833, and d. Dec. 25, 1863, aged 30. She d. at Madbury, N. H., Dec. 29, 1868, aged 35. Children: —

1287. ANNIE BERNICE DAVIS, b. Nov. 20, 1854; d. Sept. 10, 1855, aged 10 mos.
1288. JASPER WINGATE, b. Aug. 25, 1859.

1289. STEPHEN HENRY[6] [743] (Stephen[5], Daniel[4], Daniel[3], Stephen[2], Samuel[1]), served in the late war under two enlistments; first, in the Massachusetts 5th regiment, Apr. 1861, three months, being at the first battle of Bull Run; again, in the 1st Massachusetts battery, Aug. 1861. Seven previous engagements, — West Point, Va., Gaines's Mill, Savage's Station, Cross Roads, Malvern Hill, second Bull Run, and Antietam, — till finally wounded at the battle of Fredericksburg, and discharged, lame for life, Aug. 15, 1863. He is now a gold-beater, in Boston, firm of "Hood & Reynolds"; m. Lucy Adams, of Brookline, Mass., Sept. 8, 1866, at Boston. Child: —

1290. LIZZIE GERTRUDE, b. Mar. 12, 1868, at South Boston.

1291. JAMES ADDISON[6] [744) (Stephen[5], Daniel[4], Daniel[3], Stephen[2], Samuel[1]), is a shoe manufacturer, at Charlestown, N. H., now of the firm "Briggs & Co."; m. Miriam Hanson, of Madbury, Mar. 16, 1864, at Dover. She was b. Dec. 9, 1833, in Madbury. Child: —

1292. WILLIE SARGENT, b. Apr. 6, 1865, in Madbury.

1293. HANNAH JANE[6] [745] (Stephen[5], Daniel[4], Daniel[3], Stephen[2], Samuel[1]), m. Hiram Shepard Wentworth, of New Durham, N. H., Oct. 29, 1864. He was a shoemaker, lived in Dover, and there d. of consumption, May 12, 1871. Child: —

1294. EDGAR NEWLAND (Wentworth), b. Oct. 9, 1868, in Madbury.

1295. CHARLES WILLIAM[6] [746] (Stephen[5], Daniel[4], Daniel[3], Stephen[2], Samuel[1]), enlisted in the New Hampshire 5th regiment, Co. K, Oct 12, 1861; promoted to corporal; captured June 30, 1864; kept at Andersonville prison till exchanged, Dec 14, 1864; mustered out Feb. 22, 1865. He is a shoe manufacturer (1871) in

Detroit, Mich., 16 Warren Street; having m. Elizabeth C. Small-idge, Dec 20, 1866. Children: —

1296. CORA B., b. Sept. 26, 1867, in Tecumseh, Mich.
1297. GEORGE E., b. Jan. 4, 1871, in Cincinnati, O.

1298. JOSEPHINE MARIA[6] [748] (Stephen[5], Daniel[4], Daniel[3], Stephen[2], Samuel[1]), m. Joseph Frank Berry, Aug. 25, 1868, who was b. May 24, 1845, in Alton, N. H., was a shoe manufacturer, with home at Madbury, 1869, and moved to New Durham the next year to reside. Child: —

1299. GEORGE OLIVER (Berry), b. Oct. 28, 1869, in Dover.

1300. WILLIAM ADDISON[6] [753] (Addison[5], Daniel[4], Daniel[3], Stephen[2], Samuel[1]), is now (1872) a dealer in groceries, provisions, etc., 104 and 108 Southbridge Street, and 55 Madison Street, Worcester, Mass.; having m. Sarah Rebecca Deming, dau. of Thomas and Mary Noyes, of W., Jan. 8, 1862. Children: —

1301. GEORGE WILLIAM, b. Jan. 23, 1863.
1302. JENNIE, } b. July 18, 1865; d. Aug. 13, } 1865.
1303. JOSIE,   }   d. Aug. 5, }
1304. WALTER LUCIUS, b. July 12, 1869; d. July 11, 1870, aged 1 year.
1305. ALBERT ADDISON, b. Jan. 21, 1872.

1306. LIZZIE MARY[6] [754] (Addison[5], Daniel[4], Daniel[3], Stephen[2], Samuel[1]), was m. to John Forbes Sutton, by her uncle, Rev. Converse L. McCurdy [759], Nov. 18, 1856. He was the son of Thomas and Lucy Sutton; a machinist, having charge of Coe's wrench shop, in Worcester, 1870. Child: —

1307. EMMA LOUISE (Forbes), b. May 5, 1858, in Worcester.

1308. EMILY JANE[6] [756] (Addison[5], Daniel[4], Daniel[3], Stephen[2], Samuel[1]), m. James Booth, son of William and Mary Booth, of Central Falls, R. I., June 13, 1860. He is a machinist; residence in Worcester, Mass., where children were born: —

1309. HERBERT ADDISON (Booth), b. Jan. 13, 1862.
1310. WILLIE EARNEST, b. Oct. 12, 1868.

1311. CYNTHIA[6] [787] (Theodore[5], Joseph[4], Samuel[3], Samuel[2], Samuel[1]), m. William Whipple, of Bow, N. H., Oct. 17, 1841. He has since resided in Bradford, Mass.; a stock-fitter in a shoe manufactory. Child: —

1312. EMMA GEORGIANA (Whipple), b. July 4, 1846.

1313. LEONARD[6] [788] (Theodore[5], Joseph[4], Samuel[3], Samuel[2], Samuel[1]), m. Sarah M. Bradley, of Hampstead, N. H., Nov. 13, 1843; is a shoe manufacturer, residing in Bradford, Mass., where children were born: —

1314. LEVERETT AUGUSTUS, b. Mar. 23, 1847.
1315. MARY ELLA, b. Sept. 13, 1849.

1316. DANIEL LAKEMAN[6] [789] (Theodore[5], Joseph[4], Samuel[3], Samuel[2], Samuel[1]), settled as a farmer in Boxford, Mass., occupying the ancestral homestead of Samuel[2] [17] and Samuel[3] [93]; m. Abigail Perkins, of Boxford, Dec. 9, 1842. Children: —

    1317. GEORGE LAKEMAN [1595], b. Aug. 12, 1848.
    1318. AMANDA JANE [1597], b. Aug. 29, 1850.
    1319. LILLIE AUGUSTA, b. Oct. 11, 1855.
    1320. EMMA ESTELLA, b. Dec. 5, 1860.
    1321. HATTIE FLORENCE, b. Feb. 18, 1862.

1322. LORENZO[6] [790] (Theodore[5], Joseph[4], Samuel[3], Samuel[2], Samuel[1]), m. Susan Catharine Evans, Mar. 29, 1848, who was b. in Strafford, N. H., and after his death m., 2d, John K. Foster, Dec. 17, 1858. He d. Oct. 15, 1857, in his 36th year, at Bradford, where he had lived as a shoe manufacturer. Children: —

    1323. IDA JANE [1599], b. Jan. 12, 1849.
    1324. GARDNER BRYANT, b. Sept. 29, 1850; was engaged in the meat business, at Bradford, 1870.
    1325. WILLIAM WENDALL, b. Mar. 23, 1854.

1326. HORATIO[6] [791] (Theodore[5], Joseph[4], Samuel[3], Samuel[2], Samuel[1]), is a shoe manufacturer in Haverhill, Mass.; residence in Bradford; m. Augusta Marsh, of Dover, Vt., June 12, 1859. Children: —

    1327. ERNEST WILDER, b. Nov. 8, 1860, in Bradford.
    1328. MABEL HARRIET, b. Jan. 30, 1863, in Boxford.

1329. LUTHER[6] [792] (Theodore[5], Joseph[4], Samuel[3], Samuel[2], Samuel[1]), was also a shoe manufacturer, with residence in Boxford and Bradford; m. Sarah A. Carleton, of Bradford, Oct. 13, 1846, and there d. Oct. 1, 1866, aged 41. Children: —

    1330. ROSWELL HOPKINSON, b. June 6, 1848.
    1331. CHARLES ELTON, b. Mar. 27, 1850; d. Mar. 1858, aged 8.
    1332. MARY JANE, b. Aug. 22, 1851; d. June, 1856, in her 5th year.
    1333. EDSON DANA, b. June 18, 1853.
    1334. JULIA MARIA, b. Sept. 21, 1854.
    1335. SARAH ANNA, b. Aug. 11, d. Nov. 1856.
    1336. ABBY JANE, b. Oct. 11, 1860.

1337. GEORGE MOODY[6] [794] (Theodore[5], Joseph[4], Samuel[3], Samuel[2], Samuel[1]), m., 1st, Abby Kimball, of Bradford, June (July), 1853, who d. June 8, 1860; m., 2d, Lucy Bragden, of Blue Hill, Me., Apr. 9, 1863. He was enlisted for the late war, in the New Hampshire 2d regiment, and afterwards in the heavy artillery, in all, over three years; escaped unharmed; a shoe manufacturer in Bradford, 1870. Child, second wife: —

    1338. LOUIS VERNON, b. Nov. 12, 1864, in Chelsea, Mass.

1339. BETSY KIMBALL[6] [796] (Jonathan[5], Joseph[4], Samuel[3], Samuel[2], Samuel[1]), m. William Dow, Jan. 844, in Waterford, Pa. He was b. June 8, 1818, in New London, N. H.; a millwright

by trade, now residing at Drake's Mills, Crawford Co., Pa.
Children : —

1340. LYDIA ANN (DOW), b. Dec. 14, 1846, in Cambridge, Pa.
1341. CAROLINE WEST, b. Feb. 25, 1849; m. by Rev. T. B. Ernest to
       William G. Nason, Feb. 18, 1866, who was b. May 28, 1840, in
       Utica, N. Y ; a cooper by trade; present residence, Union
       City, Pa. Child : —
       1. EDGAR GIRARD (Nason), b. July 1, 1867, in Cambridge, Pa.

1342. ESTHER HERRICK[6] [797] (Jonathan[5], Joseph[4], Samuel[3],
Samuel[2], Samuel[1]), m. Alvin Houghton, of Harvard, Mass., at
Lowell, Oct. 22, 1835. He was residing, 1868, in California, and
she at Manchester, N. H. Children : —

1343. WEALTHY MARIA (Houghton), b. Feb. 8, d. Aug. 29, 1838.
1344. ALVIN OSCAR, b. Feb. 1, 1840.
1345. GEORGE ALBERT, b. Dec. 8, 1843. The two last were drowned
       together in Stevens' pond, Manchester, N. H., May 31, 1864,
       aged 24 and 20.
1346. REVILO GARDNER, b. Aug. 15, 1857; first name, "Oliver," spelled
       backwards.

1347. STEPHEN CHANDLER[6] [799] (Jonathan[5], Joseph[4], Samuel[3],
Samuel[2], Samuel[1]), m. Henrietta Crandall, at Leboeuf, Erie Co.,
Pa., July 12, 1846, where he lived as a farmer, and his five oldest
children were b. ; moved thence to Richford, Waushara Co.,
Wis. : —

1348. SYLVESTER [1601], b. July 19, 1847.
1349. WILLIAM, b. Aug. 12, 1848 ; a farmer; m. Agnes Hodge, of West-
       field, Marquette Co., Wis., Oct. 24, 1868.
1350. GARDINER [1604], b. Sept. 1, 1850.
1351. ADALINE, b. July 31, 1853 ; d. May 17, 1854, at Leboeuf, aged 10
       months.
1352. ROBERT, b. Sept. 7, 1854.
1353. ROSA, b. Nov. 15, 1858, in Richford, Wis.

1354. RHODA HOIT[6] [800] (Jonathan[5], Joseph[4], Samuel[3], Samuel[2], Samuel[1]), m. Levi Craker, Apr. 1840, in Leboeuf, Pa. He
was formerly of Waddersdon, Berkshire, Eng., b. Feb. 27, 1816.
She d. Dec. 15, 1863, aged 43, " in consequence of her unremit-
ting attentions to her brother [1396] during his war sickness."
Children : —

1355. JOHN WILLIAM (Craker), b. Mar. 19, 1842, in Waterford, Pa. ; m.
       Rose Skinner, of W., 1870.
1356. LUCY S., b. Dec. 19, 1843, in Waterford; m. at Leboeuf, by
       Francis N. Runnels, Esq., Mar. 25, 1863, to Alfred M. Barrett,
       tanner, of Waterford, who was there b. Apr. 29, 1843. Chil-
       dren, b. in Waterford : —
       1. MILES E. (Barrett), b. Dec. 17, 1864.
       2. CHARLES E., b. Jan. 24, 1867.
1357. PHEBE W. (Craker), b. July 23, 1845, in Waterford, as were all
       the following : —
1358. ESTHER H., b. July 23, 1847 ; d. Aug. 13, 1865, aged 18.
1359. BENNETT, b. June 10, 1849.
1360. MARY A., b. May 21, 1851.

1361. Francis H., b. May 10, 1853.
1362. Joseph E., b. July 30, 1855.
1363. Leon S., b. Feb. 28, 1859.

1364. Abigail.[6] [801] (Jonathan[5], Joseph[4], Samuel[3], Samuel[2], Samuel[1]), m., 1st, Calvin E. Crandall, at Leboeuf, Pa., July 31, 1838, who d. May 19, 1845 ; m., 2d, Amos T. Bishop, at Mercer, Pa., Sept. 9, 1848, and moved in 1860 to Richford, Wis., where her two youngest children were born ; the others, except the oldest, at Leboeuf : —

1365. Horace M. (Crandall), b. July 15, 1839, in Richmond, Pa. ; d. May 12, 1855, in his 16th year.
1366. Esther L., b. Dec. 2, 1841 ; d. Aug. 9, 1860, in her 19th year.
1367. Willard C., b. July 14, 1845.
1368. Flora M. (Bishop), b. Dec. 19, 1849.
1369. Miron F., b. Nov. 13, 1851.
1370. Zilpha A., b. Aug. 14, 1853.
1371. Thomas M., b. June 21, 1855.
1372. Melissa A., b. Feb. 4, 1857.
1373. Helen J., b. Sept. 13, 1859.
1374. Wiette F., b. Apr. 27, 1861.
1375. Allie V., b. Oct. 14, 1867.

1376. Fulsom Brown[6] [802] (Jonathan[5], Joseph[4], Samuel[3], Samuel[2], Samuel[1]), m. Mary Elizabeth Courtney, at Rochdale, Pa., Dec. 20, 1849, who was b. in R., Dec. 23, 1827. Children : —

1377. Burnham Sherwood, b. Dec. 24, 1850, in Leboeuf.
1378. Lois Lorilla, b. June 16, 1852, in Rochdale.
1379. James Alvin, b. May 6, 1855, in R. ; d. July 9, 1863, aged 8.
1380. Mary Lydia, b. July 10, 1858, in Leboeuf.
1381. Florence Jane, b. Apr. 22, 1866, in L.

1382. Francis Newell[6] [803] (Jonathan[5], Joseph[4], Samuel[3], Samuel[2], Samuel[1]), is a dealer in drugs, paints, groceries, and hardware, at Mill Village, Erie Co., Pa. ; m., 1st, Eunice Walker, Aug. 15, 1849, who d. Aug. 4, 1862, aged 29 ; m., 2d, Betsy Ann Parker, Dec. 1, 1864, who was b. 1832. Children : —

1383. Malinda A. (first wife), b. Mar. 27, 1852.
1384. Charles J., b. Aug. 24, 1854.
1385. John F., b. June 19, 1856; d. Aug. 23, 1862, aged 6.
1386. George W., b. June 16, 1858.
1387. William R., b. July 13, 1861; d. Sept. 13, 1862, aged 14 months.
1388. Francis N., Jr. (second wife), b. Jan. 27, 1866.
1389. Delly May, b. Aug. 23, 1868.

1390. Mary L.[6] [804] (Jonathan[5], Joseph[4], Samuel[3], Samuel[2], Samuel[1]), m. Hamilton O. Perry, of Waterford, Pa., Mar. 29, 1855, where were born : —

1391. Charlie S. (Perry), b. July 21, 1857; d. Mar. 15, 1864, in his 7th year.
1392. Willie N., b. Aug. 9, 1861; d. Mar. 16, 1864, in his 3d year. Both the two last d. of diphtheria, and were buried in one grave.
1393. Freddie I., b. Feb. 12, 1865.
1394. Halsie O., b. May 3, 1866.
1395. Eunice I., b. Apr. 19, 1868.

1396. BARTLETT DIMOND[6] [805] (Jonathan[5], Joseph[4], Samuel[3], Samuel[2], Samuel[1]), m. Marion Hadley, of Covington, N. Y., Feb. 13, 1854; served in the late war, and d. of disease thus contracted, Nov. 9, 1863, in his 32d year. Children : —

1397. JOHN FRANKLIN, b. May 8, 1855, in Cambridge, Pa.
1398. IRIS OLEVA, b. Oct. 6, 1856, in C.
1399. PERRY HENDERSON, b. May 12, 1859, in Lebocuf, Pa.
1400. EDWIN LINCOLN, b. Jan. 31, d. Dec. 30, 1860, in Cambridge.
1401. EDGAR BARTLETT, b. July 15, 1863.

1402. JEREMIAH FARNUM[6] [809] (Farnum[5], Joseph[4], Samuel[3], Samuel[2], Samuel[1]), m. Harriet M. Sawyer, of Warner, N. H., Nov. 24, 1848. Was a member of the Concord city council, and its president in 1858. Had settled on his grandfather's homestead, and had built a new house near the old one, occupied by his uncle and aunts [345, etc.], — serving also as station-master at the Mast Yard railroad depot, — where he d. of typhoid fever, Oct. 9, 1868, after a sickness of seventeen days, aged 44. He was an earnest Christian, a man greatly respected in the community, and a pillar in the Concord West Congregational Church. Attended the annual meeting of the " Kearsarge Bible Society," at Contoocookville, but the day before his final sickness commenced   Children : —

1403. NELSON IRVING, b. July 28, 1850; d. of the same disease as his father, Oct. 19, 1868, aged 18.
1404. JEROME SAWYER, b. Nov. 29, 1853.
1405. WILLIS EVERETT, b. July 7, 1856.

1406. MARIANNE JEWETT[6] [810] (Farnum[5], Joseph[4], Samuel[3], Samuel[2], Samuel[1]), m. Emulous Warren Burbank, of Boscawen, N. H., Feb. 10, 1848, and now resides in Lawrence, Mass. Children : —

1407. ALVIN H. (Burbank), b. July 30, 1851, in West Boscawen.
1408. ANNA A., b. Oct. 10, d. Dec. 10, 1861, at Lawrence.
1409. EARNEST, b. Oct. 29, 1863, in Lawrence.

1410. JERUSHA AUGUSTA[6] [811] (Farnum[5], Joseph[4], Samuel[3], Samuel[2], Samuel[1]), m. Abraham P. Burbank, Nov. 13, 1850. He is a miner, residing in California, where were born : —

1411. WALTER C. (Burbank), b. Nov. 15, 1856.
1412. SEWALL P., b. Dec. 5, 1858.
1413. ELLA M., b. Feb. 21, 1861.
1414. HELEN A., b. June 15, 1863.

1415. OSMYN EATON[6] [812] (Farnum[5], Joseph[4], Samuel[3], Samuel[2], Samuel[1]), resides in Lawrence, Mass.; a wood and coal dealer; m. Eliza Jane Eaton, of Concord, N. H., Nov. 5, 1856. Children : —

1416. CHARLES FARNUM, b. Mar. 31, 1858; d. Aug. 15, 1871, at Hopkinton, N. H., of internal inflammation, in his 14th year, thus sadly terminating his visit with beloved friends in the country.
1417. LIZZIE MAY, b. Apr. 22, 1860.

1418. HELEN CARROL[6] [813] (Farnum[5], Joseph[4], Samuel[3], Samuel[2], Samuel[1]), m. George W. French, farmer, of Hopkinton, N. H., Nov. 23, 1857. Child: —

1419. AUGUSTA JERUSHA (French), b. Mar. 23, 1860.

1420. SABRA M.[6] [822] (Moses[5], Jonathan[4], Samuel[3], Samuel[2], Samuel[1]), m. Justin E. Butler, of Pelham, Oct. 23, 1851, and d. May 31, 1853, in her 26th year, leaving : —

1421. THURSA A. (Butler), b. Sept. 23, 1852, who was making her home at her grandfather's [821], in Pelham, 1868.

1422. FARNUM J.[6] [823] (Moses[5], Jonathan[4], Samuel[3], Samuel[2], Samuel[1]), m. Letitia M. Underwood, of Nashua, N. H., Dec. 10, 1863, who d. at N., Jan. 9, 1865. He was an ensign in the U. S. Navy during the late war. Afterwards, having assisted in building a schooner, and named her the " Letitia," after his lamented wife, he commanded the same, on a voyage to Galveston, Tex., arriving at that port, Aug. 8, 1867, and there d. of yellow fever, Aug. 23, 1867, aged 28. He left: —

1423. LETITIA, b. Dec. 29, 1864, in Nashua, who was also living at her grandfather's home, in Pelham, 1868.

1424. ALMIRA[6] [830] (Samuel[5], Samuel[4], Samuel[3], Samuel[2], Samuel[1]), m. Moses E. Long, farmer, of Hopkinton, N. H., Oct. 20, 1859 ; residence in Concord, near her father's, where were born : —

1425. JOHN EDWIN (Long), b. Jan. 5, 1861.
1426. HERBERT IRA, b. June 1, 1864.
1427. MINNIE ALMIRA, b. Mar. 16, 1866.
1428. FRANK GILMAN, b. June 23, 1868.
1429. EMMA JANE FRANCES, b. Feb. 14, 1870.
1430. GEORGE PETER CYRUS, b. Apr. 11, 1872.

1431. ANNER ABBOT[6] [831] (Samuel[5], Samuel[4], Samuel[3], Samuel[2], Samuel[1]), m. Frank B. Chase, of Hopkinton, N. H., Nov. 13, 1867. He was formerly employed in a woollen mill ; is now a farmer and lumberman. Child : —

1432. SAMUEL AMBROSE (Chase), b. Feb. 1, 1872.

1433. LYDIA EMELINE[6] [838] (Jonas[5], Jonas[4], Samuel[3], Samuel[2], Samuel[1]), m. Alfred Adams, shoemaker, of Andover, Mass., Aug. 23, 1864. Child : —

1434. CHARLES FRANKLIN (Adams), b. Jan. 20, 1866.

1435. SARAH ANN[6] [849] (John[5], James[4], Benjamin[3], Ebenezer[2], Samuel[1]), m. Isaac Horn, farmer, of Hallowell, Me., Sept. 26, 1839. He was b. Oct. 3, 1815, and has lived, since marriage, in Augusta, where their children were b. : —

1436. AUGUSTA ANN (Horn), b. July 21, 1840; m. Sears Witham, of Bucksport, and resides in Augusta.
1437. HELEN MARIA, b. July 13, 1843; m. Lewis Henderson, of Hallowell; now living in Aroostook County.

1438. FRANCES ELLEN, b. Dec. 2, 1845; m. Albert A. Craig, of Windsor; resides in Aroostook County.
1439. CLARA LAWSON, b. Nov. 9, 1848.
1440. EMMA CHARLOTTE, b. Oct. 28, 1851; m. John L. Campbell, workman in an oil-cloth factory, June 11, 1871.
1441. LIZZIE PHILURA, b. May 22, 1853.
1442. GEORGE HENRY, b. Apr. 21, 1856.
1443. CHARLES MORRIS, b. May 23, 1859.
1444. IDELLA, b. Oct. 11, 1865.
1445. FREDDIE, b. Aug. 31, 1867.

1446. ELISHA WHITE[6] [851] (John[5], James[4], Benjamin[3], Ebenezer[2], Samuel[1]), m. Cordelia Smith, of Hallowell, Me., 1847; "followed the sea;" sailed on the ship "Hungarian," from Bath, 1856, and was probably lost with that vessel the same year, aged 31. She has since m. again, and moved to Connecticut. Children: —

1447. PHILURA, b. Feb. 27, d. Apr. 8, 1848.
1448. GEORGE HENRY, b. Mar. 1850.
1449. PHILURA EMMA, b. Mar. 5, 1852.
1450. LIZZIE (Ellen Maria), b. May 13, 1855.

1451. JAMES COX[6] [852] (John[5], James[4], Benjamin[3], Ebenezer[2], Samuel[1]), is a lumberman, residing (1870) at Gardiner, Me.; m. Hannah Mason, of Augusta, May 17, 1851, who was b. Aug. 30, 1827. Children: —

1452. MARY ISORA, b. Mar. 19, 1852, in Hallowell.
1453. JAMES HENRY, b. Oct. 28, 1853, in H.
1454. LEANDER, b. Sept. 12, 1855, in H.
1455. ALICE MARIA, b. Nov. 9, 1857, in H.
1456. CLARA ELLEN, b. Feb. 6, 1861, in Hallowell; d. at Augusta, forty hours after a fatal accident by fire, Mar. 6, 1862, aged 13 mos.
1457. RICHARD ELMER, b. May 28, 1863, in Augusta; d. Aug. 23, 1863, at Gardiner.
1458. RICHARD ELMER, b. July 4, 1864, in Gardiner.
1459. FRANKEY, b. Feb. 6, d. June 3, 1867, at Gardiner.
1460. EVA, b. July 23, 1869.

1461. MARY JANE[6] [854] (John[5], James[4], Benjamin[3], Ebenezer[2], Samuel[1]), m. Samuel Flood, of Ellsworth, Me., Feb. 2, 1857. He d. 1861. She d. Aug. 30, 1866, at Gardiner, in her 34th year. Child: —

1462. WILLIAM HARRISON (Flood), b. Aug. 3, 1860, in Hallowell.

1463. JOHN EDWIN[6] [855] (John[5], James[4], Benjamin[3], Ebenezer[2], Samuel[1]), was a miller; m. Sybil Mason, of Augusta, Me., Sept. 11, 1859, and d. at Hallowell, of consumption, Apr. 15, 1861, aged 26. She d. Mar. 1870. Child: —

1464. MARTHA ELLEN, b. Nov. 9, 1860, in Hallowell.

1465. MARTHA POTTER[6] [860] (Jeremiah Holmes[5], James[4], Benjamin[3], Ebenezer[2], Samuel[1]), m., 1st, Thomas Baldwin, of Hallowell, Me., July 4, 1851, who d. 1855; m., 2d, Rufus O. White, a machinist, of Hallowell, Oct. 26, 1858. Children: —

1466. CHARLES FRANKLIN (Baldwin), b. Nov. 7, 1852, in Hallowell.
1467. NELLIE (White), b. Jan. 17, 1860, in Augusta; d. Sept. 10, 1865, in her 6th year, at H.
1468. AUGUSTA SANFORD, b. Aug. 3, 1862, in H.
1469. NELLIE SALOME, b. Oct. 6, 1865, in H.

1470. CHARLES FRANKLIN[6] [862] (Jeremiah Holmes[5], James[4], Benjamin[3], Ebenezer[2], Samuel[1]), m. Elizabeth McFadden, of Bath, Me., Dec. 1854; was a lumberman, residing at Hallowell, where their children were born; a soldier in the late war, one and a half years, Maine 1st artillery, serving under Gen. Grant in all the battles around Richmond, and at the surrender of Lee; was wounded in the shoulder. Attracted by the country, he moved, with his family, to Williamsport, Penn., in the fall of 1866. Children: —

1471. CHARLES, b. Sept. 1855.
1472. WILLIAM, b. Feb., d. Sept. 1857.
1473. BENJAMIN FRANKLIN, b. July, 1860.

1474. JOHN[6] [866] (John[5], John[4], Benjamin[3], Ebenezer[2], Samuel[1]), m. Philena Roundy, of Benton, Me., Jan. 26, 1852; sent a three years' substitute to the war, at a cost of eight hundred dollars, in advance; occupies his father's homestead in Clinton, 1870. Children: —

1475. ELLA, b. Nov. 3, 1853.
1476. ROSA, b. June 21, 1855.
1477. HANNAH, b. Oct. 27, 1857.
1478. LYDIA FRANCES, b. Jan. 25, 1867.

1479. FREDERICK WINGATE[6] [867] (John[5], John[4], Benjamin[3], Ebenezer[2], Samuel[1]), settled as a farmer, near his father's, in Clinton, Me.; m., 1st, Martha A. Runnels [885], of C., Mar. 9, 1856, who d. Aug. 31, 1858, aged 23; m., 2d, Mrs. Mary B. Abbott (formerly Monk), of Winslow, Sept. 20, 1860. Children: —

1480. CLARA AMY (first wife), b. Dec. 28, 1857; d. Sept. 12, 1863, in her 6th year.
1481. FLORENCE MABEL (second wife), b. Nov. 7, 1861.
1482. FRANK, b. July 26, 1863.

1483. AUGUSTA HANNAH[6] [869] (Damon[5], John[4], Benjamin[3], Ebenezer[2], Samuel[1]), m. Increase Wyman, of Fairfield, Me., 1851, and d. Jan. 1859, aged 34, leaving: —

1484. FRANK (Wyman), b. May 8, 1852.
1485. ELIZABETH MARIA, b. Apr. 1, 1854.

1486. CLARK DAMON[6] [870] (Damon[5], John[4], Benjamin[3], Ebenezer[2], Samuel[1]), is a farmer in Benton, Me.; m., 1st, Betsy Ann Mack, of Fairfield, Nov. 15, 1854, who d. May 5, 1856; m., 2d, Maria Ward, of Troy, Me., Dec. 6, 1859. Child (adopted): —

1487. HOWARD WINSLOW, b. Mar. 27, 1865.

1488. CHARLES RANDALL[6] [871] (Damon[5], John[4], Benjamin[3], Ebenezer[2], Samuel[1]), occupies a valuable farm in Benton, Me., near Kendall's Mills, on the Kennebec River ; m. Lucinda Frances Ames, of B., Apr. 9, 1859. Children : —

1489. MARY FRANCES, b. Feb. 15, 1860.
1490. LYDIA, b. Feb. 29, 1864.
1491. BENJAMIN FRANKLIN, b. Feb. 26, 1866.
1492. ANNIE ESTELLE, b. May 8, 1869.

1493. EMELINE MORRILL[6] [872] (Damon[5], John[4], Benjamin[3], Ebenezer[2], Samuel[1]), m. Watson Burgess, farmer, of Fairfield, Me., Oct. 1858 (48), and d. Dec. 7, 1859, in her 28th year, leaving : —

1494. CHARLES SHERMAN (Burgess), b. Nov. 28, 1859.

1495. ELIZABETH FLORENCE[6] [878] (Damon[5], John[4], Benjamin[3], Ebenezer[2], Samuel[1]), m. Watson Burgess, second wife, see [1493], then residing in Benton, Sept. 9, 1865. Children : —

1496. JOSEPH (Burgess), the second of his children, b. June 22, d. July 3, 1866.
1497. HERBERT EDWARD ROSVILLE, b. Sept. 9, 1867.
1498. EMELINE, b. May 25, 1869.

1499. LYDIA ANN[6] [880] (James[5], John[4], Benjamin[3], Ebenezer[2], Samuel[1]), m. Frederick William Hansen, mariner, Dec. 31, 1851, who was b. Apr. 12, 1827, in Elsinore, Denmark ; present family residence at Searsport, Me., where all their children were born, except the two oldest : —

1500. CHARLES HENRY (Hansen), b. Oct. 10, 1852, in Frankfort, Me.; d. at Searsport, Apr. 14, 1865, in his 13th year.
1501. MARY CAROLENA, b. Oct. 3, 1855, in Frankfort.
1502. JAMES CLARENCE, b. Dec. 3, 1857.
1503. HERMAN WILLIS, b. Feb. 15, 1861; d. June 21, 1862, aged 1 year 4 months.
1504. FREDERICK ELEAZER, b. Apr. 13, 1865.
1505. LOUIS SUMNER, b. Sept. 15, 1867.

1506. WILLIAM THOMAS CURTIS[6] [881] (James[5], John[4], Benjamin[3], Ebenezer[2], Samuel[1]), is a lawyer by profession, having studied with Nehemiah Abbott, Esq., of Belfast, Me., and practised law in Searsport since 1861, where also he m. Carolena Sophia Fredcrikke Hansen, Jan. 1, 1864. She was b. Jan. 27, 1841, in Elsinore, Denmark, a sister of F. W. H. See [1499]. Child : —

1507. WILLIAM FRANKLIN, b. Feb. 18, 1865, in Searsport.

1508. CHARLOTTE[6] [890] (Washington[5], Benjamin[4], Benjamin[3], Ebenezer[2], Samuel[1]), m., 1st, Winthrop Morse Wing, merchant, of Waterville, Me., at Winslow, Jan. 1, 1838. He enlisted in the " U. S. 3d Artillery, Co. L," Aug. 16, 1845 ; participated with Gen. Taylor in the preliminary battles of the Mexican campaign, and d. Oct. 26, 1846, in the hospital at Matamoras, Mexico, after a sickness of twenty days. She m., 2d, Thomas Francis Jones, of Scituate, Mass., at Chelsea, Jan. 1, 1850, who was a cigar manufacturer and importer, and d. Sept. 1854. She was residing, 1871, in Charlestown, Mass., 4 Adams Street. Children, first husband, born in Waterville : —

1509. LUCY ANNIE (Wing). b. Sept. 24, 1839.
1510. FRANCIS MARION, b. Dec. 10, 1840; was drowned below Ticonic Falls, at Waterville, Sept. 25, 1843, in his 3d year.
1511. CHARLOTTE AUGUSTA, b. Jan. 10, 1843; m. William H. Taber, of Albion. Me., Feb. 22, 1864, who was a lieutenant in the war of the rebellion; d. July 21, 1870, at Charlestown, in her 28th year. Mrs. Taber was assistant editor of the " Waverley Magazine " (published in Boston) at the time of her death, and for some years previously. Mr. Dow, in his tribute to her memory, in the " Waverley " for Aug. 27, 1870, says : " Her education and her natural talents fitted her especially for this position. Her fine poetic taste, her love of order, and her knowledge and appreciation of the beauties of the best authors, rendered her a valuable acquisition to our editorial circle." The Rev. James B. Miles, of Charlestown, at her funeral, ascribed to her " three traits which constitute a lovely woman " : " a beauty and grace of exterior which is seldom seen; " " intellectual endowments which were far above mediocrity," and " a moral deportment and religious turn of mind which gave a finish to all." She was the secretary of the " Parker Fraternity Association," in Boston, and composed an ode which was sung at the anniversary of that society in 1870; the two last stanzas as follows : —

> " But for all true and earnest souls
>   Life wears a fadeless glow;
> For those who seek, with patient hearts,
>   Some fragrant blossoms grow;
> The trust that faints and falters not
>   Will find the blessed way —
> The golden rain of peace will fall
>   On all who work and pray.

> " Then let our hearts be glad to night;
>   Bright Pleasure, linger nigh;
> May happy meetings still be ours,
>   As years come gliding by;
> Let Hope its smiling promise give,
>   Be Faith our guiding star,
> Whose light shall lead us through the mists
>   That veil the ' gates ajar.' "

As illustrating the controlling sentiment of her own life, we add another stanza from a poem written by her for a previous anniversary of the same association : —

> " Though we meet some ' tangled crossings '
>   In the mystic web of life,
> And our years, though few or many,
>   May not all with joy be rife;
> Let the seasons, hast'ning o'er us,
>   Find our hearts still warm and true,
> Strong of faith and bravely earnest
>   In the work we have to do ! "

1512. Wellington[6] [891] (Washington[5], Benjamin[4], Benjamin[3], Ebenezer[2], Samuel[1]), is a farmer, now residing (1871) at South Albion, Me.; m. Louisa Bennett, Nov. 14, 1852, who was b. May 13, 1828 (?), in Montville. Children, b. in Montville, except the fourth: —

1513. Charles Benjamin, b. Aug. 13, 1853.
1514. Augustus Amos, b. July 7, 1855.
1515. Arthur Ellwood, b. Feb. 4, 1859.
1516. Obed, b. Aug. 14, 1862, in South Albion.
1517. Annie, b. Oct. 23, 1865.

1518. John[6] [892] (Washington[5], Benjamin[4], Benjamin[3], Ebenezer[2], Samuel[1]), m. Susan Getchel, of Winslow. Me., Sept. 8, 1852 ; business not reported, but probably a tiller of the soil, as are the majority of the Runnels sons, both East and West. Children, b. in Winslow: —

1519. Clara, b. Jan. 29, 1855.
1520. Mary Elizabeth, b. Apr. 28, 1858.

1521. Almira[6] [897] (Washington[5], Benjamin[4], Benjamin[3], Ebenezer[2], Samuel[1]), m. James Henry Coombs, farmer, of Albion, Me., Nov. 4, 1865. He was b. in A., June 21, 1842, and had served in the war, being drafted at Augusta, July 14, 1863, where he remained on detached service, one year and six months. Left Augusta, Feb. 3, 1865, joined the 17th Maine regiment in front of Petersburg, Va., Mar. 6 ; was in a number of engagements around Richmond, to the time of Gen. Lee's surrender, and discharged, Sept. 11, 1865. Children, b. in Albion : —

1522. Estella (Coombs), b. Sept. 2, 1866.
1523. James, b. Dec. 13, 1868.

1524. Emily[6] [924] (Samuel[5], Stephen[4], Benjamin[3], Ebenezer[2], Samuel[1]), m. William Henry Watson, mason, of Winslow, Me., Nov. 14, 1850. P. O. address, Waterville, Me. Children, b. in Winslow, except the oldest: —

1525. Charles Pharez (Watson), b. Jan. 25, 1852, in Waterville.
1526. Francis Lewyllen, b. Apr. 11, 1853.
1527. Clarington Leslie, b. Aug. 3, d. Nov. 6, 1856.
1528. Ellen Augusta, b. Nov. 13, 1857.
1529. Lizzie May, b. May 8, 1862.

1530. Elizabeth[6] [925] (Samuel[5], Stephen[4], Benjamin[3], Ebenezer[2], Samuel[1]), m. David Cole, Aug. 22, 1848, and d. Oct. 1, 1862, in her 34th year, leaving : —

1531. Theodore Ashley (Cole), b. Dec. 23, 1850, in Waterville, Me.
1532. Mira Ella, b. May 10, 1853, in Clinton.
1533. Ada, b. Oct. 3, 1856, in Clinton.
1534. Ellen May, b. June 24, 1862, in Waterville.

1535. Julia Ann[6] [931] (Daniel[5], David[4], Benjamin[3], Ebenezer[2], Samuel[1]), m. Hiram K. Maine, farmer, of Pittsfield, Me., Apr. 18, 1846. Children : —

1536. GEORGE WARREN (Maine), b. Oct. 17, 1849.
1537. HARRISON WOODVILLE, b. Oct. 24, 1851.
1538. LAURA ANN, b. Feb. 3, 1854.
1539. MARGARET ELLEN, b. Feb. 17, 1857.
1540. GENEVA, b. Apr. 11, 1859.
1541. SYBIL RUNNELS, b. Apr. 23, 1863.
1542. WINFIELD SCOTT, b. Oct. 19, 1865; d. Mar. 23, 1867, in his 2d year.

1543. GEORGE[6] [933] (Daniel[5], David[4], Benjamin[3], Ebenezer[2], Samuel[1]), has located (1870), as a farmer, in Pittsfield, Me., near the village; m. Frances A. Small, of P., Apr. 3, 1853. Child: —

1544. GEORGE A., b. May 17, 1856, in Pittsfield.

1545. HARRIET SMILEY[6] [934] (Daniel[5], David[4], Benjamin[3], Ebenezer[2], Samuel[1]), m. Ezra E. Town, carpenter and mechanic, Mar. 16, 1851; residence in Pittsfield, on a *farm* (1870). Children: —

1546. ABBY LUELLA (Town), b. May 18, 1853.
1547. WALTER VARIAN, b. Jan. 24, 1855.
1548. FLORA LELIA, b. Oct. 25, 1857; d. June 27, 1858, aged 8 months.
1549. CORA LELIA, b. Apr. 4, 1859.
1550. ADA SEDALIA, b. Feb. 27, 1861.
1551. ELMER ELLSWORTH, b. Jan. 12, 1864.

1552. DANIEL NELSON[6] [935] (Daniel[5], David[4], Benjamin[3], Ebenezer[2], Samuel[1]), settled in Port Huron, Mich., and there m. Mary Goodwin, a native of New York, Sept. 9, 1858. Children: —

1553. CHARLES NELSON, b. June 19, 1859.
1554. ELMER ELLSWORTH, b. June 18, 1861; d. Apr. 22, 1862, aged 10 months.
1555. HALMER EMMONS, b. May 28, 1864; d. May 6, 1865, aged 11 mos. 8 days.
1556. IDA BOTSFORD, b. May 19, 1868.

1557. MARGARET DAVENPORT[6] [936] (Daniel[5], David[4], Benjamin[3], Ebenezer[2], Samuel[1]), m. Enoch Avery Rogers, farmer and joiner, of Pittsfield, Me., Apr. 24, 1858. Children: —

1558. ERNEST HOWARD (Rogers), b. Aug. 31, 1861.
1559. SUSIE BELL, b. Jan. 5, 1865.

1560. GREENWOOD CHARLES[6] [944] (Greenwood[5], David[4], Benjamin[3], Ebenezer[2], Samuel[1]), enlisted Sept. 10, 1862: was present at the siege of Port Hudson, La., and discharged with his regiment, Maine 24th (nine months' men), Aug. 25, 1863. Has since settled near his father's in Pittsfield, Me.; a farmer; m. Philena Pushor, of P., July 2, 1865. Child: —

1561. GERTRUDE, b. Mar. 31, 1869.

1562. CARLTON KIMBALL[6] [958] (David[5], David[4], Benjamin[3], Ebenezer[2], Samuel[1]), is a merchant, now in company with his father, at Flint, Mich.; also jointly in the lumbering business at Au Sable; m Mary McKay, youngest dau. of Dr. A. McKay, of

Dumfries, Scotland, June 8, 1870, at Victoria, Norfolk Co., Dominion of Canada. Child : —

1563. JENNETT ADDIE FLORENCE, b. Nov. 12, 1871, in Flint, Mich.

1564. CELESTIA[6] [980] (Edwin[5], Stephen[4], Stephen[3], Ebenezer[2], Samuel[1]), m. Rev. George C. Hicks, Aug. 6, 1857, who labored first in Ohio, and removed to Red Oak, Iowa, 1868, where he is pastor of a church. Children : —

1565. EMMA DELL (Hicks), b. May 7, 1858, in Bloomfield, O.
1566. MARY WILLIANNA, b. Jan. 13, 1865, in Middlebury, O.

1567. ORMOND[6] [984] (Edwin[5], Stephen[4], Stephen[3], Ebenezer[2], Samuel[1]), was first a farmer in Licking Co., O , now settled in Iowa ; m. Mary Elizabeth McFarland, of Mt. Vernon, O., June 1, 1864. She was b. June 18, 1844. Children : —

1568. LORENA, b. May 26, 1865.
1569. EDWIN M., b. Aug. 4, 1867.
1570. ROLLIN, b. Oct. 3, 1869, in Hawthorne, Montgomery Co., Ia.
1571. DAVID SCOTT, b. May 3, 1871, in Hawthorne.

1572. ORLANDO LEMAN[6] [995] (Luke Brown[5], Stephen[4], Stephen[3], Ebenezer[2], Samuel[1]), is a farmer in Licking Co , O , where he m. Mary Jane Hand, Nov. 5, 1857. She was b. July 23, 1841. Children : —

1573. JOHN WESLEY, b. Jan. 15, 1860.
1574. EVERETT HARMON, b. Mar. 23, 1861.
1575. JENNIE JOANNA, b. Oct. 16, 1864.

1576. JOSEPH ALONZO[6] [996] (Luke Brown[5], Stephen[4], Stephen[3], Ebenezer[2], Samuel[1]), settled as a farmer in Licking Co., Ohio, and there m. Amanda Pike, Sept. 3, 1863. Children : —

1577. MYRTIE ELIZABETH, b. June 9, 1864.
1578. ELVADA JANE, b. Nov. 4, 1866.

1579. PURLONA JANE[6] [998] (Luke Brown[5], Stephen[4], Stephen[3], Ebenezer[2], Samuel[1]), m., 1st, Wesley J. Evans, farmer, in Licking Co., O., Sept. 2, 1863. He d. July 24, 1864, at Bermuda Hundred, Va., — a soldier, belonging to the "142d Ohio National Guards." She m., 2d, Calvin D. Hand, farmer, Oct. 19, 1865, and moved to McLean Co., Ill., 1867. Child : —

1580. MAGGIE JOANNA (Hand), b. Oct. 6, 1866, in Licking Co., O.

1581. ALZENA[6] [1000] (Luke Brown[5], Stephen[4], Stephen[3], Ebenezer[2], Samuel[1]), m. Frederick Dumbauld, farmer, Oct. 12, 1865, and moved to McLean Co., Ill., in 1867. Children : —

1582. LOAMINA (Dumbauld), b. Aug. 9, 1866, in Licking Co., O.
1583. DENNIS EVERETT, b. Apr. 9, 1868, in McLean Co., Ill.

1584. MARY J.[6] [1011] (Stephen[5], Stephen[4], Stephen[3], Ebenezer[2], Samuel[1]), m. George W. Walters, of Union Co., O., June 8,

1861. He d. as a soldier (?) July 19, 1865, at Washington, D. C. She moved to California in the spring of 1868. Children : —

1585. STEPHEN S. (Walters), b. Mar. 9, 1862; d. Sept. 14, 1866, aged 4 years 6 months.
1586. DELLIE ROSA, b. Jan. 18, 1864.

1587. VITALIS S.[6] [1012] (Stephen[5], Stephen[4], Stephen[3], Ebenezer[2], Samuel[1]), was a farmer in Union Co., O., and there m. Eliza Miller, Apr. 8, 1866 ; has since moved to California. Child : —

1588. CHARLES A., b. Mar. 31, 1867.

1589. MARTHA J.[6] [1013] (Stephen[5], Stephen[4], Stephen[3], Ebenezer[2], Samuel[1]), m. John Carpenter, farmer, in Union Co., O., Feb. 25, 1866 ; supposed to be in California with " all her father's children " ; located in or near Stockton, " at last accounts." Child : —

1590. ANNIE M. (Carpenter), b. Apr. 21, 1867.

1591. ALBINA JANE[6] [1018] (Sollis[5], Stephen[4], Stephen[3], Ebenezer[2], Samuel[1]), m. George W. Pitts, farmer, of Delaware Co., O., Feb. 22, 1865. Child : —

1592. FLORA (Pitts), b. Feb. 13, 1867.

1593. EMMA ESTELLE[6] [1129] (John S.[5], John[4], Thomas[3], Ebenezer[2], Samuel[1]), m. Frederick W. Berry, of Haverhill, Mass., June 14, 1867. Child : —

1594. WILLIE EUGENE (Berry), b. Feb. 24, 1869.

SEVENTH GENERATION.

1595. GEORGE LAKEMAN[7] [1317] (Daniel Lakeman[6], Theodore[5], Joseph[4], Samuel[3], Samuel[2], Samuel[1]), resides with his father at the ancestral home in Boxford, Mass. ; m. Anna Leslie, of West Boxford, at Plaistow, N. H., Sept. 15, 1869.   Child : —

1596. ANNIE BELLE, b. Jan. 7, 1871, in Boxford.

1597. AMANDA JANE[7] [1318] (Daniel Lakeman[6], Theodore[5], Joseph[4], Samuel[3], Samuel[2], Samuel[1]), m. Stephen G. Holt, of Andover, Mass., Jan. 19, 1865.   Child : —

1598. STEPHEN HORACE (Holt), b. Mar. 23, 1866; d. July 20, 1867, aged 1 year 4 months.

1599. IDA JANE[7] [1323] (Lorenzo[6], Theodore[5], Joseph[4], Samuel[3], Samuel[2], Samuel[1]), m. George Henry Mitchel, shoemaker, of Groveland, Mass., Dec. 31, 1868.   He was b. in G., Mar. 6, 1845.   Child : —

1600. EDITH MAY (Mitchel), b. Apr. 1, 1870, in G.

1601. SYLVESTER[7] [1348] (Stephen Chandler[6], Jonathan[5], Joseph[4], Samuel[3], Samuel[2], Samuel[1]), enlisted, 1862, in Co. I, 1st Wisconsin cavalry, and served till the close of the war.   He was employed as a scout, under Gen. E. M. McCook, and was known through the western army as the " Cumberland Scout "   Has since settled, as a farmer, at Richford, Wis., where he m. Fannie Durgin, Nov. 4, 1866.   Children : —

1602. SCOTT, b. Mar. 16, 1870.
1603. FRANCIS S., b. Dec. 3, 1871.

1604. GARDINER[7] [1350] (Stephen Chandler[6], Jonathan[5], Joseph[4], Samuel[3], Samuel[2], Samuel[1]), is a farmer in Richford, Wis. ; m. Mary Davis, Jan. 27, 1870.   Child : —

1605. ALICE MAUD, b. July 23, 1871.

PART II.

BEING A

GENEALOGICAL MEMOIR

OF

JOB RUNELS, OR RUNALS,

OF DURHAM, N. H.,

1713–1762.

INTRODUCTION.

TRADITION in Durham, N. H., and vicinity has been uniform that the earliest Runels or Runals ancestors in that town, by the names of Job and John, were brothers. This is also confirmed by the impressions of their oldest descendants, elsewhere met in later years, though not the slightest connection can be established, in this way, between these brothers and any other families of kindred name in Maine or New Hampshire, as noticed in the Appendix. There are, however, these three points of presumptive evidence that the brothers Job and John were also the brothers of Samuel, of Bradford, Mass., whose genealogy has been given in Part I.

1st. The existence of similar tradition or impressions, in both these Durham families, that their ancestors had " an older brother, Samuel, in Bradford, Mass.," with concurrent tradition in some branches of the family of Samuel, from individuals now passed away, that their ancestor had " two younger brothers who afterwards followed him from Nova Scotia to this country," and finally " settled in the New Hampshire colony."

2d. The similarity of Christian names ; the names Job and John being favorite ones with the ancestor Samuel, as three of his children were thus called ; and Samuel, on the other hand, being frequently found in the families of Job and John.

3d. The striking family resemblance which is found between many of the descendants of Samuel on the one hand, and of Job and John on the other.

For these reasons, though our relationship could not be substantiated in a court of law, yet we, the Runnelses and Reynoldses of Part I would hereby extend a cordial greeting to those of Parts II and III, as " Kinsmen and cousins, all."

FIRST GENERATION.

1606. Job[1] is first mentioned in the Rockingham Deeds, " Nov. 13, 1713," when he is said to be " of Dover," and had conveyed to him from " Joseph Davice, for £28, 3 score acres of land lying on the West side of Wensday's brook."

This is probably the time of his settling, as a young man, in the then " Oyster river Parish " of Dover, afterwards Durham, now Lee, N. H. His residence was on the now beautiful slope of land, near the above-mentioned brook, a little south of the " Mast road," and between that and the present house of Thomas Chesley, where a solitary barn was standing in 1870.

About the same time (1713), he m. his wife " Hannah," who is said to have joined the church at Durham, under the Rev. Hugh Adams, " May 5, 1723 " (see Hist. and Gen. Register, July, 1869). She was living as late as " June 28, 1731," as under that date we have " Jobe Runels and Hannah," deeding " to John Bradford of Portsmouth, one third share of land in Rochester." She was also, more probably, the " Hannah Runnels," of Durham, mentioned " Feb. 3, 1748-9," as deeding " to Joseph Smith, all her right to the estate of her grandfather, Robert Burnam " ; and if so, her maiden name *may* have been Hannah Burnam.

" May 29, 1719," his original sixty acres seems to have been increased by " 30 acres more or less, in Oyster river, in ye township of Dover, in ye Province of New Hampshire," bought of " Naphalie Kincaid " ; and " Jan. 31, 1726-7," by " a parcel of land scituate lying and being on ye south side of ye Mast path, against turtel pond, being the half of 60 acres," etc.

On the earliest town records of Durham, soon after its incorporation, " Mar. 18, 1733-4," we find a " Committee of freeholders " granting " to him his heirs and assigns forever, 25 acres of land " ; and at a meeting in the meeting-house at Durham Falls, same date, another (?) " Committee of fifteen " is mentioned, " which was then chosen to divide the common and undivided lands as the maior part of them shall grant." " The names of the Committee are as followeth, Job Runals " heading the list. He was also the owner of landed property in other towns, as " Nov. 13, 1753," he deeded to Samuel Moore, of Canterbury, for £55, one home lot in the town of C., where we elsewhere learn he possessed an " original right."

He was living " Dec. 2, 1758," as he then conveyed to " Job Runels Jun. husbandman, my son," " 100 acres of land, being all my homestead estate, whereon I now dwell." " Job Runalls Jun." is also mentioned in deeds of " July 6, 1754," and " Mar. 21, 1755"; but " Oct. 22, 1762," " Job Runells of Durham" bought of " Waldo Emerson of Wells, Me., for £60 lawful money of the Massachusetts Bay, a tract of land in Nottingham," and four days later, " Oct. 26," " Job Runels" sold the same "to Aaron Hays, for £66!" The *nature* of these two last transactions might lead us to ascribe them to the *younger* Job, in which case his father must have died before Oct. 22, 1762, so that the " Jun." had disappeared from his (the son's) name. If, however, they are ascribed to Job Runels, *Sen.*, *he* was evidently still alive and *active* in Oct. 1762, but must have d. between that time and " May 1, 1763," when " Jonathan Runels yeoman of Durham" deeded " to Joseph Sias for £100, 5 acres of land, being Lott No. 25, which was proportioned unto my father, Job Runels, *late* of *Durham deceased*, in that division called the North River Lotts." The probable year of his birth was 1685, in Nova Scotia (?) (see Introductions to Parts I and II); and his corresponding age at death would be from 74 to 77, according to the times assumed above. No probate allusions to this ancestor are found, except the inventory of his estate, taken " Apr. 25, 1765."

His children, by his wife Hannah, were born in Durham; and, as nearly as can now be ascertained, in the years and order here assigned to their names: —

1607. JOB [1615], b. 1714.
1608. ABIGAIL (Nabby) [1620], b. 1717.
1609. SUSAN [1627], b. 1719.
1610. ENOCH [1636], b. 1721.
1611. MARY [1639], b. May 15, 1724; from an old Bible at North Conway, N. H.
1612. JONATHAN [1646], b. 1726.
1613. HANNAH [1657], b. June 4, 1728.
1614. SAMUEL [1661], b. 1730.

SECOND GENERATION.

1615. Job[2] [1607] (Job[1]), inherited his father's home estate, as appears above, and is otherwise known to have occupied parts, at least, of the farms now owned in Lee, N. H. (1870), by Thomas Chesley and the widow of the late Hon. Jeremiah Smith. He afterwards divided his land between his two sons, Job and Miles, giving to the latter what is now occupied by Mrs. Smith, south of the road, as appears below. Quite early on the town records of Durham, we find him chosen one of five "Searvars of High Way"; and again "surveyor, 1762–3"; "fence viewer, 1758;" "tithing man, 1764." No later, on Durham records, than 1765, the Lee Parish being incorporated as a town, Jan. 16, 1766; after which, on the Lee records, we have "Lef. Job Runnals, Sessor." 1768 and 1769. His wife's name was Sarah; as "Apr. 29, 1771," "Job and Sarah R. of Lee," — his son Job not yet being married to Sarah Ellison, — deeded thirty-four acres of land to Jeremiah Burnam, of Durham; also "July 4, 1774," "to Simeon Taylor for £15, one half of a hundred acre lot," — probably in Canterbury, — "of which Job Runels deceased was the original grantee." "July 5, 1781," "Job Runals of Lee," to "John Colomy of New Durham," "all right to one hundred acres, in N. D." He probably died Apr. or May, 17×5, aged 71, certainly between the two dates next given; for, among the deeds, we find that "Job Runals of Lee," — then living, — conveyed "to Job R. *Jun.* certain tracts of tillage land on the Mast road, and one half his pasture," "*Mar.* 26, 1785;" and, same date, "to his son Miles, a tract of land called the upper field," — on the present Smith farm, as above, — "and half his pasture;" while, also, from the Strafford Probate records we learn that "Sarah Runels widow of the late Job Runels" relinquished "all right in his estate to her two sons Job and Miles," "*June* 8, 1785," to whom the administration of his estate was granted at the same time. His widow m. John Hill, of Nottingham, for her second husband. Proof of this appears a few years later (1790, or 1793), when J. Hill conveys to Job Runnels "his right to dower of his wife Sarah, who was mother of the said Job and former wife of Job Runels late of Lee;" whose children, there born, were: —

1616. SUSAN [1665], b. 1746.
1617. JOB [1675]. b. Jan. 12, 1749.
1618. ABIGAIL [1686], b. 1753.
1619. MILES [1695], b. Oct. 29, 1761.

1620. ABIGAIL[2] [1608] (Job[1]), m. Miles Randall, of Lee, N. H., and occupied the so-called " garrison house," on what has since been known as the " Dea. Randall place," now owned (1871) by Philip Chesley, first farm above the Hale or Smith mansion, towards Lee Hill. Mrs. Giles, of Durham [1626, 2], remembers to have seen " the log house " in which her grandparents lived, " with holes cut out of its walls for shooting the Indians." She there d. about 1784, aged 67, and he d. 1789. Their children were : —

1621. DEBORAH (Randall), b. Aug. 24, 1747, Durham records (or 1749); m. Benjamin Chesley, of Durham, who was b. Jan. 24, 1743, and d. Feb. 3, 1831, aged 88. She d. May 28, 1830, in her 83d year. Children, as by Durham records : —
   1. ABIGAIL (Chesley), b. Apr. 5, 1765.
   2. MARY, b. Oct. 17, 1767.
   3. MILES, b. Jan. 23, 1770.
   4. DEBORAH, b. Feb. 2, 1772.
   5. ISAAC, b. June 7, 1774.
   6. SUSANNAH, b. June 9, 1776.
   7. JAMES, b. Aug. 12, 1778; see [1782].
   8. BENJAMIN, b. Oct. 12, 1781.
   9. VALENTINE, b. Apr. 5, 1784.
   10. NANCY, b. Apr. 12, 1786.
   11. ISRAEL, b. Nov. 24, 1788; was a Baptist clergyman.
   12. THOMAS, b. Mar. 13, 1792.
1622. ISRAEL (Randall), b. 1751 (?); settled in Vermont.
1623. ANNA, b. 1753 (?); m. a Morrison, of Northwood, N. H.
1624. LOUISA, b. 1756 (?); m. a Huckins, of Lee.
1625. THOMAS, b. 1758; m. Mary Huckins, of Lee, 1777, who was b. 1760. He settled first as a merchant in Lee; moved to Canada, 1808, and there d. 1818, aged 60. Child : —
   1. THOMAS, b. June 18, 1778; went to sea, and visited several foreign countries; settled, on his return, in Parsonsfield, Me.; removed to Eaton, N. H., and there d. Mar. 1869, in his 91st year. He m. Lydia Mathis (Matthews), 1798, who was b. Dec. 11, 1779. Children: (1.) ANNA, b. Feb. 19, 1799. (2.) GIDEON M., b. July 3, 1801; now of Biddeford, Me. (3.) REUBEN W., b. Aug. 25, 1803. (4.) LYDIA M., b. Jan. 13, 1807; m. Stephen Allard, Esq., of East Madison, N. H., Dec. 22, 1825. He was b. Oct. 17, 1802; has been a farmer, though also engaged in "milling and lumbering." Children : I. ALANSON (Allard), b. Jan. 21, 1828. II. MARY ANN, b. Apr. 18, 1830. III. JOANNA M., b. May 16, 1832. IV. DANA, b. Mar. 26, 1836. V. MAYHEW C., b. Jan. 28, 1843. VI. HARRISON R., b. Sept. 4, 1844. (5.) SALLY (Randall), b. July 9, 1812. (6.) MARY, b. Aug. 29, 1814. (7.) THOMAS C., b. Jan. 5, 1817. (8.) ABIGAIL, b. July 21, 1819.
1626. JOB (Randall), b. June 7, 1761; settled in Lee, and m. Sarah Langley, Dec. 19, 1783, who was b. Apr. 1, 1761 (Lee records). Children : —
   1. ABIGAIL, b. Dec. 10, 1786
   2. SARAH (Sally), b. Aug. 3, 1789; m. Paul Giles, of Durham, N. H., who was b. Oct. 4, 1790, and d. Jan. 16, 1855, aged 64. She is still living at Durham (1871). Children: (1.) PAUL

(Giles), b. Nov. 29, 1812. (2.) WILLIAM, b. Sept. 19, 1814. (3.) JOHN, b. Oct. 24, 1816; d. Sept. 11, 1857, in his 41st year. (4.) SUSAN M., b. Sept. 10, 1819. (5.) ELIZABETH, b. June 2, 1822; d. Sept. 22, 1838, aged 16. (6.) SALLY, b. Nov. 21, 1824; d. Jan. 5, 1853, aged 28. (7.) CHARLES H., b. Sept. 24, 1827. (8.) JOB RANDALL, b. Aug. 6, 1829; enlisted in Co. K, 4th New Hampshire regiment, and served three years, from Sept. 18, 1861; had m. Maria Nelson, 1856. Children: I. FRANK EUGENE, b. May 20, 1857. II. MABEL, d. aged 3 mos. III. FREDDIE, d. aged 8 mos. (9.) JOSEPH, b. June 2, 1832; d. Jan. 22, 1856, in his 24th year.
3. MILES (Randall), b. Jan. 18, 1791.
4. HANNAH, b. June 29, 1794.
5. JOB, b. July 7, 1798.
6. THOMAS, b. Aug. 14, 1800.
7. ELIZA, b. Aug. 6, 1803; see [1630, 2].
8. JOHN, b. Apr. 19, 1806.
9. MARY, b. Dec. 1, 1808.

1627. SUSAN[2] [1609] (Job[1]), m., 1st, Samuel Thompson, and 2d, Jonathan Thompson, both of Durham (Lee). Children, — oldest only by first husband : —

1628. HANNAH (Thompson), b. July 25, 1750; m. Smith Emerson, of Lee, or Durham, who was a captain in the Revolutionary war, being enrolled as "Captain of Co. 6," Col. Thomas Tash's New Hampshire regiment, of "Sept. 1776, to reinforce the Continental army in New York." She d. Dec. 25, 1841, in her 92d year. Children : —
1. SAMUEL (Emerson); m. Sally Fields, and lived in Lee. Children : (1.) JOSHUA F., b. July 28, 1799; m. Sarah Durgin, 1819; now resides at Durham Point. Children: I. SMITH, b. Nov. 15, 1820; served in Co. I, 18th New Hampshire regiment, from Feb. 21 to July 29, 1865; m. Mary Abby Snell, of Lee, May 31, 1852, who was b. Aug. 20, 1828. Children: (I.) MARY ABBY, b. July 25, 1853. (II.) EDWIN SMITH, b. Nov. 10, 1855. (III.) MARTHA ANNA, b. June 25, 1858. (IV.) FLORA BELLE, b. Mar. 14, 1863. II. HANNAH, b. Aug. 20, 1823; m., 1st, a Giles; 2d, a Judkins; d. 1868, aged 45. III. MARY, b. Oct. 1, 1825; d. Jan. 1, 1835, aged 9 yrs. 3 mos. IV. GEORGE W., b. July 27, 1827; d. Dec. 15, 1856, in his 30th year. V. JOHN, b. Dec. 30, 1833; lives with his father at Durham Point. VI. SAMUEL, b. July 20, 1836; resides near his father's. VII. SARAH, b. Dec. 6, 1840; m. Stephen Rand, of Durham Point; two children. VIII. EMILY, b. Sept. 30, 1842; m. Jeremiah Langley; three children.
2. SMITH (Emerson); m. Betsy Buzzell, and lived in Barrington, N. H. (2.) TIMOTHY. (3.) JAMES. (4.) SAMUEL.
3. JONATHAN; m. Mary Davis; resided in Litchfield, Me.
4. AVIS; m. Lemuel Buzzell, of Lee.
5. BETSY; m. Joshua Fields, and lived in Merrimack, N. H.
6. SUSAN; m. Israel Tibbetts; resided in Madbury, N. H.
7. TIMOTHY; d. at Lee, aged 10 years.
8. HANNAH; m. James Pendergast; residence in Durham, N. H.
9. MARY; m. Andrew Demeritt; lived in Lee.
1629. MARY (Thompson), b. 1752; was blind for forty years; lived with her nephew, Job Thompson, Jun., in Lee [1635, 5], and d. 1832, aged 80.

630. SAMUEL, b. about 1756; m. Love Hill, and resided in Lee. Children: —
    1. SAMUEL; settled in what is now Acton, Me., and m. Miss —— Fox; three children.
    2. JONATHAN; settled as a tailor and farmer, near Lee Hill, towards Durham, and m. Eliza Randall [1626, 7], 1822. Children: (1.) Samuel, b. Apr. 17, 1823; a farmer in Nottingham; m. Rhoda Davis, 1850; enlisted in the New Hampshire 10th regiment, at Dover, July, 1862, and served three years, till the end of the war. Children: I. ELIZA, b. 1851. II. RHODA. III. BURTROUS. IV. IDA. V. HIRAM, b. 1858; d. 1864, aged 6. VI. WALTER. VII. LIZZIE. VIII. WILLIE. IX. ANNA. (2.) STEPHEN, b. Sept. 20, 1833; a farmer, residing in Lee, at the "Hook"; m. Sarah Lamos, Jan. 1859. Children: I. FRANK LESLIE, b. Mar. 1860. II. FREDDIE, b. 1862 (?); d. aged 2 years. III. MARY ELLA, b. Aug. 1864. IV. MINNIE FLORENCE, b. Dec. 1865. (3.) ELIZABETH, b. Oct. 13, 1843; m. Wright True Ellison, of Barrington, N. H., Dec. 25, 1870. He was b. Apr. 18, 1845; a shoemaker and blacksmith; enlisted in the 13th New Hampshire regiment; enrolled Aug. 30, 1862; was corporal of Co. F; discharged June 21, 1865.
    3. ABIGAIL; m. Daniel Goodwin, first wife, and settled in or near Acton, Me.; two children.
    4. LOIS; m. Stephen Twombly; settled in Dover; five children.
    5. LOVEY; m. and settled in Alton, N. H.
    6. ELIZA; m. Daniel Goodwin, second wife; now lives in Newburyport, Mass.; four children.
    7. REUBEN; moved to New York; there m. and died.

1631. JONATHAN, b. about 1760; m. Jane Kelsea.
1632. SARAH, b. about 1763; m. John McCrellis, of Nottingham, N. H.; the present John McC. of N. is her grandson.
1633. SUSANNAH, b. about 1765; m. Daniel Fox, who was among the early settlers of Acton, Me., on the so-called "Fox's Ridge."
1634. ELIZABETH, b. about 1768; m. Pelatiah Thompson, of Lee, who was b. July 15, 1766, in Lee, and d. Nov. 8, 1843, aged 77. Of their children: —
    1. PELATIAH, b. Nov. 1, 1795; see [1722].
1635. JOB, b. Sept. 2, 1772; m. Abigail Burnham, May 13, 1799, who was b. Jan. 15, 1774, and d. Oct. 21, 1859, in her 86th year. He d. Mar. 26, 1826, in his 54th year. Had resided as a farmer in Lee. Children: —
    1. SUSAN, b. June 26, 1800; m. James Buzzell, Sept. 10, 1825; resided first in Nottingham, N. H.; now in Lee. Children: (1) LUCRETIA ANN (Buzzell); d. (2.) BURNHAM; m. Mary Ann Bickford, of Newington, N. H.; three children. (3.) ABBY JANE; d. (4.) JOHN. (5.) MARY; d. (6.) JAMES.
    2. JOSEPH BURNHAM, b. Aug. 1, 1802; d. Sept. 8, 1803, aged 13 months 7 days.
    3. ELIZABETH, b. Sept. 10 (?), 1804; d. Sept. 24, 1807, aged 3.
    4. MARY, b. July 4, 1806; m. John H. Marston; lived in Manchester, N. H., and there d. 1851 (?), aged 45; three children; two living: (1.) DANIEL (Marston). (2.) ELBRIDGE.
    5. JOB, b. May 2, 1808; m., 1st, Adaline Griffin, of Durham, June, 1845, who was b. Dec. 8, 1804, and d. Feb. 1854, aged 49; m , 2d, Emma Demeritt, of Lee, Dec. 13, 1856. He retains the old homestead in Lee as a farmer, and is now (1871) a wealthy land-holder in that vicinity. Child, second wife: (1.) GEORGE JOSEPH, b. Apr. 24, 1858.
    6. JOHN, b. June 19, 1810; a farmer in Lee, occupying a very desirable situation next adjoining the paternal homestead of

his brother; m. Lydia Waterhouse, of Barrington, N. H., June 12, 1853, who was b. May 2, 1823. Children: (1.) AMANDA FLORA, b. Feb. 15, 1854. (2.) JOHN HAVEN, b. Sept. 15, 1857.

7. PARTHENA, b. Oct. 19, 1812; m. Gordon Bean, of Candia, N. H.; three children, all deceased.

8. SAMUEL, b. Mar. 30, 1815; m. Louisa Cilley, of Nottingham; now resides in Barrington. Children: (1.) ANN. (2.) VICTORIA. (3.) LE ROY. (4.) GEORGE. (5.) LOUISA. (6.) MARY. (7.) JAY. (8.) FREMONT. (9.) ELMER ELLSWORTH. (10.) EDITH.

9. DANIEL FOX, b. Mar. 19, 1817; m. Mary Frances Emerson, of Durham, Apr. 16, 1839, who was b. July 28, 1816. He d. at Braintree, Vt., Dec. 7, 1852, in his 36th year. Children: (1.) JOHN WINSLOW EMERSON, b. Apr. 16, 1840, in Deerfield, N. H.; now the station-agent of the Boston and Maine Railroad, at Durham; m. Susan Almira Clough, see [1764, 2], of Durham, at Exeter, Dec. 14, 1865. Children: I. FREDERICK WINSLOW, b. May 16, d. Aug. 30, 1867, at Durham. II. CARRIE GEORGE, b. Nov. 25, 1868. III. ALICE GERTRUDE, b. Sept. 29, 1870. (2.) ELLEN AUGUSTA, b. Sept. 17, 1841, in Nottingham. (3.) DANIEL GORDON, b. Jan. 24, 1843, in N.; m. Mary E. Gardner, Jan. 12, 1868. (4.) JENNETTE ANNALY, b. Jan. 21, 1845, in Durham; m. Frederick M. Knights, Aug. 26, 1867. (5.) CAROLINE ELIZABETH, b. May 16, 1847, in Durham. (6.) GEORGE EDWIN, b. July 31, 1851, in Durham, and there d. Jan. 4, 1852, aged 5 months 4 days.

1636. ENOCH[2] [1610] (Job[1]). Very little has been learned of him or his family, after the most persistent inquiries, except by way of *inference* from seven different registries of deeds in the county records, and from two or three allusions in the State military papers, Adj. General's office, at Concord, N. H. He is said to have been a resident " of Lee," " Oct. 23, 1766," when he bought of " Henry J. Brown, for £38, 100 acres in the town of Canterbury, westerly side of Suncook river." He had settled in Canterbury, " Loudon Parish," " May 14, 1779 ; " was still in Canterbury, " Sept. 9, 1785," when he deeded to Samuel Morrill " a certain tract of land in the parish of Loudon, belonging to the original right of Job Runnels"; is called " husbandman of Canterbury," " Nov. 22," same year, receiving from Job Runnels, his nephew, of Lee, " for £100, 100 acres, Lot No. 39, 2d division," of which, fifty acres (" East half of one hundred acre lot No. 39 ") is conveyed to Samuel Weeks by " Enoch R. of Canterbury and *Frances* his wife," " Jan. 10, 1786," — thus only we ascertain his *wife's first name;* — and finally, " Mar. 1, 1788," " to Obadiah Clough, for £37, 53 acres, in the parish of *Northfield*," — now the town of that name, — giving us the probable location of his father's " 2d division lot," above mentioned. He is known to have left Canterbury, probably soon after the last date, and to have settled and died in Canada; whence his only daughter returned and paid a visit to some of her distant relatives in New Hampshire many years ago. Tradition, in Lee and vicinity, reports him to have been a very *large man*, physically. His children were: —

1637. ENOCH, b. 1754; said to have been " a husbandman of Lee," " 21 years of age," in " List of Capt. Winborn Adams' Co.,"

"May 26, to Aug. 1, 1775;" "Miles travel 60, [5] | . "; is afterwards mentioned as "Corporal, Capt. Smith Emerson's company, at Seavey's Island;" and finally, "in Capt. Emerson's Co. for 2d regiment, to join the continental army in New York, Sept. 16, 1776." (New Hampshire Military Papers.)

1638. FRANCES (?); m. a Blair, and resided in Canada.

1639. MARY[2] [1611] (Job[1]), m. Nathaniel Randall, of Lee, N. H., who was b. Mar. 5, 1723; d. 1814 (1811), aged 90. Children : —

1640. HEZEKIAH (Randall), b. Mar. 28, 1745; m. Elizabeth Chesley, Apr. 10, 1768, who was b. Aug. 13, 1744. They were among the first settlers at North Conway, or "Pequawket," N. H., in 1772, locating on the Saco interval, just west of the village, and afterwards "moving their house up the bank on account of freshets," to the spot now occupied by their great grandson, Hezekiah Randall Seavey [1,(1), IV]. Their children were : —

1. MOLLY, b. Jan. 6, 1769; m. Simon Seavey, and inherited her father's place. Children : —
    (1.) RANDALL (Seavey), b. Apr. 11, 1792; m. Betsy Marston, Oct. 7, 1813. She was b. Mar. 8, 1788, and d. Aug. 14, 1858, in her 71st year. He d. Jan. 17, 1862, in his 70th year; both of dropsy. Children: I. DOUGLAS BEAN, b. Apr. 7, 1814; d. 1823, aged 9. II. POLLY, b. Oct. 12, 1816, d. Sept. 27, 1823, aged 7. III. STEPHEN JACKSON, b. Dec. 19, 1819; d. Sept. 20, 1823, in his 4th year. IV. HEZEKIAH RANDALL, b. May 24, 1821; retains the Randall homestead, see above; m. Elizabeth A. Hanson, of Conway, Jan. 8, 1854. Children: (I.) HERBERT ARDELL, b. Jan. 27, 1857. (II.) ERNEST ELLSWORTH, b. Oct. 21, 1863. (III.) HARRIE RANDALL, b. Aug. 25, 1866. V. STEPHEN JACKSON, b. Nov. 12, 1823; resides in Norway, Me.; five children. VI. WILLIAM, b. June 16, 1825; m. Theodora Pierce; residence in North Conway. Children: (I.) CARRIE H., b. June 30, 1855. (II.) WILLIS PIERCE, b. Oct. 1857. (III.) DE WIT CLINTON. (IV.) MINNIE MAY; d. aged 2 years. (V.) VIOLA. (VI.) JAMES. (VII.) PAULINA. (VIII.) ARTHUR. (IX.) HENRY BRAGDON, b. Dec. 1869. VII. MARY, b. Nov. 6, 1829; m. Justin Lord; resides in Biddeford, Me.
    (2.) SIMON; was a trader at North Conway; deceased.
    (3.) POLLY; m. Stephen Jackson, of Eaton, N. H.
2. BETSY, b. Feb. 2, 1775; see [1741].

1641. MOSES (Randall), b. June 20, 1747; m., 1st, Agnes Forest, who was b. Nov. 9, 1749, and d. July 4, 1784, in her 35th year, at Sanbornton, N. H. (old cemetery), where they first settled and their children were all b. (town records of Sanbornton and Conway). He m., 2d, Mrs. Lydia Ames, Sept. 9, 1784, who was b. Aug. 20, 1744, and d. Dec. 16, 1818, aged 74. He moved to North Conway about 1797, as his youngest son, at 16, is said to have "led a two-year old colt all the way from Sanbornton"; built his first log house north of his brother's on the Saco interval, and a few rods west of the present residence of his grandson Moses [5, (3)], and there d. Apr. 3, 1809, in his 62d year. Children, first wife : —

1. WILLIAM, b. Oct. 7, 1772; m. Betsy ——, and resided at North Conway. Children: (1.) ELLISON FOREST, b. Apr. 17, d. June 5, 1803. (2.) ANNE, b. Jan. 2, 1805; d. Mar. 1847, aged

42. (3.) Lydia, b. July 1, d. Nov. 27, 1808. (4.) Mary, (5.) Eliza, twins, b. Jan. 7, 1812; both residing at North Conway; Eliza having m. Samuel Willey Thompson, of Conway, Apr. 1830. He is a stage proprietor, and joint owner with his son, of the "Kiarsarge House" (1870). Children: I. William Francis (Thompson), b. July 10, 1833. II. Samuel Demerit, b. Sept. 29, 1836. III. James Willey, b. July 13, 1840. IV. Frederick, b. Sept. 13, 1845. V. Annie Eliza, b. May 27, 1851. VI. Carrie Champney, b. July 8, 1855.

2. Nathaniel (Randall), b. July 5, 1774; bore the title of "Capt."; m. Susanna Knight, of Durham, who was b. Jan. 6, 1779, and is still living, as his widow (1871), at North Conway. He d. Nov. 28, 1858, aged 79. Children: —

(1.) George Knight, b. Sept. 21, 1798; m. Martha Haynes Merrill; resides at North Conway. Children: I. James T., b. Feb. 1, 1828; in business at North Conway; m. Susan, daughter of Joshua D. Osgood, of Fryeburg, Me., Nov. 28, 1866, who d. Oct. 10, 1870, leaving: (I.) Carrie Mary, b. Nov. 1, 1867. (II.) Henry Harrison, b. May 7, 1869. II. Henry Harrison, b. June 16, 1830; d. at Fryeburg; three children, two living. III. Hannah Forest, b. Sept. 1832; d. 1861, aged 29. IV. Susan Knight, b. 1834; d. 1855, aged 21. V. Nathaniel, b. Jan. 21, 1839; a merchant with his brother [I.], at North Conway; m. Kate L. Eastman. Child: (I.) Mattie Elizabeth, b. May 4, 1866. VI. Elizabeth W., b. 1842; d. 1863, aged 21. VII. Frances Adelaide, b. 1844; m. Moses Chandler; one child.

(2.) Agnes Forest, b. Aug. 22, 1800; m. Samuel Forest, of Northfield, N. H.

(3.) Sukey K., b. Dec. 6, 1802; m. Charles Whitaker, of North Conway; two children, one living.

(4.) Hannah, b. Nov. 16, 1804; m. Abiel Lovejoy, of Conway; seven children, six living, "all West."

(5.) William Harrison, b. Mar. 14, d. Sept. 30, 1814.

(6.) Betsy Forest, b. Sept. 1, 1815; m. Luther Whitaker, of Conway; two sons.

3 Polly (Molly, on Sanbornton records), b. Feb. 5, 1777; m. Joseph Mason, of Conway. Children: (1.) Betsy Forest (Mason); m. William Page, of East Concord, N. H.; d. 1868. (2.) Hannah Randall; deceased. (3.) John Randall; m. and d. in Conway. (4.) William Randall; d. in Biddeford, Me.; nine children, three living. (5.) Moses Randall; resides in Waterford, Me.; six children. (6.) Nathaniel Randall; present proprietor of the "North Conway House"; m. Ruth Hutchins, of Fryeburg, Me. Children: I. Freeman Hutchins (Mason); resides at North Conway; keeper of the "Sunset Pavilion" hotel, with his brother [III.] II. Francis Le Roy. III. Mahlon Lee. IV. Mangum Edson; d. aged 18. V. Nathaniel; d. young.

4. Hannah (Randall), b. Nov. 26, 1779; m. Stephen Whitaker, of Conway. Child: (1.) George (Whitaker); m. and lives in the south part of the town (Conway).

5. John Forest (Randall), b. Dec. 28, 1781; m. Abiah Carleton, Apr. 13, 1809, who was b. Aug. 10, 1786. He was a blacksmith by trade, and d. Dec 1826, aged 45. Children: (1.) Samuel Carleton, b. Jan. 17, 1810. (2.) Rebekah Carleton, b. July 18, 1812; d. Dec. 1829, in her 18th year. (3.) Moses, b. Feb. 3, 1816; m. Irene Shackford, of Eaton, N. H., Jan. 1830. Children: I. Rebecca Clement, b. Dec. 30, 1840;

m. Stephen Stark, of Conway; one child. II. Elizabeth Frances, b. Aug. 1851. (4.) William, b Apr. 23, 1823; resides near the old homestead at North Conway; m. Lizzie Ann White, of Bartlett, Dec. 11, 1862.

6. Anna, b. Feb. 11, d. Feb. 22, 1784. . . .

Note. — We insert here, though a little out of its proper place, an enlarged and corrected record of 1641, 2, (2.) which came too late for insertion on the previous page : —

(2.) Agnes Forrest (Randall), m. Samuel Forrest, of Northfield, N. H. He was b. Mar. 19, 1786, in N.; was a farmer, also justice of the peace, a worthy citizen, and prominent in town affairs, for many years; d. Mar. 3, 1867, aged 81 Children, born in Northfield : I. Anne Ellison (Forrest), b. Nov. 3, 1821. II. Susan Knight, b. Nov. 2, 1823; m. Samuel B. Rogers, of Sanbornton Bridge, who d. June, 1865. Children: (I.) Orville Forrest (Rogers), b. Oct. 6, 1844; a physician; now in Dorchester, Mass. (II.) Samuel B., b. July 11, 1852. (III.) Livingston, b. June 26, 1860. III. Lafayette (Forrest), b. June 29, 1825; resides in Bangor, Me.; four children. IV. James Nathaniel, b. July 12, 1827; a farmer in Northfield on the homestead of his father and grandfather; m. Mary Augusta Eaton, of Jay, Me. Children: (I.) 'Kate, b. June 12, 1859. (II.) Samuel, b. July 8, 1861. (III.) Freddie, b. Aug. 15, 1863; d. Sept. 2, 1864, aged 1 year 18 days. (IV.) Edwin David, b. Sept. 3, 1865. (V.) Ruth, b. June 8, 1872. V. Martha Randall, b. Oct. 1, 1831; resides with her mother and eldest sister, at the old homestead, in Northfield.

1642. William (Randall), b. 1750, in Lee; settled in Canterbury, N. H., and there d.

1643. Mary (Randall), b. Aug. 19, 1753, in Lee; was m. to William Laskey, by Rev. Samuel Hutchins, Oct. 17, 1769. He was b. Oct. 28, 1745, and d. May 9, 1807, in his 62d year; was a farmer, inheriting from his father the place now owned by his grandson [10, (6)], near the mouth of "Wednesday's brook," in Lee, on the "Mast road," not far from Durham line, and just below the original homestead of her grandfather, Job Runels [1606]. The brook still meanders, — a marvel for crookedness, — through verdant meadows behind the ancestral home, in which reside (1871) representatives of the second, third, and fourth generations from herself. She d. Oct. 3, 1828, aged 75. Children (Lee Records) : —

1. Jonathan (Laskey), b. Mar. 25, 1771.
2. John, b. Mar. 4, 1772.
3. Sarah, b. Mar. 8, 1774.
4. Abigail, b. June 16, 1776.
5. Joseph, b. Jan. 12, 1778.
6. Mary, b. Apr. 24, 1780.
7. Susannah, b. Oct. 22, 1782.
8. William, b. Apr. 22, 1785, d. Nov. 1, 1786, in his 2d year.
9. Louis, b. Aug. 12, 1787.
10. Love, b. Dec. 12, 1789; m. Jonathan Bartlett, of Nottingham Square, N. H., Feb. 2, 1809, who was b. July 2, 1780. He d. and she is still living with her son in Lee, as above noted. Children : (1.) William (Bartlett), b. Aug. 2, 1813; is supposed to have d. at New Orleans, La., where last heard from, 1834. (2) Joseph, (3.) Sarah, twins, b. June 27, 1816; Joseph m. Katie Rook, of Durham, one child; Sarah m. Samuel True, of Salisbury, Mass. (4.) Enoch, b. Feb. 28, 1819; m. Jane McLane, and resides in Chelsea, Mass. Child: I. Mary Frances; m. a Briden, of Chelsea. (5.) Thomas, b. Sept. 13, 1821; a clergyman and teacher, first at

9

Andover, N. H., then at the U. C. College, Merom, Ind., now (1871) at Iola, Allen Co., Kansas; m. Elizabeth Titcomb. Children: I. DWIGHT TITCOMB; was a student at Dartmouth College; deceased. II. FRANK WHITEHOUSE; was a student at Dartmouth College, but graduated at the U. C. College, Merom, Ind. III. GEORGE TRUE. IV. ELIZABETH. V. SARAH ELLEN. VI. SUSAN. (6.) JOHN, b. May 6, 1823; occupies the old Laskey homestead in Lee, as above stated; m. Abby Haley, of Epping, N. H., Dec. 15, 1856. Children: I. JOHN FRANK, b. Apr. 9, 1859; d. Apr. 22, 1868, aged 9, by a mournful casualty at the Chelsea ferry, in Boston. II. SAMUEL HALEY, b. Dec. 14, 1863. (7.) DAVID LONGFELLOW, b. Mar. 5, 1827; was a teacher, but now a trader, residing at Amesbury Mills, Mass.; m. Lizzie C. French. Child: I. IRVING, b. July 25, 1853.

11. ANNA (Laskey), b. Jan. 14, 1792.
12. JOANNA, b. June 7, 1795

1044. JONATHAN (Randall), b. 1755, in Lee; m. a French, of Deerfield, and settled in Piermont, N. H.
1045. GIDEON (Randall), b. 1758, in Lee; m. Mary Thompson; lived first in Nottingham, N. H.; moved to North Conway with his fourth child, and "settled there the day peace was declared" (1815), on the farm above Jonathan Runnels', west side of Saco river, where he d. Dec. 1846, aged 88. Children: —
1. NATHANIEL, b. 1778; d. of throat distemper, Jan. 15, 1798, aged 20.
2. LYDIA, b. 1779; m. James Kenniston, lived in Jackson, N. H., and d. 1862, aged 83; five children.
3. NANCY, b. 1783; m. Ebenezer Lucy, of Deerfield; d. Nov. 28, 1811, aged 28; three children.
4. POLLY, b. Sept. 4, 1787; m. John Lucy, of Deerfield, Feb. 12, 1806, who was b. June 15, 1784. Lived first in Deerfield, moved back to Nottingham, and finally to Conway, with her father, as above. Children: (1.) HELEN MARIA (Lucy), b. Feb. 12, 1807; d. young. (2.) NATHANIEL RANDALL, b. May 3, 1808; d. young. (3.) NANCY, b. Nov. 14, 1811. (4.) JOHN ALFRED, b. June 1, 1815; a farmer at North Conway, near his grandfather's place; m. Caroline D. Woodis, Jan. 19, 1841. Children: I LAURA ANN. II. HELEN MARIA. III. FRANKLIN. (5.) GREENLEAF CILLEY, b. Nov. 19, 1818; was drowned 1836, aged 18, while crossing the Saco river of a Sabbath morning on his way to meeting. (6.) MARY JANE, b. Mar. 17, 1821; m. George Quint, of Conway, Aug. 17, 1842; lived at Lovell, Me., where she d. May 12, 1862, aged 41. Children: I. JAMES MONROE (Quint); killed at the battle of Gettysburg, 1863. II. ABBY; m. Charles Mark, of Brooklyn, N. Y.; one daughter. III. HENRIETTA. IV. CHARLES; killed, 1870, at Lewiston, Me., by falling from an elevator. V. MATILDA. VI. JOHN LUCY. (7.) NATHANIEL THOMPSON (Lucy), b. July 27, 1824; m., 1st, Abbie A. Redman, Nov. 28, 1852; m., 2d, Helen M. Baker, July 27, 1861. Child, first wife, I. FREDERICK; d. Apr. 3 1863. (8) CHARLES WARREN, b. Aug. 6, 1827; a confectioner in Portland, Me; m. Matilda L. Kimball, Sept. 28, 1852. Children: I. CHARLES FREDERICK. II. ADDIE. III NELLIE O.; d. aged 10 years; during the great fire in Portland, 1866, she was composed and cheerful, exhorting her father to "trust in Jesus," amidst the destruction of his property. IV. ROSCOE. (9.) GEORGE EMERSON, b. June 7, 1830; d. aged 2½ years, by scalding. (10.) GEORGE GREENLEAF. b. Oct. 31, 1836; m. Emma A. Baker, Mar. 7, 1863. Children: I. MARK ERASTUS. II. CHARLES HERBERT. III. MARY CHANDLER. IV. JOHN.

5. SALLY (Randall), b. 1789; d. aged 3 months.
6. NABBY, b. 1791; d. aged 8 years.
7. HANNAH, b. 1793; m. William Hart, of Conway; d. 1831, aged 40; three children.

1646. JONATHAN[2] [1612] (Job[1]), appears among the minor town officers of Durham in 1765, and again after Lee was set off, a fence-viewer in that town, 1779. He obtained by deed from Stephen Wille " 33 acres of land in Nottingham," N. H , " Jan. 30, 1783." Had m. Keziah Carter, 1754, who was b. Feb. 22, 1732, — " same day with George Washington," — and d. Nov. 1831, in her 100th year, having lived with her daughter, Mrs. Hines, in Nottingham, where she was lame and confined to her bed for many years. He d. prior to 1807, or early that year, aged about 81 ; as " Keziah Runels, widow of the late Jonathan R., of Lee, received right of dower April 14, 1808 " (Strafford Probate Records) ; and " Widow Jonathan Runnels " first appears on the town records of Lee, as residing in the " Centre District, 1807 "; also among the " Inventories," 1812 and 1815. The house where he lived and d. in Lee was on the spot occupied by Joseph A. Knights in 1871. Children : —

1647. HANNAH [1701], b. Feb. 28, 1755.
1648. MARTHA [1709], b. 1757.
1649. KEZIAH, b. 1758; m. John Hines, of Nottingham, who was a tanner and currier at the stand now owned (1871) by John Hill. He d. Mar. 20, 1825.
1650. ABIGAIL [1715], b. 1760.
1651. SARAH [1725], b. Aug. 3, 1762.
1652. SUSANNAH [1731], b. 1765.
1653. MOLLEY, b. 1767; m. Jonathan Harvey, of Nottingham (second wife), 1813.
1654. JONATHAN [1741], b. 1770.
1655. EUNICE, b. 1772; d. early in life.
1656. LEVI [1745], b. Mar. 31, 1774.

1657. HANNAH[2] [1613] (Job[1]), m. Samuel Langley, farmer of Lee, who was b. Jan. 5, 1724. They lived opposite the present Hale (Smith) farm, south of her father's homestead " on the other road." Children : —

1658. JONATHAN (Langley), b. Nov. 28, 1754, in Lee; m. Abigail Leathers, Dec. 30, 1773. She was b. Sept. 7, 1755. They lived in Nottingham, where their children were b., as per town records : —
   1. SAMUEL, b. Aug. 27, 1775.
   2. "VAROILL," b. Sept. 5, 1777.
   3. JONATHAN, b. Sept. 15, 1779.
   4. "MARIAM," b. Sept. 19, 1781.
   5. LYDIA, b. June 6, 1784.
   6. HANNAH, b. Sept. 3, 1786.
   7. TITUS, b. Nov. 5, 1788.
   8. JOSEPH, b. Jan. 29, 1791.
   9. MARK, b. Feb. 10, 1793.
1659. LEVI, b. Oct. 4, 1762; Abigail, his wife, was b. July 24, 1770; married Dec. 20, 1786, and settled on his father's place in Lee, where were born (town records) : —

1. HANNAH, b. Mar. 25, 1788; m. Daniel Smart, farmer, 1805, and settled in North Effingham (now Freedom), N. H., 1818, where she d. Sept. 30, 1852, aged 64. Children: (1.) LEVI L. (Smart), b. Feb. 17, 1806. (2.) OSBORN, b. May 23, 1807. (3.) JOSEPH, b. Mar. 7, 1809. (4.) EVERETT, b. Dec. 3, 1811; d. young. (5.) DANIEL, b. Oct. 15, 1812. (6.) ABIGAIL, b. Dec. 6, 1815. (7.) EVERETT, b. Mar. 18, 1816. (8.) JOHN, b. Oct. 10, 1818; resides in Freedom, N. H.; m. Amanda M. Jackson, Dec. 22, 1842. Children: I. MARY E., b. Dec. 17, 1843. II. VINA S., b. Nov. 26, 1845. III. JOHN O., b. July 10, 1851. IV. CORA A., b. Dec. 18, 1858. V. JOSEPH E., b. Sept. 4, 1861. (9.) MARY E, b. Jan. 20, 1819. (10.) SO-PHRONIA, b Jan. 11, 1823. (11.) LYDIA N., b. May 15, 1824.
2. NICHOLAS D. (Langley), b. Feb. 20, 1790.
3. SAMUEL, "Jun ," b. May 1, 1792.
4. DAVID, b. Oct. 2, 1794.
5. ORLAND, b. Jan. 19, 1797.

1660. SUSANNAH (Langley), b. May 22, 1766; m. a Woodman.

1661. SAMUEL[2] [1614] (Job[1]). Less can be ascertained of him than of his older brothers, from public records or the verbal testimony of descendants, though there remains but little doubt that he was a soldier in the old French war. He was probably the "Samuel Runnells, sentinel," "entered Apr. 30; discharged Oct. 27, 1755," and belonging to Co. 6, in the regiment of six hundred men furnished that year by New Hampshire for service against Crown Point (see Vol. II. "Military History of N. H.," p. 137). He is known to have resided chiefly in Lee, and it is the common impression of at least two aged people in that town (visited in 1871), that he moved thence to Peeling (now Woodstock), N. H., in its early settlement, and there d. soon after, about the year 1774, aged 54; also, that he was twice married, having "two or three children by his first wife, who d. soon after the birth of the youngest"; and that he "m., 2d, Love Tibbetts. just before moving to Peeling, by whom he had *no* children." "She was many years younger than he," b. about 1750; and having returned to Lee, there lived to an advanced age, "bearing the name of Love Runnels as his widow." The names of his two youngest children, and the meagre facts respecting them, are wholly on the authority of the venerable Miss Joanna Farnham, formerly of Acton, Maine, and for many years a resident at the "American House," Boston. All attempts to obtain information respecting the Drew family, if a family, from other sources, have proved abortive. Children: —

1662. SAMUEL [1753], b. 1754, in Lee.
1663. HANNAH, b. about 1756; m. a Drew, who settled "back in the country," probably in Albany, N. H., and is remembered by our informant (see above) from the circumstance of his "having no palate!"
1664. LOVEY, b. about 1759; d. early in life. Her *name* favors the supposition that she might have been a child of his second wife, but this is emphatically denied by our informants in Lee, as above.

THIRD GENERATION.

1665. SUSAN[3] [1616] (Job[2], Job[1]), m. Joseph Demeritt, Esq., of Northwood, N. H., about the year 1764. He was a farmer and justice of the peace, residing near the Nottingham line on the place more recently occupied by Samuel Bennett. See [1673.] She d. Jan. 20, 1807, aged 61. He d. Sept. 1822, aged 82. Children: —

1666. MOSES (Demeritt), b. about 1765; m. Lydia Odell (Odle), of Nottingham, May 24, 1789, and settled in Northwood. He d. 1846 (?), aged 81. She d. at the aged of 79. Children: —

  1. BETSY, b. 1791 (?); m., 1st, Thomas Furber, of Nottingham; m., 2d, Samuel Bean, of Deerfield. Children, first husband: (1.) LYDIA (Furber), m. James Bean. (2.) HARRISON. See [6, (1)]. (3.) ZEPHERUS PAGE. (4.) THOMAS. (5.) ELIZA.

  2. MOSES ODELL (Demeritt), b. Nov. 8, 1793; m. Sarah Ann Messer, of Newfield (Stratham), Apr. 10, 1820. She was b. May 30, 1802. He d. Feb. 28, 1856, aged 62. Children: (1.) BRACKETT JOHNSON; b. Nov. 12, 1821; had kept the "Northwood House," in East Northwood, for twenty-eight years, in 1871; m. Finett Welch [1672, 11], Apr. 12, 1843. Child: I. SARAH M., b. Aug. 18, 1844. (2.) LANGDON, b. Dec. 13, 1823; d. July 1, 1845, in his 22d year. (3.) ROOKSBURY BRACKETT, b. Oct. 28, 1827; m. John A. Virgin, Sept. 13, 1849. (4.) WILLIAM, b. July 28, 1830; d. May 21, 1833, in his 3d year. (5.) ELIZABETH, b. July 14, 1833; d. same day. (6.) GEORGIA PARSONS, b. Oct. 4, 1834; m. John W. Drake, Mar. 1857. Children: I. GEORGE WALTER (Drake), b. Nov. 23, 1862. II. CHARLES BRACKETT, b. Nov. 3, 1864. (7.) PHERSINA, b. Oct. 7, 1843; d. July 7, 1845, in her 2d year. (8.) APPLETON, b. Oct. 9, 1848.

  3. SALLY (Demeritt); m., 1st, Jarves Knowlton, of Northwood; m., 2d, Benjamin Hoyt; now living in Nottingham. Children: (1.) BETSY (Knowlton); m. Andrew Woodman. (2.) GILBERT G. (3.) SARAH (Hoyt); m. Charles Kingsbury, of Boston. (4.) ANNA; m. George Manning, of Northwood; three children.

  4. GORDON (Demeritt); m. Lavina Sanborn; live(d) in Nottingham. Children: (1.) ADDISON. (2.) ALMA. (3.) HAYDEN.

  5. THOMAS; m. Mary Clark, of Barnstead; live(d) in Northwood. Children: (1.) CLARK. (2.) JANE; m. George Knowlton, of Sanbornton, N. H. (3.) MARIA; m.; two children.

  6. NANCY; m. Miles Knowlton, of Northwood. Children: (1.) ROXANA (Knowlton), m., 1st, a Tuttle, of Dover; one child; m., 2d, Harrison Furber [1, (2)]; resides in Boston; one son.

     (2.) HENRY; m. a Morrison.   (3.) JAMES; m. a Morrison.
     (4.) ANGELINA; m. John Morrison.   (5.) ELIZABETH.
7.   NATHANIEL (Demeritt); was first an overseer in Dover; m. and moved to Pennsylvania, where residing as a farmer.
8.   DORCAS; m. John Batchelder, of Northwood, and moved to Sanbornton.

1067.   SALLY or SARAH (Demeritt), b. 1767(?); m. Simeon Johnson, of Northwood, who was b. 1764, and d. July 6, 1836, aged 72. She d. Nov. 1842, aged 75(?). Children: —
1.   LEVI (Johnson), b. Mar. 23, 1789; was a soldier in the war of 1812, and d. in Canada.
2.   JOSEPH, b. Sept. 10, 1791; was a farmer in Northwood; m. Mary Weeks, of N., and there d. Oct. 6, 1866, aged 75. Child: (1.) SALLY; m. Jacob Knowles Gilman, a merchant in New Market, who there d.
3.   JOHN, b. Sept. 5, 1794.
4.   BETSY, b. Sept. 16, 1797; d. Sept. 23, 1867, aged 70.
5.   SAMUEL, b. Oct. 19, 1799; deceased.
6.   THEODATE (Daty), b. Oct. 9, 1801; lived in Northwood, and there d. Sept. 30, 1871, aged 70.
7.   MATILDA, b. June 4, 1804; resides in Northwood.
8.   GILMAN, b. July 6, 1806; m. Eleanor French, of Deerfield, and d. Jan. 16, 1861, in his 55th year. Children: (1.) CHARLES; now residing in Concord, N. H.; an agent for a carriage manufactory. (2.) LOENER; a milliner in Chicago, Ill.
9.   DENNIS, b. Dec. 13, 1808; deceased.
10.   JESSIE, b. July 13, 1810; deceased.
11.   HARRISON, b. Sept. 7, 1814; now living in Northwood.

1668.   BETSY (Demeritt), b. 1768(?); m., 1st, Joseph Priest, of Nottingham; m., 2d, —— Clark, and lived in Barnstead. Children, first husband: —
1.   SAMUEL (Priest); m. Patty Jones (published), "Jan. 2, 1804"; lived in Nottingham, where his son (1.) SAMUEL now resides.
2.   SUSANNAH, b. May 3, 1787, in Nottingham; m. Andrew Daniels, of Nottingham, (published), "Nov. 20, 1803." He was b. Jan. 31, 1780, in Barrington, and d. July 3, 1862, in his 83d year. She d. Sept. 26, 1864, aged 77. Children: (1.) ELIZA (Daniels), b. June 15, 1805, in Barnstead; m. a Daniels, and d. in Barrington, leaving I. ELIZA, b. Dec. 26, 1825, who was brought up by her grandfather, and m. John Bodge, of Barrington, May 2, 1852. (2.) SALLY PRIEST, b. Dec. 5, 1806; m. a Welch, who was lost at sea; now lives at Great Falls. (3.) HENRY PRIEST, b. Feb. 23, 1809; a farmer in Nottingham, on the turnpike; see [1671, 6]. (4.) NATHAN, b. June 17, 1812; lost at sea. (5.) JOSEPH DEMERITT, b. July 16, 1816; d. Jan. 13, 1817, aged 6 months. (6.) IRA TASKER, b. Mar. 18, 1820. (7.) MARY SUSAN, b. Oct. 8, 1830, in Durham; m. John A. Buzzell, of Barrington (?), Mar. 24, 1856.
3.   SALLY (Priest), b. about 1790.
4.   NATHAN; lived "on the Great Island" (New Castle), near Portsmouth.
5.   JOSEPH.
6.   WILLIAM; m. Nancy Evans, of Barrington, and resided in New Market.
7.   HIRAM.
8.   POLLY; m. Thomas Jones, of Barrington, now residing in Portsmouth.
9.   JEFFERSON; m. Harriet True, of Pittsfield.
10.   HARRIET.
11.   NANCY; m. Daniel Clark, of Barnstead.
12.   BETSY; m., 1st, a Clark; 2d, a Proctor.

1669.   JOSEPH (Demeritt), b. 1771 (?); m. Rebecca March, and lived in
Northwood; was in the war of 1812. and d. at Greenbush, N. Y.,
from wounds received in battle.   Children: —

   1.   POLLY, b. about 1797; m. Ebenezer Chase, Jr., of Sanbornton;
now residing in Gilmanton.
   2.   MEHETABEL; m. a Chesley, of Durham; deceased.
   3.   ELEANOR; m. a Kimball, of Dover; deceased.
   4.   HARRY; d. at Dover, by drowning.
   5.   JOHN; lived first in Dover; moved thence to Philadelphia, Pa.,
and again to Manchester, N. H., where an overseer in the
print works.
   6.   SUSAN; m. a Tuttle of Dover, where still residing.

1670.   PAUL (Demeritt), b. 1774 (?), m. Martha Woodman, of Deerfield,
and lived with his father in Northwood.   Children: —

   1.   EUNICE. b. Mar. 23, 1799; m., 1st, George Seward, of Strafford,
by whom six children; m., 2d, Gilman Johnson, and now
residing near the "Bow Pond," in Strafford.
   2.   SAMUEL, b 1801; lived in Nottingham.
   3.   BETSY, b. 1803 (4); d 1817. aged 14.
   4.   SUSAN, b. Dec. 22, 1806; m. Alfred Hoitt, Oct 26, 1827.   He
was b. Jan. 11, 1806; a general in the New Hampshire
militia; keeper of a hotel in Lee for fourteen years; a member of the New Hampshire legislature, 1849–1853, being a
representative from Lee, in the House, and from District
No. 1, in the Senate.   He now resides in Durham, as a hay
merchant, doing business with his sons on Canal Street,
Boston.   All their thirteen children are now living (1871),
as here numbered, and nineteen of their twenty-five grandchildren: (1.) FRANKLIN WOODBURY (Hoitt), b. Apr. 5, 1829.
(2.) ALFRED DEMERITT, b. Oct. 14, 1830; m. and had three
children.   (3.) ALVINA AMANDA, b. Feb. 8, 1832; m. and had
four children.   (4.) SAMUEL PIPER, b. Mar. 16. 1833; occupies
his father's old stand in Lee; m. and had four children. (5.)
ELIZABETH SUSAN, b. Mar. 1, 1835; m. Samuel C. Hayes, hay
merchant, Boston; two children.   (6.) LYDIA OLIVE, b. Oct.
30, 1836; m. Rufus Willey, of Somerville, Mass.   Children:
I. EDDIE (Willey), b. May, 1854; d. Jan. 1855, aged 8 mos.
II. CLARENCE, b. Jan. 17, 1858.   III. CHARLES, b. Nov. 1865;
d. May, 1866, aged 6 months.   IV. NELLIE, b. May 30, 1867.
(7.) HENRIETTA (Hoitt), b. Feb. 28, 1838; m. Alden P. Sherburne, jeweller, Main Street, Concord, N. H.   Children:
I. ALFRED ALDEN (Sherburne).   II. ELMER DAVID.   III.
CHARLES LEWELLYN. (8.) MARY FRANCES, b. July 22, 1839;
m., 1st, Charles Bean; m., 2d, Franklin Young; four children,
of whom I. WALTER CLARK (Bean), b. Oct. 11, 1863. (9.) MAR-
THA ANN (Hoitt), b. Apr. 20, 1841; m. and had one child.
(10.) GEORGE IRVING, b. Feb. 2, 1843; enlisted for three
months in Sprague's Rhode Island cavalry, 1862, while a
member of Dartmouth College; now in the hay business
with his father, in Boston. (11.) WASHINGTON, b. Dec. 25,
1844; same business as the last. (12.) SYLVIA VICTORIA, b.
Jan. 12, 1847 (13.) CHARLES EDWARD, b. Mar. 8, 1849.
   5.   CALVIN SULDIN (Demeritt).
   6.   EDWARD.
   7.   GEORGE.
   8.   BETSY JANE.
   9.   RHODA; m. a Beales.

1671.   JOHN (Demeritt), b. Jan. 30, 1777; served three months in the
war of 1812, at the fort near Portsmouth; m. Abigail Hill, who
was b. May 13, 1781; resided in Nottingham.   Children: —

   1.   JACOB, b. July 8, 1800.

136

2.   JOSEPH, b. Nov. 11, 1802; m. Sally Colcord; resides in West Nottingham. Children: (1.) BENJAMIN WILLARD. (2.) JOSEPH EDWARD. (3.) JOHN LEONARD; now (1871) in Nevada Territory. (4.) ELIZA ANN; m. a Hoyt; deceased. (5.) SARAH JANE; deceased.

3.   SOPHIA, b. Jan. 8, 1804; m. Pelatiah Jones, of Lee. Children: (1.) DOLLY JANE (Jones). (2.) DANIEL AUGUSTUS; served in the 6th New Hampshire regiment till discharged on account of sickness; was drowned near New Market, Mar. 1866. (3.) JOHN DEMERITT; a soldier in the New Hampshire 6th regiment three years. (4.) JACOB DEMERITT. (5.) CHARLES; enlisted in the 39th Massachusetts regiment, and d. in Salisbury prison, N. C., Nov. 22, 1864. (6.) ABIGAIL ANN. (7.) MARY ELIZABETH. (8.) MARTHA JANE. (9.) LYDIA ESTHER. (10.) SARAH AUGUSTA.

4.   JOHN (Demeritt), b. Apr. 20, 1806; resides in Gilead, Mich.

5.   TIMOTHY, b. Mar. 23, 1808; lived in Nottingham, and there d. Jan. 1866, in his 58th year; m., 1st, Deborah Emerson, by whom twelve children; m., 2d, Hannah Clay, by whom four children. Of these, the six following were in the war of the rebellion, and the father said he "would go himself if that was not enough." (1.) JOHN. (2.) JACOB; d. in consequence of wounds received. (3.) EMERSON; twice enlisted. (4.) GEORGE; twice enlisted. (5.) CHARLES; d. of disease in the service. (6.) ALBERT.

6.   MEHETABEL FORD, b. Mar. 18, 1810; m. Henry P. Daniels, of Nottingham [1668, 1, (3)], May 27, 1832. Children: (1.) NATHAN EDWIN (Daniels), b. Sept. 6, 1833; m. Rachel Grant, of South Berwick, Me., Feb. 1854; resides in Nottingham; six children, one deceased. (2.) JOHN COLBY, b. Apr. 17, 1836; d. May 1, 1839, aged 3. (3.) PRIEST, b. Jan. 14, d. May 15, 1838. (4.) JOHN D., b. June 17, 1839; was in the late war; m. Esther V. Tuttle, of Nottingham, Sept. 1864; three children. (5.) MARIA SARAH, b. Jan. 2, 1842; m. William F. Holmes, of Nottingham; one child. He served with his brother-in-law, (4.), for three years, in the 13th New Hampshire regiment, Co. F.

7.   DANIEL (Demeritt), b. July 12, 1812; was a merchant at West Nottingham; m. Lorinda P. Batchelder [1674, 2], July 3, 1842, and d. Feb. 27, 1863, in his 51st year. Children: (1.) HANNAH ADALAIDE, b. Jan. 15, d. Apr. 23, 1844. (2.) GEORGE WASHINGTON, b. Jan. 26, 1845. (3.) HANNAH ABBY, b. June 28, 1846; m. Samuel A. Colcord, Mar. 28, 1868; residence at West Nottingham. Child: I. RALPH (Colcord), b. Aug. 7, 1869. (4.) JOHN WILLIAM (Demeritt), b. Jan. 4, 1848; d. Apr. 7, 1853, aged 5 years 3 months. (5.) JOHN WILLIAM, b. July 7, 1857.

8.   SAMUEL DYER, b. May 29, 1814; was in the Mexican war, being present at the taking of the capital, and is supposed there to have died.

9.   SARAH JOHNSON, b. Dec. 29, 1815; m. Levi White, of Deering, N. H., July 4, 1842; three children.

10.   MARY ANN, b. Mar. 18, 1818; m. John W. Joy, of Manchester, and d. Aug. 1857, aged 39, leaving: (1.) JOSEPHINE (Joy).

11.   BENJAMIN FRANKLIN (Demeritt), b. Jan. 15, d. Apr. 12, 1820.

12.   ANDREW JACKSON, b. Sept. 7, 1821; d. at Nottingham, Aug. 1852, aged 31.

13.   ABIGAIL FINETT, b. Jan. 12, 1825.

1672.   LOIS (Demeritt), b. about 1783; m. Jacob Welch, and settled first in Sheffield, then in Lyndon, Vt. Children: —

1.   SUSAN (Welch); m. a Miles, of Madbury, N. H.

2. DELIVERANCE; m., 1st, a French; 2d, an Elliot.
3. JOSEPH DEMERITT; m. Mary Ann Coe, and settled in Nottingham. Children: (1.) JOSEPH PRIEST. (2.) CHARLES L.
(3.) HARRISON. (4.) JACOB. (5.) MARTHA ANN; m. a
Langley, of Nottingham. (6.) ORRIN.
4. WILLIAM; resides in Lyndon, Vt.
5. HENDRICK; enlisted in the 11th Vermont regiment at the age
of 54, and was killed May 6, 1864, at the battle of the Wilderness, Va.
6. PRUDENCE.
7. MARY JANE.
8. CHARLES; d. at Lyndon, Aug. 10, 1871.
9. FREEMAN; was in Texas at the commencement of the war, and
is supposed to have been hung for the crime of being a
"Union man."
10. ISAAC; now resides in Lyndon.
11. FINETT, b. Aug. 25, 1824; see [1666, 2, (1.)]
12. HANNAH.
13. GREENLEAF; now in California.
14. LOUISA; d. young.
1673. SUSAN (Demeritt), b. Oct. 4, 1789; m. Samuel Bennett, farmer,
of Northwood, Mar. 5, 1808. He was b. Feb. 13, 1787, and d.
Apr. 25, 1852, aged 65. She d. Sept. 23, 1868, aged 79. They
lived on the original Joseph Demeritt farm, still occupied by
their daughter [10].
1. HARRIET DEMERITT (Bennett), b. Mar. 18, 1809; m. David Tuttle, of Palmyra, Me., and there d. Nov. 2, 1870, in her 62d
year; three children.
2. LUCINDA ABIGAIL, b. Jan. 16, 1811.
3. LOVINA DUSTIN, b. July 30, 1814; d. Mar. 13, 1841, in her 27th yr.
4. EMILY ANN, b. Dec. 1816.
5. SUSAN CAROLINE, b. Dec. 1818; m. Joseph Priest; d. at Great
Falls, Sept. 13, 1868, in her 50th year; one child.
6. WILLIAM PLUMMER, b. Apr. 28, 1820; d. Sept. 4, 1869, aged 49.
7. JUDITH EMELINE, b. July 15, 1823; d. Mar. 16, 1826, in her 3d
year.
8. JAMES HOLLIS, b. Jan. 19, 1825; d. Apr. 1, 1845, aged 20.
9. SARAH OLEVA, b. Jan. 18, 1827; m. a Johnson; resided in
Northwood; both deceased.
10. ELIZABETH JANE, b. Jan. 24, 1830; m. Josiah S. Willey. Jan. 8,
1870; resides on her grandfather's homestead in Northwood;
post-office, West Nottingham.
11. AMANDA MALVIRA, b. Jan. 16, 1832; m. John J. Noble, of Epping; d. Mar. 2, 1862, aged 30; one child.
12. BENJAMIN FRANKLIN, b. Jan. 9, 1835; d. May 8, 1862, aged 27.
1674. HANNAH (Demeritt), b. Aug. 23, 1793; m. William Batchelder,
house carpenter and farmer, of Nottingham, Apr. 15, 1816. He
was b. in Northwood, Apr. 27, 1788, and is still living in West
Nottingham (1871). She d. May 14, 1837 (1839), in her 44th
(46th) year; he m., 2d, Mrs. Mary Randall, who d. Dec. 13,
1862. Children, first wife: —
1. JOSEPH DEMERITT (Batchelder), b. June 12, 1817; a farmer in
West Nottingham; has been twice m.; was first selectman
and town treasurer of Nottingham in 1871. Children: (1.)
WILLIAM EDWARD, b. June 17, 1844. (2.) JOSEPH ALBERT,
b. May 2, 1849. (3.) HANNAH ELLA, b. Mar. 27, 1853. (4.)
CARRIE ABBIE, b. Aug. 1, 1866. (5.) ELMER GREENLEAF, b.
Aug. 28. 1868.
2. LORINDA PRIEST, b. Nov. 11, 1818; see [1671, 7].
3. CHARLES HENRY, b. May 28, 1820; d. Mar. 11, 1821, aged 9 mos.
11 days.

4. ORMAN, b. Feb. 4, 1822; was a tin manufacturer, residing in
    Concord, N. H., and Cleveland, O.; has now returned, as a
    farmer, to his father's homestead in West Nottingham; m.
    Susan Titus, of Vershire, Vt., Jan. 25, 1860. Child: (1.)
    WILLIE ORMAN, b. Aug. 2, 1860.
5. GREENLEAF FURBER, b. Sept. 16, 1823; m. Josephine Loomis,
    of Ohio, June, 1861; residing, as a merchant, in Kendallville,
    Noble Co., Ind., 1871. Child: (1.) KATIE, b. Jan. 1865; d.
    Feb. 1866. aged 13 months.
6. MARGARET ANN, b. Feb. 6, d. May 9, 1827.
7. SARAH JANE, b. Oct. 16, 1828; d. Jan. 14, 1832, in her 4th year.
8. JAMES MARDEN PIKE, b. July 9, 1833; resides in Kendallville,
    Ind., as principal of the high school, 1871; m. Martha Ann
    Knowlton, of Northwood, 1858. Children: (1.) VIELLA, b.
    Aug. 4, 1859. (2.) RAY, b. 1862; d. 1866, aged 4. (3.)
    LORA (?), b. Aug. 4, 1871.
9. HANNAH JANE, b. Sept. 25, 1836 ("1838" given, but less proba-
    ble, from date of her mother's death); d. Aug. 17, 1854,
    aged 18 (16).

1675. JOB[3] [1617] (Job[2], Job[1]), is styled on the town records
"Lieut." and "Job Runnels Jun." till after the death of his father;
was m. to Sarah Ellison, of Lee, by Rev. Samuel Hutchins, June
2, 1772. She was b. Apr. 3, 1751. Is reported as a "Private in
Smith Emerson's Co., at Seavey's Island, Nov. 5, 1775," in the
New Hampshire military records. "Mar. 28, 1780, Job Runnels,
Jr., and Sarah, his wife," deeded to Samuel Hill "a hundred acre
lot in the township of Canterbury;" and "May 4, 1780," they
deeded away their title "to the estate of Thomas Ellison, her
father in Barrington." He was selectman in Lee, 1781, and again
in 1787 and 1790. Said to be residing in the "Mast way district,"
1807–1815. For locality, see [1606] and [1615]. This "Mast
road," "way," or "path," found so frequently upon old records
pertaining to Lee, was the original road opened from Lee Hill to
tide-water, at Durham Falls, over which "His Majesty's pines for
the royal navy" were drawn in the winter ! This brother's part of
the ancestral estate did not probably go out of the family till after
his death, Aug. 27, 1831, in his 83d year. His widow d. Jan. 20,
1840, in her 89th year. Children, born in Lee : —

1676. SUSANNA [1761], b. July 4, 1773.
1677. THOMAS [1771], b. Feb. 2, 1775.
1678. ABIGAIL, b. Dec. 20, 1776; d. at Rochester, Oct. 1826, in her 50th
       year.
1679. SALLY [1782], b. Apr. 13, 1779.
1680. POLLY b. Nov. 2, 1781; d. in infancy.
1681. PEGGY, b. Jan. 3, 1784; d. in infancy.
1682. JOB [1788], b. Jan. 8, 1787.
1683. HANNAH [1793], b. Apr. 8, 1790.
1684. JOHN H., b. Mar. 11, 1792; settled in Portland, Me., near the
       close of the war, in 1815, where he kept a boot and shoe store
       for some time; m., 1st, widow Ellison, of Portsmouth, N. H.,
       and had one child. She d. 1820. He afterwards resided in
       Alexandria, D. C., took the management of a lottery scheme,
       authorized by Congress, and published in its interest, a news-
       paper, entitled "Runnells' Lottery Register." He m., 2d, Miss
       Dade, in Alexandria, moved thence to Washington *after* 1829,

and there d., leaving two children by his secoud wife, who were living in Washington as late as 1840, but are supposed to have d. soon after. We enter the notice of his family and children *here*, as the names and births of the latter have wholly eluded our long-continued search.

1685. BETSY [1799], b. May 21, 1794.

1686. ABIGAIL[3] [1618] (Job[2], Job[1]), m. Eliphalet Taylor, joiner, 1772; lived first in Lee, but afterwards settled in Northwood, N. H. Children: —

1687. ZACHEUS (Taylor), b. 1773, probably in Lee; m. a Burnham, of Northwood.
1688. JONATHAN, b. 1776, in Lee; m. a Fiske; settled in Tuftonborough, N. H., and moved thence to Allenstown.
1689. SALLY, b. "Mar. 11, 1779, in Lee" (Northwood records); m. John Durgin, Jr., of Northwood, who was b. Aug. 16, 1771, in N. Children, b. in Northwood: —
    1. LOUIS (Durgin), b. Mar. 3, 1796.
    2. JOB, b. Aug. 1, 1798.
    3. MILES, b. Sept. 20, 1802.
    4. SUSANNA(H), b. Mar. 22, 1805.
    5. ELIPHALET, b. June 23, 1809.
1690. DANIEL (Taylor), b. 1781; "was a seafaring man."
1691. POLLY. b. 1784; m. John Shaw, of Northwood, Oct. 18, 1803. Children (Northwood records): —
    1. "LIZZEY" (Shaw), b. Jan. 21 (26), 1805.
    2. NANCY, b. Jan. 27, 1807.
    3. SUSANNA, b. Jan. 4, 1809.
    4. JOSEPH, b. Feb. 25, 1811.
1692. JOHN (Taylor), b. 1787; m. Love Durgin, Sept. 30, 1808, and moved to Ossipee (Effingham), N. H.
1693. ABIGAIL, b. "Sept. 28, 1790"; m. Thomas Durgin, who was b. Aug. 8, 1791, and settled in Effingham. Children: —
    1. LOVEY (Durgin), b. June 24, 1811.
    2. LOUISA MEAD, b. Mar. 13, 1813.
1694. JOSEPH (Taylor), b. 1793; lived and d. in Ossipee, or Effingham.

1695. MILES[3] [1619] (Job[2], Job[1]), was a teacher as well as farmer, and disposed of his part of his father's estate in Lee, N. H., "June 5, 1790," under which date we find "Miles Runels and Margaret his wife," deeding to "Robert Parker" (the *Capt.* Parker who built the present Hale or Smith mansion), "of Portsmouth, the land in Lee which I bought of my honored father Job Runels, by his deed to me Mar. 6 (26), 1785." He remained in Lee till *after* 1815. Is called "Lieut. Miles Reynolds," of the "North River District," on town records of 1807, — though "Runnels" again on records of 1815. His is one of the few names found enrolled, for the service of his country, *both* in the war of the Revolution and in the war of 1812. The former enlistment was when a young man, before his marriage, "July 5, 1779," "Capt. Ezekiel Worthen's Co., Mooney's regiment for the defence of Rhode Island." "July 10, 1779," he is said to be "of Lee," and received "£30 bounty" and "£12 travel money"; served six months and five days; discharged "Jan. 9, 1780." Also enlisted "Oct. 5, 1814," for sixty days, in Capt. John Willey's Co., 3d regiment detached militia (New Hampshire military records). He m. Margaret Kelsea, of Nottingham, 1781, who was b. in N., Nov. 1, 1762, and d. June 5, 1851, in her 89th year. He d. Mar. 24, 1847, at Tuftonborough, in his 86th year. Their children were : —

1696. JAMES, b. July 22, 1782, in Lee, and there d. 1791, aged 9.
1697. ELIZABETH, b. Jan. 30, 1785, in Lee; d. at Dover, Mar. 1857, aged 72.
1698. JOHN [1811], b. Apr. 16, 1787, in Lee.
1699. LOIS [1817], b. Dec. 5, 1792, in Nottingham.
1700. OLIVE, b. July 31, 1797, in N.; now residing (1869) with her sister, last named, in Tuftonborough.

1701. HANNAH[3] [1647] (Jonathan[2], Job[1]), m. William McDaniels, farmer, of Nottingham, N. H., 1784. He d. June 10, 1829. She d. June 27, 1841, aged 86. Children : —

1702. JOHN (McDaniels), b. 1785; "left for parts unknown"; is supposed to have d.
1703. MARTHA, b. 1787; m. Otis Bruce; moved to Palmyra, Me., and there d.
1704. MARY, b. Mar. 17, 1789; m. Charles Bruce, farmer, of Nottingham, Nov. 1825. He occupies the old McDaniels farm in N. She d. Feb. 10, 1845, aged 56.   Child : —
    1. ANGELINA (Bruce), b. Mar. 27, 1827; m. Edward Gibbs, of Boston, 1853. He is a gas and steam fitter; has resided in Rhode Island, Wisconsin, and various other parts of the West. Children : (1.) ELDORA (Gibbs), b. July 31, 1854; m. Lorenzo Kimball Garland, of Nottingham, shoemaker, Oct. 31, 1870. (2.) CHARLES, b. June 21, 1856; d. Sept. 14, 1857, aged 15 months. (3.) CHARLES, b. Feb. 22, d. Mar. 10, 1858. (4.) MARY DORCAS, b. Jan. 18, 1863.
1705. DAVID (McDaniels), b. May 27, 1791; d. Sept. 17, 1816, aged 25.
1706. PELATIAH, b. 1793; was blown up in a fort during the war of 1812, — for which he had enlisted as a soldier, — on a 4th of July, and thus d.
1707. EUNICE, b. 1796; deceased.
1708. HANNAH, b. 1799; d. May 19, 1833, aged 34.

1709. MARTHA[3] [1648] (Jonathan[2], Job[1]), m. a Batchelder, of Nottingham, of whose family little can be ascertained. Children : —

1710. MOSES (Batchelder), m., lived, and d. in Portsmouth, N. H.
1711. ALICE (or Elsie).
1712. MARK; is said to have settled in Conway, N. H.
1713. KEZIAH; d. with her aunt Hines [1649], in Nottingham.
1714. JOHN; is supposed to have moved, with his older brother Mark, to Conway.

1715. ABIGAIL[3] [1650] (Jonathan[2], Job[1]), m. Jonathan Thompson, of Lee, N. H., 1779. He was b. Jan. 23, 1758, the son of Robert and Susannah Thompson, and d. Dec. 9 (town records "29"), 1803, in his 46th year. She d. about 1802, aged 42. They lived in Durham or Lee, on land now owned by Thomas Chesley; house removed. Children, — "arranged by pairs; two boys, then two girls, and one boy *towards* the fifth pair!" —

1716.   BENJAMIN (Thompson), b. 1780; d. 1816, in Durham, aged 36, by bleeding at the nose.
1717.   LEVI, b. Dec. 2, 1781; m. Comfort Ellison, and lived in Nottingham, where he d. June 4, 1871, in his 90th year; and she d. Aug. 7 of the same year, aged 84 years 9 months. Children: —
  1. JOHN; deceased.
  2. WILLIAM; deceased.
  3. JOSEPH; deceased.
  4. ABRAHAM; now residing at Nottingham Centre; a farmer and teamster; m. Deborah Chesley, of N., May 24, 1840.
  5. LEVI; settled in Epping.
  6. ROBERT; settled in Epping; three children.
  7. JONATHAN; lived with his father in Nottingham.
  8. CHARLES; resides in Lee.
  9. ABIGAIL; m. a Thompson; lives in Nottingham.
  10. MARY JANE; m. a Sewards, of Barrington; twelve children.
  11. KEZIAH; m. a Harvey; resides in San Francisco, Cal.; nine children.
  12. ELIZABETH; m. Robert Lucy, of Nottingham; five children.
  13. SYLVESTER; served in the late war of the rebellion; was wounded, and d. of diphtheria.
1718.   POLLY. b. 1785; m. a Speed, of Dover, and d. at New Market, N. H. Child: —
  1. ABIGAIL (Speed); m. Charles Young, of Dover; was living on Garrison Hill, 1868.
1719.   ABIGAIL (Thompson), b. 1787; d. May 25, 1808, in Lee. aged 21.
1720.   ROBERT, b. Apr. 22, 1790, in Lee. Served as "sergeant in the *State* militia" (probably of Massachusetts in Maine) during the "war of 1812;" was a farmer; resided at North Searsmont, Me., for fifty-two years, and there d. Aug. 9, 1860, aged 70, after a ten-years' sickness, — lameness ending in dropsy. He m. Susannah French, Nov. 3, 1810, in Lee, who was there b. Apr. 16, 1790, and d. at North Searsmont, Aug. 27, 1871 (?), aged 81. Children: —
  1. JONATHAN, b. Aug. 10, 1812, in Montville, Me.; a farmer; m., 1st, Elizabeth Duly, Apr. 14, 1842, in Camden. She was b. Feb. 9, 1816, and d. Mar. 4, 1845, aged 29. He m., 2d, Abigail Marion Sherman, Jan. 2, 1847, in Thomaston, Me., who was b. Nov. 27, 1823. Children: (1.) CHARLES AUGUSTUS (first wife), b. Nov. 6, 1843, in Camden; d. Nov. 10, 1844, aged 1 year 4 days. (2.) LLEWELLYN AUGUSTINE (second wife), b. Sept. 5, 1848, in Searsmont. (3.) ABBIE MARION, b. Feb. 3, 1850, in Searsmont. (4.) REGINALD ROMAINE, b. Mar. 14, 1854, in S. (5.) FRANKLIN JONATHAN, d. Sept. 3, 1856, in S. (6.) FERDINAND DE SOTO, b..Mar. 24, 1859. (7.) ARDRA HANNAH, b. July 6, 1861. (8.) MARCIA EVA, b. Apr. 23, d. Oct. 11, 1863. (9.) THEODORE BOONE, b. Dec. 21, 1866.
  2. ALFRED, b. May 11, 1814, in Montville; d. Jan. 11, 1822, at Searsmont, aged 7 years 8 months.
  3. ELIZA H., b. Mar. 20, 1816. in Searsmont, as were all the following.
  4. LEVI, b. Aug. 23, 1818; a farmer.
  5. SARAH J., b. Oct. 8, 1822; m. Albert Ring, house carpenter, of Searsmont, Dec. 28, 1846, who was b. July 21, 1818, in S. Child: (1.) GEORGE EDWIN (Ring), b. June 13, 1849, in S.
  6. WILLIAM (Thompson), b. Oct. 4, d. Oct. 10, 1823.
  7. MARY S., b. Aug. 3, 1825.
  8. JAMES F., b. Sept. 4, 1828; a farmer.
1721.   JONATHAN, b. Mar. 12, 1792; was a farmer in Durham, near New Market, till 1868; now residing in Lee with his nephew Charles Thompson [1717, 8] (?).

1722.   SUSANNAH; b. July 4, 1794; m. Pelatiah Thompson, see [1634, 1], Nov. 1, 1816, and has lived till the present in Lee, on the farm still occupied by their son Jonathan. No other individual has contributed so much information to the writer respecting the Runnelses and Thompsons of Lee. Her aid, *at first*, was indispensable. He d. Apr. 1852, in his 57th yr. Children, b in Lee: —

   1.   JOSEPH (Thompson), b. May 11, 1818; d. at Lee, Jan. 1851, in his 33d year.

   2.   ELIZABETH, b. Feb. 13, 1820; d. Apr. 1852, aged 32.

   3.   JONATHAN, b. Aug. 27, 1822; m. Lucy Moore, of Andover. Mass., June 24, 1852, who was b. Apr. 27, 1828. Children: (1.) LIZZIE LUCY, b. Aug. 4, 1853. (2.) EDWIN JONATHAN, b. Sept. 3, 1862. (3) ABBY SUSAN, b. May 25, 1864; d. July 22, 1867, aged 3 years 2 months. (4.) WILLIAM, b. Sept. 21, 1866. (5.) IRVING AUGUSTUS, b. Jan. 20, 1869. (6.) IDA BELL, b. Aug. 16, 1870

   4.   PELATIAH, b. Nov 5, 1824; lives with his brother in Lee.

   5.   SUSANNAH F., b. July 17, 1826; m. Matthew J. Harvey, of Epping, June 1, 1856. He was b. Oct. 14, 1821. Children: (1.) ABBY ELIZABETH (Harvey), b. Aug. 14, 1857. (2.) JAMES BUCHANAN. b. Dec. 3, 1858. (3.) JOSEPH THOMPSON, b. Mar. 11, 1861. (4.) MARTHA FANNIE, b. Oct. 26, 1863. (5.) NATHANIEL D , b. Aug. 8, 1865. (6) JOHN MILTON, b. Sept. 28, 1869. (7.) MATTHEW, b. Mar. 24, 1870.

   6.   ABIGAIL E., b. Dec. 20, 1827; m. Rev. George L. Becker, Oct. 1856; then a Congregational minister in Sanford, Me.; now residing in Grenada, Kansas, whither he moved Mar. 1857. Children: (1.) LIZZIE PIERSON (Becker), b. Nov. 12, 1857. (2) DANA, b. Jan. 24, 1859. (3) MARA, b. Jan 23, 1861. (4.) "SUSANNAH" (as we venture to call her, though "not named" by her parents), b. July 29, 1863; d. Mar. 27, 1864, aged 8 months. (5.) EMMA, b. June 24, 1867.

1723.   KEZIAH (Thompson), b. May 5, 1798; m. Robert Thompson, of Lee; d. Mar. 19, 1871, in her 73d year.

1724.   ASA, b. 1801; d 1804, at Durham, aged 3.

1725.   SARAH³ [1651] (Jonathan², Job¹), m. John Thompson, of Lee, and settled in Conway, N. H., west side of Saco river, opposite the north village. He was b. Mar. 29, 1762, and d. Aug. 10 (12), 1798, in his 37th year. She d. at Conway, Sept. 20, 1824, aged 62. Children: —

1726.   BETSY (Thompson), b. June 17, 1790; d. Oct. 3, 1812, aged 22.

1727.   SAMUEL, b. Sept. 1, 1792; lived on his father's place, and d. Sept. 20. 1829, aged 37. Had m. Betsy Osgood, of Conway. Children: —

   1.   CHARLES OSGOOD.

   2.   SAMUEL.

   3.   JOHN; m. Ann Thomas: lived at the old homestead in Conway, and there d. Dec. 1870.

1728.   JOHN, b. June 11, 1795; d. May 11, 1814, aged 18 years 11 mos.

1729.   KEZIAH, b. Dec. 5, 1796; d. Nov. 16. 1834, aged 38.

1730.   JONATHAN RUNNELS (middle name afterwards changed to "Reynolds"), b. Jan. 21, 1799. He graduated at Dartmouth College, 1827, and at the Dartmouth Medical School, 1831. Commenced the practice of medicine at Conway Corner, 1832, and there continued it till near his death. Represented his town in the New Hampshire legislature, 1835; held the office of town clerk ten years, and various other town offices. He was "a highly respectable citizen and successful physician; a deep thinker on all subjects which claimed his attention," and " he died in the triumphs of a Christian faith. During the last year of his life, in the investigation of Christian truth, he read the New Testament through three times in Latin and once in Greek, besides a regular use of the English translation." (From the "Class Memorial," "D. C., 1827.") He m., 1st, Abigail Hill Eastman, of Conway, Jan. 21, 1836 (his birthday), who d. Oct. 3, 1846; m., 2d, Mary Russell Hill, of Conway, Sept. 13, 1849, and d. Dec. 12, 1869, in his 71st year. Children, first wife, b. in Conway, were : —

1. SARAH ELIZABETH, b Dec. 30, 1836; m. (Rev.) Isaac S. Hamblen, of Waterville, Me., May 15, 1859. At first, principal of the Waterville Academy, he afterwards graduated from the theological seminary at Newton Centre, Mass., — class of 1868, — and has since been laboring as pastor of the Baptist church in East Abington, Mass., with much encouragement. He is a man of strong intellectual powers, and thorough in his scholarship. Children: (1.) SAMUEL WILLIS (Hamblen), b. Sept. 12. 1862. (2.) LOUISE HILL, b. Mar. 18, 1865.

2. ABBY HILL (Thompson), b. Apr. 10, 1838; m. Levi Chadbourne Quint, tanner, of Conway.

3. JONATHAN EDWARDS, b. Feb. 26, 1840; d. at Conway, Dec. 5, 1859, in his 20th year.

4. MARY EVANS, b. Sept. 30, 1841; d. Jan. 26, 1862, in her 21st year.

5. EUNICE JANE, b. Apr. 7, 1843; d. June 2, 1859, aged 16.

6. HENRY ABIATHER, b. Sept. 8, 1845; d. May 10, 1865, in his 20th year.

1731. SUSANNAH[3] [1652] (Jonathan[2], Job[1]), m., 1st., Benjamin Durgin, of Lee, farmer, 1783, who d. Oct 16, 1785 ; m., 2d, Richard Eastman, Esq., of North Conway, farmer, Aug. 27, 1791. He had eleven children by a former wife, and made the humorous remark, when on his way to Lee for a second wife, that he was after a " pullet to scratch for a dozen chickens !" His eighteen children and her two (by former husband) were all professors of religion, all but one lived to be over seventy years of age, and three lived, or are living (1871), to be nearly one hundred! He d. Dec 6, 1826. She d. May 29, 1849, aged 84. Her children were : —

1732. SUSAN (Durgin), b. Apr. 17, 1784; m. Abiather Eastman, Jr., of Conway, 1802. He was b. Aug. 1, 1781, and d. Oct. 22, 1813, aged 32, at Chatauque Four Corners, N. Y., in an army hospital, having enlisted in the U. S. service in June of the same year. She d. Apr 19, 1853, at Sweden, Me., aged 69. Children: —

1. BENJAMIN DURGIN (Eastman), b. Dec. 21, 1802. He joined the Maine Conference of the Methodist Episcopal Church, June, 1831, and labored successfully, for some twenty-six years, as a clergyman in various fields in the eastern part of Maine, from one of which he was sent two terms to the House of Representatives and once to the State Senate. Has since resided to the present (1871) in North Conway, as a local preacher, trader, and postmaster. He m., 1st, Lois Fog Averill, Nov. 19, 1831, who was b. July 23, 1812, in Machias, Me., and d. at Limestone, Jan. 20, 1849, in her 37th year; m., 2d, Nancy Fisher Whitney, Feb. 21, 1850, who was b. June 30. 1828, in Corinth, Me. Children: (1.) CAROLINE BANGS, b. Jan. 7, 1833, in Castine, Me. (2.) CHARLES WARD, b. July 17, 1834, in Brooksville, Me. (3.) DOLLY AVERILL, b. June 17, 1837, in Wesley, Me. (4.) EMMA ELLEN, b. July 21, 1840,

in Wesley. (5.) Lois Anna, b. Mar. 10, 1843, in Cooper, Me.
(6.) Susan Durgin, b. May 19, 1848, in Limestone, Me.
(7.) George Vernon (second wife), b. Nov. 24, 1851, in
Limestone. (8.) Clara Alice, b. Jan. 23, 1854, in Limestone. (9.) Olive Jeanette, b. Mar. 6, 1856, in Phillips,
Me. (10.) Ella May, b. Nov. 9, 1858, in Bartlett, N. H.

2.   Samuel, b June 17, 1804; went to South Carolina, where he
probably died.

3.   Otis, b. Apr. 15, 1806; resides in Minnesota; m. Florilla Merrill; four sons, of whom : (1.) Rufus Merrill, served in the
late war, 1st Minnesota regiment; and (2.) George, likewise, in a Maine regiment, was wounded in the James river
campaign, Va., and " maimed for life."

4.   Caroline, b. Dec. 25, 1808; m. James Evans, of Sweden, Me.
Three sons and two daughters; of the former, (1.) Samuel
Eastman (Evans) and (2.) George Meserve, both d. in the
war, being " killed or lost on the field of strife."

5.   Calvin B. (Eastman), b. Jan. 13, 1811; went to Maryland, and
probably d. there.

6.   Pollie Reynolds, b. Dec. 14, 1812; was a teacher in the ornamental branches, and d. at Portland, Me., Mar. 5, 1862,
aged 49.

1733.   Lydia (Durgin), b. Oct. 18, 1785; m. Job Eastman, of Conway,
Feb. 17, 1803. The families of their children, as follows, are *all*
located near together in the vicinity of North Conway, N. H. : —

1.   Mary Runnels (Eastman), b. Mar. 29, 1804; m. Josiah Weeks,
of Bartlett; five children; four living.

2.   Adaline, b. Feb. 14, 1806; m. Stephen Wheeler; one child.

3.   Lorenzo, b. July 14, 1808; m., 1st, Esther Holt; four children,
one living, of whom : (1.) Chauncy, d. of disease in the
Union army, at Paris, Tenn.

4.   Daniel, b. May 29, 1811; m. Sally G. Holt; three children; one
living.

5.   J. Osborn, b. Mar. 24, 1813; m. Olive Lang; three children;
two living.

6.   Abiather, b. July 12, 1815; m. Louisa Holt; eight children;
six living.

7.   Clarissa, b. May 22, 1818; deceased.

8.   Susan, b. June 2, 1820; deceased.

9.   Jeremiah Chandler, b. June 11, 1824; m. the widow of his
younger brother; one child, deceased.

10.   George Freeman, b. Oct. 9, 1827; m. Lucinda Heath; deceased;
three children.

1734.   Keziah (Eastman), b. Oct 5, 1792; m. Henry Tucker, of Conway,
farmer, Dec. 26, 1813. He was b. May 1, 1789, in Falmouth,
Eng., and d. at Conway, Aug. 18, 1830, aged 41. She moved
to Leeds, Me., Oct. 30, 1868. Children : —

1.   Lewis McMillan (Tucker), b. Jan. 30, 1815; m. Lydia Frances
Robbins, Jan. 31, 1864, who was b. June 18, 1839, in Yarmouth,
N. S. He is now a farmer in Leeds, Me. Children: (1.) Mary
Ann, b. Feb. 6, 1865, in Conway. (2.) Edwin Robbins, b.
Sept. 27. 1866, in C. (3.) Lewis Henry, b. Dec. 19, 1869, in
Leeds, Me.; d. Nov. 3, 1870, aged 10 months 15 days.

2.   Mary Ann, b. May 26, 1817; d. June 22, 1831, aged 14.

3.   Elizabeth Eastman, b. July 18, 1821; m. George W. Burbank,
of Conway, Mar. 25. 1842. Children: (1.) Lewis Laroy
(Burbank), b. Oct. 25, 1843; enlisted in the 9th New Hampshire regiment, Co. D, July, 1862; was present in several
engagements, and was finally killed in the battle of Spottsylvania Court House, Va., May 12, 1864. (2.) Laura Ann, b.
Mar. 4, 1845. (3.) Edward Luellen, b. Nov. 29, 1846; d.

Apr. 27, 1865, in his 19th year. (4.) SUSAN FABYAN, b. July 30, 1848; d. Jan. 7, 1869, in her 21st year. (5.) HORACE HERBERT, b. June 11, 1850. (6.) GEORGE WASHINGTON, b. Apr. 3, 1852. (7.) AMOS EASTMAN, b. Oct. 7, 1853. (8.) CLARA LIZZIE, b. Aug. 12, 1855. (9.) CORA ELLEN, b. Sept. 21, 1857. (10.) SARAH KEZIA, b. July 1, 1860. (11.) ALICE MARIA, b. Mar. 17, 1862. (12.) HARRIET MERILLA, b. Dec. 31, 1864.

4. SUSAN RUNNELS (Tucker), b. Oct. 1, 1823; m. Oliver B. Fabyan, Dec. 9, 1845. He was b. Feb. 27, 1817, in Durham, Me. Children: (1.) GEORGE HENRY (Fabyan), b. Jan. 18, 1847, in Leeds, Me.; d. Sept. 30, 1871, in his 25th year. "He was truly a child of God." (2.) ELLA LOUISE, b. Feb. 21, 1857, in Leeds.

5. HENRY EASTMAN (Tucker), b. Jan. 18, 1831. He embarked, Feb. 19, 1853, at New York, for California, where he engaged in mining; but was at last severely maimed by a portion of earth falling on his back while digging, causing a paralysis of the lower limbs. Reaching Conway in July, 1857, with much suffering, he was afterwards enabled to move about by means of a wheeled chair; commenced trade on a small scale in a private house; m. Susan Willey, Apr. 9, 1863; moved to the village, built a store, and carried on quite an extensive business till his death, occasioned by his injuries, Jan. 25, 1865, aged 34. Soon after his return from California, he composed the following lines: —

> "Five years have passed, since, full of hope,
>   I left this home to me so dear;
> My body, but a wreck, is brought,
>   *Now*, to those friends that still are here,
>   Sorrows begun.

> "Deep in the bowels of the earth
>   I've sought the precious, glittering ore;
> But God saw fit to change the scene,
>   And I shall never wander more,
>   Misfortune's son.

> "Crippled! Yes, for the rest of life,
>   A helpless cripple I must be;
> O God, lift up my sinking heart,
>   And give me power to say to thee,
>   'Thy will be done.'"

1735. BETSY (Eastman), b. May 11, 1795; m. John Hill, of Conway, merchant, Dec. 6, 1821. Children: —

1. POLLY FREEMAN (Hill), b. Oct. 1822; d. in infancy.
2. MARY FREEMAN, b. May 22, 1824. She and her next younger sister united with the church in 1840, and finished their course of study at the Young Ladies' Seminary, Freehold, N. J. She m. David Richardson, of Lebanon, machinist, Oct. 8, 1849; moved to Knoxville, Tenn., and there d. Mar. 10, 1856, in her 32d year. Child: (1.) GEORGE HILL (Richardson), b. Sept. 18, 1852; d. Oct. 1, 1853, aged 1 year and 13 days.
3. ELIZABETH (Hill), b. Feb. 15, 1827; see [2] above; m., 1st, Rev. Lyman Cutler, of Dorchester, Mass., Mar. 14, 1851. He d. Apr. 1854, and she m., 2d, Rev. Augustus C. Thompson, D. D., pastor of the Eliot Church, Roxbury, Mass., July 6, 1858. She d. Nov. 24, 1867, in her 41st year. Children:

10

(1.) ELIZABETH (Cutler), b 1852; d. in infancy. (2.) LYMAN
EDWARDS, b. Sept. 14, 1853; d. Jan. 16, 1864, in his 11th year.
(3.) MARY (Thompson), b. Sept. 14, 1862. (4.) WILLIAM and
(5.) CHARLES (twins); d. in infancy.

4.   GEORGE FREEMAN (Hill), b. June 2, 1829.
5.   THOMAS, b. Feb. 2, 1831; m. Louisa J. Merriam, in Boston.
Children : (1.) JANE G., b. Sept. 14, 1857. (2.) EDWARD M.,
b. Oct. 14, 1862. (3.) ARTHUR T., b. Apr. 29, 1864. (4.)
ELIZABETH C., b. Feb. 1, 1866.
6.   SUMNER CUMMINGS, b. Aug. 10, 1833.
7.   CHARLES HENRY, b. Jan. 31, 1836; d. Apr. 23, 1842, aged 6 years
3 months.
8.   SUSAN ANN, b. July 4, 1838; m. Dr. Simeon A. Evans, June 8,
1871. Child: (1.) GEORGE HILL (Evans), b. May 6, 1872.

1736.   AMOS (Eastman), b. Aug. 28, 1797; m. Betsy E. Merrill; resided
in Conway, and was killed by accident while sledding in the
woods, Jan. 30, 1854, in his 57th year; two children, of
whom : —
1.   RICHARD is supposed to be living; the other d. in infancy.

1737.   CLARISSA (Eastman), b. Oct. 28, 1799; m. Rev. Stephen Merrill,
Nov. 3, 1842; d. July 12, 1869, in her 70th year.

1738.   HARRIET (Eastman), b. Apr. 18, 1803; m. George Pendexter
Meserve, farmer, of Jackson, N. H., May 1, 1821. He ranked
as Major-General of the New Hampshire militia, at the age of
26, and has been a representative of the town of Jackson in the
State legislature. Children : —
1.   MARTHA TRICKEY (Meserve), b. Sept. 20, 1822; m. James
Monroe Meserve, teacher and farmer, May 3, 1846. Children : (1.) SARAH EDITH (Trickey), b. Apr. 27, 1848. (2.)
J. ERVING, b. Jan. 28, 1850. (3.) WILLARD ALLISON, b. July
1, 1857.
2.   ALICE PENDEXTER, b. Aug. 7, 1825; m. Joseph Burnham Trickey,
proprietor of the Jackson Falls Hotel, Mar. 29, 1849. Children : (1.) JAMES COLEMAN (Trickey), b. Apr. 27, 1850 (2.)
GEORGE PENDEXTER MESERVE, b. Feb. 23, 1852. (3.) NELSON
IRVING, b. Oct. 28, 1854. (4.) WILLIAM WALLACE, b. Dec. 11,
1857. (5.) FRANK PIERCE, b. Aug. 20, 1860; d. Apr. 2, 1863,
in his 3d year. (6.) CLARA LILLIAN, b. Mar. 30. 1862. (7.)
SARAH ALICE, b. May 30, 1868. (8.) JOSIE GERALDINE, b.
Apr. 6, 1870.
3.   SUSAN EASTMAN (Meserve), b. Jan. 7, 1828; m. Rev. George
Hayes Pinkham, of Jackson, Oct. 12, 1851. He has been
pastor of the Freewill Baptist Church, in Whitefield, N. H.,
since 1857. Children: (1.) GEORGE MESERVE (Pinkham),—
b. Jan. 14, 1853; d. Dec. 15, 1863, in his 11th year. (2.) MARY
SUSAN, b. Dec. 18, 1854; d. Dec. 16, 1863, aged 9. (3.) HAT-
TIE ALICE, b. Aug. 24, 1859; d. Dec. 24, 1863, aged 4 years 4
months. The three last — thus borne away as by one fell
swoop of the angel of death — were all "children of remarkable intelligence and promise." (4.) MARTHA GRACE, b. Nov.
8, 1864. (5.) ALBERT DAY, b. Aug. 13, 1867. (6.) CLARA
ESTELLA, b. June 10, 1871.
4.   MARY DAVIS (Meserve), b. June 18, 1831; a successful teacher
for twenty-three terms; m. William K. Quimby, of Whitefield, merchant, Dec. 31, 1859. Children: (1.) HATTIE ME-
SERVE (Quimby), b. Oct. 15, 1862. (2.) GEORGE MESERVE,
b. Nov. 13, 1864. (3.) WILLIAM EUGENE, b. Jan. 12, 1870.
5.   CLARA EASTMAN (Meserve), b. Oct. 5, 1835; a teacher for
several years; graduated at the New Hampton (N. H.)
Institution, 1863.
6.   HATTIE DOUGLAS, b. Aug. 27, 1837; graduated at New Hamp-

ton, 1862. For three years (1872), the faithful and efficient preceptress of the Littleton, N. H., High School.

7. GEORGE WASHINGTON, b. June 19, 1839; a farmer; m. Melvina Luella Eastman, of Jackson, Dec. 22, 1866. Children: (1.) VIRGIL KENT, b. Aug. 1, 1869. (2.) FRANK MARION, b. June 5, 1871.

8. LIZZIE AMELIA EVERETT, b. Sept. 6, 1842; m. Chase Burnham Perkins, of Jackson, farmer, May 19, 1872.

9. SARAH ADDIE WILLIAMS. b. Apr. 28, 1845; m. Alonzo Stillings, of Jackson, farmer, Oct. 25, 1868.

1739. JOHN LANGDON (Eastman), b. Mar 12, 1805; m. Margaret Douglass, Nov. 18, 1834, who was b. Jan. 10, 1812, in Portland, Me. He is a farmer, residing at North Conway, and deacon of the Congregational church. Children : —

1. BARNARD DOUGLASS, b. Feb. 5, 1836; graduated at a New York medical school; now (1871) first assistant physician in the Government Hospital for the Insane, Washington, D. C.; m. Carrie Ely, Oct. 12, 1865. Child: (1.) MARY STERNE, b. Aug. 1868.

2. EDWARD PAYSON, b. July 15, 1838; enlisted in the New Hampshire 1st heavy artillery, Sept. 1864, serving till the close of the war; graduated at the Bangor Theological Seminary, 1871, and ordained Apr. 20, 1871, as pastor of the Congregational church of Conway and North Conway, his old home; m. Eliza N. Sawyer, of Westbrook, Me., Mar. 8, 1868. Children: (1.) FRED LANGDON, b. June 17, 1869, at North Conway. (2.) LOUISA SNOW, b. Aug. 9, 1871, at N. C.

3. CHARLES HENRY, b. Feb. 14, 1841; enlisted in the 2d regiment N. H. volunteers, Co. F, June 4, 1861, for three years.

4. MARIA CUMMINGS. b. Apr. 16, 1844; m James M. Durham, Sept. 30, 1868, who is a lawyer in Ashley, Ill. Child: (1.) CONWAY (Durham), b. Aug. 11, 1870.

5. MARGARET DOUGLASS (Eastman), b. June 12, 1846; see [1844].

6. HARRIET ELIZABETH, b. May 16, d. June 1, 1849.

7. JOHN LANGDON, b. Feb. 3, 1851.

8. ELLSWORTH, b. Dec. 21, 1861; d. June 20, 1862, aged 6 months.

1740. IRENA (Eastman), b. Mar. 22, 1815; m. Jonathan E. Chase, of Conway. Children : —

1. GEORGE HENRY (Chase), b. 1838; d. 1845, aged 7.

2. ISABELLA EASTMAN, b. 1844; d. 1865, aged 21.

3. GEORGE MASON, b. 1849; m. Carrie Wilson, of Marblehead, Mass.; was the esteemed superintendent of the North Conway Congregational Sabbath School, and died, leaving a mournful void in many hearts, Mar. 1870, aged 21. His widow still residing at North Conway, 1871.

1741. JONATHAN[3] [1654] (Jonathan[2], Job[1]), came to North Conway in 1790 to visit his two sisters, and there finally settled, receiving, jointly, with his cousin, Hezekiah Randall [1640], from "Joseph Whipple, of Portsmouth," "the intervale lot, No. 2, westerly side of Saco river, Nov. 17, 1792." The same year he m. Betsy Randall [1640, 2], the daughter of his cousin and partner. "Mar. 11, 1796," the said Hezekiah deeded to his children, "Jonathan Runnels and Betsy his wife, for $150, the whole of said lot No. 2, with house lot included." This was the farm afterwards occupied by himself and family, now owned by Isaac F. Davis. "Oct. 11, 1798," he deeded "to Samuel Bradley all his share of the original right of Nathaniel Eastman." He d. Apr. 27, 1825, aged 55 ; she d. Apr. 1830, aged 55, both at Conway, where were born : —

1742. JONATHAN [1823], b. July 4, 1793.
1743. LEVI [1829], b. May 20, 1795.
1744. BETSY [1836], b. Oct. 30, 1799.

1745. LEVI[3] [1656] (Jonathan[2], Job[1]), was a farmer at Lee, N. H., living in a house adjoining his father's, "Centre district, 1807"; m. Mary Watson, of Nottingham, 1796, who was b. July 14, 1774. He d. at Lee, Mar. 15, 1808, aged 34, and his widow received her right of dower "Apr. 14, 1808," same date with her husband's mother, see [1646], so that the *two* widows, of father and son, must have visited the Probate office for the same purpose at the same time! She rendered her account as administratrix, "Nov. 28, 1808," and "license to sell real estate of Levi Runnels" was granted "to Polly his wife, Jan. 24, 1809." Her name is among the Lee "Inventories" as the "widow of Levi," 1812 and 1815 ; and again, 1827, as "Widow Mary Runels." She d. Aug. 23 (24), 1864, at Lee, aged 90. Their children's names are given on the Lee records, with surname changed to "Reynolds," as follows : —

1746. ASA [1845], b. July 27, 1797.
1747. BETSY [1850], b. Feb. 10, 1799.
1748. ABIGAIL [1854], b. Nov. 7, 1800.
1749. MARY [1862], b. June 14, 1802.
1750. JONATHAN [1867], b. Mar. 24, 1804.
1751. LEVI, b. Oct. 9, 1806 ; moved to Michigan ; but where at present, or whether living, is unknown. No responses, by letter, can be received.
1752. JANE, b. Nov. 15, 1808 ; d. at Lee, Oct. 2 (9), 1853, in her 45th year.

1753. SAMUEL[3] [1662] (Samuel[2], Job[1]). One of his descendants says that he was "probably the youngest" of his father's children ; but this is on the mistaken supposition that he was the "brother of Job and Miles" [1617 and 1619]. By others of his descendants, and by the few aged people, still surviving, who knew him, his pedigree is *now* well established, as here given. It is further remembered that he "migrated from Lee to Shapleigh, now Acton, Me.," that at first he "located on Acton Ridge," and "worked for Daniel Fox, who had married his cousin," see [1633], "and had previously moved from Lee ;" and that he afterwards "settled near Cesar's (Lovewell's?) pond, in the north part of the town." He m. Olive Farnham, of Acton, — sister of Ralph Farnham, "the last survivor of the battle of Bunker Hill," — in 1783 ; and d. of dropsy, Dec. 19, 1797, aged 43, in Milton, N. H., where he last resided. She d. in Lebanon, Me. Children, b. in Shapleigh : —

1754. POLLY (Mary) [1884], b. May 28, 1784.
1755. EUNICE [1890], b. May 6, 1786.
1756. SAMUEL [1900], b. June 22, 1788.
1757. PAUL [1910], b. June 4, 1790.
1758. BETSY, b. June 20, 1792 ; m. Miles Huckins, Feb. 20, 1832.
1759. OLIVE, b. 1794 (3) ; lived in Lebanon, Me., till 1850 ; d. Oct. 2, 1855, aged 61.
1760. ASA [1920], b. July, 1796.

FOURTH GENERATION.

1761. SUSANNAH[4] [1676] (Job[3], Job[2], Job[1]), m. William Clough, of Lee, 1792, who was b. Dec. 5, 1768. She d. Nov. 25, 1865, in her 93d year. Children: —

    1762. SALLY (Clough), b. Apr. 11, 1793, in Lee; resided in Durham, and there d. Apr. 19, 1869, aged 76.
    1763. DAVID, b. June 20, 1795, in Nottingham.
    1764. BENJAMIN, b. Sept. 3, 1798, in Lee; m. Eliza A. Magoon, in Danville, C. E., Feb. 8, 1837. She was b. Mar. 6, 1806, in Shipton, C. E., and there d. June 8, 1844, aged 38. He d. at Durham, Oct. 16, 1865, aged 67. Children: —
        1. LOUISA VICTORIA, b. Oct. 16, 1838, in Shipton; m. John J. Bunker, June 17, 1860.
        2. SUSAN ALMIRA, b. Mar. 7, 1840, in Shipton: see [1635, 9, (1)].
    1765. JERRY, b. Mar. 21, 1801, in Lee.
    1766. SUSANNAH, b. Feb. 19, 1806, in Lee; resided in Canada.
    1767. WILLIAM, b. June 22, 1808, in Lee; d. in infancy.
    1768. BETSY, b. Dec. 23, 1810, in Lee; m. a Fogg, and d. Mar. 1860, in her 50th year.
    1769. WILLIAM, b. Aug. 22, 1813; d. Sept. 27, 1835, aged 22.
    1770. LUCINDA, b. June 26, 1816; d. Sept. 9, 1852, aged 36.

1771. THOMAS[4] [1677] (Job[3], Job[2], Job[1]), at the age of 18, was apprenticed by his father to a tailor " in a neighboring village," probably Dover. Being the youngest apprentice, he was kept by his master at outside drudgery, and was not permitted to " learn the trade" according to agreement. He therefore left the place, after a few months, and returned home. His father approved his course, and soon after accepted his proposition to give him his time, with two hundred dollars, and allow him to " paddle his own canoe." Thus, at nineteen years of age, he located in Portland, Me. (then a part of Massachusetts), rented a shop, hired a first-class foreman, took his seat on the bench, — still as master of the establishment, — and was soon found driving a popular trade, with several hands in his employ, at what would be called, in modern parlance, " a clothing emporium." He continued in this business, with increasing success, till after the war of 1812, near the close of which the tide of his affairs turned, and he became bankrupt by losses on sea and land, though chiefly by " being surety" for some of his friends. He next resided in Durham, Me., a little more than three years ; but, in 1818, joined a colony for the "Far West," consisting of about ten families, with whom he settled in Manchester, Dearborn Co., Ind.   Here he lived as a farmer, and working at his trade winters, till his death, May 7, 1843, aged 6⁹, "in great peace, and in the blissful hope of a happy immortality." He had m. Sally True, daughter of William and Mary True, of Durham, Me., Nov. 27, 1800. She was b. May 31, 1782, and survived her husband, on the old homestead in Indiana, though in feeble health, till Nov. 28, 1847 ; when, in her 65th year, she, too, as surviving friends have every reason to believe, "exchanged her earthly home for the home of angels and the palace of her God." Children : —

1772. WILLIAM [1924], b. May 1, 1802, in Durham, Me.
1773. SARAH (Sallie) [1930], b. Mar. 28, 1804, in Portland.
1774. DAVID [1937], b. Mar. 5, 1807, in Portland.
1775. THOMAS, b. Mar. 8, 1810; d. Aug. 4, 1811, aged 1 year and 5 mos.
1776. MARY TRUE [1947], b. Mar. 31, 1813, in Portland.
1777. BENJAMIN TRUE, b. Mar. 7, 1817, in Durham; d. July 10, 1826, in his 10th year.
1778. JOHN [1953], b. July 20, 1819, in Manchester, Ind.
1779. CAROLINE T. [1957], b. Apr. 7, 1822, in M.
1780. HANNAH TUKEY [1966], b. Oct. 27, 1824, in M.
1781. BENJAMIN [1972], b. Mar. 30, 1829, in M.

1782. SALLY⁴ [1679] (Job³, Job², Job¹), m. James Chesley, of Durham [1621, 7], Feb. 27, 1803, who d. Oct. 7, 1825, aged 47. She d. Apr. 19, 1838, aged 59. Children : —

1783. WILLIAM J. (Chesley), b. Jan. 7, 1804, in Durham ; a justice of the peace; residence, Dover, N. H.
1784. VALENTINE, b. Apr. 27, 1807, in Durham ; d. Dec. 30, 1832, in his 26th year.
1785. LOUISA JANE, b. Aug. 31, 1809, in Rochester.
1786. BENJAMIN, b. May 18, d. Oct. 20, 1819, in Durham.
1787. SALLY RUNNELS, b. Jan. 15, 1821, in D.

1788. JOB⁴ [1682] (Job³, Job², Job¹), resided, as a shoe merchant, in Portland, Me., and there m. Harriet Hatch, dau. of Walter Hatch, of P., Oct. 13, 1814. He d. Sept. 29, 1823, in his 37th year, and she d. July, 1827, both in Portland. Children : —

1789. HARRIET ANN [1979], b. July 15, 1815, in Portland.
1790. WALTER, b. Aug. 7, 1817 ; d. July 4, 1845, in his 28th year.
1791. SARAH, b. Dec. 21, 1819, in Portland; d. May 1, 1838, at Windham, Me. (?), in her 19th year.
1792. MARTHA ELIZABETH [1982], b. Mar. 29, 1822, in P.

1793. HANNAH⁴ [1683] (Job³, Job², Job¹), m., 1st, Williams Tukey, Jan. 1, 1815. He was a tinman, residing in Portland, Me. ; b. Aug. 13, 1792, and d. at P., Apr. 17, 1823, in his 31st year. She m., 2d, Samuel Duran, Aug. 6, 1828, who d. June 3, 1857. She d. Aug. 8, 1855, aged 65 years 4 months. Children : —

1794. GEORGE W. (Tukey), b. Nov. 11, 1815, in Portland ; now a resident of Saco, Me.
1795. SARAH W., b. Jan. 20, 1819 ; d. at Windham, Me. (?), Sept. 28, 1840, in her 21st year.

1796. James G., b. Feb. 13, 1821, in Portland, and there still residing, as a shoe dealer, on Middle Street.
1797. Job Runnels (Duran), b. Nov. 25, 1829.
1798. Josiah, b. Feb. 15, 1836.

1799. Betsy[4] [1685] (Job[3], Job[2], Job[1]), m. Gershom Downs, of Rochester, N. H., Apr. 22, 1811. He d., and she is now living (1870) in Dover. Children : —

1800. Stephen (Downs), b. Feb. 15, 1812, in Rochester.
1801. Lydia, b. Mar. 10, 1814; d. Mar. 7, 1851, aged 37.
1802. Levi, b. Jan. 19, 1816; a soldier in the New Hampshire 13th regiment; enlisted, and d. thirty days afterwards, having been on the field fifteen days, and in the hospital fifteen.
1803. James Monroe, b. Aug. 9, 1820; m. and resides in Dover.
1804. Sarah Ann, b. 1822 (?); m. a Kenney, of Great Falls.
1805. Abigail, b. July, 15, 1827, in Rochester; m. Sylvester Ham, of Dover, at South Berwick, Aug. 22, 1844. He was corporal in the 9th N. H. volunteers; mustered in, Aug. 13, 1862; promoted to sergeant, Nov. 22, 1862; discharged on account of sickness, May 27, 1864. Children : —
  1. Abby Jane (Ham), b. July 1, 1854; d. at Great Falls, Dec. 6, 1856, in her 3d year.
  2. Edwin Forest, b. Jan. 23, 1860, at Great Falls.
1806. William Henry (Downes), b. "Oct. 27, 1829" (on his own authority), in Rochester. Date at first given "1825"; but for an obvious reason, we have him change places with his sister [1805]. He resides, as a farmer, at East Sumner, Oxford Co., Me.; m. Martha S. Robinson, May 13, 1854, who was b. July 15, 1831; served three years in the late war, Co. F, 17th Maine regiment. Children : —
  1. Mary R., b. Dec. 18, 1855.
  2. Rachel F., b. Apr. 18, 1860.
1807. John, b. 1831 (1830), d. Feb. 6, 1860, aged 29.
1808. Louisa Chesley, b. July 25, 1834; resides with her mother in Dover.
1809. Calvin Cutter, b. 1836 (?); a soldier in the New Hampshire 2d regiment; d. at Dover, Jan. 29, 1865, aged 29, having served in the army four years and nine months.
1810. Betsy Jane, b. Aug. 17, 1837; d. Oct. 15, 1858, aged 21.

1811. John[4] [1698] (Miles[3], Job[2], Job[1]), "graduated at the Gilmanton Academy," N. H., 1813; was a teacher and farmer, living first at New Durham, where all his children were born; afterwards at Strafford. Was m. at N. D. by Rev. Joseph Boody, to Hannah Bennett, of Alton, Feb. 21 (2), 1822. She d. June 5, 1850. He d. Feb. 4, 1860, in his 73d year, both at Strafford. Children : —

1812. Adaline [1987], b. Jan. 8, 1824.
1813. John Bennett, b. July 17, 1826; was engaged in the muslin delaine manufactory at Manchester, N. H., for eleven years; then went West, and is supposed to have d. at New Orleans, La., where last heard from, Oct. 1857.
1814. Betsy Jane, b. Oct. 10, 1829; d. Oct. 10, 1837, aged 8.
1815. Horatio Gates [1993], b. Mar. 30, 1836.
1816. George Harrison, b. Mar. 29, 1840; was a shoemaker; enlisted in the New Hampshire 12th regiment, Aug. 1861; was shot in action, at the battle of Chancellorsville, Va., May 3, 1863, aged 23.

1817. Lois[4] [1699] (Miles[3], Job[2], Job[1]), m. John Stevens, farmer, of Tuftonborough, N. H., Sept. 1826. He d , and she was still living on the homestead in T., 1869. Children : —

1818. DANIEL (Stevens), b. July 30, 1827; m. and succeeded his father on their farm in Tuftonborough, where he d. Apr. 2, 1868, in his 41st year.
1819. AVICE, b. Jan. 22, 1829; d. July 29, 1847, in her 19th year.
1820. CHARLES, b. Mar. 24, 1831; d. Feb. 21, 1832, aged 11 months.
1821. SARAH ANN, b. Feb. 11, 1833; m. a Young; resides in Barnstead.
1822. MARY JANE, b. Aug. 30, 1835; m. a Knox; resides in Gardner, Mass.

1823. JONATHAN[4] [1742] (Jonathan[3], Jonathan[2], Job[1]), commenced learning the printer's trade in Albany, N. Y., 1814; was afterwards in the office of one of the daily papers in New York city, and there m. Mary Farrell, of New York, 1816. His health failing, he returned to Conway, N. H., and took the home farm, at the death of his father, 1825. In his will, dated at Conway, "Sept. 26, 1832," he mentions his four oldest children as "now of New York," and the youngest as "now of Conway." We infer from this that the *home* of all his children, except the youngest, was, at the time of his death, in New York; probably with their mother's friends. He d. and was buried in C., Oct. 1832, aged 39. She afterwards returned to New York, and there d. Children : —

1824. JOHN HENRY [1995], b. 1818, in New York city.
1825. MARY JANE, b. 1820, in New York; m. a Schmanouski, who was doing business at 339 Pearl Street, N. Y., in 1853. She was also a milliner in New York at that time.
1826. BETSY, b. 1823, in New York, and there d. *prior* to July 19, 1853.
1827. FRANCES ANN, b. 1825, in Conway, and d. young, in New York, after her mother's return.
1828. JOSEPHINE, b. 1827, in Conway; lived in the family of her brother, in New York; there d. June 26, 1847, aged 20, and was buried in Greenwood Cemetery.

1829. LEVI[4] [1743] (Jonathan[3], Jonathan[2], Job[1]), m. Susan C. Foster, of Danvers, Mass., 1815; was a storekeeper and grocer, first in Jefferson, N. H., then in Dover, where he d. July, 1832, aged 37. She d. with her son, in Wareham, Mass., Aug. 26, 1865. Children : —

1830. WILLIAM AUGUSTUS [1999], b. Dec. 1816.
1831. ABIGAIL AUGUSTA, b. 1820; m. William C. Brown, merchant tailor, of Concord, Mass., 1838; d. July, 1845, aged 25.
1832. ANDREW JACKSON [2003], b. May 20, 1823.
1833. SUSAN ELIZABETH [2008], b. 1826.
1834. SARAH MELISSA, b. 1828; d. young.
1835. LEVI AUGUSTUS [2013], b. Oct. 23, 1829.

1836. BETSY[4] [1744] (Jonathan[3], Jonathan[2], Job[1]), m. Jedediah Lovejoy, of Conway, N. H., farmer, Apr. 27, 1822. He was b. Feb. 26, 1793, son of Jeremiah Lovejoy, and brother of Mrs. Samuel Willey, who perished with her family at the "slide" in the White Mountain Notch, 1826. Their first home was opposite North Conway village, near her father's; afterwards moved to the east part of the town, in the Saco valley, near Fryeburg, Me., where he d. Jan. 22, 1869, in his 76th year, and she d. July 13, 1871, in her 72d year. Children: —

1837. JEREMIAH A. (Lovejoy), b. July 8, 1823; was a teacher at Tarry-town, N. Y.; studied law in Lexington, Ky., graduating at the Transylvania Law School; practised his profession in Marion, Ark., and while a representative to the General Court of that State, d. at Little Rock, Nov. 1854, aged 31.
1838. MARY ANN, b. July 8, 1825; m. Jonathan Melvin Seavey, of North Conway, carpenter, May 7, 1868.
1839. ELIZA ANN, b. Aug. 9, 1827; m. John McMillan, Mar. 9, 1854. He was the son of Gilbert, of Conway, and grandson of An-drew McMillan, a native of Londonderry, Ireland, 1731, who m. Hannah Osgood, of Concord, N. H. He is now a farmer and pro-prietor of the "McMillan House," at No. Conway. Children: —
  1. GILBERT (McMillan), b. Aug. 15, 1855; d. Dec. 13, 1857, aged 2 years 4 months.
  2. JENNIE, b. Oct. 29, 1860.
1840. WILLIAM (Lovejoy), b. May 19, 1830; was a blacksmith in Gil-manton and Concord, N. H., till the death of his next younger brother; now (1871) a farmer on his father's place in Conway; post-office address, "Fryeburg, Me." He m., 1st, Mary Jane (Frances) Hutchinson, of Gilmanton, Apr. 27, 1854, who d. Mar. 26, 1862, in Concord; m., 2d, Elizabeth Osgood, of Con-way, Nov. 29, 1866. Children: —
  1. JENNIE, b. Aug. 28, 1861 (first wife), in Concord.
  2. FRED B., b. Sept. 17, 1867 (second wife), in Conway.
  3. CARRIE OSGOOD, b. Oct. 26, 1869, in Conway.
1841. MARSHAL, b. Apr. 5, 1832; settled with his father in Conway, and there d. Apr. 22, 1864, aged 32.
1842. SOPHIA SPRING, b. May 31, 1835; m. Charles Hazen Osgood, of North Conway, farmer and stage proprietor, Jan. 12, 1858. Children: —
  1. JENNY STEELE (Osgood), b. Feb. 7, 1859.
  2. FRED, b. Sept. 6, 1861; d. Dec. 17, 1864, aged 3 yrs. 3 ms. 11 dys.
  3. MARSHAL LOVEJOY, b. Aug. 13, 1864.
  4. GEORGIANNA SOUTHER, b. Aug. 1, 1866.
  5. CHARLES HAZEN, b. Feb. 4, 1869.
1843. EMMA (Lovejoy), b. July 15, 1837; d. July 1, 1853, aged 16.
1844. ALBION, b. June 27, 1839; m. Margaret D. Eastman [1739, 5], of Conway, Mar. 22, 1868; residence at Rantoul, Ill. Children: —
  1. BESSIE CUMMINGS, b. Mar. 1, 1869.
  2. GEORGE DOUGLASS, b. Sept. 15, 1871, in Rantoul.

1845. ASA[4] [1746] (Levi[3], Jonathan[2], Job[1]), m. Mary Ann Haley, of New Market, Mar. 17 (May 25), 1829; resided as a farmer, first at Lee, then at South New Market, where he d. Aug. 15, 1853, aged 56. She d. Aug. 24, 1867. Children: —

1846. LEVI G. [2016], b. Mar. 30, 1830, in Lee.
1847. ASA JASPER [2018], b. Jan. 7, 1834, in New Market.
1848. LUTHER CALVIN, b. Nov. 28, 1835, in Lee; a farmer, at South New Market, 1869.
1849. MARY S., b. Sept. 5, 1843, in South New Market.

1850. BETSY[4] [1747] (Levi[3], Jonathan[2], Job[1]), m. David Mathes, of Lee, July 28, 1823. He d., and her home is now (1871) with her youngest daughter, in Lee. Children: —

1851. ELIZABETH (Mathes), b. Oct. 4, 1824; m. Josiah Webber, of New Ipswich, N. H., tailor, May, 1860. Child : —
> 1. GENEVIEVE (Webber), b. Oct. 10, 1861.

1852. JUDITH (Mathes), b. Nov. 21, 1828; m. Solomon Pendergast, of Durham, N. H., May, 1850; a farmer, now living in Hutchinson, Minn. Children : —
> 1. LYDIA MARIA CHILD (Pendergast), b. Jan. 24, 1852.
> 2. MAURICE D., b. Apr. 5, 1861.

1853. LYDIA ANN (Mathes), b. Nov. 19, 1830; m. George Edward Durgin, Apr. 1854. He is a farmer in Lee, N. H., and has held every town office, including that of town clerk for several years. Was representative of Lee in the State legislature, 1871 and 1872. P. O. address, "Wadleigh's Falls, N. H." Child : —
> 1. ELLA GERTRUDE (Durgin), b. Mar. 20, 1856.

1854. ABIGAIL[4] [1748] (Levi[3], Jonathan[2], Job[1]), m. John Shaw, farmer, of Epping, N. H., Sept. 9, 1820, at Lee. He d. at Nottingham, Mar. 15, 1846. She resides at North Andover, Mass., 1871. Children : —

1855. ABIGAIL JANE (Shaw), b. July 2, 1821, in Epping; d. Sept. 18, 1843, at Nottingham, aged 22.

1856. SARAH, b. Feb. 3, 1823, in Epping; m. Henry Kenniston, mason, of North Andover, Mass., Apr. 1847. Children : —
> 1. EMMA LADORA (Kenniston), b. July 13, 1849.
> 2. MARY ABBY, b. 1851; d. young.
> 3. ETTA, b. 1853; d. 1861, aged 8.
> 4. IDA, b. 1855; d. young.
> 5. MARIA, b. July 10, 1857.
> 6. MARY LIZZIE, b. 1859; d. young.
> 7. NELLIE, b. Aug. 10, 1861.
> 8. MABEL, b. Sept. 1863.

1857. MARY ELIZABETH (Shaw), b. Feb. 6, 1828, in Epping.

1858. HARRIET ANN, b. Mar. 24, 1831, in Lee; m. Jeremiah Boughton, of Springfield, Mass., railroad machinist, 1860. Children : —
> 1. ETTA (Boughton), b. Sept. 1863; d. Aug. 1865, in her 2d year.
> 2. FREDDIE, b. Nov. 25, 1866.

1859. MARIA (Shaw), b. Apr. 11, 1833, in Lee; d. at Indian Orchard (Springfield), Mass., June 19, 1863, aged 30.

1860. EMELINE, b. Nov. 16, 1836, in Epping; m. Otis Sylvester Needham, carpenter, of Springfield, Mass., 1857; now residing in Lawrence, Mass. Children : —
> 1. MARIA (Needham), b. Aug. 10, 1858.
> 2. FRANK, b. Jan 29, 1862.

1861. SUSAN (Shaw), b. June 28, 1839, in Nottingham, and there d. Mar. 2, 1846, in her 7th year.

1862. MARY[4] [1749] (Levi[3], Jonathan[2], Job[1]), m. Dr. Stephen Brown, of Deerfield, N. H., Apr. 22, 1830. He was b. Apr. 12, 1803; a practising physician for many years in Deerfield, where she d. Jan. 26, 1842, in her 40th year. Children : —

1863. MOSES (Brown), b. May 29, 1831; m. Susan R. James, Apr. 19, 1855. Children : —
> 1. MARY L., b. Mar. 8, 1856.
> 2. CHARLES S., b. Sept. 13, 1857.

1864. JOSEPH T., b June 28, 1833; m. Mary E. Batchelder, Sept. 24, 1862. Child : —
> 1. CORA M., b. Sept. 3, 1866.

1865. MARY A., b. Aug. 3, 1837.

1866. MARTHA A., b. Jan. 3, d. May 10, 1842.

1867. JONATHAN[4] [1750] (Levi[3], Jonathan[2], Job[1]).   Having learned the carpenter's trade, he went South in the fall of 1827, settled in Mobile, Ala., and there m., 1st, Mary Elizabeth Cleveland, of New York, Mar. 25, 1834. He moved to New Orleans, La., fall of 1847, where she d. Jan. 6, 1857.   He m., 2d, Mrs. Margaret E. Thompson, of New Orleans, Feb. 2, 1858, and in May following removed to Summit, Pike Co., Miss., where still residing.   Children : —

1868.   THEODORE WATSON, b. Dec. 2, 1835 ; a farmer, 1872, at Dry Grove, Hinds Co., Miss.
1869.   ALONZO V., b. July 13, 1837 ; d. of yellow fever, Aug. 4, 1853, aged 16.
1870.   FREDERICK J., b. June 28, 1839 ; d. at Mobile, May 13, 1840, aged 10 months 15 days.
1871.   MARY JANE [2021], b. Jan. 1, 1841.
1872.   CAROLINE MADORA, b. Dec. 28, 1843 ; d. Feb. 20, 1862, aged 18.
1873.   GEORGE WASHINGTON [2029], b. Oct. 19, 1845.
1874.   EMMA, b. Mar. 19, 1848 ; d. in New Orleans, Nov. 20, 1851, in her 4th year.
1875.   ANNA GLOVER, b. Nov. 11, 1850.
1876.   JOHN, b. Sept. 24, 1852 ; d. of yellow fever, Aug. 22, 1853, aged 11 months.
1877.   CLEVELAND, b. Feb. 19, 1854.
1878.   EDWIN BRYANT (second wife), b. Dec. 6, 1858.
1879.   CORIAN, b. Mar. 1, 1860.
1880.   ROBERT LEE, b. July 8, 1863.
1881.   OCTAVIA, b. Sept. 4, 1865.
1882.   EUGENE, b. Aug. 5, 1867.
1883.   JONATHAN, b. Aug. 12, 1869 ; d. Oct. 28, 1870, aged 14 mos. 16 days.

1884.   MARY[4] [1754] (Samuel[3], Samuel[2], Job[1]), was m. at the house of her grandfather, Paul Farnham, to Stephen Hersom, Jan. 8, 1803 ; resided at Lebanon, Me., where he d. May 1, 1841, and she d July 21, 1850, aged 66.   Children, b. in Lebanon : —

1885.   SAMUEL (Hersom), b. May 22, 1804 ; now residing in Illinois.
1886.   JOHN, b. Oct. 23, 1805 ; present residence in Lebanon.
1887.   NAHUM, b. Sept. 6, 1807 ; also residing in Lebanon.
1888.   LUCIUS, b. May 29, 1809 ; see [1911] ; d. in Lebanon, June 15, 1867, aged 58.
1889.   OLIVE, b. Sept. 11, 1811 ; m. a Sherman, living in Shapleigh, Me.

1890.   EUNICE[4] [1755] (Samuel[3], Samuel[2], Job[1]), m. Simon Peter Downs, at Shapleigh, Me., Aug. 29, 1810 ; resided first at Lebanon, Me., and finally at Freedom, N. H., where he d. Sept. 25, 1854, and she d. Jan. 7, 1860, in her 74th year.   Children : —

1891.   SALLY (Downs), b. Aug. 15, 1811, in Lebanon.
1892.   PAUL, b. Aug. 8, 1813, in Lebanon ; d. Oct. 27, 1866, at Tamworth, N. H., aged 53.
1893.   EUNICE, b. June 13, 1815, in Lebanon ; d. at Freedom, May 19, 1861, in her 46th year.
1894.   SAMUEL, b. Sept. 9, 1817, in Lebanon ; d. at Eaton, N. H., June 9, 1821, in his 4th year.
1895.   MARY, b. Nov. 3, 1821, in Eaton ; d. Oct. 30, 1850, at Freedom, aged 29.
1896.   HIRAM, b. June, 1823, in Eaton, and there d. Apr. 15, 1824, aged 10 months.

1897. SIMON P., b. July 1, 1825, in Eaton.
1898. ELIZABETH ANN, b. Mar. 28, 1828, in Effingham, N. H.
1899. NATHANIEL, b. Aug. 5, 1832, in Freedom.

1900. SAMUEL[4] [1756] (Samuel[3], Samuel[2], Job[1]), m. Hannah Farnham, of Acton, Me., Jan. 3, 1811. She was the daughter of Ralph Farnham, see [1753]; was b. Mar. 20, 1788, and d. at Acton, Oct. 14, 1861, in her 74th year; on her gravestone, " My trust is in God." He was a farmer, and deacon of the Free Will Baptist Church, at Acton (Milton Mills), and there d. Mar. 29 (27), 1854, of small-pox, in his 66th year. On his gravestone, " My record is on high;" a sentiment most appropriate to himself. Children : —

1901. ASENATH [2031], b. Oct. 28, 1811.
1902. ELI [2040], b. Feb. 21, 1815.
1903. JOHN [2046], b. Mar. 9, 1817.
1904. ASA, b. Apr. 10, 1818; d. Mar. 30, 1824, in his 6th year.
1905. HOSEA [2049], b. July 11, 1820.
1906. ISRAEL [2051], b. July 5, 1823.
1907. ALVAH [2060], b. Dec. 1, 1825.
1908. WILLIAM BUZZELL [2068], b. Aug. 14, 1828.
1909. ALMIRA [2072], b. Jan. 18, 1831.

1910. PAUL[4] [1757] (Samuel[3], Samuel[2], Job[1]), m. Ann Worster, of Portsmouth, N. H., June 15, 1816. She was b. Oct. 5, 1793, in Berwick, Me., and was still living, 1869, as his widow, in Acton, Me., where he had resided, though officiating as a clergyman of the Christian denomination in various other places as well as Acton, chiefly at Sanford, Me., and at Wolfborough, Tuftonborough, and Moultonborough, N. H. He was ordained to the work of the ministry, June 17, 1829, at Lebanon, Me. (Little River Falls), and continued in the same till his health failed, Dec. 1841. After his ordination, he became pastor of a newly-formed church in Sanford, for several years, and subsequently devoted himself to visiting the churches of his order in Maine, New Hampshire, and Vermont, " which labors were blest to the conversion of many souls to Christ." He d. of dropsy, at Acton, Aug. 2, 1842, aged 52, " having labored for the cause of his Heavenly Master almost to the last." Children, b. in Acton : —

1911. MARTHA ANN, b. Mar. 16, 1817; m. Lucius Hersom, of Lebanon, Oct. 3, 1841, see [1888], and settled in North Lebanon, where she still lives.
1912. JONATHAN PRESCOTT [2076], b. Apr. 16, 1820.
1913. NATHANIEL JACKSON, b. Aug. 4, 1822; followed the sea from early youth; was first mate of a vessel; when last heard from, at Mobile, Ala., 1855, he had been to the Straits of Gibraltar, and was about sailing again for Europe; is supposed to have d. soon after, aged 33.
1914. JOANNA FARNHAM [2079], b. Mar. 22, 1825.
1915. WILLIAM WORSTER, b. Dec. 2, 1827; a clerk in the war department, at Washington, D. C., 1869; having been placed upon the pension roll " for wounds received in the service of his country." Had m. Asenath C. Bean, of Alfred, Me., Oct. 3, 1851.
1916. LUCETTA FALL [2082], b. Jan. 8, 1830.

1917.   JACOB PICKERING, b. Feb. 15, 1833; d. Aug. 7, 1837, in his 5th year.
1918.   LORENZO PARKER, b. Oct. 15, 1835.
1919.   JACOB PICKERING, b. July 7, 1838; served in the late war three
        years; "Corp., Co. F, 8th Maine regiment, Sept. 7, 1861;"
        "promoted to sergeant." Had repaired to San Francisco,
        Cal., 1869, for the restoration of his health, lost in the service.

1920.   ASA[4] [1760] (Samuel[3], Samuel[2], Job[1]), was a tanner and
currier, living first in Portsmouth, then at Wolfborough Centre,
N. H., and finally at Acton, Me., where he d Apr. 1, 1839, in his
43d year. He m. Hannah, daughter of Joseph Tarlton, of Rye,
N. H., 1821 (2), who was residing, 1871, at Dedham, Mass.
Children : —

1921.   SAMUEL [2084], b. Dec. 8, 1823.
1922.   JOHN, b. May 31, 1825; d. while serving his apprenticeship as a
        mason, in Boston, Mass., May 18, 1845, aged 20.
1923.   MARY JANE [2090], b. Aug. 14, 1827, in Wolfborough.

FIFTH GENERATION.

1924. WILLIAM[5] [1772] (Thomas[4], Job[3], Job[2], Job[1]), united
with the Methodist Episcopal Church when a child, in Maine, and
felt, after moving to Indiana, an often-recurring impression to con-
secrate himself to the gospel ministry. Resisting this positive call
to duty for several years, he was at last " thrust into the Lord's
vineyard " by the Rev. John Strange, in the spring of 1824, and
placed, as third preacher, on the Madison circuit, Indiana. The
next fall, he was admitted on trial in the old Ohio conference, then
embracing nearly the whole State of Ohio, Michigan Territory, and
portions of other States. Over much of this territory he travelled,
as an itinerant minister, for nearly thirty consecutive years. In
1828, when on the Delaware circuit in Michigan, he had thirty-
three standing appointments each month. The two following years
were spent at a station on the Sandusky bay. The glorious revival,
" beginning in the old cooper's shop," and the building of the *first*
meeting-house in what is now the beautiful city of Sandusky, —
with lumber brought in schooner from Detroit through a terrific
gale, — afford some of the most pleasant personal reminiscences of
his itinerant life. Appointed to the Tiffin station in 1837–8, he
was presiding elder of that district for the four following years ;
was delegate from the North Ohio conference to the most memor-
able of all the general conferences, at New York in 1844 ; but in
the fall of this year, being thrown from his horse, and badly
breaking his right limb, the idea of " location " was first suggested,
though not finally realized, till 1851. From this time, for fifteen
years, continuing his residence in Wellington, O., he preached to
that one people over twelve hundred times, and saw the log-cabin
meeting-house exchanged for one of the most tasty and substantial
brick church edifices in Northern Ohio ; that, too, in the face of
the expressed opinion of another, that " a local preacher of the
Methodist church is nothing but a cipher ! " (The above is substantially from the " Cincinnati Christian Advocate " of Nov. 4, 1868.)
    In 1865, he removed to Cleveland, O., his present residence, 1872,
where, at the age of 70, he is still able to work six days in the
week for a living, and gladly to preach on the seventh, " without
money and without price." He m. Clarissa House, at Perkins, O.,

Aug. 18, 1831, who was b. June 3, 1812, in Glastenbury, Conn. Children : —

1925. MARY JANE [2095], b. June 3, 1833, in Elyria, O.
1926. LUCRETIA DAY [2100], b. Jan. 11, 1836, in Wooster, Wayne Co., O.
1927. ELIZABETH EBBERT [2102], b. Dec. 11, 1838, in Tiffin City, O.
1928. LOUISE CENTENARIA [2105], b. Nov. 23 1839, in Tiffin, O.
1929. WILLIAM HENRY, b. Apr. 15, 1842, in Tiffin City. He was a member of the "Cleveland Grays," Co. A, 150th regiment Ohio National Guards; term of service in the "War for the Union," four months. Is at present (1872) of the firm of "Runnells & Manchester," underwriters, 211 Superior Street, Cleveland, O.

1930. SARAH[5] [1773] (Thomas[4], Job[3], Job[2], Job[1]), m., 1st, Major Huestis, Nov. 15, 1826, in Manchester, Ind. He was a Quaker by persuasion, and d. in Texas, Sept. 4, 1857. She m., 2d, George D. Drake, Dec. 22, 1859, in Dallas, Tex. Present residence, Fort Scott, Kansas. Children : —

1931. HENRY (Huestis), b. Aug. 2, 1828, in Manchester, Ind.; m., and has three children; present residence in Collin Co., Texas.
1932. DAVID RUNNELLS, b. Oct. 18, 1834, in Manchester; residence, Olympia, Washington Territory.
1933. CAROLINE, b. Jan. 26, 1838, in Jefferson, Ind.; m. Lyman D. Drake, Mar. 11, 1858; resides at Fort Scott, Kansas; five children.
1934. THOMAS RUNNELLS, b. Dec. 18, 1843; served in the Union army about four years, during the rebellion, in Co. K, 12th Kansas Infantry; present residence, San Antonio, Texas.
1935. STEPHEN, b. May 15, 1847, in Jefferson Co., Ind.; d. July 26, 1848, aged 14 months 11 days.
1936. ALBERT, b. Sept. 9, 1849; d. Nov. 11, 1866, in Cherokee, Kansas, aged 17.

1937. DAVID[5] [1774] (Thomas[4], Job[3], Job[2], Job[1]), resided in Manchester, Ind., till Nov. 1850, and then emigrated with all his family to Henry Co., Ill., changing his occupation as a tailor to that of farming on the Illinois prairies. "Having lived on the same farm for twenty years, he knows what can be done to supply the deficiency of timber. Of the shade, ornamental and fruit trees *planted by himself*, the largest, a silver leaf, is now six feet eight inches in circumference! These trees break off the bleak winds of winter, and afford a refreshing shade in the heat of summer, besides an abundant supply of fruits and flowers." He m., 1st, Almira Tozier, Nov. 11, 1832, in Manchester. She d. Sept. 15, 1840, and he m., 2d, Sarah B. Clark, Feb. 18, 1841. Children : —

1938. ALMIRA JANE, b. Aug. 13, 1833, in Manchester, and there d. June 22, 1834, aged 10 months 9 days.
1939. MARGARET Jane [2108], b. Apr. 7, 1835.
1940. WILLIAM ALONZO, b. Aug. 13, 1837; d. Sept. 1838, aged 13 mos.
1941. SIMEON TOZIER [2115], b. Oct. 31, 1839.
1942. MARY E. [2117], b. Jan. 27, 1842 (second wife).
1943. THOMAS H. [2119], b. Oct. 14, 1844.
1944. CALVIN R., b. Apr. 6, 1847; publisher's special agent; residing at Peoria, Ill.
1945. DAVID WESLEY, b. Feb. 2, 1850.
1946. SARAH ADELAIDE, b. Nov. 7, 1857, in Wheatland, Ill.

1947. MARY TRUE[5] [1776] (Thomas[4], Job[3], Job[2], Job[1]), m., 1st, Rollin Tyler Tozier, Dec. 25, 1831. He was b. in Maine, Aug. 16, 1809; a farmer, residing in Indiana, where he d. July 11, 1846. She m., 2d, H. Sayles; present residence in Olympia, Washington Territory, where "the flowers are blooming all through the woods and ploughing commences by the middle of March." Children, b. in Indiana: —

    1948. CHARLES T. (Tozier), b. Nov. 7, 1832.
    1949. HENRY H., b. Dec. 26, 1834; d. in Oregon, Mar. 10, 1864, in his 30th year.
    1950. HARRIET T., b. Sept. 18, 1837.
    1951. CAROLINE A., b. Dec. 19, 1839; m. a Magill.
    1952. MARY JANE, b. June 6, 1842.

1953. JOHN[5] [1778] (Thomas[4], Job[3], Job[2], Job[1]), m. Rosanna Robinson, Sept. 1, 1850, in Manchester, Ind.; present residence, Mineral, Bureau Co., Ill. He enlisted as a private in Co. H, 1st regiment of Illinois artillery; enrolled, Mar. 7, 1862, for three years; discharged, Oct. 20, 1862, at Memphis, Tenn., on surgeon's certificate, by reason of "disability from partial paralysis and constant neuralgia, contracted since enlistment." Children: —

    1954. LOUISE MERCELLA, b. June 25, 1851, in Milo, Ill.
    1955. WILLIAM DAVID, b. Jan. 22, 1854, in Milo.
    1956. CLARISSA CLEMENTINE, b. Jan. 17, 1860, at Mineral, Ill.

1957. CAROLINE T.[5] [1779] (Thomas[4], Job[3], Job[2], Job[1]), m. Stephen M. Clark, Mar. 29, 1842. The family removed to Bureau Co., Ill., Oct. 1844, where she d. Feb. 22, 1865, in her 43d year. A coincidence seldom occurring appears in the following record, the birthdays of the eldest and the youngest children being the same, with nineteen years intervening! Also seven daughters in succession: —

    1958. EDGAR A. (Clark), b. Aug. 13, 1843, in Manchester, Ind.; m. Louise Michael, Mar. 1870.
    1959. CLARA E., b. Oct. 18, 1845; m. William W. Clement, of New York, Dec. 25, 1867; residing, at present, in Caldwell Co., Mo. Children: —
       1. CLARENCE A. (Clement), b. Feb. 13, 1869.
       2. EMMA L., b. Oct. 26, 1870.
    1960. Emma A. (Clark), b. May 19, 1848; m. Levi Rich, Oct. 3, 1868, and d. in Missouri, Oct. 20, 1870, in her 23d year. Child: —
       1. WILLIAM L. (Rich), b. Aug. 1870.
    1961. SOPHIA JANE (Clark), b. Nov. 11, 1851.
    1962. MARIANNI, b. Aug. 15, 1854.
    1963. SARAH LOUISE, b. June 12, 1857.
    1964. ELLA GERTRUDE, b. Oct. 24, 1859.
    1965. FLORENCE CAROLINE, b. Aug. 13, 1862.

1966. HANNAH TUKEY[5] [1780] (Thomas[4], Job[3], Job[2], Job[1]), m. Aurel Albee, May 8, 1850, in Marshall, Ill. Children: —

    1967. WILLIAM RUNNELLS (Albee), b. Feb. 24, 1851.
    1968. EDWIN, b. Dec. 12, 1852; d. Mar. 2, 1854, in his 2d year.
    1969. FREDERICK TRUE, b. Nov. 14, 1854, in Henry, Ill.
    1970. JOSEPH TOZIER, b. Dec. 28, 1857.
    1971. MARY ELIZA, b. Jan. 1, 1861.

1972. BENJAMIN⁵ [1781] (Thomas⁴, Job³, Job². Job¹), m. Caroline Snell, Sept. 18, 1853 : a farmer, first in Wheatland, Ill., where his children were all born ; now the owner of a valuable farm in " 76 Township, Washington Co., Iowa," on a branch of the Rock Island Railroad. His crop of corn in 1871 was three thousand 'bushels. His wife d. Nov. 8, 1870. Children : —

    1973. SARAH FRANCES, b. Oct. 24, 1856,
    1974. CHARLES MAURICE, b. Feb. 28, 1859 ; d. Nov. 28, 1870, in his 12th year.
    1975. FLORENCE ADA, b. Feb. 8, 1861.
    1976. LAURA JANE, b. Feb 11, 1863.
    1977. EDNA ELIZABETH, b May 13, 1865.
    1978. ELLA MAY, b. Dec. 12, 1868.

1979. HARRIET ANN⁵ [1789] (Job⁴, Job³, Job², Job¹), m. William Henry Eastman, of Portland, Me., Nov. 20, 1840. He was a carpenter, living first in Boston, now in San Francisco, Cal. Children : —

    1980. HENRIETTA (Eastman), b. June 1, 1843, in Boston.
    1981. EDWARD, b. June 10, 1845, in B.

1982. MARTHA ELIZABETH⁵ [1792] (Job⁴, Job³, Job², Job¹), took the name of Swan, having been adopted by William Swan, of Portland, Me., at the death of her mother ; m. Rufus William Thaxter, of Portland, merchant, Aug. 7, 1844 ; now resides at Yarmouth, Me. Children : —

    1983. MARY SWAN (Thaxter), b. July 21, 1846, in Portland.
    1984. WILLIAM SWAN, b Oct. 12, 1849, in P.
    1985. MARTHA ELLA, b. Sept. 20, 1852, in P.
    1986. EDWARD RUSSEL, b. Feb. 15, 1857, in Yarmouth.

1987. ADALINE⁵ [1812] (John⁴, Miles³, Job², Job¹), was m. at New Durham, N. H., by Rev. Joseph Boody, to William Sanders, farmer, of Pittsfield, Aug. 6, 1848. Children, b. in P. : —

    1988. JENNIE E. (Sanders), b. July 17, 1849.
    1989. ALVIN W., b. Oct. 5, 1850.
    1990. MARTIN M., b. Feb. 13, 1853.
    1991. CLARA A , b. Aug. 6, 1854.
    1992. GEORGE D., b. Dec. 29, 1862.

1993. HORATIO GATES⁵ [1815] (John⁴, Miles³, Job², Job¹), m. Jennett Dingley, of Casco, Me., Feb. 1859 ; was a shoemaker ; resided in Casco, and there d. Apr. 27, 1864, aged 28. Child : —

    1994. SCOTT, b. July 12, 1860 ; d. Mar 8, 1861, aged 8 months.

1995. JOHN HENRY⁵ [1824] (Jonathan⁴, Jonathan³, Jonathan², Job¹), was a " tin maker " in New York city, and doing a prosperous business, at 101 Houston Street, in 1848 ; m. Celia ——, 1842, d. of consumption, after nine months' illness, Jan. 11, 1852, aged 34, and was buried in Greenwood Cemetery beside his beloved sister Josephine. Children : —

1996. HESTER, b. 1843.
1997. CECELIA, b. Apr. 1845.
1998. JOSEPHINE, b. May 1, 1848.

1999. WILLIAM AUGUSTUS[5] [1830] (Levi[4], Jonathan[3], Jonathan[2], Job[1]), took his degree as a physician from the Philadelphia Medical School, and is now a resident of Jonestown, Lebanon Co., Penn. Has been a member of the Pennsylvania legislature ; changed his surname to " Barry," and m. Rachel Eaches, of Reading, Pa. Children : —

2000. HENRY AUGUSTUS.
2001. MARY ; d. 1871.
2002. EMMA.

2003. ANDREW JACKSON[5] [1832] (Levi[4], Jonathan[3], Jonathan[2], Job[1]), graduated, as a physician, at the American University, in Philadelphia, Pa., 1844. Practised first in Boston, Mass., for nine years ; afterwards in Monument and Raynham, Mass. ; is now (1872) successfully established in Stoughton, Mass. He is so fortunate as to possess a " Coat of Arms " of the " Runnells " family, obtained for him by an English gentleman, " from the books of Heraldry, in the Library of the Royal College, in England " (see General Introduction). He m., 1st, Rebecca Smith Philips, of Providence, R. I., Oct. 10, 1844, who d. 1863 ; m., 2d, Susan Elder Perry, of Monument (Sandwich), Mass., Sept. 16, 1863, who was b. Sept. 16, 1836. Children : —

2004. ABBY ELIZA, b. May 2, 1847, in Dartmouth, Mass.
2005. EUGENE FOSTER, b. Mar. 7, 1850, in Providence, R. I.
2006. ANDREW FOSTER, b. Apr. 7, 1852, in Boston ; d. at Woburn, Mass., Dec. 5, 1857, in his 6th year.
2007. SUSIE C. (second wife), b. Aug. 15, 1868, at Monument, Mass.

2008. SUSAN ELIZABETH[5] [1833] (Levi[4], Jonathan[3], Jonathan[2], Job[1]), m. Josiah Johnson, of Plymouth, Mass., Sept. 2, 1848, who was b. Aug. 12, 1808. He was a cooper by trade, and lived afterwards in New Bedford, Mass., where he d. Dec. 25, 1867, aged 59, and she still resides, his widow. Children, b. in N. B. : —

2009. WILLIAM H. (Johnson), b. June 22, 1849.
2010. HENRY A., b June 22, 1851.
2011. JOSIAH E., b. Apr. 21, 1853.
2012. GEORGE H., b. Oct. 18, 1855, and LEVI R., b. Apr. 23, 1858 (record came too late to assign this youngest child a separate number).

2013. LEVI AUGUSTUS[5] [1835] (Levi[4], Jonathan[3], Jonathan[2], Job[1]), was formerly a merchant tailor, residing in Wareham, Mass. ; is now (1872) a resident of Hyde Park, Mass., in the grocery business (?). He m. Selina G. Savery, of Wareham, Nov. 24, 1853, who was b. June 19, 1833. Children : —

2014. EDGAR A., b. Mar. 22, 1855.
2015. CORA A., b. Apr. 24, 1864.

2016. LEVI G.[5] [1846] (Asa[4], Levi[3], Jonathan[2], Job[1]), was a machinist in Manchester, N. H., where he m. Angeline Cawley,

Sept. 23, 1850 ; d. Nov. 23, 1854, at Lawrence, Mass. (?), in his 25th year. Child : —

2017. EMMA J., b. Oct. 30, 1854, in Lawrence; d. Nov. 16, 1855, aged 1 year and 17 days.

2018. ASA JASPER[5] [1847] (Asa[4], Levi[3], Jonathan[2], Job[1]), now resides, as a shoemaker, in Epping, N. H., having m. Mary S. Carr, Sept. 24, 1855. Children : —

2019. HERBERT J., b. Aug. 10, 1856.
2020. FRANK C., b. Jan. 28, 1860.

2021. MARY JANE[5] [1871] (Jonathan[4], Levi[3], Jonathan[2], Job[1]), m. George Soule, of New Orleans, La., Sept. 6, 1860. He was b. in New York, May 14, 1834, his ancestors being of German and French origin, and among the early settlers of New York. He is the author of "The Analytic and Philosophic Commercial and Exchange Calculator," the most elaborate work ever published on the subject. "All the known and approved improvements and contractions in the handling of numbers, and many new and original practical problems, embracing the whole field of business life, are contained in this book." "It presents the history, and discusses and elucidates financial questions arising in connection with stocks and bonds, exchange, banking, insurance, manufacturing, merchandise, planting, etc." "It was composed, printed, and bound in New Orleans, and throughout its *eight hundred and eighty pages*, presents the rarest gems of the science of numbers." "The demand for the book by business men, teachers, and students is beyond precedent, and its superior merits win the highest encomiums from all who peruse its pages." Mr. Soule is now (1872) the principal and proprietor of "Soule's Commercial and Telegraph College," in New Orleans, founded in 1856 ; chartered in 1861. He also publishes "Soule's Commercial College Journal," in New Orleans, a monthly, now upon its fifteenth volume. He served as captain, major, and colonel in the Confederate army, for three years and nine months, during the late civil war ; was wounded and taken prisoner at the battle of Shiloh, Miss. Children : —

2022. GEORGE (Soule), b. Aug. 22, 1861, in New Orleans; d. Dec. 25, 1864, aged 3 years 4 months.
2023. MARIE LOUISE, b. Jan. 31, 1864, at Summit, Miss.; d. July 11, 1865, in her 2d year.
2024. ALBERT LEE, b. Dec. 16, 1865, in New Orleans, as were the following children.
2025. EDWIN, b. Sept. 8, 1867.
2026. MARY ELIZABETH, b. Nov. 9, 1868.
2027. WILLIAM HOLCOMBE, b. Mar. 9, 1869.
2028. FRANK, b. Sept. 11, 1871.

2029. GEORGE WASHINGTON[5] [1873] (Jonathan[4], Levi[3], Jonathan[2], Job[1]), served three years in the late war, belonging to the "8th Mississippi regiment of cavalry, Co. H"; m. Anna Mariah

Wingate, Aug. 28, 1870 ; is now a farmer, residing near Dry Grove, Hinds County, Miss.   Child : —

2030. ROBERT EDMUND LEE, b. Sept. 25, 1871, at Dry Grove.

2031. ASENATH[5] [1901] (Samuel[4], Samuel[3], Samuel[2], Job[1]), m. John Marsh, of Acton, Me., Feb. 7, 1838. He d. at A , Apr. 19, 1867. Children : —

2032. JOHN EPHRAIM (Marsh), b. Nov. 11, 1838 ; enlisted in the 2d regiment U. S. sharpshooters ; served three years nine months, and then re-enlisted in the 5th New Hampshire regiment, till the close of the war.
2033. HANNAH ELIZABETH, b. Nov. 14, 1840.
2034. THOMAS DREW, b. Oct. 12, 1843 ; enlisted in the 7th New Hampshire regiment for three years ; after which he served in the 18th N. H. regiment till the close of the war.
2035. OSCAR FITZON, b. Jan. 23, 1846.
2036. ASENATH ANNETTE, b. Dec. 8, 1848.
2037. LUCRETIA, } b. Jan. 22, 1851.
2038. LETITIA,   }
2039. MIRA (Amanda), b Dec. 4, 1854 ; d. May 17 (gravestone says "21"), 1859, in her 5th year.

2040. ELI[5] [1902] (Samuel[4], Samuel[3], Samuel[2], Job[1]), settled as a farmer in Acton, Me., near Fox's Ridge, and m. Sally M. Dore, of A., Apr. 11, 1839. Children : —

2041. MARY AUGUSTA, b. Feb. 2, 1840 ; d. Mar. 24, 1844, aged 4 years 1 month 22 days.
2042. SABINA EMILY, b. Nov. 27, 1841 ; m. Gorham Parks Boston, of St Albans, Me., Jan. 1, 1866 ; now living in Acton.
2043. CHARLES AUGUSTIN [2121], b. Oct. 18, 1845.
2044. JOSEPH FULTON, b. Mar. 30, 1851 ; now "in the picture-frame business," Boston, Mass.
2045. ANSON ELI, b. Oct. 28, 1853 ; d. Aug. 17, 1868, in his 15th year, in consequence of a fall from a swing "at the height of thirty feet" (as reported in the "Boston Journal"), "fracturing his scull," and producing other injuries which proved fatal. This distressing accident occurred at half-past nine on Saturday evening, August 15th, at the house of a neighbor ; hence the allusions in the following "Lines," being the first of several stanzas, composed on his death by his sister-in-law, Mrs. Nellie A. Reynolds [2121], and afterwards printed : —

> " 'T was evening, and his work was done, —
>   His six days' toil was o'er ;
> A happy boy he left his home, —
>   Came back, alas, no more !

> " He, with his friends, upon the hill
>   Had often met to sing ;
> But now ambition led him on
>   Into the fatal *swing*."

His brother Joseph F. [2044] also dedicated a few verses to his mother, — in view of this and her previous affliction, — of which are the following : —

" There 's been a shadow in our home, —
A dreary void within my heart, —
Since Anson, dear, went down alone
Into the shadowed valley dark.

. . . .

" A sister, too, was called, before
She ever dreamed of earthly care;
But they will meet together now,
And know and love each other there.

" Her gentle tones, — his loving smile, —
Will never, never greet us more,
Till, freed by *Christ* from earthly guile,
We meet them on that brighter shore."

2046.   JOHN[5] [1903] (Samuel[4], Samuel[3], Samuel[2], Job[1]),
obtained his academical education at the Parsonsfield (Maine)
Academy, 1835-7, and studied for the ministry at the Free Will
Baptist Theological School, same place. Was ordained Nov. 1842,
at Acton, Me.; labored as a minister of the gospel at North Berwick, Me., 1842, at Eaton, N. H., till 1846, at Milton Mills, N. H.,
and Newport, R. I., one year each, and finally commenced his
service as pastor of the Free Baptist Church, at Tamworth Iron
Works, N. H., Jan. 1852, where he has since resided, and still
continues his very acceptable and successful pastorate (1872).
He was elected chaplain of the New Hampshire House of Representatives for the June session, 1859; is a trustee of the New
Hampton Literary and Theological Institution; and being a leading clergyman, is also an associational officer of his denomination
in the State of New Hampshire. He m. Huldah Staples, of North
Berwick, Me., Dec. 15, 1842. Children: —

2047. JOHN SUMNER [2124], b. July 30, 1844.
2048. ABBY MAY, b. July 28, 1851.

2049.   HOSEA[5] [1905] (Samuel[4], Samuel[3], Samuel[2], Job[1]), is a
blacksmith by trade, residing in Wakefield, N. H. (Union Village);
m. Tryphena Davis, of W., Dec. 6, 1842, who d. Sept. 19, 1871.
He was " a soldier in the war for the Union." Child: —

2050. JOSEPHINE AUGUSTA, b. Aug. 28, 1847.

2051.   ISRAEL[5] [1906] (Samuel[4], Samuel[3], Samuel[2], Job[1]), succeeded his father as a farmer on the old homestead in Acton, Me.,
and as deacon of the Free Baptist Church at Milton Mills. N. H.,
elected 1861. He m., 1st, Sarah Lowe, of Newfield, May 15, 1850,
who was b. Sept. 29, 1829, and d. Dec. 11, 1864, aged 35; m., 2d,
Mary E. Rogers, of Parsonsfield, Me., Apr. 23, 1865, who was b.
Mar. 22, 1840. Children: —

2052. WILLIAM VICTOR, b. May 23, 1851, probably in Acton.
2053. ELLA FRANCES, b. Oct. 3, 1853.
2054. ELMER PYM, b. Apr. 29, 1856.
2055. SARAH INEZ, b. Mar 1, 1859.

2056. WALTER ELLSWORTH, b. Apr. 18, 1861.
2057. FLORA NELLIE, b. July 26, 1866 (second wife).
2058. ISETTA, b. Mar. 12, 1869, in Acton.
2059. GRACIE BELL, b. Mar. 8, 1871, in Acton.

2060. ALVAH[5] [1907] (Samuel[4], Samuel[3], Samuel[2], Job[1]), m. Martha Wentworth, of Milton, N. H., June 13, 1847, at Acton, Me. She was b. Mar. 17, 1827. He is a blacksmith, now living (1871) in Lebanon, Me. Children : —

2061. JAY [2126], b. Feb. 5, 1850, in Acton, Me.
2062. FRANCINA, b. Jan. 4, 1852, in Acton; m. John W. Trefethen, of Dover, N. H., May 8, 1870. He is a painter and paper-hanger, and was b. Aug. 1, 1841, in Dover.
2063. ELLEN HURD, b. Oct. 21, 1853, in Acton; m. Thomas A. Trefethen, Jan. 1, 1871, who was b. Dec. 29, 1846, a tin-plate and sheet-iron worker, formerly of Dover, now (1872) of Cambridgeport, Mass.
2064. SAMUEL, b. Sept. 20, 1855, in Wakefield, N. H.
2065. HANNAH, b. Oct. 14, 1857, in Milton, N. H.; d. Nov. 21, 1859, aged 2, being scalded by a boiling tea-kettle, and surviving but seven days.
2066. ABRAHAM LINCOLN, b. Sept. 25, 1859, in Milton.
2067. HANNAH, b. Oct. 29, 1865, in Milton.

2068. WILLIAM BUZZELL[5] [1908] (Samuel[4], Samuel[3], Samuel[2], Job[1]), studied medicine with private instructors, taking also one course of lectures at Bowdoin College, two at Dartmouth College, and one at Jefferson College, Philadelphia, 1856. Practised his profession at Union (Wakefield), N. H., till the breaking out of the rebellion. Enlisted, as a private, in Co. F, 2d regiment U. S. sharpshooters, in 1861 ; was promoted to second sergeant, then to assistant surgeon, and finally was appointed on the operating staff of the third division, second army corps, remaining in front of Petersburg, Va., and afterwards with the army of the James, as army surgeon, till the close of the war. He then resumed practice in Lawrence, Mass., till the death of his first wife ; again at Union, 1869, and settled as physician at Tamworth Iron Works, N. H., Jan. 1871. He was m., 1st, by his brother, Rev. John Runnells [2046], to Clara Ellen Swasey, of Milton, N. H., Nov. 14, 1851. She d. May 15, 1867, of paralysis, after twenty-five hours' illness ; m., 2d, Martha E. Lincoln, of West Medway, Mass., Mar. 9, 1870, at W. M. Children : —

2069. EVERARD GÖETHE, b. Sept. 23, 1852.
2070. HORATIO MCLEOD, b. Apr. 13, 1857.
2071. CLIFFORD LINCOLN, b. Mar. 7, 1871 (second wife), at Tamworth Iron Works.

2072. ELMIRA[5] [1909] (Samuel[4], Samuel[3], Samuel[2], Job[1]), m. John C. Grant, of Acton, farmer, Aug. 26, 1855, at Acton. He was b. Dec. 22, 1827. Children : —

2073. FRANK WILBUR (Grant), b. Apr. 4, 1859.
2074. ELMIRA (?), b. Aug. 14, d. Oct. 12, 1860.
2075. ROSCOE ERNEST, b. June 9, 1868.

2076. Jonathan Prescott[5] [1912] (Paul[4], Samuel[3], Samuel[2], Job[1]), m. Rachel E. Tupper, of Nova Scotia, Nov. 1, 1854, and resides on his father's place in Acton, Me. Children : —

2077. Edward E., b. Aug. 15, 1855.
2078. Ida Isadore, b. Apr. 8, 1860.

2079. Joanna Farnum[5] [1914] (Paul[4], Samuel[3], Samuel[2], Job[1]), m. Nathaniel C. Decker, of Boothbay, Me., Feb. 2, 1849. He had been, in 1869, for eighteen years an officer of the Boston police; residence, at that time, 12 Dexter St., South Boston. Children : —

2080. Isadore Ida (Decker), b. Mar. 6, 1851; d. May 13, 1854, aged 3 years 2 months.
2081. Walter Curtis, b. Apr. 28, 1855.

2082. Lucetta Fall[5] [1916] (Paul[4], Samuel[3], Samuel[2], Job[1]), m. John S. Jones, of Lebanon, Me., Mar. 6, 1858, at Boston, Mass., and d. at North Lebanon, Me., Dec. 12, 1860, in her 31st year, leaving : —

2083. Hiram Leslie (Jones), b. May 19, 1859; d. Oct. 20, 1863, in his 5th year.

2084. Samuel[5] [1921] (Asa[4], Samuel[3], Samuel[2], Job[1]), was settled first, as a mason and stucco worker, in Portsmouth, N. H.; purchased, in 1861, the Horn farm, near Wolfborough Centre, — one half of which was previously owned by his father, — where he has since resided, though still working part of the time at his trade, away from home. For fifteen years he taught vocal music during each winter. He m., 1st, Hannah Newsome, of Kittery, Me., Aug. 1849, at Saugus, Mass., who d. Mar. 1851, in Portsmouth; m., 2d, Lucy Maria Parker, daughter of William Parker, of Saugus, Feb. 1852, who d. Oct. 1856; m., 3d, Charlotte D. Trundy, daughter of John Trundy, Esq., of Portsmouth, Mar. 30, 1858, at P., who was b. Dec. 30, 1834. Children : —

2085. William Parker, b. Feb. 28, d. Dec. 11, 1854 (second wife).
2086. Willis Calef, b. Oct. 18, 1859, in Portsmouth (3d wife).
2087. Mary Louise, b. Aug. 26, 1861, in Portsmouth.
2088. Lucy Hannah, b. Apr. 26, 1863, in Wolfborough.
2089. Ceorim Goodhue, b. Dec. 4, 1865, in W.

2090. Mary Jane[5] [1923] (Asa[4], Samuel[3], Samuel[2], Job[1]), m. Alonzo Daniel Nute, farmer, Aug. 20, 1854, at Wolfborough, N. H. He was b. Jan. 23, 1831, in Madbury; resided first in Wolfborough; at present (1872) in Madbury. Children : —

2091. George Daniel (Nute), b. Aug. 1, 1855, in Wolfborough.
2092. Hannah Susan, b. Apr. 22, 1857, in W.
2093. Mary Abbie, b. Sept. 17, 1861, in W.
2094. John Andrew, b. Sept. 25, 1863, in Madbury.

SIXTH GENERATION.

2095. MARY JANE[6] [1925] (William[5], Thomas[4], Job[3], Job[2], Job[1]), m. J. A. Perkins, in Wellington, Ohio, Feb. 21, 1854. He is a general railroad agent; present residence, Indianapolis, Ind. Children : —

2096. EDWARD L. (Perkins), b. July 12, 1855, in Wellington.
2097. RICHARD, b. June 15, 1857; d. Dec. 6, 1862, in his 6th year.
2098. MARY LOUISE, b. July 13, 1859, in Columbus, Ohio.
2099. FRANCES HELEN, b. Jan. 29, 1861; d. Aug. 13, 1864, in her 4th year.

2100. LUCRETIA DAY[6] [1926] (William[5], Thomas[4], Job[3], Job[2], Job[1]), m. John A. Braman, farmer, Feb. 9, 1865, in Wellington, O. Child : —

2101. WILLIE R. (Braman), b. Mar. 26, 1869.

2102. ELIZABETH EBBERT[6] [1927] (William[5], Thomas[4], Job[3], Job[2], Job[1]), m. Newton E. Adams, railroad agent, Sept. 1, 1861, in Wellington, O. ; resides at Rushville, Rush Co., Ind. Children : —

2103. MABEL FRANCES (Adams), b. May 23, 1864.
2104. FLORENCE LOUISE, b. Feb. 25, 1866.

2105. LOUISE CENTENARIA[6] [1928] (William[5], Thomas[4], Job[3], Job[2], Job[1]), m. James A. Manchester, July 12, 1864, at Wellington, O. He is an insurance agent, in company with his brother-in-law, William Henry Runnells [1929], at Cleveland, O. Children : —

2106. HARRY R. (Manchester), b. Oct. 18, 1866, in Cleveland.
2107. EDITH, b. Dec. 29, 1871.

2108. MARGARET JANE[6] [1939] (David[5], Thomas[4], Job[3], Job[2], Job[1]), m. William Moles, of Henry, Marshall Co., Ill., Feb. 20, 1856, and d. Sept. 8, 1871, in her 37th year. Children : —

2109. JOHN RALPH (Moles), b. Apr. 12, 1859.
2110. ALICE JANE, b. Jan. 28, 1861.
2111. SAMUEL DAVID, b. Aug. 2, 1862.
2112. WILLIAM HENRY, b. June 1, 1865.
2113. LIZZIE LAURA, b. Nov. 8, 1867; d. Feb. 8, 1871, aged 3 yrs. 3 mos.
2114. ROBERT HERDER, b. Aug. 23, 1871.

2115. SIMEON TOZIER[6] [1941] (David[5], Thomas[4], Job[3], Job[2], Job[1]), enlisted in the 47th regiment Illinois volunteers, Co. D, and served three years, being most of the time clerk in the commissary department; was three months in the hospital at St. Louis, Mo., with severe inflammation of the eyes, and was honorably discharged. He m. Sallie Ellsbury, Dec. 1, 1869, at Lacon, Ill. Child : —

2116. DELLA, b. Nov. 4, 1870. In Sept. 1871, when ten months old, she took the ten dollars cash premium for being "the handsomest girl baby exhibited at the Marshall County Fair," in Illinois.

2117. MARY E.[6] [1942] (David[5], Thomas[4], Job[3], Job[2], Job[1]), m. Snowden Maffitt, May 30, 1866. Child : —

2118. ELMER (Maffitt), b. Oct. 22, 1869.

2119. THOMAS H.[6] [1943] (David[5], Thomas[4], Job[3], Job[2], Job[1]), enlisted in Co. K, 148th regiment Illinois volunteers, Feb. 1, 1865, and was honorably discharged, Sept. 16, 1865 ; m. Oliva Swift, Feb. 9, 1870. Child : —

2120 LILLIAN, b. July 22, 1871.

2121. CHARLES AUGUSTIN[6] [2043] (Eli[5], Samuel[4], Samuel[3], Samuel[2], Job[1]), is a farmer residing with his father in Acton, Me. ; m. Nellie Augusta Sanborn, of Portsmouth, N. H., May 25, 1868, who was b. May 24, 1844, at Great Falls. Children : —

2122. VIOLA BELONIA, b. Dec. 31, 1869, in Acton ; d. Jan. 21, 1870, aged 21 days.
2123. WILLIS LESLIE, b. Mar. 27, 1871, in A.

2124. JOHN SUMNER[6] [2047] (John[5], Samuel[4], Samuel[3], Samuel[2], Job[1]), fitted for college at the New Hampton, N. H., Academical Institute ; graduated at Amherst College, Mass., 1865 ; taught the high schools of Rochester and Dover, N. H., 1866-7 ; admitted to the bar at Des Moines, Iowa, Jan. 1869. He was the private secretary of Governor Merrill, of Iowa, for one year, meanwhile " performing the duties of secretary " of the Iowa Republican Central Committee, " with masterly and honoring ability," and doing efficient service through the State, in company with Hon. Peter Melendy, M. C., in the Grant campaign, fall of 1868. He m. Helen R. Baker (daughter of Gen. N. B. Baker, of Iowa, formerly governor of New Hampshire), Mar. 31, 1869, at Des Moines, — alluded to in the " Register " of Apr. 1, as a " noted marriage," performed in the Episcopal house of worship. He was soon after appointed U. S. Consul at Tunstall, Staffordshire (near Manchester), Eng. ; returned from England, and commenced the practice of law in Iowa, 1872 ; also noticed in the " Clinton (Iowa) Herald," of June 28, as " a gentleman of literary culture," lately " added to the editorial corps of the ' Des Moines Register.' " Child : —

2125. MABEL, b. July 8, 1870, in Tunstall, Eng.

2126. JAY[6] [2061] (Alvah[5], Samuel[4], Samuel[3], Samuel[2], Job[1]), is a blacksmith, residing, 1870, in Lowell, Mass., at 8 Ray Street ; m. Margaret Ewing Jack, of Acton, Me., at Milton, N. H., Jan. 8, 1868 ; she was b Dec. 31, 1849, in Burlington, Mass. Children : —

2127. MARY SABERY, b. Oct. 12, 1868, in Milton.
2128. EDITH, b. June 25, 1870, in Lowell.

PART III.

BEING A

GENEALOGICAL MEMOIR

OF

JOHN RUNELS, or RUNALS,

OF DURHAM, N. H.,

1718–1756.

INTRODUCTION.

It is quite certain, as shown in the former Introductions, that the ancestors Job and John, of Parts II and III, respectively, were brothers. There is also a tradition in one branch of the family of Samuel (Part I), that one of his two younger brothers who followed him to New England, "remained near him for a time" in Bradford, or Boxford, Mass., "before finally settling in New Hampshire;" that he "lived on the other side of the pond" (from his brother's), and that he "spelled his name differently."

It seems *probable* that Samuel [1] may have had a brother John, from the circumstance of his giving that name to two of his male children, [4] and [5], Part I, and that the two brothers may have been living near each other at the time of those children's births. We only *know* that John was several years later than his brother Job in settling at the Oyster River Parish, — then of Dover, — since Durham and Lee, N. H., and that he *may* have halted first in Exeter, on his way from Bradford, as seen by comparing the deeds below.

No traditional connection whatever can be found between his and the Owen Runels family also of Exeter and Stratham, as mentioned in the Appendix. The latter seems to have passed in its migrations from Stratham to Chester, N. H., and John Runals, on the supposition already given, could only be said to have crossed its track, at Exeter, moving in another direction, from Bradford, Mass., to Dover.

Tradition among the descendants of John says that "his family *originated* in Ayrshire." This substantiates the supposed Scottish origin of John and of his older brother Job; but it must refer to their *origin prior* to their grandfather's settling in Nova Scotia, on the supposition that they were also the brothers of Samuel.

The broad Scotch orthography, "Runals," and even "Ronals" (as it may have been pronounced), instead of "Runels," prevailed in the family of John more than in that of Job; so that many of his (John's) descendants, who did not change the spelling to "Reynolds," have retained that of "Runals," or "Runnals," even to the present. But, for the sake of uniformity, we make no change in the page headings, especially as "Runnels" is also found in several branches of this family, and even "Renels" appears in the two earliest deeds, as seen below.

FIRST GENERATION

2129. JOHN[1]. The earliest authentic record of this ancestor is found among "Early Marriages in Durham" (New England Historical and Genealogical Register for 1869), where he is said to have been married at Durham, N. H., "by the Rev. Hugh Adams, to Hannah Clark, Dec. 23, 1718." This was probably his second marriage, as shown below, and he was then a resident of Exeter, *if* the "John Renels of Exeter," mentioned in deed of "Aug. 26, 1719," were the same as the "John Renels of Dover," recorded "Oct. 20, 1721," as purchasing "from James Bassford, of Dover, for £12, a certain tract of land lying and being in Dover, between Lamperell river and Oyster river, near ye point, it being twenty acres which was originally granted in 1662 unto William Roberts."

On this supposition, he must have moved from Exeter to Oyster River — perhaps, back with his wife to her former home — between 1719 and 1721, and became the possessor of his first real estate in Durham, as above described. He appears, from the following, also to have owned and disposed of land, north of his brother Job's, and not far from the later "Randall place," in Lee; "April 14, 1722, John Runals, of Dover," deeded "to William Rendal, for £30, ten acres, on *south* side of Mast Path, that goeth to Little River"; and that his land in this part of the parish extended *north* of the present road towards Wheelwright's pond, is proved from the fact that "Jan. 31, 1727–8," he deeded "to Joseph Jones ten acres, more or less, being in ye township of Dover, on ye *north* side of ye mast path that leads down to Oyster River Falls, between said path and Wheelwright's pond."

The "Committee of Freeholders" of the new town of Durham granted to him, also, as to his brother Job, "twenty-five acres of the common lands," "Mar. 18, 1733–4" (Town Records); also other lands to himself in company with James Head, which he afterwards increased by buying out Head's share, "six and one fourth acres, for £12, Oct. 28, 1735;" and same amount at same price from "Richard Blanchard, July 12, 1736" (Rockingham Deeds).

His original purchase probably constituted his home in Durham, in the south part of what is now Lee. Perhaps the following indi-

cates the same location: " Oct. 27, 1748, John Runals of Durham "
deeded " to Joseph R., tanner, of Dover, his son, for £30, the tract
of land called the Hook, in Durham, south side of Lampereel river."
His non-resident estate is shown by these two deeds, "Jan. 3,
1726-7, John Rennels, and Hannah R., of Dover," " to John Pray,
of Portsmouth, one third part of one full share of the town of
Rochester, for £5 ; " and " Feb. 15, 1754, John Runnals, of Durham, to M. Connor, of Kingston, one whole share in the town of
Canterbury."

The following copy and abstract of his will are appended, as the
only sure guide to his family record : —

" June 20, 1756, I, John Ronals, of the town of Durham, in the Province
of New Hampshire, in New England, being sick and weak in body, but of
perfect memory and sound disposing mind (Thanks be given unto God
therefore); Calling unto mind the mortality of my body and knowing that
it is appointed for all men once to die; do make and ordain this my last
will and testament. That is to say, principally and first of all, I give and
recommend my soul into the hands of God, That gave it; and then my
body to the dust by a decent Christian burial, at the discretion of my executor, nothing doubting but at the general resurrection I shall receive the
same again, by the mighty power of God; and after my funeral charges
defrayed [and] my just and honest debts paid, I will, devise and dispose of
the remainder of my worldly estate, wherewith it hath pleased God to
bless me with in this life, as follows.

" To my beloved wife Hannah, two cows, my riding mare, and eight old
sheep, and one third of all my other estate. To my son John, £50 old
tennor to be paid four years after my decease. To my son Abraham, £60,
old tenor, within six months after my decease. To my son William, £50,
o. t. in 18 months. To my daughter Elizabeth Snell, £25 in 12 mos. To
my son Joseph, all my farm or homestead estate, where I now live in the
town of Durham [widow's third excepted], immediately after my decease.
To my daughter Sarah Bunker, £25 in two years. To my son Stephen,
£50, when he gets to 14 years of age, and to be maintained out of my estate and live with his mother till then. To my son Solomon [same as last]
also a gun. To my daughter Deliverance, £25 [on same conditions as
two last] and all my household movables forever. To my son Winthrop
[same as Stephen]. To Hannah Willee and Elizabeth Willee, £25 each, to
be paid 12 months after my decease. Finally, my son Joseph Runals is
ordained and constituted my sole executor in trust, to see this my last will
and testament performed and fulfilled." (Rockingham Probate Records.)

He must have died between June 20 and " Dec. 28, 1756," and
if born, as supposed, in 1689, was about sixty-seven years of age.
Under date last quoted, the inventory of his estate is reported,
" taken by Hercules Mooney and Benjamin Drew," " as shown unto
us by Joseph R., of Dover, administrator," etc. " Homestead
place valued at £2000, old tenor ; House on said place, at £700 ;
Barn, ditto, £300, and part of saw mill in Durham, £60." His son
Joseph rendered his account as administrator of above estate,
" Dec. 19, 1758," but did not himself finally settle it, as " adminis-
tration of John R's estate, with his will annexed, is again granted to
Lydia Runnals, widow and administratrix of Joseph, Feb. 25, 1767."

As the date of his son Abraham's birth is well authenticated
among the latter's descendants, as given below, and as his son

John was doubtless older than Abraham, it is safe to surmise that he — John, the father — was twice married, having the two first children, named in will, by his first wife. who died soon after, May 23, 1718 ; while he m. Hannah Clark, as his second wife, at the first date given in this record, by whom the eight remaining children.

As the Probate records tell us that " Deliverance, a minor child of John Runals, was *upwards* of fourteen years of age, Dec. 13, 1758," when " Hannah R. was appointed her guardian and gave bonds," we assign to Deliverance the place of Stephen (in the will) ; otherwise, the order of the *will* is observed in the following list of his children, their births being assumed from the will itself where not obtained from other sources : —

2130. JOHN [2141], b. 1716 (first wife (?)).
2131. ABRAHAM [2142], b. May 23, 1718.
2132. WILLIAM [2155], b. 1721 (second wife (?)).
2133. ELIZABETH [2163], b. 1724.
2134. JOSEPH [2166], b. June 10, 1727.
2135. SARAH [2175], b. Aug. 4, 1731.
2136. HANNAH [2186], b. 1734.
2137. DELIVERANCE, b. 1743.
2138. STEPHEN, b. 1744.
2139. SOLOMON, b. 1746.
2140. WINTHROP, b. 1749. The unusual coincidence is worthy of notice, that the four oldest children of his son Joseph, see [2166], were named after these four youngest of his own family. From this circumstance, and the fact that no further trace of these four youngest can be obtained, it is presumed that they all died at an early age, and soon after the date of their father's will, being *then* under fourteen years of age.

12

SECOND GENERATION.

2141.   JOHN[2] [2130] (John[1]), located in Barrington, N. H., about "Oct. 10, 1743," as we then find "John Ranells Jun. of Durham, laborer," purchasing "50 acres in B., from Thomas Snell, one half of 3d lot, 1st range." To this he added by purchase of "land in Barrington" from "George Sherburne of Portsmouth, for £20, Jan. 10, 1757." His first wife's name was Abigail, as seen by deed of conveyance dated "Apr. 20, 1757," in which we have "John Runels and Abigail his wife, of Barronton." She must have d., and he had m. Eleanor, for his second wife, *before* "Mar. 17, 1763," when we find "John and Ellenor Runels of Barrington" deeding land in B., to John Mow, for £500. From other deeds we learn that he owned one "whole right of land in Loudon," made over by himself and Elenor his wife to "Peter Rawlings, Dec. 22, 1783"; was called "*Capt.* John Runnals, Aug. 13, 1784"; increased his estate at two different times by some sixty acres, and did not die till after "June 7, 1785." He had, however, willed to his wife Eleanor, "Sept. 2, 1784, the use and improvement of his estate in Barrington until Isaac and Hannah Runnals," see [2199 and 2200], "children of Isaac, late of Barrington, come to lawful age, — his wife to bring up said children, — when one third falls to herself and two thirds to the children." His kindness to the grandchildren of his brother Abraham, and the interest both of himself and wife in those children, as made orphans by the Revolutionary war, are worthy of commendation. His widow, though appointed executrix of his will, must have died in about a year after her husband; as we find on the Probate records, appended to his will, "Aug. 16, 1786, the executrix being deceased, administration on the above is granted to Abraham Runnals *next of kin*," who afterwards received license from Judge Badger, at Gilmanton, Sept. 21, 1792, to "sell certain tracts of land which belonged to the estate of John Runnals late of Barrington," and accordingly conveyed the same, one to Thomas H. Lewis, of Kittery, Me , "Oct. 19, 1792," and another to Thomas Langley, of Lee, "Nov. 8, 1792."

2142.   ABRAHAM[2] [2131] (John[1]), was "tithing man" in Durham, 1764 and 1765; also in Lee (set off from Durham, 1766), 1767 and 1768. His name then disappears from the Lee Records, and reappears on the New Durham Records several times in 1773 and from 1780 to 1797, as "fence viewer," or "tithing man." Having exchanged his land in Lee at £80, for one hundred acres in New Durham at £60, with Gideon Mathes, of Lee, — both deeds bearing date "Apr. 25, 1772," — he soon after moved, with his numerous family, to his New Durham home. . His improvements here had scarcely commenced, when he responded to his country's call, — showing his genuine Scotch spirit against the English, — and on July 16, 1775, joined the American army at Winter Hill, when more than fifty-seven years old. "Four of his sons embarked in the same cause, — bearing the motto, 'Victory or death,' — two of whom perished in the conflict" (Rev. E. Place in "Morning Star" of Apr. 28, 1847). Some of his descendants allege that he had "*six* sons and two sons-in-law in the revolutionary war"; but this lacks confirmation; Mr. Place's is doubtless the true account. It is also stated that during the time of his service, his wife, daughters, and daughters-in-law "carried on the farm *themselves*, and made clothes or knit socks and mittens for their husbands and brothers, or for general distribution among the soldiers." We next find him (Abraham) in "Capt. John Brewster's company; from Sept. 3 to Dec. 7, 1776; 95 days; 35 miles travel; place of abode New Durham." Again, in "Col. Pierce Long's regiment, Jan. 13, 1777," when he signs a receipt ("Runls") for "£2 advance pay"; and yet once more on the alert, old as he was, the New Hampshire military records giving his name in "Capt. Gilman's company, Stickney's regiment, Stark's brigade, July 20, 1777"; on a "march to reinforce the northern army," from which, however, he was "discharged Sept. 30." This was probably "for disability," as tradition has it in his family; as also that "his son James," being free from prior engagements, "took his place."

The original one hundred acres, in New Durham which was improved at *first*, as above stated, and was afterwards occupied by him, included nearly the farm owned in 1869 by Baalis B. Tibbets, in the south part of the town. He seems to have been a practical or assistant surveyor, when he first came to New Durham, as a deposition of his is found on the Strafford records, dated "Nov. 28, 1793," that he assisted one Timothy Murray "some time before the civil war between Great Britain and the United States of America began," in running out a lot of land in New Durham; that "a certain beech tree was marked by them at corner of Lot 3, 1st division, and that a certain stone, placed by David Elkins this day, stands where the beech tree stood, or not more than six feet from it"

He m. Hannah Smith, 1744, She was b. June 30, 1718, being a granddaughter of the venerable Rev. John Buss, who was settled as second minister and physician of Oyster River parish, in 1674, continued for thirty-three years, lost his house and valuable library in the Indian attack of 1694, and d. in 1736, aged 108. She was blind for twenty years, was an eminently pious and devoted Christian, and d. Feb. 13, 1812, aged 93 years 7 months 13 days.

He had previously d. July 24, 1804, aged 86 years 2 months 1 day. Both were buried in a small and now neglected inclosure on the old homestead above mentioned. The following list of their " eight sons and four daughters," — though in part traditional, and hence uncertain, — is yet believed to be substantially correct : —

2143. ELIZA (Elizabeth) [2189], b. Apr. 1745. Her age at death, as well confirmed among her descendants in Vermont, as also the alleged years of her children's births, induce us to place her birth *before* her seven oldest brothers', though there is *some* authority for calling her younger than they.

2144. ABRAHAM, b. 1746; d. young, in Durham, or Lee, as is *most* probable; though one of the descendants of Jonathan affirms that he grew up, was m., and served and d. of sickness in the Revolutionary army; called also " Benjamin," erroneously.

2145. JOHN, b. 1748; one authority only for the name of " Peter." This was the oldest of the " four brothers " who entered the army, and he may previously have m. He was doubtless the " John Runnels in Henry Dearborn's Co., Stark's regiment," to whom " £3 " is assigned among "Losses at the battle of Charlestown, June 17, 1775 " (N. H. Military Records); probably also the " John Reynolds " enlisted July 22, 1776, for Canada, in Col. Daniel Moore's (?) regiment, losing his life soon after in that expedition, as one of the " two sons " who is known to have " perished " *early* " in the conflict."

2146. ISAAC [2198], b. 1749.
2147. JAMES [2201, b. Jan. 25, 1752.
2148. SAMUEL [2208], b. July 16, 1754.
2149. NATHANIEL [2219], b. 1756; neither himself nor his son Abram are now *remembered* in New Durham, as the son and grandson of Abraham, which makes the relationship, to some extent, a matter of doubt and of supposition merely; but see [2407].

2150. JONATHAN [2222], b. Aug. 16, 1758; is *known* to have been a " seventh son."

2151. HANNAH, b. 1760; d. young.
2152. ALICE [2230], b. Mar. 2, 1762.
2153. JUDITH (Ruth or Rhoda), b. 1765; d. young.
2154. EBENEZER [2238], b. 1768.

2155. WILLIAM[2] [2132] (John[1]). His name appears upon the Durham records as " Informer," in 1758; " Informer of killing deer," 1760–1761, and " Field Driver," 1764. His wife was Lydia, as mentioned in his will, " May 23, 1773 "; " to receive one half the farm as long as she lives." He d. before " Feb. 9, 1774," as his oldest son was at *that time* appointed administrator of his father's estate. The true definition of an " administrator," as one " who administers upon the estate of an *intestate*," seems not to be observed in many of the old records. He was a blacksmith, in Lee, and may have occupied the stand, since removed, near the present town-house on Lee Hill, which Nathan Runnels, his son, is remembered to have owned. His children, as named in the will, cannot be traced, except the oldest. They were : —

2156. MOSES [2243], b. 1752.
2157. HANNAH, b. 1754 (?); to receive, by her father's will, " £2—10 shillings and one cow."
2158. ISRAEL, b. Nov. 1757; was " under sixteen " at the time of his

father's will; to receive "£5." His name is found among twenty-one "men who went from Lee" to the Revolutionary war; was enrolled in Capt. F. M. Ball's (?) Co., "Apr. 18, 1777," as being then "nineteen years of age"; also among "men that enlisted from the parish of Lee, before the year 1778, that are now in the Continental army, *June* 30, 1781." On the military accounts, £25, 8s. 4d. is at one time credited to him for service.

2159. STEPHEN, b. 1759; same mention made of him in the will, as of his brother Israel, above, and his military record is the same, except his enrolment in Capt. Ball's company, under date, "Jan. 24, 1777," then said to be "seventeen years of age." He is also noted in "Capt. Goss' Co, Nichols' regiment, Stark's Brigade," as enlisting, "July 20, 1777," and "discharged Sept. 28," with "travel to Stillwater"; also twenty-five days from "Aug. 6, 1778," going in Dan (?) Emerson's Co., Nichols' regiment, to Rhode Island, and finally he is noticed twice ("Stephen Runels, of Lee"), as serving in Capt. A. Perkins's company, at Portsmouth, 2 mos. 18 days at one time, 1 mo. 30 (?) days at another, receiving for the latter £2.

2160. NATHAN, b. 1761 (?); £5 by his father's will; was settled as a blacksmith at Lee Hill, see above; hence, "Oct. 16, 1793," he is called "Nathan Runels of Lee, blacksmith," receiving from Joseph Meeder, "13½ acres near land of Elijah Cartland," which he deeded to James Jenkins, "Feb. 15, 1796." He also deeded to William Runals, of Lee, probably his nephew [2244], his blacksmith's shop and tools, "Nov. 13, 1797." He is *reported* to have had a son Israel.

2161. DEBORAH, b. 1764 (?); to receive by her father's will "£2—10s." "against she is eighteen."

2162. BETTY, b. 1766 (?); had the same bequest by will.

2163. ELIZABETH[2] [2133] (John[1]), m. Solomon Snell, of Barrington, 1743; hence mentioned accordingly in her father's will, 1756. Children: —

2164. SAMUEL (Snell), b. 1744; is called "a minor upwards of fourteen years of age" in 1758; when his uncle Joseph Runnels was appointed his guardian, his father, "Solomon Snell, late of Barrington, yeoman," having previously "deceased."

2165. EDWARD, b. 1748; was in the Revolutionary war, Dearborn Drew's Co. (?); was "wounded," and probably died; in consideration of which, his brother "Samuel Snell received pay from the Treasurer, 1777." (N. H. Military Records.)

2166. JOSEPH[2] [2134] (John[1]), was a tanner, and settled at first in Durham, "Oyster River," where his three oldest children were born of his wife Lydia, whom he m. 1749. Received land from E. Davis, in Durham, "at a place called the Hook," "July 8, 1751." But "Feb. 11, 1754, Joseph Runels, of *Dover*," deeded "the Hook in Durham, to Samuel Burley, of New Market, for £500." He is called "Joseph R., tanner, of Dover," in four other real estate transactions, up to "Nov. 2, 1763." He d. in Dover, 1765, aged 38. Administration of his estate granted to Lydia, his widow, "Apr. 3, 1766"; inventory taken "April 30," including "forty-five acres of land in Durham, with orchards and buildings thereon," probably inherited from his father, "at £180," and "five acres of land, with house and barn, bark-house, work-house, tanyard and orchard," — probably in Dover, — at only " £60 " ! (perhaps a mistake of the transcriber). License to sell his real estate granted to the said Lydia, " Feb. 12, 1767 "; but as she m., 2d, James Libbey, of Dover, Aug. 31, 1768, a similar license was renewed to Libbey, in respect to the sale of fifteen and one half acres of his land in Lee, " May 12, 1779." His estate was not finally settled till more than ten years after. His old account-book, as a tanner, in Dover, is now in the possession of his grandson George [2605], of Bangor, Me.; a choice and truly valuable relic, as in it is found the following complete and well authenticated list of his children, with their birth dates, — the four oldest being evidently named *after* the four youngest of John[1], as elsewhere shown ; see [2137-40] : —

2167. STEPHEN, b. Feb. 10, 1750, in Durham; supposed to have d. young.
2168. SOLOMON, b. Nov. 5, 1751; appears from the Lee records to have been living in the " Centre District " of that town as late as 1815; but there is no evidence that he had or left a family. He was in the Revolutionary war the first year, as, among the New Hampshire military papers, we find in " Capt. Winburn Adams's Co., June 2, 1775, Solomon Runals, tanner, of Durham, aged 23." His business is thus identified. John Smith, selectman of Durham, under date " May 1, 1776," certifies to " Solomon Runals," among " the names of non-commissioned officers and soldiers from Durham, who were in the Continental service the summer past, and have engaged for the current year."
2169. DELIVERANCE, b. Mar. 25, 1753; "1752" on the record must be a mistake; is also supposed to have d. early in life.
2170. WINTHROP [2247], b. Feb. 28, 1754 (elsewhere 1755), in Durham.
2171. MARY [2261], b. Apr. 27, 1755 (6), in Dover.
2172. HANNAH [2264], b. June 8, 1757.
2173. JOSEPH [2274], b. Aug. 4, 1759, in Dover.
2174. BENJAMIN [2285], b. July 21, 1765, in Rochester.

2175. SARAH[2] [2135] (John[1]), m. Jonathan Bunker, of Durham (Lee), Dec. 1749, and moved with her husband to Barnstead, N. H., in 1770, when her sixth child was ten years old. He built the first mill on Suncook River, in B., at what is now Barnstead Parade. She was a Quaker by persuasion, and of most estimable character. After settling in Barnstead, she used to go over into Pittsfield, nearly two miles, by spotted trees, to do her *baking*, till, in the course of three or four years, an oven of rock was built near her own dwelling. At the age of 94, " she spun and reeled one skein of cotton yarn in a single hour," notice of which exploit was given to a newspaper by her neighbor, the Rev. Enos George, much to her annoyance. " I would not have spun it," said she, " if I had known Friend George would put it in the papers." All her sons were soldiers in the Revolutionary war, except Eli. on account of his being a miller, and Obadiah on account of his youth ; also two sons-in-law. He d. Sept. 1796, aged 67 ; she d. Jan. 26, 1826, in her 95th year. Children, all born in Durham except the youngest : —

2176. ISAIAH (Bunker), b. Oct. 1750; a soldier in the Revolution; m. Betsy Smith, and settled in Maine.

2177. BRADBURY, b. 1752; m. Sarah Tibbetts; a drummer in the Revolutionary war, and d. of fever while in service.

2178. SOBRIETY, b. 1755; m. Samuel Williams, of Barnstead, Apr. 7, 1777; a Revolutionary soldier, afterwards settled in B.

2179. SARAH, b. 1756; m., 1st, Bradbury Sinkler, June 26, 1777. He d. in the Revolutionary service soon after enlisting. She m., 2d, Henry Tibbetts, of Barnstead, Dec. 15, 1778, and settled in Northfield, N. H.

2180. JOSEPH, b. 1758; d. as a soldier in the Revolutionary war, 1776, aged 18.

2181. ELI, b. Apr. 22, 1760. At the age of 10, he drove the ox team which carried his mother and the younger children from Durham to Barnstead. He gave the land for Barnstead Parade, on condition that a Congregational meeting-house should always stand upon it, and built the first foundry at Gilmanton Iron Works. The Rev. Mr. George says of him, "He was one of the first settlers in Barnstead, and lived to see a wilderness changed to a fruitful field." He m. Anna Gordon, of New Hampton, N. H., Jan. 30, 1783, and d. Aug. 3, 1842, aged 82. Children : —

1. JOSEPH, b. Nov. 1, 1783; d. at Barnstead, May 22, 1830, in his 47th year.

2. ABRAHAM RUNNELS, b. Dec. 13, 1785. He "was named for his grandmother's brother, and was *her* favorite," with whom she lived till her death. He m. Polly C. Sinclair, of Barnstead, July 2, 1807, and d. Sept. 14, 1861, in his 76th year. She resided with her youngest daughter, at Barnstead Parade, and there d. Mar. 29, 1870. Children: (1.) HANNAH THING, b. Feb. 9, 1809; m. Hiram Tibbetts, of Northfield, and there d. Jan. 15, 1852, in her 43d year. (2.) CHARLES SINCLAIR, b. Dec. 26, 1811; d. at Rumney, N. H., 1860, aged 49. (3.) BETSY HODGDON, b. Feb. 2, d. Apr. 1814. (4.) ELISHA GORDON, b. Feb. 14, 1815; d. June 19, 1816, aged 1 yr. 4 mos. (5.) MARY ANN, b. Apr. 2, 1817, in Barnstead; m., 1st, George Stevens, of Deerfield, May 19, 1842, who d. July 4, same year. She m., 2d, Jeremiah Elkins, who was b. in Andover, N. H., Aug. 31, 1795; graduated at Dartmouth College, 1817; admitted to the bar in Virginia, May 17, 1821; practised law in Barnstead and Laconia, N. H.; was Register of Probate for Belknap Co., eight years, and d. Feb. 24, 1854, in his 59th year. She m., 3d, Rev. Jeremiah Blake, M. D., Mar. 29, 1860. He was b. Apr. 17, 1800, in Pittsfield, N. H., son of Enoch Blake, a soldier in the Revolution; graduated at the Dartmouth Medical College, 1826; commenced practice in Pittsfield, and continued ten years; hopefully experienced religion in 1832; entered the Gilmanton Theological Seminary, 1836, and was licensed to preach the gospel by the Deerfield Association, Jan. 1838. He has proved a successful laborer in *both* professions, being ordained and installed over the Congregational church at Wolfborough, N. H., five years, and at Tamworth seven years; preached and practised medicine in Lowell and Dracut, Mass., Barnstead, Pittsfield, and Gilmanton Iron Works, N. H. (since Dec. 1865), besides performing missionary and revival labor in several other places. "He has preached in sixty towns and cities in five States, and has practised medicine and surgery in three States; has labored in thirty revivals of religion, some of great power, and has witnessed the conversion of scores and hundreds." Her children were: I. SARAH FRANCES (Elkins), b. May 23, 1852. II. BELL D., b. Sept. 28, 1854. III. JOHN CARROLL (Blake), b. Sept. 28, 1862, in Pittsfield. (6.) ENOCH

AUGUSTUS (Bunker), b. Aug. 3, 1819; lives in Minnesota.
(7.) CYRUS EDWIN, b. Feb. 23, 1823; resides at Bethlehem,
N. H.   (8.) JOHN ELBRIDGE, b. May 27, 1827; lives in Minnesota.   (9.) ELIZA SINCLAIR, b. Jan. 22, 1832; m. D. F.
Davis, Mar. 1850, and resides at Barnstead Parade. Children: I. MARY (Davis), b. 1857. II. CHARLES F , b. 1859.
3.   GORDON (Bunker), b. Apr. 16, 1788.
4.   ANNA GORDON, b. Apr. 20, 1791.
5.   ELISHA GORDON, b. Aug. 28, 1793.
6.   TIMOTHY, b. Aug. 13, 1796; d. Dec. 30, 1840, aged 44.
7.   JONATHAN, b. July 20, 1798.
8.   ELI, b. Nov. 8, 1800.
2182.   ELIJAH, b. 1761; a Revolutionary soldier; afterwards settled in
Maine, in or near the town of Corrinna.
2183.   JONATHAN, b. 1763; a soldier in the Revolutionary war near
its close; was approbated as " a suitable person to keep a
public house in the town of Barnstead, Sept. 20, 1795 " (Town
Records).
2184.   HANNAH, b. 1767; d. 1780. aged 13.
2185.   OBADIAH, b. 1770, in Barnstead; m. Judith Collins, of Barnstead,
and settled in Starksboro', Vt.   The Bunker brothers, and
especially this youngest, were all reputed as " men of great
bodily strength."

2186.   HANNAH[2] [2136] (John[1]), m. a Willee, as we infer from
her father's will, and d. prior to the date of that instrument, " June
20, 1756," leaving : —

2187.   HANNAH (Willee).
2188.   ELIZABETH, who were each to receive a legacy from their grandfather; see [2129].

THIRD GENERATION.

2189. ELIZA[3] [2143] (Abraham[2], John[1]), m. George Chesley 1773, who is thought by some to have been a Revolutionary soldier with his wife's brothers, though this is denied by others. He was " a farmer through life " ; settled first in Barnstead, N. H. ; moved to Vershire, Vt., 1802, and finally to Waterbury, Vt., 1833, where he d. Mar. 1836, and she d. Sept. 17, 1838, aged 93. Children : —

2190. TIMOTHY (Chesley), b. 1774; m. Patty Pervier, in Barnstead, 1800; moved to Vershire, Vt., a year or two before his father, thence to Waterbury *with* his father, and there d. Sept. 11, 1855, aged 81.
2191. REBECCA, b. 1776; see [2323].
2192. HANNAH, b. 1779; m. Ichabod Watson, in Barnstead; settled in Thetford, Vt. He d. suddenly in Williamstown, — "dropping dead in the road, on a journey." She d. with her daughter [2], in Pittsfield, N. H., 1846 (?), aged 67. Children : —
    1. TIMOTHY (Watson). 2. MARGARET (Peggy); m. Stephen Libbey; moved back to New Hampshire, and settled in Pittsfield. 3. GEORGE. 4. POLLY. 5. JOHN. 6. ENOCH. 7. NANCY.
2193. ELIZABETH (Chesley), b. 1780; m. Abram Greene, in Pittsfield, N H., and there lived till her death, 1847 (?), aged 67. Six children, — four sons, two daughters.
2194. AVICE, b. Apr. 11, 1782; m. Joseph Moody, farmer, in Vershire, 1803; moved to Waterbury, spring of 1822, where she d. Sept. 1, 1848, aged 66, and he d. Apr. 15, 1857. Children : —
    1. DANIEL (Moody), b. Sept. 20, 1805, in Vershire; m. Eliza Wallace, of V.; a farmer in Waterbury; four children, of whom (1.) HARTWELL, served three years in the 2d Vermont regiment, from Waterbury. (2.) DEXTER, two years in the 11th Vermont regiment, from W.; and (3.) WILLIAM was a nine months' man from Thetford.
    2. NATHANIEL, b. June 6, 1807; was a farmer and drover; now retired, at Waterbury St.; m. Huldah Chandler, of Strafford, Vt.
    3. WILLIAM, b. Oct. 7, 1809; m. Julia Gilman, of Strafford; lived at Waterbury Street; d. Sept. 6, 1865, in his 56th year; five children, of whom, his only son, (1.) JUSTIN WILLIAM, has been postmaster in Waterbury for eight years (1872).
    4. BETSY, b. June 6, 1811; see [2732].
    5. ELISHA, b. Mar. 7, 1813; has been a farmer; now residing at Waterbury Street; m., 1st, Hannah Gilman, sister of Julia [3]; m., 2d, Julia Sears ; m., 3d, Mrs. Julianna (Smith) Dillingham; eight children, two deceased. One of his sons, (1.) CHARLES, was a soldier in the late war, 11th Vermont regiment.
    6. JOSEPH, b. July 27, 1815; resides at St. Paul, Minn.; m. Cordelia Towne, of Waterford, Vt.; now deceased; five children.

7. AVICE (Avis), b. July 27, 1817; m. Ephraim Kenney, of Barre;
        d. of consumption, Jan. 18, 1842, in her 25th year
8. GEORGE WASHINGTON, b. Sept. 20, 1822; a farmer; m. Lucia
        Eddy, of Waterbury; seven children, of whom: (1.) EMMA,
        b. Oct. 10, 1852, and d. at Waterbury, Oct. 9, 1872, aged 20.
9. ANGELINE, b. Sept. 29, 1828; m. George Duncan, of Jericho,
        Vt.; five children, one deceased.
2195. JONATHAN (Chesley), b. 1784; m. Phebe West; lived in Vershire,
        moved thence to Waterloo (Geneva), N.Y.; was there drowned
        while watering a horse on the ice in a stream, about the year
        1867, aged 83 (?); five children.
2196. ELSIE (Alice), b. 1786, m. John Colomy [2231]; moved to Thetford,
        Vt., and d in Hanover, N. H., Oct. 1837(?), aged 51. Child:—
    1. SALLY (Colomy), b. Oct. 14, 1803, in Farmington, N. H.; see
        [2714].
2197. ENOCH (Chesley). b. 1788; m. Aziah Ayers; resided in Waterbury,
        and there d. Mar. 1836, æ. 48. She m., 2d, [2323]. Children:—
    1. TIMOTHY.   2. LIZZIE.   3. ALMIRA.   4. GEORGE.   5. PATTY.
        6. LYDIA.   7. PERVILLA; m. Cyrus Kenyon, farmer. of Wa-
        terbury; now residing in Stowe, Vt.   8. JONATHAN.   9. LU-
        THERA; m. Almeron Goodell, now of Waterbury, farmer.

2198. ISAAC[3] [2146] (Abraham[2], John[1]), settled in Barrington,
near his uncle John's [2141], and m. Anna Ham, daughter of Joseph Ham, of B., 1770, who was b. 1750. He responded to his
country's call soon after the breaking out of the Revolutionary
war, see [2142], and is noticed in the New Hampshire military
records as " Ensign in Co. Six, Capt. John Hill's Co., on Seavy's
Island," for the defence of Portsmouth, " Nov. 5, 1775." Was
afterwards " Lieutenant in Capt. Daniel McDuffee's Co., Col.
Evans' regiment." " Entered Sept. 8, 1777," and " died Nov. 15,
1777 " (aged 28). " Time" of service, " 2 months 8 days ';
" travel" awarded " to New Windsor and Bennington," showing
that he was with the " Northern Army," and " sum due, £18 7s.
2d." Referring to the same service, he is elsewhere mentioned
as " 2d lieutenant of Co. Four, in Whipple's Brigade," which
" marched to Saratoga and assisted in compelling the surrender of
Burgoyne, Oct. 17, 1777." He is reported by some of his descendants to have been " killed in battle" on this expedition ; but he
was only wounded, probably in the " second severe engagement"
which preceded the surrender, when the British General Fraser was
killed, and he seems to have died of lingering sickness, connected
with the wounds thus received, as the New Hampshire military
treasurer reported among " sums paid for sick and wounded soldiers, as follows ": (. . .) " To Ann Runnels, for Lieut. Isaac R.,
" Evans's regiment, £14 6s." His wife is said to have " died of grief,"
probably at Barrington, soon after receiving news of his death ; see
also the will of John Runnels [2141]. His brother Samuel was
administrator of his estate, and presented inventory of " 34 acres
of land in Barrington, May 8, 1786," the same, doubtless, that he
purchased of Jane Larey, of Somersworth, for £50, " Apr. 16, 1773 "
(Rockingham Deeds). His children, b. in Barrington, were : —

2199. ISAAC [2294], b. 1771.
2200. HANNAH [2309], b. 1773.

2201. JAMES[3] [2147] (Abraham[2], John[1]), being present at the marriage of his brother Isaac, in Barrington, he there became acquainted with the bride's sister, Tamson Ham, whom he afterwards m., 1774. She was b. 1748. He was chosen " Fence Viewer " and " Tidden man " at New Durham, Mar. 6, 1775, but entered his country's service the following season with his father and brothers, see [2142]. He is thought to have served continuously as a soldier till 1779–80, as he is not mentioned on the town records again till Mar. 1780, when he was chosen one of the " Sevars upon the rodes." No record of that army service is found among the New Hampshire military papers, till " July 20, 1779," when he enlisted in his brother's company, " Co. Six, Col. Hercules Mooney's regiment, continental service, under Gen. Sullivan, for the defence of Rhode Island. A sergeant at first, he was promoted to ensign, in the same company, " Sept. 16, 1779," and so continued till " Jan. 17, 1780," " 4 months 2 days." He was the only soldier in that expedition from New Durham, — beside his brother Capt. Samuel, — as we have a " Record for *one* soldier who served in R. I. for New Durham, six months, and traviling fees, £42," with his name appended, as " James Runnells." It is *certain*, however, that he served under various enlistments prior to 1779, once for " about six months, taking the place of his father Abraham, who returned on account of disability " ; this is according to tradition in the family, the validity of which is not impaired by the mere *absence* of his name before 1779, from the confessedly confused and imperfect " military papers " in the Adjutant General's office of New Hampshire. He remained in New Durham till after 1783, being " drawn, as grand juror," that year (Town Records) ; but soon after moved to Ossipee, N. H. ; there resided as a farmer, and subsequently at Tuftonborough, where he d. Apr. 9, 1844, aged 92. He was a firm, consistent member of the Free Will Baptist Church for sixty years, having joined the first church of that order ever organized, and being appointed a " Ruling Elder " in the days of Randall. She d. at Tuftonboro', 1847, aged 99. Children : —

2202. JOHN [2320], b. 1774 (5), in New Durham.
2203. JOSEPH [2323], Jan. 5 (6), 1777.
2204. MARY [2332], b. Dec. 18, 1780.
2205. SAMUEL [2336], b. Jan. 6, 1783 (2).
2206. ANNA [2345], b. Nov. 11, 1785.
2207. TAMSON, b. Nov. 24, 1789 ; d. at her sister's, last named, in Tuftonboro', Oct. 15, 1854, in her 65th year.

2208. SAMUEL[3] [2148] (Abraham[2], John[1]). The following is, in part, an abstract of the sketch of his life, by Rev. E. Place, in the " Morning Star " of Apr. 28, 1847. " When sixteen years of age, he heard Whitefield preach his last sermon, at Exeter, Sept. 29, 1770, from 2d Cor. xiii. 5. The preacher died the next morning at Newburyport ; his young auditor was left under powerful conviction, but afterwards became careless as before. At the age of 21, he joined the American army at Winter Hill," as before

188   RUNNELS AND REYNOLDS MEMORIALS.

stated, [2142]. "In July, 1776, he was with Gen. Sullivan at
Crown Point, N. Y., and was left by the General for some time at
that place, in charge of all his baggage and papers. Was also with
Sullivan at the bloody battle of the Brandywine, Sept. 11, 1777,
and at Germantown, Oct. 4. With the same General again in
Rhode Island, in 1778 ; and the next winter was sent to Geneva,
N. Y., from which expedition he returned home, bearing (without
knowing it) a captain's commission for himself in a letter to Gov.
Meshech Weare." Hence his name now first appears in the Adjt.
General's (published) Report, — in which names of Revolutionary
officers only are given, — as "Captain of a Co. in Col. Hercules
Mooney's regiment for the defence of Rhode Island," serving from
"June 30, 1779, to Jan. 16, 1780, 6 months, 18 days, (£) 48 | ."
Also on the New Hampshire Provincial Records, "July 17, 1780
made out commission for Capt. Samuel Runnels appointed to com
mand a company on the western frontiers" ; and July 18, the same
ordered to proceed to Haverhill on Connecticut River, and take
under his command one of the companies [of Rangers] raised for
defence of the frontier." One account among different branches of
his descendants, makes him to have continued in the service longer,
to have acted as aide-de-camp of Gen. Washington, and to have
been *with* him at the surrender of Cornwallis. But, if so, it must
have been a special service subsequently entered, for Mr. Place
informs us that in November, of 1780, "he resigned his commission, and immediately enlisted as a soldier under the Prince of
Peace, with Randall as sub-leader instead of Washington." After
finally returning home, he received various tokens of respect from
his fellow-townsmen of New Durham, being elected assessor two
years, 1784-5 ; moderator of town meeting two years, 1786-7, and
first selectman four years, 1788-91. He received a justice's commission, in 1795, — first noted on the town books, 1797, — and in
this capacity he decided, during his life, seven hundred and forty-
five cases, only eight of which were ever appealed to a higher court.
Being a leading member and ruling elder of the new Free Will
Baptist denomination, he obtained an act from the General Court
of New Hampshire, Dec. 11, 1812, for a "Charitable Society" for
the widows and orphans of deceased ministers, and continued President of that Society for twenty years. From the Dover Registry
of Deeds, we learn that he purchased land *in Rochester*, — perhaps
intending to settle there, — at five different times, in all one hundred and thirty-nine acres, between "May 7, 1781," and "Apr. 29,
1786," a portion of which he sold in the meantime. His homestead
in New Durham was two or three miles north of his father's,
and one mile from the present Downing's Mills. Whether this was
the "100 acres, in N. D.," deeded to him by his father, "for £300,
Feb. 19, 1787," or a part of two hundred and thirty acres, probably
in N. D., received from Paul March, of Portsmouth, Mar. 2, same
year, is uncertain ; but the time of his first occupying his homestead is thus reasonably fixed. He bid off twenty-five acres for
taxes in the "Gore of New Durham" (now Alton), added to his

N. D. estate at three different times, up to 1795, — a portion of which he conveyed to Joseph L. Wille, "Aug. 6, 1793," but was still left an extensive land-holder in New Durham, at a time, however, when land was very cheap. He also came in possession of Lot No. 81, in Barrington, "the original right of Job Runnells," which he sold to John Foss, 4th, of B., Dec. 17, 1789. The final result of these transactions was not to enrich *himself*, though he also received a pension of three hundred dollars annually, and so late as Oct. 26, 1841, when nearly eighty-eight years of age, he made the following peculiar record of his worldly estate : —

"Accumulated in sixty years		$28,510,
Expenses of family, said time . .	$18,405,	
Given to family, on settlement . .	6,515,	
Given to the poor and needy, and to various		
benevolent societies . . .	1,750	
Lost in bad debts	1,257	
Property on hand, real and personal .	583 !	
Total as above	$28,510."	

"The general character of this eminent servant of God was worthy of all praise. His success was owing, under God, to his perseverance in whatever he undertook. In all religious exercises he was marked by true devotion, and great humility, with frequent falling tears." His acceptable efforts at religious meetings in his old age, are still remembered in many places, as at Andover, N. H., where he was accustomed to visit his daughter residing in that place. "He was always at public worship on the Sabbath ; heard, in later life, more than two thousand sermons, as by record kept, and travelled seventeen thousand miles to monthly, quarterly, and yearly meetings, and to general conference." He was the intimate friend and co-laborer of the Rev. Benjamin Randall, and superintended his funeral, Oct. 26, 1808, which is said to have been " conducted with great quietness, decorum, and simplicity," though " few, if any funerals, in New Hampshire, ever have had so large an attendance " (Dr. Joseph Fullonton in " Morning Star" of July 31, 1872). In stature he stood six feet, of large size, a commanding countenance and dignified deportment. He d. at N. Durham, Mar. 21, 1847, in his 93d year. His funeral was attended by several ministers, — sermon by Rev. E. Place, — and he was buried near his house, his gravestone bearing this appropriate inscription : " Precious in the sight of the Lord is the death of his saints." He m., 1st, Mary, daughter of Paul March, Esq., of Portsmouth, 1783. She was b. Nov. 16, 1754, and d. Dec. 16, 1843, aged 89 ; (gravestone) : —

> " Rest, mother, rest; life's toils are o'er,
>   Now death has set thee free;
> Though thou art seen by friends no more,
>   With Jesus thou shalt be."

He m., 2d, Mrs. Dorcas Ricker, Nov. 26, 1844, who d. June 8, 1847, aged 78 years 4 months; (gravestone) : —

> "From mortal cares to seats of love
> The sacred spirit flies;
> On wings of faith she soars above,
> And rests beyond the skies."

Children, all b. in New Durham, as per town records : —

2209. SARAH (Sally) [2350], b. Feb. 1, 1784.
2210. NATHANIEL BRACKETT [2357], b. Nov. 18 (19), 1785.
2211. POLLY (Mary) [2364], b. Apr. 19, 1787.
2212. BETSY [2369], b. Sept. 18, 1788.
2213. PAUL MARCH [2376], b. June 6, 1790.
2214. HANNAH [2378], b. June 1, 1792.
2215. JOHN SMITH [2382], b. July (Feb.) 27, 1794.
2216. NANCY BURTON [2389], b. Mar. 23, 1797.
2217. DEBORAH, b. Jan. 9, 1799; d. of fever at New Durham, Jan. 27, 1816, aged 17.
2218. SAMUEL [2394], b. Oct. 15, 1801.

2219. NATHANIEL[3] [2149] (Abraham[2], John[1]), was *not* in the Revolutionary war, but is supposed to have settled in New Durham, as he is *known* to have had the two following children, born in New Durham : —

2220. ABRAM [2407], b. Mar. 1797.
2221. HANNAH, "who was younger, and lived at least to the age of seventeen." Also "one other son and one other daughter," whether younger or older, does not appear, "who died in infancy."

2222. JONATHAN[3] [2150] (Abraham[2], John[1]). There is a tradition among some of his descendants, that he earnestly desired to join his father and brothers in the Revolutionary war, and was only dissuaded by the entreaties of his friends, being but sixteen years of age at the breaking out of hostilities. Afterwards, being still prevented by circumstances from entering the army, he seems to have led, through his disappointment, a somewhat restless life, for a few years, and at last found his way to Concord, N. H., where he m. Dorothy Dimond, 1779. She was b. July 27, 1758, the daughter of Ezekiel and Miriam Dimond. He "was once more in readiness to enlist," for the campaigns of 1779 and 1780, and was again prevented by the sickness of his wife, which continued for more than a year. "He used to pray most devoutly to the God of armies, that his dear wife might recover her health, and he thus be permitted to fight the battles of his country." He was a very sympathetic man, and never spoke of his brothers, lost in the war, without tears. "Was never known to speak a harsh or unpleasant word." Being the "seventh son" of his father's family, he was consulted, according to the custom of the times, by hundreds of people, for the cure of scrofula and other diseases. A deed among the Rockingham Records speaks of him as a "Clothier of Concord," receiving "May 1, 1787," from Ezekiel Dimond, "a certain part of the stream called Turkey river, begin-

ning at the mouth of Great Turkey pond, and extending down
stream to the head of the lesser pond; also one half of the fulling
mill on said premises, — all Dimond's right and title to the same,
— together with a dwelling-house near by." He also bought of
D. Carter, "Oct. 21, 1799," " a small piece of land in Concord,
lying upon Turkey Upper Falls, so called." He soon after moved
to Deering, where he d. Apr. 18, 1804, in his 46th year. She d. at
Deering, July 10, 1825, aged 67. The following register of their
children — born in Concord except the fifth — is mostly from
Bouton's History of Concord : —

2223. SAMUEL [2411], b. July 30, 1781.
2224. MIRIAM [2423], b. July 3, 1783.
2225. EZEKIEL DIMOND [2434], b. Jan. 21 (22), 1786.
2226. ABNER [2440], b. Mar. 2, 1789.
2227. JAMES [2448], b. Mar. 28, 1791, in Pembroke, N. H.
2228. ISRAEL [2454], b. July 14, 1793.
2229. JONATHAN CURRIER [2463], b. Sept. 29, 1795.

2230. ALICE³ [2152] (Abraham², John¹), m. Daniel Colomy, of
New Durham, N. H., Dec. 1, 1780, and d. Feb. 15, 1830, in her
68th year. He d. Mar. 22, 1830. Children : —

2231. JOHN (Colomy), b. May 20, 1782; see [2196].
2232. ABRAHAM, b. Dec. 10, 1784.
2233. ISAAC, b. June 28, 1788.
2234. JACOB, b. May 16, 1790; d. Oct. 23, 1834, aged 44, being killed by
the caving in of a well.
2235. DANIEL, b. Aug. 9, 1792; m. Rebecca Pinkham, July 11, 1819, who
was b. May 15, 1799. Children : —
  1. JOHN, b. Feb. 29, 1820; see [2794].
  2. CHARLES, b. Feb. 3, 1822; a carpenter at Alton Bay, N. H.; m.
    Augusta Nute.
  3. GEORGE WASHINGTON, b. Sept. 25, 1824; a shoemaker and
    farmer in Farmington, N. H.; m. Hattie Richardson; three
    children.
  4. ELSIE ("Elcy"), b. Aug. 8, 1826; d. Nov. 10, 1834, aged 8.
  5. JONAS, b. May 5, 1828; a "stitcher" in the shoe business; m.
    Maria Pinkham; three children.
  6. DANIEL, b. Feb. 19, 1830; a shoemaker in Dover, N. H.; m.
    Dorothy Locke; one daughter.
  7. STEPHEN, b. Mar. 27, 1832; a shoemaker in New Durham;
    m. Experience Sumner; three children, — two daughters
    living, one deceased.
  8. MARY JANE, b. Jan. 30, 1835; see [2809].
  9. SARAH ELIZABETH, b. May 16, 1837; m. John Plummer, of
    Sandwich, N. H.; two sons.
  10. JAMES PINKHAM, b. Feb. 7, 1843; was a soldier in the 4th Co.
    New Hampshire cavalry, and d. Jan. 7, 1862, in his 19th year.
2236. PEGGY, b. Mar. 9, 1795.
2237. MOLLY, b. May 2, 1797.

2238. EBENEZER³ [2154] (Abraham², John¹), received by deed
from " Amos Place, of Rochester, thirty acres of land in Middleton," N. H., " Nov. 4, 1786." He is called in this deed " Ebenezer
Runals, of Barrington," showing that he first lived in that town.
The *time* of his settling in Middleton is thus approximately ascer-

tained, where he m. Betsey Stanton, of M., 1788. He afterwards located in New Durham, and there d. Sept. 1847, aged 79. She d. at N. D. with her youngest daughter, Oct. 1836. Children, born Middleton : —

2239. PATIENCE [2475], b. 1789.
2240. ALICE (Elsey) [2481], b. Mar. 11, 1793.
2241. JAMES [2489], b. Oct. 26, 1794.
2242. ELIZABETH [2495], b. June 13, 1799.

2243. MOSES[3] [2156] (William[2], John[1]), m. Sarah Crosby, the adopted child of Paul Tasker, of Barrington, 1771, and after " administering " upon his father's estate, 1774, see [2155], receiving by will " one half the farm," " a colt, a cow and blacksmith's tools," he entered the Revolutionary service. Is noticed among the " soldiers from Lee " in connection with his brothers [2158] and [2159] ; has " £35 15s. 4d." against his name on account ; said to be " twenty-five years of age, Apr. 18, 1777," when a member of " Capt. F. M. Bell's Co." ; enrolled in " 2d Co., 2d regiment, Col. George Reed's, for the years 1777-9 " ; " amount of depreciation, $171.50 " ; " amount of wages, 1780-1, $80," and lastly, noted as " *now* in the Continental army, June 30, 1781 " (N. H. military papers). Soon *after* this latter date, he was discharged, went to procure his pay, and was never heard from afterwards. He is supposed, therefore, to have d., perhaps, by violence, 1781-2, in his 30th year. His wife was b. 1752, and d., his widow, Apr. 18, 1814, aged 62. Their children, b. in Lee, were : —

2244. WILLIAM [2500], b. May 25, 1772.
2245. POLLY [2514], b. 1774.
2246. SARAH [2521], b. 1777.

2247. WINTHROP[3] [2170] (Joseph[2], John[1]), was a joiner by trade, and is said by his descendants to have been early " in the Revolutionary war at Ticonderoga." The military records say he was " mustered at Kingston, by Josiah Bartlett, Aug. 13, 1780," and that he " enlisted for Barrington to recruit the New Hampshire regiments in the Continental service, Dec. 31, 1780." This proves he had settled in B. prior to that date. He lived, finally, in the east part of Barrington, on a small farm given him by his last wife's father, and was there killed by the falling of a tree, Jan. 13 (gravestone), more probably, as by family record, Feb. 15, 1832 (1), aged 78. He was four times m. ; 1st, to a daughter of the Rev. Samuel Hutchins, of Lee, 1780, by whom his oldest child. She d. 1781, near the birth of her son. He m., 2d, —— Ricker, of Somersworth, 1782, by whom his second child ; m., 3d, Lucy Stone, of Ipswich, Mass., 1783, by whom third and fourth children ; m., 4th, Hannah Locke, of Barrington, 1791, who was b. Dec. 16, 1767, in B., and there d. Aug. 21, 1846, in her 79th year. Her will appears on the Strafford Probate records ; abstract as follows : To her sons Winthrop (" my oldest "), Jacob K., and Ephraim F., $3.00 each ; to George F. and Samuel L., $1.00 each ;

to Elizabeth L. Weeks, a bed, and other articles of furniture; to Job F., " all my real estate, or in case he is without heirs, the same to Winthrop Reynolds, son of my son Winthrop, now residing in Boston"; also " to Hannah L. Reynolds, of Boston, daughter of Winthrop, my black silk," and other articles of apparel. His children, as here given, are mostly from the Barrington records, on which the name is spelled " Runnels," though " Reynolds " has since been adopted by the family : —

2248.　JOHN [2523], b. 1781, in Lee (first wife).
2249.　ELEANOR (Lucy) [2527], b. 1782 (second wife).
2250.　HANNAH [2529], b. Mar. 2, 1784, in Lee (third wife).
2251.　EDWARD T. [2540], b. July 17, 1785, in Durham.
2252.　WILLIAM, b. Sept. 23, 1792. in Barrington, and there d. of brain fever, Dec. 1813, aged 21.
2253.　WINTHROP [2542], b. Mar. 2, 1794, in Barrington.
2254.　SAMUEL LOCKE [2552], b. Sept. 16, 1795.
2255.　GEORGE FOOTMAN, b. Jan. 26, 1797; d. 1798, aged 1 year.
2256.　GEORGE FOOTMAN [2554], b. Oct. 9, 1799.
2257.　JOB FOSS [2559], b. Feb. 19, 1801.
2258.　JACOB KITTREDGE [2561], b. Apr. 8, 1803.
2259.　EPHRAIM FOSS [2567], b. Dec. 27, 1804.
2260.　ELIZABETH LOCKE [2572], b. Mar. 12, 1807.

2261.　MARY[3] [2171] (Joseph[2], John[1]), was m. to Jacob Garland, of Durham, Dec. 25, 1774, by the Rev. Jeremy Belknap, D. D., at Dover. They resided in Durham, near New Market, where he d. of spotted fever, about 1820, and she soon after, aged 66. Children : —

2262.　FRANCIS (Garland), b. about 1778; resided in Kennebec County, and Portland, Me., and in Boston, Mass.
2263.　JACOB, b. about 1780; resided at Great Falls, N. H., and Sanford, Me.

2264.　HANNAH[3] [2172] (Joseph[2], John[1]), m. David Ham, of Dover, N. H., July 9, 1776, at D. He was the ninth son and eleventh child of Dea. Daniel Ham; baptized, 1756; was a soldier in the Revolution, " leaving his two oldest as young children at home." hence, probably, not earlier than the year 1780; d. 1811. The following list of their children agrees, mainly, with the published record of the " Ham Family in Dover," by John R. Ham, M. D., " N. E. Genealogical Register," Oct. 1872, p. 392 : —

2265.　JOSEPH (Ham), b. Jan. 28, 1779; was a boatman on the Cocheco river, and d. at Dover, Jan. 1852, aged 73; eleven children.
2266.　HANNAH, b. Mar. 3, 1780, at Dover Neck; m. John Young, of D., and moved to Tuftonboro', N. H , where she was still living, with her son, in 1870. Of her children : —
　　1.　JOHN H. (Young); resides at Tuftonboro', " Mackerel Corner."
　　2.　MARK F.; resides in Stratham, N. H.
2267.　BETSY or ELIZABETH (Ham), b. June 3, 1783; m. Jonathan Gage, of Dover Neck, 1817, and there d. July 11, 1862, aged 79. Her son :—
　　1.　MOSES (Gage), still occupies the homestead on Dover Neck.
2268.　SARAH (Ham), b. 1788 (?); m. Moses Sawyer, of Dover, and d. in Ossipee, where her son, —
　　1.　DAVID (Sawyer), now resides.

2269. LYDIA (Ham), b. Apr. 10, 1791; m. Samuel Pinkham, of Dover; was residing with her son, at Great Falls, 1870. Children:—
    1. NATHANIEL J. (Pinkham), b. Oct. 15, 1821.
    2. EDWARD J., b. Apr. 16, 1823; a merchant in Somersworth (Great Falls).
2270. DAVID (Ham), b. 1793; went to sea in 1814, and d. in Liverpool, Eng., soon afterwards, aged 21.
2271. ROBERT, b. June 8, 1796; lived at Great Falls, and there d. Aug. 1861 (?), aged 65. His widow still living with her daughter:—
    1. REBECCA, who m. Charles H. Gilman.
2272. DANIEL (Ham), b. 1798 (?); resided in Dover; d. suddenly on his way home from Barrington, 1833, aged 35 (?). Children:—
    1. ABIGAIL; m. Stephen Otis, of Springvale, Me.
    2. RUFUS; resides in Boston, Mass.
2273. MARY (Ham), b. 1805; m. Nicholas Tripe, of Dover; resided in Charlestown, Mass., and d. at Dover, June 21, 1866, aged 61.

2274. JOSEPH³ [2173] (Joseph², John¹), appears as a Revolutionary soldier among the "twenty-one men from Lee"; afterwards as "enlisted for three years from New Durham" (at which place he must have been temporarily living), "in Capt. Drew's Co."; also, referring, probably, to the same enlistment, among those "raised for Canada, Col. Evans, 1776"; again, "in the Continental service returned by Capt. Boody," and finally, "Jan. 12, 1781," after his term of service had expired, he is noticed among soldiers entitled to "extra pay" on account of "depreciation" (N. H. Military Papers). He was also enlisted as a privateer's man at one time during the Revolution, on the testimony of his surviving children, who further say of him, — what is verified by his early enlistment at the age of 17, — that "he was of an enterprising nature, and of rather a military turn through life." His business was that of a tanner, like most of his father's family. He m. Abigail Pinkham, at Dover, Dec. 17 (19), 1780; all his own children are said to have been b. in that part of Rochester which is now Farmington, where he first settled. He afterwards lived in Dover, and there d. Mar. 20, 1846, in his 87th year. His family record is found on that choice old "account book" of his father's, see [2166] and [2605], as follows:—

2275. WILLIAM, b. June 11, 1781; was a shoemaker in Dover, and there d.
2276. JOHN [2576], b. June 24, 1783.
2277. MARTHA [2589], b. Feb. 13, 1785.
2278. JOSEPH [2593], b. Aug. 18, 1787.
2279. JEREMIAH, b. Mar. 21, 1790; d. in infancy.
2280. JAMES, b. Oct. 6, 1791; d. in infancy.
2281. ANNA, b. July 15, 1794; has been a school-teacher and milliner; residing in Bangor, Me., 1870.
2282. SAMUEL [2600], b. Mar. 17, 1797.
2283. GEORGE [2605], b. Feb. 16, 1800.
2284. OLIVER [2607], b. Jan. 1, 1810, in Madbury, N. H. (adopted).

2285. BENJAMIN³ [2174] (Joseph², John¹), m. Rebecca Wentworth, Sept. 17, 1787. She was b. June 7, 1766 (5), in Rochester, N. H., where they lived till Oct. 15, 1798, and then moved to

China, afterwards to Vassalboro', Kennebec County, Me. His father's old account book, see [2166], says "Benjamin left for the State of Maine, Mar. 7, 1802," probably after a subsequent visit at his parents' home. He d. in Vassalboro', Dec. 27, 1834, aged 69, where also she had d. Mar. 6, 1833, in her 67th year. Children : —

2286. LYDIA [2611], b. Apr. 15, 1789.
2287. HANNAH [2619], b. Apr. 7, 1791.
2288. DANIEL [2623], b. "6th month" (June) 20, 1793.
2289. BENJAMIN [2631], b. May 7, 1796.
2290. LOIS [2641], b. Oct. 11, 1798.
2291. REBECCA, b. Nov. 12, 1802; d. Dec. 9, 1805, aged 3.
2292. JONATHAN D. [2646], b. Jan. 5, 1805, in China, Me.
2293. ISAAC RANDALL [2651], b. July 13, 1808, in China.

FOURTH GENERATION.

2294. ISAAC[4] [2199] (Isaac[3], Abraham[2], John[1]), was brought up by his Uncle Samuel [2208], after the death of his parents, "till old enough to shift for himself." "Apr. 23, 1799," together with his sister Hannah, he deeded the land in Barrington, — "thirty-four acres, owned by our late honored father," — to Jonathan Glass, of Nottingham, for $204; having previously purchased fifty acres in Gilmanton of David Ames, for $360 ("Mar. 18, 1799"), which he sold to John Mooney, of New Durham, for $400, about two years later. Gilford, N. H., was afterwards his home, from which place he enlisted for one year, "Mar. 26, 1813, in Capt. L. B. Mason's Co."; was at Portsmouth, as a soldier, and drew a pension, accordingly, in after-life. He again lived in Gilmanton after his third marriage. He m., 1st, Mary Thurston, of Gilford, — mother of his eight oldest children, — 1798, who d. 1815; m., 2d, Eunice Eaton, of Tuftonboro', — mother of his ninth child, — 1817, who d. 1818; m., 3d, Sophia Leavitt, of Gilmanton ("Province road"), Feb. 28, 1820, at G., who was b. Dec. 15, 1792, and d. Nov. 17, 1846, aged 54, having been the mother of his five youngest children; m., 4th, Mrs. Susan Weeks, of Gilford, Nov. 1847, who d. July, 1862; and, "last of all," he d. at Sanbornton, N. H., with his daughter, Mrs. Buzzell, Jan. 14, 1864, aged 93; funeral attended by Rev. C. Curtice, Congregational pastor at Sanbornton Bridge. Children: —

2295. ISAAC [2657], b. June 2, 1799, in Gilmanton.
2296. LYDIA, b. Jan. 14, 1801; m. Levi Lovett, 1842, in Gilford; was residing, 1870, in Laconia, N. H., having been deaf and dumb from her earliest childhood, and yet enabled to lead a very useful life.
2297. POLLY [2663], b., Apr. 26, 1803, in Gilford.
2298. SAMUEL, b. 1805; d. young.
2299. JOSIAH, b. 1806; d. 1814, aged 8, at Gilford (now Laconia Village), being killed by mill-logs while at play in the mill-yard with his younger sister.
2300. BETSY [2669]. b. Oct. 3, 1808.
2301. LUCINDA, b. 1810; d. 1814, aged 4, by the same distressing casualty as her brother, above.
2302. JOHN [2677], b. Apr. 15, 1814, in Gilford.
2303. JOSIAH, b. 1818 (second wife); d. 1839, of consumption, aged 21.

2304. JULIA ANN [2685], b. Apr. 29, 1821 (third wife), in Gilmanton.
2305. FREEMAN, b. 1825; "led a free life;" joined the U. S. army; is supposed to have d.
2306. JESSE SANBORN, b. Jan. 27, 1830, in Gilmanton; name now changed to "Joseph George Gerrish"; is employed on the Amoskeag corporation in Manchester; residence at Pittsfield, N. H.; m. Lucy White Blaisdell, of P., Aug. 4, 1861.
2307. SAMUEL HENRY [2697], b. Nov. 3, 1831, in Gilmanton.
2308. ALMIRA RACHEL [2701], b. Nov. 3, 1833, in Gilmanton.

2309. HANNAH[4] [2200] (Isaac[3], Abraham[2], John[1]), was also, like her brother, brought up under the charge of her uncle, Esquire Samuel Runnals, of New Durham, and m. Nathaniel Witham, 1803; resided in Alton, and there d. Jan. 1831, aged 58. No less than three conflicting records of this family have come to hand, from which the following is arranged as *most probably* correct. Children: —

2310. ABIGAIL RUNNELS (Witham), b. 1804; is said to have "joined the Shakers," about 1818.
2311. ABRAHAM, b. May 26, 1806; m. a Gage.
2312. HANNAH RUNNALS, b. Nov. 3, 1808; m. Gage Horn, a farmer living in the lower part of Farmington (Place's Station), N.H. Their daughter: —
     1. H. MARIAH (Horn), m. a Downs.
2313. LOUISA [Eliza] (Witham), b. Mar. 29, 1810; m. Luther Ricker, of Farmington, and there d. Aug. 7, 1870, in her 61st year. Children: —
     1. ELIZA JANE (Ricker); m. James D. Place, of Farmington.
     2. THOMAS; m. Maria Randall, of Farmington.
2314. NANCY (Witham), b. Apr. 4, 1812; m., 1st, a Rogers; 2d, a Willey; 3d, a Witham; resides (1870) with her son: —
     1. JAMES (Rogers), at Farmington.
2315. MOSES (Witham), b. Dec. 6, 1814, in Alton; a farmer at New Durham, and there d. Dec. 24, 1859, aged 45; three children.
2316. NATHANIEL, b. Dec. 6, 1816, in Alton; farmer in New Durham; there d. Nov. 14, 1859, in his 43d year.
2317. ISAAC RUNNELS, b. 1819; d. at sea.
2318. SARAH ANN, b. Aug. 28, 1821, "a week or two before the great September gale, Sept. 9, 1821"; m. Moses Randall, of New Durham; d. Nov. 3, 1868, aged 47; six children.
2319. MARY SOPHIA, b. 1822; m. a Kenney.

2320. JOHN[4] [2202] (James[3], Abraham[2], John[1]), was a house joiner; m. Mary Horn, of Farmington, N. H., 1795; enlisted in the United States' service, autumn of 1812, and d. while a soldier, at Sackett's Harbor, N. Y., Jan. 4, 1813, aged 39. Children: —

2321. PAUL [2709], b. June 10, 1798, in Farmington.
2322. NANCY, b. Sept. 5, 1801, in New Durham; m. Capt. Thomas Frisbie, master mariner, May, 1847; now resides (1870) at Kittery, Me.

2323. JOSEPH[4] [2203] (James[3], Abraham[2], John[1]), was a farmer, residing, successively, at New Durham, Tuftonboro', and Lyme, N. H.; m., 1st, Rebecca Chesley [2191], Mar. 19, 1799, at New Durham, who d. Mar. 21, 1842. He m., 2d, Mrs. Aziah Chesley, of Waterbury, Vt., Dec. 14, 1843. She was the widow of his first wife's brother, Enoch [2197], and d. 1861.   He d. with his daughter [2754], at North Thetford, Vt., Jan. 3, 1867, aged 90.   Children :—

2324. ELIZABETH, b. Dec. 26, 1799, in New Durham; d. Jan. 3, 1800, aged 1 week.
2325. JEREMIAH [2714], b. July 16, 1801, in N. D.
2326. SALLY [2723], b. June 4, 1803, in N. D.
2327. SAMUEL [2732], b. Dec. 5, 1804, in N. D.
2328. DANIEL [2738], b July 2, 1808, in Tuftonboro'.
2329. JOHN HANSON [2747], b. Feb. 1, 1811, in T.
2330. POLLY [2754]. b Oct. 14, 1814, in T.
2331. JAMES. b. Nov. 23, 1816, in T. ; was a farmer; settled in Hanover, N. H.; m. Louvisa Jenks, of Lyme. N. H., Sept. 1838, and d. at Hanover, Aug. 11, 1850, in his 34th year. She d. at Haverhill, N. H., Aug. 16, 1869, aged 53.

2332. MARY[4] [2204] (James[3], Abraham[2], John[1]), m. Ephraim Perkins, of Hope, Me. ; afterwards moved West. *He* had nine children, but no more than *three*, it is presumed. by this, his second wife, as follows : —

2333. STAPLES (Perkins).
2334. RUNNELS.
2335. MARY (?).

2336. SAMUEL[4] [2205] (James[3], Abraham[2], John[1]), m. Ursula Randall, of New Durham, N. H., Dec. 1800. She was the daughter of the Rev. Benjamin Randall, founder of the Free Will Baptist denomination ; was b. Oct. 15, 1780, and d. at Portland, Me., Jan. 8. 1828, aged 47.   He settled first as a merchant in New Durham ; then as a stevedore in Portland, Me., 1803–4, where he d. Aug. 22, 1821, in his 39th year.   Children : —

2337. MARGARET [2757], b. Dec. 19, 1801, in New Durham.
2338. URSULA, b. Sept. 2, 1803, in New Durham; m. a Hayes, and is supposed to have d.
2339. ANNA, b. 1805, in North Yarmouth, Me.; d. Nov. 27, 1859, aged 54.
2340. SAMUEL DANA [2767], b. Dec. 12, 1806, in Portland.
2341. BENJAMIN RANDALL [2776], b. Sept. 12, 1809, in Portland.
2342. JAMES, b. Feb. 29, 1812, in P., and there d. July, 1813, aged 1 y. 5 m.
2343. JOANNA ORAM [2778], b. Apr. 9, 1814, in New Durham.
2344. MARY, b. Aug. 13, 1816, in Portland; d. at Great Falls, N. H., May 7, 1833, in her 17th year.

2345. ANNA[4] [2206] (James[3], Abraham[2], John[1]), m. Peter Glidden, Sept. 11, 1809 He was a shoemaker and tanner, resided at Tuftonboro', N. H., and there d. July 7, 1861, aged 83. having been " an acceptable member of the Free Will Baptist church for twenty-two years."   She was still residing with her son at T. (Melvin's Village), 1870.   Children : —

2346. HARRIET CONANT (Glidden), b. Feb. 5, 1811, in Tuftonboro'; m. Benjamin Bodge.
2347. JAMES RUNNELS, b. June 28, 1814, in T.; m. Mary E. Neal. He "followed the sea seven years, was the mate of a vessel, and sailed round the world." Present residence (1870), Melvin's Village, N. H.

2348. MARY ANN, b. Dec. 21, 1820, in T., and there d. Aug. 18, 1848, in her 28th year, of consumption, "borne with much patience and Christian resignation."

2349. ABBY TAMSON, b. Oct. 26, 1825, and d. at Tuftonboro', Feb. 20, 1853, in her 28th year. She was an excellent Christian of the Free Will Baptist denomination. "Lines composed by her in her last sickness," appeared in print, — first two stanzas as follows : —

"I will not murmur; let sickness come,
Its waves and its billows will bear me home.
Sure I must suffer, — this frame must decay, —
But I will not murmur, — 'tis the breaking of day.

"It is the warm spirit that pants to be free, —
Pants its bright home in heaven to see.
In all this anguish, this trouble and pain,
I would not murmur, I would not complain."

2350. SARAH⁴ [2209] (Samuel³, Abraham², John¹), m., 1st, John Hanson, blacksmith and farmer, of Rochester, N. H., Oct. 9, 1806 ; was m. at New Durham by Elder Benjamin Randall. He was b. Apr. 7, 1777, and d. at Rochester, Mar. 12, 1844, in his 67th year. She m., 2d, Simon Locke, Mar. 15, 1853, who d. Apr. 7, 1854 She continued to reside with her youngest son on the old homestead in R., above Great Falls, till her death, June 4, 1871, in her 88th year. Having "experienced religion at the early age of 16," she "held fast her profession" for more than seventy years. Children, b. in Rochester : —

2351. ABIGAIL CLEMENTS (Hanson), b. Aug. 13, 1807; d. Dec. 20, 1824, aged 17.
2352. SARAH ANN, b. Dec. 6, 1808; m. Charles W. Varney; d. Aug. 22, 1835, in her 27th year.
2353. MARY ADALINE, b. July 16, 1810; m. Samuel Meserve, of Rochester.
2354. JACOB CLEMENTS, b. Sept. 29, 1812; commenced the study of medicine with Dr. Charles Trafton, of South Berwick, Me., 1833; continued with Prof. R. D. Mussey, of Hanover, N. H., and graduated at the Dartmouth Medical College, 1839, since which he has practised his profession constantly, — from 1845 to 1873, in Great Falls, N. H. He m. Hannah M. Brown, of South Berwick, June 6, 1837. Children : —
1. JOSEPH WARREN, b. Nov. 9, 1838.
2. JOHN BAKER, b. Apr. 29, 1840; studied medicine with his father, and d. Jan. 18, 1871, in his 31st year. His death was finally occasioned by a piece of whalebone, about one-half an inch long, which he "carried in his left lung upwards of twenty-seven years."
3. JACOB CLEMENTS, Jr., b. Mar. 12, 1844.
4. ANN SARAH, b. Aug. 5, 1849; d. Dec. 10, 1866, aged 17.
2355. DEBORAH SMITH, b. Aug. 20, 1815; m. Benjamin Wentworth, of Somersworth, N. H., and d. Feb. 12, 1872, in her 57th year.
2356. SAMUEL RUNNALS, b. Jan. 19, 1818; a farmer on the old homestead; m. Elizabeth C. Furber.

2357. NATHANIEL BRACKETT⁴ [2210] (Samuel³, Abraham², John¹), m. Nancy Folsom, of Rochester, N. H., public records say "June 7"; family, "July 2," 1812. He was first a merchant in

New Durham, where also he kept a public house; removed to Exeter, Me., there arriving June 1, 1828; again moved to Garland, Me., Apr. 1834, and there d. June 8, 1836. in his 51st year. She d. in Garland, Dec. 27, 1847. Children, all b. in New Durham : —

2358. NATHANIEL B., b. Sept. 15, 1813; d. at Garland, Dec. 29, 1841, aged 28.
2359. LEONORA F., b. Oct. 24, 1814; m. William W. French, of Exeter, Me., May 8, 1842, and d. at Bangor, May 25, 1851, in her 37th yr.
2360. JOHN S. [2782], b Sept. 3, 1816.
2361. ROXANA [2792], b. Jan 7, 1818.
2362. SAMUEL NEWMARCH, b. Dec. 29, 1820; d. Aug. 29, 1825, in his 5th year.
2363. JOSIAH FOLSOM, b. Jan. 13, 1823; d. Aug. 25, 1825, in his 2d year.

2364. POLLY[4] [2211] (Samuel[3], Abraham[2], John[1]), m. Moses Kimball, farmer, of Dover, N. H., Nov. 8, 1808. He d. June 7, 1854 ; she d. Nov. 14, 1855, in her 69th year. Children, all b. in Dover : —

2365. EZRA (Kimball), b. Apr. 25, 1810; d. Nov. 3, 1866, in his 57th year.
2366. SAMUEL RUNNALS, b. Nov. 3, 1811; d. Aug. 19, 1840, in his 29th year.
2367. NANCY L., b. Nov 9, 1814; d. Mar. 7, 1827, in her 13th year.
2368. CLARISSA, b. July 14, 1818; was residing on her father's estate in Dover, 1869, as the sole survivor of his family; has since m. Rev. William Davis (?), formerly a clergyman of the Free Will Baptist denomination, living in Massachusetts.

2369. BETSY[4] [2212] (Samuel[3], Abraham[2], John[1]), m. Ebenezer Blazo, merchant, of Parsonsfield, Me., Jan. 1, 1815. He d. Sept. 10, 1855, and she d. Sept. 24, 1870, aged 82, both in Parsonsfield. "Her consistent life told on the side of righteousness and truth." Children, all b. in P. : —

2370. JOSEPH (Blazo), b. Mar. 26, 1816.
2371. NANCY, b. Aug. 22, 1818; d. Aug. 14, 1819, aged 1 year.
2372. NANCY, b. Mar. 20, 1820.
2373. BETSY, b. Mar. 13, 1824.
2374. AMOS, b. Aug. 20, 1828.
2375. ANNA, b. May 5, 1830.

2376. PAUL MARCH[4] [2213] (Samuel[3], Abraham[2], John[1]), enlisted for sixty days in Capt. Reuben Hayes's Co., "Oct. 3, 1814," and was stationed at Fort Washington for the defence of Portsmouth. He was engaged in trade (a merchant) first in New Durham, afterwards in Nachitoches, La.; m. Eliza Waldron, of Farmington, Oct. 3, 1828 ; returned to New Durham, and there d. Jan. 13, 1830, in his 40th year. His will bears date, "Dec. 12, 1829." She was appointed guardian of her son, "Jan. 19, 1836"; her will dated "Sept. 10, 1836." Child : —

2377. BENJAMIN MARCH, b. Feb. 26, 1830; d. Mar. 5, 1841, aged 11.

2378. HANNAH[4] [2214] (Samuel[3], Abraham[2], John[1]), m. Joseph Berry, Jr., hotel-keeper, of New Durham, May 9, 1813. He d.

July 4, 1862, and she is still living (1872) at their old stand in New Durham. Children : —

2379. LAVINA (Berry), b. Aug. 23, 1814 ; d. May, 1815, aged 9 months.
2380. JOSEPH, b. Feb. 23, 1816 ; m. Laurentina Glidden, see [2398], and
     d. May 14, 1857, aged 41. Children : —
     1. CHARLES FRANK, b. Jan. 24, 1850 ; m. Martha Trickey, of
         Rochester, N. H., and there residing as a shoe manufacturer.
     2. GEORGE ERVING, b. Jan. 19, 1851 ; present residence in De-
         troit, Mich.
     3. CYRUS, b. Aug. 18, 1852 ; d. Aug. 5, 1870, aged 18.
     4. JOHN KENISON, b. Jan. 10, 1855 ; resides in Rochester.
     5. JOSEPHINE LAVINA, b. Dec. 18, 1857 ; now living in Lynn, Mass.
2381. SAMUEL MARCH, b. Oct. 20, 1833 ; d. Apr. 1835, aged 1 year 6 mos.

2382. JOHN SMITH[4] [2215] (Samuel[3], Abraham[2], John[1]), m. Susan McCann, at Poland, Me., May 29, 1831. Having previously resided at P., he was ordained as a Free Will Baptist clergyman, in 1842, by the Wolfborough, N. H., Quarterly Meeting, and preached for several years in various parts of New Hampshire and Maine. During the winter of 1853-4, he spent some time in the eastern part of Maine, in scenes of revival, and returning home, was immediately confined by a lung fever ; " lingered about three weeks, and then bade his family and friends farewell, in the triumphs of faith, and the hope of a glorious resurrection," Mar. 22, 1854, in his 60th year. Funeral discourse, on the following Sabbath, by the Rev. John Pinkham, from Numb. xxiii. 10. His widow d. July 15. 1861, at New Durham, N. H. Children, all b. in Poland, except the third : —

2383. JOHN SMITH, b. June 8, 1832 ; d. Apr. 2, 1854, in his 22d year.
2384. MARY SUSAN [2794], b. Dec. 12, 1834.
2385. CHARLES EARLE, b. Jan. 1, 1837, in New Durham ; m., 1st, Mary
     B. Stanton, of Poland, Me., in Casco, Nov. 14, 1861 ; resided
     in P., where she d. of consumption, Nov. 8, 1864. He enlisted
     in Poland a few days before the close of the war, 1865. He m.,
     2d, Lydia A. Savage, of New Durham, N. H., at Casco, Me.,
     Aug. 7, 1868. She was the tenth and youngest child of Capt.
     Benjamin and Mrs. Lois (Davis) Savage, b. July 2, 1842. He
     occupied the estate of her father in New Durham, as a farmer,
     till 1873
2386. DAVID HANSON, b. Dec. 1, 1839 ; d. Nov. 11, 1841, in h s 2d year.
2887. GEORGE ADDISON, b. Apr. 4, 1842 ; m. Clara Jane Tash, Jan. 1,
     1863, at Sanford, Me. ; owns a valuable farm in Poland, with
     orchards producing no less than twenty-three varieties of
     grafted fruit.
2388. BENJAMIN FRANKLIN, b. Mar. 20, 1847 ; d. Dec. 15, 1849, in his
     3d year.

2389. NANCY BURTON[4] [2216] (Samuel[3], Abraham[2], John[1]), m., 1st, Joseph Philbrick, Jr., of Andover, N. H., Jan. 9, 1820. He was b. Feb. 16, 1785 (by age on headstone), and d Dec. 20, 1826, in his 42d year. She m , 2d, David Sleeper, of Andover, Apr. 8, 1832, who was b Apr. 11, 1807, and was killed by the falling of a tree while fencing on Ragged Mountain, Apr. 11, 1833, aged 26. She m., 3d, John Shaw, Oct. 1843 ; first lived, and had their house burned, in West Boscawen. N. H. ; afterwards lived in Salisbury, near East Andover, where she d. Aug. 7, 1865, aged 68. Children : —

2390. DEBORAH SOPHRONIA (Philbrick), b. Oct. 22, 1820; resides with her sister, on Boston Highlands, 1872.

2391. SAMUEL RUNNALS (Philbrick), b. Dec. 22, 1822; studied medicine in South Berwick, Me., with Dr. Charles Trafton; took his medical degree at the University of Pennsylvania, receiving also a diploma from the "Medical Society of Massachusetts," "June 12, 1856." He was first established as an apothecary and manufacturing chemist in Boston, firms of "Colcord & Philbrick," and "Philbrick & Trafton." His attention being early called to the manufacture of coal oil, he became one of a company for that purpose in Waltham, Mass. He was afterwards the leader of a colony which formed a settlement called Merrimack, near the Asphaltum lake on the island of Trinidad, S A., for manufacturing oil from the contents of the lake; but the enterprise was only partially successful. He m. Almira T. Gilmore, of Boston, 1850, who was the daughter of Eliab Gilmore, a well-known railroad contractor, and d. spring of 1857, on Trinidad Island, but was buried in her native land, at the Forest Hills Cemetery, beside her oldest child. After finally returning to this country, he assisted in establishing the "Portland Kerosene Oil Company," and was its business manager till his death, at Portland, Nov. 23, 1859, in his 37th year. On the beautiful monument erected to his memory at Forest Hills, we find this inscription : "A family reunited." "By his chemical discoveries, he made valuable contributions to the art of dyeing," and procured several patents on the products resulting from the coal oil manufacture, in the interest of which he visited Europe twice, and also the Island of Cuba. "For his intelligence and fine character, he was greatly esteemed." His death was called "the complement of his life"; and it was further said of him, "Truly a *man* has passed by." Children : —
  1. FRANK, b. June, 1852; d. 1853, aged 1 year.
  2. HENRY MARCH, b. Apr. 1854; d. Feb. 1858, in his 4th year; "a very promising son."

2392. ELIZABETH ANN, b. June 24, 1824; graduated at the Mount Holyoke Institution, in the *last* of Miss Lyon's classes, 1848, and m. Asa Cheney Partridge, Oct. 17, 1852, in Wheeling, Va., whither she had previously gone as a teacher. He was b. July 9, 1820, in Stockbridge, Vt.; was at first an eminent teacher of penmanship; commenced the business of a daguerreian artist in 1841, and is now, 1872, one of the oldest living artists, if not *the* oldest, in the country. He was the first operator in St. Johnsbury, Vt., and Lancaster, N. H.; travelled in different parts of the United States and Canada, and settled in Wheeling, Va., 1848. He claims to have been the *first* to take pictures on glass, afterwards styled ambrotypes. Having previously moved to Winchester, Mass., he opened a studio in Boston, 351 Washington Street, in the fall of 1871. Present residence on Boston Highlands. Children : —
  1. FRANCIS CHARLES (Partridge), b. Aug. 2, 1853, in Wheeling,Va.; was admitted with his next younger brother [3] to the "Massachusetts Institute of Technology," in Boston, 1872.
  2. ELLA SOPHRONIA, b. Feb. 4, 1855, in Wheeling; was a member of the "Jubilee Chorus," from Winchester, 1872; also of the graduating class in the "New England Conservatory of Music," 1872 3.

   3. Edward Joseph, b. May 18, 1856, in Wheeling, see [1] above;
      a "proficient in mathematics, for his years."
   4. Flora Almira, b. Oct. 1, 1857, in Wheeling.
   5. William Henry. b. Sept. 21, 1858, in Wheeling.
   6. Anna Eliza, b. Jan. 29, d. Dec. 28, 1861, in Wheeling.
   7. Samuel Cheney, b. May 9, 1864, in Wheeling.
   8. Asa, b. June 9, 1865, in Boston; d. Aug. 31, 1865, in Winchester.
   9. Jessie Elizabeth, b. Oct. 19, 1868, in Winchester.
2393. David March (Sleeper), b. Mar. 5, 1833; m. Julia A. Norton,
      1854-5; engaged, unfortunately, in the Trinidad enterprise,
      see [2391]. and d. in New York City, two or three days after
      arriving from that island, May 15, 1858, aged 25. His widow
      is now Mrs. Atwood, of Portland, Me. Child: —
   1. Helena (Sleeper), b. May 18, 1856; now residing with her
      mother in Portland.

2394. Samuel[4] [2218] (Samuel[3], Abraham[2], John[1]), first resided in New Durham, and m. Eliza Ricker, of N. D., Dec. 9, 1822.
He migrated to East Tennessee, Nov. 1852, but was driven out by
the rebels with a great sacrifice of the personal comfort and property of himself and family, early in the war of 1861–64. Now
resides at Parker's Landing (Martinsburg), Butler County, Penn.
Children, b. in New Durham : —

2395. John Smith, b. May 10, 1824; d. Aug. 30, 1826, aged 2 years 8
      months 20 days.
2396. Jonas [2799]. b. June 20, 1825.
2397. Samuel [2806], b. Sept. 28, 1827.
2398. Caleb Ricker, b. Feb. 15, 1830; resides in New Durham; a farmer;
      m. Mrs. Laurentina D. Berry, widow of [2380], Aug. 14, 1861.
2399. Paul March [2809], b. Apr. 14, 1832.
2400. Andrew Jackson, b. Dec. 18, 1834; d. Sept. 1848, in his 14th
      year, being caught in the shaft of a saw-mill, and thus fatally
      injured, so as to live but five and a half hours.
2401. Eliza, b. July 9, 1837; d. July 20, 1840, aged 3.
2402. Martin Van Buren [2813], b. Sept. 15, 1839.
2403. Syrena [2820], b. Apr. 9, 1842.
2404. John Smith [2822], b June 12, 1844.
2405. Eliza Smith, b. Nov. 12, 1846; d. Oct. 14, 1851, in her 5th year.
2406. Eliza Rachel. b. Apr. 9, 1852; m. Lewis Herrick, Feb. 4, 1870,
      who is a coal miner and engineer at Parker's Landing, Pa.

2407. Abram[4] [2220] (Nathaniel[3], Abraham[2], John[1]), is alleged
to have come from New Durham, N. H., to Saugus, Mass., about
the year 1820, as a young man ; was a carpenter, and was subsequently engaged in the woollen factory at Saugus, where he m.
Lucy Smith, Apr. 1822, and d. Jan. 21, 1826, in his 29th year, in
consequence of being kicked by a horse. His widow still resides
at Clifton Dale, Saugus, 1872. Her decided affirmations that her
husband "was a native of New Durham. the son of Nathaniel. and
the probable grandson of Abraham"; that he "was visited by *his
cousin*, March Runnels [2376]. just before his death," and that he
"was intending to re-visit his New Durham friends the following
season," are, altogether, our chief authority for connecting this
family with that of Abraham, of New Durham, see [2149] and
[2219]; otherwise this supposed connection would be rendered

quite improbable by the ignorance respecting it, which now prevails among the descendants of Abraham [2142] in New Durham and vicinity. Children : —

2408. LUCY JANE, b. Mar. 1823; d. Oct. 30, 1841, in her 19th year.
2409. ABRAM [2825], b. Oct. 3 (4), 1824.
2410. HANNAH, b. Dec. 2, 1825, being seven weeks old at the time of her father's death; d. Apr. 1826, aged 4 months.

2411. SAMUEL[4] [2223] (Jonathan[3], Abraham[2], John[1]), m. Eliza Nevens Lovejoy, Apr. 26, 1809 ; was a millwright, and repaired, among others, the mills of Elder M. Clark, at Union Bridge (Sanbornton), N. H. ; of Gov. Badger, at Gilmanton, and of John Wilson, at Lee. He resided successively at Bradford, Hopkinton, West Boscawen, Meredith Bridge, Union Bridge, New Market, Kensington, and finally at Concord, where he d. Jan. 14, 1859, in his 78th year. She d. Oct. 1, 1862. Children : —

2412. ALBERT [2828], b. Dec. 23, 1809, in Bradford; named "Samuel Albert," at first.
2413. JOHN BURBANK [2831], b. May 9, 1811, in Hopkinton.
2414. ELIZABETH CLINTON, b. Feb. 22, 1813, in Hopkinton; m. Eri Colby, of Sutton, N. H., Dec. 10, 1832. He was b. Mar. 15, 1807, in Danville, Vt. ; lived first in Concord, N. H., as a mechanic, then at Charlestown, Vt., Newark, Vt. (three years), Lowell, Mass. (eighteen years), Concord again, 1856-60, and at Sutton again, as a farmer and speculator, 1860-72. The writer would acknowledge himself as highly indebted to Mrs. Colby for aid in collating the records of her grandfather's family.
2415. ASA DARWIN [2836], b. Dec. 30, 1814.
2416. HANNAH DOW [2839], b. Feb. 21, 1817.
2417. ROBERT KNOWLTON, b. Feb. 21, 1820; resides in Lowell, Mass. ; a wholesale and retail grocer; m. Huldah Doe, of Highgate, Vt., July 4, 1850, at Lowell.
2418. SARAH CAROLINE, b. Sept. 7, 1822; d. June 10, 1825, in her 3d year.
2419. MARY ROXCILANA, b. Oct. 11, 1824 ; m. Alvin Williams, shoemaker, Nov. 4, 1849, at Hampton. N. H. ; lived in Lynn, Mass., and there d. Apr. 10, 1854, in her 30th year.
2420. FRANKLIN LOVEJOY [2842], b. May 17, 1827.
2421. HAMILTON DIMOND, b. Aug. 20, 1829 ; d. Aug. 15, 1834, aged 5.
2422. CAROLINE FRANCES, b Apr. 19, 1832; d. Apr. 3, 1863, at Concord, aged 31.

2423. MIRIAM[4] [2224] (Jonathan[3], Abraham[2], John[1]), m. William McFerson, at Bradford, N. H., 1802. He was b. Oct. 17, 1784, in Henniker (or Goffstown) ; settled first in Newport ; afterwards " moved West," and d. at Freedom, Cattaraugus Co., N. Y., May, 1825, in his 41st year. She d. in Lee Co., Iowa, 1848, aged 65. Children : —

2424. ROSWELL SMITH (McFerson), b. Apr. 15, 1803, in Bradford; d. at Freedom, N. Y., Nov. 1823, in his 21st year.
2425. ROXANA, b. Mar. 24, 1805, in Newport, then "Cheshire Co.," N H ; d. at Freedom, Mar. 4, 1825, aged 20.
2426. EMERY WOOD, b. Apr. 18, 1807, in Newport; m., 1840, and resided in Lee Co., Ga.

2427. DIMON(D), b. June 15, 1809, in Newport; m., 1st, Amilla Savage, Feb. 17, 1839, in Caldwell Co., Mo., who there d. May 1, 1841; m., 2d, Mary Ann Neas, Nov. 29, 1845, in Nauvoo, Hancock Co., Ill. He united with the "Latter-Day Saints" in 1834, and has followed their various fortunes to the present, "leaving New York in 1836; being driven from the State of Missouri, and afterwards from Illinois; travelling more than one thousand miles westward, with ox teams, carrying provisions and tools, in 1851, and keeping constant guard for months together against the Indians." He now resides (1872) in Kaysville (between Salt Lake City and Ogden), Davis Co., Utah Territory; is a prosperous farmer, a member of the city council, and "an Elder in Israel"; "has been justice of the peace, orderly sergeant and color-bearer"; "did not leave the military ranks till he was fifty-nine years old." Children : —

  1. THOMAS JEFFERSON, b. May 8, 1840, and d. same day in Caldwell Co., Mo.

  2. AMILLA JANE, b. May 1, 1841, in Calwell Co.; m. Reddick Newton Allred, Jan. 11, 1857, at Salt Lake City, and resides in Saupete Co., U. T. Children : (1.) NERON ALONZO (Allred), b. July 2, 1858, in Nephi, U. T.; d. Sept. 7, 1859, aged 14 months. (2.) WILLARD NEAS, b. Jan. 8, 1860, in Spring City, U. T.; d. Oct. 6, 1870, in his 11th year. (3.) ALBERT MILTON, b. Aug. 23, 1862, in Spring City; d. Aug. 23, 1863, aged 1 year. (4.) MIRIAM AMILLA, b. Apr. 5, 1865. (5.) CHARLES RICH, b. Sept. 24, 1867. (6.) PRATT. DIMON, b. Aug. 22, 1870.

  3. SARAH ELLEN (McFerson), b. Oct. 20, 1846 (second wife), in Kanesville, Pottowatomie Co., Ia.; m. Peter Van Orden, at Salt Lake City, Oct. 10, 1870; resides in Cache Co., U. T. Child : (1.) WILLIAM DIMON RUNNALS (Van Orden), b. Oct. 30, 1871.

  4. WILLIAM (McFerson), b. May 10, 1848, and d. same day in Pottowatomie Co., Ia.

  5. ABNER, b. Sept. 14, 1849, in Kanesville, Ia.

  6. DELILA, b. Jan. 5, 1852, in Kaysville, U. T., as were the eight following.

  7. LYDIA, b. Aug. 26, 1853.

  8. ISRAEL, b. Sept. 14, d. Dec. 31, 1855.

  9. JEDIDIAH, b. Dec. 7, 1856.

  10. MIRIAM, b. Oct. 12, 1858.

  11. MORGAN, b. Nov. 4, 1860.

  12. RHODA MATILDA, b. May 6, 1862.

  13. DOLLY, b. Mar. 7, 1865.

  14. DAVID, b. Mar. 31, 1867.

2428. BATHSHEBA (McFerson), b. Apr. 5, 1812, in "Cheshire Co.," (Newport), N. H.; m. Thomas Green, Nov. 1832, in Cattaraugus Co., and lived in Livingston Co., N. Y., where he probably died. Children : —

  1. GEORGE M. (Green), b. Apr. 25, 1835, in Pittsford, N. Y.

  2. WILLIAM, b. July 24, 1837, in P.

  3. MIRIAM, b. Oct. 12, 1840, in Mendon, N. Y.

  4. AMELIA, b. Apr. 24, 1843, in Barre.

  5. JAMES, b. June 16, 1846, in Mendon.

  6. MARY ANN, b June 26, d. Sept. 26, 1850, in M.

  7. ORLOW DIMOND b. Jan. 2, 1854, in M.

2429. SALLY DIMOND (McFerson), b. May 2, 1815, in Newport, N. H.; d. in Clark Co., Mo., 1847, aged 32.

2430. WILLIAM, b. May 10, 1818, and d. same day in Freedom, N. Y.

2431. ORLOW HARTWELL, b. May 13, 1819, in Freedom; m. Eliza J. Johnson, in Lee Co., Ia.; eight children (?), all b. in Croton,

Ia., four of whom were daughters, one daughter deceased; but one child's name reported : —

    1. SULIA ANN, b. Nov. 28, 1850.

2432. RUSHEAUN, b. Jan. 1822, in Freedom; m. Thomas Johnson, 1840, in Caldwell Co., Mo.; subsequent residence in Iowa; eight children in all, — two deceased, of whom : —

    1. GEORGE (Johnson), b. 1842, and d. Oct. 1842, at Mount Rose, Lee Co., Ia.

    2. MARY ANN, b. 1844, in Lee Co.

    3. HENRY CLAY.

2433. PRISCILLA (McFerson), b. Aug. 5, 1825, in Freedom, N. Y.; m. William Welden, of Clark Co., Mo., 1843. Had two children in 1846; residing in Iowa.

2434. EZEKIEL DIMOND[4] [2225] (Jonathan[3], Abraham[2], John[1]), migrated from Concord, N. H., to the " Holland Purchase," — Western New York, — in 1810, and first located in what is now Freedom, Cattaraugus Co., with only his axe and rifle, several miles from any other white settler. Built him a shanty on the borders of a beautiful sheet of water, since called " Fish Lake," subsisting on its spotted denizens with wild game from the woods, while he cleared his land with the aid of a horse which he had ridden from New Hampshire, having also for company during the season a young bear caught one morning near his premises ! Here he remained most of the time till 1816, when, having m. Rebecca Parker, Apr. 12, 1815, he sold out and took up his abode at her home, in what is now Arcade, Wyoming Co., N. Y. Received his deed from the " Holland company" for one hundred and thirty-eight acres of land, July 17, 1819, " being the first farm deeded in the town "; afterwards increased this farm to two hundred and fifty acres ; bought another of one hundred and eighteen acres, two miles distant ; gained other property in Racine, Wis ; moved thither in Sept. 1846, and there d. Jan. 28, 1847, aged 61. He was a hard-working farmer, and a man universally respected for his sound judgment and excellence of character. In religious views he sympathized with the Quakers. His wife was b. Apr. 8, 1782, in Westford, Mass.; afterwards lived with her parents in Cavendish, Vt., and moved with them to the Holland Purchase in 1810. She taught the first schools in Warsaw and Sheldon (now Arcade), N. Y. After years of poor health, she became a very *devoted* Christian. The following, from her pen, was given as advice to her oldest son, while away at school : " Repentance towards God, and faith in our Lord Jesus Christ, is the only foundation which is laid, or can be laid, for man's salvation." " Thus did Christ and his apostles preach, as you may find in Matt. iv. 17 ; Mark i. 15 ; Acts xvi. 31, etc. I wish you to examine these texts, accept them, and resign yourself into the hands of God, praying Him earnestly, for Christ's sake, to forgive your sins, and yourself forgiving your erring fellow-men, as you hope to be forgiven." She d. Oct. 30, 1839, in her 58th year. Children, b. in China (now Arcade) : —

2435. REBECCA, b. Apr. 1, d. Apr. 3, 1816.

2436. LEONARD PARKER [2846], b. May 26, 1817.
2437. ADNA WALLACE, b. Mar. 19, d. Nov. 30, 1819.
2438. DOLLY FORSTER [2852], b. Sept. 10, 1820.
2439. EDMOND LUCIEN [2857], b. Dec. 28, 1825.

2440. ABNER[4] [2226] (Jonathan[3], Abraham[2], John[1]), settled in Pike Hollow, Alleghany Co., N. Y., previously to 1810, or the time of his brother Ezekiel's first arrival in that vicinity; returned to New Hampshire, on a visit, but was never heard from after leaving Concord for his final journey West He m. Diodema Rocelia Griffeth, at Pike, N. Y., where all their children were born : —

2441. ELI GRIFFETH [2859], b. Jan. 26, 1815.
2442. MARY ANN, b. 1817 (?); m. Benjamin Adams; d. about 1852, aged 35 (?).
2443. ABNER ABELIONO, b. 1819 (?); resides in Peoria, Ill.
2444. MARIA [2864], b. 1820 (?).
2445. SUSAN M. [2870], b. 1822 (?).
2446. JOHN D. [2875], b. July 5, 1824.
2447. HENRY [2880], b. 1826 (?).

2448. JAMES[4] [2227] (Jonathan[3], Abraham[2], John[1]), m. Rebecca Lovejoy, at Concord, N. H., June 19, 1814, and settled first in the State of New York; afterwards moved to Ohio, as inferred from the births of his youngest children. He d. Aug. 16, 1827, aged 36. She was b. Sept. 14, 1793, and d. Apr. 5, 1858, in her 65th year. Children : —

2449. MARY ELIZA [2886], b. Mar. 4, 1815.
2450. JEREMIAH AMES [2894], b. Sept. 22, 1816, in Freedom, N. Y.
2451. STELLA ALMIRA [2901], b. May 18, 1819, in Mentor, Lake Co., O.
2452. SOPHRONIA MARIA [2905], b. Jan. 11, 1823.
2453. WILLIAM CARL [2912], b. Oct. 2, 1824, in Mentor, O.

2454. ISRAEL[4] [2228] (Jonathan[3], Abraham[2], John[1]), m. Anna Cheney, Jan. 20, 1819, who was b. Jan. 30, 1796. He settled with his brothers in New York, where he d. Nov. 9, 1849, aged 56, and she d. Mar. 29, 1856, aged 60, both at Portageville. (Most of *his* children have adopted the " Reynolds " orthography; those of his *oldest* brothers retained " Runals, or Runnals "; of his *youngest*, " Runnels.") Children : —

2455. LORENZO DOW [2917], b. Nov. 29, 1820, in Freedom, N. Y.
2456. PHILANDER MORTIMER, b. Oct. 20, 1822, in Freedom; d. June 9, 1844, in his 22d year, at Manchester, Dearborn Co., Ind.
2457. BENJAMIN CHENEY, b. Jan. 9, 1825, in Perry, N. Y.; was a hotel-keeper for twelve years, and was twice married; had one child by first wife; m., 2d, Catharine Post, of Gainesville, Wyoming Co., N. Y., Dec. 30, 1855. He d. Nov. 26, 1869, in his 45th year, at Attica, N. Y., and was there buried with Masonic honors.
2458. ISRAEL MORRIS [2921], b. Mar. 31, 1827, in Freedom.
2459. JONATHAN, b. May 26, 1829, in Perry; was drowned, at Portageville, in the Genesee River, May 5, 1834, aged 5.
2460. WARREN WILLIAM [2925], b. June 7, 1831, in Freedom.
2461. LOUISA ANN [2927], b. May 25, 1833, in Perry.
2462. GEORGE WILLIAMS [2930], b. Nov. 17, 1836, in Portageville.

2463. JONATHAN CURRIER[4] [2229] (Jonathan[3], Abraham[2], John[1]), resided in Deering, N. H.; by occupation a miller; m., 1st, Mary Dimond, of Concord, Dec 31, 1822. She was the mother of his six oldest children; was b. June 1, 1805, and d. Apr. 12, 1836, in her 31st year. He m, 2d, Ruth Dimond, of Concord, Sept. 26, 1836, who was b. Sept. 23, 1805. He d. at Weare, Dec. 19, 1861, aged 66. Children, all b. in Deering : —

2464. JOHN LORENZO, b. Mar. 8, 1824; d. Sept. 17, 1827, in his 4th year.
2465. MARY ANN [2932], b. July 9, 1826.
2466. ALMIRA BARTLETT [2934], b. Dec. 8, 1828.
2467. GEORGE SULLIVAN [2937], b. Jan. 27, 1832.
2468. HORACE HERRICK [2941], b. Jan. 16, 1834.
2469. HARVEY HARTSON, b. Mar. 3, 1836; was a lawyer by profession, and d. Sept. 21, 1858, in his 23d year, at Fort Madison, Iowa.
2470. ARVILA JANE [2944] (second wife), b. Nov. 27, 1837.
2471. LAURA AUGUSTA [2951], b. May 1, 1839.
2472. AMANDA MALVINA, b. Apr. 14, 1842; m. William H. Gilmore, carriage manufacturer, Feb 26, 1865, at Hillsborough, N. H.
2473. SAMANTHA FRYE, b. Nov. 10, 1844.
2474. ELVIRA JOSEPHINE, b. Oct. 2, 1846.

2475. PATIENCE[4] [2239] (Ebenezer[3], Abraham[2], John[1]), m. Joseph Watson, of Farmington, N. H., 1808; lived first in Middleton, and then in Alton, where she d. Aug. 9, 1816, aged 27, " a little before the deaths of her youngest children " : —

2476. LOVEY (Watson), b. June 20, 1809, in Middleton; m. John Willey, of New Durham, Apr. 23, 1827; a farmer in N. D., where they are still living, 1872.
2477. LOUISA, b. Apr. 22, 1811; m. Daniel Sargent, of Gilmanton, farmer, Dec. 3, 1828, and there residing, — north part of the town, — 1869.
2478. SALLY, b. May, 1812; d. of spotted fever, at Alton, Sept. 1816, aged 4 years 4 months.
2479. LAVINA, b. May, 1814; d. same as last, aged 2 years 4 months.
2480. PATIENCE, b. Aug. 5, 1816; d. Jan. 1817, aged 5 months.

2481. ALICE[4] [2240] (Ebenezer[3], Abraham[2], John[1]), m. Jonathan Pinkham, farmer, of New Durham, Dec. 10, 1812. He was b. July 28, 1784. Children, all but the first, b. in New Durham : —

2482. LUTHER HALE (Pinkham), b. June 16, 1815, in Alton, N. H.; was a farmer, now residing in Farmington; m., 1st, Ann Randall, Apr. 8, 1836, who d. Apr. 1838; m., 2d, Mary C. Wallis, of Moultonborough, May 8, 1839, who d. Jan. 22, 1866; m., 3d, Mrs. Hannah R. Tibbetts, Aug. 13, 1869. Children : —
    1. ANN DORCAS (first wife), b. Sept. 4, 1837.
    2. CHARLES LUTHER (second wife), b. Nov. 18, 1840.
    3. GEORGE HALE, b. July 3, 1843.
    4. NATHANIEL EDWIN, b. June 2, 1846.
    5. HORACE JONATHAN, b. Dec. 30, 1850.
    6. SETH TAYLOR, b. May 8, 1852.
    7. ISAAC DEARBORN, b. Apr. 10, 1858.
2483. EMELINE, b. Oct. 21, 1816.
2484. THOMAS, b. Mar. 30, 1820.
2485. CHARLES, b. Aug. 14, 1822; d. Aug. 14, 1823, aged 1 year.
2486. JONATHAN ROBERTS, b. Sept. 26, 1826.

2487. HANNAH AVERY, b. Aug. 19, 1830; m., 1st, a Wallace, of Alton Corner; m., 2d, a Sherman.

2488. NATHAN PRATT, b. Sept. 17, 1833; d. Mar. 8, 1858, in his 25th year.

2489. JAMES[4] [2241] (Ebenezer[3], Abraham[2], John[1]), was a farmer in New Durham; m. Sally W. Herd, of that town, Mar. 5, 1821, and there d. Oct. 2, 1862, aged 68. She was b. July 20, 1797, and d. at N. D., Oct. 19, 1867, aged 70. Children : —

2490. MARY JANE, b. Oct. 20, 1822, and d. at New Durham, Aug. 19, 1845, in her 23d year.

2491. SETH TAYLOR HERD, b. Sept 17, 1824; a shoemaker and farmer in New Durham; m. Lydia Olive Hayes, at Dover, Apr. 13, 1853.

2492. ABIGAIL ANN [2953], b. July 24, 1830.

2493. ORLANDO JAMES [2957], b. July 28, 1834.

2494. SARAH ELIZABETH [2959], b. Aug. 25, 1836.

2495. ELIZABETH[4] [2242] (Ebenezer[3], Abraham[2], John[1]), m. Willard Pinkham, farmer, of New Durham, Sept. 29, 1824. Residing, 1872, with [2378]. Children, b. in New Durham, except the youngest : —

2496. MARY ADALINE (Pinkham), b. Nov. 11, 1825.

2497. VINCENT T., b. June 1, 1827.

2498. LAURA JANE, b. Mar. 31, 1833.

2499. THOMAS FRANCIS GREENE, b. Mar. 10, 1839, in Chelsea, Mass.

2500. WILLIAM[4] [2244] (Moses[3], William[2], John[1]), remained in Lee, N. H., till after " Nov. 13, 1797," when his uncle, " Nathan Runals, of Lee," deeded to him (" William R., of Lee "), his " blacksmith's shop and tools." Within two years after this, he sold out, and " moved from Lee to Bingham, Me.," where he m., 1st, Abigail Jackson, of Moscow, 1799, or 1800, — " the year that Washington died." She was b. Dec. 1778, became the mother of his five oldest children, and d. at Moscow, May 2, 1814, in her 36th year. In 1816, he moved still farther north, to Carritunk, Me., " taking up wild land forty miles from any grist-mill." He there m., 2d, Mrs. Lydia (Rowe) Ellis, 1817, who was b. Mar. 18, 1788, in Barrington, N. H., and d. Mar. 12. 1846, aged 58, at Carritunk. He d. at C., July 25, 1855, aged 83. Children : —

2501. ABIGAIL [2961], b. May 4, 1802, in Moscow, Me.

2502. SARAH CROSBY [2969], b. Aug. 28, 1804, in Concord, Me.

2503. WILLIAM, b. Oct. 15, 1806, in Concord; d. Apr. 1823, in his 17th year, being drowned from a raft in Kennebec river; body found the following June, below Carritunk Falls.

2504. ELIZABETH RANDALL [2978], b. July 15, 1809, in Concord.

2505. POLLY [2985], b. Oct. 13, 1811, in Concord. The remaining children, by second wife, and all b. in Carritunk.

2506. MOSES CROSBY [2989], b. Jan. 12, 1819.

2507. GEORGE JOHNSON [2997], b Feb. 18, 1822.

2508. STEPHEN OTIS [3001], b. Apr. 2, 1824.

2509. OLIVE BALL [3005], b. Mar. 3, 1826.

2510. RACHEL BRIGGS [3015], b. May 25, 1828.

2511. RHODA, b. Dec. 1829; d. Mar. 1830, aged 3 months.

2512. WILLIAM BALL [3020], b. May 22, 1832.

2513. JOSEPH SPAULDING [3026], b. May 31, 1835.

14

210   RUNNELS AND REYNOLDS MEMORIALS.

2514.   POLLY[4] [2245] (Moses[3], William[2], John[1]), m. Solomon
Knights, of Bingham, Me. Children : —

2515.   SOLOMON (Knights), who was probably the father of
  1. AMOS (Knights), livery stable keeper, at South Berwick,
      Me., 1870.
2516.   POLLY ; deceased.
2517.   ABRAHAM.
2518.   WILLIAM.
2519.   HANNAH.
2520.   CHANDLER.

2521.   SARAH[4] [2246] (Moses[3], William[2], John[1]), m. Alfred
Parlin, of Bingham, Me.   Child : —

2522.   POLLY (Parlin).

2523.   JOHN[4] [2248] (Winthrop[3], Joseph[2], John[1]). It is only
known that he was m., lived in Lee, N. H.. and there went by the
undignified title of " Guff," though a grandson of the first clergyman in Lee ! He resided in the " Centre district, 1807," and his
name again appears among the " Inventories " on town records,
" 1815 " ; soon after which time he is supposed to have d. " His
two oldest sons were married, but neither left children " : —

2524.   SAMUEL HUTCHINS, — named after the Rev. Samuel H., — was
      residing in Lee, " 1827," " 1834," and " 1846 " (records).
2525.   GEORGE ; was living in Lee, " 1834 " and " 1846 "; m. Mrs. Sarah
      York, of Pittsfield, Nov. 26, 1865, but d. before 1868.
2526.   DANIEL ; supposed to have d. young.

2527.   ELEANOR[4] [2249] (Winthrop[3], Joseph[2], John[1]), is said to
have m. Samuel Austin, of Madbury, N. H., who lived in Somersworth and moved to Canada about 1814.   One of her children : —

2528.   JACOB KITTREDGE (Austin), visited Newington, N. H., in 1837 ;
      afterwards resided for some time in Boston, and then returned
      to Canada.

2529.   HANNAH[4] [2250] Winthrop[3], Joseph[2], John[1]), m. James
Twombly, at Dover, N. H., 1807. He was b. Nov. 1787 ; lived, as
a farmer, after marriage, at Wolfboro', Dover, Durham, and Newington, and d. at N., May 7, 1866, in his 79th year. She d. at N.,
Aug. 18, 1869, aged 85.   Children : —

2530.   ELHANAN CHARLES (Twombly), b. Apr. 24, 1808, in Wolfborough ;
      now lives at Newington.
2531.   LUCY STONE, b. Oct. 3, 1809, in Newington, and there d. Mar. 29,
      1833, in her 24th year.
2532.   ABIGAIL SARAH GREENLEAF, b. July 10, 1811, in Dover ; m. Gil-
      man Upham, of Newington. Of her children : —
  1. WINTHROP (Upham), served on board the ship of war " Ports-
      mouth " during the late rebellion, at New Orleans, La., and
      there d. of ship fever.
  2. SARAH A. ; see [2535, 6].
2533.   EZEKIEL WINGATE (Twombly), b. Feb. 3, 1813, in Dover ; a farmer,
      now residing in Newington.
2534.   ISAAC JAMES, b. Oct. 4, 1814, in Dover.

2535. Eliza(beth) Hannah, b. May 18, 1816, in Dover; m. Benjamin
Swain, farmer and teamster, Jan. 12, 1837. He d. at Exeter,
of heart disease, Sept. 28, 1870. Children: —

1. Lucy Elizabeth (Swain), b. Oct. 1, 1838, in Saugus, Mass.;
m. Almon Sylvanus Langley, blacksmith, of Exeter, Apr. 17,
1857. He served in the army, Co. B, 11th regiment New
Hampshire volunteers, from Sept. 1863 till the close of the
war, and d. of disease thus contracted, Apr. 17, 1866, at
Exeter. She also d. of consumption, Dec. 5, 1871, aged 33.
Children: (1.) Emma Grace (Langley), b. Oct. 14, 1858.
(2.) Annie Mabelle, b. Aug. 16, 1860. (3.) Freddy, b.
Mar. 14, 1862; d. Apr. 1864, aged 2. (4.) Charles Almon,
b. Dec. 1, 1865.

2. William Henry (Swain), b. Mar. 14, 1841, in Newington, and
there d. June 21, 1847, aged 6.

3. Lavinia Antoinette, b. Apr. 11, 1843, in Newington; d. Aug. 5,
1850, aged 7, in Amesbury, Mass.

4. Albert Ephraim, b. June 14, 1845, in Newington; served three
years in the army; is now m. (1872), and resides in Boston,
Mass., 5 Rochester Street.

5. Eugene Margarenia, b. Aug. 9, 1847; in Newington; d. at
Amesbury, Aug. 19, 1850, aged 3.

6. James William, b. Mar. 30, 1849, in West Amesbury, Mass.;
m. Sarah A. Upham [2532, 2], July 28, 1872, present residence
in Boston.

7. Clara Octavia, b. Feb. 20, 1852, in Newington; d. in Exeter,
June 23, 1855, aged 3 years 4 mos.

8. Hariet Ann, b. May 6, 1854, in Newington; d. at Exeter, June
20, 1855, aged 13 months 14 days.

9. Edgar Clarence, b. Apr. 26, 1856, in Exeter.

2536. Clara Augusta (Twombly), b. Aug. 18, d. Oct. 1, 1817 (18), in
Dover.

2537. James Runnels, b. Nov. 2, 1819, in Durham; "attended the U. S.
Military Academy at West Point, N. Y., and was in the Mexican war"; d. July 22, 1851, in his 32d year, at Malden, Mass.,
being "killed by the cars when crossing a railroad."

2538. Simes Frinck, b. May 29, 1822, in Newington; "was in the
Mexican war, and also in the last war at Fortress Monroe"; a
carpenter; now lives in Malden, Mass.

2539. William Henry Winthrop, b. May 9, 1824, in Newington, and
there d. July 22, 1850, aged 26.

2540. Edward T.[4] [2251] (Winthrop[3], Joseph[2], John[1]), was
twice married; first wife is said to have "joined the Shakers;
second wife was from Maine." "He used to go about the country,
as a pack-peddler, a scissors grinder," and sometimes as a "temperance lecturer"! At one time he "drew his little son to Barrington on a hand-sled"; d. 1857 at Woodstock, N. H., aged 72.
One child, second wife: —

2541. Edward, b. about 1843; is supposed to have d. young.

2542. Winthrop[4] [2253] (Winthrop[3], Joseph[2], John[1]), was first
a truckman, afterwards a "glass manufacturer" in Boston, and
there m. Elizabeth Coldin Jones, of B., Nov. 8, 1817. He d. at
Barrington, N. H., Aug. 7, 1849, aged 55. She was residing with
her oldest daughter, at Longwood, Mass., 1870. Children, all b.
in Boston: —

2543. SARAH JONES [3028], b. May 5, 1819.
2544. ELIZABETH ADALINE, b. Nov. 18, 1820; m. Joseph Windsor, Jr., of Boston, Oct. 9, 1839. He was a fish dealer and book-keeper in B. She d. May 20, 1840, in her 20th year.
2545. SUSAN CAROLINE [3084], b. Jan. 6, 1824.
2546. WINTHROP, b. Aug. 24, 1826; was m. and soon after d. of consumption at Boston, Oct. 9, 1846, aged 20.
2547. HANNAH ADAMS [3042], b. Dec. 16, 1828.
2548. ROBERT JONES, b. June 16, 1831; d. of consumption, at Chelsea, Mass., June 28, 1850, aged 19.
2549. MARY JANE VEAZIE, b. Mar. 26, 1836; d. Sept. 28, 1855, aged 19 years 6 months.
2550. JOSEPH ALLEN, b. Aug. 12, d. Nov. 14, 1838.
2551. JOSEPH ALLEN, b. Dec. 26, 1839; d. Aug. 1, 1840, aged 7 ms. 6 ds.

2552. SAMUEL LOCKE[4] [2254] (Winthrop[3], Joseph[2], John[1]), m., 1st, Adaline Smith, of Boston, 1820, who d 1827. Having moved to Georgia, he there m., 2d, and there d. 1848 or 1849, aged 53. One child, first wife : —

2553. HENRY HILL, b. Dec. 20, 1821. After the death of his mother, he lived three years with his aunt [2572], at Strafford Corner, N. H. Leaving that place "in search of his father," he is known to have enlisted in the U. S. Navy, and was last heard from at Rio Janeiro, S. A. There is, however, other evidence that he was a soldier, or marine, in the last war, and that he d. in a hospital.

2554. GEORGE FOOTMAN[4] [2256] (Winthrop[3], Joseph[2], John[1]), m. Abigail Locke, of Boston, and now resides in Victoria (Peoria), Knox Co., Ill. Children : —

2555. GEORGE.
2556. CHARLES.
2557. JOHN WILLIAM.
2558. JULIA ANN.

2559. JOB FOSS[4] [2257] (Winthrop[3], Joseph[2], John[1]), was a farmer, and m., 1st, Eunice Jones, of Milton, Mass., Oct. 11, 1827. She was b. July 12, 1798 ; moved with her husband to Barrington, N. H., but returned to Milton, and there d. Dec. 6, 1842. He m., 2d, Ann Tibbetts, of Brookfield, N. H., Sept. 1843, and remained on his father's homestead, in Barrington, till his death, Mar. 22, 1853, aged 52. Administration of his estate granted, Apr. 1, 1853 His second wife d. at Brookfield, 1863. One child, first wife : —

2560. MARY ESTHER, b. July 12, 1828, in Milton, Mass., where still residing (1870).

2561. JACOB KITTREDGE[4] [2258] (Winthrop[3], Joseph[2], John[1]), m., 1st, Sarah Jones, of Boston (half sister of his brother Winthrop's wife, see [2542]), 1834. He afterwards lived and followed his trade as a blacksmith at Haverhill, N. H., where she d. He m., 2d, Mehetabel Stevens, in Maine, who d. about 1856. Having returned to Barrington, he there d. Sept. 26, 1865, aged 62. Children, — four oldest by first wife : —

2562. WILLIAM HENRY, b. 1835; was a soldier in the late war; a teamster in Boston, 1869, stand at 50 North Market Street; m.
Elizabeth L. Low, of B., Sept. 4, 1870.

2563. CHARLES H.; was wounded in the war of the rebellion, and d. in
Boston.

2564. GEORGE.

2565. HENRY; was also in the late war; at Sandy Island, Mobile Bay,
when last heard from.

2566. PHINEHAS; "killed in the war."

2567. EPHRAIM FOSS[4] [2259] (Winthrop[3], Joseph[2], John[1]), was
a farmer; m. Mary Pinkham Locke, of Barrington, N. H., Apr.
14, 1825, and d. Aug. 15, 1851, in his 47th year. She was b.
Apr. 4, 1807, and m., 2d, William Henry Dearborn, Apr. 3, 1859,
who is a native of Jackson, N. H, and a farmer, now living in
Barrington, near the old Winthrop Reynolds place. Children of
[2567], b. in Barrington : —

2568. HORACE [3044], b. July 2, 1826.
2569. SOPHIA LOCKE [3047], b. Nov. 5, 1827.
2570. LUCY LOCKE [3052], b. Feb. 26, 1830.
2571. WINTHROP [3055], b. Oct. 8, 1834.

2572. ELIZABETH LOCKE[4] [2260] (Winthrop[3], Joseph[2], John[1]),
m. Joseph Potter Weeks, hatter and farmer, of Strafford, N. H.,
Mar. 13, 1831. He was b. May 3, 1809. Children : —

2573. LEROY (Weeks), b. Oct. 17, 1833; began to learn the machinist's
trade, at Berwick, Me., and d. Oct. 12, 1854, aged 21.
2574. HANNAH ELIZABETH, b. Dec. 3, 1835; d. Sept. 12, 1859, in her
24th year; "a faithful instructor, to the last, in the Sabbath
school," at Strafford Corner.
2575. MARY FRANCES, b Nov. 29, 1836; d. May 13, 1849, in her 13th
year, of typhoid fever, the same disease of which her brother
and sister afterwards died.

2576. JOHN[4] [2276] (Joseph[3], Joseph[2], John[1]), m. Mary Harriman, of Bangor, Me., Dec. 24, 1807, at B She was b. Jan. 5,
1793, in Pittston, Me., and d. at Bangor, Apr. 20, 1866, aged 73.
He resided at Bangor, as a clothier and tailor; was also com-
mander of a company of cavalry, and d. Aug. 13, 1869, aged 86.
Children, all b. in Bangor : —

2577. NANCY, b. Jan. 31, d. Feb. 11, 1809.
2578. CHARLES AUSTIN [3057], b. Feb. 10, 1810.
2579. ORCHARD COOK, b. Jan. 2, 1812; residing in Bangor, 1870.
2580. ELIZA [3065], b. Sept. 11, 1814.
2581. MARY PINKHAM b. Aug. 23, 1816; m. E. N. Torrey, of Bangor,
Aug. 23, 1835; was residing, 1870, in San Francisco, Cal.,
516 Dupont Street.
2582. JOHN EMERSON [3067], b. Oct. 13, 1818.
2583. MARTHA ANN [3071], b. Oct. 11, 1820.
2584. EMELINE, b. Sept. 9, 1822; resides in Bangor.
2585. GEORGE WASHINGTON b. Sept. 14, 1824; was a miner in California;
afterwards an apothecary in San Francisco, and there d. Sept.
13, 1860, aged 36.
2586. EDWARD HATCH [3074], b. July 23, 1826.

2587. ABIGAIL HATCH, b. Oct. 3, 1828; m. Albion K. P. Wilson, of Bangor, June 1, 1853. He was a captain in the 2d Maine regiment during the late war.

2588., FRANCIS AUGUSTUS, b. Aug. 8, 1830; resides, as an instructor, in San Francisco, Cal.

2589. MARTHA[4] [2277] (Joseph[3], Joseph[2], John[1]), m. Jeremy Washington Orange, of Milton, N. H., at Rochester, May 5, 1809. He was b. Oct. 25, 1788; was a joiner, and owned a farm in Milton; moved to Great Falls, N. H., July, 1823, and had been in the employ of the "Great Falls Manufacturing Company" for forty-seven years, continuously (1870), still holding his place at the age of 82! He was also deacon of the Congregational church at Great Falls. She d. Feb. 3, 1860, aged 75. Children: —

2590. FRANKLIN (Orange), b. Oct. 25, 1810, in Milton, where he still resides.

2591. GEORGE WASHINGTON, b. Dec. 22, 1812, in Milton; is now in the employ of the "Erie Railroad Company," at Waverly, Tioga Co., N. Y.

2592. HENRY SMITH, b. Feb. 12, 1815, in Milton; at present (1870) a grocer and flour merchant in Lowell, Mass., Merrimack Street.

2593. JOSEPH[4] [2278] (Joseph[3], Joseph[2], John[1]), was "an officer in the war of 1812, but not in the regular service"; settled as a shoemaker in Dover (and Rochester), N. H., having previously m. Phebe A. Walker, of Newington. He d Mar. 16, 1826, in his 39th year, at Dover, and was there buried, but his remains were afterwards removed to Manchester. She d. Apr. 12, 1856, aged 64. A monument over their graves and the graves of their two youngest children, in the Manchester cemetery, has this inscription: "Loved on earth, — will be loved in heaven." Children: —

2594. OLIVE [3077], b. June 20, 1812, in Dover.
2595. JOHN, b. 1814; "was last heard of near Boston."
2596. WILLIAM [3081], b. Sept. 6, 1816, in Dover.
2597. LYDIA, b. Sept. 8, 1818, in Dover; m. Robert Gilchrist, of Goffstown, N. H., Nov. 1851. He was a crockery dealer in Manchester, and there d. Dec. 25, 1865. She still continues the business, 1870.
2598. SUSAN ABBY, b. Jan., d. Apr. 10, 1821.
2599. MARY JONES, b. 1823; d. Dec. 18, 1825, aged 2 years.

2600. SAMUEL[4] [2282] (Joseph[3], Joseph[2], John[1]), was enlisted at the age of 16 in the war of 1812, for the defence of Portsmouth. "Served the term of his draft," and was afterwards captain of a company of infantry, in Portland, Me., where he settled, as a shoemaker, and m Hannah Gove, a native of Berwick, Me. Moved to Bangor, 1825, and there resided till his death, Feb. 16, 1865, in his 68th year. Children: —

2601. DEXTER BREWER [3084], b. Apr. 25, 1822, in Portland.
2602. GEORGE WASHINGTON, b. 1825 (?); was drowned at Bangor, in Penobscot river, about 1834, aged 9 years.
2603. ANTOINETTE FAUSTINA, b. about 1827; d. 1851 (?), aged 24.
2604. ANNA ELIZA [3088], b. Aug. 28, 1831.

2605. GEORGE[4] [2283] (Joseph[3], Joseph[2], John[1]), has been for many years a worthy citizen in Bangor, Me.; by original occupation, a tanner, now also (1870) a somewhat extensive owner of real estate in that city. He m. Martha Nowell, of Sanford, Me.; Oct. 3, 1842, who was there b. May 8, 1812. He has taken great interest in the prosecution of this work, materially assisting to solve the problem of his grandfather's genealogy, by old records in his possession, see [2166] and [2274]. One child (adopted) : —

2606. MARTHA CAROLINE, b. May 13, 1845, in Sanford.

2607. OLIVER[4] [2284] (Joseph[3], Joseph[2], John[1]), resided, as a machinist, in Dover, N. H.; there m. Sarah Hanson Watson, of D., June 9, 1831, and there d. July 23, 1862, in his 52d year. Children : —

2608. CECELIA AMANDA, b. Mar. 13, 1832, in Dover; d. Mar. 1, 1850, aged 18.
2609. JULIETTE, b. Nov. 29, 1833, in Dover, where now residing (1870) with her mother, and also employed as a teacher in one of the city schools.
2610. BENJAMIN OLIVER, b. Dec. 3, 1836, in Hopkinton, Mass.; is a sea captain by employment; was on a voyage to China, 1870, in the ship "Mindaro."

2611. LYDIA[4] [2286] (Benjamin[3], Joseph[2], John[1]), m. John Jepson, of China, Me., Oct. 23, 1806. She d. at C., May 30 (3), 1822, aged 33. He was b. Aug. 24, 1782; a farmer; d. Sept. 22, 1822, aged 40. Children, all b. and five youngest d. in China : —

2612. JEDIDIAH (Jepson), b. Sept. 8, 1807; m. Rebecca Meader, Nov. 27, 1828. Children : —
  1. WILLIAM, b. May 12, 1829; m. Sarah Nye, May 16, 1869.
  2. GEORGE, b. Nov. 24, 1830; m. Ellen Winslow, May 27, 1866; one child.
  3. CHARLES H., b. Mar. 12, 1833; m. Lucy Clark, 1855.
2613. BENJAMIN RUNNELS, b. July 24, 1809; m., 1st, Patience Meader, 1832, who d. Mar. 2, 1866, aged 56; m., 2d, Hannah R. Briggs, Dec. 2, 1868. Children, first wife : —
  1. ELIJAH D., b. Sept. 1, 1833; married; two children.
  2. BENJAMIN F., b. Aug. 27, 1838; married; one child.
  3. LYDIA R., b. May 14, 1844; d. Oct. 14, 1822, aged 4, — three
2614. DANIEL, b. Dec. 27, 1811; d. Nov. 12, 1822, in his 11th year.
2615. ISAAC, b. Feb. 24, 1814; d. Aug. 31, 1831, in his 18th year.
2616. ELIJAH D., b. Aug. 15, 1816; d. Sept. 5, 1822, aged 6.
2617. WILLIAM, b. Aug. 31, 1818; d. Oct. 14, 1822, aged 4, — three children, with their parents, "passing away" the same year.
2618. JOHN, JR., b. Aug. 4, 1820; d. June 24, 1859, in his 39th year.

2619. HANNAH[4] [2287] (Benjamin[3], Joseph[2], John[1]), m. William Moody, a farmer in Vassalborough, Me., and there d. Aug. 11 (26), 1839, aged 48. He d. at V., May 30, 1830. Children : —

2620. FRANKLIN (Moody); resides in Boston.
2621. AMOS; deceased.
2622. ELIZABETH; deceased.

2623. Daniel[4] [2288] (Benjamin[3], Joseph[2], John[1]), belonged
to the Society of "Friends," in which his family were brought up;
residence, China, Me. We cheerfully conform to their scruples in
reference to the *names* of the months, in the following record. He
m. Mary Allen, 11th mo., 28, 1822, and d. 7th mo., 24, 1859,
aged 66. Children: —

    2624. Peter A. [3092], b. 2d mo., 27, 1824.
    2625. Lydia [3095]. b. 3d mo., 9, 1826.
    2626. Mary A. [3099], b 5th mo , 13, 1828.
    2627. Alvina P. [3104], b. 12th mo., 7, 1830.
    2628. Clara C. [3108], b. 1st mo., 30, 1833.
    2629. Rebecca M. [3110], b. 2d mo , 11, 1836.
    2630. Emma R. [3114], b. 8th mo., 15, 1838.

    2631. Benjamin[4] [2289] (Benjamin[3], Joseph[2], John[1]), was a
farmer and justice of the peace, with residences as indicated by
children's births; m. Sally Webb, of China, Me., and d. Jan. 5 (1),
1843, in his 47th year. Children: —

    2632. Benjamin Franklin [3118], b. Jan. 18, 1822, in China, Me.
    2633. Samuel Webb, b. Sept. 11, 1823, in China; d. at Chelsea, Me.,
            Nov. 18, 1844, aged 21.
    2634. John Wentworth Ireland [3122], b. Apr. 23, 1825, in Vassal-
            boro', Me.
    2635. Isaac Randall [3124], b. Mar. 16, 1827, in V.
    2636. William Moody, b. July 11, 1830; m. Henrietta B. Runnels [2648],
            Sept. 1852; was a farmer; residence, Wilton, Waseca County,
            Minn.; is now deceased; four children, all d.
    2637. Albert Prescott [3128], b. June 3, 1832, in Vassalboro'.
    2638. Joseph Emerson, b. Apr. 10, 1835, in Chelsea, Me.; there d. May
            19, 1854, aged 19.
    2639. Sally Omenia, b. Nov. 11, 1839, and d. Sept. 8, 1841, aged 1 year
            10 months, in Chelsea.
    2640. Sarah Omenia [3135], b. Sept. 18, 1843, in Chelsea.

    2641. Lois[4] [2290] (Benjamin[3], Joseph[2], John[1]), m. Aaron
Brown, farmer, and d. Feb. 1869, in her 71st year. He had preceded her a few months, June 7, 1868. Children: —

    2642. John M. (Brown), b. Aug. 5, 1829; m. Mary Gardiner.
    2643. Rebecca, b. June 11, 1830; m. a Bessey; one child, deceased.
    2644. Benjamin, b. Oct. 11, 1832; d. Apr. 11, 1850, in his 18th year.
    2645. Omena, b. Aug. 11, 1841; married.

    2646. Jonathan D.[4] [2292] (Benjamin[3], Joseph[2], John[1]), m.
Hannah Clark, Mar. 2, 1828, who was b. Aug. 31, 1806. He was
a blacksmith; held a captain's commission in the Maine militia,
and was for a time postmaster at Togus' Mills (East Hallowell),
Me ; now resides in Portland, corner of St. Lawrence and Sher-
brooke streets. Children: —

    2647. Elizabeth S. [3138], b. Jan. 19, 1829, in Belfast, Me.
    2648. Henrietta B., b. Feb. 20, 1832, in Hallowell, see [2636].
    2649. Frances H. [3143], b. Feb. 18, 1834, in Vassalboro'.
    2650. William A., b. Nov. 14, 1837, in Hallowell; m. Kate Burgit, Jan.
            10, 1866, who d. Aug. 1867; is a cabinet maker in Faribault,
            Rice Co., Minn.

2651. ISAAC RANDALL[4] [2293] (Benjamin[3], Joseph[2], John[1]) m , 1st, to Hannah Moody, at Vassalboro', Me., by Rev. W. S Bray, Apr. 19, 1831. She was b. Dec. 4, 1814, in Nobleboro', Me , and d. at V., July 4, 1849, aged 39 years 7 months. He m., 2d, Coretha Kendall, 1850, in Lowell, Mass., who there (?) d. ; m., 3d, Mary D. Whitehouse, Dec. 8, 1858, who was b. Mar. 29, 1815, in Vassalboro', and survives as his widow, now living at South Vassalboro'. He d. at Vassalboro', his residence, July 4, 1864, aged 56. Children : —

2652. ABBY J., b. Aug. 23, 1832, in Vassalboro'; d. at Lowell, Mass., Mar. 1, 1852, in her 20th year.
2653. WILLIAM S. B. [3145], b. May 6, 1835, in V.
2654. ISAAC A., b. July 22, 1839, in V., and there d. Apr. 28, 1841, in his 2d year.
2655. ISAAC A., b. Dec. 31, 1842, in Lowell, and there d. Oct. 13, 1843, aged 10 months.
2656. ANNABELLA [3148] (second wife), b. Nov. 16, 1851.

FIFTH GENERATION.

2657. ISAAC[5] [2295] (Isaac[4], Isaac[3], Abraham[2], John[1]), m., 1st, Mehetabel P. Sargent, June 16, 1822, at Gilmanton, N. H. She was b. Jan. 2, 1802, in Loudon. He settled as a farmer first in Gilmanton, then at Loudon, Bennington, Vt. (N. Y.), and finally at Warrensville, Ill., where she d. Apr. 18, 1867, aged 65, and he m., 2d, Mrs. Anna Vaughn, July 26, 1868. Children, first wife : —

2658. JOHN SARGENT [3150], b. Nov. 7, 1823, in Gilmanton.
2659. RICHARD SANBORN SARGENT [3158], b. May 31, 1825, in Loudon.
2660. BEDELIA ELVIRA [3168], b. Oct. 30, 1827, in Bennington.
2661. MARY SOPHRONIA [3172], b. Oct. 19, 1832, in B.
2662. ISAAC THOMAS CHARLES [3174], b. Apr. 26, 1837, in Warrensville.

2663. POLLY[5] [2297] (Isaac[4], Isaac[3], Abraham[2], John[1]), m. Samuel Brown, farmer, Jan. 14, 1826, at Gilmanton, N. H. He resided first in G., afterwards in Northfield, and there d. Aug. 2, 1837. Children : —

2664. HARRIET JANE (Brown), b. Oct. 26, 1826, in Gilmanton; m. a Mawrey, and now resides in Providence, R. I.
2665. MARY E., b. Feb. 28, 1828, in G.
2666. FRANCES A., b. Jan. 24, 1831, in Northfield.
2667. MEHETABEL B., b. Mar. 28, 1833, in N.
2668. ABBIE S., b. May 4, 1835, in N.

2669. BETSY[5] [2300] (Isaac[4], Isaac[3], Abraham[2], John[1]), m. Elias Smith Buzzell, farmer, of Sanbornton, N. H., July 26, 1833. He was b. Aug. 6, 1810 ; furnished three sons and two sons-in-law for the late war, as recorded below. Children : —

2670. MARY (Buzzell), b. June 12, 1835 ; d. Aug. 20, 1847, aged 12.
2671. CHARLES WESLEY, b. Mar. 6, 1837 ; enlisted in the New Hampshire 15th regiment, Co. H, fall of 1862 ; was at New Orleans. He was m., by the compiler, to Caroline E. Morrison, of New Hampton, N. H., Jan. 2, 1866 ; settled as a farmer in New Hampton. Child : —
    1. NELLIE ETTA, b. Dec. 1, 1867.
2672. SARAH CARTER, b. Oct. 15, 1839 ; m. George Dawson, Feb. 25, 1858. He was b. Apr. 18, 1836 ; was in the New Hampshire 15th regiment, Co. H ; now a railroad employé, at Lathrop. Clinton Co., Mo. Children : —

1. Mary Hannah (Dawson), b. Aug. 18, 1859.
2. Joseph Allen, b. Dec. 6, 1861.
3. Georgia, b. Sept. 3, 1865.

2673. Henry Clay (Buzzell), b. Aug. 15, 1842; enlisted in the 12th New
    Hampshire regiment, Co. D, 1862; promoted to sergeant;
    remained in the army two years; wounded in the breast and
    thigh at the battle of Cold Harbor, June 3, 1864, and d. of
    hemorrhage, in the hospital at Washington, D. C., June 29,
    1864, in his 22d year.

2674. James Monroe, b. Sept. 14, 1844; enlisted in the 26th Vermont
    regiment, 1863; served at the gulf of Mexico, and continued
    till the end of the war. He is now an engineer on the Vermont
    Central Railroad; residence at Northfield, Vt.; m. Arlette L.
    Briggs, June 3, 1870. Child : —
    1. Jessie May, b. May 1, d. July 1, 1871.

2675. Emma Tilton, b. July 18, 1847; m. Sylvester D. Hunt, Apr.
    9, 1865, who was b. Jan. 23, 1844, and was in the 15th New
    Hampshire regiment, Company G; now a railroad employé,
    Tilton, N. H.

2676. Clara Hunkins, b. May 10, 1849; m. Augustus Shaw, farmer,
    now of Tilton, N. H., Dec. 15, 1864. Children : —
    1. Henry Elmer (Shaw), b. Sept. 12, 1865.
    2. Frankie, b. Apr. 3, d. May 30, 1868.
    3. Bertie Edward, b. Apr. 9, 1869.
    4. Amos Cornelius, b. Nov. 4, 1872.

2677. John[5] [2302] (Isaac[4], Isaac[3], Abraham[2], John[1]), m., 1st,
Sally Gilman, of Sanbornton, 1831. She was the mother of his
three first children, and d. Oct. 20, 1837. He m., 2d, Artemesia
Stewart Whitcher, of Northfield, Feb. 22, 1839; resided in North-
field and the south part of Sanbornton till 1869; then moved to
Canterbury. Children : —

2678. Josiah George, b. 1832; d. 1834, aged 1 year and 6 months.
2679. Ann, b. Aug. 23, 1833, in Sanbornton (Gilford); joined the
    Canterbury Shakers, 1841, with whom she still continues,
    " maintaining a good reputation."
2680. Sally [3178], b. July 23 (Aug. 25), 1835, in Northfield.
2681. Josiah George (second wife), b. Apr. 3, d. Nov. 26, 1840.
2682. Frances Jane, b. June 3, d. July 31, 1842.
2683. John, b. June 9, d. July 28, 1845, in Sanbornton (town records).
2684. Horace Sanborn, b. July 20, 1848, in Sanbornton.

2685. Julia Ann[5] [2304] (Isaac[4], Isaac[3], Abraham[2], John[1]),
m., 1st, Benjamin Kimball Mason, Oct. 13, 1838. He was b. May
24, 1819, in Chichester, N. H., and there d. June 12, 1854, aged 35.
She m., 2d, John Samuel Hussey, Feb. 4, 1856. He was b. Mar. 1,
1825, in Dover, where they still reside. Children : —

2686. David Brown (Mason), b. Nov. 16, 1839, in Chichester, with the
    seven following; enlisted in the 7th New Hampshire regiment,
    Co. G, Nov. 23, 1861; served with his regiment at the Dry
    Tortugas, Port Royal, and St. Augustine; discharged for disa-
    bility, Jan. 7, 1863; returned home sick, and d. at Northfield,
    May 28, 1865, in his 26th year.
2687. Elvira, b. Apr. 6, 1841; d. Apr. 16, 1842, aged 1 year 10 days.
2688. James Monroe, b. Aug. 24, 1842; enlisted in Co. F, 12th New
    Hampshire regiment; d. on his passage home from Fredericks-
    burg, Va., Jan. 15, 1863, in his 21st year.

2689. CHARLES FRANK, b. July 25, 1844; served in Co. F, 12th New
Hampshire regiment, and fell at the battle of Chancellorsville,
Va., May 3, 1863, in his 19th year.
2690. JOHN COLBY, b. Apr. 20, 1846; enlisted in Company G, New
Hampshire 15th regiment; d. at Cleveland, O., Aug. 7, 1863,
aged 17.
2691. LEWIS CASS, b. June 30, 1847.
2692. BENJAMIN LEROY, b. June 14, 1850.
2693. RHODA ELVIRA, b. June 13, 1852.
2694. ABBY JANE (Hussey), b. Sept. 24, 1857 (probably in Dover, with
the two following); d. July 14, 1860, in her 3d year.
2695. GILBERT EUGENE, b. Oct. 28, 1859.
2696. ELLA MARIETTA, b. Sept. 9, 1861.

2697. SAMUEL HENRY[5] [2307] (Isaac[4], Isaac[3], Abraham[2],
John[1]), m., 1st, Eliza Ann Shaw, of Canterbury, N. H., June 22,
1852. Served in the 1st New Hampshire infantry, Co. D, three
months, enlisting " from Loudon," May 2, 1861; mustered out
Aug. 9, 1861. Afterwards in the 4th New Hampshire regiment,
sergeant Co. A, mustered in Sept. 18, 1861; wounded May 16,
1864; mustered out Sept. 27, 1864, having served two years and
eight months as color-bearer of the regiment   His second cousin
[2822], who stood beside him, bears testimony to his eminent
bravery as a soldier. He m., 2d, Mary E. Currier, of Concord,
Mar. 10, 1864, and was there residing, near Fisherville, 1869.
Children, two oldest by first wife: —

2698. JOHN NASON, b. Oct. 22, 1853, in Canterbury.
2699. HENRY, b. Oct. 30, 1854, in Canterbury.
2700. IRA WILLIE (second wife), b. Nov. 23, 1865, in Concord.

2701. ALMIRA RACHEL[5] [2308] (Isaac[4], Isaac[3], Abraham[2],
John[1]), m. Stephen Fletcher Weeks, Jan. 7, 1849. He is a cooper
and farmer; residences at Gilmanton, Loudon, and Epsom, N. H.
(1864–69); served ten months in the New Hampshire 15th regiment, 1863, being at New Orleans and Port Hudson, La., till the
surrender of the latter place, July 8, 1863. Children: —

2702. MARY ELIZABETH (Weeks), b. Jan. 7, 1850, in Gilmanton.
2703. SARAH ADELAIDE, b. May 17, 1851, in G.; m. H. D. Foss, 1869.
2704. STEPHEN FRANCIS, b. Aug. 7, 1855, in Loudon.
2705. ALBERT EUGENE, b. Oct. 8, 1857, in L.
2706. WALTER HARRIMAN, b. Jan. 23, 1864, in Epsom.
2707. ADDISON TRUE, b. Jan. 23, d. Feb. 11, 1866, in Epsom.
2708. ALMIRA, b. Feb. 12, 1867.

2709. PAUL[5] [2321] (John[4], James[3], Abraham[2], John[1]), m.
Sally Ranlet, Oct. 15, 1818, " both of Farmington." Resided,
first, in Tuftonborough, N. H., where his children were all born;
for several years past, in Milton (south part), as a shoemaker and
farmer. Children: —

2710. SARAH ABBA [3183], b. Jan. 6, 1824.
2711. JAMES ORIN [3186], b. Nov. 30, 1826.
2712. MARY ANN [3192], b. Oct. 3, 1832.
2713. ANDREW TETHERLY [3198], b. July 27, 1835.

2714. JEREMIAH[5] [2325] (Joseph[4], James[3], Abraham[2], John[1]), m. Sally Colomy [2196, 1], Feb. 27, 1821, at Vershire, Vt. He was a farmer; resided at Thetford, Vt., at Hanover, N. H. (after 1831), and finally at Lyme, where he d. Feb. 8, 1867, in his 66th year. Children : —

2715. MARTHA JANE, b. Aug. 21 (29), 1823, in Thetford; d. at Lyme, Aug. 30, 1858, aged 35.
2716. MARY ANN, b. Oct. 23, 1825, in Thetford, and there d. Aug. 23, 1829, in her 4th year.
2717. ELSA [3202], b. Mar. 1, 1828. in Thetford.
2718. SARAH ANN [3208], b. Jan. 23, 1830, in T.
2719. GEORGE WASHINGTON [3210], b. May 14, 1832, in Hanover.
2720. JAMES MONROE, b. Oct. 26, 1835, in Hanover.
2721. MARY [3214], b. Apr. 20, 1839, in H.
2722. HARLAN PAGE, b. Dec. 20, 1841, in H.

2723. SALLY[5] [2326] (Joseph[4], James[3], Abraham[2], John[1]), m. Richard Everett, farmer, Nov. 16, 1829; lived at time of marriage in Hanover, N. H.; afterwards in Lyme, Hanover again, and Fairlee, Vt. (Bradford P. O. 1843–1870). Children : —

2724. AMOS (Everett), b. Aug. 26, 1830, in Lyme; d. at Fairlee, Feb. 5, 1852, in his 22d year.
2725. MARIA, b. Sept. 2, 1831, in Lyme; m. Carlos Waterman, Hillsboro', Wis.
2726. JOSEPH RUNNELS, b. Nov. 16, 1833, in Hanover; a farmer in Fairlee, Vt. (Bradford P. O.), 1870.
2727. LUCY ANNA, b. May 16, 1835, in Hanover; m. Henry K. Wilkins, Lowell, Mass.
2728. LUCRETIA, b. Jan. 20, 1837, in Lyme; m. Nelson Prescott, Washington, Vt.
2729. ETHERLINDA, b. Oct. 4, 1842, in Hanover; m. Wesley Chamberlain, Thetford, Vt.
2730. ELLEN REBECCA, b. Apr. 19, 1844, in Fairlee; resides in Lowell, Mass., 1870.
2731. ELLOVISA, b. Apr. 11, 1846, in F.; d. Jan. 14, 1848, in her 2d year.

2732. SAMUEL[5] [2327] (Joseph[4], James[3], Abraham[2], John[1]), m., 1st, Elsie Colomy, of Vershire, Vt., Mar. 1823, and settled in V., near Strafford, where she d. from injuries received in the great hurricane, Aug. 31, 1825, being caught between two timbers of the falling house, and so injured as to live but five hours. Her child, — oldest of the following list, — was saved alive in her arms. He m., 2d, Betsy Moody [2194, 4], Aug. 11, 1829, and now resides (1873), as a farmer, in Duxbury, Vt., — Waterbury P. O. Children : —

2733. LOUISA [3218], b. Jan. 16, 1825, in Vershire (first wife).
2734. PHILENA FAIRFIELD [3222], b. Jan. 1, 1831, in Vershire (second wife).
2735. GEORGE CHESLEY [3226], b. Aug. 11, 1835, in Thetford, Vt.
2736. HARRIET ANGELINE [3234], b. May 6, 1837, in T.
2737. FLORA ARMINA [3238], b. May 23, 1840, in Waterbury, Vt.

2738. DANIEL[5] [2328] (Joseph[4], James[3], Abraham[2], John[1]), m. Susan Everett, at Hanover, N. H., May 23, 1830. She was b.

Nov. 15, 1807, in Lyme. He resided latterly in Strafford, Vt.' and there d. Jan. 27, 1858, in his 50th year. She m., 2d, Thomas Clogston, farmer, and now resides in Strafford. Children : —

2739. CHARLOTTE ANN [3242], b. Oct. 5, 1832, in Thetford, Vt.
2740. HEMAN JASON [3244], b. Apr. 8, 1834, in Hanover.
2741. WILLIAM ADDISON [3246], b. Nov. 20, 1837, in Hanover.
2742. DANIEL HARTWELL, b. May 4, 1840, in Thetford; served in the New Hampshire cavalry four years; mustered in (Troop I) Dec. 17, 1861; appointed blacksmith, and transferred to Troop L, Apr. 1, 1863; re-enlisted Jan. 5, 1864; was twice taken prisoner, — first at Dutch Gap, — and was detained in the Libbey prison, Richmond, Va., and at Belle Island. He is now an iron smith in Lowell, Mass.; m., 1st, Lucy L. Wilmot, Sept. 14, 1865, who d. June 4, 1867; m., 2d, Hannah Margaret Elliot, of Lowell, Jan. 28, 1870, a native of Fairfax Co., Va.
2743. LYMAN HINCKLY, b. Aug. 15, 1842; d. Oct. 9, 1858, aged 16.
2744. CHARLES CARROL, b. Nov. 6, 1844, in Thetford; was in the 9th regiment Vermont volunteers, Co. G, from Aug. 1862 to its dismemberment; now a farmer in Strafford; m. Frances Morey, of Vershire, Mar. 31, 1869.
2745. SUSAN ADALINE, b. June 9, 1848, in Vershire; m. Joseph White, of Lowell, Mass., July 20, 1870, who was b. Jan 19, 1848, in Boston, and is now a clothing dealer in L., 3 Central Street.
2746. EDWIN LAFRANCE, b. July 25, 1850, in Lyme, N. H.

2747. JOHN HANSON[5] [2329] (Joseph[4], James[3], Abraham[2], John[1]), m., 1st, Diana Pingree, Apr. 1835, and settled in Hanover, N. H., near Connecticut river, as a farmer and shoemaker. She d. Mar. 1840, and he m., 2d, Beulah Pingree, in H., Mar. 6, 1841. Children, second wife, b. in Hanover : —

2748. JOHN RANSOM, b. June 24, 1842; enlisted Aug. 7, 1862, in the New Hampshire 9th regiment; three times promoted to corporal, sergeant, and first sergeant; mustered out at the end of the war, June 10, 1865; was in several severe battles, with repeated hair-breadth escapes, losing only his little finger, probably when "wounded, May 12, 1864." He was m. to Frances J. Burnham, of Hanover, by Rev. B. Smith, Nov. 26, 1868; now settled in H. as a farmer.
2749. HIRAM EUGENE, b. May 14, 1844; enlisted in the 11th New Hampshire regiment, Co. H, Aug. 21 ("mustered Sept. 2"), 1862; d. Jan. 2, 1863, in his 19th year, — of fever contracted by exposure at and after the battle of Fredericksburg, Va., — at the "Harewood Hospital," Washington, D. C., "trusting in Jesus Christ, and with strong love for his God."
2750. JAMES ALLISON, b. Oct. 7, 1846; enlisted in the New Hampshire 17th regiment, Nov. 29, 1862; served three months, till its disbandment and consolidation with the 2d regiment; then in another, the 2d (?) New Hampshire regiment, six months; afterwards, being in Poughkeepsie, N. Y., at the commercial college, enlisted for one year in the 150th New York regiment, joined Gen. Sherman at Atlanta, Ga., and remained under his command till the end of the war.
2751. DIANA REBECCA, b. May 1, 1851; an invalid for many years at her father's in Hanover.
2752. FREDERICK AUGUSTUS, b. Jan. 1, 1855.
2753. APPLETON COLBURN, b. Aug. 4, 1859; d. Mar. 6, 1860, aged 7 months.

2754. POLLY[5] [2330] (Joseph[4], James[3], Abraham[2], John[1]), m. Putman Webster Silver, farmer, of Orford, N. H., Feb. 14, 1832, at Hanover; has since resided at North Thetford, and now at Strafford (West Faïrlee), Vt. Children: —

    2755. HARRIET MARIA (Silver), b. Nov. 13, 1833, at Orfordville, N. H.; m. James Cummings; residence at Bunker Hill, Ill., 1870.
    2756. DEXTER FREEMAN, b. Nov. 11, 1835. at Orfordville; now (1870) a farmer in Strafford, Vt.; post-office, West Fairlee.

2757. MARGARET[5] [2337] (Samuel[4], James[3], Abraham[2], John[1]), m. David K. Perkins, stone-cutter, of New Durham, N. H , Feb. 22 (Mar. 4), 1819. He was b. Sept. 3, 1797, in N. D., and d. at Manchester, Dec. 4, 1862, aged 65. Children: —

    2758. NATHANIEL (Perkins), b. Apr. 21, 1820, in New Durham; a hatter and horse dealer; settled first in Manchester; m. Elizabeth T. Summers, Oct. 1842, who was a native of Norfolk, Va. He now resides in Brighton, Mass. Seven children, of whom five d. in infancy: —
        1. NATHANIEL; was residing with his parents in Brighton, 1869.
        2. MARY ANN, b. May 26, 1847; m. John E. Collins, formerly of Fall River, Mass.; now (1872) of Manchester, N. H. Children: (1.) NATHANIEL JOHN (Collins), b. Nov. 7, 1869. (2.) ELIZABETH ISABELLA, b. July 13, 1871.
    2759. SAMUEL RUNNELS (Perkins), b. May 2 (21), 1822, in Middleton, N. H.; was a stone-cutter and horse dealer, but is now (1869) in the hotel business at Brighton, Mass.; m. Mary Abbott, of Londonderry, N. H., Aug. 1840. Children: —
        1. ELIZABETH THERESA, b. 1842, in Manchester, N. H.; m. a Pratt, of Epping.
        2. MARY ANTIONETTE, b. 1843, in Somersworth; m. Loren Hunt, 1864; residences, Hartford, Ct., and Brighton, Mass.
        3. SAMUEL R., b. 1845, in Manchester; served in the late war, and d. in a military prison, Georgia, 1863-4, aged 19.
        4. DANA, b. 1847, in Manchester; d. 1861, aged 14.
    2760. MARY ANN, b. July 29, 1824, in Middleton; m. James Eastman, mason, of Londonderry, 1841, and has resided chiefly in Manchester. Children: —
        1. FRANCES ANGELA (Eastman), b. June 24, 1843, in Manchester; d. Feb. 23, 1846, in her 3d year.
        2. JAMES AUGUSTINE, b. Sept. 7, 1845, in Springfield, Mass.; a mason by trade, as also the two following.
        3. ALAYSIUS, b. Aug. 10, 1848, in Springfield.
        4. WILLIAM DAVID, b. Sept. 11, 1850, in S.
        5. IGNATIUS DANA. b. Sept. 5, 1852, in Manchester; a student in college, 1869.
        6. RICHARD STEPHEN, b. Dec. 25, 1854, in Manchester; attending school, 1869.
        7. JOHN, b. June 20, d. Dec. 25, 1857.
        8. GEORGE WHITMAN, b. Apr. 3, 1860; d. Jan. 8, 1862, aged 1 year 9 months.
    2761. MANASSEH HOLMES (Perkins), b. June 18, 1826, in Middleton; is a mason; resides at Manchester; m. Louisa Dwinals, of Londonderry, 1845. Children: —
        1. MARY EMMA, b. June, 1847, in M.
        2. ISABELLA, b. 1848; d. in infancy.
    2762. NATHAN RANDALL, b. Dec. 13, 1828, in Middleton; a blacksmith and farmer; m. Elizabeth Hicks, of Jefferson, N. H., 1853. Child: —
        1. MANASSEH, b. 1855.

2763. WILLIAM DANA. b. Feb. 27, 1831, in Jefferson; was first a mason; moved to California about 1850; there m. and has three
children. He was the State collector of California in 1869.

2764. JONANNA RANDALL (or Runnals), b. Jan. 27, 1834, in Whitefield, N. H.; m., 1st, Richard H. A. Burnes, of Manchester, Sept.
1854. He d. Mar. 1859, and she m., 2d, M. M. Drew, in California; one child, first husband: —
  1. MARY HOPE (Burnes); d. aged 1 year 6 months

2765. JANE (Perkins), b. Apr. 7, d May 1, 1837. in Whitefield.

2766. DAVID. b. Apr. 10, 1838, in Whitefield; a hotel-keeper; m. Annette E. Stanley, 1861, at Manchester. Children: —
  1. DAVID WALTER, b. Jan. 14, 1862.
  2. FREDERICK, b. Apr. 10, 1864.
  3. GERTRUDE HOPE, b. Mar. 17, 1866.

2767. SAMUEL DANA[5] [2340] (Samuel[4], James[3], Abraham[2],
John[1]), m., 1st, Jane Greene, of Portland, Me., Nov. 24, 1830.
She was b. Nov 17, 1809, and d. Nov. 29, 1835, aged 26. He m.,
2d, Mrs. Emeline (Greene) Rogers, of Portland, 1838, who there
d. Mar. 1871. Children, — two oldest by first wife : —

2768. SAMUEL, b. Dec. 17, 1831; d. Jan. 17, 1832, aged 1 month.
2769. EMILY JANE, b. Dec 22, 1834; d. Feb. 13, 1835, aged 1 mo. 22 days.
2770. LUCY JANE, b. June 10, 1839 (second wife); m. William G. Read,
of Portland, carpenter, June 11, 1868.
2771. KATE [3251], b. Mar. 18, 1841.
2772. GEORGE ALBERT [3254], b. Jan. 2, 1843.
2773. DANA, b. Apr. 29, 1845; enlisted from Manchester, N. H., 4th
New Hampshire regiment, Co. G, Sept. 18, 1861; re-enlisted,
Feb. 16, 1864. He is now residing in Portland, Me., as an
engineer, engaged at Sebago Luke, for the city, in 1870.
2774. FREDERICK GATES, b. Feb 5, 1849; enlisted Mar. 3, 1864, Maine
18th (?) regiment; wounded Apr. 2, and discharged June 6,
1865; is now an engineer in Portland, employed like his
brother above; m. Lizzie Lawrence, of P., Jan. 1, 1870.
2775. ALICE LUCE, b. May 12, 1853.

2776. BENJAMIN RANDALL[5] [2341] (Samuel[4], James[3], Abraham[2],
John[1]), received the additional name of " Paul," on being confirmed
by the Bishop of Mobile in 1835. He was first a mariner and carpenter; resided in Mobile, Ala., and there m. Margaret M. J.
Dawling. Jan. 7 (8), 1837. She was b. in Kerry Co, Ireland, her
father afterwards moving to this country, and being killed, as supposed, at the battle of New Orleans. Returning from the South,
he settled in Strafford, N. H. where she d (?). His present residence (1870) is in Manchester, 46 Concord Street. Child : —

2777. MARY URSULA, b. Feb. (Jan.) 15, 1843, in Strafford; d. Feb. 17,
1846, aged 3.

2778. JOANNA ORAM[5] [2343] (Samuel[4], James[3], Abraham[2],
John[1]), m. Col. Zechariah Boody, of New Durham, farmer, Feb.
19, 1837. He was there b. June 20, 1813. Children : —

2779. CHARLES HAYES (Boody). b Dec. 27, 1838; a lawyer residing in
New Durham, of which town he has been selectman, and was
representative in the State Legislature in 1869.

2780. DANIEL EDWIN, b. Aug. 25, d. Nov. 27, 1840.
2781. ELLEN AURILLA, b. Jan. 3, 1847; m. Francis W. Colbath, Sept. 25, 1867.

2782. JOHN S.[5] [2360] (Nathaniel Brackett[4], Samuel[3], Abraham[2], John[1]), m. Asenath Burnham, of Garland, Me., Dec. 25, 1842. Himself a farmer in G., his four oldest sons are machinists, in both iron and wood, now living (1872) in Pittsfield, Me. Children, all b. in Garland : —

2783. LEONORA F., b. Oct. 31, 1843.
2784. NATHANIEL B. [3256], b. May 16, 1845.
2785. SAMUEL, b Oct. 15, 1847.
2786. JOHN S., b. Oct 17, 1849.
2787. WILLIAM F., b. May 20, 1852.
2788. CHARLES, b. Apr. 6, 1855; d. Jan. 14, 1856, aged 9 months 8 days.
2789. FRANK, b. Oct. 10, 1857.
2790. CHARLES H., b. Jan. 2, 1860; d. June 18, 1864; aged 4½ years.
2791. MABEL E., b. Oct. 8, 1862.

2792. ROXANA[5] [2361] (Nathaniel Brackett[4], Samuel[3], Abraham[2], John[1]), m. Amos Dow, Jr., of Hampden, Me., Mar. 1842, and d. July 3, 1844, in her 27th year, leaving : —

2793. ANNA R. (Dow), b. Feb. 3, 1843; m. Burnham W. Hinds, of North Vassalboro', Me.

2794. MARY SUSAN[5] [2384] (John Smith[4], Samuel[3], Abraham[2], John[1]), m. John Colomy, shoemaker, of New Durham [2235, 1], May 23, 1852. He is now a farmer in Poland, Me., removing thither after the birth of their youngest child : —

2795. JOHN FRANK (Colomy), b. Jan. 15, 1854; d. Nov. 4, 1865, in his 12th year.
2796. WALTER McCANN, b. Sept. 18, 1858.
2797. JAMES ADDISON, b. Oct. 27, 1861.
2798. CARL ERVINE, b. Apr. 22, 1867.

2799. JONAS[5] [2396] (Samuel[4], Samuel[3], Abraham[2], John[1]), was m., 1st, to Hannah Young Corson, of Milton, N. H., by Rev. J. Bodge, at Middleton, Dec. 22, 1845. She d. Mar. 19, 1854, at New Durham. He m., 2d, Sophia E. Austin, of South Berwick, Me., 1856. Enlisted, first, in the 1st New Hampshire regiment, Co. B, Apr. 21, 1861; mustered in May 2, mustered out Aug. 9, 1861. Enlisted, second, in the 17th Maine, July 22, 1862, and served till the capture of General Lee, June, 1865, including the battles of Fredericksburg, Chancellorsville (the "midnight charge"), Gettysburg, Wilderness, Petersburg, Coal Harbor, and the battles around Richmond, till it was taken. Though present in all the above, he was only once wounded, on the head. He is now a shoemaker, residing in Dover. Children, three by each wife : —

2800. AUGUSTA ELLEN, b. June 4, 1847, in Farmington.
2801. GEORGIANNA MARILLA, b. Oct. 7, 1849, in New Durham.
2802. JONAS MARCH, b. July 11, 1851, in Farmington; was a shoemaker; m. Mary Tuttle, of Dover, Feb. 1872, and d. Apr. 11, 1872, in his 21st year. She d. Sept. 1872.

15

2803. SCOTT MONTEZ. b. Oct. 18, 1857, in Rollinsford.
2804. LUELLA GERTRUDE, b. Jan. 11, 1860, in R.; d. at Farmington,
Aug. 7, 1861, aged 1 year 7 months.
2805. LEANDER WINFIELD, b. Dec. 7, 1861, in South Berwick, Me.

2806. SAMUEL[5] [2397] (Samuel[4], Samuel[3], Abraham[2], John[1]),
migrated to Tennessee in 1846, and has resided chiefly at Nashville, as a shoemaker; m., 1st, Eliza Burns, at N., 1848, who was
a native of Alabama, and d. Sept. (?) 1863; m., 2d, Emily Crockett,
of Montgomery Co., Tenn., 1866. He entered the rebel army (by
compulsion), "May, 1861, and served two years in the 1st Tennessee (confederate) cavalry"; enlisted in the Union army, 1864,
10th Tennessee cavalry, in which he " served one year till the war
was over." Children, second wife : —

2807. N. B. FORREST, b. July 25, 1868.
2808. MARY ELIZA, b. May 12, 1870, to whose number must also be
assigned a younger sister, — reported too late for a number of
her own : —
DIXEY, b. Nov. 13, 1871.

2809. PAUL MARCH[5] [2399] (Samuel[4], Samuel[3], Abraham[2],
John[1]), m. Mary Jane Colomy, of New Durham [2235, 8], Dec.
28, 1856; served in the 4th company New Hampshire cavalry,
Capt. William P. Ainsworth's, for eleven months; afterwards in
the New Hampshire heavy artillery, till the end of the war. He
now resides in New Durham, as a shoemaker, on the place formerly
occupied by his father. Children, b. in N. D. : —

2810. FORREST LEROY, b. Sept. 20, 1857.
2811. ARA BERTIE, b. Aug. 1, 1863.
2812. IDA MAY, b. Dec. 13, 1871; d. at N. D., May 2, 1872, aged 4 mos.
19 days.

2813. MARTIN VAN BUREN[5] [2402] (Samuel[5], Samuel[4], Abraham[2], John[1]), m. Mary Catharine Crockett, sister of his brother's
second wife [2806], Dec. 16, 1853. She d. Mar. 1, 1868, of measles,
when their youngest child was nine days old; residence, Nashville,
Tenn. He " served in the rebel army"; " is at present in Miss."
Children : —

2814. JONAS CALVIN, b. Oct. 1854; d. Apr. 1856, aged 18 months.
2815. WILLIAM FRANKLIN, b. Aug. 1860.
2816. MARTHA ANN, b. July, 1862.
2817. LUELLA MARIA, b. 1864.
2818. SAMUEL, b. 1866.
2819. CHARLES HENRY, b. Feb. 22, d. July, 1868.

2820. SYRENA[5] [2403] (Samuel[5], Samuel[4], Abraham[2], John[1]),
m. Charles Herrick, of Salamanca, Cattaraugus Co., N. Y., who
was afterwards a soldier in the 7th (?) Indiana light artillery
through the war. He is now engineer in an oil mill in Warren Co.,
Penn., where they reside. Child : —

2821. SOPHRONIA (Herrick), b. Mar. 28, 1860.

2822. JOHN SMITH[5] [2404] (Samuel[4], Samuel[3], Abraham[2], John[1]), served in the 4th New Hampshire regiment, Co. A ; mustered in Sept. 18, 1861 ; re-enlisted Feb. 15, 1864 ; wounded by a ball, June 15, 1864, losing his thumb and fore-finger. He m. Elizabeth F. Evans, of New Durham, Jan. 18, 1865. Children, b. in N. D. : —

  2823. JOHN NEWMARCH, b. Mar. 3, 1867.
  2824. EDWIN EVANS, b. Jan. 1, 1869.

  2825. ABRAHAM[5] [2409] (Abram[4], Nathaniel[3], Abraham[2], John[1]), m. Eliza Ann Skinner, of Lynnfield Centre, Mass., Mar. 9, 1845 ; resided in Saugus, as a shoemaker, and there d. Apr. 28, 1855, in his 31st year. She has m., 2d, R. H. Goodwin, whose residence is in Malden, and place of business 37 Haverhill Street, Boston. Children : —

  2826. CHARLES MILTON, b. Aug. 20, 1846 ; d. Apr. 9, 1854, in his 8th year.
  2827. CLARENCE ABRAM, b. Apr. 11, 1851, now residing in Malden; business in Boston.

  2828. ALBERT[5] [2412] (Samuel[4], Jonathan[3], Abraham[2], John[1]), settled as a farmer, with other extended business relations, in the south part of Boscawen (now Webster), N. H. ; m., 1st, Ann Myra Colby, of Concord, Jan. 7, 1835. She d. Oct. 22, 1866. He m., 2d, Lucy Jane Holmes, of Webster, Oct. 3, 1867. Children, first wife : —

  2829. MARY MARIA, b. June 10, 1836 ; d. of paralysis, at Webster, Feb. 20, 1872, in her 36th year.
  2830. MARCIA E. [3259], b. July 14, 1838.

  2831. JOHN BURBANK[5] [2413] (Samuel[4], Jonathan[3], Abraham[2], John[1]), m. Louisa Towne, Sept. 20, 1835, at Milford, N. H. She was a native of Lyndeborough. He is a carpenter, now residing, as for several years past, in Concord. Children : —

  2832. ALONZO, b. May 20, 1837, in Nashua; m. Carrie Ward, of Concord, Dec. 19, 1864, and d. at C., Dec. 26, 1864, in his 28th year. She was residing, 1870, in Portland, Me.
  2833. MELISSA, b. Jan. 13, 1840, in Concord; m. James Martin Hook, of C., Oct. 27, 1859, and d. at Concord, Aug. 16, 1863, in her 24th year.
  2834. JOHN MASON, b. Sept. 11, 1850, in Concord ; was established, 1870, as a druggist and apothecary, firm of " Hildreth & Runals," at Suncook, N. H.
  2835. HATTIE LOUISA, b. Mar. 10, 1854, and d. at Concord, Aug. 2, 1867, aged 13.

  2836. ASA DARWIN[5] [2415] (Samuel[4], Jonathan[3], Abraham[2], John[1]), first settled as a farmer, in Sebago, Me., and there m. Hannah B. Pike, of Sebago, who was b. in S , Feb. 27, 1823. He was residing, 1869, in Andover, Mass., three miles from Lawrence. Children : —

  2837. JOSEPHINE, b. Oct. 10, 1852, in Sebago.
  2838. FRANK, b. Jan. 8, 1865, in S.

2839. HANNAH DOW[5] [2416] (Samuel[4], Jonathan[3], Abraham[2], John[1]), m. Eli Searles, wheelwright, Feb. 1836, and d. at Bradford, N. H. (?), Aug. 7, 1841, aged 24 years 6 months. Children : —

    2840. JEFFERSON ROCKWOOD (Searles), b. Jan. 2, 1837, in Nashua, N. H.; enlisted in the New Hampshire 7th regiment, Co. E, Nov. 7, 1861; "missing at Olustee, Fla., Feb. 20, 1864" (Mil. Hist.); is supposed to have been taken prisoner, and soon after to have d. at the Andersonville prison, aged 27.

    2841. HANNAH JANE, b. 1839, in Merrimack; d. 1840, aged 1 year.

2842. FRANKLIN LOVEJOY[5] [2420] (Samuel[4], Jonathan[3], Abraham[2], John[1]), is an extensive wood and coal dealer in Lawrence, Mass., occupying a new and costly residence, in 1869 ; m. Charlotte Durgin, of Lee, N. H., Feb. 5, 1850, at Lawrence. Children : —

    2843. IDA JANE, b. Apr. 12, d. Nov. 7, 1855.
    2844. ELLA ESTELLE, b. Sept. 16, 1859; d. Sept. 24, 1861, aged 2.
    2845. CARRIE CLEON, b. May 5, 1863.

2846. LEONARD PARKER[5] [2436] (Ezekiel D[4], Jonathan[3], Abraham[2], John[1]), still owns and occupies the homestead in Arcade, first settled by his grandfather, Leonard Parker, and owned by his father over thirty years. Was a merchant in A. two years, in company with James Wadsworth; afterwards in Strykersville, N. Y., four years, where also postmaster. Health failing, he returned to Arcade, where, for twenty-five years (1872), he has been justice of the peace, and also session justice (or side judge), the latter being an elective office in New York. As a farmer, he has been quite successful in raising horses and cattle, taking several "first prizes" at agricultural fairs, and devoting one farm of one hundred and eighty-four acres to the raising of stock, — some for distant markets, — besides his homestead of two hundred and sixty acres. He m. Emily M. Bolcom, Sept. 1, 1841, at Strykersville. Children : —

    2847. JAMES. b. July 31, 1842; d. Mar. 21, 1843, aged 7 months 21 days.
    2848. WILLIAM, b Nov. 13, 1843; d. July 10, 1844, aged 8 months.
    2849. WILLARD, b. Aug. 20, 1846; d. July 1, 1847, aged 10 mos. 11 days.
    2850. EZEKIEL DEAN, b. Aug. 11, d. Aug. 13, 1852.
    2851. LEONARD EARL, b. Oct. 8, 1854.

2852. DOLLY FORSTER[5] [2438] (Ezekiel D.[4], Jonathan[3], Abraham[2], John[1]), m. Charles Williams Arnold, June 25, 1843. He was b. June 30, 1816, in China (now Arcade), N. Y., and has there resided as a farmer. Children : —

    2853. JAMES HENRY (Arnold), b. Oct. 2, 1845 ; d. Mar. 2, 1846, aged 5 mos.
    2854. LAVINIA REBECCA, b. Jan. 11, 1848; has been engaged as a teacher in the vicinity of Arcade.
    2855. CHARLES EDMUND, b. May 12, 1854.
    2856. GEORGE HARVEY, b. July 9, 1863.

2857. EDMOND LUCIEN[5] [2439] (Ezekiel D.[4], Jonathan[3], Abraham[2], John[1]), moved to Ripon, Wis., or vicinity, Sept. 1846, where now a practising attorney-at-law, — firm of "Runals & Reed," 1872.

Had previously obtained his education at Bethany and Strykersville, N. Y., and m. Dorlesca Avery, of Livonia, Mich., July 15, 1847. Growing up with Ripon, from nothing to a city (1869) of five thousand inhabitants, he held the offices of assessor, school commissioner, town superintendent, and alderman, three years each, and of city attorney five years. Was two years a member of the State legislature, and four years judge of the municipal court. He also owned, published, and edited the " Ripon Spur " (newspaper), and the " Ripon Home," two years. Child : —

2858. WILLIE T., b. Oct. 10, 1849 ; a printer at Ripon, and proprietor of the " Prairie City Local," in 1869.

2859. ELI GRIFFETH[5] [2441] (Abner[4], Jonathan[3], Abraham[2], John[1]), m. Hellen Charrilla Murray, June 7, 1844, in Pike, N. Y., where she was b. Mar. 28, 1817. He was first a hatter in New York, serving his apprenticeship in Pike ; moved to Kenosha, Wis., in 1846, where he has since resided, chiefly as a dealer in real estate. Children : —

2860. ELI GRIFFETH, Jr., b. Jan. 2, 1846, at Honey Falls, N. Y., and there d. Oct. 13, 1848, in his 3d year.
2861. IDA BELLE, b. Jan. 6, 1850, in Kenosha ; m. Charles W. Weyl, June 15, 1869, and d. at K., June 16, 1871, aged 21 years 5 mos. 10 dys.
2862. FRANK ADELBERT, b. Mar. 7, 1853, in K.
2863. LILLY MAUDE, b. Mar. 14, 1855, in K.
   NOTE. — Fuller records of the next younger sister and brother of [2859] coming too late for insertion in their proper places, are here given : —
      MARY ANN (Adams) [2442] left three children ; one son, deceased ; one daughter, living in Toledo, O., and one daughter, supposed to be in Denver City, Col.
      ABNER A. [2443], b. May 30, 1819, in Alleghany, N. Y. ; settled in Lorain Co., O., with his uncle, 1829 ; lived and learned the trade of harness-maker at Elyria, O. ; m. Elizabeth A. Stevison, of Mt. Vernon, O., 1847, and is now a farmer in Illinois, located seven miles from the city of Peoria.

2864. MARIA[5] [2444] (Abner[4], Jonathan[3], Abraham[2], John[1]), has been twice married ; 2d, to S. Franklin Comstock, merchant tailor, of Chicago, Ill., at Newburg, O. Children : —

2865. EUGENE (Comstock (?)), b. about 1836.
2866. ELIZA, b. about 1842.
2867. HENRY, b. about 1847.
2868. FREDERICK, b. about 1854.
2869. FRANCES MARIA, b. 1856 (?) ; d., aged 1 year 9 months.

2870. SUSAN M.[5] [2445] (Abner[4], Jonathan[3], Abraham[2], John[1]), m. Asaph Shattuck, at Newburg, O. He d. and she now lives, as his widow, in Toledo, O. Children : —

2871. CHARILLA (Shattuck), b. 1848 (?) ; d., aged 2 years.
2872. LEGRAND, b. 1849 (?).
2873. ANNETTE, b. 1851 (?).
2874. MARIA, b. Aug. 16, 1852, in Newburg, O.

2875. JOHN D.[5] [2446] Abner[4], Jonathan[3], Abraham[2], John[1]), came to Newburg, O., at the age of 15, probably with his parents, where he has since made it his home, with the exception of two years, since 1870, while he has been in business_ at Auburn, Ala., under the firm of " Runals, Switz & Taylor," forming the " Auburn Furniture Company," " manufacturers of chairs, bedsteads, etc." He m. Annette Brainard, only daughter of Dudley Brainard, at Newburg, Oct. 20, 1853, who was b. Apr. 1, 1826, in N. Children, b. in Newburg : —

2876.   ADA ANNETTE, b. May 8, 1855.
2877.   MARY ESTHER, b. Sept. 30, 1857 ; d. Aug. 17, 1858, aged 10 mos. 18 days.
2878.   MARY ELIZA, b. June 18, 1859.
2879.   FANNIE SUSAN, b. Sept. 4, 1861.

2·80.   HENRY[5] [2447] (Abner[4], Jonathan[3], Abraham[2], John[1]), resides in Lagrange, Lorain Co., O., having m. Jane Jackson, 1850. (We regret that the records of his and of other branches of his father's family, not coming to hand for the first time till a late day, are necessarily left so imperfect.)   Children, — the *years* of whose births, even, we will not venture to *guess:* —

2881.   HATTIE.
2882.   DIODEMA.
2883.   MARY ANN.
2884.   JANE.
2885.   ELI GRIFFETH.

2886.   MARY ELIZA[5] [2449] (James[4], Jonathan[3], Abraham[2], John[1]), m., 1st, Abel Travers, Dec. 23, 1831, at Dunkirk, N. Y. He was b. Sept. 22, 1811, was a farmer in Pomfret, Chautauque Co., N. Y., and there d. from an accident with a threshing machine, Aug. 19, 1839, in his 28th year.   She m., 2d, David Hufstader, farmer, Dec. 16, 1841, at Ellicottsville, N. Y.   He was b. July 20, 1809 ; d. Jan. 12, 1862, in his 53d year.   Children : —

2887.   JAMES (Travers), b. June 2, 1835, in Pomfret; m. Helen Kent, Oct. 8, 1857.
2888.   ELLEN, b Apr. 21, 1838, in Pomfret; m. James Austin, mechanic, Sept. 16, 1857, at Ellicottsville   Children : —
    1.   EARNEST (Austin), b. in Ellicottsville.
    2.   WALTER, b in Ashtabula Co., O.
    3.   LILIE, b. in Kingsville, O.
2889.   MARY A. (Travers), b. Apr. 20, 1840, in Pomfret; m. Harvey C. Armstrong, farmer, Sept. 16, 1857, at Ellicottsville. Children : —
    1.   JEDDIE (Armstrong), and
    2.   KOSIE, both b. in East Otto, Cattaraugus Co., N. Y.
2890.   FRANCIS (Hufstader), b. Mar. 9, 1844, in Ashford, N. Y.; m. Temperance Cross, Nov. 1, 1866.
2891.   ELMIRA, b. Apr. 15, 1846, in Ellicottsville; m. George O. Sacket, farmer, of East Otto, Feb. 28, 1866.   Child : —
    1.   CARRIE B. (Sacket), b. Feb. 19, 1869.
2892.   CHARLES J. (Hufstader), b. Apr. 3, 1848, in Ellicottsville ; a farmer.
2893.   OSCAR, b. June 5, 1851, in Ellicottsville ; a farmer.

2894.   JEREMIAH AMES[5] [2450] (James[4], Jonathan[3], Abraham[2], John[1]), m. Arvilla Winchester, Nov. 4, 1839, at Ellicottsville, N. Y., where he resided as a farmer ; afterwards at East Otto.   Children, all b. in Ellicottsville : —

2895. SOPHRONIA [3262], b Aug. 9, 1840.
2896. LEVERETT B., b. Mar. 27, 1842; d. May 1, 1862, at E. Otto, aged 20.
2897. GEORGE W., b. Mar. 15, 1846; d. May 9, 1862, at E. O., aged 16.
2898. MARY A., b. Feb. 13, 1848; m. William H. Winchester, Nov. 11, 1865, at Gonanda, N. Y.
2899. IDA B., b. Jan. 17, 1854; d. Apr. 27, 1862, at E. Otto, aged 8.
2900. ADA B., b. Oct. 10, 1861.

2901. STELLA ALMIRA⁵ [2451] (James⁴, Jonathan³, Abraham², John¹), m. Jacob W. Travers, Jan. 10, 1833, at Fredonia, N. Y. He was b. Aug. 29, 1814, in Rensselaer Co.; a mariner for thirty years; afterwards a farmer; residence, Monroe Centre, O. (1872). Children: —
2902. CAROLINE (Travers), b. Jan. 4, 1834, in Huron Co, O.
2903. WILLIAM GILBERT, b. May 18, 1836, in Dunkirk, N. Y.
2904. CHARLES HENRY, b. Apr 28, 1838, in Sandusky City, O.; d. at Monroe, July 3, 1862, aged 24.

2905. SOPHRONIA MARIA⁵ [2452] (James⁴, Jonathan³, Abraham², John¹), m. Leverett Barker Goldsmith, Dec. 5, 1839, at Portland, N.Y. He was a steamboat captain for thirty years prior to 1869; residence, as now, at Conneaut, Ashtabula Co., O. Children, all b. in C.: —
2906. JAMES LEVERETT, b. Mar. 4, 1841; d. Aug. 22, 1842, aged 1 year 5 months 18 days.
2907. CHARLES WILLIAM, b. Dec. 10, 1844.
2908. HENRY LAKE, b. Nov. 5, 1847.
2909. CECELIA REBECCA, b. Sept. 27, 1849.
2910. JENETTE EMELINE, b. Feb. 21, 1852.
2911. GEORGE DERBY, b. Aug. 13, 1860.

2912. WILLIAM CARL⁵ [2453] (James⁴, Jonathan³, Abraham², John¹), has resided as a farmer in Ellicottsville and East Otto, N. Y.; m. Mary M. Ballou, Jan. 6, 1848, at Ashford, Cattaraugus Co. Children: —
2913. HOMER C., b. Nov. 3, 1848, in Ellicottsville; d. June 5, 1866, at East Otto, in his 18th year.
2914. WILLIAM B., b. Sept. 23, 1850, in E., and there d. Mar. 28, 1851, aged 6 months.
2915. INEZ R., b. Jan. 31, 1853, in E.
2916. MINNIE M., b. June 18, 1865, in East Otto.

2917. LORENZO DOW⁵ [2455] (Israel⁴, Jonathan³, Abraham², John¹), was a hotel-keeper and farmer for twenty-one years; m. Jane Scott, of Hume, Alleghany Co., N. Y., Sept. 20, 1842. She was b. Sept. 24, 1826. He now resides at Wiscoy, N. Y. Children: —
2918. ALONZO MANLY [3264], b. Jan. 9, 1844, in Hume.
2919. RINALDO SCOTT [3267], b. May 9, 1849, in Sharon, Penn.
2920. FRED BRONELLO, b. Nov. 25, 1857, in Caneadia, N. Y.

2921. ISRAEL MORRIS⁵ [2458] (Israel⁴, Jonathan³, Abraham², John¹), m. Angeline Esther Rhodes, of Hume, N. Y., Aug. 13, 1848, at Sharon Centre, Pa. She was b. Aug. 3, 1832. He is a hotel-keeper at Emporium, Cameron Co., Pa. Children: —
2922. FRANCES MARY [3269], b. Aug. 13, 1849.
2923. LOUISA ANN, b. Feb. 12, 1854; d. Oct. 7, 1865, in her 12th year, at Scio, N. Y.
2924. ALICE JANE, b. July 11, 1858.

2925. WARREN WILLIAM⁵ [2460] (Israel⁴, Jonathan³, Abraham²,
John¹), m., 1st, Alice Rosebrooks, of Rochester, N. Y., May 2,
1855. She d. at R., June 7, 1856, aged 19. He m. a 2d wife,
a Canadian lady, 1860, and now resides at Peterborough, Ontario
Co., C. W. Had one child by second wife, who d., aged 9 months ;
also : —

2926. GEORGE WILLIAMS (first wife), b. Feb. 27, 1856, in Rochester.

2927. LOUISA ANN⁵ [2461] (Israel⁴, Jonathan³, Abraham²,
John¹), m. Andrew Jacobs, June 22, 1856, at Sharon Centre, Pa.,
where he is now residing, as a farmer, — formerly of Warren,
Bradford Co. He served nine months in Company F, 210th
regiment Pennsylvania volunteers, second division, fifth army
corps. Children : —

2928. CHARLES BENJAMIN (Jacobs), b. June 3, 1858, at Sharon Centre.
2929. KATY ANNA, b. Aug. 5, 1866, at S. C.

2930. GEORGE WILLIAMS⁵ [2462] (Israel⁴, Jonathan³, Abraham², John¹), m. Martha Colton, of Attica, N. Y., Dec. 23, 1861,
who was b. May 20, 1845. He is a merchant in Attica. Child : —

2931. ROSE GROVENOR, b. Mar. 16, 1863.

2932. MARY ANN⁵ [2465] (Jonathan C.⁴, Jonathan³, Abraham²,
John¹), m. Silas McKellips, Mar. 26, 1856, at Manchester, N. H.
He is a farmer, residing in Weare. Child : —

2933. WILBUR H. (McKellips), b. Apr. 30, 1858.

2934. ALMIRA BARTLETT⁵ [2466] (Jonathan C ⁴, Jonathan³,
Abraham², John¹), m. Jacob N. Flanders, Feb. 14, 1850, at Deering,
N. H. He is a farmer, residing in Concord. Children : —

2935. LUCIA ANN (Flanders), b. Jan. 15, 1851.
2936. MARY AUGUSTA, b. Oct. 5, 1862; d. Mar. 26, 1865, at Concord, in
her 3d year.

2937. GEORGE SULLIVAN⁵ [2467] (Jonathan C.⁴, Jonathan³,
Abraham², John¹), is a miller ; settled first in the State of New
York, but has since returned to New Hampshire ; m. Mary A.
Brierly, July 4, 1855, at Little Falls, N. Y. Children : —

2938. MARTHA J., b. Sept. 5, 1856, in Stratford, N. Y.
2939. BERTHA P., b. Sept. 13, 1860, in Deering, N. H.
2940. ANNA MAY, b. Aug. 5, 1862, in Weare, N. H.

2941. HORACE HERRICK⁵ [2468] (Jonathan C.⁴, Jonathan³,
Abraham², John¹), resides in Deering, N. H., as a miller ; m. Mary
F. Carter, Feb. 12, 1862, at Henniker. Children : —

2942. NETTIE E., b. Sept. 2, 1866, in Deering.
2943. DALTON S., b. June 15, 1868, in D.

2944. ARVILLA JANE⁵ [2470] (Jonathan C.⁴, Jonathan³, Abraham², John¹), m. John O. Clark, of Deering, 1854, at Weare. He

has resided in D. as a dealer in produce, since 1856, where all the children were b. except the oldest : —

2945. LUCY J. (Clark), b. July 28, 1855, in Weare; d. at Deering, June 9, 1858, in her 3d year.
2946. FRED A., b. Aug. 7, 1857.
2947. H. GILLIE, b. Sept. 1, 1859.
2948. LUCY E , b. Dec. 8, 1862; d. Aug. 9, 1864, aged 1 year 8 months.
2949. WARREN J., b. Apr. 12, 1865; d. July 17, 1866, aged 1 year 3 mos.
2950. ELLIE RUTH, b. Sept. 7, 1871.

2951. LAURA AUGUSTA[5] [2471] (Jonathan C.[4], Jonathan[3], Abraham[2], John[1]), m., 1st, Warren H. Emery, 1859, at Deering. He was a sash and blind manufacturer in D.; enlisted in the 14th New Hampshire regiment, Co. D, Aug. 12, 1862 ; was stationed with his regiment in and around Washington, D. C., till Mar. 1864 ; then, after a short furlough, sailed on the "Daniel Webster" for New Orleans, encountering a terrible gale; came up the river to Morganza, where he was taken sick in June ; was transferred, two weeks later, to the U. S. General Hospital in Natchez, Miss., and there d. July 25, 1864. She m., 2d, Charles Dow, of North Weare, railroad engineer, Dec. 19, 1869, at New Boston. Child : —

2952. SILBIE J. (Emery), b. Nov. 29, 1860, in Deering.

2953. ABIGAIL ANN[5] [2492] (James[4], Ebenezer[3], Abraham[2], John[1]), m. George Newton Wallace, Dec. 25, 1858, at Alton, N. H. He is a farmer on New Durham Ridge, though he had been an invalid for some years, in 1870. Children : —

2954. ALMENA AUGUSTA (Wallace) (adopted child), b. Aug. 8, 1851, in New Durham; m. Trask W. Averill, Dec. 15, 1870, in Farmington.
2955. GEORGE MELVIN, b. Apr. 13, 1860, in New Durham.
2956. EDGAR FENTON, b. Oct. 10, 1861, in N. D.

2957. ORLANDO JAMES[5] [2493] (James[4], Ebenezer[3], Abraham[2], John[1]), was a shoemaker ; m. Maria Antoinette Young, of Wolfborough, Mar. 8, 1860 ; enlisted in the 8th New Hampshire regiment, Dec. 7, 1861 (mustered in Dec. 20, Co. I) ; d. of disease at New Orleans, La., July 6, 1862, aged 28. Child : —

2958. CAPITOLA, b. Aug. 2, 1861.

2959. SARAH ELIZABETH[5] [2494] (James[4], Ebenezer[3], Abraham[2], John[1]), m. Elijah Wallace, July 8, 1860, and d. Feb. 10, 1862, in her 26th year. Child : —

2960. SARAH FRANCES (Wallace), b. Sept. 2, 1861; d. Oct. 9, 1862, aged 1 year 1 month 1 week.

2961. ABIGAIL[5] [2501] (William[4], Moses[3], William[2], John[1]), m. William Adams, of Madison, Me., Aug. 26, 1817. Children, b. in Carritunk, Me., except the fourth and fifth : —

2962. ERASTUS (Adams), b. Apr. 9, 1824; was in the late war, and has since d. in consequence of wounds received.

2963. JUSTUS, b. July 29, 1827; also in the war, and badly wounded.
2964. ORILLA, b. Mar. 13, 1830; m. Joseph Adams. of Carritunk.
2965. FLAVILLA, b. Mar. 22, 1833, at the Forks (of the Kennebec river), Me.
2966. PRISCILLA, b. June 11, 1836, at the Forks.
2967. ELEANOR, b. Jan. 11, 1839.
2968. ALMEDA, b. June 14, 1843.

2969. SARAH CROSBY[5] [2502] (William[4], Moses[3], William[2], John[1]), m. Joseph Bean, Oct. 1, 1822. He was b. July 23, 1799; settled first as a farmer in Carritunk, Me., where all their children were b.; moved to Norridgewock, 1852, and to Waterville (West), 1866, where still residing in 1870. Children: —

2970. ELIZABETH EASTMAN (Bean), b. Oct. 21, 1823; m. Reuben Ham, Fayette, Me.
2971. SELDEN, b. July 16, 1825; a clergyman, in Vienna, Me.
2972. LEVI HERBERT, b. Aug. 7, 1827; now residing at Danvers, Mass.
2973. SARAH, b. Nov. 22, 1829; d. Mar. 18, 1832, in her 3d year.
2974. ISAAC HANSON, b. Sept. 2, 1831; present residence, Danvers Centre, Mass.
2975. JACOB EMERSON, b. Apr. 6, 1834; now in West Waterville.
2976. WILLIAM RUNNELS, b. Oct. 15, 1836; enlisted in the 7th Maine battery, Dec 1863; wounded at the Spottsylvania battle by a ball in the ankle, May 12, 1864; discharged, in consequence, Aug. 20, 1864, and has since lost his leg   Resides at New Sharon, Me.
2977. SARAH BATES, b. May 26, 1841; now at West Watervile.

2978. ELIZABETH RANDALL[5] [2504] (William[4], Moses[3], William[2], John[1]), m., 1st, William Forsythe, farmer, of Carritunk, Me., Sept. 10, 1835. He d. Oct. 15, 1836, and she m., 2d, Thomas Doyle, farmer, of C., Jan. 22, 1837, who was b. Nov. 14, 1806. Present address, " Bingham, Me." Children: —

2979. ELIZABETH RANDALL (Doyle), b. Oct. 8, 1838, in Carritunk; m. Dudley L. Rollins, of C.
2980. CATHARINE MALVINA, b. Dec. 14, 1840; m. William Cate, of Carritunk, who was b. Nov. 8, 1834. Children: —
    1. ELVIRA LYDIA (Cate), b. July 3, 1861.
    2. MILES MANLEY, b. Apr. 8, 1863.
    3. MALORA ELIZABETH, b. Nov 11, 1864.
    4. MALVINA ELLEN, b. May 16, 1867.
2981. THOMAS STEWART (Doyle), b. Feb. 12, 1843; m. Victoria L. Meserve; resides at the Forks, Me.
2982. ALBERT SMITH, b. Apr. 23, 1845, in Lower Canada; m. Mary Ann Williams; residence, Harlem, Ill.
2983. NANCY BELL, b. July 24, 1847; m. Samuel S. Cate, of Carritunk, Me.
2984. WILLIAM RUNNELS, b. May 25, 1850, at Moose river, Me.

2985. POLLY[5] [2505] (William[4], Moses[3], William[2], John[1]), m. Isaac Hanson, June, 1830. Children: —

2986. AMOS W. (Hanson), b. Dec. 1, 1831; d. in Ohio, Aug. 1868, in his 37th year.
2987. MARY ANN, b. Sept. 6, 1833.
2988. JOSEPH BEAN, b. Oct. 19, 1835; served in the late war three years.

2989. MOSES CROSBY[5] [:506] (William[4], Moses[3], William[2], John[1]), m. Mary A. Cate, of Carritunk, Me., May 16, 1847. She was b. June 15, 1826. He resided at Carritunk till 1855, where the four oldest children were b.; since then at Richmond, Me., where the three youngest were b. Business, first, that of a teamster; now (1872) a dealer in groceries, etc., at Richmond. Children: —

2990. WILLIS SMITH, b. Feb. 20, d. Sept. 6, 1848.
2991. SARAH FRANCES [3272], b. Sept. 16, 1849.
2992. ELVIRA ANN, b. Aug. 19, 1851.
2993. ANSIL THURSTON, b. June 12, 1853; d. May 12, 1854, aged 11 mos.
2994. CHARLES WILLIAM, b. July 13, 1857; d. Oct. 7, 1858, aged 1 yr. 3 ms.
2995. WILLIAM CATE, b. Oct. 15, 1867.
2996. ARTHUR CROSBY, b. Nov. 15, 1870.

2997. GEORGE JOHNSON[5] [2507] (William[4], Moses[3], William[2], John[1]), was a farmer; m., 1st, Rosanna Rice, of Vassalboro', Me., June 14, 1844, who d. May 2, 1851. He m., 2d, Sarah Forbuss, of Brighton, Me., Jan. 1852, and d. at B., Feb. 1854, aged 32. Children, first wife: —

2998. EDWIN CROSBY, b. July 2, 1845, in Carritunk, Me.; enlisted Mar. 17, 1864, in the 31st Maine regiment, Co. G; "on detached service"; discharged July 15, 1865; m. Laura Greene, of Rockland, Dec. 19, 1865; was a stone-cutter at Hallowell, in 1870.
2999. LYDIA ANN [3274], b. July 23, 1848, in Augusta.
3000. ALBERT, b. Apr. 3, 1851, in Brighton; d. Mar. 1852, aged 11 mos.

3001. STEPHEN OTIS[5] [2508] (William[4], Moses[3], William[2], John[1]), m. Emily Pierce, of Brewer, Me., Oct. 1857; resided at B., and there d. Mar. 6, 1865, in his 41st year. Children: —

3002. IDA, b. Feb. 1860.
3003. CHARLES, b. Jan. 6, 1862.
3004. WILLIAM, b. Feb. 8, 1864.

3005. OLIVE BALL[5] [2509] (William[4], Moses[3], William[2], John[1]), m. Jonathan Emery, of Carritunk, Me., Nov. 11, 1844 (P. O., "Bingham, Me."). He is a farmer, and was b. Dec. 3, 1815, in Concord, Me. Children, all but one, b. in Carritunk: —

3006. OLIVE BALL (Emery), b. Feb. 12, 1846.
3007. SILAS, b. Nov. 24, 1847; d. Dec. 25, 1848, aged 1 year 1 mo. 1 day.
3008. JANE ANN, b. Apr. 5, 1849.
3009. CLARA ELLA, b. Aug. 24, 1850; d. Aug. 10, 1863, aged 13.
3010. SILAS, b. Mar. 29, 1852.
3011. WILLIAM CATES, b. Feb. 14, 1854.
3012. SARAH AUGUSTA, b. July 22, 1856; d. Aug. 1, 1863, aged 7.
3013. MOSES CROSBY, b. Feb. 27, 1860.
3014. JOSEPH KINGMAN, b. Dec. 5, 1864; d. Aug. 16, 1869, in his 5th year.

3015. RACHEL BRIGGS[5] [2510] (William[4], Moses[3], William[2], John[1]), m. Seth Adams, of Carritunk, Me, Dec. 1851, and is now deceased. His P. O. address is "Forks, Me." Children: —

3016. ORTANN (Adams).
3017. RACHEL.
3018. JOHN.
3019. SARAH.

3020. WILLIAM BALL[5] [2512] (William[4], Moses[3], William[2], John[1]), m. Almira Ham, of Richmond, Me., Apr. 26, 1855. She was b. Sept 16, 1836, in Medford, Mass. Present residence at Bath, Me. He enlisted May 1, 1861, in Co. G, 4th regiment Maine volunteers; served in the army twenty months; was engaged in seven battles, and was wounded in the face, occasioning the loss of his right eye. Children: —

3021. CHANDLER BAKER, b. Feb. 21, 1856, in Richmond.
3022. WILLIAM EVERETT, b. Feb. 28, 1858, in Richmond; was drowned in Back river, Georgetown, July 1, 1870, in his 13th year.
3023. SMITH SPALDING, b. Mar. 31, 1865, in Bowtown, Me.
3024   LEVI HOLMAN, b. Apr. 9, 1867, in Bath.
3025. ANNIE CORA SIMPSON, b. June 10, 1869, in Bath.

3026. JOSEPH SPALDING[5] [2513] (William[4], Moses[3], William[2], John[1]), m. Esther M. Williams, of Forks, Me., 1858, at Carritunk. She was b. Dec. 9, 1840, and was residing, as his widow, at Skowhegan, 1870; he having d. May 4, 1867, aged 32, leaving: —

3027. ALLEN W., b. Jan. 22, 1859, at the Forks.

3028. SARAH JONES[5] [2543] (Winthrop[4], Winthrop[3], Joseph[2], John[1]), m. Robert Newman, of Boston, Mass., a merchant tailor, June 5, 1836; present residence, Longwood. Children, all b. in Boston: —

3029. ROBERT (Newman), b. July 12, 1838; enlisted in the 1st Massachusetts cavalry, spring of 1861. Time of service, one year; was at the first battle of Bull Run; has since m. Mary J. Herriman [3036 (?)].
3030. ELIZABETH ADALINE, b. Apr. 22, 1841; was baptized by the Rev. Baron Stow, at the age of 15. "Amiable by nature, grace added adornments to her character, and made her one of the loveliest of earth." She d. July 25, 1861, aged 20 years 3 mos., and was buried in Forest Hills cemetery. From the "In Memoriam" of a friend: —

> "O! never was a purer gem
> Committed to its trust;
> A fairer form of maidenhood
> Ne'er mingled with the dust."

3031. HENRY JONES, b. June 23, 1844; m. Emma P. Hanford; was in the commission business, Chicago, Ill., 1870.
3032. MARSHAL PERRY, b. May 5, 1848; enlisted Sept. 1, 1862, with a company formed chiefly from the Baptist church, Charlestown, Mass. ("Co. E, Putnam Blues, Massachusetts 47th regiment"), in the capacity of drummer. Discharged for disability, Dec. 17, 1862. Afterwards enlisted in the navy, — U. S. frigate "Sabine," — Aug. 4, 1864, for three years. Having been transferred to the U. S. steamer "Wabash," he was at the storming of Fort Fisher, Jan. 15, 1865; had nine hours' hard fighting with the storming party, and being captain's clerk, he took lists of the killed and wounded, and made the report of the battle for the squadron. Has since m. Louisa Walther (German), and is now (1870) in business with his father, in Boston.
3033. FRANK ALBERT, b. Jan. 7, 1854.

3034. Susan Caroline[5] [2545] (Winthrop[4], Winthrop[3], Joseph[2], John[1]), m., 1st, James Babbit, hatter, of Boston, July, 1842 ; who d. Oct. 18, 1843. She m , 2d, Charles Herriman, marine captain, Feb. 27, 1847, who d. June 9, 1858 ; she m., 3d, John Gregory Beecher, trunk-maker, Feb. 20, 1861, in Boston, where now residing, Pleasant Street, near corner of Carver. Children : —

3035. Sarah Elizabeth (Babbit), b. July 12, 1843, in Boston ; m. an
Oliver, and d. Mar. 7, 1870, in her 27th year.
3036. Mary Jane (Herriman), b. July 19, 1848, in Chelsea ; see [3029].
3037. Charles Winthrop, b. July 14, 1850, in Chelsea.
3038. Robert Reynolds, b. May 20, 1852, in C.
3039. Willie Wheeler, b. Nov. 23, 1855, in C.
3040. Henry Ward (Beecher), b. Oct. 14, 1862, in Chicago, Ill., and
there d. Jan. 20, 1864, aged 1 year 3 months.
3041. Lilian Grace, b. Aug 31, 1864, in Chicago.

3042. Hannah Adams[5] [2547] (Winthrop[4], Winthrop[3], Joseph[2], John[1]), m. John Godbold, of Chelsea, Mass., shipsmith, Jan. 1846. He d Apr. 3, 1847. She d. Aug. 9, 1863, in her 35th year. Child : —

3043. Annie Elizabeth (Godbold), b. Jan. 1847 ; d. Jan. 9, 1852, aged 5.

3044. Horace[5] [2568] (Ephraim F.[4], Winthrop[3], Joseph[2], John[1]), is a shoemaker, residing in Barrington, N. H. (1870) ; m. Sarah Elizabeth Young, of Durham, June 18, 1849, who was b. Nov. 11, 1819. Children : —

3045. Mary Josephine, b. May 18, 1852, in Barrington ; m. Orin W.
Canney, of Dover, July 2, 1871.
3046. George Hamilton, b. May 27, 1855, in B.

3047. Sophia Locke[5] [2569] (Ephraim F.[4], Winthrop[3], Joseph[2], John[1]), m. William Holmes Babb, of Barrington, Jan. 1, 1850. He is a farmer in B., b. May 3, 1822. Children : —

3048. Mary Sophia (Babb), b. Mar. 20, d. Apr. 2, 1851, in Rochester.
3049. Ida Florence, b. Jan. 1, 1852, in R.
3050. Fred Sumner, } b. Nov. 20, 1857, in Durham.
3051. Frank Ozell,   }
It is said of these twins that their own mother could scarcely
tell them apart. The latter d. Nov. 25, 1858, aged 1 year 5 days.

3052. Lucy Locke[5] [2570] (Ephraim F.[4], Winthrop[3], Joseph[2], John[1]), m. Charles H. Ranlett, carpenter. Nov. 5, 1850. He was b Mar. 24, 1828 ; resided in Durham, where were b. : —

3053. Frank Edward (Ranlett), b. July 6, 1853.
3054. Mary Abby, b. Mar. 26, 1856.

3055. Winthrop[5] [2571] (Ephraim F.[4], Winthrop[3], Joseph[2], John[1]), first entered the U. S. Navy, Aug. 1849, on board the frigate "St. Lawrence," with which he cruised in the South Pacific and around the world. At the commencement of the late war, he served first on the U. S. frigate "Wabash"; next on the gun-boat "Isaac Smith," Capt. Nicholson. Participated in seven naval engagements, including that at Port Royal, Nov. 7, 1861; was wounded in the leg by guerrillas while cruising up St. Johns River, in Florida; was confined twenty-three weeks on hospital ship and in the Brooklyn, N. Y., Hospital, and was finally discharged from the navy, Sept. 12, 1863. Is at present (1869) a shoemaker, in Barrington; m., 1st, Olive Hoyt, July, 1854; m., 2d, Olive Willey, June, 1864. Child, first wife: —

3056. MARY SOPHIA, b. Apr. 2, 1855, in Barrington.

3057. CHARLES AUSTIN[5] [2578] (John[4], Joseph[3], Joseph[2], John[1]), like his father, a clothier and tailor in Bangor, Me., and also a popular staff and drill officer in the art military; was m. to Marianna Gould, of Bangor, Sept. 2, 1832, by Rev. Mr. Huntoon, in the Unitarian house of worship. Children: —

3058. CHARLES FREDERICK, b. Aug. (?) 6, 1834, in Bangor; d. on his passage to California, within four days' sail of San Francisco, Aug. (?) 27, 1853, aged 19 years 21 days.
3059. MARIA LOUISA, b. Sept. 16, 1836, in Bangor; d. at Levant, Me., 1837, aged 1 year.
3060. JAMES AUGUSTUS, b. Aug. 1, 1838, in Levant; d. at Bangor, Aug. 7, 1839, aged 1 year 6 days.
3061. HENRY AUGUSTUS, b. Nov. 9, 1839, in Bangor. At the commencement of the rebellion, he was attending medical lectures at the Harvard University (Mass.), where he received his diploma, as M D., two years before the war closed; he then had an appointment from the governor of Maine, as assistant surgeon in the first Maine heavy artillery; commissioned, "Apr. 6, 1864"; started for the front, and there remained till the end of the war; mustered out, "Sept. 11, 1865." Now resides, as a physician, in Bangor, having previously been located in Winn, Me., for a few years.
3062. FRANK SANFORD, b. May 8, 1844, in Houlton; d. at Bangor, Dec. 1847, aged 3 years 9 months.
3063. FREDERICK ARTHUR, b. May 21, 1850, in Bangor.
3064. MAMIE ALLEN, b. Sept. 8, 1862.

3065. ELIZA[5] [2580] (John[4], Joseph[3], Joseph[2], John[1]), m. Greenleaf Bray, of Bangor, May 21, 1835, at Levant, Me. He was b. Oct. 19, 1816, in Minot, Me.; a dealer in horses, having resided in Burlington, Vt., Minot and Portland, Me.; now (1870) in South Boston, Mass., 560 Seventh Street. Child: —

3066. HATTIE ELIZA (Bray), b. July 17, 1837, in Burlington, Vt.; m. Isaac H. Thompson, Feb. 7, 1863, at Portland, Me.

3067. JOHN EMERSON[5] [2582] (John[4], Joseph[3], Joseph[2], John[1]), m., 1st, Martha A. Dearborn, of Portland, June 20, 1843. She d. and he m., 2d, Melissa B. Veazie, of Bangor, Dec. 4, 1853, at Corinna, Me. Was commissioned adjutant of the 2d regiment Maine infantry, May 6, 1861; promoted to captain in the 17th U. S. infantry, Feb. 19, 1862; transferred into the 20th Maine, as captain and brevet major. He was present at the battle of Bull Run. Business, that of a tailor, in Bangor, Me. Children: —

3068. HELEN LOUISA, b. June 2, 1845 (first wife); d. June 6, 1847, aged
2 years 4 days.
3069. FRED LAWLER, b. Jan. 8, 1855 (second wife); d. Aug, 19, 1857, in
his 3d year.
3070. HETTA LOUISE, b. Nov. 16, 1858.

3071. MARTHA ANN[5] [2583] (John[4], Joseph[3], Joseph[2], John[1]),
m. William Bryant, of Bangor, Oct. 17, 1844, who d. at B., Mar.
20, 1866, aged 47 years 7 months. Children : —

3072. MARY CAROLINE (Bryant), b. July 25, 1845; d. June 17, 1847, in
her 2d year.
3073. GEORGE FRED, b. Apr. 23, 1848.

3074. EDWARD HATCH[5] [2586] (John[4], Joseph[3], Joseph[2], John[1]),
resides in Belfast, Me. ; m Margaretta J. Clark, Dec. 20, 1849.
He was adjutant in the 8th regiment Maine infantry, commissioned
Jan. 8, 1862 ; promoted captain Co. A. Apr. 27, 1864 ; mustered
out, Jan. 18, 1866. He was highly commended by Col. H. Boynton, of the 8th Maine regiment, for his "gallant conduct in the
battle of Sept. 29, 1864" (perhaps at Fort Harrison (?), near
Richmond, under Gen. Butler), "when in command of the skir-
mish line, consisting of three companies of the same regiment, he
so bravely and successfully charged over the enemy's earth-works."
"This was a very brilliant affair, and reflected high credit upon
[his] courage and management, as a careful examination of the
captured works afterwards proved." Children : —

3075. FRANK C., b. May 11, 1851, in Lincoln, Me.
3076. EDWARD W., b. May 23, 1858, in Belfast.

3077. OLIVE[5] [2594] (Joseph[4], Joseph[3], Joseph[2], John[1]), m.
William Potter, of Great Falls, N. H., Jan 1, 1·33. He was b.
Nov. 5, 1808, in Newport, R. I. ; a machinist, and now (1870) an
overseer, Appleton corporation, Lowell, Mass. Children : —

3078. JOSEPH WILLIAM (Potter), b. Apr. 24, 1834, at Great Falls; m.
Lois McLellan, June 7, 1857 ; now a machinist in Lowell.
Children : —
   1. LIZZIE OLIVE, b. Mar. 6, 1858, in Dayton, O.
   2. WILLIAM HENRY, b. Aug. 25, 1861, in Newton, Mass.
   3. BLANCH, b. Oct. 1868, in Lowell.
3079. ELIZABETH, b. July 29, 1835, at Great Falls.
3080. HENRY, b. Nov. 26, 1837, at G F. ; a pipe-layer, residing in Lowell;
m. Mary Elizabeth Winn. Oct. 1864. Children : —
   1. CHARLES HENRY, b. Oct. 15, 1865.
   2. ALICE ANN. b. June 29, 1868.
   3. JENNIE, b. Jan. 1870.

3081. WILLIAM[5] [2596] (Joseph[4], Joseph[3], Joseph[2], John[1]),
was a manufacturer in Rochester, N. H., 1834–1845 ; in Manches-
ter, 1845–1870. He has received patents on "Parallel Shuttle
Motion" for looms in cotton machinery, and on a "Burglar
Alarm," in progress 1870. He m , 1st, Mary Jane Cross, of
Rochester, Nov. 12, 1838. She was b. May 8, 1817, and d. at R.,

Sept. 12, 1844, aged 27 years 4 months. On her headstone in the Manchester cemetery : —

> " Fare thee well; with hopes of meeting
> In yon bright world above,
> Where parting scenes will never enter,
> And ' fare thee well ' be heard no more."

He m., 2d, Sarah Smith Bean, of Woodstock, Vt., Jan. 7, 1849, at Manchester. She was b. Mar. 30, 1828, in Salisbury, N. H. Children, first wife : —

3082. ELIZA ANN, b. Mar. 26, d. Mar. 29, 1841, in Rochester.
3083. MARY JOSEPHINE, b. Aug. 21, d. Sept. 7, 1842, in R.

> " Sweet buds of being, for a moment given
> To show how pure young spirits are in heaven."

3084. DEXTER BREWER[5] [2601] (Samuel[4], Joseph[3], Joseph[2], John[1]), has been in business as a merchant tailor in Boston since 1843, excepting one year at Fitchburg, Mass. Present residence in B., 44 Tennyson Street. He was m. to Ann Colby Tracy, of Boston, June 4, 1845, by the Rev. Dr. Blagden. She was b. July 22, 1825, in B., as were all their children : —

3085. GEORGE DEXTER, b Aug. 13, d. Dec. 20, 1846.
3086. CHARLES GORDON GREENE, b. Sept. 19, 1850; now (1870) a book-keeper in Boston.
3087. GEORGIE ANTOINETTE, b. Dec. 8, 1855; d. Dec. 1, 1857, aged 2 years, wanting 7 days.

3088. ANNA ELIZA[5] [2604] (Samuel[4], Joseph[3], Joseph[2], John[1]), m. Benjamin H. Morrill, carriage maker, of Bangor, Me., Sept. 20, 1849. Resided in B. till June, 1864; in Bolton, Mass., till Mar. 1868, and in Chelmsford, Mass., till Apr 1870. She d. Nov. 29, 1869, aged 38, " an exemplary Christian, — a true and faithful mother." He m., 2d, Abbie A. W. Lawrence. Children, first wife : —

3089. FREDERICK HERBERT (Morrill), b. Aug. 5, 1852.
3090. GEORGE WILLIAM, b. Aug. 17, 1855.
3091. LUCY ANTOINETTE, b. Feb. 28, 1858; d. May 17, 1859, aged 1 year 3 months.

3092. PETER A.[5] [2624] (Daniel[4], Benjamin[3], Joseph[2], John[1]), m. Martha A., widow of J. W. I. Runnels [3122], 11th mo. 1, 1855. Residence, South China, Me. Children : —

3093. JOHN H., b. 8th mo. 26, 1856; d. 4th mo. 8, 1857, aged 7 mos. 12 dys.
3094. DORA M., b. 7th mo. 21, 1866.

3095. LYDIA[5] [2625] (Daniel[4], Benjamin[3], Joseph[2], John[1]), m. John Jones, 9th mo. 30, 1847. Children : —

3096. ELIZABETH M. (Jones), b. 12th mo. 9, 1848.
3097. CYRUS, b. 4th mo. 10, 1851.
3098. DANIEL R., b. 8th mo. 6, 1860.

3099. Mary A.⁵ [2626] (Daniel⁴, Benjamin³, Joseph², John¹), m. William A. Jones, 3d mo. 23, 1851. She is a preacher in the Society of Friends. Children: —

3100. Ellwood W. (Jones), b. 6th mo. 9, 1852.
3101. Franklin E., b. 5th mo. 7, 1854.
3102. Josiah A., b. 6th mo. 21, 1859.
3103. Arthur W., b. 11th mo. 31, 1864.

3104. Alvina P.⁵ [2627] (Daniel⁴, Benjamin³, Joseph², John¹), m. Clarkson Jones, 5th mo. 18, 1853, and d. 1st mo. 1, 1865, aged 34. Children: —

3105. Lindley Y. (Jones), b. 4th mo. 26, d. 11th mo. 8, 1854.
3106. Frederick D., b. 11th mo. 30, 1855.
3107. Isaac L., b. 12th mo. 25, 1864.

3108. Clara C.⁵ [2628] (Daniel⁴, Benjamin³, Joseph², John¹), m. Eli Jepson, 12 mo. 19, 1854. Child: —

3109. Herbert O. (Jepson), b. 3d mo. 21, 1859.

3110. Rebecca M.⁵ [2629] (Daniel⁴, Benjamin³, Joseph², John¹), m., 1st, James P. Jones, 9th mo. 15, 1857. He was captain of Co B, 7th Maine regiment, 1861; promoted to Major, 1863; d. from wounds received in battle, 7th mo. 12, 1864. She m., 2d, Rev. Moses W. Newbert, of Waldoboro', Me., 9th mo. 29, 1867. Children: —

3111. James L. (Jones), b. 3d mo. 6, d. 9th mo. 25, 1859.
3112. James A., b. 2d mo. 16, 1861; d. 8th mo. 14, 1864, aged 3 yrs. 6 mos.
3113. Alice M., b. 8th mo. 6, d. 8th mo. 11, 1864.

3114. Emma R.⁵ [2630] (Daniel⁴, Benjamin³, Joseph², John¹), m. Eben P. Goddard, of Vassalboro', Me., 9th mo. 4, 1857. Children: —

3115. Frank E. (Goddard), b. 1st mo. 2, 1859.
3116. Charles E., b. 11th mo. 4, 1860.
3117. Mary R., b. 9th mo. 26, 1865.

3118. Benjamin Franklin⁵ [2632] (Benjamin⁴, Benjamin³, Joseph², John¹), m. Naomi Freeman Dearborn, Nov. 2, 1843, in Hallowell (now Chelsea), Me. His principal business was the manufacturing of lumber, at Chelsea, Me, till his removal to California. He first arrived in San Francisco, Jan. 15, 1857; his family joined him Aug. 1864, and he still resides there. Children, b. in Chelsea: —

3119. Benjamin Franklin, Jr., b. Aug. 3, 1844; his present business, "photographing."
3120. William Howard, b. Nov. 8, 1848; present business, "mercantile agency."
3121. Clara Augusta, b. Aug. 12, 1851; m. Edward J. Baxter, of San Francisco (1109 Howard Street), Oct. 18, 1871; had a son b. Oct. 1, 1872, name not reported.

3122. John Wentworth Ireland⁵ [2634] (Benjamin⁴, Benjamin³, Joseph², John¹), was a farmer in Chelsea, Me., and clerk of the Free Will Baptist church; m. Martha A. Woodbury, Jan. 3, 1849, and d. at Chelsea, Dec. 27, 1853, in his 29th year. Child: —

3123. Letitia Olive, b. May 26, 1850, in Chelsea; resides at South China.

3124. Isaac Randall⁵ [2635] (Benjamin⁴, Benjamin³, Joseph²,

John[1]), was married Jan. 3, 1847; removed to California, and d. at Sonora, June 8, 1857, aged 30. Children: —

3125. SILAS HOLMAN, b. Feb. 27, 1849, in Chelsea, Me.
3126. PEARLY RANDALL, b. Aug. 14, 1850, in C.
3127. CHARLES, b. Sept. 20, 1856 (?), in Sonora, Cal.

> NOTE. — The children of [2636], received too late for insertion in the usual form, are here given: —
> 1. EVA SEADORA, b. May 3, 1854, in Chelsea, Me.; there d. Jan. 31, 1855, aged 8 months.
> 2. ABBIE FRANCES, b. Aug. 22, 1856, in Medford, Minn.; d. Nov. 12, 1863, aged 7.
> 3. WILLIE FREEMAN, }
> 4. ETTA FLORA,   } b. July 16, 1862; { d. Mar. 28, 1863,
>   { d. Mar. 24, 1863,
> in Medford, aged 8 months.

3128. ALBERT PRESCOTT[5] [2637] (Benjamin[4], Benjamin[3], Joseph[2], John[1]), has resided in Minnesota since 1854, now at Freedom, Waseca Co. (P. O., Alma City); occupation, farming; m. Rachel Melissa Clay, June 22, 1858, the daughter of Jonathan and Abigail S. Clay, of Kennebec Co., Me. Children: —

3129. ELLA FRANCES, b. July 5, 1859, in Minnetonka, Hennepin Co., Minn.; d. at Deerfield, Minn., Oct. 27, 1863, in her 5th year.
3130. ELLIAN ALBERT, b. Feb. 18, 1861, in Minnetonka.
3131. MABEL MELISSA, b. Nov. 17, 1863, in Deerfield, Steele Co., Minn.
3132. FREDERIC OSCAR, b. Dec. 5, 1866, in Alton, Waseca Co.
3133. ABBY ELLA, b. Oct. 20, 1868, in Freedom.
3134. BENJAMIN JOSEPH, b. Nov. 2, 1870, in Freedom, and there d. Feb. 23, 1872, in his 2d year.

3135. SARAH OMENIA[5] [2640] (Benjamin[4], Benjamin[3], Joseph[2], John[1]), m. Emery Merrill Gatchell, Feb. 22, 1858. He is a blacksmith, now residing in Hudson, Minn. (?) (1872). Children: —

3136. LESLIE EMERY (Gatchell), b. Dec. 1, 1858, in Medford, Minn.
3137. PRESTON ELLSWORTH, b. Feb. 16, 1862, in M.

3138. ELIZABETH S.[5] [2647] (Jonathan D.[4], Benjamin[3], Joseph[2], John[1]), m. George Gray, Jr., May 29, 1851. He is a painter and dealer in paints, Commercial St., Portland, Me. Children, b. in P.: —

3139. EDWIN AUGUSTUS (Gray), b. Apr. 9, 1852.
3140. ANNA FRANCES, b. May 5, 1854.
3141. CARRIE ETHEL, }
3142. EMMA NEAL,   } b. Sept. 22, 1871.

3143. FRANCES H.[5] [2649] (Jonathan D.[4], Benjamin[3], Joseph[2], John[1]), m. William S. Smith, Jan. 4, 1860. He was a machinist in South Boston, Mass.; d. Apr. 15, 1872, leaving: —

3144. CORA BELLE (Smith), b. Aug. 31, 1861.

3145. WILLIAM S. B.[5] [2653] (Isaac R.[4], Benjamin[3], Joseph[2], John[1]), was m. at Vassalboro', Me., by Warren Percival, Esq., to Alvira A. Hall, Apr. 22, 1860. She was b. June 7, 1840, in Belmont, Me. His present residence is in Lowell, Mass.; employment at the bleachery. Children: —

3146. CHARLES E., b. May 6, 1864.
3147. GEORGE G., b. Aug. 22, 1868.

3148. ANNABELLA[5] [2656] (Isaac R.[4], Benjamin[3], Joseph[2], John[1]), m. Justin Buzzell, farmer, of Canaan, Me., N█ 18, 1869. Child: —

3149. OREGON (Buzzell), b. Nov. 28, 1871.

SIXTH GENERATION.

3150. JOHN SARGENT[6] [2658] (Isaac[5], Isaac[4], Isaac[3], Abraham[2], John[1]), settled as a farmer in Illinois, having m. Emma M. Fountain, Mar. 13, 1851, at St. Charles, Ill.; residences as below. Children : —

3151. CALVIN P., b. Dec 6, 1852, in Warrensville.
3152. MARY E., b. Apr. 5, 1854, in W.
3153. ALBERT J., b. Apr. 25, 1856, in Batavia.
3154. MEHETABEL C., b. Mar. 30. 1859, in W.
3155. JULIA A., b. Apr. 21, 1862, in Batavia; d Feb. 20, 1863, aged 10 mos.
3156. EFFIE R., b. Dec. 2, 1863, in B.
3157. HENRY C., b. Dec. 13, 1866, in Warrensville; d. Feb. 14, 1867, aged 2 months.

3158. RICHARD SANBORN SARGENT[6] [2659] (Isaac[5], Isaac[4], Isaac[3], Abraham[2], John[1]), has also been a farmer in Illinois, mostly at Warrensville, near his father's, where his seven oldest children were born. He m. Julia Graves, Sept. 28, 1845, at W., who was b. Apr. 2, 1829. Children : —

3159. MARY E., b. Mar. 27, 1848; d. Apr. 24, 1851, aged 3.
3160. ISAAC P. P., b. Aug. 11, 1852.
3161. ANNA M., b. Aug. 30, 1854.
3162. CHARLIE R. L., b. Mar. 20, 1857.
3163. MARY E., b. Mar. 31, 1859.
3164. IDA, b May 6, 1861; d. same day.
3165. AMOS S., b. Aug. 6, 1862.
3166. EMMA G., b. Oct. 9, d. Oct. 14, 1865, in Campton, Ill.
3167. MAGGIE, b. May 21, 1867; d. Mar. 14, 1869, in her 2d year.

3168. BEDELIA ELVIRA[6] [2660] (Isaac[5], Isaac[4], Isaac[3], Abraham[2], John[1]), m. Calvin P. Johnson, farmer, Sept. 25, 1845, at Warrensville, Ill. He was b. Nov. 16, 1815, in Sodus, N. Y. Children, b. in W. : —

3169. CLARA M. (Johnson), b. Nov. 22, 1847; m. N. M. Triplett, merchant, Feb. 23, 1868. Child : —
    1. HARRY M. (Triplett), b. Feb 5, 1869, in Princeton, Ill.
3170. ETTIE M. (Johnson), b. Jan. 8, 1863.
3171. HATTIE M., b. July 18, 1866.

3172. MARY SOPHRONIA[6] [2661] (Isaac[5], Isaac[4], Isaac[3], Abraham[2], John[1]), m. William S. Lindsay, mason, Aug. 27, 1848, at Winfield, Ill He was b. Dec. 1, 1826, at Middlebury, Vt. She d. Nov. 5, 1849, aged 17, leaving : —

3173. MARY B. (Lindsay), b. Sept. 30, 1849, in Winfield, who there d. Jan. 7, 1863, her 14th year.

3174. Isaac Thomas Charles[6] [2662] (Isaac[5], Isaac[4], Isaac[3], Abraham[2], John[1]), is a farmer ; m. Elizabeth A. Vaughn, Dec. 23, 1860, at Princeton, Ill. She was b. Nov. 29, 1838, in Cape Breton. Children : —

3175. Mary L., b. Dec. 18, 1861, in Winfield.
3176. Harry O., b. July 4, 1864, in Warrensville.
3177. Eva M., b. Sept. 19, 1868, in W.

3178. Sally[6] [2680] (John[5], Isaac[4], Isaac[3], Abraham[2], John[1]), m. Alpheus Washington Chaplain, shoemaker, of Canterbury, N. H., July 28, 1854. Children : —

3179. George Franklin (Chaplain), b. July 19, 1855.
3180. Martha Ann, b. June 28, 1857.
3181. Horace Sanborn, b. May 9, 1861.
3182. Thomas Alpheus, b. Sept. 1, 1867.

3183. Sarah Abba[6] [2710] (Paul[5], John[4], James[3], Abraham[2], John[1]), m. Robert Brown, of Ossipee, N. H., Mar. 18, 1854. He is a farmer and shoemaker, now residing (1870) at Milton Three Ponds. Children, b. in Milton : —

3184. Everett Eugene (Brown), b. July 20, 1855.
3185. Elmer Ellsworth, b. May 4, 1861.

3186. James Orin[6] [2711] (Paul[5], John[4], James[3], Abraham[2], John[1]), is an extensive and prosperous shoe manufacturer in Dover, N. H. (1870) ; m., 1st, Mary E. Cooke, of Wakefield, Nov. 10, 1856, at Great Falls. She d. at W., July 4, 1858, and he m., 2d, Myra J. Hill, of Strafford, at Northwood, Nov. 8, 1860. Children, second wife : —

3187. Adella May, b. June 8, 1862.
3188. Emma Augusta, b. May 29, 1865.
3189. Arthur Dudley, b. Apr. 7, 1867.
3190. James Fred, b. Oct. 12, 1869, in Dover.
3191. Bertha Myra, b. Aug. 28, 1872, in D.

3192. Mary Ann[6] [2712] (Paul[5], John[4], James[3], Abraham[2], John[1]), m. Benjamin Herrick, Jr., shoe-cutter, Dec. 15, 1850, at Topsfield, Mass. ; residence in Danvers. He served in the 13th Massachusetts regiment nearly four years during the late civil war. Children : —

3193. Charles Edgar (Herrick), b. Apr. 14, 1852, in Topsfield, Mass.
3194. Ida Florence, b. Feb. 19, 1855, in Milton, N. H.
3195. William Henry, b. Oct. 17, 1856, in M.
3196. Adelaide, b. June 25, 1858, in Danvers, Mass.
3197. Cora May, b. Oct. 26, 1859, in Milton.

3198. Andrew Tetherey[6] [2713] (Paul[5], John[4], James[3], Abraham[2], John[1]), was a shoemaker ; m. Elvina Augusta Runnels, of Tuftonborough, N. H., Aug. 26, 1854, at Milton. She was the adopted daughter of [1700], Part II. He enlisted for two years in the 5th New Hampshire volunteers, and d. May 29, 1868, in his 33d year, as the effect of his army service. Children : —

3199. FRANK ALLIS, b. Oct. 1, 1855, in Milton.
3200. CORA MAY, b. Aug. 20, 1858, in Milton; d. Oct. 1, 1859, aged 13 months 11 days.
3201. LIZZIE ESTELLE, b. Aug. 5, 1860, in Dover.

3202. ELSIE[6] [2717] (Jeremiah[5], Joseph[4], James[3], Abraham[2], John[1]), m. George Minkler Childs, farmer, July 3, 1850. Settled first in Lyme, N. H., where their children were b. Has since removed to Springfield, Ill. Children: —

3203. JULIUS MINKLER (Childs), b. Feb. 1, 1853.
3204. AMELIA HENRY, b. Apr. 8, 1855.
3205. GEORGIANNA, b. Apr. 30, 1857.
3206. JAMES ARTHUR, b. Jan. 28, 1860.
3207. WILLEY CHANDLER.

3208. SARAH ANN[6] [2718] (Jeremiah[5], Joseph[4], James[3], Abraham[2], John[1]), m. James Alexander Hammond Grout, Sept. 1, 1864. He was b. June 16, 1833; resided in Lyme, N. H., till 1869, then in Manchester, where he d. of consumption, July 23, 1871, aged 38. The author was greatly aided by him in *this* part of the work. Child: —

3209. WALTER JAMES HAMMOND (Grout), b. June 26, 1867, in Lyme.

3210. GEORGE WASHINGTON[6] [2719] (Jeremiah[5], Joseph[4], James[3], Abraham[2], John[1]), a farmer in Lyme, N. H.; m. Mary E. Tyler, of L., Dec. 1. 1858 Children: —

3211. ABBY FRAYDILLA, b. June 23, 1860.
3212. WILLIE HENRY, b. Aug. 2, 1862.
3213. EMMA ALMIRA, b. Jan. 21, 1866.

3214. MARY[6] [2721] (Jeremiah[5], Joseph[4], James[3], Abraham[2] John[1]), m. David Carrol Stark, farmer, of Lyme, Mar. 19, 1861; now settled in Springfield, Ill. Children: —

3215. FRANK DAVID (Stark), b. July 5, 1862, in Lyme.
3216. MARTHA JANE, b. Mar. 8, 1866, in L.
3217. IDA, b. May 8, 1867, in Springfield, Ill.

3218. LOUISA[6] [2733] (Samuel[5], Joseph[4], James[3], Abraham[2], John[1]), m. Clark J. Elliot, of Orford, N. H., May 6, 1847. She was residing at North Thetford, Vt., 1870. Children: —

3219. MARY (Elliot), b. Jan. 15, 1849, in Orford; d. 1864, at Tewksbury, Mass., aged 5.
3220. ELLA, b. June 25, 1852, in Waterbury, Vt.
3221. BENJAMIN FRANKLIN, b. Mar. 17, 1856, in Duxbury, Vt. (name changed to Shaw, by adoption).

3222. PHILENA FAIRFIELD[6] [2734] (Samuel[5], Joseph[4], James[3], Abraham[2], John[1]), m., 1st, Daniel Nelson, farmer, of Waterbury, Vt., Dec. 1853; m., 2d, William Adams, tinman and farmer, of Moretown, now of Worcester, Vt., Aug. 1865. Children: —

3223. ANGELLO DELBERT (Nelson), b. Apr. 23, 1855, in Waterbury, and there d. Mar. 4, 1859, in his 4th year.
3224. CURTIS WELLS, b. July 17, 1858.
3225. FREDDIE (Adams), b. May 20, 1866, in Moretown.

3226. George Chesley[6] [2735] (Samuel[5], Joseph[4], James[3], Abraham[2], John[1]), m Sarah Pervier, of Stowe, Vt., Apr. 23, 1855, who was b. Dec. 9, 1833, in Epsom, N. H.; resides as a farmer, with his father, in Duxbury. Children : —

3227. Joseph Andrew, b. Apr. 23, 1856, in Stowe; d. at Duxbury, July 6, 1864, aged 8. His moral nature was uncommonly developed for one of his age. Much of his conversation with his grandmother, a few hours before his death, is, for sentiment, embodied in the following lines, afterwards addressed to her by a friend, the first being in imitation of Pope, " The Dying Christian's Address to his Soul" : —

> " What is this that stealeth o'er me?
> Drowns my spirit, draws my breath,
> Chills my heart with dewy dampness?
> Tell me, grandma, is this death?

> " Shall I soon pass o'er that river, —
> Not dark, but bright with Jesus' love,
> As when he blessed the little children,
> And gained for them a home above?

> " ' In my Father's house are many mansions,'
> There I shall surely find a home;
> Surrounded by the holy angels,
> I 'll wait there, grandma, till you come.

> " I know, when spring again shall open,
> And bright flowers are all in bloom,
> 'T is then you 'll miss your little Andrew,
> Sleeping sweetly in the tomb.

> " Not there will be the loving spirit, —
> No, ah, no! *that* dwells on high;
> Returned again to God who gave it,
> No more to sin, no more to die.

> " O, glorious hope! do not reject it;
> That Christ our sins has washed away;
> With his own blood he gave the ransom,
> Then from *His* arms I would not stay."

3228. Clara Mandana, b. June 7, 1858, in Waterbury.
3229. Charles Freeman, b. Jan. 21, 1861, in Duxbury.
3230. Jane Towne, b. Oct. 3, 1863.
3231. Samuel George, b. May 5, 1866.
3232. Eugene William, b. May 11, 1869.
3233. Betsy Ann, b. May 11, 1872.

3234. Harriet Angeline[6] [2736] (Samuel[5], Joseph[4], James[3], Abraham[2], John[1]), m. Albert Phillips, farmer, of Duxbury, Vt., Sept. 30, 1861. Children : —

3235. Willis Albert (Phillips), b. Apr. 24, 1864, in Waterbury.
3236. Carrie Hattie, b. Nov. 1869, in Duxbury.
3237. Jesse, b. June 6, 1871, in D.

3238. FLORA ARMINA[6] [2737] (Samuel[5], Joseph[4], James[3], Abraham[2], John[1]), m. Desten D. Griffith, of Duxbury, farmer, — now living in Waterbury, — Mar. 6, 1861. Children : —

3239. VERNON DESTEN (Griffith), b. Nov. 6, 1862.
3240. NETTIE BETSY DIANA, b. June 17, 1867.
3241. JULIA ERMINA, b. Jan. 27, 1872.

3242. CHARLOTTE ANN[6] [2739] (Daniel[5], Joseph[4], James[3], Abraham[2], John[1]), m James Adams. Feb. 26. 1862, at Manchester, N. H. He was b. in Lunenburg, Vt. ; a machinist ; now residing in Lowell, Mass., 21 Franklin Street. Child : —

3243. WALTER ARTHUR (Adams), b. July 29, 1869, in Lowell.

3244. HEMAN JASON[6] [2740] (Daniel[5], Joseph[4], James[3], Abraham[2], John[1]), went to California, there m. Annora Scannall, and d. Jan. 1, 1870, in his 36th year. Her present address is Bernicia, Salona Co., Cal., where he is supposed to have lived. Child : —

3245. SUSAN ADALINE, b. Apr. 1858, and one other, a twin with the last, who d. young.

3246. WILLIAM ADDISON[6] [2741] (Daniel[5], Joseph[4], James[3], Abraham[2], John[1]), was a soldier in the 9th regiment Vermont volunteers, Co. G ; mustered in, July 9, 1862 ; also as a " recruit" in the same regiment from Feb. 1864 till Nov. 1865 ; engagements, " siege of Suffolk," May, 1863. Chapin's farm, Va., Sept. 29, 1864, with several others, and finally at the taking of Richmond. He had m. Susan Savage, of Strafford, Vt., Apr. 1, 1862, who was b. Dec. 7, 1840, in Hartford, Vt. He is now a farmer in Strafford, where were born : —

3247. FLORENCE ESTELLA, b. Dec. 15, 1863.
3248. BELLE, b. June 29, 1867.
3249. WILLIAM ADDISON, b. Mar. 8, 1869.
3250. CHARLES CARROL, b. Aug. 1870.

3251. KATE[6] [2771] (Samuel D.[5], Samuel[4], James[3], Abraham[2], John[1]), m. John H. Farrell, shoemaker, of Portland, Me., Oct. 4, 1858. Children : —

3252. CHARLIE (Farrell), b. July 20, 1859.
3253. LEILA ANGIE, b. Mar. 20, 1867.

3254. GEORGE ALBERT[6] [2772] (Samuel D.[5], Samuel[4], James[3], Abraham[2], John[1]), enlisted from Manchester. N. H., corporal Co. G, New Hampshire 4th regiment, Sept. 18, 1861 ; promoted to first sergeant ; wounded severely in left leg, when attempting to storm the confederate works at Petersburg, Va., July 30, 1864 ; mustered out, Sept. 27, 1864. He m. Mary Greene, Sept. 3, 1866 ; was a carpenter, resided in Portland, and there d. Jan. 11, 1869, aged 26. Child : —

3255. GEORGE WASHINGTON, b. Feb. 22, d. Apr. 26, 1868.

3256. NATHANIEL B.[6] [2784] (John S.[5], Nathaniel B.[4], Samuel[3], Abraham[2], John[1]). Being apprenticed as a machinist in Worces ter, Mass., during the war, he enlisted July, 1864, in Co. E, 42d regiment Massachusetts volunteers, under a call for one hundred days' men, with which regiment he served and returned. He m. Eliza V. Warren, of Charlestown, Mass., July 29, 1868 ; now resides in Pittsfield, Me. (?). Children : —

3257. MAUD, b. Mar. 5, 1870.
3258. LILIAN, b. Nov. 30, 1871.

3259. MARCIA E.[6] [2830] (Albert[5], Samuel[4], Jonathan[3], Abraham[2], John[1]), m. Andrew P. Bennett, of Concord, N. H., farmer, Jan. 1, 1856, and d. May 16, 1863, in her 25th year. Children : —

3260. FRANK ROBERTS (Bennett), b. Aug. 28, 1857.
3261. EUGENE ALBERT, b. Nov. 16, 1862.

3262. SOPHRONIA[6] [2895] (Jeremiah A.[5], James[4], Jonathan[3], Abraham[2] John[1]), m. Edwin Quackenbush, Jan. 1, 1857, at Spring- ville, N. Y. Child : —

3263. HARLIN S. (Quackenbush), b. June 5, 1863, in Ellicottsville, N. Y.

3264. ALONZO MANLY[6] [2918] (Lorenzo D.[5], Israel[4], Jonathan[3], Abraham[2], John[1]), is a dentist, now residing (1869–1872) in Cou- dersport, Potter Co., Penn. ; m. Jenny Lenora Ellis, of Caneadea, N. Y., Sept. 9, 1865. Children : —

3265. FRED EUGENE, b. Feb. 1, 1867, in Whitesville, N. Y.
3266. MARY EDITH, b. Aug. 24, 1868, in W.

3267. RINALDO SCOTT[6] [2919] (Lorenzo D.[5], Israel[4], Jonathan[3], Abraham[2], John[1]), m. Charlotte Lorena Pratt, of Eagle, Wyoming Co., N. Y., Jan. 3, 1868. Child : —

3268. JESSY BELL, b. Dec. 1, 1869, in Caneadea, N. Y.

3269. FRANCES MARY[6] [2922] (Israel M.[5], Israel[4], Jonathan[3], Abraham[2], John[1]), m. Samuel Stoddard, Sept. 7, 1867, at Empo- rium, Cameron Co., Pa. He " was from Steuben Co., N. Y.," b. Apr. 27, 1846. Children : —

3270. WILLIAM HENRY (Stoddard), b. Mar. 1, d. Mar. 15, 1869.
3271. LOUISA ESTELLE, b. in the autumn of 1870.

3272. SARAH FRANCES[6] [2991] (Moses C.[5], William[4], Moses[3], William[2], John[1]), m. James Kimball Hathorn, of Richmond, Me., Oct. 18, 1865. Child : —

3273. FLORENCE KIMBALL (Hathorn), b. Mar. 21, 1867, in Richmond.

3274. LYDIA ANN[6] [2999] (George J.[5], William[4], Moses[3], Wil- liam[2], John[1]), m. George Alden Dailey, Oct. 16, 1868, at East Weymouth, Mass. He was b. July 29, 1849, in E. W., and has there resided, first as a " nailer," now (1870) as a boot-maker. Child : —

3275. ETTA WHITCOMB (Dailey), b. Oct. 15, 1871, in East Weymouth.

APPENDIX.

APPENDIX.

INTRODUCTORY NOTE.

THE chief object of this Appendix is to preserve in a permanent form, for the aid of future genealogists, such notes and items respecting other Reynolds and Runnels families as came to hand *incidentally*, while the author was collecting materials for the main body of his work. These families, of course, could *not* be *fully* traced without swelling the book to an inordinate size, and delaying its issue far beyond the expectations of those interested in the preceding parts. The records are, therefore, fragmentary, desultory, and imperfect; mere names are given in many cases, and there has been no opportunity to substantiate the doubtful or reconcile the conflicting allusions; but the author flatters himself that the more laborious and competent annalists of the numerous Reynolds families in our land, who may yet appear, will feel grateful for the notes and suggestions herein contained.

The remark has been well made, that any attempt to trace and *connect all* the Reynolds families, even in this country, would prove almost as fruitless a task as to do the same with the families of Smith or Brown. Still it is to be hoped that different individuals may yet be encouraged to trace out different branches of that truly honorable name.

A.

THE EARLIEST REYNOLDS FAMILIES OF NEW ENGLAND;
WITH RECORDS AND NOTICES OF THE DESCENDANTS OF
ROBERT REYNOLDS, OF BOSTON, 1632–1659.

SAVAGE's Genealogical Dictionary mentions the *twenty-two* following as being heads of families in New England prior to 1690,
and as bearing the names, chiefly, of " Reynolds, Renold, or
Renolds." Here given in chronological order, and numbered con-
secutively for reference. The notes in quotations directly *after*
the names are from Savage.

3276. RICHARD, "passenger, 1634"; probably the same mentioned in
the "N. E. Gen. Register," Vol. 9, as "Richard Reynolds,
passenger to New England, Mar. 24, 1633."
3277. JOHN, "Watertown, 1634; freeman, May 6, 1635; wife's name
Sarah (?)." This is probably the John who is known, from
other sources, to have been the brother of Robert [3278], to
have moved *with* his brother from Boston to Watertown, and
afterwards, in 1636, to Weathersfield, Conn. Savage says he
"removed again before 1644 to Stamford," Ct. Bond's Hist.
of Watertown spells his name "Reinolds," and says he "went
from Weathersfield to Saybrook, and d. as early as 1662."
3278. ROBERT [3298], "Watertown, 1635."
3279. WILLIAM, "Duxbury, 1636; m. Alice Kitson, Aug. 30, 1638."
3280. WILLIAM, "Providence, 1637."
3281. WILLIAM, "Salem, 1640." We elsewhere learn that he was admitted to the church in Salem, 1640, and moved to Providence,
perhaps following Roger Williams, in 1641. From these ancestors and others mentioned below, who settled in Providence
and vicinity, the very numerous Reynolds families now in
Rhode Island are doubtless descended. No less than *seventy*
individuals of this name were found in the Providence city
directory in 1871.
3282. HENRY, "Salem, 1642, Lyme, 1647"; perhaps returned to Salem,
as Henry Renolds deeded land in Salem to Thomas West,
"Apr. 29, 1665," and may have been the "Henry Reinoles, on
petition against imposts, Massachusetts, 1668" (N. E. Gen.
Reg., Vol. 9). The "Inventory of Henry Renolds, of Salem,"
was rendered "May 13, 1693, £19– 19s." (Essex Prob. Recs.).
3283. JAMES ("Renell"), "Plymouth, 1643. To Wickford, R. I." The
N. E. Gen. Reg., Vol. 4, also says "James Renell, Plymouth,
Aug. 1643."
3284. JOHN, "Isle of Shoals, 1647."
3285. NATHANIEL [3299], "son of Robert [3278], Boston, 1657."
3286. JOHN, "Saybrook to Norwich, 1659"; probably the "Raynolds"
mentioned in N. E. Gen. Reg., Vol. 2, as found "among the first
inhabitants of Saybrook," and afterwards "in Norwich," Ct.
3287. JOHN, "Weymouth, 1660."
3288. THOMAS, "New London, 1664"; may also have been the "Thomas
Rennolds, Westerly, R I., 1669" (N. E. Gen. Reg., Vol. 10).
3289. JOHN, "Weathersfield, 1667"; probably son of [3277].

3290. JONATHAN, " Stamford, 1667 "; perhaps the same as " Jonathan Renalds " in list of citizens in Greenwich, Ct., 1672 (N. E. Gen. Reg., Vol. 4), and probably another son of [3277].

3291. ROBERT, " Boston, 1670 "; cannot be identical with Robert [3278]; see [3298]; was probably a fisherman, lived at Pulling Point.

3292. JOHN.

3293. JOSIAH and

3294. SAMUEL (" Ronalls "), " perhaps brothers at Wickford, 1674, may have spelled variously."

3295. JOHN, " Providence, 1676."

3296. FRANCIS, " also "

3297. HENRY, " probably a brother, Kingstown (Naraganset country), 1686."

From the above ample storehouse of genealogical material, in the names of ancestors, as afforded by Savage, we are now only able to select, for more particular mention, —

3298. ROBERT[1] [3278]. From well authenticated private " records of long ago," he is *known* to have been in Boston in 1632, where he is mentioned as a " shoemaker and freeman, Sept. 3, 1634 "; shortly after to have moved to Watertown, Mass , — hence Savage's allusion [3278], — and finally to have migrated " with his brother John " to Weathersfield, Conn., — hence " was dismissed by the church, Mar. 29, 1636, to form a church at Weathersfield." He soon returned, however, to Boston, and there lived and d. Apr. 27, 1659. Hence his will is referred to, " N. E. Gen. Reg., Vol. 9," " Boston, 1658-9." His wife's first name was Mary. She d. Jan. 18, 1663. Children, all b. in England : —

3299. NATHANIEL [3304].

3300. RUTH; m. John Whitney.

3301. TABITHA; m. Matthew Abdy.

3302. SARAH; m. a Mason.

3303. MARY; m. a Sawyer (" Richard Sanger," according to Savage).

3304. NATHANIEL[2] [3299] (Robert[1]), was designated as " Captain Nathaniel R.," probably for service in Philip's war " at Chelmsford, Feb. 25, 1676 "; was also a " shoemaker " and " freeman, 1665 "; was m., 1st, by Gov. John Endicott, to Sarah, daughter of John Dwile, or " Dwite " (Savage says " Dwight "), of Dedham, Nov. 30, 1657. She d. July 8, 1663. He m., 2d, Priscilla, daughter of Peter Brackett, " a well-to-do tradesman in Boston," previously to Feb. 21, 1666. He moved to Bristol, R. I., in 1680 ; was recognized in the first town-meeting at Bristol, " and became one of the principal men of that town," where he d. July 10, 1708. Children : —

3305. SARAH, b. July 26, 1659 ; m. John Fosdick, — thus named in her father's will.

3306. MARY, b. Nov. 20, 1660; d. Jan. 28, 1663, aged 2 years 2 months.

3307. NATHANIEL [3316], b. Mar. 3, 1662-3.

3308. JOHN, b. Aug. 4, 1668 (second wife); d. Jan. 30, 1757, in his 89th year. His will, dated " Mar. 10, 1749," leaves his property to brothers, nephews, and cousins.

3309.   PETER [3319], b. Jan 26, 1670.
3310.   PHILIP, b. Sept. 15, 1672; d. previously to 1706.
3311.   JOSEPH, b. Jan. 9, 1677; d. Jan. 16, 1759, aged 82 years 7 days.
3312.   HANNAH, b Jan. 15, 1682; m. Samuel Rayall.
3313.   MARY, b. 1684 (?); m. Nathaniel Woodbury, — thus named in her
           father's will.
3314.   BENJAMIN [3321], b. May 10, 1686, in Bristol; "sixth son and
           ninth or tenth child."
3315.   RUTH, b. Dec. 9, 1688; m. Josiah Cary.

3316.   NATHANIEL[3] [3307] (Nathaniel[2], Robert[1]). For a long
time we had supposed *this* Nathaniel to have been the *father* of the
two sons who settled in North Bridgewater; but his birth now
being established between twenty and thirty years earlier than our
first reckoning, we are constrained to call him their *grandfather*.
If so, he doubtless lived in Bristol, and there d. " Oct. 29, 1719,"
aged 56. His wife's name is said to have been Ruth, and he is
thought to have had *seven* children, of whom we have the names of
only two. " The oldest was," probably, —

3317.   NATHANIEL [3330], "b. Sept. 11, 1689," thus confirming the state-
           ment of one of his descendants that he was b. "*about* 1690, in
           Bristol."
3318.   JOHN [3333], b. Mar. 29, 1696.

3319.   PETER[3] [3309] (Nathaniel[2], Robert[1]), was styled " Capt.
Peter Reynolds, of Bristol," d. before May 26, 1732, and *may* have
been the father of —

3320.   PETER, b. 1700, in Bristol; called Rev. Peter *Raynolds* in Sprague's
           Annals; graduated at Harvard College, 1720; settled as pastor
           of the church in Enfield, Ct., 1724; m. Elizabeth Taylor, the
           granddaughter of Rev. Edward Taylor, of Westfield, Mass ,
           1727, and d. 1768, aged 68.

3321.   BENJAMIN[3] [3314] (Nathaniel[2], Robert[1]), m. Susanna,
eldest daughter of the Rev. Grindall Rawson, of Mendon, Mass.,
1709. He resided in Bristol, R. I., and d. Aug. 4, 1770, aged 84.
Children : —

3322.   PRISCILLA, b. Apr. 13, 1711; m. Edward Ransom.
3323.   ANN,   } b. July 12, 1715; { d. unmarried.
3324.   MARY,   }   { d., probably, very young.
3325.   MARY, b. Nov. 20, 1716.
3326.   JOHN [3338], b. Apr. 1, 1718.
3327.   BENJAMIN, b. Nov. 15, 1722; "moved to Ciquecto, N. S., but
           came back and served in the Revolutionary war."
3328.   GRINDALL [3347] (given also, erroneously, as Wendal), b. July
           11, 1726; settled in Putney, Vt.
3329.   SARAH; m. Seth Chapin.

3330.   NATHANIEL[4] [3317] (Nathaniel[3], Nathaniel[2], Robert[1]),
m. a Snell, 1712; came from Bristol to Boston, 1735; there owned
a store, and d. 1740, aged 51, after which his widow settled in
North Bridgewater, Mass., with her two sons : —

3331.   NATHANIEL [3354], b. 1716–17; though Kingman's Hist. of North
           Bridgewater gives to Nathaniel the date following.
3332.   THOMAS [3365], b. Mar. 19, 1718.

3333.   JOHN[4] [3318] (Nathaniel[3], Nathaniel[2], Robert[1]), m. Anna
Blanch, Oct. 10, 1717, and settled in Marblehead.   Two oldest
children only are made sure by our informant; but by the Essex
Deeds we know positively that he had a son John, as "John Raynolds and Anne, his wife," of Marblehead, conveyed property to
"their son John" in 1754.   He had d. before "Nov. 6, 1769,"
when the "Inventory of John Reynolds, late of Marblehead," was
presented.   Children : —

3334.   RUTH, b. Oct. 16, 1719.
3335.   ANNA, b. May 17, 1721.
3336.   JOHN (see above). He or his son may have been the "John Ren-
    nel, of Marblehead," in list of men taken in the "Grand Turk's
    Prize," and committed to "Old Mill Prison." England, during
    the war of the Revolution, 1781–2 (N. E. Hist. and Gen. Reg.).
3337.   NATHANIEL [3374], b. in Beverly, is also supposed to have been
    the son of John [3333], or of John [3336], as a grandson of the
    said Nathaniel, Jotham G. [3463], of Lubec, Me., says his
    great-grandfather's name was John, and that he "migrated to
    Beverly, Mass."

3338.   JOHN[4] [3326] (Benjamin[3], Nathaniel[2], Robert[1]), m., 1st,
Susanna Giles, Jan. 11, 1743.   She d. and he m., 2d, Dorothy
Weld, of Roxbury, May 3, 1753.   He may have been the "*Capt.*
J. (S.) Reynolds, of Bristol," somewhere noticed ; but is known to
have moved first to Providence, "and again, Feb. 12, 1765, to
Boston."   He d. 1801, aged 83.   Children : —

3339.   PRISCILLA, b. June 3, 1745 (first wife); d. about 1763 or 1765,
    aged 19 (?).
3340.   SAMUEL, b. Apr. 3, 1754 (second wife); served in the Revolu-
    tionary war; was wounded for life by a bayonet "at the time
    of Lee's capture," and afterwards d. "in early manhood."
3341.   GRINDALL [3384], b. Oct. 12, 1755.
3342.   BENJAMIN, b. Nov. 17, 1757; moved to Norfolk. Va.; d. Dec. 5,
    1842, aged 85, and there left numerous descendants.
3343.   JOHN, b. Feb. 3, 1759; resided in Strafford, Vt., and d. Jan. 11,
    1848, in his 89th year.
3344.   EDWARD [3388], b. Mar. 28, 1761.
3345.   WILLIAM, b. June 3, 1763; d. without children.
3346.   THOMAS; d. young.

3347.   GRINDALL[4] [3328] (Benjamin[3], Nathaniel[2], Robert[1]),
moved from Bristol to Putney, Vt, about 1755 or 1760, where
some of his descendants were still supposed to be, in 1869.
Children : —

3348.   BENJAMIN ("oldest"), b. about 1760; was deacon of the church
    in Putney, and there d. about 1848, aged 88.
3349.   NATHANIEL; "raised a family, in or near Putney"
3350.   SAMUEL; after the close of the Revolutionary war, migrated to
    Canada; lived and d. at Sutton, C. E., and left many descendants.
3351.   SALLY; m. a Gilson; settled, lived and d. in Barnet, Vt., her
    children still occupying the homestead.
3352.   GRINDALL [3395], b. about 1767 ("fourth son").
3353.   CONSTANT [3406]; "other daughters probably younger."

3354.   NATHANIEL[5] [3331] (Nathaniel[4], Nathaniel[3], Nathaniel[2],

Robert[1]), is said in the History of North Bridgewater to have settled near his brother Thomas " at the West Shares, North Parish.".
Was known as " Nathaniel Reynolds, Esq." He m., 1st, Hannah,
daughter of Samuel Hartwell, 1739, who d. Aug. 12, 1742 ; m., 2d,
Mary Tolman, of Stoughton, Mass., June 14, 1744. He afterwards
moved to Vassalboro', Me., with his five youngest children : —

3355. Philip [3410], b. Sept. 19, 1740.
3356. Jonas [3415], b. Jan. 28, 1742.
3357. Timothy, b. Oct. 29, 1746 (second wife); m. Rebecca ——. Has
        descendants in Sidney, Me.
3358. Hannah, b. Mar. 4, 1750; m. William Packard, June 8, 1769.
3359. Mary, b. Mar. 23, 1754; m. Dea. Ebenezer Packard, Mar. 31, 1774.
3360. Nathaniel [3423], b. Apr. 26, 1757.
3361. David [3437], b. Mar. 9, 1759.
3362. Silence, b. Oct. 30, 1760
3363. Jonathan [3443], b. May 17, 1764.
3364. Cynthia, b. Oct. 9, 1769. Her descendants are now found in
        Vassalboro', Me.

3365. Thomas[5] [3332] (Nathaniel[4], Nathaniel[3], Nathaniel[2],
Robert[1]), m. Elizabeth Turner, Nov. 3, 1748, and probably raised
up his family in North Bridgewater, — from the history of which
town his family record is taken, — though there are now said to
be descendants of his in Winslow, Me. He d. 1795, aged 77.
Children : —

3366. Amy. b. Oct. 29, 1749; d. May 9, 1752, in her 3d year.
3367. Joseph [3447], b. June 22, 1751 ; m. Jemima Perkins. Sept. 17, 1772.
3368. Amy, b. Feb. 25, 1753 ; m. Silas Dunbar, July 2, 1772.
3369. Elizabeth, b. June 22, 1755.
3370. Susanna, b. Apr. 24, 1757; m. Oliver Howard, 1780.
3371. Martha (Patty), b. Mar. 23, 1759; m. Parmenas Packard,
        Apr. 9, 1798.
3372. Thomas, b. Jan. 27, 1762; m. Tabitha Thayer, 1785.
3373. Josiah, b. July 1, 1766; m. a Phillips, and removed to Vermont.

3374. Nathaniel[5] [3337] (John[4], Nathaniel[3], Nathaniel[2], Robert[1]). Whose son he was is not certainly known. His pedigree is
thus given. on the supposition that he may have been a son of
John[4] [3333], as before stated. He m. Lydia Raymond, and settled in Marblehead (or Beverly), Mass , as per birth of oldest son ;
moved to Amherst, N. S., in 1762. He had been a sea captain,
but left his home in Nova Scotia, at the commencement of the
Revolutionary war, to fight for the freedom of the colonies. He
could not return till after peace was declared, when he found his
wife dead, his children scattered, and his property confiscated In
the meantime, however (probably about 1780), he once vainly
attempted to rescue his family from Amherst by a bold strategy.
Single-handed, he captured a small vessel in the night, boarding it
from a log canoe, securing the watch, demanding the cabin key of
the captain, pistol in hand, and quietly locking him in ! The captain supposed he had several men with him. This was in Cumberland Bay. He then attempted to work the vessel towards Amherst,
but with slow progress, being really alone, so that the guns of Fort

Cumberland were turned upon him by daylight, and he was obliged to escape by his canoe, in the fog, and paddle his way to Machias, Me. The officers of the fort, suspecting he might be secreted near his home, sought to intimidate his wife to divulge his hiding-place, one of them firing his pistol, killing her lap-dog under her chair, and thus throwing her into a death-like swoon, as her youngest son well remembered.

He was a captain in the Revolutionary army, and had a township of land granted to him, on which Marietta, O., now stands, being sold soon after his death "for thirty pieces of silver." After the war, collecting his children, the oldest son now married, he made, with them, a pioneer settlement, in the then howling wilderness, at Lubec, District of Maine; revisited Marblehead, where he again married; returned to Lubec " to prepare for his bride," and was soon after drowned on his final passage to Marblehead, thus closing his eventful life. (Letter of Mrs. Clara J. Reynolds [3481], Pembroke, Me.) His children were : —

3375. LYDIA; m. Elisha Freeman, and settled in the State of New York.
3376. BENJAMIN [3459], b. 1753, in Marblehead or Beverly.
3377. MARY; m. a Campbell.
3378. SARAH; m. a Pond.
3379. JOHN; went with his brother Nathaniel to New York, soon after the close of the Revolutionary war, and their father's death; settled in or near Cherry Valley, and finally built a cotton factory of his own, in which he was burned to death, July 4, 1827(8).
3380. NATHANIEL; settled in New York (see last number).
3381. PARKER; lost at sea.
3382. JONATHAN [3470], b. Mar. 7, 1774, in Amherst, N. S.
3383. EUNICE, b. 1776; d. 1860, aged 84.

3384. GRINDALL[5] [3341] (John[4], Benjamin[3], Nathaniel[2], Robert[1]), was the father of at least nine children, of whom the names of only three have been given, and the two youngest, or " eighth and ninth" (brothers), only, are said to be " surviving" : —

3385. CYNTHIA, b. May 12, 1821, in Franconia, N. H.; d. at Boston, Mass., Mar. 18, 1870, in her 49th year.
3386. GRINDALL [3485], b. Dec. 22, 1822, in Franconia.
3387. HENRY RUSSELL [3489], b. Apr. 1, 1830, in Boston.

3388. EDWARD[5] [3344] (John[4], Benjamin[3], Nathaniel[2], Robert[1]), was a merchant in Boston, owned more or less shipping, and run the first line of packets between Boston and Philadelphia. He m., 1st, Deborah Belcher, June 20, 1790 ; m., 2d, Ann Foster, May 28, 1819, ▓▓▓ Nov. 2, 1848, in his 88th year. Children (first wife) : —

3389. JANE THOMPSON, b. Aug. 28, 1791.
3390. EDWARD [3493], b. Feb. 28, 1793.
3391. FRANCES McKAY, b. Dec. 2, 1795.
3392. WILLIAM BELCHER [3496], b. Jan. 16, 1797.
3393. CHARLES GREENE, b. July 10, 1802.
3394. EMILY AUGUSTA, b. Apr. 7, 1807.

3395. GRINDALL[5] [3352] (Grindall[4], Benjamin[3], Nathaniel[2], Robert[1]), served for a time in the Revolutionary army, near the

17

close of the war, " at the early age of sixteen years," and soon
after migrated with his younger brother, on foot, over mountains
and through the wilderness, from Putney, Vt., to the new town of
Grand Isle, in Lake Champlain. He m. Dorcas Sandon, of South
Hero, 1789. Children : —

3396. AMELIA, b. June, 1791; m. a Thomas; now residing at Sun
    Prairie, Wis.
3397. JESSE, b. 1793 (?); d. at Grand Isle, 1818 (?), aged 25.
3398. SALLY, b. 1795; m. a Streeter; d. at Fort Covington, N. Y., 1867,
    aged 72.
3399. GUY, b. 1797; a farmer on Grand Isle; "has a numerous family
    widely scattered." He represented his town in the State legis-
    lature two years.
3400. AMANDA [3504]. b. 1799.
3401. HENRY HARDY [3506], b. Feb. 24, 1801.
3402. JULIA, b. 1803 (?); m. a Fuller; d. at Milton, Vt., about 1849,
    aged 46, "leaving a large family."
3403. ELIZABETH, b. 1805 (?); m. a Seymour; d. at Newark, Ill., 1861,
    aged 56 (?); "several children."
3404. JOHN [3511]; b. April, 1807.
3405. WILLIAM V. [3516].

3406. CONSTANT[5] [3353] (Grindall[4], Benjamin[3], Nathaniel[2],
Robert[1]), m. Margaret Graham ; was a farmer in South Hero, Vt.,
till 1830 ; then moved to Pierpont, N. Y., and there d. about 1844.
Several children and grandchildren " scattered over the West " ; of
the former : —

3407. EDWARD; was formerly a Congregational minister in Omro, Wis.
3408. SEARLE; resides in Minnesota.
3409. GRINDALL; d. about 1864, in Michigan.

3410. PHILIP[6] [3355] (Nathaniel[5], Nathaniel[4], Nathaniel[3], Nathaniel[2], Robert[1]), m. Hannah Packard, Oct. 29, 1765, settled in
North Bridgewater, and d. Jan. 1775, in his 35th year. She m.,
2d, a Thayer, and d. 1831, " over ninety years old." The following traditionary account from one of his descendants, besides
confirming, adds somewhat to the history already given. " Our
ancestors by the names of Snell and Reynolds came from England
to Shawmut (now Boston), and afterwards went out to a township
of domesticated Indians, bought the title, and paid them in merchandise, part of which was large buttons! This township was
incorporated by the name of Bridgewater, now four towns, — East,
West, North, and South (?)." Children : —

3411. WILLIAM [3518], b. 1767.
3412. PHILIP [3527].
3413. CHARITY [3530], b. 1771.
3414. MARY (Polly), m. Oliver Belcher; settled in Easton, Mass., and
    d. soon after in 1832.

3415. JONAS[6] [3356] (Nathaniel[5], Nathaniel[4], Nathaniel[3], Nathaniel[2], Robert[1]), m. Anna Perkins, 1768. Children : —

3416. JONAS.
3417. ISAAC [3532].

3418. JOHN [3534].
3419. DAVID.
3420. JONATHAN.
3421. ANNA; m. a Perkins.
3422. POLLY; m. a French.

3423. NATHANIEL[6] [3360] (Nathaniel[5], Nathaniel[4], Nathaniel[3], Nathaniel[2], Robert[1]), m., 1st, Bethiah, daughter of Levi Keith, Apr. 20, 1777. She d. and he m., 2d, Mary Adams, 1786. Children : —

3424. LUTHER [3536].
3425. NATHANIEL [3547].
3426. ZILPHA [3552].
3427. EDWARD (second wife), b. 1787; d. 1826, aged 39.
3428. BETHIA [3560], b. 1790.
3429. MOSES [3564], b. 1793.
3430. SARAH [3571], b. 1795.
3431. ELIZA [3575], b. 1797.
3432. CALVIN [3577], b. 1799.
3433. NEWTON [3586], b. 1801.
3434. JONATHAN [3592], b. 1805.
3435. STEPHEN [3597], b. 1807.
3436. MARY [3605], b. 1809.

3437. DAVID[6] [3361] (Nathaniel[5], Nathaniel[4], Nathaniel[3], Nathaniel[2], Robert[1]), settled in Sidney, Me., where his descendants are now found. His wife's name was Mary; b. May 3, 1766, and d. 1815, aged 49. He d. 1842, aged 83. Children ; —

3438. ELISHA [3609], b. May 3, 1796.
3439. LYDIA [3614], b. Dec. 14, 1797.
3440. HANNAH; b. Mar. 4, 1800; now residing in Sidney.
3441. NARCISSA [3621], b. Jan. 12, 1802.
3442. CHARLES [3625], b. Jan. 17, 1809.

3443. JONATHAN[6] [3363] (Nathaniel[5], Nathaniel[4], Nathaniel[3], Nathaniel[2], Robert[1]), m. Anna Thayer, Oct. 18, 1794, and moved to Sidney, Me. Children : —

3444. BETSY.
3445. MIRA.
3446. CYNTHIA [3629], b. 1806; besides another daughter, who d. in infancy.

3447. JOSEPH[6] [3367] (Thomas[5], Nathaniel[4], Nathaniel[3], Nathaniel[2], Robert[1]), m. Jemima Perkins, Sept. 17, 1772. Children : —

3448. ICHABOD [3634].
3449. JOSEPH.
3450. DANIEL.
SIMEON.
AZEL.
3453. THOMAS.
3454. OLIVE; m. a Macomber.
3455. AMY; m. a Howard.
3456. VESTA; m. a Clapp.
3457. SUSANNA.
3458. JEMIMA.

3459. BENJAMIN[6] [3376] (Nathaniel[5], John[4], Nathaniel[3], Nathaniel[2], Robert[1]), was styled "Captain"; m. Lydia Watson, of

Nova Scotia, a native of England; settled at Lubec, Me., and there d. 1835, aged 82. Children : —

3460. JOHN W. [3646], b. 1779, or "sometime afterwards."
3461. BENJAMIN.
3462. BETSY; m. a Smith.
3463. JOTHAM G., b. Sept. 17, 1790; was in the war of 1812, and still resides at Lubec.
3464. LYDIA; m. a Billings; d. 1871.
3465. NATHANIEL, b. 1795; was also a soldier in the war of 1812; "has a family in Pembroke, Me."
3466. MARY; m. a Simpson; d. 1870.
3467. HOPLEY.
3468. EUNICE, b. 1805; m. a Reynolds.
3469. HANNAH, b. 1808; m. a Reynolds.

3470. JONATHAN[6] [3382] (Nathaniel[5], John[4], Nathaniel[3], Nathaniel[2], Robert[1]), m. Persis, daughter of Capt. Theophilus Wilder, formerly of Hingham, Mass.; settled in Pembroke, Me. (?), and there d. 1866, aged 92. Of this numerous family, as a whole, in Maine, with their descendants and collateral branches, it may be added, " they are honest, industrious, influential, and comfortable livers ; not one bearing the name (Reynolds) has ever been amenable to the laws, and no more than one intemperate man has been known among them." Children : —

3471. LYDIA, b. 1795; m. a Lawrence; d. 1839, aged 44.
3472. BELA R. [3654], b. 1797.
3473. PERSIS, b. 1799; m. an Avery; d. 1821, aged 22.
3474. JONATHAN, b. 1801.
3475. NATHANIEL [3657], b. 1803.
3476. BENJAMIN G. [3659], b. 1805.
3477. MARIA S., b. 1806; m. a Wilder; d. 1871, aged 65.
3478. MARY, b. 1808; m. a Reynolds.
3479. WILLIAM H., b. 1810; is said to have built the St. John's Suspension Bridge.
3480. PARKER R., b. 1812; d. 1837, aged 25.
3481. CLARA J., b. 1814; m. Simeon H. Reynolds, a *great*-grandson of Capt. Nathaniel [3374].
3482. ELISHA T., b. 1817.
3483. LEMUEL T., b. 1819.
3484. ALFRED, b. 1824; d. 1827, aged 3.

3485. GRINDALL[6] [3386] (Grindall[5], John[4], Benjamin[3], Nathaniel[2], Robert[1]), is residing, 1873, as the minister of the First Parish, in Concord, Mass., where he was settled, July, 1858, having previously been minister of a parish at Jamaica Plain (West Roxbury), Mass., from Jan. 1848 until May, 1858. He m▓▓▓y Maria, daughter of Nathaniel P. and Lucy G. Dodge, Feb. ▓▓▓. She was b. Sept. 15, 1827. Children, b. in West Roxbury : ▬

3486. EDWARD GRINDALL, b. Apr. 3, 1850.
3487. LUCY GILMORE, b. Apr. 26, 1852.
3488. ALICE, b. Mar. 26, 1856.

3489. HENRY RUSSELL[6] [3387] (Grindall[5], John[4], Benjamin[3], Nathaniel[2], Robert[1]), was m. Sept. 11, 1854, to Susan Duncan, daughter of John Reynolds and Mary Ann Preston, his wife, of

Strafford, Vt.; see [3343]. She was b. Sept. 10, 1830. He is now residing in Boston, Mass. (1179 Washington Street, in 1871), where he has been treasurer of the Boston Penny Savings Bank for some years. Children, b. in Boston : —

3490. JOHN, b. Oct. 4, 1857.
3491. HENRY RUSSELL, b. Dec. 30, 1862.
3492. SUSAN ADELAIDE, b. Feb. 26, 1869.

3493. EDWARD[6] [3390] (Edward[5], John[4], Benjamin[3], Nathaniel[2], Robert[1]), graduated at Harvard in 1811 ; has been in active practice as a physician of distinguished reputation, till within a year or two, and was the founder of the Boston " Eye and Ear Infirmary" in 1824. He was twice married ; 2d, to Margaret Wendall, daughter of Hon. John Phillips, of Boston. Of his children : —

3494. JOHN PHILLIPS, is now a physician in Boston, having graduated at Harvard in 1845.
3495. AUGUSTA THERESA, the " youngest daughter" (first name afterwards dropped); m. the Rev. William R. Huntington, of Worcester, Mass., and is now deceased.

3496. WILLIAM BELCHER[6] [3392] (Edward[5], John[4], Benjamin[3], Nathaniel[2], Robert[1]), m. Elizabeth Margaret Carter, Apr. 24, 1821, and d. Feb. 19, 1866, aged 69 ; was in active business through life, having entered his father's office in 1811, " keeping up the same general business," and being for many years, till his death, senior partner of the well-established firm, " William B. Reynolds & Co.," commission merchants, 201 State Street, Boston. He was also " one of those who started St. Paul's (Episcopal) Church," in Boston, " and was its senior warden for many years." Children : —

3497. WILLIAM THOMAS, b. Sept. 1, 1822.
3498. GEORGE DUNCAN, b. Feb. 1, 1825; d. Jan. 7, 1828, in his 3d year.
3499. ELIZABETH DUNCAN, b. June 22, 1829.
3500. ELLEN MARIA POTTER, b. Jan. 7, 1832.
3501. CAROLINE MARGARET, b. Feb. 23, 1834; d. Feb. 13, 1857, aged 23.
3502. FRANK WAYLAND [3663], b. Apr. 28, 1836.
3503. ANNA THAXTER, b. Nov. 15, 1840.

3504. AMANDA[6] [3400] (Grindall[5], Grindall[4], Benjamin[3], Nathaniel[2], Robert[1]), m. —— Bullis, and has of late been residing in Decorah, Iowa. Her only son : —

3505. HENRY (Bullis), is a doctor of medicine in Iowa, and had been for two years, in 1869, a member of the Iowa State Senate.

6. HENRY HARDY[6] [3401] (Grindall[5], Grindall[4], Benjamin[3], iel[2], Robert[1]), has practised medicine in the county of Isle, Vt., for forty years (1869) ; now residing at Alburg Springs. Children, still living : —

3507. ANN ELIZA; m. B. W. Reynolds, who moved from New York; now living in Grand Isle; one son and one daughter.
3508. MARIA; m. Henry C. Adams, Esq., of St. Albans, Vt.; was assessor of internal revenue, third district of Vermont, in 1869.
3509. JULIA; residing in Brattleborough, Vt., 1869.
3510. HARDY L., b. Jan. 1855.

3511. JOHN[6] [3404] (Grindall[5], Grindall[4], Benjamin[3], Nathaniel[2], Robert[1]), resides as a farmer in Georgia, Vt. Children, living : —

3512. CHARLES.
3513. HOMER.
3514. SWIFT.
3515. GEORGE.

3516. WILLIAM V.[6] [3405] (Grindall[5], Grindall[4], Benjamin[3], Nathaniel[2], Robert[1]), has been a trader in Winooski Village, Vt. Three sons and one daughter living. His third son : —

3517. WILLIAM B., was a major in the war of the rebellion, and "fell at the head of the 17th Vermont regiment, which he was then commanding, in a charge after the blowing up of the fort at Petersburg, Va."; from which charge but one commissioned officer of his regiment came out alive. "No better officer or braver man went from Vermont" than Maj. Reynolds. His sash and field-glass are now in possession of his uncle [3506].

3518. WILLIAM[7] [3411] (Philip[6], Nathaniel[5], Nathaniel[4], Nathaniel[3], Nathaniel[2], Robert[1]), m. Martha Snell, of North Bridgewater, Mass. ; was a joiner and architect; afterwards resided in Hebron, in Buckfield, and (1802) in Minot (now Auburn), Me. She d. in Garland, Me., 1847, aged 77. He d. in Winthrop, 1854, aged 87. Children : —

3519. WILLIAM, b. 1794, in North Bridgewater; m. Abigail Roberts; was a carriage maker in Minot, Me , and d. 1837, aged 43.
3520. NATHAN [3667], b. 1796, in N. B.
3521. ZOPHAR [3670], b. 1797-8, in N. B.
3522. ZEBEDEE SNELL [3672], b. Oct. 2, 1800, in Buckfield, Me., — name afterwards changed to "Charles," as elsewhere entered.
3523. DAVID, b. in Minot, Me., and there d.
3524. MARTHA, b. in Minot; m. Thomas J. Howard, of M., and d. leaving one son.
3525. MARY, b. in Minot; d. at North Bridgewater, aged 23.
3526. LEONARD ORCUTT, b. 1814, in Minot; m. Ellen Stevens, of Portland, and there settled as a trader; two daughters.

3527. PHILIP[7] [3412] (Philip[6], Nathaniel[5], Nathaniel[4], Nathaniel[3], Nathaniel[2], Robert[1]), was twice married, and settled in Stoughton, Mass. Six children, — two by first wife, — of whom : —

3528. WILLIAM, and one sister, are now living in Grafton, Wis.
3529. PHILIP, and another sister, in North Bridgewater.

3530. CHARITY[7] [3413] (Philip[6], Nathaniel[5], Nathaniel[4], Nathaniel[3], Nathaniel[2], Robert[1]), m. Leonard Orcutt, and settled Winthrop, Me   She d. 1863, aged 92. Six daughters, of only three are living : —

3531. LYDIA (Orcutt), m. Alvin Leighton, of Bangor, Me.; one other resides in Auburn, Me.; the third in Winthrop.

3532. ISAAC[7] [3417] (Jonas[6], Nathaniel[5], Nathaniel[4], Nathaniel[3], Nathaniel[2], Robert[1]), m. a Ford. Children, among others : —

3533. FRANKLIN [3679].

3534. JOHN[7] [3418] (Jonas[6], Nathaniel[5], Nathaniel[4], Nathaniel[3], Nathaniel[2], Robert[1]), was the father of : —

3535. JOSHUA W., who now resides, 1872, in Stoughton, Mass. We regret that fuller returns from this and the preceding family have not been received.

3536. LUTHER[7] [3424] (Nathaniel[6], Nathaniel[5], Nathaniel[4], Nathaniel[3], Nathaniel[2], Robert[1]), m. Sarah Faught, of Sidney, Me. Children : —

3537. ALFRED; deceased.
3538. LUTHER; deceased.
3539. FANNY; m. William Robbins (first wife), and d. leaving three children.
3540. SUSAN; m. William Robbins (second wife); d. and left children.
3541. PHILIP [3685].
3542. JANE FRANCE [3687].
3543. MARTIN; m. Frances Coney, of Augusta, Me.
3544. SUMNER; m. Sarah Pullen, and d. leaving two children.
3545. WILLIAM; m. Elizabeth Spinny, and d. leaving two clildren.
3546. SARAH; m. Nathan Pinkham; deceased.

3547. NATHANIEL[7] [3425] (Nathaniel[6], Nathaniel[5], Nathaniel[4], Nathaniel[3], Nathaniel[2], Robert[1]), m. Hannah Porter, of Bridgewater, 1811. Children : —

3548. JULIA ANN [3690].
3549. SARAH; m. a Mosier; one child.
3550. CYRUS; never married.
3551. CAROLINE [3696].

3552. ZILPHA[7] [3426] (Nathaniel[6], Nathaniel[5], Nathaniel[4], Nathaniel[3], Nathaniel[2], Robert[1]), m. Joshua Howard, 1805. Children, all who survive, living in Dexter, Me., as farmers : —

3553. DULCENA (Howard); m. and d.
3554. ZILBA; m. Moses Jose. Child : —
    1. LEWIS (Jose); m. Isubell Shaw.
3555. HORACE (Howard); m. and has one child : —
    1. FANNY.
3556. ANNA.
3557. REYNOLDS.
3558. SCOTT.
3559. JENNIE; m. Charles G. Wing.

3560. BERTHA[7] [3428] (Nathaniel[6], Nathaniel[5], Nathaniel[4], Nathaniel[3], Nathaniel[2], Robert[1]), m. Dea. Paul Bailey, of Sidney, Me. Children : —

3561. ELIZA PORTER (Bailey), b. 1831; m. Greenleaf Boynton. Children : —
    1. BERTHA B. (Boynton).
    2. DANIEL.
3562. PAUL (Bailey); d. 1859.
3563. BETHIA; d. 1862.

3564. MOSES[7] [3429] (Nathaniel[6], Nathaniel[5], Nathaniel[4], Nathaniel[3], Nathaniel[2], Robert[1]), m. Betsy Reynolds, who was b. 1797, and d. 1845, aged 48. Children : —

3565. ELVIRA, b. 1816; m., 1st, Sumner Dyer; m , 2d, B. Bicknell, all
now deceased. (Also "a child," who d. 1818, and "a son,"
who was b. 1820.)

3566. JONATHAN [3700], b. 1822.

3567. FRANK B. [3706], b. 1825.

3568. EDWARD A., b. and d. 1828.

3569. S. EDWARD [3711], b. 1830.

3570. MOSES F., b. 1835; d. 1854, aged 19.

3571. SARAH[7] [3430] (Nathaniel[6], Nathaniel[5], Nathaniel[4], Nathaniel[3], Nathaniel[2], Robert[1]), m. Jacob Faught, and d. 1871, aged
76. Children, all deceased : —

3572. NANCY (Faught).

3573. BETHIA.

3574. JACOB ; d. 1828 ; besides one other son, who d. an infant.

3575. ELIZA[7] [3431] (Nathaniel[6], Nathaniel[5], Nathaniel[4], Nathaniel[3], Nathaniel[2], Robert[1]), m Daniel D. Dailie. Child : —

3576. SARAH (Dailie), b. 1835 ; m. Charles Stevens, mason, of Hallowell,
Me. Child : —
  1. RUTH D. (Stevens), b. 1869.

3577. CALVIN[7] [3432] (Nathaniel[6], Nathaniel[5], Nathaniel[4],
Nathaniel[3], Nathaniel[2], Robert[1]), m. Caroline B., daughter of
Capt. Shubael Baker, of Sidney, Me., 1826. She was b. 1807,
and d. of consumption, 1850, aged 43. Children : —

3578. MARY ADAMS, b. 1827.

3579. ELIZA A. [3714], b. 1830.

3580. GILBERT B. [3721], b. 1832.

3581. ABBIE H. [3723], b. 1835.

3582. MERCY A., b. 1837; d. 1854, aged 17.

3583. ANN M., b. 1840; m. Willard A. Field, farmer, 1871.

3584. MULFARD B., b. 1843; enlisted in Co. C, 1st Maine cavalry, 1862;
served during the war; was a prisoner five months, "living
four months of that time in Andersonville on half a pint of
meal per day"!

3585. NETTIE, b. 1846; m. John B. Scouller, farmer, of North East,
Penn., 1871.

3586. NEWTON[7] [3433] (Nathaniel[6], Nathaniel[5], Nathaniel[4],
Nathaniel[3], Nathaniel[2], Robert[1]), m. Lydia, daughter of Capt.
Shubael Baker, 1828. Children : —

3587. SARAH JANE [3726], b. 1829.

3588. HANNAH PORTER, b. 1831; d. 1848, aged 17.

3589. CLARISSA, b. 1833; d. young.

3590. WILLIAM HENRY, b. 1842; served during the war 1862-1865, and
is now in the regular army.

3591. LYDIA; d. 1852.

3592. JONATHAN[7] [3434] (Nathaniel[6], Nathaniel[5], Nathaniel[4],
Nathaniel[3], Nathaniel[2], Robert[1]), m. Emily Spinny, of Phipsburg,
Me., 1833 ; both d. 1870, he aged 65. Children : —

3593. ALEANOR [3729].

3594. GEORGE S.

3595. ANN E. ; m. Isaac Pray, farmer, of Belgrade, Me. ; two children.

3596. HENRY O.

3597. STEPHEN[7] [3435] (Nathaniel[6], Nathaniel[5], Nathaniel[4], Nathaniel[3], Nathaniel[2], Robert[1]), m. Aurelia P. Davis, 1831. Children : —

3598. HELEN MAR [3732], b. 1832.
3599. ADA B., b. 1835; d. 1868, aged 33.
3600. ALBERLINE A. [3735], b. 1837.
3601. GEORGIANNA [3737], b. 1841.
3602. LLEWELLYN, b. 1843; started for Montana in 1867 (1), and has not since been heard from.
3603. A. LETTA [3739], b. 1846.
3604. FREDERIKA JANE, b. 1851; m. Albert N. Lord, cooper, of Upper Stillwater, Me., 1871.

3605. MARY[7] [3436] (Nathaniel[6], Nathaniel[5], Nathaniel[4], Nathaniel[3], Nathaniel[2], Robert[1]), m. Reuben (?) Burgess, 1831. Children : —

3606. ALBERT (Burgess), b. 1832; d. 1852, aged 19.
3607. ORIANN, b. 1833; m. Albert Arnold, shoemaker, and moved to North Bridgewater, Mass. Children : —
    1. FRANK (Arnold). 2. HENRY. 3. EDWIN. 4. ANNIE LOUISE.
3608. ANGELIE(C) (Burgess), b. 1835; m. Henry Woodbury, mason, of Massachusetts. He d. leaving : —
    1. EMMA (Woodbury). 2. GEORGE.

3609. ELISHA[7] [3438] (David[6], Nathaniel[5], Nathaniel[4], Nathaniel[3], Nathaniel[2], Robert[1]), m. Susan Hayward, and d. 1857, aged 61. Children : —

3610. LORENZO.
3611. HATTIE; m. a Weymouth, of Braintree, Mass.
3612. CHARLES.
3613. ORO; m. a Dimmick, of Braintree.

3614. LYDIA[7] [3439] (David[6], Nathaniel[5], Nathaniel[4], Nathaniel[3], Nathaniel[2], Robert[1]) ; m. Samuel Hayward, of Sidney; now residing in Springvale, Me. Children : —

3615. MARY (Hayward); m. Lewis Smiley, now of Amesbury, Mass.
3616. SUSAN; m. Rev. Henry Stetson, now of Waldoboro', Me.
3617. ALMIRA; m. L. Moulton, of Springvale, Me.
3618. HANNAH.
3619. PAULINA; m. William Brown, of Amesbury, Mass.
3620. OREN; m. Sarah Trussell.

3621. NARCISSA[7] [3441] (David[6], Nathaniel[5], Nathaniel[4], Nathaniel[3], Nathaniel[2], Robert[1]), m. Nathan Bragg, of Sidney, Me. Children : —

3622. LAURA A. (Bragg); m. Luther Hutchinson, of Sidney.
3623. DELIA C.
3624. LORING; m. Abbie Grant, of Sidney.

3625. CHARLES[7] [3442] (David[6], Nathaniel[5], Nathaniel[4], Nathaniel[3], Nathaniel[2], Robert[1]), m. Anne Bragg, of Sidney, and d. 1864, aged 55. Grandchildren, fourteen in number. Children : —

3626. ARVILLA.
3627. ANNIE; m. Herbert Freeman, of Boston, Mass.
3628. AUGUSTA; m. Edward Sibley, of Sidney.

3629. CYNTHIA[7] [3446] (Jonathan[6], Nathaniel[5], Nathaniel[4], Nathaniel[3], Nathaniel[2], Robert[1]), m. Shubael Baker, 1826. Children : —

3630. JOHN C. (Baker); m., 1st, Margaret Robinson; one child, who d. young. She d. and he m., 2d, Delia Manning; six children.
3631. SHUBAEL A.; m. Lydia Berrie, of Paris, Me.
3632. ANN M.; m. Alonzo T. Jones, paper-hanger, of Boston, 1857. Children : —
    1. EDDIE FRANCIS (Jones), b. 1859.
    2. JONATHAN; d. young.
3633. JAMES L. (Baker).

3634. ICHABOD[7] [3448] (Joseph[6], Thomas[5], Nathaniel[4], Nathaniel[3], Nathaniel[2], Robert[1]), m. Polly Brett, and moved to Minot, now North Auburn, Me. Children : —

3635. OTIS.
3636. ICHABOD.
3637. MADISON.
3638. LUKE.
3639. SAMUEL L.
3640. ADONIRAM J.
3641. POLLY; m. a Kinsley.
3642. NANCY; m. a Bird.
3643. BETSY; m. a Farrington.
3644. CLARA; m. a Kinsley.
3645. LAURA; m. Franklin Reynolds [3679].

3646. JOHN W.[7] [3460] (Benjamin[6], Nathaniel[5], John[4], Nathaniel[3], Nathaniel[2], Robert[1]), held a captain's commission in the war of 1812, and d. at Eastport, Me., June, 1844, aged 65. Children : —

3647. SIMON M., b. 1807; d. at sea, 1826, aged 19.
3648. BENJAMIN R., b. 1808; was captain of a ship; d. on the island of St. Thomas, W. I., 1840, aged 32.
3649. JAMES W., b. 1812; was drowned, April, 1830, aged 18.
3650. JOHN C., b. 1814 (?); was first mate of a ship, and d. at St. Thomas, W. I., 1838, aged 24.
3651. NATHANIEL C. [3741], b. July 30, 1816, in Lubec.
3652. SARAH B.; was married, and is now residing as a widow in Boston, Mass.
3653. GEORGE W., b. 1830 (?); was also first mate of a ship, and d. at New Orleans, La., 1853, aged 23.

3654. BELA R.[7] [3472] (Jonathan[6], Nathaniel[5], John[4], Nathaniel[3], Nathaniel[2], Robert[1]), is presumed to have settled in Pembroke, Me., and d. by drowning, 1853, aged 56. Of his children : —

3655. BELA, was a soldier in the war of the rebellion, enlisting in the 6th Maine regiment, 1861.
3656. CHARLES E., also enlisted in Co. K, 1st Maine artillery, 1862; d. Aug. 1871, as the final result of "injuries received in his last battle."

3657. NATHANIEL[7] [3475] (Jonathan[6], Nathaniel[5], John[4], Nathaniel[3], Nathaniel[2], Robert[1]), is only known to the writer as the father of : —

3658. FREEMAN, who "enlisted in the 2d Massachusetts cavalry, 1862, went to New Orleans, and after nearly three years' fighting, was taken prisoner, and d. at Tyler, Texas. He was present at the taking of Columbus, Miss., and had previously been engaged in the Red River expedition. His letters from those places were full of interest."

3659. BENJAMIN G.[7] [3476] (Jonathan[6], Nathaniel[5], John[4], Nathaniel[3], Nathaniel[2], Robert[1]), resided in Pembroke, Me., and was the father of thirteen children, — five sons and eight daughters, — all but one of whom lived to grow up. Of these : —

3660. BENJAMIN WESLEY [3743], b. Sept. 15, 1837.
3661. JOHN W., was a soldier in the Maine 6th regiment from 1861; returned at the close of the war, but d. in six weeks after, of consumption, caused by his exposure.
3662. JONATHAN S., was also in the war with his brother, and is now the "only one of the fourth generation" (from Nathaniel[5]) who remains "settled in business in the town of Pembroke."

3663. FRANK WAYLAND[7] [3502] (William B.[6], Edward[5], John[4], Benjamin[3], Nathaniel[2], Robert[1]), is a commission merchant, in the old firm of his father, 201 State Street, Boston. During the late war, he "spent several weeks in garrison duty at Fort Independence, Boston harbor, as a member of the 4th battalion, and afterwards as captain, Co. K, 44th Massachusetts volunteers, a nine months' regiment, with which he "went to North Carolina." He m. Cordelia Frances Weld, Sept. 16, 1863. Children : —

3664. MARION, b. Mar. 16, 1867.
3665. EDITH, b. June 14, 1870; d. Aug. 31, 1871, aged 1 yr. 2 ms. 17 ds.
3666. DUNCAN HARDING, b. Oct. 27, 1872.

3667. NATHAN[8] [3520] (William[7], Philip[6], Nathaniel[5], Nathaniel[4], Nathaniel[3], Nathaniel[2], Robert[1]), was a trader in Lewiston, Me. ; m. Elizabeth Briggs ; both deceased. Children : —

3668. NELSON BRIGGS.
3669. CHARLES HORACE.

3670. ZOPHAR[8] [3521] (William[7], Philip[6], Nathaniel[5], Nathaniel[4], Nathaniel[3], Nathaniel[2], Robert[1]), m. Mary Pollard, 1820 ; settled as a trader in Portland, Me., and d. 1847, aged 50. Child : —

3671. CHARLES HENRY ; a physician ; residing, with his mother, in Gorham, Me.

3672. CHARLES[8] [3522] (William[7], Philip[6], Nathaniel[5], Nathaniel[4], Nathaniel[3], Nathaniel[2], Robert[1]), settled as a trader in Garland, Me., 1827, and there m. Harriet L. Fairfield, 1828 ; moved to Bangor, 1850, where she d. June, 1855, aged 47. Children : —

3673. SUSAN HELEN, b. Mar. 1830; m. Daniel B. Head; d. at Bangor, 1859, aged 29, leaving one son.
3674. CHARLES TAPPAN, b. Apr. 1834; m. Eliza G. Storer; is a currier, and lives in Saco, Me.
3675. MARY ELIZA, b. 1836; a dress and cloak maker, residing in Bangor.
3676. HENRY GRENVILLE, b. 1841; now residing in Bangor; was a soldier in the 2d Maine regiment, army of the Potomac, 1861; wounded in both legs, and discharged in 1865.
3677. FRANK ORVILLE, b. 1847; entered the army of the Potomac, Apr. 1862; discharged, after four months, on account of sickness.

Entered the U. S. Navy, 1864, steamer "Santiago de Cuba"; was a volunteer in the bombardment of Fort Fisher, Jan. 15, 1865; discharged at the close of the war. He now lives in Portland, Me., as a cigar-maker.
3678. FREDERICK ARTHUR, b. Nov. 10, 1850; d. at Bangor, 1861, aged 11.

3679. FRANKLIN[8] [3533] (Isaac[7], Jonas[6], Nathaniel[5], Nathaniel[4], Nathaniel[3], Nathaniel[2], Robert[1]), m. Laura Reynolds [3645], his third cousin. Children: —

3680. ISAAC.
3681. CASANDER.
3682. CHARLES.
3683. MARY.
3684. FRED.

3685. PHILIP[8] [3541] (Luther[7], Nathaniel[6], Nathaniel[5], Nathaniel[4], Nathaniel[3], Nathaniel[2], Robert[1]), m. Mercy C. Davis. Child : —

3686. LEMUEL; d., aged 21 years.

3687. JANE FRANCE[8] [3542] (Luther[7], Nathaniel[6], Nathaniel[5], Nathaniel[4], Nathaniel[3], Nathaniel[2], Robert[1]), m. Jacob H. Faught. Children : —

3688. L. ORENT (Faught).
3689. NELLIE.

3690. JULIA ANN[8] [3548] (Nathaniel[7], Nathaniel[6], Nathaniel[5], Nathaniel[4], Nathaniel[3], Nathaniel[2], Robert[1]), m. Wally Ellis. Children : —

3691. ANN (Ellis).
3692. WILLIAM; deceased.
3693. SARAH.
3694. JAMES.
3695. CARRIE; deceased.

3696. CAROLINE[8] [3551] (Nathaniel[7], Nathaniel[6], Nathaniel[5], Nathaniel[4], Nathaniel[3], Nathaniel[2], Robert[1]), m. a Whitman, of Bridgewater, Mass. Children, all deceased : —

3697. NATHANIEL (Whitman).
3698. HANNAH.
3699. BETHIA.

3700. JONATHAN[8] [3566] (Moses[7], Nathaniel[6], Nathaniel[5], Nathaniel[4], Nathaniel[3], Nathaniel[2], Robert[1]), m. Susan Square. Children : —

3701. BETSY; d., aged 20.
3702. GEORGE; deceased.
3703. GEORGE.
3704. ALBERT.
3705. FRED W.

3706. FRANK B.[8] [3567] (Moses[7], Nathaniel[6], Nathaniel[5], Nathaniel[4], Nathaniel[3], Nathaniel[2], Robert[1]), is a druggist in California, where he m. Mary Picket. Children : —

3707. NETTIE.
3708. ELVIRA; d. young.
3709. BETSY; d. young.
3710. MARY FRANK.

3711. S. EDWARD[8] [3569] (Moses[7], Nathaniel[6], Nathaniel[5], Nathaniel[4], Nathaniel[3], Nathaniel[2], Robert[1]), m. Isabella Waterman, of Middleboro', Mass., and d. of consumption, 1858, aged 28. Children : —

3712. CHARLIE.
3713. FRANK.

3714. ELIZA A.[8] [3579] (Calvin[7], Nathaniel[6], Nathaniel[5], Nathaniel[4], Nathaniel[3], Nathaniel[2], Robert[1]), m. Abram Moore, 1850. Children : —

3715. FRED L. (Moore), b. 1851.
3716. FRANK C., b. 1853.
3717. ENOS L., b. 1858.
3718. MINNIE C., b. 1861.
3719. ALICE M., b. 1864.
3720. NETTIE R., b. 1868.

3721. GILBERT[8] [3580] (Calvin[7], Nathaniel[6], Nathaniel[5], Nathaniel[4], Nathaniel[3], Nathaniel[2], Robert[1]), m. Rose Ballard, 1860. Children : —

3722. LUTIE ELLA, b. 1861, and a son who d. in infancy.

3723. ABBIE H.[8] [3581] (Calvin[7], Nathaniel[6], Nathaniel[5], Nathaniel[4], Nathaniel[3], Nathaniel[2], Robert[1]), m. William M. Burgess, 1860. He served in the first Maine cavalry, Co. C, during the war. Children : —

3724. CHARLIE H. (Burgess), b. 1861.
3725. HATTIE F., b. 1868.

3726. SARAH JANE[8] [3587] (Newton[7], Nathaniel[6], Nathaniel[5], Nathaniel[4], Nathaniel[3], Nathaniel[2], Robert[1]), m. Whitman M. Thayer, proprietor of the "Mansion House," Augusta, Me. Children : —

3727. ALBERT (Thayer).
3728. NELLIE M.

3729. ALEANOR[8] [3593] (Jonathan[7], Nathaniel[6], Nathaniel[5], Nathaniel[4], Nathaniel[3], Nathaniel[2], Robert[1]), m., 1st, Webster Hutchinson. He d., and she m., 2d, Frank Colby, of Augusta, Me. Children, first husband : —

3730. CHARLIE (Hutchinson).
3731. GEORGE.

3732. HELEN MAR[8] [3598] (Stephen[7], Nathaniel[6], Nathaniel[5], Nathaniel[4], Nathaniel[3], Nathaniel[2], Robert[1]), m. William A. Ellis, merchant, of Upper Stillwater, Me., 1851 ; moved to Peshtigo, Wis., after birth of first child, and were burned out in the great fire of October, 1871 ; being obliged, with their family, to "lodge

with their faces to the ground" during all that terrific night of
Oct. 8, to preserve their lives. Children : —

3733. EDWARD D. (Ellis), b. 1852.
3734. WILLIAM, b. 1857.

3735. ALBERLINE A.⁸ [3600] (Stephen⁷, Nathaniel⁶, Nathaniel⁵,
Nathaniel⁴, Nathaniel³, Nathaniel², Robert¹), m. Thomas Googins,
of Bangor, Me., 1865, and afterwards moved to Boston, Mass.
Children : —

3736. STEPHEN (Googins), b. 1868, and another son, b. 1871.

3737. GEORGIANNA⁸ [3601] (Stephen⁷, Nathaniel⁶, Nathaniel⁵,
Nathaniel⁴, Nathaniel³, Nathaniel², Robert¹), m. Charles H. Roberts, millman, of Upper Stillwater, Me., 1866, and moved to
Stillwater, Minn. He had served in the war, and was burned to
death by the explosion of a kerosene lamp, 1868. She afterwards
moved to Peshtigo. Wis., and was there at the great conflagration,
1871, with her child : —

3738. CHARLIE LLEWELLYN (Roberts), b. 1868.

3739. A. LETTA⁸ [3603] (Stephen⁷, Nathaniel⁶, Nathaniel⁵,
Nathaniel⁴, Nathaniel³, Nathaniel², Robert¹), m. Coney Hodgkins,
merchant, of Upper Stillwater, Me., 1867. Child : —

3740. BYRON (Hodgkins), b. 1869.

3741. NATHANIEL C.⁸ [3651] (John W.⁷, Benjamin⁶, Nathaniel⁵,
John⁴, Nathaniel³, Nathaniel², Robert¹), was residing in Ellsworth,
Me., in 1872, having moved thither in 1850. Child : —

3742. JAMES S., b. Apr. 10, 1840, in Eastport; served two years in the
late war, Co. G, 8th regiment Maine volunteers.

3743. BENJAMIN WESLEY⁸ [3660] (Benjamin G.⁷, Jonathan⁶,
Nathaniel⁵, John⁴, Nathaniel³, Nathaniel², Robert¹), now resides at
Princeton, Me., " in the carriage business," having m. Susan E.
Daggett, July 8, 1861. Children : —

3744. NELLIE MARIA, b. May 23, 1863.
3745. EMMA JANE, b. Sept. 20, 1867.

B.

NOTICES OF OTHER REYNOLDS FAMILIES ORIGINATING IN
NEW ENGLAND.

The connection of these families cannot be certainly established
with any of the ancestors previously named from Savage.

3746. JACOB (Reynolds), b. Jan. 25, 1692; settled near New
Bedford, Mass., and d. Jan. 31, 1755, aged 63. He is said to have
had a brother who settled in Vermont. They " were church of
England people and Quakers." His son : —

3747. JACOB, Jr., b. May 8, 1731 ; settled in Killingly, Windham, Co., Ct., and d. 1785, aged 54. Children : —

3748. PHEBE [3759].
3749. JACOB, " was in the Revolutionary war with two of his brothers, under Gen. Sullivan, while marching through western New York; afterwards settled in Gilford, Chenango Co., N. Y.
3750. SIBEL.
3751. DAVID ; was in the Revolutionary war, as above.
3752. SORANA.
3753. SQUIRE ; probably, also in the Revolutionary war.
3754. OBADIAH.
3755. MARTHA.
3756. LUCY [3763], b. 1774, in Killingly.
3757. SULLIVAN ; lived in Gilford, N. Y.

From one of the above is descended : —

3758. N. S. REYNOLDS (Rev.), a clergyman, residing at Blossburg, Pa., 1870.

3759. PHEBE[3] [3748] (Jacob[2], Jacob[1]), m. her cousin, by the name of Reynolds, and moved to Vermont (from Connecticut). Children : —

3760. JOSHUA (Reynolds).
3761. JOHN.
3762. GILBERT. Also a daughter, who m. Abel Close, and moved to Chatham, Tioga Co., Penn.

3763. LUCY[3] [3756] (Jacob[2], Jacob[1]), m. Daniel Hopkins, Jan. 1794; moved to Otsego Co., N. Y., 1796, and d. at Steuben, Crawford Co., Pa., Aug. 9, 1857, aged 83. Children : —

3764. LUCINA (Hopkins), b. Oct. 16, 1794; resides in Pittsburg, Pa.
3765. THOMAS, b Feb. 14, 1797; d. Nov. 1851, in his 55th year.
3766. AVIS, b. Mar. 5, 1801; now residing in St. Joseph Co., Mich.
3767. DANIEL, b. Mar. 15, 1803; d. Feb. 1872, in his 69th year.
3768. ALEXANDER H., b. May 6, 1805; present residence in Crawford Co., Pa.
3769 LUCY A., b. Apr. 7, 1807 ; "Crawford Co., Pa."
3770. JEREMIAH, b. Oct. 23, 1809; now residing as postmaster (1872), in Worth, Tuscola Co., Mich.
3771. MARY ANN, b. Mar. 30, 1812 ; residing in Michigan.

3772. JAMES (Reynolds); resided in Hancock, Mass., and followed his oldest son to Canada, a few years after the latter's settlement there. Children : —

3773. CLARK ; moved to the vicinity of Missisquoi Bay (Vermont or Canada) about 1794.
3774. GRIFFIN.
3775. DAVID.
3776. JAMES ; all three of the last " settled in some of the Western States."
3777. H. N. (Reynolds), now of St. Armand West, Missisquoi Co., P. Q., is the son of [3773].
3778. J. HENRY, undertaker in Lawrence, Mass. (1869), 155 Elm Street, formerly from Franklin, Vt., is also of this family.

3779. BENJAMIN, was a brother of James [3772], who also moved from Hancock, Mass., to Canada, in 1807. Children : —

3780. WILLIAM; settled in Cambridge, Vt.
3781. JOHN.
3782. BENJAMIN.
3783. THOMAS; the three last all settled in St. Armand, P. Q.

3784. BENJAMIN, of still *another* family, moved from Pownal, Vt., about 1830, and settled in Durham, C. E.   His son is the present —

3785. BENJAMIN (Rev.), a clergyman, now of St. Armand, P. Q.

The following family *may* be descended from one of Savage's original Reynolds ancestors in New England ; or, possibly, from the Owen Runels family, see [3820].

3786. LUCIUS (Reynolds) is said to have moved from the vicinity of Manchester, N. H., to that of Plattsburg, N. Y., " in its early settlement, before 1800, bringing his sons with him," as here given : —

3787. BENJAMIN; d. without children.
3788. HENRY [3791].
3789. STEPHEN [3793].
3790. REUBEN [3797].

3791. HENRY[2] [3788] (Lucius[1]), has(d), as " his only surviving child " : —

3792. LOYAL L. ; now residing near Plattsburg, N. Y.

3793. STEPHEN[2] [3789] (Lucius[1]), left children : —

3794. STEPHEN; lives in Peru, N. Y.
3795. LAURA ; m. a Fisk; resides near Plattsburg.
3796. ELIZA ; m. a Day; residence, Peru, N. Y.

3797. REUBEN[2] [3790] (Lucius[1]), lived and d. in Nicholville, St. Lawrence Co., N. Y.   Children : —

3798. REUBEN.
3799. AUGUSTUS; resides in the same place.

Not connected with any of the above, as known, nor yet with the Pennsylvania family at Chateaugay Lake, N. Y., see [3810], and hence supposed to be of New England origin, were : —

3800. CHARLES (Reynolds), who formerly lived in the vicinity of Plattsburg, N. Y., and —

3801. THOMAS, who was a pensioner for service in the war of 1812. and lived on Isle La Mott, Lake Champlain, where others of the name are still residing.   Of his sons were : —

3802. ROSS.
3803. NOEL, who now resides in Beekmantown, Clinton Co., N. Y.

C.

NOTICES OF CERTAIN REYNOLDS FAMILIES THAT SETTLED ORIGINALLY IN AMERICA, OUTSIDE OF NEW ENGLAND.

We have it on the authority of a descendant, Mrs. Thomas Reynolds, assistant P. M. at Reynoldsville, Jefferson Co., Pa., that —

3804. HENRY (Reynolds) came from Chichester, Eng., and settled at Burlington, N. J., after a twenty-two weeks' voyage in 1676. Mrs. R., above, has a brief record of his posterity, who are very numerous in that vicinity.

Another descendant, M J. Reynolds, a nephew of Mrs. Thomas, resides at Chateaugay Lake, northern New York, from whom we learn that this ancestor was of the Quaker persuasion, and came over with William Penn, having previously been a king's collector for Charles II ; also, that the family, or a branch of it, settled in Chester Co., Pa. This would make his arrival six years later than the above, or 1682. In a later generation we have three brothers : —

3805. THOMAS [3808].
3806. ABRAHAM; resided in New York city, and had a family.
3807. SAMUEL; also of New York city; no children.

3808. THOMAS [3805] (—— Henry[1]), is said to have had six sons and daughters, of whom : —

3809. THOMAS, residing in Reynoldsville, Pa. (see above), is the only survivor (1868).
3810. ABRAHAM, b. in Wilmington, Del.; settled at Chateaugay Lake, or vicinity, in New York; is said to have been a very large man, six feet ten inches in height, and weighing 396 pounds. He was probably the father of —
3811. M. J. (Reynolds), mentioned above.

It is presumed that —

3812. JOHN F., a distinguished general in the late civil war, may have been a descendant of Henry [3804], as he was b. 1820, in Lancaster, Pa. He entered the U. S. army in 1846, and first served his country in Mexico and California. Early in the late war he commanded a brigade of the " Pennsylvania Reserves," with which he distinguished himself at the battle of Gaines' Mills, in 1862, though afterwards taken prisoner. Again in most daring and heroic service at the battle of Gainesville (or second Bull Run), in August of that year; a leader of two corps in " the main attack in front," at Fredericksburg, in the following December, and finally falling in defence of the soil of his native State, and almost in sight of his home, near the commencement of the great battle at Gettysburg, July 1, 1863. He had dismounted and gone forward to reconnoitre; and while observing the enemy through a fence, was struck in the neck by a sharp-shooter's bullet, and d. in a few moments. His age was 43.

18

We are furnished with the following items respecting another Reynolds family, traced from England to Nova Scotia : —

3813. WILLIAM (Reynolds), and his brother, two years younger, by the name of
3814. THOMAS, were b. and bred in Leicestershire, Eng., where they lived with their mother and one younger sister, owning a house and a small piece of land. The latter (Thomas) left England just before the first American war, and, being on the high sea when war was declared, he was "pressed" and put on board an English man-of-war. Was finally landed and discharged at Halifax, N S.; went thence to Pictou, was m., and at last moved into the wilds of Musquodoboit, where he made him a home, lived, and d. at the age of 96. No tidings from friends or property in the old country were ever obtained. He had eight children, none of whom ever left Nova Scotia. Of these —
3815. WELLWOOD, b. 1783, now resides in Upper Musquodoboit, N. S. (1869), having reared a family of six sons and six daughters, "now alive," — of whom
3816. JAMES, was living in the same place, 1869.

D.

NOTICES OF OTHER RUNNELS FAMILIES IN NEW HAMPSHIRE.

We now propose to add a few notes on certain individuals and families of the Renels, Renals, or Runels name in southeastern New Hampshire, not connected with those of Parts II and III. These notes are taken from the earliest town and county records in Rockingham County, and may prove of some service or satisfaction, especially to the descendants of Owen [3820].

The *earliest* allusion to any of these, or similar names, is found on the Portsmouth town records, where we have —

3817. JOHN ("Renals") on a committee and among the town officers, in notice of a town meeting held "Aug. 15, 1646."

The next allusion is among the Rockingham deeds, to one

3818. JAMES ("Rennell") "of ye same Portsmouth carpenter," who received by deed, "July 21, 1668, from Joseph Mason of Portsmouth in ye river of Piscataquack in N. E., his dwelling house and lands (gardens, orchards, marishes, arable lands, floodings, etc.), for £270 7s. lawful money, lying and being in ye Little Harbor, within Piscataquack aforesaid."
    This James *may* have been a *grocer* as well as carpenter, as he had conveyed to him, "Nov. 12," of the same year, "six and a half barrels of good molasses"! We have also
3819. SARAH (Rennels), "of Portsmouth, only heir of her father Stephen Craffit, deceased," in deed of "May 28, 1692, third year of William and Mary."

We can only conclude from the above that there *were* one or
more families of this name very early in Portsmouth, from which
may have been descended —

3820. OWEN[1] or "OWIN" ("Renalls"), first noticed as a
"Planter in Exeter, May 29, 1706," and also "of Quamscott"
(the same as Exeter), "July 6, 1715." His children were : —

3821. OWEN, who settled in Stratham; as he is called "Owen Runalls,
Jun., of Stretham, May 21, 1720," and "Feb. 16, 1721-2." He
appears, also, in *twelve* other deeds, with varied and sometimes
grotesque orthographies ("Runnels, Renels, Runals, Renes,"
and even, in one or two cases, "Oen Renls"), but always "of
Stretham or Stratham," till "May 10, 1749." From other allusions to his brothers, and especially from the "Report of committee appointed for the division of Owen Runnels' estate into
four parts," and signed "Stratham, Jan. 28, 1755," by "Jona.
Dearborn, Jona. Robinson, and Samuel Lane," we learn that he
left no children, and was probably unmarried. The administration of his estate had been previously granted to Thomas
Runnels, his brother, in said Stratham, "Sept. 30, 1752," —
marking, *nearly*, the time of his death. The four divisions of
his estate, just referred to, indicate the four additional children
of Owen, Sen. [3820], as follows : —
3822. ROBERT [3826].
3823. "JOHN (Runnels), deceased, late brother of said Owen"; his
"heirs and legal representatives" to receive "one fourth part
of his land, 5 + acres, bounded," etc. He must therefore have
d. prior to "Jan. 28, 1755," date of report.
3824. MARY; "sister of said Owen," one fourth part of land as above,
"also lower room and cellar at westerly end of his house."
She is elsewhere called "singel woman and spinner."
3825. THOMAS [3829].

3826. ROBERT[2] [3822] (Owen[1]), resided in Stratham till "Oct.
3, 1728, when he received from Thomas Packer, of Portsmouth,
"all right to Lot No. 30 in ye new township commonly known by
ye name of Chester or Chestnut country," "on condition of settlement and improvement." Accordingly he is afterwards reported
in five other deeds prior to "Nov. 10, 1749," as being "of Chester," selling off parts of his land in C., buying one half a share in
the town of Bow of his brother Owen, 1738, and selling the same
to Samuel Emerson, of Chester, in 1740. He had d. like his
brother John prior to "Jan. 28, 1755," as he is alluded to in the
same terms in committee's report, and "his heirs and legal representatives" receive one fourth part of his brother Owen's estate in
Stratham. His children were : —

3827. "JUDETH," alluded to in her aunt Mary's will, "Jan. 15, 1755," as
"my kindswoman daughter to my brother Robert deceased,"
and made sole legatee. Probably, also, —
3828. ROBERT, as a "Robert Runnels and Susanna his wife" were
living "in Chester, Feb. 16, 1795," and then deeded a parcel of
land in C. to T. Webster.

3829. THOMAS[2] [3825] (Owen[1]), was probably occupying a part
of his brother Owen's house in Stratham at the time of the latter's

death, as by report of committee for division he receives, besides
the remaining fourth part of the said Owen's land, the " East lower
room and cellar and garret in said house to be his part of the
buildings."

Thomas " Reanols" bought twenty acres of land in Chester from
Samuel Rymes, of Portsmouth, in 1729, but sold it to his brother
Robert, in 1741, for £45.   He finally sold out in Stratham, " Feb.
13, 1761," as we have, under that date, Thomas Runnels, of S.,
and Elizabeth, his wife, conveying a lot of land to Satchell Clark,
of S., " lying and being within the estate which was my brother
Owen Runnels's, late of Stratham, yeoman, deceased ; also some
which fell to Mary, sister of deceased, to heirs of John, his brother,
and also that which fell to Judith, daughter of Robert, brother of
said deceased, twenty-one and one fourth acres in all "; thus confirming our previous records.

He moved to the " Parish of Deerfield, N. H.," and there under
date " Jan. 27, 1766 "; name " Thomas Runils," and condition
" being very sick in body," he wills to Elizabeth, his dearly beloved
wife, all his real and personal estate, and makes her his executrix.
He d. between that time and " Feb. 17, 1769," when Elizabeth
Runels, *widow*, of Deerfield, sold out to P. Simpson, thirty-five
acres for £25.   Their children were named in will with legacies as
follow, each styled " my son " : —

3830. OWEN, " Five shillings."
3831. THOMAS, " A yoke of white-faced steers."
3832. SAMUEL, " Five shillings."
3833. JOHN, " Five shillings."

One of the four last mentioned children, — probably Samuel, —
was the father of —

3834.   OWEN, b. Oct. 29, 1790 ; lived in Candia, perhaps,
also in Raymond ; d. Mar. 25, 1835, in his 45th year.   He m.
Susan L. Roberts, of Raymond, Nov. 7, 1811, who was b. Mar. 13,
1794, and d. Feb. 15, 1854, in her 60th year.   Children : —

3835. THOMAS F. [3846], b. Feb. 24, 1813, in Raymond.
3836. CHARLES W. [3851], b. Mar. 4, 1815.
3837. HENRIETTA P., b. Feb. 22, 1817; d. Apr. 9, 1835, aged 18.
3838. OWEN, b. Mar. 15, 1819, in Candia; m. Betsy Keniston, of Barn-
        stead; was a blacksmith in Pittsfield for many years, and was
        sent to the New Hampshire legislature for two years, probably
        from that town.   He d. at P., Apr. 2, 1872, aged 53 years 18
        days.   His "Obituary" appeared in the "Morning Star."
3839. SUSAN C., b. June 15, 1821; m. David Lovejoy; d. Nov. 1, 1860,
        aged 39.
3840. SAMUEL R. [3856], b. Jan. 12, 1824.
3841. JOHN [3859], b. June 2, 1828.
3842. ROBERT CRAWFORD, b. May 29, 1830; d. Sept. 30, 1857, aged 27.
3843. OLIVE M. [3861], b. Jan. 9, 1826.
3844. CYRUS S., b. Apr. 10, 1833; was married; d. Oct. 18, 1861, aged
        25 years 6 months.
3845. HENRIETTA M. [3866], b. June 10, 1835.

3846. THOMAS F.[5] [3835] (Owen[4], Samuel (?)[3], Thomas[2], Owen[1]), was a Free Will Baptist clergyman; ordained about 1849, and pastor of the second Free Will Baptist church in Candia for fourteen years. He m., 1st, Hannah Currier, of Raymond, Feb. 21, 18 9, who d. one year later; m., 2d, Mary Currier, sister of first wife, Sept. 16, 1841. She was the mother of his children, and d. at Chester, of pneumonia, Apr. 8, 1860. He m., 3d, Nancy L. Dennett, of Pittsfield, Nov. 1, 1860, who survives him, and now lives in Deerfield. His will is found in the Rockingham Probate records, dated "Chester, Aug. 23, 1864"; "to each of my three sons," as below, "one dollar each"; "to my wife Nancy L. Reynolds all the rest of my estate, provided she adopt and educate as her own, my daughter, Mary Jane R., till eighteen years of age, but no longer." He d. Aug. 27, 1864, aged 51 years 6 months. Children : —

3847. THOMAS O. [3869], b. Dec. 24, 1842.
3848. WILLIAM O., b. Sept. 15, 1844.
3849. GEORGE F., b. Oct. 8, 1846.
3850. MARY JANE, b. Sept. 13, 1849.

3851. CHARLES W.[5] [3836] (Owen[4], Samuel[3], Thomas[2], Owen[1]), was twice married, — second wife, Nancy Clifford, — and d. July 18, 1850, aged 35. Children : —

3852. HENRIETTA P.; m. Benjamin Page.
3853. LAURA A.; m. John K. Simpson.
3854. CHARLES W.
3855. SUSAN (second wife); was married, but husband's name unknown.

3856. SAMUEL R.[5] [3840] (Owen[4], Samuel[3], Thomas[2], Owen[1]), m. Sarah Dearborn; d. July 3, 1858, aged 34 years 6 months. Children : —

3857. GEORGE.
3858. SARAH ALICE; m. D. Bean.

3859. JOHN[5] [3841] (Owen[4], Samuel[3], Thomas[2], Owen[1]), m. Cynthia Buzzell, of Barnstead, and d. Feb. 8, 1855, in his 27th year. One child : —

3860. MARY H.

3861. OLIVE M.[5] [3843] (Owen[4], Samuel[3], Thomas[2], Owen[1]), has been twice married; once to Ed(ward) Rowell; the only one of her father's children still living (1873). Her children were : —

3862. NORRIS (Rowell (?)).
3863. CHARLES.
3864. SUSAN.
3865. WILLIE.

3866. HENRIETTA M.[5] [3845] (Owen[4], Samuel[3], Thomas[2], Owen[1]), m. Benjamin Sanborn, of Candia; d. Oct. 31, 1865, aged 30. Children : —

3867. NELLIE M. (Sanborn).
3868. MARTHA.

3869.   THOMAS O.[6] [3847] (Thomas F.[5], Owen[4], Samuel[3], Thomas[2], Owen[1]), graduated at the Danville, Ky., Seminary, and in medicine at the Albany Medical College, Dec. 24, 1866. He first practised as a physician in Port Huron, Mich., but returned East, and commenced his professional labors at Kingston, N. H., Feb. 20, 1870, where he already enjoys an extensive and lucrative practice. He m. M. Fanny Smith, formerly of Raymond, preceptress of the Mystic Valley English and Classical Institute, at Mystic Bridge (Stonington), Conn., July 13, 1870. Child : —

3870. MABEL, b. May 5, 1871.

Still another Runnels family, which can neither be connected with any of the preceding, nor traced to any descendants of their own, appears in Barrington, N. H., as follows : —

3871.   WILLIAM, said to be "of Barrington, Jan. 4, 1766," and had previously m. Eleanor Cavenoe, as the last date is that of the deed by which "Arthur Cavenoe, of Durham," conveyed to him sixty acres of land in B., Lot 256, "for and in consideration of ye love and affection that I (Cavenoe) have and do bar towards my daughter Eleanor Runnells, wife of William R."
        There is similar evidence from two or three other deeds, — in one called William Ronalls, — that he was still living in Barrington, "Apr. 1, 1772," and "Mar. 18" and "Apr. 14, 1775," in the last of which he conveyed "certain tracts of land to John Cavernoe." His children, as proved below, were : —
3872. MICHAEL and
3873. RICHARD, to whom, jointly, John Caverno deeded "certain tracts of land in Barrington," "Sept. 14, 1781"; and Richard Runnels, of B., exchanged land with Michael R., of B , "Feb. 26 and 27, 1793," — "one half the land deeded by *our father, William Runnels*, to John Caverno, and by Caverno to ourselves," for "one half the land on which the said Michael" ("Runnalls") was then living. Michael again appears in deed of "Oct. 12, 1793," between which and "Dec. 12, 1793," he must have d. ; as under last date, "administration of the estate of Michael Runnels, of Barrington, *tayler*, deceased, intestate, is granted to *Sarah* R., his wife." His brother also d. before "Dec. 14, 1795," as administration of the estate of "Richard Runnels, of Barrington, deceased," is then "granted to Jonathan Dame."

Another isolated personage is found, from the Strafford Records, in —

3874. PELEG ("Pelek") Runnels, of New Durham Gore (Alton), receiving from Daniel McDuffee "five acres of land, more or less, beginning on Merrymeeting river," etc., "July 2, 1796." He may have lived in that vicinity till near "Oct. 5, 1835," and thus have been identical with "Peleg Runnals, late of Alton," whose "Dower" at the last date "was appointed to his widow, Martha Runnals."

E.

OTHER RUNNELS FAMILIES IN MAINE.

Passing over into the State of Maine, we find the following Runnels family, whose origin is unknown. Names of descendants, mostly without dates, as here given, were furnished by George E. Fogg [3922], of Saco. The earliest ancestor was —

3875. CHARLES (Runnels), said to have been b. in Scarboro', Me.; d. and was buried in Saco. His children were: —

3876. JOHN [3882].
3877. CHARLES [3893].
3878. GRACE.
3879. MARY.
3880. SARAH.
3881. HANNAH.

3882. JOHN[2] [3876] (Charles[1]), m. Rhoda Edgecomb, of Scarboro'; served in the Revolutionary war; d. and was buried in Saco. His widow was a pensioner till her death, Mar. 1864, aged 96. She was hence b. 1768. Children: —

3883. SALLY [3898].
3884. GRACE [3907], b. about 1796.
3885. ISAAC [3914].
3886. ELIZA [3919].
3887. MARY; d. of consumption, Dec. 1842.
3888. HANNAH; m. Jonathan Fogg, of Scarboro, where now living, his widow.
3889. CHARLES [3923], b. about 1805.
3890. JOSEPH; m. Mary Mann; d. in New Portland, Me.
3891. JAMES; d. of consumption, in Portland, when quite young.
3892. WILLIAM; m. Deborah Wedgwood; was a tinman by trade; lived and d. in Portland. Had one child, now deceased.

3893. CHARLES[2] [3877] (Charles[1]), m. Abigail Cleaves, of Saco. Children: —

3894. ROBERT.
3895. SUSAN [3930].
3896. CHARLES.
3897. JANE.

3898. SALLY[3] [3883] (John[2], Charles[1]), m. Gibbins Edgcomb, of Saco, and soon after moved to Gardiner, Me., where still residing. Children: —

3899. RACHEL (Edgcomb)
3900. ELIZA.
3901. BURNHAM.
3902. RHODA.
3903. EMMA JANE.
3904. ENOS.
3905. WILLIAM.
3906. SARAH.

3907. GRACE³ [3884] (John², Charles¹), m. Rufus Coolbroth, of Scarboro'; there lived and d. at an interval of two or three weeks from each other, Feb. 1866, " at or near their 70th year." Children : —

3908. SAMUEL (Coolbroth).
3909. RHODA.
3910. FRANK.
3911. JOHN
3912. EUNICE.
3913. EDWARD.

3914. ISAAC³ [3885] (John², Charles¹), m. Sally Seavy, of Saco, and lived at the time of his death (Aug. 1866), at Union Falls (Buxton), Me. Children : —

3915. BETSEY.
3916. SALINDA.
3917. SARAH FRANCES.
3918. MAY ANNA.

3919. ELIZA³ [3886] (John², Charles¹), m. George Fogg, of Saco, " and are now both living." Children : —

3920. JOSEPH ARTHUR (Fogg), b. Mar. 12, 1835.
3921. EPHRAIM H., b. Nov. 26, 1837 ; d. of consumption, 1843, aged 6.
3922. GEORGE E., b. Mar. 1, 1839.

3923. CHARLES³ [3889] (John², Charles¹), m., 1st, Ann Dearborn, who d. in Buxton ; m., 2d, Lucy Jose, of B., who d. Mar. 1862 ; m., 3d, Ruth E. Hungerford, of Saco, where he now resides. Children, first wife : —

3924. MARY ELIZABETH.
3925. LOUISA.
3926. WILLIAM; " enlisted, and served his time in the army " of the late war ; now resides in Saco.
3927. LAWRISTAN; d. Jan. 21, 1861.
3928. HENRY B.; was also in the service of his country, and was shot mortally in battle.
3929. GEORGE; served the time of his enlistment in the army ; " afterwards shipped to go a whaling voyage, and was drowned."

3930. SUSAN³ [3895] (Charles², Charles¹), m. Samuel Grace, of Saco, and d. Mar. 1870. Children, all deceased, except the youngest : —

3931. AARON (Grace).
3932. SUSAN.
3933. MOSES.
3934. CHARLES.
3935. ORIN.

———

Yet another unconnected Runnels family is reported from the vicinity of Dennysville, Me. The earliest of this family known, was another —

3936. SAMUEL [3938], said to have been "of Scotch descent";
first settled near Portland, Me., and migrated thence to Dennysville, in the east part of the State. "There was a brother of his
by the name of"

3937. "JOHN."

3938. SAMUEL [3936] had the following children : —

3939. THOMAS [3944].
3940. SAMUEL.
3941. ROBERT.
3942. JOHN.
3943. SARAH.

3944. THOMAS² [3939] (Samuel¹), was the father of

3945. SARAH (?), the "eldest daughter"; m. Capt. Rufus Ames, of
Orland, Me.
3946. SAMUEL; was residing at Prospect, Me., till 1870, then went to
Omaha, Neb.
3947. SUSAN F.; m. George E. Ordway, of the "Essex House," Lawrence, Mass., 1870; afterwards moved to Omaha.

F.

A GENEALOGY OF THE FAMILY OF VALENTINE RUNNALLS, OR RUNNELS, IN MASSACHUSETTS.

This family is proved to be of independent origin, and entirely
distinct from any other Runnels or Reynolds family in this country.
Its earliest known ancestor was —

3948. VALENTINE¹ (Runnalls), b. as stated below; "cast away
on his passage to America" (?); soon after settled in Marblehead,
and m. Hannah Townshend. An old prayer-book, with version of
the Psalms by Tate and Brady, Edinburg, 1772, — now in possession of his family, — tells its own story and his, in his handwriting,
upon one of its fly-leaves, as follows: "This book I picked up in
the wrack of the Argo, when I ware cast away, in the year of our
Lord 178 ', Nov. 22d day." On the same leaf, "Valentine Runnall, his book, born Sept. 2ʸ, in the year of our Loard 1748, in
Great Britain, in the county of Coarnwel (Cornwall), with in 19
miles of the Lands End, in the parrish of Golvail."
His immediate *English* origin is thus established, and we must
concede this as a seeming exception to the general conclusion,
arrived at in the Introduction, that Runnels or Runnals is invariably Scotch, though even in this case an earlier ancestor may have
emigrated from Scotland into England.
If, as by one well authorized account, his daughter Hannah was
the oldest child, he was perhaps m. and this child was b. in England,

and both wife and child suffered shipwreck, and were saved *with* him on their passage hither. We give the following, therefore, as the only authenticated *order* of his children, the birth date of the second only being known; though it seems a little singular that the pronoun "we" should not have been used instead of "I" on the leaf of the prayer-book, if his wife and child were cast away with him. On the supposition that he was *alone* when cast away, he must have married at Marblehead soon after reaching that place from "the wrack of the Argo," and his son Valentine must have been his oldest child; or, he may previously have established his family at M., and was taking a subsequent cruise upon the "Argo," not being at that time on his passage to this country. Children : —

3949. HANNAH; m. William Jaffrey, of Salem, and lived in or near
    Worcester.
3950. VALENTINE [3952], b. Oct. 8, 1783.
3951. WILLIAM; d. young.

3952. VALENTINE[2] [3950] (Valentine[1]), was a painter in Salem ; m. Nancy Perkins, of Wenham, and d. July, 1842, in his 59th year. She was b. 1786, and was found by the author on the eve before St. Valentine's day, 1873, residing at Beverly, at the age of 87, in the enjoyment of most remarkable health and vigor, both of body and mind. She naively remarked that she 'never had but one Valentine in her life, and *that* she kept till the death of her good husband.' Children : —

3953. GEORGE WASHINGTON [3960], b. Nov. 12, 1805, in Salem.
3954. JOHN PERKINS [3962], b. Sept. 22, 1807, in Salem.
3955. CATHARINE ALLEY, b. Nov. 29, 1809, in S.; d. at Boston, Feb. 15,
    1825, in her 16th year.
3956. NANCY [3970], b. Oct. 22, 1812, in S.
3957. LYDIA [3973], b. Sept. 26, 1815, in Wenham, the family having
    moved thither on account of the war.
3958. THOMAS [3978], b. Apr. 7, 1818, in W.
3959. EDWARD PERKINS, b. Sept. 29, 1820, in W.; d. at Beverly, Aug.
    24, 1840, in his 20th year.

3960. GEORGE WASHINGTON[3] [3953] (Valentine[2], Valentine[1]), m. Elizabeth Herrick, of Beverly ; went to California in 1849, and there still resides. She d. Mar. 1850, leaving : —

3961. GEORGE, b. 1834, who joined his father in California, after his
    mother's death, and there continues.

3962. JOHN PERKINS[3] [3954] (Valentine[2], Valentine[1]), was a mason in Salem, residing at 13 Northey Street, where his son now lives. He m. Sarah Rebecca Roberts, Jan. 10, 1833, and d suddenly, by a casualty on the railroad track, near his home, May 4, 1865, in his 58th year. She was b. Oct. 3, 1808, and d. Aug. 28 (25), 1866, in her 58th year. Children, b in Salem : —

3963. SARAH ELIZABETH [3982], b. Nov. 2, 1833.
3964. JOHN PERKINS, b. June 25, 1836; d. Oct. 27, 1837, aged 1 yr. 4 ms.
3965. JOHN PERKINS [3984], b. June 4, 1840.
3966. MARY SAUNDERSON, b. Nov. 11, 1843; d. May 28, 1861, in her 18th yr.

3967. EDWARD PERKINS, b. July 8, d. Oct. 17, 1846.
3968. LUCY ELLEN, b. Oct. 14, 1849.
3969. CHARLOTTE ALICE, b. Apr. 24, 1853.

3970. NANCY[3] [3956] (Valentine[2], Valentine[1]), m. Joseph Porter, of Beverly, and there d. Apr. 8, 1836, in her 24th year, leaving : —

3971. CATHARINE (Porter) ; m. Adoniram Judson Hood ; two children, both deceased.
3972. JOSEPH VALENTINE ; is a painter in Beverly ; m. Helen Wallace ; three children.

3973. LYDIA[3] [3957] (Valentine[2], Valentine[1]), m. John Lowe, a native of Essex, Apr. 19, 1835 ; now residing (1873) in Beverly. Children : —

3974. ABBY (Lowe), b. Mar. 8, 1836 ; m. Benjamin Carrico ; four children, three living.
3975. NANCY (Lowe), b. Apr. 27, 1837 ; m. George Wilson, of Danvers ; four children.
3976. JOHN (Lowe), b. Jan. 12, 1839.
3977. REBECCA, b. Nov. 15, 1840 ; d. of dropsy on the brain, 1853, aged 13.

3978. THOMAS[3] [3958] (Valentine[2], Valentine[1]), was first a mariner, afterwards a shoemaker, in Beverly, and there d. of lung fever, Feb. 11, 1857, in his 39th year. He m. Abigail Mears, of Essex, 1847. Children : —

3979. EDWARD WARREN, b. July 15, 1848.
3980. MARY LIZZIE, b. May 19, 1851.
3981. ABBY BUTLER, b. Aug. 18, 1853.
         Thanks to Miss Abby for so kindly and promptly procuring the old prayer-book and large family Bible on the 13th of February, 1873 !

3982. SARAH ELIZABETH[4] [3963] (John P.[3], Valentine[2], Valentine[1]), m. Dennison P. Moore, Feb. 1, 1863, at Salem. He was a mariner ; now a watchman, residing in Peabody, Mass. Child : —

3983. MARY EMMA (Moore), b. July 25, d. Aug. 23, 1871.

3984. JOHN PERKINS[4] [3965] (John P.[3], Valentine[2], Valentine[1]), was a brave and able officer in the late civil war, first entering as a corporal in Co. I (Salem Light Infantry), Massachusetts 8th regiment, for three months, " May 18, 1861 " (enlisted " Apr. 17, 1861 "). Mustered out " Aug. 1, 1861." Was commissioned as a lieutenant in the 19th Massachusetts volunteers, " Aug. 28, 1861 " ; promoted to captain in the same regiment ; shared in all its previous battles ; was twice wounded at the battle of Antietam, " Sept. 17, 1862," and resigned on account of his wounds, " Nov. 13, 1863." He was afterwards on duty in the veteran reserved corps at Kalamazoo, Mich., and in command of the post at New Albany, Ind , from Aug. 1864 to Sept. 1865 ; was finally mustered out of the service, " June 30, 1866," and is now, as a militia captain, in command of the same company in Salem, with which he first enlisted. Since the war, Capt. Reynolds has been engaged in the very commendable occupation of "designer and emblazoner of military and naval coats of arms, for perpetuating the record of soldiers and sailors" in our country's service. He received a patent in this enterprise, "July 14, 1868," and his facilities for its prosecution are unrivalled. Judging from the rich beauty and appropriateness of his own coat of-arms, we feel inclined to commend the work and the *patronage* of Capt. R. to the living soldiers in our "Roll of Honor." Residence and head-quarters, 13 Northey Street, Salem, Mass. He m. Mary Ellen Henville, Nov. 5, 1863, who was b. in New York city, Nov. 5, 1843. Children : —

3985. AUGUSTUS GOVEA, b. July 30, 1865, in New Albany, Ind.
3986. SARAH MAY, b. June 29, 1867, in Salem; d. July 17, 1869, aged 2
       years 18 days.
3987. JOHN PERKINS, b. Sept. 28, 1871.

G.

NAMES OF INDIVIDUALS AND OF SMALL FAMILY GROUPS NOT AS YET CERTAINLY CONNECTED WITH ANY OF THE PRECEDING.

"Mere mention," in conclusion, may be made of other *names*, as follows : —

3988. CAPT. REINOLDS, of the "Speedwell" (Pilgrim fathers), 1620;
       may be the same as "Mr. Runolds, maker of the Speedwell"
       (see Vol. 1, N. E. Gen. Register).
3989. "CHR." (Christopher) (Reinolds), age 24, passenger for Virginia
       in the "Speedwell," May 28, 1635 (Vol. 2, N. E. Gen. Register).
3990. BENJAMIN (Reynolds); m. Elizabeth Bradford.
3991. "NICO." (Nicholas) Reinolds and
3992. "TH." (Thomas) Reynolds, "passengers for Virginia."
3993. ELECTIACUS (Renolds), "son of the same. b. Feb. 2, 1706-7, at
       Middleboro'." (All four of the last from Vol. 4, N. E. Gen. Reg.)

3994. HARMON (Runnels), alluded to near the close of Introduction to Part I (see p. 4), is only known to have been a colonel in the Revolutionary war, but is supposed to have been descended, as there stated, from an older brother of Samuel [1] who "settled in the South" His son —

3995. HIRAM G. was governor of the State of Mississippi, afterwards
       removed to Houston, Texas, and there d. Dec. 15, 1857. His
       widow signs her name "O. A. Runnels," in letter of Nov. 16,
       1868, and states that he left an only son, who also has an only
       son; but their names, and further information respecting the
       family, we have sought in vain to obtain, seemingly through an
       unwillingness, on their part, to acknowledge a connection with
       aught pertaining to the North!

Another son of Col. Harmon *may* have been —

3996. HARDIN W.

Who may, in turn, have been the father of —

3997. HIRAM RICHARD; known to have been the nephew of Ex-Gov. Hiram G., to have resided in the north part of Texas, and to have been himself the governor of that State, about the years 1855–7.

———

3998. DEBORAH (Runnels) is alluded to in Sprague's Annals, Vol. II, p. 373, as m. to Abijah Wines, Sen., of L. I., and as being the mother of —

3999. ABIJAH (Wines), Rev., b. May 27, 1766, at Southold, L. I.; afterwards a resident and pastor of the Congregational church at Newport, N. H., 1796–1816; d. Feb. 11, 1833, at Charlestown, Mass., in his 67th year.

———

4000. JAMES (Runnels), "late of Newburyport, mariner, deceased, intestate; administration granted Feb. 4, 1806" (Essex Probate Records).

———

4001. WILLIAM HOOPER (Reynolds), administration granted "Apr. 20, 1809," said to be "of Marblehead"; hence probably descended from [3336]; as also
4002. MARY (Reynolds), "of Marblehead"; administration granted 1812.

———

4003. GIDEON (Reynolds) is an old man in Hartford, Ct., 1870; "family in Westchester Co., N. Y.; originally from Ireland to Connecticut, two or three generations back."

———

4004. WILLIAM (Runnels) [perhaps the same as 3750] was the father of —

4005. SAMUEL and
4006. WILLIAM, brothers in Westford, Vt., 1870.

———

4007. JOSHUA (Runnels), now of Hillsborough, N. H., is said to be descended from a family in Newburyport, Mass., of which, however, no traces can be obtained in the records of Newburyport or Newbury.

———

4008. WILLIAM (Reynolds), of Peoria, Ill., is well known through all the West, and especially in Illinois, as a most earnest and successful Christian and Sabbath-school worker.

4009.   DANIEL (Reynolds), b. about 1756 ; moved from Vermont to the town of Burnham, Me., and there d. 1831, aged 75. His son : —

4010.   JOHN, b. 1796; m. Betsy ——, and d. in Burnham, Sept. 1868, aged 72. Respecting his widow and family, we quote the following from the " New England Historical and Genealogical Register," for October, 1870 ; —

> " A few months since a resolve was presented in the legislature of Maine, in favor of granting a pension to Mrs. Betsy Reynolds, widow of John Reynolds, of Burnham, and the following facts were stated in support of the resolve "; viz, that she "sent four sons, two sons-in-law, and one grandson to the war, neither of whom returned to tell their story. They all died defending our flag When the war closed, she was left with thirty-one orphan grandchildren, made so by the war. Her only surviving son, who is lame, volunteered, but was rejected on account of his lameness. Mrs. Reynolds is now depending on her own labor for her livelihood. Seven of her orphan grandchildren were taken into the Bath asylum."

We have made strenuous efforts, while waiting for the printers, to obtain the names of *all* the patriotic sons of this family, but can get only the following : —

4011.   CHRISTOPHER, " b. Sept. 1823 ; d. in the army, of consumption."
4012.   GILMAN H., " b. Oct. 23, 1825 ; d. in the army, of neuralgia."
4013.   JESSE S., " b. Oct. 19, 1839 ; never enlisted, but was enrolled and stricken from the rolls on account of lameness." The names of the " two sons-in-law " who went to the war, were : —
1.   CHANDLER K. CHURCH ; d. of disease in the service.
2.   JAMES T. CARR ; still living, and a preacher, in the State of Maine.
The " grandson," who enlisted, was shot in battle, name not given.

This list (of Appendix G) might be indefinitely increased by adding soldiers of the Reynolds name, not previously noted in this genealogy, especially from the late adjutant generals' reports of Maine, New Hamsphire, Massachusetts, and other States ; as also from the triennial catalogues of several colleges, — ten of the name having graduated at Yale College (prior to 1852), three at Harvard University, and two, besides those already mentioned in this work, at Dartmouth College.

ADDENDA.

ADDENDA.

I.

For the future genealogists of the Reynolds families, we re-enter and *add* the following citations, chiefly from Savage's Genealogical Dictionary, not previously noted : —

4014. JAMES [3283], of Wickford, was doubtless the father of these four sons : —

4015. FRANCIS [3296], of Kingstown.
4016. HENRY [3297], of Kingstown; m. Sarah, daughter of James Greene.
4017. JAMES, Jr., of Wickford; m. Mary, daughter of James Greene, Feb. 19, 1685.
4018. JOSEPH, of Wickford, 1687.

4019. JOHN [3286], of Saybrook and Norwich; d. at N., 1702; had eleven children, of whom, — according to Caulkin's History of Norwich, —

4020. JOHN, b. Aug. 1655, at Saybrook; was killed by the Indians, probably in King Philip's war, Jan. 28, 1676, in his 21st year.
4021. SARAH, b. Nov. 1656: m. John Post.
4022. SUSANNA, b. Oct. 1658.
4023. JOSEPH, b. Mar. 1660.
4024. MARY, b. 1664; m. a Lothrop.
4025. ELIZABETH, b. 1666; m. a Lyman.
4026. STEPHEN, b. Jan. 1669.
4027. LYDIA, b. 1671; m. a Miller.

4028. JOHN [3287], of Weymouth ; sold his estate in W., 1664, and probably removed at the same time. His wife's name was Ann. Child : —

4029. MARY, b. Mar. 15, 1660.

4030. JOHN^2 [3289] (John^1), of Weathersfield ; d. 1682; wife's name was Mary. Children : —

4031. KEZIA, b. 1667.
4032. ANN (Anna), b. 1669.
4033. REBINA, b 1671.
4034. JOHN, b. 1674.
4035. JONATHAN, b. 1677.

4036. JONATHAN[2] [3290] (John[1]), of Stamford; representative in 1667; d. 1673. Children, at that time living, as by will:—

4037. REBECCA, b. 1656.
4038. JONATHAN, b. 1660.
4039. JOHN, b. 1662.
4040. SARAH, b. 1665.
4041. ELIZABETH, b. 1667.
4042. JOSEPH, b. 1669.

4043. ROBERT [3291], of Boston; wife's name Elizabeth. Children:—

4044. ELIZABETH, b. Jan. 2, 1669.
4045. ANN, b. Aug. 11, 1670.

II.

Just as the work of the printers was being completed, the author was favored with material for the following genealogy of *Henry* and *Sarah (Bunker) Tebbetts*, with the desire at least *suggested*, by some branches of the family, that it be herewith inserted. Having invariably complied with such suggestions hitherto, he is very happy to make this, as the *latest possible* addition to his work, especially as several of the families here traced are found living near his home, and are reckoned among his most valuable acquaintances. He only regrets that their records did not come to hand early enough to be incorporated in their proper place in the main body of the work, under [2179]. He also avails himself of the opportunity thus afforded of explaining more fully, as promised in the Preface (p. ix), how the "female lines," generally, through the book, are entered and carried out.

Re-entering, from p. 183, the name of

4046. SARAH (Bunker) [2179], she thus appears among the consecutive numbers as being of the second generation from (*i. e.* a child of) the common female ancestor, Sarah Runnels [2175]. She was b. Jan. 7, 1759, not 1750, as before given, and should therefore change places with her brother Joseph [2180]. She m., 2d, Henry Tebbetts, as before stated, the name being found upon the old Barnstead records as "Tibbetts" and "Tibbits." He was three years older than his wife, and d. May 19, 1818, in his 63d year. The additional facts have been gathered that this second husband was also in the Revolutionary service before marriage, that he stood beside her first husband, Bradbury Sinkler (or Sinclair), in his dying moments, and afterwards married her, as the widow of his deceased comrade. Their original location, on settling in Northfield, N. H., was near the present "Shaker road," a little north of the residence of her grandson,

George S. Tebbetts [4046, 1, (4)]. She there d. Dec. 22, 1836,
in her 78th year. At least 5 of her descendants, in the Tebbetts name, have taken the degree of M. D. Children, — being
of the third generation from the common ancestress [2175];
here entered with the cardinal numbers 1, 2, and 3, falling
under each other on the left margins of the pages, and appearing in Index No. 2, with the same numbers following the consecutive number here employed [4046, 1, etc.] : —

1. BRADBURY (Tebbetts), b. Oct. 23, 1779; m. Polly Clough, who
was b. Jan. 7, 1785. He was a farmer and storekeeper in
Northfield; d. Nov. 22, 1833, aged 54. She d. Dec. 1, 1846,
in her 62d year. Children, — entered like all others of the
fourth generation from [2175], with cardinals in parentheses,
(1), (2), (3), etc., and appearing in the Index with the same numbers directly after those previously given [4046, 1, (1), etc.] : —

(1.) NATHAN CLOUGH, b. Jan. 28, 1802; pursued preparatory studies
at Gilmanton Academy, 1818–20; studied medicine with Drs.
William Prescott and R. D. Muzzey, graduating at the Dartmouth Medical College, 1825; practised his profession in
Gilmanton, and was the representative of that town in 1841
and 1842. He m. Hannah, daughter of Maj. Rufus Parish,
Feb. 28, 1826; d. in Louisiana, Feb. 15, 1848, aged 46. Chil-
dren, — entered like all others of the *fifth* generation from
[2175], with Roman figures I, II, etc., and appearing in the
Index with the same figures directly after those previously
given [4046, 1, (1), I, etc.] : —I. GEORGE PARISH; resides in
California; four children living. II. RUFUS BRADBURY; m.
Mary Addie Shannon; present residence, Pittsfield, N. H.
III. MARY BADGER; m. a Lake; now resides in California.

(2.) MELINDA, b. Aug. 18, 1803; m. Noah L. Merrill, a native of
Deerfield, N. H.; resided in Manchester, and there d. Mar.
1847, in her 44th year, leaving: I. BRADBURY TEBBETTS
(Merrill); d. in the U. S. naval service at Cairo, Ill., near
the beginning of the war. II. NOAH L.; d. at Hartford, Ct.,
being a student at the Episcopal Theological Seminary,
III. ARTHUR TEBBETTS; m. Arianna Elizabeth Dearborn, of
Northfield, Sept. 16, 1862; was a Union soldier during the last
year of the late civil war; afterwards engaged in the shoe
business at the South, and d. near New Orleans, Mar. 7, 1868.
She also had previously d. at Northfield, within thirty hours
of the death of her husband. Children, — left doubly orphans,
and now being brought up by their grandmother Dearborn ; —
here entered, like all others of the *sixth* generation from their
great-great-great grandmother of the Runnels name before
marriage [2175], with Roman figures in parentheses (I), (II,)
etc.; appearing in the Index with same figures directly after
those previously given [4046, 1, (1), I, (I), etc.] : — (I.) FAN-
NIE LANE (Merrill), b. July 25 (?), 1863. (II.) WILLIE ARTHUR,
b. Mar. 22, 1867. IV. DE WITT CLINTON; only surviving son;
resides in Haverhill, Mass.; is m. and has two children.

(3.) JOHN CLOUGH (Tebbetts), b. Jan. 19, 1805; was a merchant in
Boston; m. Mrs. Sophia (Williams) Whitman, of B.; she has
since d. He is now residing (1873) chiefly in New York city.

(4.) GEORGE SULLIVAN (called "Henry," at first), b. Apr. 16, 1807;
has been a farmer in Northfield, near the place first occupied
by his grandfather; m. Olive Curry, daughter of Robert and
Olive Curry, of Northfield, who was b. Dec. 6, 1811, and d.
Oct. 19, 1872, in her 61st year, leaving a precious memory for
the excellence of her character as a wife, mother, sister, and
in all the other relations of life. Children : I. SAMUEL BRAD-
BURY, b. Aug. 31, d. Sept. 23, 1836. II. ADALAIDE CURRY,

b. June 12, 1838 ; d. Dec. 14, 1842, aged 4 years 6 months. III.
GEORGE WALTER (afterwards changed to " Walter George "),
b. Apr. 1, 1840 ; m. Elizabeth Elvira Belden, of Chicago, Ill..
May 10, 1863; resides in C. as a "packer and provision
dealer," firm of "R. Puddy & Co.," 250 S. Des Plains Street;
is also an active and influential member of the third Presbyterian church, and has been superintendent of its Sunday
school. Child : (I.) ARTHUR BRADBURY, b. Oct. 4, 1866, in
Chicago. IV. CHARLOTTE MCFARLAND, b. Aug. 21, 1842 ; m.
Richard Puddy, Oct. 19, 1870. He was b. July 28, 1845, in
Somersetshire, Eng.; is now in business with his brother-
in-law [III], at Chicago. V. JOHN CLOUGH, b. Jan. 24, 1849 ;
graduated at Dartmouth College, 1871 ; is now (1873) a member of the "General Theological Seminary" (Episcopal), in
New York city.

(5.) HANNAH, b. Feb. 26, 1809 ; m. Benjamin Curry, farmer, of
Northfield ; who was the son of Robert and Olive Curry ; b.
Jan. 30, 1800, and d. June 22, 1852, in his 53d year. Children :
I. MARY ELIZABETH (Curry), b. Dec. 26, 1829 ; m. David
La Rue Clifford, of Loudon, N., H.. shoemaker, May 2, 1853 ;
now residing in Tilton. Children: (I.) HELEN FRANCES
(Clifford), b. Feb. 3, 1854, in Northfield. (II.) GEORGIE
AUGUSTA, b. Dec. 4, 1861, at Sanbornton Bridge, now Tilton.
II. JOHN WILLIAMS (Curry), b. Sept. 12, 1832 ; d. in Califor-
nia, Mar. 8, 1857, in his 25th year. III. OLIVE AUGUSTA, b.
Sept. 7, 1834 ; d. of consumption, Nov. 18, 1846, aged 12.
IV. FRANCES SUSAN, b. May 31, 1836 ; m. George Ezra Spen-
cer, M. D., Dec. 1, 1858. He graduated at the Dartmouth
Medical College, 1846, practised medicine in Gilmanton, and
d. at Hanover, Jan 6, 1866, aged 48. V. SOPHIA TEBBETTS
(Curry), b. Mar. 27, 1838 ; graduated at the Conference
Seminary, Sanbornton Bridge ; m. Charles Carroll Rogers,
Esq , an attorney-at-law in Sanbornton (now Tilton), Aug.
27, 1860. Children : (I.) JOHN WILLIAM (Rogers), b. Oct. 1,
1861. (II.) CARROLL BURBANK, b. Apr. 28, 1863. (III.) AR-
THUR, b. Jan. 25, 1870. VI. GEORGIANNA BRADLEY, VII.
JOSEPHINE BRADBURY (Curry), twins, b. June 27, 1841 ; the
former d. Mar. 22, 1861, in her 20th year ; Josephine B. grad-
uated at the Sanbornton Bridge Conference Seminary ; was
a teacher in New York, and on the Island of Cuba for one
year ; m. Joseph Board, of Chester, N. Y. (first wife), June
3, 1868 ; d. of consumption, Apr. 6, 1869, in her 28th year.
Child : (I.) CHARLES (Board), b. Mar. 4, 1869 ; d. same day.
VIII. ANNETTE CARROLL, IX. ARABELLA CLOUGH (Curry),
twins, b. Aug. 11, 1845 ; Annette C. m., 1st, Samuel Bean
Noyes, clerk at Meredith Village, afterwards a merchant in
Chicago, Mar. 15, 1866 ; he d. Jan. 15, 1870, and she m., 2d,
Clinton Sawyer Mason, May, 1872. Children: (I.) HARRY
LINCOLN (Noyes), b. Aug. 29, 1868. (II.) MARY JOSEPHINE,
b. Feb. 14, 1870 ; d. Mar. 1, 1871, aged 1 year 15 days. Ara-
bella C. m. Enoch George Rogers, farmer, of Columbia, N. H.,
July 12, 1865, a brother of the husband of [V]. X. HANNAH
AUGUSTA (Curry), b. July 15, 1848 ; graduated at the Confer-
ence Seminary, Sanbornton Bridge ; m. Joseph Board (sec-
ond wife), see [VII]. Nov. 3, 1870. Child : (I.) JOSEPH
ORTEN (Board), b. Sept. 4; 1872.

(6.) HIRAM BRADBURY }
(7.) HORACE BRADLEY } (Tebbetts), b. Feb. 2, 1812.

    Hiram B. took his degree at the Boston Medical College
about 1836 ; was a physician, and afterwards a planter in
Louisiana ; now resides (1873) in Concord, N. H., 44 Main

Street. He m. Mrs. Laura Sophia (Watson) Boone, Mar. 31, 1842. . She was b. Mar. 14, 1816, in Claiborne Co., Miss. Children, b. in Carroll Parish, La.: I. HIRAM WATSON, b. Dec. 22, 1845; studied medicine, and took a medical degree at Dartmouth College, 1867, but is now employed in the service of the U. S. signal corps, near Washington. II. LAURA SOPHIA, b. Oct. 17, 1847; m. Howard Fremont Hill, printer and editor, of Concord, Oct. 17, 1870. He graduated at Dartmouth College, 1867. Child: (I.) JOHN McCLARY (Hill), b. Oct. 30, 1871; d. Dec. 4, 1872, aged 13 months 4 days. III. MARIA DIX (Tebbetts), b. Feb. 7, 1852; d. May 19, 1863, aged 11 years 3 months. IV. WILLIE BRADBURY, b. Mar. 10, 1855; is now (1873) a member of the Scientific Department of Dartmouth College.

HORACE B. [(7)]; m. Mrs. Keene, of Louisiana; present residence in New York city.

(8.) CHARLES CARROLL, b. Jan. 14, 1813; m. Harriet Kimball Sibley, of Laconia, N. H.; was a physician, graduating at the Dartmouth Medical College, 1845; settled at Iron Dale, Mo., and d. in the U. S. service as a surgeon, in Missouri, May 19, 1863, aged 50; was buried near Springfield. Only living child, besides three or four who d. in infancy: I. GEORGE HARRISON, b. Aug. 19, 1854; is an artist in Laconia; m. Emma Porter, of L., Dec. 28, 1870. Child: (I.) HATTIE C., b. Nov. 30, 1872.

(9.) ARTHUR BEEDE, b. Dec. 16, 1816; d. July 5, 1836, in his 20th year.

2. HANNAH (Tebbetts), b. Mar. 16, 1781; m. Edward Osgood, of Northfield, and d. Sept. 22, 1807, aged 26. Children, both reared by their grandmother Tebbetts: —

(1.) SALLY (Osgood), b. Apr. 5, 1805; m. Chase Ring.
(2.) HENRY T., b. Feb. 5, 1807; m. Hannah Tebbetts [4046, 3 (5)]; d. Mar. 28, 1841, aged 34.

3. HENRY (Tebbetts), b. Nov. 23, 1783; was a farmer in Northfield; m. Polly Beck, of Canterbury, 1800, who was b. Apr. 8, 1783, and d. Dec. 13, 1851, in her 69th year. He d. Mar. 15, 1856, in his 73d year. Children: —

(1.) SARAH, b. Jan 1, 1801; m. Chauncey Garvin, of Concord; a farmer in Northfield for the last twenty years (1873). Children: I. MARTHA (Garvin), b. May 21, 1838; m. James Kennard, of Manchester. II. SARAH JANE, b. Oct 10, 1840; d. Dec. 31, 1843, aged 3.
(2.) ABIEL FOSTER (Tebbetts), b. 1802; d. at the age of 6 months.
(3.) ALICE, b. Apr. 4, 1804; m. John Langdon Leach, of Weare, N. H.; two children, living.
(4.) HIRAM, b. Apr. 28, 1806; was a farmer on his father's homestead in Northfield; m. Hannah T. Bunker [2181, 2, (1)], of Barnstead, Dec. 25, 1856; d. Oct. 19, 1868, aged 62. Children: I. MARY A., b. Oct. 6, 1837. II. CHARLES A., b. July 22, 1839. III. HARRIET D., b. Aug. 22, 1842. IV. ALBERT H., b. Dec. 1, 1845; still owns the old homestead; one other child d. young. V. ELIZA W., b. Dec. 15, 1847; was a young lady of excellent spirit, and a successful teacher; is gratefully remembered by the author as the instructor of his children, in Sanbornton, 1868. She d. of consumption, Sept. 6, 1870, in her 23d year.
(5.) HANNAH, b. Nov. 3, 1808; m., 1st, Henry T. Osgood [4046, 2, (2)]; m., 2d, Asa K. Osgood (1st wife), brother of Edward [4046, 2], of Canterbury; she afterwards d., leaving two sons, one by each husband.

(6.) MARY, b. Oct. 27, 1810; m. Joseph Babb, of Barrington; two
    sons. I. HENRY (Babb); d. in the army. II. HORACE T.;
    m. Carrie Nute, and resides in Farmington.
(7.) ROSANNA, b. Feb. 11, 1813; d. June 6, 1861, aged 48.
(8.) HARRIET, b. Mar. 6, 1815; m. Thomas Dennis, of Lowell, Mass.;
    d. 1838, aged 23.
(9.) MELINDA, b. Apr. 16, 1817; m. Asa K. Osgood, of Northfield
    (second wife); d. Feb. 23, 1872, aged 55.
(10.) HENRY BRADBURY, b. May 16, 1819; studied medicine with Dr.
    Hoyt, of Northfield; graduated at the Dartmouth Medical
    School, 1846; practised his profession for a time in Weare,
    N. H., and d. about 1849, aged 30.
(11.) CLEMENTINA, b. Oct. 25, 1823; d. July 27, 1836, in her 13th year.
(12.) MANDANA, b. Sept. 25, 1827; m. Stephen Bean, of Piermont,
    N. H.; now resides in Bradford, Vt.

ROLL OF HONOR.

THE names of all persons referred to in the foregoing records, who are known to have been engaged *for* the American colonies, or the United States government, in their several wars against foreign or intestine foes, are here inserted in alphabetical order, with their respective consecutive numbers. At the same numbers in the main body of the work, more full and definite allusions to their military services may usually be found.

Many others, especially in the female lines, were, doubtless, engaged in a similar service, which has not come to the knowledge of the compiler.

Those marked with an asterisk (*) are known to have lost their lives in their country's defence, or as the speedy effect of their sufferings in the wars for which enlisted.

The whole number in this catalogue is 291. — Belonging to Part I, 100; belonging to Part II, 56; belonging to Part III, 95; belonging to the Appendix, 40.

KING PHILIP'S (INDIAN) WAR. — 1675-6.

Whole number (Appendix), 2.

REYNOLDS, JOHN,* 4020 ; REYNOLDS, Capt. NATHANIEL, 3304.

FRENCH WAR. — 1755-60.

Whole number, 4. — Part I, 3 ; Part II, 1.

RUNNELS, JOHN,	22	RUNNELS, Maj. SAMUEL,	93
RUNNELS, Lieut. SAMUEL,	17	RUNNELS, SAMUEL,	1661

WAR OF THE AMERICAN REVOLUTION. — 1775-1783.

Whole number, 48. — Part I, 12 ; Part II, 4 ; Part III, 22 ; Appendix, 10.

Ayer, William,	146	Reynolds (Runnels), Win-	
Bunker, Bradbury,	2177	throp,	2247
Bunker, Elijah,	2182	Runnals, Abraham,	2142
Bunker, Isaiah,	2176	Runnals, Ens. Isaac,*	2198
Bunker, Jonathan,	2183	Runnals, Ens. James,	2201
Bunker, Joseph,*	2180	Runnals, John,*	2145
Buswell, Daniel,	118	Runnals, Capt. Samuel,	2208
Chesley, George,	2189	Runnels, Benjamin,	123
Emerson, Capt. Smith,	1628	Runnels, Billey,*	67
Gage, Abel,	205	Runnels, Corp. Enoch,	1637
Ham, David,	2264	Runnels, Col. Harmon,	3994
Reynolds, Benjamin,	3327	Runnels, Israel,	2158
Reynolds (Runnels), Col.		Runnels, Job,	1675
Daniel,	82	Runnels, John,	22
Reynolds, David,	3751	Runnels, John,	3882
Reynolds (Runnels), Ens.		Runnels, Joseph,	341
Enos,	215	Runnels, Joseph,	2274
Reynolds, Grindall,	3395	Runnels, Moses,	2243
Reynolds, Jacob,	3749	Runnels, Lieut. Samuel,	93
Reynolds, John,	3336	Runnels, Solomon,	2168
Reynolds (Runnels),		Runnels, Sergt. Stephen,	136
Miles,	1695	Runnels, Stephen,	2159
Reynolds, Capt. Nathan-		Runnels, William,	74
iel,	3374	Sinkler, Bradbury,*	2179
Reynolds, Samuel,	3340	Snell, Edward,*	2165
Reynolds, Squire,	3753	Tebbetts, Henry,	4046
		Williams, Samuel,	2178

ENGLISH WAR. — 1812–14.

Whole number, 27. — Part I, 11; Part II, 7; Part III, 5; Appendix, 4.

Demeritt, John,	1671	Reynolds (Runnels), Jo-	
Demeritt, Joseph,*	1669	seph,	2593
Drew, John,	405	Reynolds, Jotham G.	3463
Eastman, Abiather, Jr.,*	1732	Reynolds (Runnels),	
Johnson, Levi,	1667, 1	Miles,	1695
McDaniels, Pelatiah,*	1706	Reynolds, Nathaniel,	3465
Reynolds, Capt. John W.,	3646		

Reynolds (Runnels), Sam-
uel, 2600
Reynolds, Maj. Stephen, 282
Reynolds, Thomas, 3801
Reynolds (Runnels),
Thomas K., 334
Runnels, Ebenezer, 198
Runnels, Isaac, 780
Runnels, Isaac, 2294

Runnels, Jeremiah H., 859
Runnels, John, 848
Runnels, John,* 2320
Runnels, Paul M., 2376
Runnels, Sergt. Samuel, 366
Spear, Robert,* 414
Thompson, Sergt. Robert, 1720
Whidden, Benjamin, 383
Whidden, David, 385

Mexican War. — 1846-7.

Whole number, 5. — Part I., 1; Part II., 1; Part III., 2; Appendix, 1.

Demeritt, Samuel D.,* 1671, 8
Reynolds, John F., 3812
Wing, Winthrop M., 1508
Twombly, James R., 2537
Twombly, Simes F., 2538

War of the Rebellion. — 1861-5.

Whole number, 205. — Part I., 73; Part II., 43; Part III., 66; Appendix, 23.

Adams, Erastus,* 2962
Adams, Justus, 2963
Ayer, Royal, 152, 8
Babb, Henry,* 4046, 3 (6), I.
Bean, William R., 2976
Blood, Franklin, 1093
Brown, Charles,* 1157
Burbank, Lewis L.,* 1734, 3 (1)
Burgess, William M., 3723
Buswell, Isaac,* 118, 9 (2)
Buswell, Isaac J.,* 118, 12
Buswell, James E., 119, 4 (2)
Buswell, Thomas A.,* 118, 9 (1)

Butler, Henry, 213, 2
Buzzell, Charles W., 2671
Buzzell, Sergt. Henry C.,* 2673
Buzzell, James M., 2674
Carr, James T., 4013, 2
Carris, Edward,* 1084
Church, Chandler K.,* 4013, 1
Colomy, James P.,* 2235, 10
Cook, Jesse M., 478, 1
Coombs, James H., 1521
Cutting, David,* 237, 5
Daniels, John D., 1671, 6 (4)
Danielson, Frederick, 1159
Dawson, George, 2672

Demeritt, Albert, 1671, 5 (6)
Demeritt, Charles,*
    1671, 5 (5)
Demeritt, Emerson, 1671, 5 (3)
Demeritt, George, 1671, 5 (4)
Demeritt, Jacob,* 1671, 5 (2)
Demeritt, John, 1671, 5 (1)
Dodge, George S., 843
Downs, Calvin C.,* 1809
Downs, Levi,* 1802
Downs, William H., 1806
Dunfield, George T.,
    154, 2 (2)
Dunfield, William, 154, 2
Dunfield, William N.,*
    154, 2 (1)
Eastman, Charles H., 1739, 3
Eastman, Chauncy,*
    1733, 3 (1)
Eastman, Edward P., 1739, 2
Eastman, George, 1732, 3 (2)
Eastman, Rufus M., 1732, 3 (1)
Eaton, Melzar, 1210
Ellison, Corp. Wright T.,
    1630, 2 (3)
Emerson, Smith, 1628, 1 (1), I.
Emery, Warren H.,* 2951
Evans, George M.,*
    1732, 4 (2)
Evans, Samuel E.,*
    1732, 4 (1)
Evans, Wesley J.,* 1579
Fox, George I.,* 365, 3
Foye, Albert, 1159
Gage, Capt. Aaron H., 207, 6
Gage, William L., 207, 4 (1)
Getchell, Henry, 416, 1
Getchell, Sebastian S., 416, 2
Giles, Job R., 1626, 2 (8)
Gilmore, Edward C., 779

Goodhue, Charles W., 356, 7
Goodhue, David H.,* 356, 8
Greenwood, Calvin W.,
    239, 2 (3)
Greenwood, Capt. Frank
  W., 239, 2 (1)
Ham, Sergt. Sylvester, 1805
Hanson, Joseph B., 2988
Herrick, Benjamin, Jr., 3192
Herrick, Charles, 2820
Hoitt, George I., 1670, 4 (10)
Holmes, William F.,
    1671, 6 (5)
Hopkins, George W., 356, 5 (1)
Huestis, Thomas R., 1934
Hunt, Sylvester D., 2675
Jacobs, Andrew, 2927
Jones, Charles,* 1671, 3 (5)
Jones, Daniel A., 1671, 3 (2)
Jones, Maj. James P.,* 3110
Jones, John D., 1671, 3 (3)
Jordan, William, 845
Kinsley, Capt. E. B., 764
Langley, Almon S.,* 2535, 1
Littlefield, Capt. Roger
  S., 1214
Marsh, John E., 2032
Marsh, Thomas D. 2034
Mason, Charles F.,* 2689
Mason, David B.,* 2686
Mason, James M.,* 2688
Mason, John C.,* 2690
McCurdy, Lieut. Charles
  W., 762
Merrill, Arthur T.,
    4046, 1 (2), III.
Merrill, Bradbury T.,*
    4046, 1 (2), I.
Millett, Capt. Alonzo D., 953
Moody, Charles, 2194, 5 (1)

MOODY, DEXTER, 2194, 1 (2)
MOODY, HARTWELL, 2194, 1 (1)
MOODY, WILLIAM, 2194, 1 (3)
NEWMAN, MARSHALL P., 3032
NEWMAN, ROBERT, 3029
PERKINS, SAMUEL R.,* 2759, 3
QUINT, JAMES M.,* 1645, 4 (6), I.
READ, Sergt. HIRAM A., 520
READ, Sergt. JAMES D., 522
REYNOLDS, ALFONZO S., 732
REYNOLDS, BELA, 3655
REYNOLDS, CHARLES C., 2744
REYNOLDS, CHARLES E.,* 3656
REYNOLDS, CHARLES H., 2563
REYNOLDS, Corp. CHARLES W., 1295
REYNOLDS, CHRISTOPHER,* 4011
REYNOLDS, DANIEL H., 2742
REYNOLDS, Capt. EDWARD H., 3074
REYNOLDS, FRANK O., 3677
REYNOLDS, Capt. FRANK W., 3663
REYNOLDS, FREEMAN,* 3658
REYNOLDS, GEORGE H.,* 1816
REYNOLDS, GILMAN H.,* 4012
REYNOLDS, HENRY, 2565
REYNOLDS, Surg. HENRY A., 3061
REYNOLDS, HENRY G., 3676
REYNOLDS, HENRY H.,* 2553
REYNOLDS (RUNNELS), HOSEA, 2049
REYNOLDS, Sergt. JACOB P., 1919
REYNOLDS, JAMES S., 3742
REYNOLDS, Maj. JOHN E., 3067
REYNOLDS, Gen. JOHN F.,* 3812
REYNOLDS, Capt. JOHN P., 3984
REYNOLDS, JOHN W.,* 3661
REYNOLDS, JONATHAN S., 3662
REYNOLDS, LUCIUS A.,* 758

REYNOLDS, MULFARD B., 3584
REYNOLDS, NASON F., 1263
REYNOLDS, PHINEHAS,* 2566
REYNOLDS, STEPHEN H., 1289
REYNOLDS, WILLIAM A., 1261
REYNOLDS, WILLIAM A., 3246
REYNOLDS (RUNNELS), Surg. WILLIAM B., 2068
REYNOLDS, Maj. WILLIAM B.,* 3517
REYNOLDS, WILLIAM H., 2562
REYNOLDS, WILLIAM H., 3590
REYNOLDS, WILLIAM W., 1915
REYNOLDS, WINTHROP, 3055
ROBERTS, CHARLES H., 3737
RUNNALS, CHARLES E., 2385
RUNNALS, DANA, 2773
RUNNALS, FREDERICK G., 2774
RUNNALS, JOHN S., 2822
RUNNALS, JONAS M., 2799
RUNNALS, PAUL M., 280⁹
RUNNALS, SAMUEL, 2806
RUNNELS, ANDREW T.,* 3198
RUNNELS, BARTLETT D.,* 1396
RUNNELS, BENJAMIN F.,* 858
RUNNELS, BENJAMIN F.,* 893
RUNNELS, CHARLES F., 1470
RUNNELS, DANIEL, 896
RUNNELS, EDWIN C., 2998
RUNNELS, Ens. FARNUM J., 1422
RUNNELS, GEORGE, 3929
RUNNELS, Sergt. GEORGE A., 3254
RUNNELS, GEORGE F.,* 886
RUNNELS, GEORGE M., 1337
RUNNELS, GREENWOOD C., 1560
RUNNELS, HENRY B.,* 3928
RUNNELS, HIRAM E.,* 2749
RUNNELS, JAMES A., 2750
RUNNELS, JOHN, 1953

RUNNELS, JOHN R. *   981
RUNNELS, Sergt. JOHN R.,   2748
RUNNELS, JOHN S.,*   1126
RUNNELS, NATHANIEL B.,   3256
RUNNELS, ORLANDO J.,*   2957
RUNNELS, Sergt. SAMUEL
    H.,   2697
RUNNELS, SANFORD E.,*   864
RUNNELS, SIMEON T.,   2115
RUNNELS, STEPHEN W.,*   997
RUNNELS, SYLVESTER,   1601
RUNNELS, THOMAS H.,   2119
RUNNELS, Lieut. THOMAS
    L.,   964
RUNNELS, WILLIAM,   3926
RUNNELS, WILLIAM B.,   3020
RUNNELS, WILLIAM F.,   943
RUNNELS, WILLIAM H.,   1929
SEARLES, JEFFERSON R.,*   2840
SPEAR, STEPHEN,*   421, 2
SPEAR, WILLIAM,*   421, 1
SWAIN, ALBERT E.,   2535, 4

TABER, Lieut. WILLIAM H., 1511
TEBBETTS, Surg. CHARLES
    C.,*   4046, 1 (8)
THOMPSON, SAMUEL, 1630, 2 (1)
THOMPSON, SYLVESTER,*
                                 1717, 13
TIBBETTS, FREDERICK,*   419, 2
TIBBETTS, SUMNER,*   419, 1
TURNER, JAMES R.,   1084
TWOMBLY, SIMES F.,   2538
UPHAM, WINTHROP,*   2532, 1
WALTERS, GEORGE W.,*   1584
WATKINS, GEORGE R., 152, 3 (1)
WATSON, JAMES C.,   1236
WEEKS, STEPHEN F.,   2701
WELCH, HENDRICK,*   1672, 5
WEST, JAMES G.,*   548
WHIPPLE, WILLIAM H.,   203, 1
WILSON, Capt. ALBION K.
    P.,   2587
WORTHEN, ARTHUR E.,   597
WORTHEN, GEORGE B.,*   596

INDEX I.

EXPLANATION AND SUMMARY.

THIS Index includes all the Christian names, in the foregoing records, with which the surnames Runnels or Reynolds, in some styles of their orthography, are to be supplied.

The figures *before* the names indicate years of birth, as found in the main body of the work.

Where these years were not known the spaces are usually left blank; though in several cases, mostly in the Appendix, the year of earliest mention is given instead, or the *supposed* year of birth, when any data were found from which to reckon it, approximately.

The figures *after* each name denote the consecutive number at which the birth is recorded, or the name first occurs. (See Preface, pp. VII and VIII).

The whole number of names in this Index is 2,081; of which 24, marked thus (†), are the names of females, "marrying into the family," whose maiden surnames were unknown, and who, therefore, could not be specified in Index II.

Deducting these, we have left, as original ancestors, and their descendants, bearing the same or similar patronymics, 2,057; distributed as follows: —

						adding those marked with (†),				total,	
Ancestor and descendants of Part I,				747;		"	"	"	" " 3;	"	750
"	"	"	"	" II,	212;	"	"	"	" " 3;	"	215
"	"	"	"	" III,	555;	"	"	"	" " 4;	"	559
Ancestors "		."	" the App.,	543;		"	"	"	" " 14;	"	557
Sums total, as above,		.	.	2,057;		"	"	"	" " 24;		2,081

Births.	Names.	Cons. Nos.	Births.	Names	Cons. Nos.
1849	Abbie Anna................	929	1776	Abigail....................	1678
1856	Abbie Frances............	3127, 2	1778	Abigail....................	130
1835	Abbie H....................	3581	1780	Abigail....................	·78
1853	Abby Butler...............	3981	1796	Abigail	379
1847	Abby Eliza.................	2004	1800	Abigail....................	1748
1868	Abby Ella..................	3133	1802	Abigail....................	2501
1859	Abby Ettie.................	1132	1823	Abigail	801
1860	Abby Fraydilla............	3211	.	Abigail (†)................	2141
1832	Abby J.....................	2652	1830	Abigail Ann...............	2492
1860	Abby Jane.................	1336	1820	Abigail Augusta...........	1831
1851	Abby May..................	2048	1828	Abigail Hatch.............	2587
1834	Abby Minerva	274	1826	Abigail Jane	725
1831	Abby Perkins..............	736	1789	Abner.......	2226
1717	Abigail (Nabby)...........	1608	1819	Abner Abeliono............	{ 2443 2863
1722	Abigail	8			
	Abigail (†)................	20	1718	Abraham...................	2131
1734	Abigail.	21	1746	Abraham...................	2144
1753	Abigail....................	1618		Abraham...............	3806
1755	Abigail	63		Abraham...................	3810
1760	Abigail...................	52	1859	Abraham Lincoln..........	2066
1760	Abigail....................	1650	1797	Abram.....................	2220
1773	Abigail...................	135	1824	Abram	2409

Births.	Names.	Cons. Nos.
1855	Ada Annette	2876
1835	Ada B	3599
1861	Ada B	2900
1815	Adaline	463
1824	Adaline	1812
1833	Adaline	894
1853	Adaline	1351
1815	Adaline Ann	337
1808	Addison	309
1831	Addison	727
1862	Adella May	3187
1862	Adie Anna	700
1819	Adna Wallace	2437
1826	Adoniram J	3640
1837	Alberline A	3600
1809	Albert	2412
1850	Albert	3704
1851	Albert	3000
1872	Albert Addison	1305
1856	Albert J	3153
1832	Albert Prescott	2637
1845	Albina Jane	1018
1846	Albion	945
1834	Aleanor	3593
1846	A. Letta	3603
1846	Alfonzo Scott	732
1811	Alfred	283
1814	Alfred	3537
1824	Alfred	3484
1839	Alfred Wesley	755
1844	Alfred Wesley	757
1762	Alice	2152
1793	Alice (Elsey)	2240
1856	Alice	3488
1858	Alice Iane	2924
1853	Alice Luce	2775
1857	Alice Maria	1455
1871	Alice Maud	1605
1859	Allen W	3027
1809	Almira	199
1831	Almira	1909
1841	Almira	830
1843	Almira	897
1828	Almira Bartlett	2466
1825	Almira Goodwin	734
1833	Almira Jane	1938
1833	Almira Rachel	2308
1837	Alonzo	2832
1844	Alonzo Mauly	2918
1837	Alonzo V	1869
1864	Alson Winter	1049
1825	Alvah	1907
1853	Alvah Ernest	963
1830	Alvina P	2627
1845	Alzena	1000
1799	Amanda	3400
1850	Amanda Jane	1318
1842	Amanda Malvina	2472
1791	Amelia	3396
1840	Amelia Elizabeth	563
1831	Amos	510
1862	Amos S	3165
1749	Amy	3366
1753	Amy	3368
1788	Amy	3455
1852	Andrew Foster	2006
1823	Andrew Jackson	1832
1834	Andrew Jackson	2400

Births.	Names.	Cons. Nos.
1866	Andrew Justin	1277
1835	Andrew Tetherly	2713
1840	Angenette	942
1839	Angenora	982
	Ann (†)	4028
1669	Ann (Anna)	4032
1670	Ann	4045
1715	Ann	3323
1833	Ann	2679
1839	Ann E	3595
1835	Ann Eliza	3507
1832	Ann Maria	586
1840	Ann M	3583
1721	Anna	3335
	Anna	3421
1748	Anna	19
1785	Anna	2206
1794	Anna	2281
1803	Anna	370
1805	Anna	2339
1846	Anna Adaline	772
1831	Anna Eliza	2604
1850	Anna Glover	1875
1854	Anna M	3161
1862	Anna May	2940
1840	Anna Thaxter	3503
1851	Annabella	2656
1843	Anne	876
1844	Anner Abbot	831
1807	Annie	435
1834	Annie	3627
1865	Annie	1517
1871	Annie Belle	1596
1869	Annie Cora S	3025
1869	Annie Estelle	1492
1857	Annie Louise	949
1845	Annie Philoma	986
1826	Annis C	490
1853	Ansil Thurston	2993
1853	Anson Eli	2045
1827	Antoinette Faustina	2603
1859	Appleton Colburn	2753
1863	Ara Bertie	2811
1806	Arthur	185
1870	Arthur Crosby	2996
1867	Arthur Dudley	3189
1859	Arthur Ellwood	1516
1870	Arthur Samuel H. L.	835
1837	Arvila Jane	2470
1831	Arvilla	3626
1737	Asa	14
1796	Asa	1760
1797	Asa	1746
1818	Asa	1904
1814	Asa Darwin	2415
1834	Asa Jasper	1847
1811	Asenath	1901
1840	Atemiza	882
1836	Augusta	3628
1847	Augusta Ellen	2800
1824	Augusta Hannah	869
1832	Augusta Theresa	3495
	Augustus	3799
1855	Augustus Amos	1514
1865	Augustus Govea	3985
1850	Aurelia Adelaide	883
1782	Azel	3452
1831	Azro Dennison	493

Births.	Names.	Cons. Nos.
1813	Bartlett	188
1832	Bartlett Dimond	805
1827	Bedelia Elvira	2660
1826	Bela	3655
1797	Bela R.	3472
1867	Belle	3248
1861	Belle Maude	1117
1686	Benjamin	3314
1722	Benjamin	3327
1748	Benjamin	46
1750	Benjamin	3779
1753	Benjamin	3376
1757	Benjamin	3342
1760	Benjamin	3348
1765	Benjamin	2174
1773	Benjamin	127
1783	Benjamin	3461
1796	Benjamin	2289
1806	Benjamin	394
1829	Benjamin	1781
	Benjamin	3782
	Benjamin	3784
	Benjamin (Rev.)	3785
	Benjamin	3787
	Benjamin	3990
1825	Benjamin Cheney	2457
1822	Benjamin Franklin	2632
1823	Benjamin Franklin	467
1830	Benjamin Franklin	893
1844	Benjamin Franklin	858
1844	Benjamin Franklin, Jr.	3119
1847	Benjamin Franklin	2388
1860	Benjamin Franklin	1473
1866	Benjamin Franklin	1491
1805	Benjamin G.	3476
1870	Benjamin Joseph	3134
1830	Benjamin March	2377
1836	Benjamin Oliver	2610
1833	Benjamin Pencin	863
1809	Benjamin Randall	2341
1808	Benjamin R.	3648
1817	Benjamin True	1777
1837	Benjamin Wesley	3660
1849	Bernice Ann	751
1872	Bertha Myra	3191
1860	Bertha P.	2939
1790	Bethia	3428
1800	Bethia	168
1785	Betsy	92
1786	Betsy	3462
1788	Betsy	2212
1792	Betsy	1758
1794	Betsy	1685
1795	Betsy	3444
1798	Betsy	174
1799	Betsy	1744
1799	Betsy	1747
1800	Betsy (†)	4010
1808	Betsy	400
1808	Betsy	2300
1823	Betsy	1826
1832	Betsy	3643
1844	Betsy	3701
1860	Betsy	3709
	Betsy	3915
1872	Betsy Ann	3233
1819	Betsy Augusta	338
1829	Betsy Jane	1814
1813	Betsy Kimball	796
1766	Betty	2162
1763	Billey	67
1850	Burnham Sherwood	1377
1867	Cady Alberta	1181
1830	Caleb Ricker	2398
1799	Calvin	3432
1839	Calvin	909
1852	Calvin P.	3151
1847	Calvin R.	1944
1861	Capitola	2958
1620	Capt.	3988
1863	Carleton	1048
1847	Carlton Kimball	958
1826	Caroline	3551
1850	Caroline	912
1832	Caroline Frances	2422
1843	Caroline Madora	1872
1834	Caroline Margaret	3501
1818	Caroline Matilda	644
1843	Caroline Stearn	1017
1828	Caroline Stearns	491
1862	Caroline Stearns	1051
1822	Caroline T.	1779
1853	Carrie Augusta	775
1863	Carrie Cleon	2845
1864	Cary Homer	1281
1857	Casander	3681
1814	Catharine	375
1809	Catharine Alley	3955
1868	Catharine Baker	1054
1845	Cecelia	1997
1832	Cecelia Amanda	2608
1834	Celestia	980
	Celia (†)	1995
1865	Ceorim Goodhue	2089
1771	Chandler Baker	3021
1771	Charity	3413
1800	Charles	3672
1805	Charles	3889
1809	Charles	3442
1817	Charles	196
1830	Charles	3612
1833	Charles	3512
1846	Charles	558
1846	Charles	607
1849	Charles	627
	Charles	2556
1855	Charles	1471
1855	Charles	2788
1856	Charles	3127
1859	Charles	3682
1862	Charles	3003
	Charles	3800
	Charles	3875
	Charles	3877
	Charles	3896
1867	Charles A.	1588
1835	Charles Alfred	907
1845	Charles Augustine	2043
1810	Charles Austin	2578
1858	Charles Bartlett	670
1853	Charles Benjamin	1513
1844	Charles Carrol	2744
1870	Charles Carrol	3250
1828	Charles E.	3656

Births.	Names.	Cons. Nos.
1864	Charles E.	3146
1837	Charles Earle	2385
1830	Charles Eben	585
1850	Charles Elton	1331
1860	Charles Everett	1262
1858	Charles Farnum	1416
1832	Charles Franklin	862
1834	Charles Frederick	3058
1861	Charles Freeman	3229
1850	Charles Gordou G.	3086
1802	Charles Greene	3393
	Charles H.	2563
1860	Charles H.	2790
1861	Charles Hamilton	1280
1825	Charles Henry	3671
1868	Charles Henry	2819
1830	Charles Horace	3669
1854	Charles J.	1384
1834	Charles Leach.	737
1848	Charles Lewis.	685
1859	Charles Maurice	1974
1846	Charles Milton	2826
1859	Charles Milton	950
1859	Charles Nelson	1553
1831	Charles Pearl	650
1829	Charles Randall.	871
1831	Charles Smith.	513
1818	Charles Swan	190
1834	Charles Tappan	3674
1815	Charles W.	3836
	Charles W.	3854
1840	Charles William	746
1857	Charles William	2994
1854	Charlie.	3712
1857	Charlie R. L.	3162
1822	Charlotte.	890
1853	Charlotte Alice.	3969
1832	Charlotte Ann	2739
1821	Charlotte Matilda	638
1787	Chloe	140
1611	Christopher	3989
1823	Christopher	4011
1834	Clara	3644
1855	Clara.	1519
1857	Clara Amy.	1480
1851	Clara Augusta	3121
1833	Clara C.	2628
1861	Clara Ellen.	1456
1814	Clara J.	3481
1852	Clara Jean	667
1858	Clara Mandana.	3228
1851	Clarence Abram.	2827
1855	Clarence William	669
1833	Clarissa	3589
1860	Clarissa Clementine.	1956
1774	Clark	3773
1827	Clark Damon	870
1854	Cleveland	1877
1871	Clifford Lincoln	2071
1799	Columbus	402
	Constant	3353
1864	Cora A.	2015
1867	Cora B.	1296
1855	Cora Ella	1131
1856	Cora Ella	966
1858	Cora Eva.	1279
1858	Cora May	3200
1860	Corian	1879

Births.	Names.	Cons. Nos.
1840	Corwin	983
1769	Cynthia	3364
1806	Cynthia	3446
1816	Cynthia	787
1821	Cynthia	3385
1823	Cyrus	3550
1832	Cyrus	827
1833	Cyrus S.	3844
1868	Dalton S.	2943
1800	Damon	391
1845	Dana	2773
1742	Daniel	16
1756	Daniel	4009
1771	Daniel	85
1773	Daniel	57
1775	Daniel	58
1777	Daniel	77
1778	Daniel	3450
1793	Daniel	2288
1799	Daniel	305
1803	Daniel	434
1808	Daniel	2328
1828	Daniel	735
1839	Daniel	896
1841	Daniel	622
	Daniel	2526
1833	Daniel Frederick	514
1801	Daniel George	193
1840	Daniel Hartwell.	2742
1835	Daniel Henry	621
1820	Daniel Lakeman	789
1836	Daniel Nelson.	931
1828	Daniel Thomas.	726
1757	David	3751
1759	David	3361
1776	David	3419
1778	David	3775
1783	David	132
1805	David	3523
1807	David	1774
1821	David	439
1839	David Hanson.	2386
1871	David Scott	1571
1850	David Wesley	1945
1745	Deborah.	3998
1764	Deborah.	2161
1799	Deborah.	2217
1743	Deliverance	2137
1753	Deliverance	2169
1870	Della.	2116
1868	Delly May.	1389
1846	Denison.	1030
1822	Dexter Brewer	2601
1851	Diana Rebecca	2751
	Diodema	2882
1871	Dixey.	2808
1820	Dolly Forster.	2438
1866	Dora M.	3094
1797	Dorcas	350
1872	Duncan Harding.	3666
1726	Ebenezer	9
1750	Ebenezer	47
1768	Ebenezer	2154
1771	Ebenezer	134

Births.	Names.	Cons. Nos.
1778	Ebenezer	59
1794	Ebenezer	165
1800	Ebenezer	183
1811	Ebenezer	200
1840	Ebenezer	556
1803	Ebenezer Thompson	307
1855	Edgar A.	2014
1863	Edgar Bartlett	1401
1870	Edith	2128
1870	Edith	3665
1825	Edmond Lucien	2439
1865	Edna Elizabeth	1977
1853	Edson Dana	1333
1851	Edson Rodolf	1246
1761	Edward	3344
1787	Edward	3427
1793	Edward	3390
	Edward	3407
1836	Edward	371
1843	Edward	2541
1828	Edward A.	3568
1855	Edward E.	2077
1825	Edward Everett	647
1843	Edward Gilman	814
1850	Edward Grindall	3486
1826	Edward Hatch	2586
1838	Edward Jackson	634
1851	Edward Parker	686
1820	Edward Perkins	3959
1846	Edward Perkins	3967
1785	Edward T.	2251
1858	Edward W.	3076
1848	Edward Warren	3979
1807	Edwin	459
1858	Edwin Bryant	1878
1853	Edwin Burget	990
1845	Edwin Crosby	2908
1869	Edwin Evans	2824
1850	Edwin Lafrance	2746
1860	Edwin Lincoln	1400
1867	Edwin M.	1569
1863	Effie R.	3156
	Eleanor (†)	2141
1782	Eleanor (Lucy)	2249
1833	Eleanor Analette	641
1707	Electiacus	3993
1815	Eli	1902
1815	Eli Griffeth	2441
1846	Eli Griffeth, Jr.	2860
	Eli Griffeth	2885
1789	Eliphalet	219
1796	Elisha	3438
1817	Elisha T.	3482
1825	Elisha White	851
1745	Eliza (Elizabeth)	2143
1797	Eliza	3431
	Eliza	3796
	Eliza	3886
1809	Eliza	310
1814	Eliza	2580
1816	Eliza	285
1837	Eliza	2401
1827	Eliza A.	566
1830	Eliza A.	3579
1835	Eliza Alice	918
1841	Eliza Ann	3082
1851	Eliza L.	1014
1852	Eliza Rachel	2406
1845	Eliza Sargent	684
1846	Eliza Smith	2405
1826	Eliza Waitt	442
1666	Elizabeth	4025
1667	Elizabeth	4041
1669	Elizabeth	4044
	Elizabeth (†)	3829
1724	Elizabeth	2133
1743	Elizabeth	26
1748	Elizabeth	27
1755	Elizabeth	3369
1785	Elizabeth	1697
1799	Elizabeth	2242
1799	Elizabeth	2324
1805	Elizabeth	3403
1829	Elizabeth (Betsy)	925
	Elizabeth (†)	4043
1820	Elizabeth Adaline	2544
1813	Elizabeth Clinton	2414
1829	Elizabeth Duncan	3499
1838	Elizabeth Ebbert	1927
1850	Elizabeth Florence	878
1811	Elizabeth Foster	258
1829	Elizabeth Foster	272
1807	Elizabeth Locke	2260
1806	Elizabeth Louisa	335
1834	Elizabeth Maria	873
1861	Elizabeth Murr	967
1809	Elizabeth Randall	2504
1826	Elizabeth S.	508
1829	Elizabeth S.	2647
1853	Ella	1475
1855	Ella	1063
1859	Ella Estelle	2844
1853	Ella Frances	2053
1859	Ella Frances	3129
1849	Ella Jane	624
1868	Ella May	1978
1849	Ellen Frances	1128
1853	Ellen Hurd	2063
1828	Ellen Mar	290
1832	Ellen Maria P.	3500
1861	Ellian Albert	3130
1861	Elmer Ellsworth	1554
1856	Elmer Pym	2054
1802	Elnathan	392
1828	Elsa	2717
1859	Elva Estelle	888
1866	Elvada Jane	1578
1816	Elvira	3565
1858	Elvira	3708
1851	Elvira Ann	2992
1846	Elvira Josephine	2474
1821	Emeline	466
1822	Emeline	2584
1832	Emeline Morrill	872
1835	Emeline Sophia	495
1864	Emer	1036
1824	Emily	923
1826	Emily	924
1838	Emily	829
1853	Emily	610
1807	Emily Augusta	3394
1845	Emily Brown	877
1841	Emily Elizabeth	498
1834	Emily Jane	2769
1841	Emily Jane	756
1847	Emma	626

306 INDEX.

Births.	Names.	Cons. Nos.
1848	Emma	1874
	Emma	2002
1866	Emma Almira	3213
1865	Emma Augusta	3188
1860	Emma Estella	1320
1851	Emma Estelle	1129
1865	Emma G.	3166
1854	Emma J.	2017
1867	Emma Jane	3745
1838	Emma R.	2630
1721	Enoch	1610
1754	Enoch	1637
1757	Enos	64
1804	Ephraim Foss	2259
1869	Ernest	690
1860	Ernest Wilder	1327
1734	Esther	13
1768	Esther	70
1782	Esther	79
1814	Esther Herrick	797
1783	Esther S.	91
1862	Etta Flora	3127, 4
1867	Eugene	1882
1850	Eugene Foster	2005
1869	Eugene William	3232
1761	Eunice	66
1772	Eunice	1655
1776	Eunice	3383
1786	Eunice	1755
1805	Eunice	3468
1854	Eunice Matilda	1247
1869	Eva	1460
1868	Eva M.	3177
1854	Eva Seadora	3127, 1
1831	Eveline	631
1852	Everard Göethe	2069
1861	Everett Harmon	1574
1851	Everett Hazen	819
1852	Ezekiel Dean	2850
1786	Ezekiel Dimond	2225
1847	Ezra Bartlett	591
1857	Fannie Eliza	1226
1861	Fannie Susan	2879
1818	Fanny	3539
1863	Fanny Huntington	1052
1838	Fanny Wells	497
1794	Farnum	348
1795	Farnum	349
1839	Farnum J.	823
1851	Flora	609
1863	Flora	1118
1840	Flora Armina	2737
1866	Flora Nellie	2057
1861	Florence Ada	1975
1863	Florence Estella	3247
1866	Florence Jane	1381
1861	Florence Mabel	1481
1852	Florentine Scott	784
1857	Forrest Leroy	2810
1838	Fraisette	555
	Frances (†)	1636
	Frances	1638
1825	Frances Ann	1827
1827	Frances Ann D.	648
1829	Frances Ellen	853
1834	Frances H.	2649

Births.	Names.	Cons. Nos.
1842	Frances Jane	2652
1853	Frances Jane	1033
1833	Frances Joues	553
1849	Frances Mary	2922
1795	Frances McKay	3391
1852	Francina	2062
1686	Francis	3296 / 4015
1828	Francis	782
1830	Francis Augustus	2588
1854	Francis Lewis	965
1828	Francis Newell	803
1866	Francis N., Jr.	1388
1871	Francis S.	1603
1856	Frank	3713
1857	Frank	2789
1861	Frank	1233
1863	Frank	1482
1865	Frank	2838
1853	Frank Adelbert	2862
1855	Frank Allis	3199
1825	Frank B.	3567
1851	Frank C.	3075
1860	Frank C.	2020
1838	Frank Mellen	681
1847	Frank Orville	3677
1844	Frank Sanford	3062
1836	Frank Wayland	3502
1867	Frankey	1459
1830	Franklin	502
1832	Franklin	3533
1854	Franklin Benjamin	1034
1827	Franklin Lovejoy	2420
1863	Fred	3684
1853	Fred Augustus	959
1857	Fred Bronello	2920
1867	Fred Eugene	3265
1855	Fred Lawler	3069
1852	Fred W.	3705
1866	Frederic Oscar	3132
1785	Frederick	217
1792	Frederick	164
1850	Frederick Arthur	3063
1850	Frederick Arthur	3678
1855	Frederick Augustus	2752
1870	Frederick Daniel	1121
1849	Frederick Gates	2774
1839	Frederick J.	1870
1856	Frederick Warren	698
1830	Frederick Wingate	867
1851	Frederika Jane	3604
1825	Freeman	2305
1830	Freeman	3658
1858	Fremont	1025
1825	Fulsom Brown	802
1850	Gardiner	1350
1850	Gardner Bryant	1324
1816	Gardner Kimball	798
1831	Gayton Osgood	273
1800	George	2283
1815	George	189
1823	George	197
1827	George	583
1829	George	943
1834	George	3961
1844	George	557

Births.	Names.	Cons. Nos.
1844	George	3515
1846	George	3702
1848	George	3703
	George	2525
	George	2555
	George	2564
	George	3857
	George	3929
1856	George A.	1544
1842	George Addison	2387
1843	George Albert	2772
1847	George Albert	750
1835	George Chesley	2735
1846	George Dexter	3085
1825	George Duncan	3498
1871	George E.	1297
1867	George Edward E. L.	834
1846	George F.	3849
1837	George Farrington	886
1797	George Footman	2255
1799	George Footman	2256
1849	George Francis.	608
1868	George G.	3147
1855	George Hamilton	3046
1840	George Harrison	1816
1834	George Hazen	587
1850	George Henry	1448
1822	George Johnson	2507
1848	George Lakeman	1317
1849	George Milton	946
1829	George Moody	794
1836	George S.	3594
1832	George Sullivan	2467
1830	George W.	3653
1846	George W.	2897
1858	George W.	1386
1827	George Warren	903
1870	George Warren	1148
1805	George Washington	3953
1824	George Washington	2585
1825	George Washington	2602
1832	George Washington	2719
1837	George Washington	895
1845	George Washington	1873
1868	George Washington	3255
1822	George William	850
1863	George William	1301
1836	George Williams	2462
1856	George Williams	2926
1854	Georgia Ella	785
1840	Georgiana	920
1841	Georgianna	3601
1849	Georgianna Marilla	2801
1855	Georgie Antoinette	3087
1869	Gertrude	1561
1800	Gideon	4003
1780	Gilbert	3762
1832	Gilbert B.	3580
1825	Gilman H.	4012
	Grace	3878
1796	Grace	3884
1871	Gracie Bell	2059
1816	Greenwood	437
1844	Greenwood Charles	944
1776	Griffin	3774
1726	Grindall	3328
1755	Grindall	3341
1767	Grindall	3352

Births.	Names.	Cons. Nos.
1822	Grindall	3386
	Grindall	3409
1797	Guy	3399
1864	Halmer Emmons	1555
1836	Hamilton	738
1773	Hamilton Davidson	86
1829	Hamilton Dimond	2421
1850	Hamilton Eugene	1272
1682	Hannah	3312
1728	Hannah	1613
1734	Hannah	2136
1750	Hannah	3358
1754	Hannah	2157
1755	Hannah	1647
1756	Hannah	1663
1757	Hannah	2172
1758	Hannah	65
1760	Hannah	2151
1764	Hannah	68
1773	Hannah (Anna)	100
1773	Hannah	2200
1776	Hannah	88
1781	Hannah	3949
1783	Hannah	60
1784	Hannah	2250
1787	Hannah	61
1787	Hannah	141
1790	Hannah	1683
1791	Hannah	2287
1792	Hannah	2214
1796	Hannah	166
1797	Hannah	304
1800	Hannah	3440
1802	Hannah	194
1808	Hannah	3469
1820	Hannah	505
1825	Hannah	2410
1857	Hannah	1477
1857	Hannah	2065
1865	Hannah	2067
	Hannah (†)	1133
	Hannah	2221
	Hannah	3881
	Hannah	3888
1828	Hannah Adams	2547
1817	Hannah Dow	2416
1801	Hannah Eveline	225
1837	Hannah Jane	588
1838	Hannah Jane	745
1831	Hannah Porter	3588
1811	Hannah Smith	187
1824	Hannah Tukey	1780
1788	Hardin W.	3996
1855	Hardy L.	3510
1841	Harlan Page	2722
1755	Harmon	3994
1799	Harriet	182
1799	Harriet	223
1837	Harriet Angeline	2736
1815	Harriet Ann	1789
1838	Harriet Ann	562
1838	Harriet Ann	739
1841	Harriet Ann	887
1830	Harriet Augusta	649
1823	Harriet Eliza	646
1837	Harriet Isabella	642

Births.	Names.	Cons. Nos.
1836	Harriet Mariah	496
1833	Harriet Smiley	934
1835	Harriette	633
1845	Harrison	1029
1864	Harry O.	3176
1836	Harvey Hartson	2469
1828	Hattie	3611
	Hattie	2881
1862	Hattie Florence	1321
1854	Hattie Louisa	2835
1869	Hattie Maria A. C.	835
1801	Hazen	351
1820	Hazen	191
1834	Hazen	561
1857	Hazen Fayette	617
1845	Helen	623
1839	Helen Carrol	813
1845	Helen Louisa	3068
1832	Helen Mar	3598
1834	Heman Jason	2740
1825	Henrietta	501
1832	Henrietta B.	2648
1835	Henrietta M.	3845
1817	Henrietta P.	3837
	Henrietta P.	3852
1642	Henry	3282
1676	Henry	3804
1686	Henry	3297 / 4016
1826	Henry	2447
1852	Henry	628
1854	Henry	2699
	Henry	2565
	Henry	3788
1839	Henry Augustus	3061
	Henry Augustus	2000
	Henry B.	3928
1866	Henry C.	3157
1848	Henry Elwin	773
1841	Henry Grenville	3676
1801	Henry Hardy	3401
1821	Henry Hill	2553
1841	Henry O.	3596
1830	Henry Russell	3387
1862	Henry Russell	3491
1856	Herbert J.	2019
1858	Herbert Sargent	699
1869	Herbert Sewall	1106
1843	Hester	1996
1858	Hetta Louise	3070
1831	Hiram	560
1866	Hiram	1134
1831	Hiram Crammer	905
1844	Hiram Eugene	2749
1796	Hiram G.	3995
1810	Hiram Richard	3997
1815	H. N.	3777
1836	Homer	3513
1848	Homer C.	2913
1800	Hopley	3467
1826	Horace	2568
1848	Horace Edward	961
1834	Horace Herrick	2468
1848	Horace Sanborn	2684
1822	Horatio	791
1836	Horatio Gates	1815
1857	Horatio McLeod	2070
1820	Hosea	1905

Births.	Names.	Cons. Nos.
1865	Howard Winslow	1487
1774	Ichabod	3448
1817	Ichabod	3636
1860	Ida	3002
1861	Ida	3164
1854	Ida B.	2899
1850	Ida Belle	2861
1854	Ida Blanchard	1206
1868	Ida Botsford	1556
1860	Ida Isadore	2078
1849	Ida Jane	1323
1855	Ida Jane	2843
1861	Ida Maria	688
1871	Ida May	2812
1853	Inez R.	2915
1859	Ira Augustus	687
1865	Ira Willie	2700
1856	Iris Oleva	1398
1855	Irving	1023
1749	Isaac	2146
1771	Isaac	2199
1772	Isaac	3417
1783	Isaac	343
1799	Isaac	2295
1823	Isaac	440
1855	Isaac	3680
	Isaac	3885
1839	Isaac A.	2654
1842	Isaac A.	2655
1852	Isaac P. P.	3160
1808	Isaac Randall	2293
1827	Isaac Randall	2635
1837	Isaac Thomas C.	2662
1849	Isabel Gertrude	1204
1853	Isadore Frances	1130
1869	Isetta	2058
1757	Israel	2158
1793	Israel	2228
1823	Israel	1906
1840	Israel Fox	875
1827	Israel Morris	2458
1692	Jacob	3746
1731	Jacob, Jr.	3747
1753	Jacob	3749
1803	Jacob Kittredge	2258
1833	Jacob Pickering	1917
1838	Jacob Pickering	1919
1643	James	3283 / 4014
1685	James, Jr.	4017
1748	James	3772
1752	James	2147
1769	James	124
1780	James	3776
1782	James	1696
1791	James	2227
1791	James	2280
1794	James	2241
1804	James	393
1806	James	4000
1812	James	2342
1816	James	2331
1842	James	2847
	James	3816

Births.	Names.	Cons. Nos.
	James.......................	3818
	James.......................	3891
1836	James Addison.............	744
1868	James Alexander..........	1209
1846	James Allison.............	2750
1855	James Alvin...............	1379
1838	James Augustus...........	3060
1827	James Cox.................	852
1869	James Fred................	3190
1839	James Harris..............	276
1853	James Henry..............	1453
1829	James Lawrence...........	492
1824	James Monroe.............	468
1835	James Monroe.............	2720
1826	James Orin................	2711
1840	James S...................	3742
1812	James W..................	3649
1808	Jane.......................	1752
1825	Jane.......................	915
	Jane.......................	2884
	Jane.......................	3897
1824	Jane France...............	3542
1791	Jane Thompson............	3389
1863	Jane Towne................	3230
1850	Jay........................	2061
1793	Jemima....................	3458
1871	Jennett Addie F.	1563
1865	Jennie.....................	1302
1856	Jennie Elizabeth...........	1064
1864	Jennie Joanna.............	1575
1790	Jeremiah..................	2279
1801	Jeremiah..................	2325
1816	Jeremiah Ames............	2450
1824	Jeremiah Farnum.........	809
1794	Jeremiah Holmes..........	378
1853	Jerome Sawyer............	1404
1831	Jerusha Augusta...........	811
1793	Jesse......................	3397
1808	Jesse......................	373
18.9	Jesse......................	4013
1830	Jesse Sanborn..............	2306
1864	Jessie.....................	614
1869	Jessy Bell.................	3268
1839	J. Henry..................	3778
1829	Joanna....................	826
1843	Joanna Brooks.............	999
1825	Joanna Farnham..........	1914
1834	Joanna Farnum...........	806
1814	Joanna Oram.............	2343
1685	Job........................	1606
1712	Job........................	6
1714	Job........................	1607
1749	Job........................	1617
1787	Job........................	1682
1801	Job Foss...................	2257
1634	John......................	3277
1647	John......................	3284
1655	John......................	4020
1659	John......................	3286 / 4019
1660	John......................	3287 / 4028
1662	John......................	4039
1667	John......................	3289 / 4030
1668	John......................	3308
1674	John......................	3292
1674	John......................	4034

Births.	Names.	Cons. Nos.
1676	John......................	3295
1689	John......................	2129
1696	John......................	3318
1710	John......................	4
1711	John......................	5
1716	John......................	2130
1718	John......................	3326
1736	John......................	22
1748	John......................	2145
1752	John......................	48
1756	John......................	50
	John......................	3336
1759	John......................	3343
1771	John......................	126
1774	John......................	2202
1774	John......................	3418
1778	John......................	3761
1781	John......................	2248
1783	John......................	2276
1786	John......................	80
1787	John......................	1698
1792	John......................	377
1796	John......................	173
1796	John......................	389
1796	John......................	4010
1807	John......................	3404
1814	John......................	2302
1814	John......................	2595
1817	John......................	1908
1819	John......................	1778
1825	John......................	1922
1827	John......................	892
1828	John......................	866
1828	John......................	3841
1845	John......................	2683
1852	John......................	1876
1857	John......................	3490
	John......................	3379
	John......................	3781
	John......................	3817
	John......................	3823
	John......................	3833
	John......................	3876
	John......................	3937
	John......................	3942
1826	John Bennett.............	1813
1811	John Burbank.............	2413
1814	John C....................	3650
1854	John Corliss..............	820
1824	John D....................	2446
1835	John Edwin...............	855
1818	John Emerson.............	2582
1820	John F....................	3812
1856	John F....................	1385
1855	John Franklin.............	1397
1792	John H....................	1684
1856	John H....................	3093
1811	John Hanson.............	2329
1818	John Henry...............	1824
1824	John Lorenzo.............	2464
1850	John Mason...............	2834
1853	John Nason...............	2698
1867	John Newmarch...........	2823
1807	John Perkins.............	3954
1836	John Perkins.............	3964
1840	John Perkins.............	3965
1871	John Perkins.............	3987
1825	John Phillips.............	3494

Births.	Names.	Cons. Nos.
1842	John Ransom	2748
1833	John Rice	632
1836	John Ryland	981
1816	John S.	2360
1826	John S.	532
1849	John S.	2786
1823	John Sargent	2658
1794	John Smith	2215
1824	John Smith	2395
1832	John Smith	2383
1844	John Smith	2404
1844	John Sumner	2047
1845	John Tilton	749
1779	John W.	3460
1839	John W.	3661
1825	John Wentworth I.	2634
1860	John Wesley	1573
	John William	2557
1742	Jonas	3356
1770	Jonas	3416
1775	Jonas	101
1825	Jonas	2396
1854	Jonas Calvin	2814
1851	Jonas March	2802
1660	Jonathan	4038
1667	Jonathan	{ 3290 4036
1677	Jonathan	4035
1726	Jonathan	1612
1758	Jonathan	2150
1760	Jonathan	95
1764	Jonathan	3363
1765	Jonathan	97
1770	Jonathan	1654
1774	Jonathan	3382
1778	Jonathan	3420
1791	Jonathan	346
1793	Jonathan	1742
1801	Jonathan	3474
1804	Jonathan	1750
1805	Jonathan	3434
1822	Jonathan	3566
1829	Jonathan	2459
1869	Jonathan	1883
1795	Jonathan Currier	2229
1805	Jonathan D.	2292
1820	Jonathan Prescott	1912
1841	Jonathan S.	3662
1660	Joseph	4023
1669	Joseph	4042
1677	Joseph	3311
1687	Joseph	4018
1727	Joseph	2134
1751	Joseph	3367
1758	Joseph	94
1759	Joseph	2173
1776	Joseph	3449
1777	Joseph	2203
1778	Joseph	89
1782	Joseph, Jr.	342
1787	Joseph	2278
	Joseph	3890
1838	Joseph Allen	2550
1839	Joseph Allen	2551
1837	Joseph Alonzo	996
1856	Joseph Andrew	3227
1847	Joseph Dwight	817
1835	Joseph Emerson	2638

Births.	Names.	Cons. Nos.
1839	Joseph Franklin	839
1851	Joseph Fulton	2044
1867	Joseph Hazen	615
1833	Joseph Jackson	906
1835	Joseph Spaulding	2513
1827	Josephine	1828
1848	Josephine	1998
1852	Josephine	2837
1847	Josephine Augusta	2050
1843	Josephine Maria	748
1776	Joshua	3760
	Joshua	4007
1826	Joshua W.	3535
1674	Josiah	3293
1766	Josiah	3373
1792	Josiah	347
1806	Josiah	2299
1818	Josiah	2303
1832	Josiah George	2678
1840	Josiah George	2681
1823	Josiah Folsom	2363
1865	Josie	1303
1790	Jotham G.	3463
	Judeth	3827
1765	Judith (Ruth)	2153
1803	Julia	3402
1847	Julia	3509
1862	Julia A.	3155
1815	Julia Ann	3548
1821	Julia Ann	2304
1824	Julia Ann	931
1828	Julia Ann	904
	Julia Ann	2558
1843	Julia Fidelia	499
1854	Julia Maria	1334
1833	Juliette	2609
1851	Justin	1032
1841	Kate	2771
1868	Kate Sarah	1120
1667	Kezia	4031
1758	Keziah	1649
1802	King Lapham	176
1836	Laura	3645
	Laura	3795
	Laura A.	3853
1839	Laura Augusta	2471
1863	Laura Jane	1976
1861	Lawrence Arthur	1066
	Lawristan	3927
1855	Leander	1454
1861	Leander Winfield	2805
1847	Lemuel	3686
1819	Lemuel T.	3483
1818	Leonard	788
1854	Leonard Earl	2851
1814	Leonard Orcutt	3526
1817	Leonard Parker	2436
1814	Leonora F.	2359
1843	Leonora F.	2783
1827	Leverett	793
1847	Leverett Augustus	1314
1842	Leverett B.	2896
1774	Levi	1656

Births.	Names.	Cons. Nos.
1795	Levi	1743
1806	Levi	1751
1822	Levi	922
1829	Levi Augustus	1835
1830	Levi G.	1846
1867	Levi Holman	3024
1847	Lewis Harmon	1001
1871	Lilian	3258
1871	Lillian	2120
1858	Lillie	1065
1855	Lillie Augusta	1319
1855	Lilly Maude	2863
1855	Lizzie (Ellen M.)	1450
1860	Lizzie Estelle	3201
1868	Lizzie Gertrude	1290
1836	Lizzie Mary	754
1839	Lizzie May	1417
1843	Llewellyn	3602
1768	Lois (Louisa)	98
1792	Lois	1699
1798	Lois	368
1798	Lois	2290
1852	Lois Lorilla	1378
1865	Lorena	1568
1822	Lorenzo	790
1826	Lorenzo	3610
1820	Lorenzo Dow	2455
1835	Lorenzo Parker	1918
1864	Louis Vernon	1338
1800	Louisa	175
1810	Louisa	460
1825	Louisa	2733
	Louisa	3025
1833	Louisa Ann	2461
1854	Louisa Ann	2923
1827	Louisa G.	509
1811	Louisa Hamilton	312
1835	Louisa Jane	828
1834	Louisa M.	994
1839	Louise Centenaria	1928
1851	Louise Mercella	1954
1759	Lovey	1664
	Loyal L.	3792
1830	Lucetta Fall	1916
1810	Lucinda	2301
1832	Lucinda	917
	Lucius	3786
1845	Lucius Addison	758
1836	Lucretia Day	1926
1774	Lucy	3756
1826	Lucy	289
1820	Lucy Ann	531
1865	Lucy Ann	1146
1864	Lucy Colby	689
1849	Lucy Ellen	3968
1852	Lucy Gilmore	3487
1863	Lucy Hannah	2088
1823	Lucy Jane	2408
1839	Lucy Jane	2770
1830	Lucy Locke	2570
1846	Lucy Orlinah	603
1860	Luella Gertrude	2804
1864	Luella Maria	2817
1822	Luke	3638
1811	Luke Brown	461
1838	Lurinda Means	856
1778	Luther	3424
1816	Luther	3538
1825	Luther	792
1835	Luther	783
1835	Luther Calvin	1848
1861	Lutie Ella	3722
1671	Lydia	4027
1751	Lydia	3375
1789	Lydia	2286
1792	Lydia	3464
1795	Lydia	3471
1797	Lydia	3439
1801	Lydia	2296
1815	Lydia	3957
1818	Lydia	2597
1826	Lydia	2625
1842	Lydia	605
1844	Lydia	3591
1864	Lydia	1490
	Lydia (†)	2155
	Lydia (†)	2166
1830	Lydia Abigail	512
1831	Lydia Ann	880
1848	Lydia Ann	2999
1837	Lydia Ellen	516
1836	Lydia Emeline	838
1867	Lydia Frances	1478
1813	Lydia Jane	462
1833	Lydia Margaret	742
1849	Lyman Beecher	818
1842	Lyman Hinckly	2743
1870	Mabel	2125
1871	Mabel	3870
1862	Mabel E.	2791
1863	Mabel Harriet	1328
1863	Mabel Melissa	3131
1819	Madison	3637
1867	Maggie	3167
	M. J.	3811
1852	Malinda A.	1383
1809	Malvina Abigail	336
1862	Mamie Allen	3064
1838	Marcia E.	2830
1801	Margaret	2337
1843	Margaret	910
1839	Margaret Davenport	936
1812	Margaret Davis	436
1835	Margaret Jane	1939
1820	Maria	2444
1840	Maria	3508
1854	Maria Dunn	1225
1836	Maria Louisa	3059
1806	Maria S.	3477
1827	Marianne Jewett	810
1867	Marion	3664
1852	Marion Parker	1020
1732	Martha	12
1750	Martha	28
1757	Martha	1648
1759	Martha (Patty)	3371
1770	Martha	3755
1785	Martha	2277
1805	Martha	3524
	Martha (†)	3874
1835	Martha Amy	885
1817	Martha Ann	1911
1820	Martha Ann	2583
1862	Martha Ann	2816

Births.	Names.	Cons. Nos.
1845	Martha Caroline	2606
1822	Martha Elizabeth	1792
1860	Martha Ellen	1464
1847	Martha J.	1013
1856	Martha J.	2938
1823	Martha Jane	2715
1845	Martha Louisa	767
1827	Martha Potter	860
1826	Martin	3543
1839	Martin Van Buren	2402
1632	Mary (†)	3298
1660	Mary	3306
1660	Mary	4029
1664	Mary	4024
1684	Mary	3313
1715	Mary	3324
1716	Mary	3325
1724	Mary	1611
1737	Mary	23
1754	Mary	3359
1755	Mary	2171
1755	Mary	3377
1770	Mary	125
1773	Mary	3414
1780	Mary	2204
1797	Mary	3466
1801	Mary	306
1802	Mary	1749
1807	Mary	179
1808	Mary	3478
1809	Mary	3436
1810	Mary	3525
1816	Mary	2344
1833	Mary	444
1839	Mary	2721
1861	Mary	3683
1865	Mary	1067
	Mary	2001
	Mary	3303
	Mary	3824
	Mary	3879
	Mary	3887
	Mary	4002
	Mary (†)	3437
	Mary (†)	4030
1828	Mary A.	2626
1848	Mary A.	2898
1835	Mary Abigail	515
1827	Mary Adams	3578
1865	Mary Ainsworth	1053
1817	Mary Ann	2442 / 2863
1818	Mary Ann	286
1822	Mary Ann	506
1825	Mary Ann	2716
1826	Mary Ann	2465
1827	Mary Ann	639
1828	Mary Ann	861
1828	Mary Ann	916
1832	Mary Ann	2712
1847	Mary Ann	911
	Mary Ann	2883
1840	Mary Augusta	2041
1832	Mary Clough	620
1784	Mary Crocker	138
1842	Mary E.	1942
1848	Mary E.	3159
1854	Mary E.	3152
1859	Mary E.	3163
1861	Mary Eaton	1207
1868	Mary Edith	3266
1815	Mary Eliza	2449
1836	Mary Eliza	3675
1859	Mary Eliza	2878
1870	Mary Eliza	2808
1821	Mary Elizabeth	269
1829	Mary Elizabeth	584
1832	Mary Elizabeth	741
1858	Mary Elizabeth	1520
	Mary Elizabeth	3924
1849	Mary Ella	1315
1851	Mary Ella	774
1811	Mary Emeline	374
1828	Mary Esther	2560
1857	Mary Esther	2877
1843	Mary Exeline	985
1834	Mary Frances	728
1860	Mary Frances	1489
1862	Mary Frank	3710
	Mary H.	3860
1824	Mary Harris	270
1807	Mary Isabella	227
1839	Mary Isabella	602
1852	Mary Isora	1452
1843	Mary J.	1011
1820	Mary Jane	1825
1822	Mary Jane	2490
1827	Mary Jane	1923
1833	Mary Jane	854
1833	Mary Jane	1925
1841	Mary Jane	1871
1849	Mary Jane	3850
1851	Mary Jane	1332
1865	Mary Jane E. V.	833
1836	Mary Jane V.	2549
1823	Mary Jones	2599
1842	Mary Josephine	3083
1852	Mary Josephine	3045
1829	Mary L.	804
1861	Mary L.	3175
1838	Mary Lamson	926
1866	Mary Lenora	1105
1851	Mary Lizzie	3980
1861	Mary Louise	2087
1833	Mary Lucretia	494
1858	Mary Lydia	1380
1836	Mary Maria	2829
1826	Mary Mariah	469
1809	Mary Merrill	186
1841	Mary Morrill W.	590
1858	Mary Piccolomina	612
1816	Mary Pinkham	2581
1824	Mary Roxcilaua	2419
1843	Mary S.	1849
1868	Mary Sabery	2127
1843	Mary Saunderson	3966
1855	Mary Sophia	3056
1832	Mary Sophronia	2661
1834	Mary Susan	2384
1813	Mary True	1776
1843	Mary Ursula	2777
1787	Matilda	218
1830	Matilda Euela	630
1870	Maud	3257
1866	Maud Lelia	1208
	May Anna	3918

Births.	Names.	Cons. Nos.
1859	Mehetabel C.	3154
1764	Mehiteball	121
1840	Melissa	2833
1837	Mercy A.	3582
1861	Merrill Fremont	613
	Michael	3872
1761	Miles	1619
1865	Minnie M.	2916
1797	Mira	181
1798	Mira	3445
1856	Mira	611
1852	Miranda L.	1002
1783	Miriam	2224
1767	Molley	1653
1758	Molly (Mary)	51
1752	Moses	2156
1793	Moses	3429
1801	Moses	363
1837	Moses	908
1805	Moses Clement	178
1819	Moses Crosby	2506
1821	Moses Cross	339
1835	Moses F.	3570
1790	Moses Thurston	142
1828	Moses Thurston	473
1830	Moses Thurston	474
1848	Moses Thurston	988
1870	Moses Thurston	1055
1835	Moses W.	568
1843	Mulfard B.	3584
1864	Myrta Belle	1119
1864	Myrtie Elizabeth	1577
1801	Nancy	2322
1809	Nancy	2577
1812	Nancy	3956
1830	Nancy	3642
1797	Nancy Burton	2216
1802	Narcissa	3441
1841	Nason Freemen	731
1761	Nathan	2160
1796	Nathan	3520
1657	Nathaniel	3285 / 3299
1663	Nathaniel	3307
1689	Nathaniel	3317
1717	Nathaniel	3331
1756	Nathaniel	2149
1757	Nathaniel	3360
1766	Nathaniel	3380
1780	Nathaniel	3425
1795	Nathaniel	3465
1803	Nathaniel	3475
1844	Nathaniel	606
	Nathaniel	3337
	Nathaniel	3349
1813	Nathaniel B.	2358
1845	Nathaniel B.	2784
1785	Nathaniel Brackett	2210
1816	Nathaniel C.	3651
1822	Nathaniel Jackson	1913
1771	Nathaniel Stevens	56
1868	N. B. Forrest	2807
1863	Nellie Maria	3744
1828	Nelson Briggs	3668
1850	Nelson Irving	1403
1846	Nettie	3585

Births.	Names.	Cons. Nos.
1856	Nettie	3707
1866	Nettie E.	2942
1801	Newton	3433
1640	Nicholas	3991
	Noel	3803
1830	N. S. (Rev.)	3758
	O. A. (Mrs.) (†)	3995
1766	Obadiah	3754
1862	Obed	1516
1865	Octavia	1881
1785	Olive	3454
1794	Olive	1759
1797	Olive	1700
1812	Olive	2594
1826	Olive Ball	2509
1826	Olive M.	3843
1798	Oliver	390
1810	Oliver	2284
1847	Orange Scott	987
1812	Orchard Cook	2579
1834	Orlando James	2493
1836	Orlando Leman	995
1842	Ormond	984
1832	Oro	3613
1836	Osmyn (Osmond)	807
1834	Osmyn Eaton	812
1815	Otis	3635
1706	Owen (Owin)	3820
1720	Owen	3821
1790	Owen	3834
	Owen	3830
1819	Owen	3838
1770	Parker	3381
1812	Parker R.	3480
1859	Parley	1035
1789	Patience	2239
1790	Paul	1757
1798	Paul	2321
1790	Paul March	2213
1832	Paul March	2399
1850	Pearly Randall	3126
1784	Peggy	1681
1796	Peleg (Pelek)	3874
1859	Perry Henderson	1399
1798	Persis	167
1799	Persis	3473
1670	Peter	3309
1700	Peter	3320
1824	Peter A.	2624
1739	Phebe	24
1752	Phebe	3748
1766	Phebe	69
1771	Phebe	122
	Phebe (†)	120
1822	Philander Mortimer	2456
1831	Philena Fairfield	2734
1672	Philip	3310
1740	Philip	3355
1769	Philip	3412
1822	Philip	3541
1834	Philip	3529
1848	Philura	1447
1852	Philura Emma	1449
	Phinehas	2566

Births.	Names.	Cons. Nos.
1773	Polly	87
1774	Polly	2245
1781	Polly	1680
1782	Polly	3422
1784	Polly (Mary)	1754
1787	Polly (Mary)	2211
1803	Polly	2297
1811	Polly	2505
1814	Polly	2330
1828	Polly	3641
1711	Priscilla	3322
1745	Priscilla	3339
1799	Priscilla	369
1837	Prudence Lavinia	275
1842	Purlona Jane	998
1671	Rabina	4033
1782	Rachel	131
1828	Rachel Briggs	2510
1870	Ralph Nason	1264
1840	Randolph Marshal	927
1656	Rebecca	4037
1802	Rebecca	2291
1816	Rebecca	2435
	Rebecca (†)	3357
1801	Rebecca Adaline	224
1803	Rebecca Eveline	226
1836	Rebecca M	2629
1773	Rebekah	75
	Reuben	3790
	Reuben	3798
1763	Rhoda	96
1829	Rhoda	2511
1820	Rhoda Hoit	800
1634	Richard	3276
1781	Richard	3873
1849	Richard Corydon	1019
1863	Richard Elmer	1457
1864	Richard Elmer	1458
1825	Richard Sanborn S.	2659
1849	Rinaldo Scott	2919
1839	Ripley	874
1632	Robert	3298
1670	Robert	3291 / 4043
	Robert	3822
	Robert	3828
	Robert	3894
	Robert	3941
1854	Robert	1352
1830	Robert Crawford	3842
1871	Robert Edmund L.	2030
1831	Robert Jones	2548
1820	Robert Knowlton	2417
1863	Robert Lee	1880
1869	Rollin	1570
1855	Rosa	1476
1858	Rosa	1353
1857	Rosa E.	1015
1863	Rose Grovenor	2931
	Ross	3802
1848	Roswell Hopkinson	1330
1818	Roxana	2361
1837	Roxana Alden	554
1819	Rufus Anderson	268
1688	Ruth	3315
1689	Ruth (†)	3316

Births.	Names.	Cons. Nos.
1719	Ruth	3334
1776	Ruth	129
	Ruth	3300
1861	Ryland	1027
1825	Sabina	781
1841	Sabina Emily	2042
1827	Sabra M.	822
	Salinda	3916
1809	Sallie Webster	257
1769	Sally	84
1779	Sally	1679
1795	Sally	3398
1803	Sally	2326
1810	Sally	195
1835	Sally	2680
	Sally	3351
	Sally	3883
1802	Sally Hazen	184
1839	Sally Omenia	2639
1832	Samantha	471
1844	Samantha Frye	2473
1674	Samuel	1
1674	Samuel	3294
1706	Samuel	3
1730	Samuel	18
1730	Samuel	1614
1754	Samuel	1662
1754	Samuel	2148
1754	Samuel	3340
1767	Samuel	54
1770	Samuel	99
1781	Samuel	2223
1783	Samuel	2205
1788	Samuel	1756
1796	Samuel	367
1797	Samuel	2282
1801	Samuel	2218
1802	Samuel	403
1804	Samuel	2327
1805	Samuel	170
1805	Samuel	2298
1818	Samuel	504
1823	Samuel	1921
1827	Samuel	2397
1828	Samuel	825
1831	Samuel	2768
1847	Samuel	2785
1855	Samuel	2064
1866	Samuel	2818
	Samuel	3350
	Samuel	3807
	Samuel	3832
	Samuel	3936
	Samuel	3940
	Samuel	3946
	Samuel	4005
1821	Samuel Archer	645
1824	Samuel B.	507
1806	Samuel Dana	2340
1866	Samuel George	3231
1831	Samuel Henry	2307
	Samuel Hutchins	2524
1824	Samuel L.	3639
1795	Samuel Locke	2254
1820	Samuel Newmarch	2362
1824	Samuel R.	3840

Births.	Names.	Cons. Nos.
1791	Samuel Spofford	220
1823	Samuel Webb	2633
1839	Sanford Eli	864
1634	Sarah (†)	3277
1656	Sarah	4021
1659	Sarah	3305
1665	Sarah	4040
1716	Sarah	7
1731	Sarah	2135
1758	Sarah	3378
1759	Sarah	29
1762	Sarah	1651
1770	Sarah	71
1777	Sarah	2246
1784	Sarah (Sally)	2209
1788	Sarah	345
1791	Sarah	81
1793	Sarah	143
1795	Sarah	3430
1796	Sarah	222
1804	Sarah (Sallie)	1773
1819	Sarah	1791
1819	Sarah	3549
1822	Sarah	288
1832	Sarah	3546
	Sarah (†)	1615
	Sarah	3302
	Sarah	3329
	Sarah	3819
	Sarah (†)	3872
	Sarah	3880
	Sarah	3943
	Sarah	3945
1824	Sarah Abba	2710
1857	Sarah Adelaide	1946
	Sarah Alice	3858
1820	Sarah Ann	849
1829	Sarah Ann	443
1830	Sarah Ann	2718
1856	Sarah Anna	1335
1822	Sarah B.	3652
1854	Sarah Bartlett	668
1822	Sarah Caroline	2418
1817	Sarah Clement	636
1804	Sarah Crosby	2502
1833	Sarah Elizabeth	3963
1836	Sarah Elizabeth	729
1836	Sarah Elizabeth	2494
1840	Sarah Elizabeth	517
1842	Sarah Elizabeth	1123
1824	Sarah Farrar	340
1849	Sarah Frances	2991
1856	Sarah Frances	1973
	Sarah Frances	3917
1830	Sarah George	619
1859	Sarah Inez	2055
1835	Sarah Isabella	651
1829	Sarah Jane	567
1829	Sarah Jane	3587
1861	Sarah Jane	1026
1819	Sarah Jones	2543
1845	Sarah Lavancia	816
1867	Sarah May	3986
1828	Sarah Melissa	1834
1841	Sarah Mitchell	747
1843	Sarah Omenia	2640
1860	Scott	1994
1870	Scott	1602

Births.	Names.	Cons. Nos.
1857	Scott Montez	2803
1830	S. Edward	3569
	Searle	3408
1850	Seraphine	947
1871	Seth Albert	1107
1824	Seth Taylor H.	2491
1797	Sewall	145
1861	Seward	1047
1851	Sherwin Tip	989
1850	Shubal Dixon	962
1755	Sibel	3750
1849	Silas Holman	3125
1760	Silence	3362
1780	Simeon	3451
1839	Simeon Tozier	1941
1807	Simon M.	3647
1865	Smith Spalding	3023
1797	Sollis	144
1819	Sollis	465
1854	Sollis	1021
1867	Sollis Shelton	1069
1746	Solomon	2139
1751	Solomon	2168
1794	Sophia	172
1804	Sophia	398
1845	Sophia Frances	928
1827	Sophia Locke	2569
1840	Sophronia	2895
1823	Sophronia Maria	2452
1759	Sorana	3752
1761	Squire	3753
1849	Stanley Woodbury	1245
1819	Stella Almira	2451
1669	Stephen	4026
1703	Stephen	2
1729	Stephen	11
1744	Stephen	2138
1750	Stephen	2167
1754	Stephen	49
1759	Stephen	2159
1768	Stephen	83
1775	Stephen	76
1775	Stephen	128
1782	Stephen	216
1783	Stephen	137
1785	Stephen	139
1805	Stephen	308
1807	Stephen	3435
1817	Stephen	464
1820	Stephen	287
1842	Stephen	683
	Stephen	3789
	Stephen	3794
1818	Stephen Chandler	799
1835	Stephen Henry	743
1824	Stephen Otis	2508
1840	Stephen Walter	997
1776	Sullivan	3757
1828	Sumner	3544
1719	Susan	1609
1746	Susan	1616
1803	Susan	169
1820	Susan	3540
1837	Susan	910
	Susan	3855
	Susan	3895
1821	Susan Abby	2598
1848	Susan Adaline	2745

Births.	Names.	Cons. Nos.
1858	Susan Adaline	3245
1869	Susan Adelaide	3492
1821	Susan C.	3839
1824	Susan Caroline	2545
1826	Susan Elizabeth	1833
	Susan F.	3947
1830	Susan Helen	3673
1822	Susan M.	2445
1658	Susanna	4022
1757	Susanna	3370
1773	Susanna	1676
1791	Susanna	3457
	Susanna (†)	3828
1765	Susannah	1652
1868	Susie C.	2007
1839	Swift	3514
1802	Sybil	397
1819	Sybil	438
1847	Sylvester	1348
1842	Syrena	2403
	Tabitha	3301
1789	Tamson	2207
1786	Theodore	344
1835	Theodore Watson	1868
1640	Thomas	3992
1664	Thomas	3288
1718	Thomas	3332
1741	Thomas	25
1762	Thomas	3372
1763	Thomas	53
1769	Thomas	55
1775	Thomas	1677
1784	Thomas	3453
1810	Thomas	1775
1818	Thomas	3958
	Thomas	3346
	Thomas	3783
	Thomas	3801
	Thomas	3805
	Thomas	3809
	Thomas	3814
	Thomas	3825
	Thomas	3831
	Thomas	3939
1830	Thomas Brown	470
1813	Thomas F.	3835
1847	Thomas Gage	1127
1844	Thomas H.	1943
1780	Thomas K	90
1819	Thomas King	530
1825	Thomas Lewis	441
1842	Thomas O.	3847
1848	Thomas Taylor	1031
1746	Timothy	3357
1803	Ursula	2338
	Valentine	3948
1783	Valentine	3950
1790	Vesta	3456
1869	Viola Belonia	2122
1845	Vitalis S.	1012

Births.	Names.	Cons. Nos.
1817	Walter	1790
1856	Walter	1024
1861	Walter Ellsworth	2056
1869	Walter Lucius	1304
1826	Walter McDonald	932
1831	Walter Scott	640
1849	Walter Sweeny	696
1804	Warren	177
1805	Warren	399
1853	Warren	948
1843	Warren Hazen	564
1852	Warren Henry	913
1831	Warren William	2460
1800	Washington	396
1824	Wellington	891
1783	Wellwood	3815
1846	Willard	2849
1636	William	3279
1637	William	3280
1640	William	3281
1721	William	2132
1740	William	15
1763	William	3345
1766	William	3871
1767	William	3411
1772	William	2244
1781	William	2275
1785	William	3951
1792	William	2252
1794	William	221
1794	William	3519
1802	William	1772
1806	William	2503
1814	William	284
1816	William	2596
1829	William	3528
1830	William	3545
1838	William	569
1840	William	682
1843	William	2848
1848	William	1349
1857	William	1472
1864	William	3004
	William	3780
	William	3813
	William	3892
	William	3926
	William	4004
	William	4006
	William	4008
1837	William A.	2650
1834	William Addison	753
1837	William Addison	2741
1839	William Addison	730
1869	William Addison	3249
1837	William Alonzo	1940
1816	William Augustus	1830
1836	William B.	3517
1850	William B.	2914
1832	William Ball	2512
1826	William Bartlett	271
1797	William Belcher	3392
1862	William Brown	1227
1828	William Buzzell	1908
1824	William Carl	2453
1867	William Cate	2995
1854	William David	1955
1858	William Everett	3022

Births.	Names.	Cons. Nos.
1852	William F.	2787
1842	William Franklin	943
1860	William Franklin	2815
1865	William Franklin	1507
1810	William H.	3479
1839	William Harrison	857
1835	William Henry	2562
1842	William Henry	1929
1842	William Henry	3590
1867	William Henry	1147
	William Hooper	4001
1848	William Howard	3120
1814	William James	313
1819	William James	637
1849	William James	768
1868	William Lewis	968
1830	William Moody	2636
1844	William O.	3848
1854	William Parker	2085
1861	William R.	1387
1835	William S. B.	2653
1822	William Thomas	3497
1835	William Thomas C.	881
1809	William V.	3405
1851	William Victor	2052

Births.	Names.	Cons. Nos.
1851	William Walter S.	1205
1854	William Wendall	1325
1827	William Worster	1915
1863	Willie Franklin	1104
1862	Willie Freeman	3127, 3
1862	Willie Henry	3212
1865	Willie Sargent	1292
1849	Willie T.	2858
1855	Willie Waldo	697
1866	Willis	1282
1859	Willis Calef	2086
1856	Willis Everett	1405
1871	Willis Leslie	2123
1848	Willis Smith	2990
1749	Winthrop	2140
1754	Winthrop	2170
1794	Winthrop	2253
1826	Winthrop	2546
1834	Winthrop	2571
1800	Zebedee Snell	3522
1783	Zilpha	3426
1798	Zophar	3521

INDEX II.

EXPLANATION AND SUMMARIES.

THIS Index includes the names of all lineal descendants, male and female, of the original ancestors in the foregoing records, who bore *other names;* also, the names of all persons who became connected by marriage with the heads or any of the branches of the families traced.

The surnames are first alphabetically arranged, and under each the Christian names, also in alphabetical order, followed by the *consecutive numbers* at or under which each name is found with dates of births or marriages, if ascertained. When the Christian name of the person uniting in marriage is unknown, its place in the Index is supplied by the contractions "Mr.," "Mrs.," or "Miss."

The whole number of names in this Index is 4,835, distributed as follows:—

Descendants in Part I	1,294	
" " II	995	
" " III	668	
" in the App.	116	
Whole number of descendants		3,073
Connected by marriage in Part I	685	
" " " " II	394	
" " " " III	459	
" " " in the App.	224	
Whole number connected by marriage		1,762
Sum total, as above		4,835

Adding to these numbers those found in Index I, we have a final summary as follows: —

The ancestor and his descendants of every name in Part I . . 2,041
    "   "   "   "   "   "   " II . . 1,207
    "   "   "   "   "   "   " III . . 1,223
    " ancestors and their   "   "   " in the App. . . 659
    Whole number of ancestors and their descendants 5,130
Persons connected by marriage in Part I 688
    "   "   "   "   " II 397
    "   "   "   " III 463
    "   "   " in the App. 238
    Whole number of persons connected by marriage 1,786

Total number of individuals whose names are recorded in the book and
    referred to in the Indexes 6,916

Names.	Cons. Nos.
Abbot Anner	824
Abbott Mary	2759
Mary B. (Mrs.)	1479
Abdy Matthew	3301
Adams Alfred	1433
Almeda	2968
Benjamin	2442
Charles Franklin	1434
Eleanor	2967
Erastus	2962
Flavilla	2965
Florence Louise	2104
Freddie	3225
George K.	203, 3
Henry C.	3508
James	3242
John	3018
Joseph	2964
Justus	2963
Lucy	1289
Mabel Frances	2103
Mary	3423
Newton E.	2102
Oriann	3016
Orilla	2964
Priscilla	2966
Rachel	3017
Sarah	3019
Seth	3015
Walter Arthur	3243
William	2961
William	3222
Akers Arthur W.	237, 6, (1)
Ettie P.	237, 6, (3)
Fred C.	237, 6, (4)
Henry S.	237, 6, (5)
Leslie M.	237, 6, (2)
Samuel	237, 6
Albee Aurel	1966
Edwin	1968
Frederick True	1969
Joseph Tozier	1970
Mary Eliza	1971
William Runnells	1967
Alden Nancy	552
Allard Alanson	1625, 1, (4), I
Dana	1625, 1, (4), IV

Names.	Cons. Nos.
Allard Harrison R.	1625, 1, (4), VI
Joanna M.	1625, 1, (4), III
Mary Ann	1625, 1, (4), II
Mayhew C.	1625, 1, (4), V
Stephen	1625, 1, (4)
Allen Mary	2623
Mary Denton	207, 4
Allred Albert Milton	2427, 2, (3)
Charles Rich	2427, 2, (5)
Miriam Amilla	2427, 2, (4)
Neron Alonzo	2427, 2, (1)
Pratt Dimon	2427, 2, (6)
Reddick Newton	2427, 2
Willard Neas	2427, 2, (2)
Alward Margaret	914
Ames Arthur Edwin	1168
Asa	1166
Ezra Asa	1169
Lucinda Frances	1488
Luella Pamelia	1167
Lydia (Mrs.)	1641
Rufus	3945
Anderson Charles Carlton	211, 2, (2), II
Charles Robert	211, 2, (2)
David Albert	211, 2, (2), IV
Frank Herbert	211, 2, (2), III
Mr.	424
Nancy	207
William H.	211, 2, (2), I
Armstrong Harvey C.	2889
Jeddie	2889, 1
Kosie	2889, 2
Arnold Albert	3607
Alice E.	229, 1, (2), II
Annie Louise	3607, 4
Betsy T.	229, 4
Charles Edmund	2855
Charles Williams	2852
Clara A.	229, 1, (8)
Edith V.	229, 1, (9)
Edwin	3607, 3
Eunice Runnels	229, 1, (4)
Eunice Runnels	229, 2
Flora	229, 1, (2), I
Frank	3607, 1
George Harvey	2856
Hannah C.	229, 3

Names.	Cons. Nos.
Arnold Henry	3607, 2
James Henry	2853
Joseph A.	229, 1, (6)
Lavina Rebecca	2854
Lottie C.	229, 1, (5)
Maria G.	229, 5
Martha M.	229, 1, (7)
Mary E.	229, 1, (3)
Samuel B.	229, 1, (2)
Samuel M.	229, 1
Sherebiah	229
Sherebiah M.	229, 1, (1)
Atwood Mr.	2393
William	43
William, Jr.	44
Austin Earnest	2888, 1
Jacob Kittredge	2528
James	2888
Lilie	2888, 3
Samuel	2527
Sophia E.	2799
Walter	2888, 2
Averill Lois Fog	1732, 1
Trask W.	2954
Avery Dorlesca	2857
Mr.	3473
Ayer Abbie E.	152, 8, (2)
Abby A.	152, 12
Adalaide	155, 9
Adaliza	155, 11
Addison	155, 14
Alexander A.	152, 11
Alma Ann	155, 7
Almedia	155, 10
Andrew J.	152, 5, (1)
Ann Caroline	155, 4
Ann Caroline	155, 5
Annie	155, 14, (3)
Benjamin	155
Benjamin Franklin	155, 12
Betsy	150
Caroline S.	147, 4
Carrie F.	152, 8, (3)
Charles J.	152, 8, (5)
Clarissa	154
Cyrus	151, 10
Delia	147, 2
Ella Vesta	152, 8, (4)
Elmond	152, 1
Elton	155, 14, (1)
George Washington	152, 7
Hannah	147, 1
Hannah	155, 2
Harriet	151, 3
Hazen	151, 2
Henrietta	155, 6
James	148, 1
James	151
John	148
John	155, 1
John Alvin	151, 11
John Hodgman	148, 3
John Q.	152, 10
Jonathan B.	151, 9
La Fayette	155, 16
Leonard	151, 1
Loren	155, 14, (2)
Louisa	152, 3

Names.	Cons. Nos.
Ayer Lucy	151, 3
Lucy	152, 13
Lucy A.	152, 8, (1)
Mary	149
Mary	152, 2
Mary	155, 3
Mary B.	151, 6
Mary R.	147, 3
Martha M.	152, 9
Matilda	151, 4
Moses	152
Moses, Jr.	152, 4
Nancy	152, 6
Nancy	156
Roena F.	147, 5
Roxana P.	151, 7
Royal	152, 8
Sally Banden	155, 13
Samuel	157
Sarah	153
Sherman	155, 14, (4)
Simon	151, 5
William	146
William, Jr.	147
William	148, 2
William	155, 8
William P.	152, 5
Willie E.	152, 5. (2)
Zeroida	155, 15
Ayers Aziah	2197
Babb Frank Ozell	3051
Fred Sumner	3050
Henry	4046, 3, (6), I
Horace T.	4046, 3, (6), II
Ida Florence	3049
Joseph	4046, 3, (6)
Mary Sophia	3048
William Holmes	3047
Babbit James	3034
Sarah Elizabeth	3035
Bailey Bethia	3563
Cyrus Nichols	154, 6, (2)
E. A. (Miss)	155, 8
Eliza Porter	3561
Elva Julia	154, 6, (3)
Eva Jane	154, 6, (4)
Herman Alonzo	154, 6, (1)
Jacob C.	154, 6
Mary	192
Paul (Dea.)	3560
Paul	3562
S. P. (Miss)	155, 12
Willis Newton	154, 6, (5)
Baker Ann M.	3632
Caroline B.	3577
Emma A.	1645, 4, (10)
Fannie Maria	1050
Helen M.	1645, 4, (7)
Helen R.	2124
James L.	3633
John C.	3630
Lovina	884
Lydia	3586
Mr.	431
Shubael	3629
Shubael A.	3631

Names.	Cons. Nos.
Baldwin Charles Franklin	1466
Harriet Matilda	654
Joshua	652
Sarah Eveline	653
Susan Isabella	656
Thomas	1465
William	655
Ballard Rose	3721
Ballou Mary M.	2912
Bancroft Charles	359
Barker Clarence Sprague	244, 4, (1)
James	244, 1
Jedidiah	244
John Sprague	244, 3
Mary Stickney	244, 2
Warren White	244, 4
Barnard Ezekiel F.	155, 13
Sarah A.	155, 14
Barnes George	152, 9, (1)
George W.	152, 9
Barney Daniel W.	155, 9
Barrett Alfred M.	1356
Charles E.	1356, 2
Miles E.	1356, 1
Bartlett David Longfellow	1643, 10, (7)
Dwight Titcomb	1643, 10, (5), I
Elizabeth	1643, 10, (5), IV
Enoch	1643, 10, (4)
Frank Whitehouse	1643, 10, (5), II
George True	1643, 10, (5), III
Irving	1643, 10, (7), I
John	1643, 10, (5)
John Frank	1643, 10, (6), I
Jonathan	1643, 10
Joseph	1643, 10, (2)
Mary Frances	1643, 10, (4), I
Samuel Haley	1643, 10, (6), II
Sarah	1643, 10, (3)
Sarah Ellen	1643, 10, (5), V
Susan	1643, 10, (5), VI
Thomas	1643, 10, (5)
William	1643, 10, (1)
Batchelder Alice (Elsie)	1711
Carrie Abbie	1674, 1, (4)
Charles Henry	1674, 3
Elmer Greenleaf	1674, 1, (5)
Greenleaf Furber	1674, 5
Hannah Ella	1674, 1, (3)
Hannah Jane	1674, 9
James Marden P.	1674, 1
John	1666, 8
John	1714
Joseph Albert	1674, 1, (2)
Joseph Demeritt	1674, 1
Katie	1674, 5, (1)
Keziah	1713
Lora	1674, 8, (3)
Lorinda Priest	1674, 2
Margaret Ann	1674, 6
Mark	1712
Mary E.	1864
Moses	1710
Mr.	1709
Orman	1674, 4
Ray	1674, 8, (2)
Sarah Jane	1674, 7
William	1674
William Edward	1674, 1, (1)

Names.	Cons. Nos.
Batchelder Willie Orman	1674, 4, (1)
Viella	1674, 8, (1)
Bates Byron	154, 8, (1)
Clarabell	154, 8, (2)
Samuel	154, 8
Baxter Edward J.	3121
Beales Mr.	1670, 9
Bean Asenath C.	1915
Charles	1670, 4, (8)
D.	3858
Elizabeth Eastman	2970
Gordon	1635, 7
Isaac Hanson	2974
Jacob Emerson	2975
James	1666, 1, (1)
Joseph	2969
Levi Herbert	2972
Samuel	1666, 1
Sarah	2973
Sarah Bates	2977
Sarah Smith	3081
Selden	2971
Stephen	4046, 3, (12)
Walter Clark	1670, 4, (8), I
William Runnels	2976
Beck Polly	4046, 3
Becker Dana	1722, 6, (2)
Emma	1722, 6, (5)
George L. (Rev.)	1722, 6
Lizzie Pierson	1722, 6, (1)
Mara	1722, 6, (3)
Susannah	1722, 6, (4)
Beecher Henry Ward	3040
John Gregory	3034
Lilian Grace	3041
Belcher Deborah	3388
Oliver	3414
Belden Elizabeth Elvira	4046, 1, (4), III
Bennett Amanda Malvira	1673, 11
Andrew P.	3259
Benjamin Franklin	1673, 12
Elizabeth Jane	1673, 10
Emily Ann	1673, 4
Emma E.	356, 8
Eugene Albert	3261
Frank Roberts	3260
Hannah	1811
Harriett Demeritt	1673, 1
James Hollis	1673, 8
Judith Emeline	1673, 7
Louisa	1512
Lovina Dustin	1673, 3
Lucinda Abigail	1673, 2
Samuel	1673
Sarah Oleva	1673, 9
Susan Caroline	1673, 5
William Plummer	1673, 6
Berrie Lydia	3631
Berry Charles Frank	2380, 1
Cyrus	2380, 3
Frederick W.	1593
George Erving	2380, 2
George Oliver	1299
John Kenison	2380, 4
Joseph	2378
Joseph	2380
Joseph Frank	1298
Josephine Lavina	2380, 5

Names.	Cons. Nos.
Berry, Lavina	2379
Samuel March	2381
Willie Eugene	1594
Bessey, Mr.	2643
Bickford, Mary Ann	1635, 1, (2)
Bicknell, B.	3565
Billings, Mr.	3464
Bird, Mr.	3642
Bishop, Allie V.	1375
Amos T.	1364
Flora M.	1368
Helen J.	1373
Melissa A.	1372
Miron F.	1369
Thomas M.	1371
Wiette F	1374
Zilpha A.	1370
Bixby, Earnest Merle	212, 3, (2)
Moses H. (Rev.)	212, 3
William	212, 3, (1)
Blair, Mr.	1638
Blaisdell, Lucy White	2306
Blake, Jeremiah (Rev.)	2181, 2, (5)
John Carroll	2181, 2, (5), III
Blanch, Anna	3333
Blanchard, Abby Hersey	1219
Carrie Wilder	1221
Charles Kimball	1195
Charles William	1202
Charlotte Hannah	1201
Clara Lilla	1200
Elizabeth Robins	1199
Emma Frances	1220
George	455, 1
Isaac Archer	1223
Isaac Wilder	1217
Isabella Arietta	1198
Mary Maria	1197
Mary Thomas	1222
Marjery Catharine	1196
Origen	455, 3
Samuel Wilder	1218
Blazo, Amos	2374
Anna	2375
Betsy	2373
Ebenezer	2369
Joseph	2370
Nancy	2371
Nancy	2372
Blood, Adaline	1102
Addison	1100
Almeron	1099
Amanda Melinda	1098
Charles Sewall	1094
Edwin	1097
Franklin	1093
Guy	1101
Lenora Ellen	1103
Lewis P.	1092
Nathan Lewis	1095
Seth	1096
Bly, J. Peabody	155, 2
Board, Charles	4046, 1, (5), VII. (I)
Joseph	4046, 1, (5), VII
Joseph Orten	4046, 1, 5), X, (I)
Bodge, Benjamin	2346
John	1668, 2, (1), I
Bodwell, Dolly F.	237, 1

Names.	Cons. Nos.
Bodwell, Ede	118
Bolcom, Emily M.	2846
Boody, Charles Hayes	2779
Daniel Edwin	2780
Ellen Aurilla	2781
Zechariah	2778
Boone, Laura Sophia (Mrs.). 4046, 1, (6)	
Booth, Herbert Addison	1309
James	1308
Willie Earnest	1310
Boston, Gorham Parks	2042
Boughton, Etta	1858, 1
Freddie	1858 2
Jeremiah	1858
Bowers, Augustus	769
Willie Fred R.	770
Boynton, Bertha B.	3561, 1
Betsy	150, 3
Clarissa	150, 8
Daniel	3561, 2
Eleazer	150, 9
Greenleaf	3561
Hazen	150, 1
Moses	150
Moses, Jr.	150, 4
Nancy	150, 6
Nathaniel	150, 7
Samuel	150, 5
William	150, 2
Brackett, Frederick	155, 7
Priscilla	3304
Bradford, Elizabeth	3990
Olive	212
Bradley, Hephzibah	123
Sarah M.	1313
Bragden, Lucy	1337
Bragg, Anne	3625
Delia C.	3623
H.	422
Laura A.	3622
Loring	3624
Nathan	3621
Sarah (Mrs.)	865
Brainard, Annette	2875
Braman, John A.	2100
Willie R.	2101
Brashier, Mr.	424
Brawder, Malinda J.	1010
Bray, Greenleaf	3065
Hattie Eliza	3066
Brett, Polly	3634
Brewster, Mary Jennett	782
Briden, Mr.	1643, 10, (4). I
Brierly, Mary A.	2937
Briggs, Arlette L.	2674
Elizabeth	3667
Hannah R.	2613
Brockway, Annis	148
Harriet	154. 4
Jonathan	156
Lucy	151
Brooks, Adolphus L.	1006
Amanda M.	1007
Delilah D.	1008
Joanna	993
Mary Jane	1004
Rosetta M.	1005
Ruhama	981

Names.	Cons. Nos.
Brooks, Sarah C.	1009
Solomon	1003
Brown, Aaron	2641
Abbie S.	2668
Benjamin	2644
Charles	1157
Charles S.	1863, 2
Cora M.	1864, 1
Ella Maria	1158
Elmer Ellsworth	3185
Everett Eugene	3184
Frances A.	2666
Hannah	868
Hannah M.	2354
Harriet Jane	2664
Jane	458
John M.	2642
Joseph T.	1864
Martha A.	1866
Mary	388
Mary A.	1865
Mary E.	2665
Mary L.	1863, 1
Mehetabel B.	2667
Moses	1863
Omena	2645
Rebecca	2643
Robert	3183
Samuel	2663
Sarah Maria	1224
Stephen (Dr.)	1862
William	3619
William C.	1831
Bruce, Angelina	1704, 1
Charles	1704
Otis	1703
Bryant, George Fred	3073
Mary Caroline	3072
William	3071
Bullard, Aaron	294
Bullis, Henry	3505
Mr.	3504
Bunker, Abraham Runnels	2181, 2
Anna Gordon	2181, 4
Betsy Hodgdon	2181, 2, (3)
Bradbury	2177
Charles Sinclair	2181, 2, (2)
Cyrus Edwin	2181, 2, (7)
Eli	2181
Eli	2181, 8
Elijah	2182
Elisha Gordon	2181, 5
Elisha Gordon	2181, 2, (4)
Eliza Sinclair	2181, 2, (9)
Enoch Augustus	2181, 2, (6)
Gordon	2181, 3
Hannah	2184
Hannah Thing	2181, 2, (1)
Isaiah	2176
John Elbridge	2181, 2, (8)
John J.	1764, 1
Jonathan	2175
Jonathan	2181, 7
Jonathan	2183
Joseph	2180
Joseph	2181, 1
Louisa	478
Lucina	479

Names.	Cons. Nos.
Bunker, Mary Ann	2181, 2, (5)
Obadiah	2185
Sarah	2179 / 4046
Sobriety	2178
Timothy	2181, 6
Burbank, Abraham P.	1410
Alice Maria	1734, 3, (11)
Alvin H.	1407
Amos Eastman	1734, 3, (7)
Anna A.	1408
Clara Lizzie	1734, 3, (8)
Cora Ellen	1734, 3, (9)
Earnest	1409
Edward Luellen	1734, 3, (3)
Ella M.	1413
Emulous Warren	1406
George W.	1734, 3
George Washington	1734, 3, (6)
Harriet Merilla	1734, 3, (12)
Helen A.	1414
Horace Herbert	1734, 3, (5)
Laura Ann	1734, 3, (2)
Lewis Laroy	1734, 3, (1)
Sarah Kezia	1734, 3, (10)
Sewall P.	1412
Susan Fabyan	1734, 3, (4)
Walter C.	1411
Burchard, Eliza Ellen	1028
Burgess, Albert	3606
Alonzo John	952, 4
Angelie	3608
Charles Sherman	1494
Charlie H.	3724
Emeline	1498
Hattie F.	3725
Herbert Edward R.	1497
John	952
Joseph	1496
Oriann	3607
Reuben	3605
Watson	1493
William M.	3723
Burgit, Kate	2650
Burnam, Hannah	1606
Burnes, Mary Hope	2764, 1
Richard H. A.	2764
Burnham, Abigail	1635
Asenath	2782
Frances J.	2748
Miss	1687
Burns, Benajah	100
Eliza	2806
Burpee, David	116, 4
Buswell, Abigail	118, 1
Ann Seaton	118, 8
Ascenath	119, 3
Benjamin Pearl	119, 5
Betsey	116
Charles Elliot	119, 4, (1)
Charles Spofford	119, 6
Charlotte	118, 3
Daniel	115
Daniel	118
Eliza	119, 2
Eliza Elma	118, 10
Eliza Messer	118, 11
Emily	119, 10

Names.	Cons. Nos.
Buswell, Fidelia	119, 7
Isaac	118, 9, (2)
Isaac James	118, 12
James	119
James Eustace	119, 4, (2)
James Otis	119, 9
John Runnels	119, 4
Jonathan W	155, 5
Joshua	118, 5
Marianne	119, 8
Priscilla	118, 6
Sally	118, 2
Sally	119, 1
Sarah	117
Thomas	118, 4
Thomas Alfred	118, 9, (1)
William Alfred	118 ,9
Zelinda	118, 7
Butler, Albert Steele	213, 1, (2)
Arthur Milton	213, 1, (1)
Blanche Maria	213, 1, (4)
Charles Henry	213, 2, (3)
Clara Adella	213, 1, (3)
Emma Maria	213, 2, (2)
Henry	213, 2
James Milton	213, 1
Joel	213
Justin E	1420
Linnie Frances	213, 2, (1)
Nellie Martenah	213, 2, (4)
Thursa A	1421
Butterworth, John	639
Buzzell, Abby Jane	1635, 1, (3)
Betsy	1628, 2
Burnham	1635, 1. (2)
Charles Wesley	2671
Clara Hunkins	2676
Cynthia	3859
Elias Smith	2669
Emma Tilton	2675
Henry Clay	2673
James	1635, 1
James	1635, 1, (6)
James Monroe	2674
Jessie May	2674, 1
John	1635, 1, (4)
John A	1668, 2, (7)
Justin	3148
Lemuel	1628, 4
Lucretia Ann	1635, 1, (1)
Mary	1635, 1, (5)
Mary	2670
Nellie Etta	267l, 1
Oregon	3149
Sarah Carter	2672
Call, Charles Henry	1185
Emma Frances	1187
Frank Hanson	1183
Jere C	1182
Mary Ellen	1184
Willie F	1186
Callaham, James	119, 10
Campbell, Isabell	821
John L	1440
Mr	3377
Cannavan, Sarah Jane	1271
Canney, Orin W	3045
Carleton, Abiah	1641, 5
Sarah A	1329
Carlton, Abbie E	230, 5, (5)
Albion	230, 8
Ari	230, 4. (1)
Betsy P	230, 5, (3)
Catharine B	230, 9
Celenda Hovey	211, 2, (2)
Charles Warren	211, 2, (1)
Charlotte	230, 7
Charlotte	230, 5, (1)
Daniel R	230, 5, (2)
Deborah	230, 1
Elijah	230, 3, (2)
Elizabeth	230, 3, (1)
Elmer E	230, 5, (10)
Etta A	230, 5, (11)
Evens A	230, 5, (9)
James	211, 2
John F	230, 5, (6)
Joseph	230, 2
Joseph S	230
Leona E	230, 5, (8)
Leonard	79
Leroy P	230, 5, (4)
Levi	230, 4, (4)
Lewis A	211, 2, (3)
Louisa	230, 5, (7)
Marcilla	230, 4, (3)
Mary	230 3, (3)
Mary W	229, 1
Sally	230, 6
Samuel S	230, 4
Sewall	230, 4, (2)
Thomas	230, 5
Viola	230, 4, (5)
William M	230, 3
William P	230, 5, (12)
Carpenter, Annie M	1590
John	1589
Carr, James T	4013, 2
Mary S	2018
Carrico, Benjamin	3974
Carris, Albert Wyeth	1004, 3
Edward	1084
Eldridge Greenleaf	1004, 2
Eva May	1004, 8
Fanny Edith	1085
Hila Ann	1004, 1
John Smith	1004, 6
Mary	1004, 9
Rosetta Melvina	1004, 5
Rufus Tupper	1004
Ulysses S. Grant	1004, 7
William Henry	1004, 4
Carter, Benjamin	325
Benjamin	330
Benjamin Adolphus	331
Benjamin Franklin	1108
Benjamin Garvin	1115
Charles	328
Charles Franklin	1110
Daniel Reynolds	327
Elizabeth Margaret	3496
Frederick Runnels	1109
George W	329
Hamilton	333

Names.	Cons. Nos.
Carter, Hannah	326
Henry Wells	1114
John Hall	1112
Keziah	1646
Mary F.	2941
Mary Louisa	1113
Matilda C.	382, 7
Sarah Elizabeth	1111
Stephen Hamilton	332
Cary, Josiah	3315
Cate, Elvira Lydia	2980, 1
Malora Elizabeth	2980, 3
Malvina Ellen	2980, 4
Mary A.	2989
Miles Manley	2980, 2
Samuel S.	2983
William	2980
Cavenoe, Eleanor	3871
Cawley, Angeline	2016
Chamberlain, Abbie Gray	211, 3, (5)
Celenda Gage	211, 3, (2)
Daniel	211, 3
Daniel Arthur	211, 3, (6)
Edward Gage	211, 3, (1)
George William	211, 3, (4)
Grace Mabel	1235
Gustavus	1234
Hannah	503
Harriet Eliza	211, 3, (3)
Mr. (Rev.)	534
Wesley	2729
Chandler, H. C.	942
Huldah	2194, 2
Moses	1641, 2, (1), VII
Chapin, Seth	3329
Chaplain, Alpheus Washington	3178
George Franklin	3179
Horace Sanborn	3181
Martha Ann	3180
Thomas Alpheus	3182
Chase, Ebenezer, Jr.	1669, 1
Frank B.	1431
George Henry	1740, 1
George Mason	1740, 3
Isabella Eastman	1740, 2
Jonathan E.	1740
Samuel Ambrose	1432
Cheney, Anna	2454
Chesley, Abigail	1621, 1
Almira	2197, 3
Avice	2194
Benjamin	1621
Benjamin	1621, 8
Benjamin	1786
Deborah	1621, 4
Deborah	1717, 4
Elizabeth	1640
Elizabeth	2193
Elsie (Alice)	2196
Enoch	2197
George	2189
George	2197, 4
Hannah	2192
Isaac	1621, 5
Israel	1621, 11
James	1621, 7
James	1782
Jonathan	2195

Names.	Cons. Nos
Chesley, Jonathan	2197, 8
Lizzie	2197, 2
Louisa Jane	1785
Luthera	2197, 9
Lydia	2197, 6
Mary	1621, 2
Mary Frances	1203
Miles	1621, 3
Mr.	1669, 2
Nancy	1621, 10
Patty	2197, 5
Pervilla	2197, 7
Rebecca	2191
Sally Runnels	1787
Susanna	1621, 6
Thomas	1621, 12
Timothy	2190
Timothy	2197, 1
Valentine	1621, 9
Valentine	1784
William J. (Esq)	1783
Chickering, Adda L.	239, 2, (1)
Henry T.	239, 9
William Henry	239, 9, (1)
Childs, Amelia Henry	3204
George Minkler	3202
Georgianna	3205
James Arthur	3206
Julius Minkler	3203
Willey Chandler	3207
Church, Chandler K.	4013, 1
Cilley, Hiram	456
Louisa	1635, 8
Claggett, Susan	207, 1
Clapp, Mr.	3456
Clark, Abbie A.	940
Clara E.	1959
Daniel	1668, 11
Edgar A.	1958
Ella Gertrude	1964
Ellie Ruth	2950
Emma A.	1960
Florence Caroline	1965
Fred A.	2946
Hannah	2129
Hannah	2646
H. Gillie	2947
Isadora	987
John O.	2944
Lucinda Elvira	601
Lucy	2612, 3
Lucy E.	2948
Lucy J.	2945
Margaretta J.	3074
Marianni	1962
Mary	1666, 5
Mr.	1668
Mr.	1668. 12
Sarah B.	1937
Sarah Louise	1963
Sarah Tyler	214, 4
Sophia Jane	1961
Stephen M.	1957
Warren J.	2949
Clay, Hannah	1671, 5
Rachel Melissa	3128
Cleaves, Abigail	3893
Clement, Clarence A.	1959, 1

Names.	Cons. Nos.
Clement, Emma L	1959, 2
Henry	201
Mary Runnels	202
Sarah Louisa	203
William Henry	204
William W	1959
Cleveland, Mary Elizabeth	1867
Clifford, David La Rue	4046, 1, (5), I (II)
Georgie Augusta	4046, 1, (5), I (II)
Helen Frances	4046, 1, (5), I, (I)
Nancy	3851
Clogston, Thomas	2738
Close, Abel	3762
Clough, Benjamin	1764
Betsy	1768
David	1763
Jane S	599
Jerry	1765
Louisa Victoria	1764. 1
Lucinda	1770
Polly	4046. 1
Sally	1762
Susan Almira	1764, 2
Susannah	1766
William	1761
William	1767
William	1769
Coburn, John A	336
Coe, Mary Ann	1672, 3
Colbath, Francis W	2781
Colburn, Sarah	153, 1, (1)
Zabina	153
Zerah	153, 1
Colby, Ann Myra	2828
Annah Mariah	680
Eri	2414
Frank	3729
Samuel W	154, 10
Thomas	382
Colcord, Ralph	1671, 7, (3), I
Sally	1671, 2
Samuel A	1671, 7, (3)
Cole, Abbie R	214, 6
Abby Lavinia	662
Abigail	264
Ada	1533
Benjamin	201
David	1530
Ellen May	1534
Ephraim Foster	262
John Kimball	265
Kimball	259
Mary	665
Mehetabel Barker	263
Mira Ella	1532
Morris Lee	664
Norman Seaver	663
Rebecca	261
Sarah Foster	260
Theodore Ashley	1531
William Kimball	661
William Runnels	266
Collins, Elizabeth Isabella	2758, 2, (2)
John E	2758. 2
Judith	2185
Nathaniel John	2758, 2, (1)
Colomy, Abraham	2232
Carl Ervine	2798
Colomy, Charles	2235, 2
Daniel	2230
Daniel	2235
Daniel	2235, 6
Elsie (Eloy)	2235, 4
Elsie	2732
George Washington	2235. 3
Isaac	2233
Jacob	2234
James Addison	2797
James Pinkham	2235, 10
John	2231
John	2235, 1
John Frank	2795
Jonas	2235, 5
Mary Jane	2235, 8
Molly	2237
Peggy	2236
Sally	2196, 1
Sarah Elizabeth	2235, 9
Stephen	2235, 7
Walter McCann	2796
Colton, Martha	2930
Comstock, Eliza	2866
Eugene	2865
Frances Maria	2869
Frederick	2868
Henry	2867
S. Franklin	2864
Coney, Frances	3543
Cook, Jesse M	478, 1
Mabel Louisa	478, 1, (1)
Monroe	508
Cooke, Mary E	3186
Coolbroth, Edward	3913
Eunice	3912
Frank	3910
John	3911
Rhoda	3909
Rufus	3907
Samuel	3908
Coombs, Estella	1522
James	1523
James Henry	1521
Copp, Hannah	680
Corliss, Sarah E	815
Corser, Adelbert M	152, 13, (3)
Alfred	152, 13. (2)
Erastus T	152, 6
Frank E	152, 13, (1)
George E	152, 13, (4)
Maria N	152, 6, (1)
Mary E	152, 13, (5)
Rachel	618
Corson, George	386, 4
Hannah Young	2799
Courtney, Mary Elizabeth	1376
Cox, Arabella Ophelia	478, 1
Daniel Edwin	484, 3
Daniel Walter	488
Edwin Fuller	484
Elias	482
Elias Walter	486
Ella	484, 4
Eva	484, 2
Francina	479, 1
Henrietta Maria	478. 3
Huldah Maltby	477

Names.	Cons. Nos.
Cox, Jennie Ardelle	488, 1
Lizzie A.	938
Louisa	484, 1
Lucy Maria	487
Mary Jane	483, 2
Moses Thurston R.	478
Nettie Y.	483, 3
Phebe Louisa'	478, 2
Phebe M.	481
Salina Sawin	480
Sewall Fuller.	479
Sollis Runnels	483
Stephen Runnels	485
William, Jr.	475
William Arthur	483, 1
William R.	476
William Wallace	488, 2
Craffit, Sarah.	3819
Crafts, Lucy Flagg	594
Craig, Albert A.	1438
Craker, Bennett.	1359
Esther H.	1358
Francis H.	1361
John William	1355
Joseph E.	1362
Leon S.	1363
Levi.	1354
Lucy S.	1356
Mary A.	1360
Phebe W.	1357
Cram, John S.	299
Sarah Jane.	666
Crammer, Hiram S.	398
Crandall, Calvin E.	1364
Esther L.	1366
Henrietta	1347
Horace M.	1365
Willard C.	1367
Crane, Rhoda Adaline.	523
Crawford, Samuel	429
Crockett, Albina J.	255, 4
Emily	2806
Mary Catharine	2813
Crook, Alice	576, 5
Effie	576, 3
George Edward	576, 6
Gertrude	576. 4
Julia	576, 1
Louise	576, 2
Rufus	576
Crosby, Sarah	2243
Cross, Mary Jane.	3081
Temperance	2890
Crowley, Daniel	231, 4, (1)
Ralph L.	231, 4, (1), I
Cummings, James.	2755
Currie, Andrew	229, 1, (4)
Currier, Hannah	38:6
Mary.	3846
Mary E. (Mrs.)	1245
Mary E.	2697
Nettie Ardell.	1245, 1
Curry, Annette Carroll.4046,1,(5),VIII
Arabella Clough.	4046, 1. (5), IX
Benjamin	4046, 1, (5)
Frances Susan	4046. 1, (5). IV
Georgianna Bradley.4046,1,(5), VI
Hannah Augusta	4046, 1, (5), X

Names.	Cons. Nos.
Curry, John Williams.	4046, 1, (5), II
Josephine Bradbury.4046,1,(5),VII
Mary Elizabeth	4046, 1, (5), I
Olive.	4046, 1, (4)
Olive Augusta.	4046, 1, (5), III
Sophia Tebbetts	4046, 1, (5), V
Curtis, Abbie.	302
Cushing, Maria Louisa	679
Cutler, Elizabeth	1735, 3, (1)
Lyman (Rev.)	1735, 3
Lyman Edwards	1735, 3. (2)
Cutter, Abiah	213, 4
Amelia.	213, 3
Seth.	213
Cutting, Adra Lora.	237, 1, (5)
Agnes Eda	237, 1, (6)
Alura E.	237, 2, (2)
Betsy E.	237, 3, (1)
Caleb O.	237, 14
Charles E.	237, 3, (3)
Charles H.	237, 3
Charley Brown.	237, 1, (7)
Cora M.	237, 3 (6)
David	237, 5
David Homer.	237, 5, (2)
Ebenezer	237
Ebenezer M.	237, 1
Eliza C.	237, 4
Ella Adelia.	237, 1, (2)
Ella J.	237, 2, (1)
Eunice O.	237, 8
Fred Milton.	237, 1, (9)
George M.	237, 11
George M.	237, 3, (7)
Harriet M.	237, 9
Ida Mira	237, 5, (1)
Katie Elvie.	237, 1, (4)
Lizzie E.	237, 3, (5)
Louisa M.	237, 13
Lucinda	231, 1
Luella E.	237, 3, (2)
Moses Nelson.	237, 1, (3)
Moses P.	237, 12
Nellie Adelia.	237, 1, (8)
Nellie E.	237, 3, (4)
Oscar Winfred.	237, 1, (1)
Persis B.	237, 10
Rose E	237, 7, (2)
Samuel E.	237, 7
Sarah B.	237, 6
Sherman U.	237, 2, (4)
Walter J.	237, 7, (1)
William A.	237, 2, (3)
William H.	237, 2
William W.	237, 3, (8)

Dade, Miss.	1684
Daggett, Susan E.	3743
Dailey, Etta Whitcomb.	3275
George Alden	3274
Dailie, Daniel D.	3575
Sarah	3576
Daniels, Andrew.	1668, 2
Eliza	1668, 2, (1)
Eliza	1668, 2, (1), I
Henry Priest.	1668, 2, (3)
Ira Tasker.	1668, 2, (6)

Names.	Cons. Nos.
Daniels, John Colby	1671, 6, (2)
John D.	1671, 6, (4)
Joseph Demeritt	1668, 2, (5)
Maria Sarah	1671, 6, (5)
Mary Susan	1668, 2, (7)
Mr.	1668, 2 (1)
Nathan	1668, 2, (4)
Nathan Edwin	1671, 6, (1)
Priest	1671, 6, (3)
Sally Priest.	1668, 2, (2)
Danielson, Frederick	1159
Gracie Marshal.	1165
Katie Mabel.	1164
Darling, Mr.	1125
Davenport, Ammi	940
Charity	921
Georgiana	939
Nathaniel	937
Stephen Franklin	938
Davis, Annie Bernice	1287
Aurelia P.	3597
Charles F.	2181, 2, (9), II
Charlie B.	229, 5
D. F.	2181, 2. (9)
Elizabeth Lee	1122
Jasper Wingate	1288
John M.	1286
Mercy C.	3685
Mary	1604
Mary	1628, 3
Mary	2181, 2, (9), 1
Rhoda	1630, 2, (1)
Sarah	372
Tryphena	2049
William (Rev.)	2368
Dawling, Margaret M. J.	2776
Dawson, George	2672
Georgia	2672, 3
Joseph Allen	2672, 2
Mary Hannah	2672, 1
Day, Mr.	3796
Dearborn, Ann	3923
Arianna Elizabeth	4046, 1, (2), III
Louisa	212, 2
Martha A.	3067
Naomi Freeman	3118
Sarah	3856
William Henry	2567
Decker, Isadore Ida	2080
Nathaniel C.	2079
Walter Curtis.	2081
Delano, Ann M.	231, 4
Demeritt, Abigail Finett	1671, 13
Addison	1666, 4, (1)
Albert	1671, 5, (6)
Alma	1666, 4, (2)
Andrew	1628, 9
Andrew Jackson	1671, 12
Appleton	1666, 2, (8)
Benjamin Franklin	1671, 11
Benjamin Willard	1671, 2, (1)
Betsy	1666, 1
Betsy	1668
Betsy	1670, 3
Betsy Jane	1670, 8
Brackett Johnson	1666, 2, (1)
Calvin Sulden	1670, 5
Charles	1671, 5, (5)

Names.	Cons. Nos.
Demeritt, Clark	1666, 5, (1)
Daniel	1671, 7
Dorcas	1666, 8
Edward	1670, 6
Eleanor	1669, 3
Eliza Ann	1671, 2, (4)
Elizabeth	1666, 2, (5)
Emerson	1671, 5, (3)
Emma	1635, 5
Eunice	1670, 1
George	1670, 7
George	1671, 5, (4)
George Washington	1671, 7, (2)
Georgia Parsons	1666, 2, (6)
Gordon	1666, 4
Hannah	1674
Hannah Abby	1671, 7, (3)
Hannah Adalaide	1671, 7, (1)
Harry	1669, 4
Hayden	1666, 4, (3)
Jacob	1671, 1
Jacob	1671, 5, (2)
Jane	1666, 5, (2)
John	1671
John	1669, 5
John	1671, 4
John	1671, 5, (1)
John Leonard	1671, 2, (3)
John William	1671, 7, (4)
John William	1671, 7. (5)
Joseph	1665
Joseph	1669
Joseph	1671, 2
Joseph Edward	1671, 2, (2)
Langdon	1666, 2, (2)
Lois	1672
Maria	1666, 5, (3)
Mary Ann	1671, 10
Mehetabel	1669, 2
Mehetabel Ford	1671, 6
Moses	1666
Moses Odell	1666, 2
Nancy	1666, 6
Nathaniel	1666, 7
Paul	1670
Phersina	1666, 2, (7)
Polly	1669, 1
Rhoda	1670, 9
Rooksbury Brackett	1666, 2, (3)
Sally	1666, 3
Sally (Sarah)	1667
Samuel	1670, 2
Samuel Dyer	1671, 8
Sarah	1666, 2, (1), F
Sarah Jane	1671, 2, (5)
Sarah Johnson	1671, 9
Sophia	1671, 3
Susan	1670. 4
Susan	1669, 6
Susan	1673
Thomas	1666, 5
Timothy	1671, 5
William	1666, 2, (4)
Deming, Sarah Rebecca	1300
Dennett, Nancy L.	3846
Dennis, Thomas	4046, 3, (8)
Dewitt, Lydia Ann	521
Dillingham, Julianna (Mrs.)	2194, 5

Names.	Cons. Nos.
Dimmick, Mr.	3613
Dimond, Dorothy	2222
Mary	2463
Ruth	2463
Dingley, Jennett	1993
Dixon, Elizabeth Moor	960
Dodge. George Stanwood	843
Lucy Maria	3485
Doe, Huldah	2417
Dole, Jane	154, 3, (2)
Donnell, Ann Jane	582
Nathaniel	1153
Octavius	1154
Dore, Sally M.	2040
Doughty, Clarissa Ann	900
Isaac	898
Louisa Maria	901
Mahala	899
Douglass, Margaret	1739
Dow, Amos, Jr.	2792
Anna R.	2793
Caroline West	1341
Charles	2951
Lydia Ann	1340
William	230, 6
William	1339
Downs, Abigail	1805
Betsy Jane	1810
Calvin Cutter	1809
Elizabeth Ann	1898
Eunice	1893
Gershom	1799
Hiram	1896
James Monroe	1803
John	1807
Levi	1802
Louisa Chesley	1808
Lydia	1801
Mary	1895
Mary R.	1806, 1
Mr.	2312, 1
Nathaniel	1899
Paul	1892
Rachel F.	1806, 2
Sally	1891
Samuel	1894
Sarah Ann	1804
Simon P.	1897
Simon Peter	1890
Stephen	1800
William Henry	1806
Doyle, Albert Smith	2982
Catharine Malvina	2980
Elizabeth Randall	2979
Nancy Bell	2983
Thomas	2978
Thomas Stewart	2981
William Runnels	2984
Drake, Charles Brackett	1666, 2, (6), II
George D.	1930
George Walter	1666, 2, (6), I
John W.	1666, 2, (6)
Lyman D.	1933
Drew, John	405
M. M.	2764
Mr.	405
Mr.	1663
Stephen	119, 8

Names.	Cons. Nos.
Duly, Elizabeth	1720, 1
Dumbauld, Dennis Everett	1583
Frederick	1581
Loamina	1582
Dunbar, Silas	3368
Duncan, George	2194, 9
Dunfield, Carrie E.	154, 2, (2), I
George T.	154, 2, (2)
Lizzette L.	154, 2, (3)
Lizzie E.	154, 2, (2), II
William	154, 2
William N.	154, 2, (1)
Willie C.	154, 2, (1), I
Dunn, Henry Claude	231, 1, (1), II
Henry W.	231, 1, (1)
Duran, Job Runnels	1797
Josiah	1798
Samuel	1793
Durgin, Benjamin	1731
Charlotte	2842
Eliphalet	1689, 5
Ella Gertrude	1853, 1
Fannie	1601
George Edward	1853
Job	1689, 2
John, Jr.	1689
Louis	1689, 1
Louisa Mead	1693, 2
Love	1692
Lovey	1693, 1
Lydia	1733
Miles	1689, 3
Sarah	1628, 1, (2)
Susan	1732
Susanna	1689, 4
Thomas	1693
Durham, Conway	1739, 4, (1)
James M. (Esq.)	1739, 4
Dutch, Mary A.	895
Dwelley, Mary Elizabeth	879
Dwight, or Dwile, Sarah	3304
Dwinals, Louisa	2761
Dwinell, Abigail	244
James	245
Jonathan	243
Polly	246
Stephen	247
Dyer, Harriet K.	1145
Sumner	3565

Names.	Cons. Nos.
Eaches, Rachel	1999
Eastman, Abiather, Jr.	1732
Abiather	1733, 6
Abigail Hill	1730
Adaline	1733, 2
Alaysius	2760, 3
Amos	1736
Barnard Douglass	1739, 1
Benjamin Durgin (Rev.)	1732, 1
Betsy	1735
Calvin B.	1732, 5
Caroline	1732, 4
Caroline Bangs	1732, 1, (1)
Charles Henry	1739, 3
Charles Ward	1732, 1, (2)
Chauncy	1733, 3, (1)
Clara Alice	1732, 1, (8)

Names.	Cons. Nos.
Eastman, Clarissa	1733, 7
Clarissa	1737
Daniel	1733, 4
Dolly Averill	1732, 1, (3)
Edward	1981
Edward Payson (Rev.)	1739, 2
Ella May	1732, 1, (10)
Ellsworth	1739, 8
Emma Ellen	1732, 1, (4)
Frances Angela	2760, 1
Fred Langdon	1739, 2, (1)
George	1732, 3, (2)
George Freeman	1733, 10
George Vernon	1732, 1, (7)
George Whitman	2760, 8
Harriet	1738
Harriet Elizabeth	1739, 6
Helen R.	318
Henrietta	1980
Ignatius Dana	2760, 5
Irena	1740
J. Osborn	1733, 5
James	2760
James Augustine	2760, 2
Jeremiah Chandler	1733, 9
Job	1733
John	2760, 7
John Langdon	1739
John Langdon	1739, 7
Kate L.	1641, 2, (1), V
Keziah	1734
Lois Anna	1732, 1, (5)
Lorenzo	1733, 3
Louisa Snow	1739, 2, (2)
Margaret Douglass	1739, 5
Maria Cummings	1739, 4
Mary Runnels	1733, 1
Mary Sterne	1739, 1, (1)
Melvina Luella	1738, 7
Olive Jeanette	1732, 1, (9)
Otis	1732, 3
Pollie Reynolds	1732, 6
Richard	1731
Richard	1736, 1
Richard Stephen	2760, 6
Rufus Merrill	1732, 3, (1)
Samuel	1732, 2
Susan	1733, 8
Susan Durgin	1732, 1, (6)
William David	2760, 4
William Henry	1979
Eaton, Abigail	147
Annie Lawrie	322, 1, (4)
Edward Melzar	1213
Elisha H.	147, 5
Eliza Jane	1415
Eunice	2294
Fannie Fisher	322, 1, (1)
Grace Harper	322, 1, (2)
Hannah P.	1244
Harriet Ella	322, 3
Harry Wilmarth	1212
Jesse	322
Jessie Reynolds	322, 1, (3)
Lydia	979
Martha	311
Mary Augusta	1641, 2 & 6, (2), IV
Mary Estelle	322, 1, (5)
Eaton, Mary Rogers	322. 2
Melzar	1210
Samuel	322, 1
Walter Reynolds	1211
Eddy, Lucia	2194, 8
Edgates, Philinda	293
Edgcomb, Burnham	3901
Eliza	3900
Emma Jane	3903
Enos	3904
Gibbins	3898
Rachel	3899
Rhoda	3882
Rhoda	3902
Sarah	3906
William	3905
Ela, Sarah	282
Elder, Annie Gertrude	1285
Levi Leighton	1283
Willie Lincoln	1284
Eldridge, Shepard	928
Elkins, Bell D.	2181, 2, (5), II
Jeremiah	2181, 2, (5)
John	382
Sarah Frances	2181, 2, (5), I
Elliot, Benjamin Franklin	3221
Clark J.	3218
Ella	3220
Hannah Margaret	2742
Mary	3219
Mr.	1672, 2
William	116, 7
Ellis, Ann	3691
Carrie	3695
Edward D.	3733
James	3694
Jenny Lenora	3264
Lydia (Mrs.)	2500
Sarah	3693
Wally	3690
William	3692
William	3734
William A.	3732
Ellison, Comfort	1717
Mrs.	1684
Sarah	1675
Wright True	1630, 2, (3)
Ellsbury, Sallie	2115
Elmer, Eva Estelle	455, 4
Frances Adella	455, 5
George Eugene	455, 6
George Washington	455
Luella Maria	455, 2
Louisa	454
Louisa H	455, 1
Myra L.	455, 3
Richard	453
Richard Fowler	457
Roxana	456
William	445
Ely, Carrie	1739, 1
Emerson, Avis	1628, 4
Betsy	1628, 5
Deborah	1671, 5
Edwin Smith	1628, 1, (1), I, (II)
Emily	1628, 1, (1), VIII
Flora Belle	1628, 1, (1), I, (IV)
George W.	1628, 1, (1), IV

Names.	Cons. Nos.
Emerson, Hannah	17
Hannah	1628, 1, (1), II
Hannah	1628, 8
James	1628, 1, (3)
John	1628, 1, (1), V
Jonathan	1628, 3
Joshua F.	1628, 1, (1)
Margaret S.	212, 1, (1)
Martha Anna	1628, 1. (1), I, (III)
Mary	1628, 1. (1), III
Mary	1628, 9
Mary Abby	1628, 1, (1), I, (I)
Mary Frances	1635, 9
Samuel	1628, 1
Samuel	1628, 1, (4)
Samuel	1628, 1, (1), VI
Sarah	1628, 1, (1), VII
Smith	1628
Smith	1628, 1, (1), I
Smith	1628, 2
Susan	1628, 6
Timothy	1628, 1, (2)
Timothy	1628, 7
Emery, Alexander	430
Betsy	433
Clara Ella	3009
George W.	428
Hephzibah	424
Jane Ann	3008
Jonathan	3005
Joseph	423
Joseph	427
Joseph Kingman	3014
Julia A.	425
Mary	431
Melinda (Belinda)	426
Miranda	429
Moses Crosby	3013
Olive Ball	3006
Reuben	899
Sarah Augusta	3012
Silas	3007
Silas	3010
Silbie J.	2952
Susan	432
Warren H.	2951
William Cates	3011
Enos, Ann Eliza	1180
Evans, Elizabeth F.	2822
George Hill	1735, 8, (1)
George Meserve	1732, 4, (2)
James	1732, 4
Nancy	1668, 6
Samuel Eastman	1732, 4, (1)
Simeon A (Dr.)	1735, 8
Susan Catharine	1322
Wesley J.	1579
Everett, Amos	2724
Ellen Rebecca	2730
Ellovisa	2731
Etherlinda	2729
Joseph Runnels	2726
Lucretia	2728
Lucy Anna	2727
Maria	2725
Richard	2723
Susan	2738

Names.	Cons. Nos.
Fabyan, Ella Louise	1734, 4, (2)
George Henry	1734, 4, (1)
Oliver B	1734, 4
Fairfield, Harriet L.	3672
Farley, Sarah E.	1116
Farnham, Hannah	1900
John E.	212, 1, (2)
Olive	1753
Farnsworth, Addie	152, 2, (2)
Daniel	152, 2
Lucy M.	152, 2, (1)
Verona	152, 2, (3)
Farnum, Adaliza A.	957
Joanna	341
Ruth	362
Farrell, Charlie	3252
David	1140
John H.	3251
Leila Angie	3253
Mary	1823
Warren Matthias	1141
Farrington, Mr.	3643
Faught, Bethia	3573
Jacob	3571
Jacob	3574
Jacob H.	3687
L. Orent	3688
Nancy	3572
Nellie	3689
Sarah	3536
Field, Willard A.	3583
Fields, Joshua	1628, 5
Sally	1628, 1
Fish, Charles Hazen	1136
Frank Henry	1139
Hiram Francis	1137
John Ellsworth	1138
John R.	1135
Fisher, Adello	322, 1
Fisk. Mr.	3795
Sarah Blanchard	815
Fiske, Miss	1688
Flanders, Jacob N.	2934
Lucia Ann	2935
Mary Augusta	2936
Flint, Alvin	361
Flood, Samuel	1461
William Harrison	1462
Fogg, Ephraim H.	3921
George	3919
George E.	3922
Jonathan	3888
Joseph Arthur	3920
Mr.	1768
Folsom, Nancy	2357
Forbuss, Sarah	2997
Ford, Miss	3532
Forrest, Agnes	1641
Anne Ellison	1641, 2 & 6, (2), I
Edwin David	1641, 2 & 6, (2), IV, (IV)
Freddie	1641, 2 & 6, (2). IV, (III)
James Nathaniel	1641, 2 & 6, (2), IV
Kate	1641, 2 & 6, (2), IV, (I)
Lafayette	1641, 2 & 6, (2), III
Martha Randall	1641, 2 & 6, (2), V
Ruth	1641, 2 & 6, (2), IV, (V)
Samuel	1641, 2 & 6, (2)
Samuel	1641, 2 & 6, (2), IV, (II)

Names.	Cons. Nos.
Forrest,Susan Knight,1641, 2 & 6,(2),11	
Forsythe, William	2978
Fosdick, John	3305
Foss, H. D	2703
Foster, Ann	3388
Caroline Bartlett	211, 1
John K	1322
Rebekah	74
Susan C.	1829
Fountain, Emma M	3150
Fowler, Emeline	455
Fox, Daniel	1633
Diana L.	365, 2
George I.	365, 3
Joseph V.	365
Martha M.	365, 1
Miss	1630, 1
Foye, Albert	1159
Charles Eben	1161
Edward Drew	1162
Henry Albert	1160
Nellie Alberta	1163
Freeman, Elisha	3375
Herbert	3627
Freeze, Joseph M	829
French, Augusta Jerusha	1419
Eleanor	1667, 8
Elvina E.	447, 3
George W.	1418
Lizzie C.	1643, 10, (7)
Miss	1644
Mr.	1672, 2
Mr.	3422
Susannah	1720
William W.	2359
Frisbie, Capt. Thomas	2322
Frost, Susan	358
Fuller, Mr.	3402
Furber, Eliza	1666, 1, (5)
Elizabeth	2356
Harrison	1666, 1, (2)
Lydia	1666, 1, (1)
Thomas	1666, 1
Thomas	1666, 1, (4)
Zepherus Page	1666, 1, (3)
Furplus, Mr.	432
Gage, Aaron Hardy	207, 6
Abbie Frances	207, 3, (4)
Abby H.	1126
Abel	205
Abel	214
Abigail	207, 5
Abigail	211, 2
Alice Augusta	207, 3, (2)
Alice May	214, 6, (2)
Amos	211
Amos	211, 6
Angelina Matilda	214, 1
Annie S.	207, 3, (3)
Arthur Augustus	214, 2
Arthur Edward	214, 2, (1)
Ascenath	212, 5
Billy Runnels	207
Caleb	207, 1
Caroline	212, 1
Carrie Alice	214, 4, (2)

Names.	Cons. Nos.
Gage, Carrie Madora	211, 1, (4)
Celenda	211, 7
Charles	207, 2
Charles Augustus	207, 3, (1)
Charles F.	207, 7, (3)
Charles Henry	207, 1, (2), II
Charles Henry H	207, 4, (3)
Deborah	213
Elizabeth Denton	207, 4, (5)
Ella F.	207, 7, (1)
Ellen Isabel	211, 1, (1)
Ellen Isabel	214, 8
Ellen Isadore	214, 2, (3)
Emma Addie	214, 4, (1)
Emma Isadore	214, 7
Frank Hermon	207, 1, (4) II
Frederic Allen	207, 4, (6)
Frederic William	207, 1, (4) I
George	211, 4
George F.	207, 1, (3)
George Warren	211, 1, (3)
Hannah	209
Harriet Reynolds	211, 3
Hattie Tenney	211, 1, (5)
Henrietta Philena	214, 5
Henry Willis	211, 1, (6)
Herbert Edwin	214, 6, (1)
John Anderson	207, 7
Jonathan	2267
Julia Angie	214, 4, (3)
Laura Ann	212, 3
Leander	207, 4
Leander	207, 1, (2)
Louisa D.	212, 2, (1)
Lydia P.	207, 7, (5)
Lyman Berkley	214, 4
Mary Ann	211, 5
Mary Anna	214, 2, (2)
Mary Kimball	211, 1, (2)
Mehetabel	208
Mehetabel	210
Melinda Claggett	207, 1, (1)
M. Florence	207, 7, (2)
Miss	2311
Moses	2267, 1
Nancy Jane	207, 7, (4)
Otis Allen	214, 10
Rebecca Eveline	212, 4
Richard Allen	207, 4, (2)
Richard Allen	207, 4, (4)
Roscoe Wisner	214, 6
Sarah	206
Sarah F.	212, 2, (2)
Stephen	212
Susan Ardell	207, 1, (2), I
Sydney Payson	214, 9
Walter Edwards	214, 3
Warren	211, 1
William B.	212, 2
William Claggett	207, 1, (4)
William L.	207, 4, (1)
William Washington	207, 3
William Washington	207, 3, (5)
Gardiner, Mary	2642
Gardner, Joanna Angeline	522
Mary E.	1635, 9, (3)
Garfield, Laura E.	154, 2, (1)
Garland, Francis	2262

Names.	Cons. Nos.
Garland, Jacob	2261
Jacob	2263
Lorenzo Kimball	1704, 1, (1)
Sally	740
Garret, Catharine	1133
Garvin, Chauncey	4046, 3, (1)
Martha	4046, 3, (1), I
Sarah Jane	4046, 3, (1), II
Gatchell, Emery Merrill	3135
Leslie Emery	3136
Preston Ellsworth	3137
Gay, Mehetabel	147
Gayety, Edwin C.	477, 4
Francis	477, 2
Huldah Ann	477, 3
John A.	477
Mary C.	477, 6
Sarah Elizabeth	477, 5
William C.	477, 1
William Edwin	477, 7
George, Chloe	192
Lucy	484
Luella F.	483
Gerrish, Matilda	568
Getchel, Susan	1518
Getchell, Asa	416
Henry	416, 1
Sebastian S.	416, 2
Gibbs, Charles	1704, 1, (2)
Charles	1704, 1, (3)
Edward	1704, 1
Eldora	1704, 1, (1)
Julia A. M.	119, 4, (2)
Mary Dorcas	1704, 1, (4)
Gilchrist, Robert	2597
Giles, Charles H.	1626, 2, (7)
Elizabeth	1626, 2, (5)
Frank Eugene	1626, 2, (8), I
Freddie	1626, 2, (8), III
Job Randall	1626, 2, (8)
John	1626, 2, (3)
Joseph	1626, 2, (9)
Mabel	1626, 2, (8), II
Mr.	1628, 1, (1), II
Paul	1626, 2
Paul	1626, 2, (1)
Sally	1626, 2, (6)
Susan M.	1626, 2, (4)
Susanna	3338
William	1626, 2, (2)
Gillingham, J. T. (Miss)	155, 1
Gilman, Charles H.	2271, 1
Hannah	2194, 5
Hannah N.	151, 5
Jacob Knowles	1667, 2, (1)
Julia	2194, 3
Sally	2677
Gilmore, Almira T.	2391
Edward Clarence	779
Ellen Augusta	777
Helen Lexera	778
William	776
William H.	2472
Gilson, Mr.	3351
Glanden, Mary Ann	1068
Glidden, Abby Tamson	2349
Harriet Conant	2346
James Runnels	2347
Glidden, Laurentina	2380
Mary Ann	2348
Peter	2345
Simeon D.	151, 6
Glines, Corysand A.	1278
Glover, Ira F.	152, 12, (1)
Janet	152, 12, (2)
William R.	152, 12
Godbold, Annie Elizabeth	3043
John	3042
Goddard, Charles E.	3116
Eben P.	3114
Frank E.	3115
Mary R.	3117
Goldsmith, Cecelia Rebecca	2909
Charles William	2907
George Derby	2911
Henry Lake	2908
James Leverett	2906
Jenette Emeline	2910
Leverett Barker	2905
Goodell, Almeron	2197, 9
Goodhue, Adaline	356, 3
Agnes	356, 2
Charles W.	356, 7
Daniel	356
Daniel J.	356, 6
David H.	356, 8
Emma E.	356, 8, (1)
Imla	356, 4
Mary Jane	356, 5
Ozias	356, 1
Samantha A.	356, 9
Goodwin, Daniel	1630, 3 & 6
Mary	1552
R. H.	2825
Googins, Stephen	3736
Thomas	3735
Gordon, Anna	2181
Gorrell, Hannah	604
Gosling, William Alfred	1140
Gould, Marianna	3057
Gove, Hannah	2600
Grace, Aaron	3931
Charles	3934
Moses	3933
Orin	3935
Samuel	3930
Susan	3932
Graham, Margaret	3406
Grant, Abbie	3624
Elmira	2074
Frank Wilbur	2073
John C.	2072
Rachel	1671, 6, (1)
Roscoe Earnest	2075
Graves, Julia	3158
Gray, Anna Frances	3140
Carrie Ethel	3141
Edwin Augustus	3139
Emma Neal	3142
George, Jr.	3138
Gregg, Clarinda	299
Daniel R.	301
David A.	769
Eliza Reynolds	300
Esther	295
Hannah	292

Names.	Cons. Nos.
Gregg, Jonathan	293
Joseph (Capt.)	291
Joseph Ladd	302
Lucinda	298
Polly	294
Sally	296
Sophia	297
Green, Amelia	2428, 4
George M.	2428, 1
James	2428, 5
Mary Ann	2428, 6
Miriam	2428, 3
Orlow Dimond	2428 7
Thomas	2428
William	2428, 2
Greene, Abram	2193
Jane	2767
Laura	2998
Mary	3254
Mary	4017
Sarah	4016
Greenwood, Alvin	239, 1
Calvin	239
Calvin Washburn	239, 2, (3)
Caroline	239, 9
Dexter	239, 8
Frank Waldo	239, 2, (1)
George	239, 3
George	239, 7
Lucinda	239, 6
Mary Louisa	239, 4
Maude Sarah	239, 2, (3), I
Orlan	239, 2
Oscar	239, 5
Ursula Newell	239, 2, (2)
Walter	239, 10
Griffeth, Diodema Rocelia	2440
Griffin, Adaline	1635, 5
Nathaniel	29
Sarah W.	207, 3
Griffith, Desten D.	3238
Julia Ermina	3241
Mason K.	455, 2
Nettie Betsy D.	3240
Vernon Desten	3239
Grout, James Alexander H.	3208
Walter James H.	3209
Guppey, Benjamin Wilder	1219, 2
Caroline Warren	1219, 1
Joseph Warren	1219
Guptil, Lydia	865
Hadley, Marion	1396
Haggett, Benjamin	158
Ebenezer	161
Hannah	162
Lydia	159
Polly	160
Hale, Lydia (Mrs.)	511
Haley, Abby	1643, 10, (6)
Mary Ann	1845
Hall, Abigail	207
Alvira A.	3145
Charles Henry	207, 5
Hannah	635
Lucy A.	231, 4
Luella	589

Names.	Cons. Nos.
Ham, Abby Jane	1805, 1
Abigail	2272, 1
Almira	3020
Anna	2198
Betsy (Elizabeth)	2267
David	2264
David	2270
Daniel	2272
Edwin Forrest	1805, 2
Hannah	2266
Joseph	2265
Lydia	2269
Mary	2273
Rebecca	2271, 1
Reuben	2971
Robert	2270
Rufus	2272, 2
Sarah	2268
Sylvester	1805
Tamson	2201
Hamblen, Isaac S. (Rev.)	1730, 1
Louise Hill	1730, 1, (2)
Samuel Willis	1730, 1, (1)
Hammond, Morton	447, 9
S. Anna	239, 2, (3)
Hancock, Letitia	597
Hand, Calvin D.	1579
Maggie Joanna	1580
Mary Jane	1572
Hanford, Emma P.	3031
Hansen, Carolena Sophia F.	1506
Charles Henry	1500
Frederick Eleazer	1504
Frederick William	1499
Herman Willis	1503
James Clarence	1502
Louis Sumner	1505
Mary Carolena	1501
Hanson, Abigail Clements	2351
Amos W.	2986
Ann Sarah	2354, 4
Deborah Smith	2355
Elizabeth	1640, 1, (1), 1V
Isaac	2985
Jacob Clements	2354
Jacob Clements	2354, 3
John	2350
John Baker	2354, 2
Joseph Bean	2988
Joseph Warren	2354, 1
Mary Adaline	2353
Mary Ann	2987
Miriam	1291
Samuel Runnals	2356
Sarah Ann	2352
William	918
Hardy, Abigail	366
Anna	316
Harlow, Jane	229, 1, (2)
Harnden, Eben	230, 1
Eben, Jr.	230, 1, (1)
Elizabeth	230, 1, (3)
John	230, 1, (5)
Joseph	230, 1, (7)
Samuel	230, 1, (4)
Thomas	230, 1, (6)
William	230, 1, (2)
Harriman, Mary	151

Names.	Cons. Nos.
Harriman, Mary	2576
Harris, Prudence	267
Hart, William	1645, 7
Hartshorn, Albert Henry	939, 1
Edwin	939
Frank Davenport	939, 2
Hartwell, Hannah	3354
Hartzell, Bruce P.	1078
Charles Dennison	1082
Ira S.	1079
John R.	1076
Mary E.	1080
Nellie M.	1081
Sollis Runnels	1077
Thomas Arthur H.	1083
Harvey, Abby Elizabeth	1722, 5, (1)
James Buchanan	1722, 5, (2)
John Milton	1722, 5, (6)
Jonathan	1653
Joseph Thompson	1722, 5, (3)
Martha Fannie	1722, 5, (4)
Matthew	1722, 5, (7)
Matthew J.	1722, 5
Mr.	1717, 11
Nathaniel D.	1722, 5, (5)
Haskell, Margaret C.	331
Hassam, Laura Ann	1271
Hatch, Harriet	1788
Hathorn, Florence Kimball	3273
James Kimball	3272
Hayes, Lydia Olive	2491
Mr.	2338
Samuel C.	1670, 4, (5)
Hayward, Almira	3617
Dodge	369
Hannah	3618
Mary	3615
Oren	3620
Paulina	3619
Samuel	3614
Susan	3609
Susan	3616
Head, Daniel B.	3673
Healy, John Plummer (Esq.)	244, 2
Joseph	244, 2, (1)
Heath, Lucinda	1733, 10
Hemphill, Joseph (Rev.)	317
Henderson, Lewis	1437
Heuville, Mary Ellen	3884
Herd, Sally W.	2489
Herrick, Adelaide	3196
Benjamin, Jr.	3192
Charles	2820
Charles Edgar	3193
Cora May	3197
Elizabeth	3960
Ida Florence	3194
Lewis	2406
Sophronia	2821
William Henry	3195
Herriman, Charles	3034
Charles Winthrop	3037
Mary Jane	3036
Robert Reynolds	3038
Willie Wheeler	3039
Hersom, John	1886
Lucius	1888
Nahum	1887

Names.	Cons. Nos.
Hersom, Olive	1889
Samuel	1885
Stephen	1884
Hibbard, Benjamin	571
George	570
Hannah Jennette	575
Mira	576
Moses	573
Sarah A.	572
William	574
Hicks, Elizabeth	2762
Emma Dell	1565
George C. (Rev.)	1564
Mary Willianna	1566
Hill, Abigail	1671
Arthur T.	1735, 5, (3)
Charles Henry	1735, 7
Edward M.	1735, 5, (2)
Elizabeth	1735, 3
Elizabeth C.	1735, 5, (4)
George Freeman	1735, 4
Howard Fremont	4046, 1, (6), II
Jane G.	1735, 5, (1)
John	1615
John	1735
John McClary	4046, 1, (6), II, (1)
Kate L.	273
Love	1630
Mary Freeman	1735, 2
Mary Russell	1730
Mina A.	203, 1
Myra J.	3186
Polly Freeman	1735, 1
Sumner Cummings	1735, 6
Susan Ann	1735, 8
Thomas	1735, 5
Hinds, Burnham W.	2793
Hines, John	1649
Hodge, Agnes	1349
Hodgkins, Byron	3740
Coney	3739
Hoitt, Alfred	1670, 4
Alfred Demeritt	1670, 4, (2)
Alvina Amanda	1770, 4, (3)
Charles Edward	1670, 4, (13)
Elizabeth Susan	1670, 4, (5)
Franklin Woodbury	1670, 4, (1)
George Irving	1670, 4, (10)
Henrietta	1670, 4, (7)
Lydia Olive	1670, 4, (6)
Martha Ann	1670, 4, (9)
Mary Frances	1670, 4, (8)
Samuel Piper	1670, 4, (4)
Sylvia Victoria	1670, 4, (12)
Washington	1670, 4, (11)
Holmes, Lucy Jane	2828
William F.	1671, 6, (5)
Holt, Abby Hattie	1270
Charles Hamilton	1269
Esther	1733, 3
Frank Oliver	1267
Freddie Eugene	1268
Louisa	1733, 6
Mira Eva	1266
Oliver Wetherbee	1265
Sally G.	1733, 4
Stephen G.	1597
Stephen Horace	1598

Names.	Cons. Nos.
Hood, Adoniram Judson	3971
Hook, James Martin	2833
Hopkins, Alexander H.	3768
Alma Ethael	1045
Amanda Jane	1039
Amelia Caroline	1041
Avis	3766
Cary Mead	1042
Cortland Runnels	1038
Daniel	3763
Daniel	3767
Emma E.	356, 5, (4)
George W.	356, 5, (1)
Jeremiah	3770
Joseph B.	356, 5
Laura Dukes	1043
Lucina	3764
Lucy A.	3769
Mary A.	356, 5, (3)
Mary Ann	3771
Matthew Eli	1037
Meroa Mariah	1040
Norah Dell	1044
Sarah J.	356, 5, (2)
Thomas	3765
Horn, Augusta Ann	1436
Charles Morris	1443
Clara Lawson	1439
Emma Charlotte	1440
Frances Ellen	1438
Freddie	1445
Gage	2312
George Henry	1442
Helen Maria	1437
H. Mariah	2312, 1
Idella	1444
Isaac	1435
Lizzie Philura	1441
Mary	2320
Houghton, Alvin	1342
Alvin Oscar	1344
George Albert	1345
Revilo Gardner	1346
Wealthy Maria	1343
House, Clarissa	1924
Hovey, Celenda	211
Esther	10
Luke	10
Howard, Anna	3556
Dulcena	3553
Fanny	3555, 1
Horace	3555
Jennie	3559
Joshua	3552
Mr.	3455
Oliver	3370
Reynolds	3557
Scott	3558
Thomas J.	3524
Zilba	3554
Howarth, Elizabeth	231, 3, (1)
Thomas	231, 3
Thomas J.	231, 3, (2)
Howlitt, Enoch	153
Hoyt, Anna	1666, 3, (4)
Benjamin	1666, 3
Mr.	1671, 2, (4)
Olive	3055

Names.	Cons. Nos.
Hoyt, Sarah	1666, 3, (3)
Hubbard, Martha	953
Huckins, Mary	1625
Miles	1758
Mr.	1624
Huestis, Albert	1936
Caroline	1933
David Runnells	19; 2
Henry	1931
Major	1930
Stephen	1935
Thomas Runnells	1934
Hufstader, Charles J.	2892
David	2886
Elmira	2891
Francis	2890
Oscar	2893
Hull, Gilman	202
Humphrey, Hannah	207, 6
Hungerford, Ruth E.	3923
Hunt, Loren	2759, 2
Sylvester D.	2675
Huntington, William R. (Rev.).	3495, 1
Huse, George R.	1130
Hussey, Abby Jane	2694
Ella Marietta	2696
Gilbert Eugene	2695
John Samuel	2685
Hutchins, Carlton	237, 10
Eben F.	237, 10, (3)
Edgar H.	237, 10, (2)
Edward C.	237, 10, (1)
John L.	237, 10, (4)
Miss	2247
Ruth	1641, 3, (6)
Hutchinson, Charlie	3730
George	3731
Luther	3622
Mary Jane	1840
Webster	3729
Huzzy, Enos H.	386, 1
Hyatt, Mary A.	541
Jack, Margaret Ewing	2126
Jackman, Clarissa	149, 5
Eliza	149, 4
Elmond	149, 2
Gilman	149, 1
Humphrey	149
Humphrey	149, 3
Lavinia	149, 6
Jackson, Abigail	2500
Amanda M.	1659, 1, (8)
Jane	2880
Nancy	152, 8
Stephen	1640, 1, (3)
Susan	629
Jacobs, Andrew	2927
Charles Benjamin	2928
Katy Anna	2929
Jaffrey, William	3949
James, Susan R.	1863
Jaques, Eliza J.	323, 2
Jenks, Lorenzo	524
Louvisa	2331
Mary Abbie	524, 1
Jepson, Benjamin F.	2613, 2

Names.	Cons. Nos.
Jepson, Benjamin Runnels	2613
Charles H.	2612, 3
Daniel	2614
Eli	3108
Elijah D.	2616
Elijah D.	2613, 1
George	2612. 2
Herbert O.	3109
Isaac	2615
Jedidiah	2612
John	2611
John, Jr.	2618
Lydia R.	2613, 3
William	2617
William	2612, 1
Jewell, Mr (Rev.)	535
Johnson, Anna Moody	214
Betsy	1637, 4
Calvin P.	3168
Charles	1667, 8, (1)
Clara M.	3169
Dennis	1667, 9
Eliza J.	2431
Ettie M.	3170
George	2432, 1
George H.	2012
Gilman	1667, 8
Gilman	1670, 1
Harrison	1667, 11
Hattie M.	3171
Henry A.	2010
Henry Clay	2432, 3
Jessie	1667, 10
John	1667, 3
Joseph	1667, 2
Josiah	2008
Josiah E.	2011
Levi	1667, 1
Levi R.	2012
Loener	1667, 8, (2)
Mary Ann	2432, 2
Matilda	1667, 7
Mr.	1673, 9
Sally	1667, 2, (1)
Samuel	1667, 5
Simeon	1667
Theodate (Daty)	1667, 6
Thomas	2432
William H.	2009
Jones, Abigail Ann	1671, 3, (6)
Alice M.	3113
Alonzo T.	3632
Arthur W.	3103
Charles	1671, 3, (5)
Clarkson	3104
Cyrus	3097
Daniel Augustus	1671, 3, (2)
Daniel R.	3098
Dolly Jane	1671, 3, (1)
Eddie Francis	3632, 1
Elizabeth Coldin	2542
Elizabeth M.	3096
Ellwood W.	3100
Eunice	2559
Franklin E.	3101
Frederick D.	3106
Hannah D.	447, 5
Hiram Leslie	2083

Names.	Cons. Nos.
Jones, Isaac L.	3107
Jacob Demeritt	1671, 3, (4)
James A.	3112
James L.	3111
James P.	3110
John	3095
John Demeritt	1671, 3, (3)
John S.	2082
Jonathan	3632, 2
Josiah A.	3102
Laura A.	1272
Lindley Y.	3105
Lydia Esther	1671, 3, (9)
Martha Jane	1671, 3, (8)
Mary Elizabeth	1671, 3, (7)
Nellie	207, 1, (4)
Patty.	1668, 1
Pelatiah	1671, 3
Sarah	2561
Sarah Augusta	1671, 3, (10)
Thomas	1668, 8
Thomas Francis	1508
William A.	3099
Jordan, Mr.	718
William	845
Jose, Lewis	3554, 1
Lucy	3923
Moses	3554
Joy, John W.	1671, 10
Josephine	1671, 10, (1)
Judkins, Mr.	1628, 1, (1), II
Stephen B.	229, 3
Keene, Ella	1154
Mrs.	4046, 1, (7)
Keith, Bethiah	3423
Kelsea, Jane	1631
Margaret.	1695
Kendall, Benjamin	384
Coretha	2651
Waldo	384, 1
Keniston, Betsy	3838
Kennard, James	4046, 3, (1), I
Kenne, Cordelia B.	207, 1, (2)
Kennedy, Amelia B.	239, 2, (1)
Kenney, Ephraim	2194, 7
Mr.	1804
Mr.	2319
Kenniston, Emma Ladora	1856, 1
Etta.	1856, 3
Henry.	1856
Ida	1856, 4
James	1645, 2
Mabel	1856, 8
Maria	1856, 5
Mary Abby.	1856, 2
Mary Lizzie	1856, 6
Nellie	1856, 7
Kent, Helen	2887
Lucie Montgomery	709
Richard.	708
Sallie Lois.	710
Kenyon, Cyrus	2197, 7
Kilgore, John	386, 8
Kimball, Abby	1337
Abraham	24
Amos	114

Names.	Cons. Nos.
Kimball, Bette	112
Clarissa	2368
Esther Runnels	240
Ezra	2365
Hannah	239
James	238
Jeremiah	109
Jeremiah	111
Lois	242
Matilda L.	1645, 4,(8)
Michael	27
Moses	2364
Mr.	1669, 3
Nancy L.	2367
Rebecca (Mrs.)	22
Richard	110
Sally	241
Samuel Runnals	2366
Sarah	22
Sarah	113
Kingsbury, Charles	1666, 3, (3)
Kinsley, E. B.	764
Mr.	3641
Mr.	3644
Kitson, Alice	3279
Kittredge, Charles Henry	382, 7, (7)
Edward Paul	382, 7, (9)
George Bradley	382, 7, (2)
George Whitten	382, 2
Harriet Melvina	382, 7, (3)
Henry Runnels	382, 1
Horace Vesper	382, 7, (1)
Horatio Gates	382, 5
Laura Amelia	382, 7, (5)
Luther Bradley	382, 4
Mary Elizabeth	382, 7, (4)
Morania Jane	382, 7, (6)
Nahum	382
Timothy B.	382, 7
Timothy Eugene	382, 7, (8)
Walter Swain	382, 3
William	382, 6
Knight, Susanna	1641, 2
Knights, Abraham	2517
Amos	2515, 1
Chandler	2520
Frederick M.	1635, 9, (4)
Hannah	2519
Polly	2516
Solomon	2514
Solomon	2515
William	2518
Knowlton, Angelina	1666, 6, (4)
Betsy	1666. 3, (1)
Elizabeth	1666, 6, (5)
George	1666, 5, (2)
Gilbert G.	1666, 3, (2)
Henry	1666, 6, (2)
James	1666, 6, (3)
Jarves	1666, 3
Martha Ann	1674, 8
Miles	1666, 6
Roxana	1666, 6, (1)
Knox, Mr.	1822
Lake, Mr.	4046, 1, (1), III
Lakeman, Abigail	35

Names.	Cons. Nos.
Lakeman, Amos	40
Daniel	39
Ebenezer	37
Elizabeth	31
Esther	38
Job	41
Mary	34
Mary	42
Nathaniel	30
Nathaniel	36
Samuel	32
Sarah	33
Lambert, Annie Cuyler	575, 4
Edward Augustus	575
Edward Hibbard	575, 1
Jennette Hibbard	575, 3
Rufus Crook	575, 2
Lamos, Sarah	1630, 2, (2)
Lang, Olive	1733, 5
Langley, Abigail	1659
Almon Sylvanus	2535, 1
Annie Mabelle	2535, 1, (2)
Charles Almon	2535, 1, (4)
David	1659, 4
Emma Grace	2535, 1, (1)
Freddy	2535, 1, (3)
Hannah	1658, 6
Hannah	1659, 1
Jeremiah	1628, 1, (1), VIII
Jonathan	1658
Jonathan	1658, 3
Joseph	1658, 8
Levi	1659
Lydia	1658, 5
Mariam	1658, 4
Mark	1658, 9
Mr.	1672, 3, (5)
Nicholas D.	1659, 2
Orland	1659, 5
Samuel	1657
Samuel	1658, 1
Samuel	1659, 3
Sarah	1626
Susannah	1660
Titus	1658, 7
Varoill	1658, 2
Lane, Hannah	198
Lapham, Lucy	171
Laskey, Abigail	1643, 4
Anna	1643, 11
Joanna	1643, 12
Jonathan	1643, 1
John	1643, 2
Joseph	1643, 5
Louis	1643, 9
Love	1643, 10
Mary	1643, 6
Sarah	1643, 3
Susannah	1643, 7
William	1643
William	1643, 8
Lawrence, Abbie A. W.	3088
Lizzie	2774
Mr.	3471
Leach, John Langdon	4046, 3, (3)
Leathers, Abigail	1658
Leavitt, Sophia	2294
Leighton, Alvin	3531

22

338

INDEX.

Names.	Cons. Nos.
Leighton, Elizabeth	303
Leslie, Anna	1595
Lewis, John W.	595
Melissa	1271
Libbey, Arthur	956, 2
Herbert Alonzo	956, 1
Ira	956
James	2166
Stephen	2192, 2
Lincoln, Martha E.	2068
Lindsay, Mary B.	3173
William S.	3172
Littlefield, Clara Isabella	1215
Roger Sherman	1214
Walter	1216
Littlehale, Abbie M.	231, 1, (2)
Locke, Abigail	2554
Cora Belle	1260
Dorothy	2235, 6
George Edgar	1258
Hannah	2247
Mary Pinkham	2567
Simon	2350
Walter Herbert	1257
William H.	1256
Willie Henry	1259
Loker, Halina Maria	1276
Long, Emma Jane F.	1429
Frank Gilman	1428
George Peter C.	1430
Herbert Ira	1426
John Edwin	1425
Minnie Almira	1427
Moses E.	1424
Longfellow, Mr.	425
Loomis, Josephine	1674, 5
Lord, Albert N.	3604
Edith Viola	229, 1, (3), I
George	229, 1, (3)
Justin	1640, 1, (1), VII
Matta E.	229, 1, (3), II
Lothrop, Mr.	4024
Lovejoy, Abiel	1641, 2, (4)
Albion	1844
Bessie Cummings	1844, 1
Carrie Osgood	1840, 3
David	3839
Eliza Ann	1839
Eliza Nevens	2411
Emma	1843
Fred. B.	1840, 2
George Douglass	1844, 2
Jedediah	1836
Jennie	1840, 1
Jeremiah A. (Esq.)	1837
Marshal	1841
Mary Ann	1838
Rebecca	2448
Sophia Spring	1842
William	1840
Lovett, Levi	2296
Low, Elizabeth L.	2562
Lowe, Abby	3974
John	3973
John	3976
Nancy	3975
Rebecca	3977
Sarah	2051

Names.	Cons. Nos.
Luce, Rosilla	879
Lucy, Addie	1645, 4, (8), II
Charles Frederick	1645, 4, (8), I
Charles Herbert	1645, 4, (10), II
Charles Warren	1645, 4, (8)
Ebenezer	1645, 3
Franklin.	1645, 4, (4), III
Frederick.	1645, 4, (7), I
George Emerson	1645, 4, (9)
George Greenleaf	1645, 4, (10)
Greenleaf Cilley	1645, 4, (5)
Helen Maria	1645, 4, (1)
Helen Maria	1645, 4, (4), II
John	1645. 4
John	1645, 4, (10), IV
John Alfred	1645, 4, (4)
Laura Ann	1645. 4, (4), I
Mark Erastus	1645, 4, (10), I
Mary Chandler	1645, 4, (10), III
Mary Frances	214, 2
Mary Jane	1645, 4, (6)
Nancy	1645, 4, (3)
Nathaniel Randall	1645, 4, (2)
Nathaniel Thompson	1645, 4, (7)
Nellie O.	1645, 4, (8), III
Robert	1717, 12
Roscoe	1645, 4, (8), IV
Lull, Greenleaf.	1151
Lund, Mary Isabella	659
Matilda Barker	658
William	657
Lyman, Mr.	4025
Mack, Betsy Ann	1486
Macomber, Mr.	3454
Maffitt, Elmer	2118
Snowden	2117
Magill, Mr.	1951
Magoon, Eliza A.	1764
Mahoney, Louisa	941
Maine, Geneva	1540
George Warren	1536
Harrison Woodville	1537
Hiram K.	1535
Laura Ann	1538
Margaret Ellen	1539
Sybil Runnels	1541
Winfield Scott	1542
Manchester, Edith	2107
Harry R.	2106
James A.	2105
Mann, Mary	3890
Manning, Delia	3630
George	1666, 3, (4)
Orlando L.	816
March, B. F.	412
Henry	206
Mary	2208
Rebecca	1669
Mark, Charles	1645, 4, (6), II
Marsh, Asenath Annette	2036
Augusta	1326
Hannah Elizabeth	2033
John	2031
John Ephraim	2032
Letitia	2038
Lucretia	2037

Names.	Cons. Nos.
Marsh, Mira (Amanda)	2039
Oscar Fitzon	2035
Thomas Drew	2034
Marshal, Faustina	1263
Marshall, Sabra	821
Marston, Abel Gage	231, 2
Abigail G.	231, 7
Alma G.	231, 4, (3)
Anna	235
Arvilla W.	231, 2, (7)
Ascenath Perris	231, 1, (5)
Betsy	1640, 1, (1)
Catie S.	231, 6, (2)
Celinda G.	231, 2, (4)
Charles H.	231, 4, (2)
Charles Harding	231, 5
Charlotte	236
Clara E.	231, 6, (3)
Daniel	1635, 4, (1)
David Alonzo	231, 1, (3)
Deborah	230
Elbridge	1635, 4, (2)
Eliza	237
Ellen I.	231, 2, (11)
Elmer N.	231, 4. (10)
Emma A.	231, 4, (5)
Ethel M.	231, 4, (6)
Francena P.	231, 2, (5)
George L.	231, 6, (4)
Hannah	229
Hannah Ermina	231, 1, (4)
Hannah M.	231, 2, (1)
Haunah Pearl	231, 3
Herbert H.	231, 4, (11)
Ida H.	231, 6, (1)
John H.	1635, 4
John W.	231, 2, (3)
Laura C.	231, 2, (9)
Leander A.	231, 2, (2)
Leander Arnold	231, 6
Lettie A.	231, 4, (9)
Lucinda Melvina	231, 1, (1)
Lucy V.	231, 4, (1)
Martha H.	231, 2, (10)
Mary F.	231, 4, (8)
Matilda Barker	231, 8
Molly	234
Nellie F.	231, 4, (7)
Nora M.	231, 2, (6)
Samuel	228
Samuel	231
Samuel	231, 1
Samuel Warren	231, 1, (2)
Sarah	233
Walter E.	231, 2, (8)
William H.	231, 4, (4)
William Runnels	231, 4
William Runnels	232
Martin, Caroline	119, 6
Mason, Benjamin Kimball	2685
Benjamin Leroy	2692
Betsy Forest	1641, 3, (1)
Charles Frank	2689
Clinton Sawyer	4046, 1, (5), VIII
David Brown	2686
Elvira	2687
Francis Le Roy	1641, 3, (6), II
Freeman Hutchins	1641, 3, (6), I

Names.	Cons. Nos.
Mason, Hannah	1451
Hannah Randall	1641, 3, (2)
James Monroe	2688
John Colby	2690
John Randall	1641, 3, (3)
Mason Joseph	1641, 3
Lewis Cass	2691
Mahlon Lee	1641, 3, (6), III
Mangum Edson	1641, 3, (6), IV
Moses Randall	1641, 3, (5)
Mr.	3302
Nathaniel	1641, 3, (6), V
Nathaniel Randall	1641, 3, (6)
Rhoda Elvira	2693
Sybil	1463
William Randall	1641, 3, (4)
Masterman, Alice	231, 7, (1)
Benjamin J.	230, 9
Eva	231, 7, (2)
Mathes, David	1850
Elizabeth	1851
Judith	1852
Lydia Ann	1853
Mathis, Lydia	1625, 1
Mawrey, Mr.	2664
McCann, Susan	2382
McCrellis, John	1632
Sally	155
McCurdy, Charles Wesley	762
Converse L. (Rev.)	759
Elizabeth R.	760
George Sumner	761
Hannah Nason	764
Harriet Newell	763
Marianne	765
McDaniels, David	1705
Eunice	1707
Hannah	1708
John	1702
Martha	1703
Mary	1704
Pelatiah	1706
William	1701
McDonald, Beulah Reed	1230
Charles Allison	1228
Charles Edward A.	1229
Samuel Allison	1231
Sarah	433
Sybil	930
McFadden, Elizabeth	1470
McFarland, Charles	986
Mary Elizabeth	1567
McFerson, Abner	2427, 5
Amilla Jane	2427, 2
Bathsheba	2428
David	2427, 14
Delila	2427, 6
Dimon (d)	2427
Dolly	2427, 13
Emery Wood	2426
Israel	2427, 8
Jedidiah	2427, 9
Lydia	2427, 7
Miriam	2427, 10
Morgan	2427, 11
Orlow Hartwell	2431
Priscilla	2433
Rhoda Matilda	2427, 12

Names.	Cons. Nos.
McFerson, Roswell Smith	2424
Roxana	2425
Rusheann	2432
Sally Dimond	2429
Sarah Ellen	2427, 3
Sulia Ann	2431, 1
Thomas Jefferson	2427, 1
William	2423
William	2430
William	2427. 4
McKay, Mary	1562
McKellips, Silas	2932
Wilbur H.	2933
McLane, Jane	1643, 10, (4)
McLellan, Lois	3078
McMaster, Emma	212, 1, (3)
McMasters, Betsy Ann	118, 9
McMillan, Gilbert	1839, 1
Jennie	1839, 2
John	1839
McMullen, Elizabeth	152, 5
Meader, Patience	2613
Rebecca	2612
Mears, Abigail	3978
Melvin, Anna E.	447
Chloe	451
Jackson	452
Mary	449
Moses	445
Moses	448
Nathan	446
Stephen	450
Menser, Emily Jane	1028
Merriam, Louisa J.	1735, 5
Merrill, Anna (Nancy)	372
Arthur Tebbetts	4046, 1, (2), III
Betsy E.	1736
Bradbury Tebbetts	4046, 1, (2), I
Clarissa B.	231, 6
DeWitt Clinton	4046, 1, (2), IV
Ella J.	591
Fannie Lane	4046, 1, (2), III, (I)
Florilla	1732, 3
Joel	231, 2, (1)
Martha Haynes	1641, 2, (1)
Noah L.	4046, 1, (2)
Noah L.	4046, 1, (2), II
Polly	180
Stephen (Rev.)	1737
William	257
Willie Arthur	4046, 1, (2), III, (II)
Merrow, Asa	417
Meserve, Alice Pendexter	1738, 2
Clara Eastman	1738, 5
Frank Marion	1738, 7, (2)
George Pendexter	1738
George Washington	1738, 7
Hattie Douglas	1738, 6
James Monroe	1738, 1
J. Erving	1738, 1, (2)
Lizzie Amelia E.	1738, 8
Martha Trickey	1738, 1
Mary Davis	1733, 4
Samuel	2353
Sarah Addie W.	1738, 9
Sarah Edith	1738, 1, (1)
Susan Eastman	1738, 3
Victoria L.	2981
Meserve, Virgil Kent	1738, 7, (1)
Willard Allison	1738, 1. (3)
Messer, Adelbert	255, 4
Edwin	255, 2
Hezekiah	249
Jacob	255
Joseph	248
Joseph	251
Mary Ann	255, 3
Mehetabel	250
Putney	255, 1
Rebekah	254
Sarah Ann	1666, 2
William	252
William	253
Metcalf, Harriet A.	616
Michael, Louise	1958
Middleton, Abigail	1
Miles, Mr.	1672, 1
Miller, Eliza	1587
Mr.	4027
Sarah	997
Millett, Adoniram	951
Albro	953, 1
Alonzo Dixon	953
Isaac Runnels	955
John Cook	954
Lucy Stinson	956
Melissa Jane	952
Mills, Maria Jennie	814
Mitchell, Edith May	1600
George Henry	1599
Moffith, Eva	1039, 1
Joab	1039
Moles, Alice Jane	2110
John Ralph	2109
Lizzie Laura	2113
Robert Herder	2114
Samuel David	2111
William	2108
William Henry	2112
Monroe, Hiram	147, 2
Montgomery, Fanny	704
Joseph	703
Lizzie	705
Lucy	707
Nellie	706
Moody, Amos	2621
Angeline	2194, 9
Avice (Avis)	2194, 7
Betsey	2194, 4
Charles	2194, 5, (1)
Daniel	2194, 1
Dexter	2194, 1, (2)
Elisha	2194, 5
Elizabeth	2622
Emma	2194, 8, (1)
Franklin	2620
George Washington	2194, 8
Hannah	2651
Hartwell	2194, 1, (1)
Joseph	2194
Joseph	2194, 6
Justin William	2194, 3, (1)
Nathaniel	2194, 2
William	2194, 3
William	2194, 1, (3)
William	2619

Names.	Cons. Nos.
Moore, Abram	3714
Alice M.	3719
Dennison P.	3982
Enos L.	3717
Frank C.	3716
Fred L.	3715
George	701
Joseph B.	1072
Lucy	1722, 3
Mary Emma	3983
Mary Harriet	1074
Mary Helen	702
Minnie O.	3718
Nettie R.	3720
Robert Dennison	1073
Sollis Albert	1075
Morey, Frances	2744
Louisa Angeline	447, 1
Morrill, Benjamin H.	3088
Frederick Herbert	3089
George William	3090
Lucy Antoinette	3091
Mary Ann	625
Morrison, Caroline E.	2671
John	1666, 6, (4)
Miss	1666, 6, (2)
Miss	1666, 6, (3)
Mr.	1623
Thomas	116, 1
Morse, Charlotte	551
Hattie J.	237, 7
Mosier, Mr.	3549
Moulton, L.	3617
Munsell, Anna	1173
Emma	1172
George	1170
Henry C.	1171
William	1174
Murdough, William J.	147, 4
Murr, Adelia Caroline	964
Rhoda Eliza	964
Murray, Helen Charrilla	2859
Nash, Eliza G.	1016
Nason, Caroline Augusta	715
Cordelia	718
Daniel	711
Daniel	717
Edgar Girard	1341, 1
Elizabeth Hooton	716
Hannah	713
James	720
Joshua Pierce	722
Matilda	714
Olivia	712
Raymond Lee	723
Stephen Hamilton	721
Sylvester	719
William G.	1341
Neal, Mary E.	2347
Neas, Mary Ann	2427
Needham, Frank	1860, 2
Maria	1860, 1
Otis Sylvester	1860
Nelson, Angello Delbert	3223
Curtis Wells	3224
Daniel	3222

Names.	Cons. Nos.
Nelson, Maria	1626, 2, (8)
Newbert, Moses W. (Rev.)	3110
Newman, Elizabeth Adaline	3030
Frank Albert	3033
Henry Jones	3031
Marshall Perry	3032
Robert	3028
Robert, Jr.	3029
Newsome, Hannah	2084
Newton, Charlie M.	237, 8, (3)
George	237, 9
Harvey L.	231, 4, (3)
John D.	237, 8
John F.	237, 8, (1)
J. Orville	237, 8, (2)
Mary	207, 2
Nichols, Alice J.	154, 7, (5)
Alilian	154, 3, (10)
Benjamin	154
Benjamin	154, 3, (2)
Calista	154, 3, (1)
Charles N.	154, 3, (7)
Clara J.	154, 4, (5)
Clara J.	154, 5, (3)
Clarissa	154, 6
Edwin	154, 7
Eliza	154, 8
Ella F.	154, 7, (1)
Emma J.	154, 7, (2)
Etta F.	154, 4, (4)
Eugene S.	154, 5, (1)
Frank	154, 3, (9)
George	154, 3, (8)
George A.	154, 5, (2)
George H.	154, 4, (3)
Gilman S.	154, 7, (7)
Hattie E.	154, 4, (2)
Henry B.	154, 5, (4)
Henry D.	154, 5
Henry H.	154, 3, (3)
Hiram	154, 4
Hubbard Newton	154, 3
Jefferson D.	154, 3, (12)
John O.	154, 4, (1)
Joseph	154, 1
Julia	154, 9
Loren E.	154, 7, (6)
Lucy A.	154, 7, (4)
Mary	154, 5
Mary A.	154, 3, (5)
Minnie K.	154, 7, (8)
Nancy Ayer	154, 2
Nancy M.	154, 7, (3)
Nellie	154, 3, (11)
Sarah J.	154, 10
Silas D.	154, 3, (13)
Soranus G.	154, 3, (6)
William A.	154, 3, (4)
William E.	926
Noble, John J.	1673, 11
Norton, Alfred	901
James	853
Julia A.	2393
Nowell, Martha	2605
Noyes, Harry Lincoln	4046, 1, (5), VIII, (1)
Mary Josephine	4046, 1, (5), VIII, (II)

Names.	Cons. Nos.
Noyes, Samuel Bean..4046, 1, (5), VIII	
Nute, Alonzo Daniel	2090
Augusta	2235, 2
Carrie	4046, 3, (6), II
George Daniel	2091
Hannah Susan	2092
John Andrew	2094
Mary Abbie	2093
Nutting, Eben	236
Jason S.	236, 1
Nye, Sarah	2612, 1
Odell, Lydia	1666
Odlin, Emma	886
Oliver, Mr.	3035
Orange, Franklin	2590
George Washington	2591
Henry Smith	2592
Jeremy Washington	2589
Orcutt, Leonard	3530
Lydia	3531
Ordway, George E.	3947
Osgood, Asa K.	4046, 3, (5), & (9)
Betsy	1727
Charles Hazen	1842
Charles Hazen	1842, 5
Edward	4046, 2
Elizabeth	1840
Fred	1842, 2
Georgianna Souther	1842, 4
Henry T.	4046, 2, (2)
Jenny Steele	1842, 1
Marshall Lovejoy	1842, 3
Sally	4046, 2, (1)
Susan	1641, 2, (1), I
Otis, Stephen	2272, 1
Outhank, Mary Ann	640
Packard, Ebenezer (Dea.)	3359
Hannah	3410
Parmenas	3371
William	3358
Page, Anna	529
Benjamin	3852
Caleb	105
Hannah	103
Joseph	106
Joseph	116, 5
Joshua	102
Moses	108
Sally	107
Samuel	104
William	1641, 3, (1)
Parish, Hannah	4046, 1, (1)
Parker, Aaron	118, 6
Betsy Ann	1382
Hannah	230, 5
Lucy Maria	2084
Mary D.	489
Rebecca	2434
Parlin, Alfred	2521
Polly	2522
Partridge, Abby	542
Anna Eliza	2392, 6
Asa	2392, 8
Asa Cheney	2392

Names.	Cons. Nos.
Partridge, Edward Joseph	2392, 3
Ella Sophronia	2392, 2
Flora Almira	2392, 4
Francis Charles	2392, 1
Jessie Elizabeth	2392, 9
Samuel Cheney	2392, 7
William Henry	2392, 5
Pattee, Mary F.	905
Patterson, Mr.	538
Payson, Harriet H.	119, 4
Peabody, Amanda Malvina	365
Amasa	352
Amasa	355
Eliza	359
Frederick	358
Jonathan	354
Rhoda	360
Rhoda	361
Rufus	357
Sarah	353
Tryphena	356
Pearl, Hannah	62
Sarah	119
Pearson, Benjamin H.	300
Simon	179
Pearsons, Clark	353
Peaslee, Daniel G.	155, 15
Peck, Sewall	451
Peckett, Ada Isabelle	593, 1
George Franklin	593, 2
Hattie Lewis	593, 3
William Edwin	593
Pendergast, Caroline Frances	1261
James	1628, 8
Lydia Maria O.	1852, 1
Maurice D.	1852, 2
Solomon	1852
Perkins, Abiel Jacob	1059
Abigail	1316
Anna	3415
Chase Burnham	1738, 8
Dana	2759, 4
David	2766
David K.	2757
David Walter	2766, 1
Edgar Moore	1060
Edward S.	2096
Elizabeth Theresa	2759, 1
Ephraim	2332
Frances Helen	2099
Frederick	2766, 2
Gertrude Hope	2766, 3
Hiram P.	1056
Isabella	2761, 2
J. A.	2095
Jane	2765
Jemima	3367
Jemima	3447
Joanna Randall	2764
Lawrence Taft	1061
Manasseh	2762, 1
Manasseh Holmes	2761
Marilla E.	1058
Mary	2335
Mary Ann	2760
Mary Ann	2758, 2
Mary Antoinette	2759, 2
Mary Emma	2761, 1

Names.	Cons. Nos.
Perkins, Mary Louise	2098
Mr.	3421
Nancy	3952
Nathan Randall	2762
Nathaniel	2758
Nathaniel, Jr.	2758, 1
Parker Hazen	1057
Richard	2097
Runnels	2334
Samuel R.	2759, 3
Samuel Runnels	2759
Staples	2333
William Dana	2763
Perry, Charlie S.	1391
Eliza B.	565
Eunice I.	1395
Freddie I.	1393
Halsie O.	1394
Hamilton O.	1390
Susan Elder	2003
Willie N.	1392
Pervier, Patty	2190
Sarah	3226
Pevere, James	159
Philbrick, Deborah Sophronia	2390
Elizabeth Ann	2392
Frank	2391, 1
Henry March	2391, 2
Joseph	2389
Samuel Runnals	2391
Philips, Mehetabel	786
Rebecca Smith	2003
Phillips, Albert	3234
Carrie Hattie	3236
Jesse	3237
Margaret Wendall	3493
Miss	3373
Willis Albert	3235
Philo, William	447, 7
Pickering, Charles Elwood	1157
Picket, Mary	3706
Pierce, Augusta A.	356, 2, (1)
Emily	3001
Flora E.	356, 2, (3)
John	356, 2
John M.	356, 2, (2)
Theodora	1640, 1, (1), VI
Pike, Amanda	1576
Hannah B.	2836
Pillsbury, Adams Dix	1190
Charles S.	1188
Charles George	1189
John Arthur	1191
Sally Moody	334
Pingree, Beulah	2747
Diana	2747
Roxilana	255
Pinkham, Abigail	2274
Albert Day	1738, 3, (5)
Ann Dorcas	2482, 1
Charles	2485
Charles Luther	2482, 2
Clara Estella	1738, 3, (6)
Edward J.	2269, 2
Emeline	2483
George Hale	2482, 3
George Hayes (Rev.)	1738, 3
George Meserve	1738, 3, (1)
Pinkham, Hannah Avery	2487
Hattie Alice	1738, 3, (3)
Horace Jonathan	2482, 5
Isaac Dearborn	2482, 7
Jonathan	2481
Jonathan Roberts	2486
Laura Jane	2498
Luther Hale	2482
Maria	2235, 5
Martha Grace	1738, 3, (4)
Mary Adaline	2496
Mary Susan	1738, 3, (2)
Nathan	3546
Nathan Pratt	2488
Nathaniel Edwin	2482, 4
Nathaniel J.	2269, 1
Rebecca	2235
Samuel	2269
Seth Taylor	2482, 6
Thomas	2484
Thomas Francis G.	2499
Vincent T.	2497
Willard	2495
Pitts, George W.	1591
Flora	1592
Place, James D.	2313, 1
Platts, Joanna	93
Plummer, John	2235, 9
Pollard, John Worthen	600, 1
Luther B.	609
Mary	3670
Mira Hibbard	600, 2
William	592
Pond, Mr.	3378
Poole, John Henry	516
Poor, Emma Rowena	599, 4
Frank Clough	599, 1
Hattie Clarabelle	599, 2
Joseph W.	673
Lincoln	676
Mary Louisa	599, 3
Minnie White	675
William George	674
Porter, Benjamin	277
Catharine	3971
Emma	4046, 1, (8), I
John Tyler	279
Joseph	3970
Joseph Valentine	3972
Hannah	3547
Martha Osgood	281
Sarah	280
Stephen Runnels	278
William	861
Post, Catharine	2457
John	4021
Potter, Alice Ann	3080, 2
Blanch	3078, 3
Charles Henry	3080, 1
Elizabeth	3079
Henry	3080
Jennie	3080, 3
Joseph William	3078
Lizzie Olive	3078, 1
Salome	859
William	3077
William Henry	3078, 2
Pratt, Charlotte Lorena	3267

Names.	Cons. Nos.
Pratt, James	380
Martha R.	766
Mr.	2759, 1
Pray, Isaac	3595
Prescott, Nelson	2728
Pressy, Lydia	795
Preston. Adaline (Mrs.)	875
Priest, Betsy	1668, 12
Harriet	1668, 10
Hiram	1668, 7
Jefferson	1668, 9
Joseph	1668
Joseph	1668, 5
Joseph	1673, 5
Lucy	401
Lydia	395
Nancy	1668, 11
Nathan	1668, 4
Polly	1668, 8
Sally	1668, 3
Samuel	1668, 1
Samuel	1668, 1, (1)
Susannah	1668, 2
William	1668, 6
Proctor, Aaron	409
Abigail	152
Abigail	407
Asa A.	233, 1
Charles A.	233, 1, (1)
Dolly A.	233, 1
Eliza	410
James	406
Jeremiah	413
Joseph	404
Josiah	408
Mary A.	233, 1, (2)
Mr.	233
Mr.	1668, 12
Rhoda	412
Syrena	411
Puddy, Richard	4046, 1, (4), IV
Pulcifer, Sarah E.	237, 2
Pullen, Sarah	3544
Pumphrey, Mahala D.	1046
Punchard, Ellennora	541, 1
Pushor, Philena	1560
Putney, Laura Ann	255
Mary	255
Quackenbush, Edwin	3262
Harlin S.	3263
Quimby, George Meserve	1738, 4, (2)
Hattie Meserve	1738, 4, (1)
William Eugene	1738, 4, (3)
William K.	1738, 4
Quint, Abby	1645, 4, (6) II
Charles	1645, 4, (6), IV
George	1645, 4, (6)
Henrietta	1645, 4, (6), III
James Monroe	1545, 4, (6), I
John Lucy	1645, 4, (6), VI
Levi Chadbourne	1730, 2
Matilda	1645, 4, (6), V
Rand, Alonzo N.	237, 13
John G.	237, 13, (2)

Names.	Cons. Nos.
Rand, Lluellyn A.	237, 13, (1)
Stephen	1628, 1, (1), VII
Randall, Abigail	1625, 1, (8)
Abigail	1626, 1
Agnes Forrest	1641, 2. (2)
Ann	2482
Anna	1623
Anna	1625, 1, (1)
Anna	1641, 6
Anne	1641, 1, (2)
Betsy	1640, 2
Betsy	1641, 1
Betsy Forrest	1641, 2, (6)
Carrie Mary	1641, 2, (1), I (I)
Deborah	1621
Eliza	1626, 7
Eliza	1641, 1, (5)
Elizabeth Frances	1641, 5, (3), II
Elizabeth W.	1641, 2, (1), VI
Ellison Forrest	1641, 1, (1)
Frances Adalaide	1641, 2, (1), VII
George Knight	1641, 2, (1)
Gideon	1645
Gideon M.	1625, 1, (2)
Hannah	1626, 4
Hannah	1641, 4
Hannah	1641, 2, (4)
Hannah	1645, 7
Hannah Forrest	1641, 2, (1), III
Henry Harrison	1641, 2, (1), I, (II)
Henry Harrison	1641, 2, (1), II
Hezekiah	1640
Israel	1622
James T.	1641, 2, (1), I
Job	1626
Job	1626, 5
John	1626, 8
John Forrest	1641, 5
Jonathan	1644
Louisa	1624
Lydia	1641, 1, (3)
Lydia	1645, 2
Lydia M.	1625, 1, (4)
Maria	2313, 2
Mary	1625, 1, (6)
Mary	1626, 9
Mary	1641, 1, (4)
Mary	1643
Mary (Mrs.)	1674
Mattie Elizabeth	1641, 2, (1), V, (I)
Miles	1620
Miles	1626, 3
Molly	1640, 1
Moses	1641
Moses	1641, 5, (3)
Moses	2318
Nabby	1645, 6
Nancy	1645, 3
Nathaniel	1639
Nathaniel	1641, 2
Nathaniel	1641, 2, (1), V
Nathaniel	1645, 1
Polly (Molly)	1641, 3
Polly	1645, 4
Rebecca Clement	1641, 5, (3), I
Rebekah Carleton	1641, 5, (2)
Reuben W.	1625, 1, (3)
Sally	1625, 1, (5)

Names.	Cons. Nos.
Randall, Sally	1645, 5
Samuel Carleton	1641, 5, (1)
Sarah (Sally)	1626, 2
Sukey K.	1641, 2, (3)
Susan Knight	1641, 2, (1), IV
Thomas	1625
Thomas, Jr.	1625, 1
Thomas	1626, 6
Thomas C.	1625, 1, (7)
Ursula	2336
William	1641, 1
William	1641, 5, (4)
William	1642
William Harrison	1641, 2, (5)
Ranlet, Sally	2709
Ranlett, Charles H.	3052
Frank Edward	3053
Mary Abby	3054
Ransom, Edward	3322
Rawson, Susanna	3321
Ray, Lizzie	1232
Rayall, Samuel	3312
Raymond, Henry	398
Lydia	3374
Read, Abbie Ethel	522, 6
Bertha Ettie	522, 1
Calvin Richardson	521
Claudie Gertrude	521, 2
Dana Dunbar	523
Ebenezer Runnels	519
Effie Jenette	522, 2
Elmer Augustus	523, 2
Gertrude Dexter	522, 5
Gracie Darling	521, 1
Hannah Abigail	524
Harry Lyman	523, 3
Hattie Maud	523, 5
Hiram Augustus	520
James Dexter	522
James R.	518
Llewellyn James	522, 4
Lottie Josephine	523, 4
Raymond Dexter	522, 3
Tessie Mary	521, 3
Walter Sidney	523, 1
William G.	2770
Redman, Abbie A.	1645, 4, (7)
Reed, Abbie Hattie	1274
Addie Cora	1275
Beulah	643
Clara J.	154, 5, (1)
John Augustus	1273
Reynolds, Betsy	3564
B. W.	3507
Mr.	3468
Mr.	3469
Mr.	3478
Mr.	3759
Simeon H.	3481
Susan Duncan	3489
Rhodes, Angeline Esther	2921
Rice, Rosanna	2997
Rich, Levi	1960
William L.	1960, 1
Richardson, Albert H.	212, 1, (6)
Charley	212, 1, (3), I
Charley B.	212, 1, (5)
David	1735, 2

Names.	Cons. Nos.
Richardson, Frank W.	212, 1, (7)
Freddie Emerson	212, 1, (1), I
George Asa	672
George Hill	1735, 2, (1)
Hattie	2235, 3
Justin W.	212, 1, (4)
Lizzie William	678
Louise Caroline	212, 1, (2)
Orlando W.	212, 1, (3)
Russell	212, 1
Russell Ozro	212, 1, (1)
William George	671
Ricker, Dorcas (Mrs.)	2208
Eliza	2394
Eliza Jane	2313, 1
George	887
Luther	2313
Miss	2247
Thomas	2313, 2
Ring, Albert	1720, 5
Chase	4046, 2, (1)
George Edwin	1720, 5, (1)
Robbins, John	147, 1
Lydia Frances	1734. 1
Philura	848
Samuel	411
Sarah L.	154, 2, (2)
Willard	407
William	3539
Roberts, Abigail	3519
Abigail A.	237, 3
Almira	237, 5
Charles H.	237, 4, (2)
Charles H.	3737
Charlie Lewellyn	3738
Lauretta E.	237, 4, (1)
Sarah Rebecca	3962
Susan L.	3834
Sylvester	237, 4
Robie, Alfred M.	581
Robinson, John	118, 8
Margaret	3630
Martha S.	1806
Rosanna	1953
Rogers, Arthur	4046, 1, (5), V, (III)
Bertha Alice	978
Carroll Burbank	4046, 1, (5), V, (II)
Charles Carroll (Esq.)	4046, 1, (5), V
Daniel	315
Daniel	324
Dorabelle	975
Eliza Jane	319
Elizabeth Winship	752
Emeline (Mrs.)	2767
Enoch Avery	1557
Enoch George	4046, 1, (5), IX
Ernest Howard	1558
George Lincoln	976
Hannah Ophelia	317
Harriet Eliza	323
Ida Emma	974
James	2314, 1
John	314
John	973
John Adams	318
John William	4046, 1, (5), V, (I)
Kate May	977
Livingston	1641, 2 & 6, (2), II, (III)

Names.	Cons. Nos.
Rogers, Malvina Bordwell	320
Maria	316
Mary E.	2051
Mr.	2314
Orville Forrest 1641, 2 & 6, (2), II, (I)	
Rebecca	321
Samuel B.	1641, 2 & 6, (2), II
Samuel B.	1641, 2 & 6, (2), II, (II)
Stephen Reynolds	321
Susan Hemphill	322
Susie Bell	1559
Rollins, Dudley L.	2979
Rook, Katie	1643, 10, (2)
Rosebrooks, Alice	2925
Rosecrans, Charles W.	1070
Mary Lucretia.	1071
Roundy, Philena	1474
Rowell, Charles	3863
Edward	3861
Norris	3862
Susan	3864
Willie	3865
Runnels, Elvina Augusta	3198
Sacket, Carrie B.	2891, 1
George O.	2891
Sampson, Alfred.	229, 1, (5)
Mitie.	229, 1, (5), I
Sanborn, Benjamin.	3866
Lavina	1666, 4
Martha	3868
Nellie Augusta.	2121
Nellie M.	3867
Sanders, Alvin W.	1989
Clara A.	1991
George D.	1992
Jennie E.	1988
Martin M.	1990
William	1987
Sandon, Dorcas.	3395
Sargent, Abigail	76
Asa	73
Daniel	2477
Mehetabel P.	2657
Moses	72
Mr.	537
Sarah	695
Savage, Amilla.	2427
Lydia A.	2385
Susan	3246
Savery, Selina G.	2013
Roxana G.	507
Sawyer, David.	2268, 1
Eliza N.	1739, 2
Harriet M.	1402
John H.	572
Moses	2268
Sawyer (or Sanger) Richard	3303
Sayles, H.	1947
Scannall, Annora.	3244
Schmanouski, Mr.	1825
Scott, Jane.	2917
Scouller, John B.	3585
Scribner, Esther	993
Searles, Eli	2839
Hannah Jane	2841

Names.	Cons. Nos.
Searles, Jefferson Rockwood	2840
Sears, Julia	2194, 5
Seaton, Alma Etta	1089
Amanda Virginia.	1088
George Edward.	1090
Joseph P.	1087
Robert E. Lee	1091
Seavey, Arthur.	1640, 1, (1), VI, (VIII)
Carrie H.	1640, 1, (1), VI, (I)
DeWitt Clinton 1640, 1, (1), VI, (III)	
Douglas Bean	1640, 1, (1), I
Earnest Ellsworth 1640, 1, (1), IV, (II)	
Harrie Randall 1640, 1, (1), IV, (III)	
Henry Bragdon 1640, 1, (1), VI, (IX)	
Herbert Ardell.	1640, 1, (1), IV, (I)
Hezekiah Randall.	1640, 1, (1), IV
James	1640, 1, (1), VI, (VI)
Jonathan Melvin.	1838
Mary	1640, 1, (1), VII
Minnie May.	1640, 1, (1), VI, (IV)
Paulina.	1640, 1, (1), VI, (VII)
Polly	1640, 1, (3)
Polly	1640, 1, (1), II
Randall	1640, 1, (1)
Sally	3914
Simon	1640, 1
Simon	1640, 1, (2)
Stephen Jackson.	1640, 1, (1), III
Stephen Jackson	1640, 1, (1), V
Viola	1640, 1, (1), VI, (V)
William	1640, 1, (1), VI
Willis Pierce.	1640, 1, (1), VI, (II)
Sessions, Anna (Mrs.)	17
Seward, George.	1670, 1
Sewards, Mr.	1717, 10
Seymour, Mr.	3403
Shackford, Irene	1641, 5, (3)
Shannon, Mary Addie.	4046, 1, (1), II
Shattuck, Annette	2873
Asaph.	2870
Charrilla.	2871
Legrand	2872
Maria	2874
Shaw, Abigail Jane	1855
Amos Cornelius	2676, 4
Augustus	2676
Bertie Edward	2676, 3
Edward Charles	1196, 1
Eliza Ann.	2697
Emeline	1860
Frankie	2676, 2
Harriet Ann	1858
Henry Elmer.	2676, 3
Isabell	3554, 1
James T.	1196
John	1691
John	1854
John	2389
Joseph	1691, 4
Lizzey	1691, 1
Maria	1859
Mary Elizabeth.	1857
Nancy.	1691, 2
Sarah	1856

Names.	Cons. Nos.
Shaw, Susan	1861
Susanna	1691, 3
Sheldon, Ezra	241
Sherburn, Abigail	527
George W.	528
George Washington	525
Samuel	526
Sherburne, Alden P.	1670, 4, (7)
Alfred Alden	1670, 4, (7), I
Charles Lewellyn	1670, 4, (7), III
Elmer David	1670, 4, (7), II
Sherman, Abigail Marion	1720, 1
Angeline	1237
Charles	1238
Charles Henry	1240
Converse McCurdy	1239
Henry	1236
Mr.	1889
Mr.	2487
Shoemaker, Hannah	1062
Sibley, Edward	3628
Harriet Kimball	4046, 1, (8)
Silsby, Anna Shepherd	292, 2
Hamilton Reynolds	292, 4
Ithiel	292
Ithiel Homer	292, 3
Levi Hayward	292, 1
Mary Bullard	292, 5
Silver, Dexter Freeman	2756
Harriet Maria	2755
Putman Webster	2754
Simmons, Sarah	215
Simpson, Bradford	386, 3
Charles	1150
David	386, 7
Elvira	386, 9
George	386, 2
Harriet	386, 1
James	1149
John K.	3853
Mary Ann	386, 4
Mr.	3466
Olive	386, 6
Reuben	386
Sarah	386, 8
Uriah	386, 5
Sinclair, Polly C.	2181, 2
Sinkler, Bradbury	2179
Skilton, William Eustis	648
Skinner, Eliza Ann	2825
Rose	1355
Sleeper, Andrew J.	487, 9
Annabelle	487, 4
Carrie W.	487, 2
Cora G.	487, 6
David	2389
David March	2393
Helena	2393, 1
James	487
James Burton	487, 8
Katie I.	487, 3
Luetta	487, 5
Myrtie L.	487, 7
Sewall I.	487, 1
Small, Frances A.	1543
Smallidge, Elizabeth C.	1295
Smart, Abigail	1659, 1, (6)
Cora A.	1659, 1, (8), IV
Smart, Daniel	1659, 1
Daniel	1659, 1, (5)
Everett	1659, 1, (4)
Everett	1659, 1, (7)
John	1659, 1, (8)
John O.	1659, 1, (8), III
Joseph	1659, 1, (3)
Joseph E.	1559, 1, (8) V
Levi L.	1659, 1, (1)
Lydia N.	1659, 1, (11)
Mary E.	1659, 1, (8), I
Mary E.	1659, 1, (9)
Osborn	1659, 1, (2)
Sophronia	1659, 1, (10)
Vina S.	1659, 1, (8), II
Smiley, Lewis	3615
Smith, Abigail	163
Adaline	2552
Alfred E.	239, 2, (2) I
Belinda	213, 2
Betsy	2176
Caroline Elizabeth	535
Charles Otis	536
Charles W.	1199
Cora Belle	3144
Cordelia	1446
Francis	154, 3, (1)
Hannah	45
Hannah	2142
Herbert Augustine	539
H. M.	239, 2, (2)
Jane Underhill	537
Joseph Elbridge	1124
Lucy	2407
Mary	154, 3, (1), I
Mary Lucy	538
Mary Lucy	1125
M. Fanny	3869
Mr.	3462
Olive (Mrs.)	74
Peter Elkins	533
Sophia Runnels	534
William S.	3143
Snell, Caroline	1972
Edward	2165
Martha	3518
Mary	3330
Mary Abby	1628, 1, (1), I
Samuel	2164
Solomon	2163
Sollis, Abigail	45
Soule, Albert Lee	2024
Edwin	2025
Frank	2028
George	2021
George	2022
Marie Louise	2023
Mary Elizabeth	2026
William Holcombe	2027
Spalding, Sewall	118, 2
Thomas	156
Spear, Alfred	420
Charlotte	416
Eliza	417
Hephzibah	419
Mary Ann	422
Nehemiah	418
Robert	414

Names.	Cons. Nos.
Spear, Stephen	421
Stephen	421, 2
William	415
William	421, 1
Speed, Abigail	1718, 1
Mr.	1718
Spencer, George Ezra (Dr.)	4046, 1, (5), IV
Spinny, Elizabeth	3545
Emily	3592
Spofford, Hannah	82
Sprague, Betsy Copeland	244, 4
Sarah Baker (Mrs.)	244, 4
Square, Susan	3700
Stanley, Annette E.	2766
Stanton, Betsey	2238
Mary B.	2385
Staples, Huldah	2046
Stark, David Carrol	3214
Frank David	3215
Ida	3217
Martha Jane	3216
Stephen	1641, 5, (3), I
Stearns, Caroline	472
Steele, Sarah Jane	213, 1
Stetson, Henry (Rev.)	3616
Stevens, Anne	889
Avice	1819
Charles	1820
Charles	3576
Daniel	1818
Ellen	3526
George	2181, 2, (5)
John	1817
Jonathan P.	236
Mary Jane	1822
Mehetabel	2561
Ruth D.	3576, 1
Sarah Ann	1821
Stevison, Elizabeth A.	2443 & 2863
Stiles, Caroline Thompson	847
Charles Franklin	841
Elijah	840
Everett	846
Henry Everett M.	844
Henry Leverett	842
Israel	845
Julia Jeanette	843
Lydia	837
Stillings, Alonzo	1738, 9
Stoddard, Louisa Estelle	3271
Samuel	3269
William Henry	3270
Stokesbury, Eliza Ellen	1179
Flora Ethel	1178
George Arthur	1176
John W.	1175
Mary Jane	1177
Stone, Lucy	2247
Storer, Eliza G.	3674
Stowell, Abner	155, 7
Annie Gracia	155, 6, (3)
Benjamin Frank	155, 6, (1)
Elgin Ware	155, 6, (2)
Henry Fisher	155. 6
Streeter, Mr.	3398
Stroud, William	1197
Stuart, Almira	154, 7

Names.	Cons. Nos.
Sullivan, Mr.	263
Summers, Elizabeth T.	2758
Sumner, Experience	2235, 7
Sutton, John Forbes	1306
Emma Louise	1307
Swain, Albert Ephraim	2535, 4
Benjamin	2535
Clara Octavia	2535, 7
Edgar Clarence	2535, 9
Eugene Margarenia	2535, 5
Harriet Ann	2535, 8
James William	2535, 6
Lavinia Antoinette	2535, 3
Lucy Elizabeth	2535, 1
William Henry	2535, 2
Swan, Mary Ann	488
Swasey, Clara Ellen	2068
Sweat, Ann	235, 1
Benjamin	234, 6
Charlotte	235, 4
Clara	235, 6
Daniel	235
Daniel	235, 3
Elizabeth R.	234, 4
Elvira	235, 5
Frederic	235, 2
Hiram	234, 7
James	234, 8
John	234
John A.	234, 1
Joshua	234, 9
Martha	234, 11
Mary	230, 2
Mary A.	234, 2
Matilda	235, 7
Persis	234, 5
Sarah B.	234, 3
Sophia	234, 10
Sweetzer, Charles	970
Eliza	972
Martha	971
William B.	969
Swift, Oliva	2119
Taber, William H.	1511
Talbot, Charles P.	323
Edward Reynolds	323, 2
Fannie Melburn	323. 1
Gertrude	323, 2, (2)
Harriet	323, 2, (1)
Julian	323, 3
Tarbox, Abner	577
Charles	578
David	480, 3
George Minot	480, 4
Harriet R.	580
Lucy Ann	480, 5
Mira Ann	579
Rodney Carr	480
Rodney Walter	480. 2
Sarah Jane	581
William Fellows	480. 1
Tarlton, Hannah	1920
Tash, Clara Jane	2387
Taylor, Abigail	1693
Daniel	1690
Edward Reynolds	692

Names.	Cons. Nos.
Taylor, Eliphalet	1686
Elizabeth	3320
Frank Montgomery	693
George Warren A.	694
John	1692
Jonathan	1688
Joseph	1694
Mary E.	1152
Polly	1691
Robert	691
Sally	1689
William	1151
Zacheus	1687
Tebbetts, Abiel Foster	4046, 3, (2)
Adalaide Curry	4046, 1, (4), II
Albert H.	4046, 3, (4), IV
Alice	4046, 3, (3)
Arthur Beede	4046, 1, (9)
Arthur Bradbury	4046, 1, (4), III, (I)
Bradbury	4046, 1
Charles A.	4046, 3, (4), II
Charles Carroll	4046, 1, (8)
Charlotte McFarland	4046, 1, (4), IV
Clementina	4046, 3, (11)
Eliza W.	4046, 3, (4), V
George Harrison	4046, 1, (8), I
George Parish	4046, 1, (1), I
George Sullivan	4046, 1, (4)
Hannah	4046, 1, (5)
Hannah	4046, 2
Hannah	4046, 3, (5)
Harriet	4046, 3, (8)
Harriet D.	4046, 3, (4), III
Hattie C.	4046, 1, (8), I, (I)
Henry	2179 & 4046
Henry	4046, 3
Henry Bradbury	4046, 3, (10)
Hiram	4046, 3, (4)
Hiram Bradbury	4046, 1, (6)
Hiram Watson	4046, 1, (6), I
Horace Bradley	4046, 1, (7)
John Clough	4046, 1, (3)
John Clough	4046, 1, (4), V
Laura Sophia	4046, 1, (6), II
Mandana	4046, 3, (12)
Maria Dix	4046, 1, (6), III
Mary	4046, 3, (6)
Mary A.	4046, 3, (4), I
Mary Badger	4046, 1, (1), III
Melinda	4046, 1, (2)
Melinda	4046, 3, (9)
Nathan Clough	4046, 1, (1)
Rosanna	4046 3, (7)
Rufus Bradbury	4046, 1, (1), II
Samuel Bradbury	4046, 1, (4), I
Sarah	4046, 3, (1)
Walter George	4046, 1, (4), III
Willie Bradbury	4046, 1, (6), IV
Tenney, Martha	207, 7
Thaxter, Edward Russel	1986
Martha Ella	1985
Mary Swan	1983
Rufus William	1982
William Swan	1984
Thayer, Albert	3727
Anna	3443
Anna Maria	1156
Thayer, Emma Florence	1155
Levi P.	1153
Mr.	3410
Nellie M	3728
Tabitha	3372
Whitman M.	3726
Thomas, Ann	1727, 3
Mr.	3396
Nathaniel R.	231, 1, (1)
Warren Nathaniel	231, 1, (1), I
Thompson, Abbie Marion	1720, 1, (3)
Abby Hill	1730, 2
Abby Susan	1722, 3, (3)
Abigail	1630, 3
Abigail	1717, 9
Abigail	1719
Abigail E.	1722, 6
Abraham	1717, 4
Alfred	1720, 2
Alice Gertrude	1635, 9, (1), III
Amanda Flora	1635, 6, (1)
Ann	1635, 8, (1)
Anna	1630, 2, (1), IX
Annie Eliza	1641, 1, (5), V
Ardra Hannah	1720, 1, (7)
Asa	1724
Augustus C. (Rev.)	1735, 3
Benjamin	1716
Betsy	1726
Burtrous	1630, 2, (1), III
Caroline Elizabeth	1635, 9, (5)
Carrie Champney	1641, 1, (5), VI
Carrie George	1635, 9, (1), II
Charles	1717, 8
Charles	1735, 3, (5)
Charles Augustus	1720, 1, (1)
Charles Osgood	1727, 1
Daniel Fox	1635, 9
Daniel Gordon	1635, 9, (3)
Edith	1635, 8, (10)
Edwin Jonathan	1722, 3, (2)
Eliza	1630, 6
Eliza	1630, 2, (1), I
Eliza H.	1720, 3
Elizabeth	1630, 2, (3)
Elizabeth	1634
Elizabeth	1635, 3
Elizabeth	1717, 12
Elizabeth	1722, 2
Ellen Augusta	1635, 9, (2)
Elmer Ellsworth	1635, 8, (9)
Eunice Jane	1730, 5
Ferdinand De Soto	1720, 1, (6)
Frank Leslie	1630, 2, (2), I
Franklin Jonathan	1720, 1, (5)
Freddie	1630, 2, (2), II
Frederick	1641, 1, (5), IV
Frederick Winslow	1635, 9, (1), I
Fremont	1635, 8, (8)
George	1635, 8, (4)
George Edwin	1635, 9, (6)
George Joseph	1635, 5, (1)
Hannah	1628
Henry Abiather	1730, 6
Hiram	1630, 2, (1), V
Ida	1630, 2, (1), IV
Ida Bell	1722, 3, (6)
Irving Augustus	1722, 3, (5)

Names.	Cons. Nos.
Thompson, Isaac H.	3066
James F.	1720, 8
James Willey	1641, 1, (5), III
Jay	1635, 8, (7)
Jennette Annaly	1635, 9, (4)
Job	1635
Job	1635, 5
John	1635, 6
John	1717, 1
John	1725
John	1727, 3
John	1728
John Haven	1635, 6, (2)
John L.	712
John Winslow E.	1635, 9, (1)
Jonathan	1627
Jonathan	1630, 2
Jonathan	1631
Jonathan	1715
Jonathan	1717, 7
Jonathan	1720, 1
Jonathan	1721
Jonathan	1722, 3
Jonathan Edwards	1730, 3
Jonathan Runnels (Dr.)	1730
Joseph	1717, 3
Joseph	1722, 1
Joseph Burnham	1635, 2
Joseph P. (Capt.)	312
Julia	230, 4
Keziah	1717, 11
Keziah	1723
Keziah	1729
Le Roy	1635, 8, (3)
Levi	1717
Levi	1717, 5
Levi	1720, 4
Lizzie	1630, 2, (1), VII
Lizzie Lucy	1722, 3, (1)
Llewellyn Augustine	1720, 1, (2)
Lois	1630, 4
Louisa	1635, 8, (5)
Lovey	1630, 5
Marcia Eva	1720, 1, (8)
Margaret E.	1867
Mary	1629
Mary	1635, 4
Mary	1635, 8 (6)
Mary	1645
Mary	1735, 3, (3)
Mary Ella	1630, 2, (2), III
Mary Evans	1730, 4
Mary Jane	1717, 10
Mary S.	1720, 7
Minnie Florence	1630, 2, (2), IV
Mr.	1717, 9
Parthena	1635, 7
Pelatiah	1634
Pelatiah	1634, 1
Pelatiah	1722, 4
Polly	1718
Reginald Romaine	1720, 1, (4)
Reuben	1630, 7
Rhoda	1630, 2, (1), II
Robert	1717, 6
Robert	1720
Robert	1723
Roxanna	230, 8
Thompson, Samuel	1627
Samuel	1630
Samuel, Jr.	1630, 1
Samuel	1630, 2, (1)
Samuel	1635, 8
Samuel	1727
Samuel	1727, 2
Samuel Demerit	1641, 1, (5), II
Samuel Willey	1641, 1, (5)
Sarah	1632
Sarah Elizabeth	1730, 1
Sarah J.	1720, 5
Susan	1635, 1
Susannah	1633
Susannah	1722
Susannah F.	1722, 5
Stephen	1630, 2, (2)
Sylvester	1717, 13
Theodore Boone	1720, 1, (9)
Thomas	118, 11
Victoria	1635, 8, (2)
Walter	1630, 2, (1), VI
William	1717, 2
William	1720, 6
William	1722, 3, (4)
William	1735, 3, (4)
William Francis	1641, 1, (5), I
Willie	1630, 2, (1), VIII
Thurston, Chloe	136
Mary	2294
Tibbetts, Ann	2559
Frederick	419, 2
Israel	1628, 6
Hannah R. (Mrs.)	2482
Leonard	419
Love	1661
Sarah	2177
Sumner	419, 1
Titcomb, Elizabeth	1643, 10, (5)
Stephen	447, 4
Titus, Susan	1674, 4
Tolman, Mary	3354
Torrey, E. N.	2581
Towers, Miles	917
Town, Abby Luella	1546
Ada Sedalia	1550
Betsey	357
Cora Lelia	1549
Elmer Ellsworth	1551
Ezra E.	1545
Flora Lelia	1548
Mr.	260
Walter Varian	1547
Towne, Cordelia	2194, 6
Louisa	2831
Susan	841
Townshend, Hannah	3948
Tozier, Almira	1937
Caroline A.	1951
Charles T.	1948
Harriet T.	1950
Henry H.	1949
Mary Jane	1952
Rollin Tyler	1947
Tracy, Ann Colby	3084
Trafton, Anna	507
Trask, Ann	116, 6
Eliza	116, 4

Names.	Cons. Nos.
Trask, Ezra	116
Irena	116, 7
Mary (Polly)	116, 2
Matilda	116, 3
Sarah	116, 5
Sophia	116, 1
Travers, Abel	2886
Caroline	2902
Charles Henry	2904
Ellen	2888
Jacob W.	2901
James	2887
Mary A.	2889
William Gilbert	2903
Trefethen, John W.	2062
Thomas A.	2063
Trickey, Clara Lillian	1738, 2, (6)
George Pendexter M.	1738, 2, (2)
Frank Pierce	1738, 2, (5)
James Coleman	1738, 2, (1)
Joseph Burnham	1738, 2
Josie Geraldine	1738, 2, (8)
Martha	2380, 1
Nelson Irving	1738, 2, (3)
Sarah Alice	1738, 2, (7)
William Wallace	1738, 2, (4)
Tripe, Nicholas	2273
Triplett, Harry M.	3169, 1
N. M.	3169
True, Harriet	1668, 9
Sally	1771
Samuel	1643, 10, (3)
Trundy, Charlotte D.	2084
Trussell, Gracia	808
Sarah	3620
Tucker, Edwin Robbins	1734, 1, (2)
Elizabeth Eastman	1734, 3
Henry	1734
Henry Eastman	1734, 5
Lewis Henry	1734, 1, (3)
Lewis McMillan	1734, 1
Lucy Maria	832
Mary Ann	1734, 1, (1)
Mary Ann	1734, 2
Susan Runnels	1734, 4
Tukey, George W.	1794
James G.	1796
Sarah W.	1795
Williams	1793
Tupper, Rachel E.	2076
Turner, Elizabeth	3365
James R.	1084
Sewall A.	1086
Tuttle, Alvah	1252
Clara Durgin	1255
David	1673, 1
David D.	1248
Esther V.	1671, 6, (4)
Ivory Burten	1250
Manson	1251
Mary	2802
Mary Hannah	1254
Mr.	1666, 6, (1)
Mr.	1669, 6
Nettie Jane	1253
Woodbury Durgin	1249
Twombly, Abigail Sarah G.	2532
Clara Augusta	2536
Twombly, Elhanan Charles	2530
Elizabeth Hannah	2535
Ezekiel Wingate	2533
Isaac James	2534
James	2529
James Runnels	2537
Lucy Stone	2531
Simes Frinck	2538
Stephen	1630, 4
William Henry W.	2539
Tyler, Mary E.	3210
Phinehas	915
Underwood, Letitia M.	1422
Upham, Gilman	2532
Sarah A.	2532, 2 & 6
Winthrop	2532, 1
Van Orden, Peter	2427, 3
William Dimon R.	2427, 3, (1)
Varney, Betsy	326, 5
Charles	326, 3
Charles W.	2352
George Carter	326, 1
Hannah Reynolds	326, 2
Mary Elizabeth	326, 4
Stephen	326
William Henry	326, 6
Vaughn, Anna (Mrs.)	2657
Elizabeth A.	3174
Veazie, Melissa B.	3067
Virgin, John A.	1666, 2, (3)
Waldron, Eliza	2376
Walker, Eunice	1382
Phebe A.	2593
William J.	916
Wallace, Almena Augusta	2954
Edgar Fenton	2956
Elijah	2959
Eliza	2194, 1
George Melvin	2955
George Newton	2953
Helen	3972
Mr.	2487
Sarah Frances	2960
Waller, Viann (Mrs.)	500
Wallis, Mary C.	2482
Walters, Dellie Rosa	1586
George W.	1584
Stephen S.	1585
Walther, Louisa	3032
Ward, Carrie	2832
Maria	1486
Warren, Eliza V.	3256
Washburn, Eunice	239, 2
William	713
Waterhouse, Lydia	1635, 6
Waterman, Carlos	2725
Isabella	3711
Watkins, Albert E.	152, 3, (2)
Eliza Ann	152, 3, (3)
Emma Jane	152, 3, (9)
George R.	152, 3, (1)
Lucy Viola	152, 3, (5)

Names.	Cons. Nos.
Watkins, Mary Eldora	152, 3, (6)
Olon Ayer	152, 3, (4)
Orick William	152, 3, (7)
Otis G(ould)	152, 3
Otis Gould, Jr.	152, 3, (8)
Watson, Charles Pharez	1525
Clarington Leslie	1527
Ellen Augusta	1528
Enoch	2192, 6
Eunice Matilda	1241
Francis Lewyllen	1526
George	2192, 3
Grace	1243
Herbert	1242
Ichabod	2192
James Clinton	1236
John	2192, 5
Joseph	2475
Laura Sophia (Mrs.)	4046, 1, (6)
Lavina	2479
Lizzie May	1529
Louisa	2477
Lovey	2476
Lydia	3459
Margaret (Peggy)	2192, 2
Mary	1745
Nancy	2192, 7
Patience	2480
Polly	2192, 4
Sally	2478
Sarah	724
Sarah Hanson	2607
Timothy	2192, 1
William Henry	1524
Way, Lorrin	316
Webb, Sally	2631
Webber, Genevieve	1851, 1
Jerusha	808
Josiah	1851
Webster, Ella Frances	213, 4, (2)
Eliza Ball	213, 4, (5)
James	213, 4, (4)
Julia Anna	213, 4, (7)
Kimball	213, 4
Kimball C.	213, 4, (3)
Lizzie Jane	213, 4, (1)
Lydia	256
Lutina Ray	213, 4, (6)
Mary Newton	213, 4, (8)
Wedgwood, Deborah	3892
Weed, Dolly	618
Weeks, Addison True	2707
Albert Eugene	2705
Almira	2708
Hannah Elizabeth	2574
Joseph Potter	2572
Josiah	1733, 1
Le Roy	2573
Mary	1667, 2
Mary Elizabeth	2702
Mary Frances	2575
Sarah Adelaide	2703
Susan (Mrs.)	2294
Stephen Fletcher	2701
Stephen Francis	2704
Walter Harriman	2706
Welch, Charles	1672, 8
Charles L.	1672, 3, (2)

Names.	Cons. Nos.
Welch, Deliverance	1672, 2
Finett	1672, 11
Freeman	1672, 9
Greenleaf	1672, 13
Hannah	1672, 12
Harrison	1672, 3, (3)
Hendrick	1672, 5
Isaac	1672, 10
Jacob	1672
Jacob	1672, 3, (4)
Joseph Demeritt	1672, 3
Joseph Priest	1672, 3, (1)
Louisa	1672, 14
Martha Ann	1672, 3, (5)
Mary Jane	1672, 7
Mr.	1668, 2, (2)
Orrin	1672, 3, (6)
Prudence	1672, 6
Susan	1672, 1
William	1672, 4
Weld, Cordelia Frances	3663
Dorothy	3338
Welden, William	2433
Wells, Ann (Mrs.)	559
Wentworth, Benjamin	2355
Edgar Newland	1294
Hiram Shepard	1293
Martha	2060
Rebecca	2285
West, Adelaide	551, 2
Ann H.	545
Ann M.	231, 2
Anna P.	231, 8, (3)
Arvilla	231, 8, (1)
Asa A.	231, 8
Ben Lapham	551
Charles O.	544
Diontha	231, 8, (2)
Edward Henry	542, 1
Elbridge G.	542
Ellen	543
Emma L.	549
George Hyatt	541, 1
James G.	548
Leonard	147, 3
Lizzie F.	231, 8, (4)
Mary E.	547
Mary Louisa	541, 2
Orestes	541
Phebe	2195
Richard H.	540
Richard Hazen	551, 1
Sarah Page	550
Scott C.	231, 8, (5)
Walter	546
Wetherbee, Abijah	240
William	240, 1
Weyl, Charles W.	2861
Weymouth, Mr.	3611
Wheeler, Benjamin Franklin	991
Fidelia	513
Louisa	992
Stephen	1733, 2
Wheelwright, Harriet E.	766
Whidden, Benjamin	383
David	385
George	380
George	381

Names.	Cons. Nos.
Whidden, Nancy	384
Olive	382
Samuel	387
Sarah	386
Whipple, Emma Georgiana	1312
George Albert	203, 1, (1)
John Albert	203, 4
Lyman	203
Lyman Holbrook	203, 2
Mary Louise	203, 3
William	1311
William Henry	203, 1
Whitaker, Charles	1641, 2, (3)
George	1641, 4, (1)
Luther	1641, 2, (6)
Stephen	1641, 4
Whitcher, Artemesia Stewart	2677
White, Augusta Sanford	1468
Joseph	2745
Levi	1671, 9
Lizzie Ann	1641, 5, (4)
Marshall W.	760
Nellie	1467
Nellie Salome	1469
Rufus O.	1465
Whitehouse, Mary D.	2651
Whitman, Bethia	3699
Hannah	3698
Mr.	3696
Nathaniel	3697
Sophia Williams (Mrs.)	4046, 1, (3)
Whitney, Horace	167
John	3300
Nancy Fisher	1732, 1
Whitten, Sarah	376
Wilder, Persis	3470
Mr.	3477
Wiley, Isaac	900
Wilkins, Henry K.	2727
Willee, Elizabeth	2188
Hannah	2187
Mr.	2186
Willetts, Adoniram Wilson	952, 1
Charles	952
Charles	952, 3
Francis Coburn	952, 2
Willey, Adaline	472
Charles	1670, 4, (6), III
Clarence	1670, 4, (6), II
Eddie	1670, 4, (6), I
John	2476
Josiah S.	1673, 10
Malinda	500
Mr.	2314
Nellie	1670, 4, (6), IV
Olive	3055
Rufus	1670, 4, (6)
Susan	1734, 5
Williams, Alvin	2419
Esther M.	3026
Mary Ann	2982
Samuel	2178
Willard	579
Wilmarth, Arthur Reynolds	1193
Edward Nathan	1194
Henry Dan	1192
Wilmot, Lucy L.	2742
Wilson, Albion K. P.	2587

Names.	Cons. Nos.
Wilson, Carrie	1740, 3
Elizabeth (Mrs.)	529
George	3975
Mr.	712
Rebecca	207
Winchester, Arvilla	2894
William H.	2898
Windsor, Joseph, Jr.	2544
Wines, Abijah	3998
Abijah (Rev.)	3999
Wing, Charles G.	3559
Charlotte Augusta	1511
Francis Marion	1510
Lucy Annie	1509
Winthrop Morse	1508
Wingate, Alfred Seymour	1140
Anna Mariah	2029
Emma	732
Henry Herrick	1143
Maria	1142
Walter Raymond	1144
Winn, Mary Elizabeth	3080
Winship, Adaline	230, 3
Winslow, Ellen	2612, 2
Witham, Abigail Runnels	2310
Abraham	2311
Hannah Runnals	2312
Isaac Runnels	2317
Louisa (Eliza)	2313
Mary Sophia	2319
Moses	2315
Mr.	2314
Nancy	2314
Nathaniel	2309
Nathaniel	2316
Sarah Ann	2318
Sears	1436
Wolcott, Alonzo	447, 5
Alphonso	447, 6
Carrie Louisa	447, 6, (2)
Charlotte Lemira	447, 7
Chloe Annette	447, 9
Eddie Seward	447, 1, (5)
Edwin	447, 2
Emma Jane	447, 1, (3)
Horace Eddie	447, 6, (1)
Ida Ann	447, 1, (2)
Martha	447, 1, (7)
Milton Daniel	447, 1, (4)
Milton John	447
Newell Nason	447, 10
Norman Maltby	447, 8
Sarah Jane	447, 4
Sewall Albert	447, 3
Sollis Alconder	447, 1
Sollis Alfred	447, 1, (6)
Solomon	447, 1, (1)
Woodbury, Emma	3608, 1
George	3608, 2
Hannah	355
Henry	3608
Martha A.	3122
Nathaniel	3313
Woodis, Caroline D.	1645, 4, (4)
Woodman, Andrew	1666, 3, (1)
Martha	1670
Mary	20
Mr.	1660

Names.	Cons. Nos.
Woodward, Lyman	454
Woodworth, Lucy Ann	447, 6
Worster, Ann	1910
Worthen, Adams Merrill	599
Arthur Enoch	597
Frank Fayette	594, 1
George Arthur	597, 1
George B.	596
Harriet	595
Inez Emma	597, 2
Jane Elizabeth	600
John Adams	592
John Adams	594
Mary Ann	593
Mira Jenette	598
Susie S.	594, 2
Wright, Henry	242

Names.	Cons. Nos.
Wright, Savira	242, 1
Wyatt, Abigail	733
Wyeth, Lucy Snow	1022
Wyman, Elizabeth Maria	1485
Frank	1484
Increase	1483
York, Sarah (Mrs.)	2525
Young, Charles	1718, 1
Franklin	1670, 4, (8)
John	2266
John H.	2266, 1
Maria Antoinette	2957
Mark F.	2266, 2
Mr.	1821
Sarah Elizabeth	3044

ERRATA.

Page 64, eighth line from the bottom, after "592 Mary," for "Morrill" read "Merrill."

Page 63, eighth line from the bottom, for "th efirm" read "the firm."

Page 94, twenty-first line from the bottom, after "1167 Luella Pamelia" insert "(Ames)."

Page 102, eighteenth line from the bottom [1307], for "(Forbes)" read "(Sutton)."

Page 124, eleventh line from the bottom to be read as the thirteenth, inserting "(2.) Timothy. (3.) James. (4.) Samuel" directly *after* "1628, 1, (1), VIII," and the words "three children."

Page 125, first line, for "630" read "1630."

Page 133, eighth line, for "aged" read "age."

Page 136, twenty-seventh line, after "Nottingham" for "[1668, 1, (3)]," read "[1668, 2, (3)]."

Page 141, eighteenth line from the bottom, after "(5) Franklin Jonathan" for "d. Sept. 3," read "b. Sept. 3."

Page 146, twenty-ninth line, after "1738, 1, (1) Sarah Edith," for "(Trickey)" read "(Meserve)."

Page 183, fifth and ninth lines, "2179 Sarah" should change places with "2180 Joseph," reading "2179 Joseph, b. 1757," instead of "1758"; and "2180 Sarah, b. 1759," instead of "1756."

Page 206, fourth line, after "2432," for "Rusheaun" read "Rusheanu."

Page 231, twenty-first line after "2906 James Leverett" insert "(Goldsmith)."

Page 262, seventh line, for "5515" read "3515."

Page 290, eighteenth line from the bottom, instead of "(p. IX)" read "(p. VII)."

Index I, eleventh line, instead of "pp. VII and VIII," read "pp. V and VI."

NOTE. — For peculiarities and variations in the spelling of certain names, especially Christian names, individuals and families *furnishing the records* are mainly responsible.